Labours Lost

This is a unique account of the hidden history of servants and their employers in late eighteenth-century England and of how servants thought about and articulated their resentments. It is a book which encompasses state formation and the maidservant pounding away at dirty nappies in the back kitchen; taxes on the servant's labour and the knives he cleaned, the water he fetched, and the privy he shovelled out. Carolyn Steedman shows how deeply entwined all of these entities, objects and people were in the imagination of those doing the shovelling and pounding and in the political philosophies that attempted to make sense of it all. Rather than fitting domestic service into conventional narratives of 'industrial revolution' or 'the making of the English working class' she offers instead a profound re-reading of this formative period in English social history which restores the servant's lost labours to their rightful place.

CAROLYN STEEDMAN is Professor of History at the University of Warwick. Her previous publications include *Master and Servant: Love and Labour in the English Industrial Age* (2007) and *Dust* (2001).

Frontispiece. Doing all sorts, in W. H. Pyne, *Microcosm; or a Pictoresque Delineation of the Arts, Agriculture and Manufactures of Great Britain*, London, 1806. Reproduced by kind permission of the Syndics of Cambridge University Library

Labours Lost

Domestic Service and the Making of Modern England

Carolyn Steedman

Steedman
Maloney
Sambrook
Lethbridge
Delap
Todd.
Brayßon & Summerfield
Giles
Buckley
Fleming
Read

Arthur
light
Davidson

pooley

CAMBRIDGE
UNIVERSITY PRESS

⨂ Gd J clismann
change.
footnote.
80 in final

⨂ 119 footnote

CAMBRIDGE UNIVERSITY PRESS
Cambridge, New York, Melbourne, Madrid, Cape Town, Singapore,
São Paulo, Delhi, Dubai, Tokyo

Cambridge University Press
The Edinburgh Building, Cambridge CB2 8RU, UK

Published in the United States of America by
Cambridge University Press, New York

www.cambridge.org
Information on this title: www.cambridge.org/9780521736237

First published 2009

Printed in the United Kingdom at the University Press, Cambridge

A catalogue record for this publication is available from the British Library

Library of Congress Cataloguing in Publication data
Steedman, Carolyn.
Labours lost : domestic service and the making of modern England / Carolyn
Steedman.
   p.   cm.
Includes bibliographical references and index.
ISBN 978-0-521-51637-2 (hardback)
1. Domestics – Great Britain – History – 18th century.   2. Country homes –
Great Britain – History – 18th century.   3. Great Britain – Social life and
customs – 18th century.   I. Title.
HD8039.D52S74   2009
331.7′6164046094109033 – dc22   2009031008

ISBN 978-0-521-51637-2 Hardback
ISBN 978-0-521-73623-7 Paperback

Signposts left at random in the no-man's land between what can and cannot be represented, they indicate only that the other side of the border is inhabited.

Bruce Robbins, The Servant's Hand (1993)

None of us has time to live the true dramas of the life that we are destined for. This is what ages us – this and nothing else. The wrinkles and creases on our faces are the registration of the great passions, vices, insights, that called on us; but we, the masters, were not at home.

Walter Benjamin, Illuminations (1972)

Mary: 'Do People reason so much about Servants?'

Jonas Hanway, Virtue in Humble Life (1774)

CARRYING... It is good for a Servant to dream he is carried by his Master, and for the mean Man to be carried by the rich.

Anon., Nocturnal Revels (1706)

Contents

viii   Contents

Illustrations

Tables

Abbreviations

BCRO	Berkshire County Record Office
BCLA	Birmingham Central Library Archives
BUL	Birmingham University Library
BL	British Library
CRO	Cambridgeshire Record Office
CCA	Cheshire and Chester Archives and Local Studies Service
DCRO	Derbyshire County Record Office
DRO	Devon Record Office
DMA	Doncaster Metropolitan Archives
ESCRO	East Sussex County Record Office
HCRO	Hertfordshire County Record Office
KU	Keele University Special Collections and Archives
LRO	Lancashire Record Office
LIL	Lincoln's Inn Library
LMA	London Metropolitan Archives
NMM	National Maritime Museum
NCRO	Norfolk County Record Office
NA	Nottinghamshire Archives
SA	Shropshire Archives
SP	Scone Palace
SCRO	Somerset County Record Office
SHC	Surrey History Centre
TNA	The National Archives
WCRO	Warwickshire County Record Office
WYAS	West Yorkshire Archive Services
WRO	Wiltshire Record Office

Acknowledgements

A therapist might say that I have a good relationship with the state, in the way that relationships with parents, employers, and other forms of authority are described as being 'good'. This would mean that I do not experience the relationship as onerous, or oppressive; that I have a cheerful-seeming, passive, and somewhat childlike acceptance of its place in my life and consciousness. (A psychoanalyst on the other hand, might well make me plumb the depths of my desire to express self-identity in such terms. I am, by the way, entirely with the psychoanalyst here, not the therapist.) The state gave me good teeth and strong bones (National Health orange juice, school milk, many jars of Virol); the state taught me to read, got me away from home and sent me to university. In the shape of the then Social Science Research Council, the state funded my PhD and made me a historian. It is *in* me; the state is imprinted *on* me; I carry it with me, as the person it has made me. This is not an entirely unusual attitude for children born, reared and educated in the early years of the National Health Service and as beneficiaries of the Education Act of 1948.[1] I have never asked for welfare benefits, been imprisoned, or subjected to military service; if any of these things had happened to me, no doubt my attitude would be different. As it is, I shall always be some kind of child who knows that the morning break-time milk and, later, the university grant cheque are provided by some distant but kindly force. I shall always be grateful to the state. But to describe myself as being married to the state for three years past, is probably taking things too far. This is how I explained my coming absence from the University of Warwick to a group of students in the autumn of 2004, shortly after I had been awarded an Economic and Social Research Council Professorial Fellowship to work on this book: 'you won't be seeing much of me over the next three years;

---

[1] Carolyn Steedman, *Landscape for a Good Woman*, Virago, London, 1986; Michael Wadsworth, *The Imprint of Time: Childhood, history, and adult life*, Clarendon Press, Oxford, 1991.

from 1st October I shall be married to the state'.[2] They did not laugh; I enjoy my own jokes far too much for them to be at all funny. One of many things that I have discovered from the work here presented, is where my jokes come from. They come from the eighteenth century. Employers thought through (the therapist would say, *dealt with*) the great questions of state and society, and social and class formation that their domestic servants embodied, by making servant-jokes. Sometimes they laughed self-deprecatingly at themselves for suffering the depredations of the lower orders represented by their servant. Alison Light reports Virginia Woolf making this kind of joke about her servants in the 1920s and 1930s; she did not know that their form was at least 200 years old.[3]

How I learned this form of deeply unpleasant self-regard dressed as self-deprecation, is a different matter: I have been doing it since my teens, long before I knew what the eighteenth century *was*. However, my idea of marriage to the state was prescient (though as this book will show, I would have done better to describe the relationship as a contractual one, *tout court*. But then nobody would have laughed, not even I.) I have worried a great deal about my obligations to the state (in its aspect as the ESRC) over the past three years: whether I am doing what I said I would do, writing the book it wants (*might* want – what *does* the State want?); whether I am keeping my promises. I have invented the state's needs and wants, to express my anxieties ('They'll want tables! My only tables are kitchen tables!'; actually, there are tables of the first sort in this book). In my pitch to the Fellowship interview panel I said, somewhat piously, that I took my responsibilities as a historian seriously; that most disciplines in the human and social sciences are grounded in an overt or implied history of state and class formation in the UK that . . . isn't quite right . . . ; that histories of the working class, and accounts of modern social structure based on these histories miss out the waged domestic workers who comprised a majority of working people. I said that I could rectify this to some extent, and provide a new and better history. That here and now I have been able to tell the story of writing this book in this way is my acknowledgement of the interest, support, and – yes – distant kindliness of the ESRC over the three years it took (and expression of a profound gratitude for its allowing me to get on with the work in the first place). What I didn't know back in 2004, and do know now, is how useful was going to be my childlike belief that the state manifests

[2] ESRC RES-051-27-0123 (2004–2007), 'Service, Society and the State: The making of the social in England 1760–1820'.
[3] Alison Light, *Mrs Woolf and the Servants*, Fig Tree, London, 2007. But one modern mistress does know the antiquity of servant-jokes: Kate Clanchy, *What Is She Doing Here? A refugee's story*, Picador, London, 2008, p. 243.

itself in the ordinary things of everyday life. That is why this is a book about state formation *and* the maidservant pounding away at the dirty nappies in the back kitchen; about the tax on the servant's labour *and* the knives he cleaned, the water he fetched, and the privy he shovelled out. It is about those entities, objects and people; how they related to one another; how deeply intertwined they were, in the imagination of those doing the shovelling and the pounding and in the many philosophies that attempted to account for it all.

Prologue: The servant's dream

Eighteenth-century employers knew that thinking about the servants was an ancient activity. Myth, history and the Holy Scriptures demonstrated that elite masters and mistresses had always embodied questions of state and society, of personhood and identity, in their domestics. In Genesis for example, Joseph interprets the dreams of Pharaoh's servants. He has been sold into slavery by his jealous brothers. Bought by Potiphar, one of Pharaoh's captains of the guard, he is imprisoned after a false charge of rape made by Potiphar's wife. Incarcerated, he is accorded the same trust he enjoyed as Potiphar's house-steward, and is put in charge of the other prisoners. When the Pharaoh's butler and baker arrive – they have offended their master – they are given into his care. The two servants have a dream, one each, both on the same night. Joseph's magisterial interpretation predicts that one of the servants will live and find himself in service and in favour again; and that the other – the baker – will not be forgiven, and will be hanged. The swift fulfilment of these prophecies – both are realised within three days – is the reason for Joseph's release to interpret a dream of the Pharaoh himself. As Joseph reads it, Pharaoh's dream is about organisation of the food supply during famine to come. (Genesis, xxxvii–xli) The meaning he gives to the kingly dream is resolutely social, to do with economy and society; it is by way of marked contrast with his earlier interpretation of the servants' dreams, as merely individual fates.

Joseph is both house slave and superior servant in Potiphar's establishment. Incarcerated, he is still enslaved, but also warden of the other prisoners, whom he serves. (Genesis, xl, 4) He is prophet and seer whose labour in interpreting the servants' dreams appears to be for no purpose other than to demonstrate his fitness to perform the same service for a king, for which he is rewarded with governorship of Egypt, much wealth, and a wife. Eighteenth-century legal theorists and philosophers explained some of these shifts in status and persona in their discussions of Ancient World and Old Testament slavery. Paramount was the message of history and anthropology, that slavery and servitude were conditions

1

from which modern commercial society had arisen. 'In the Infancy of our Constitution, the Common People of England were little better than Slaves' said one legal guidebook; 'But since the abolition of Vassalage . . . the Tyranny of Nobility is restrained; the Commonality are upon the same Footing as to Liberty and Property as the Gentry; and Servants of the lowest Class, being under the Protection of the Laws, if mal-treated, have the same Remedy and Redress as their Masters.'[1]

The legal philosopher's aim might be to point up the differences between English common law and Roman law; then the contrast between the house slave of classical antiquity and the modern domestic servant was highly useful. In his *Elements of Civil Law* (1767) the Reverend Taylor provided a sociology of Roman slavery in relation to 'the customs and manners of the Roman people'.[2] Modern English people did not need to be reminded that here and now, in the 1760s, 'Hired or Domestic servants . . . is the true, proper and natural Contemplation, and prevails with us at this Day'. In the great, inequitable world that God had made, there was certainly 'an inferiority' attached to the servant, 'but not such an Inferiority, as includes a Civil Subjection. And the terms of the Covenant [contract] convey to the Master a right over the Offices of his servant, but I think, not over his Person.'[3] There were many sources like this for understanding the great differences between present times and the legal and social organisation of the historically remote, the strange shifts in the Biblical Joseph's status and identity, and for noting the unimportance of the servants' dreams. Comparison between the slave (ancient and modern, Biblical, Classical and New World) and the contracted girl dusting the parlour and mopping the floor, provided the insistent base note to these discussions.

A servant's dreams were unimportant to eighteenth-century employers – except when it concerned them or their family.[4] One morning in 1781, Margaret Rice told her mistress Hester Thrale that she had

[1] Anon., *The Laws Relating to Masters and Servants: With Brief Notes and Explanations to Render them easy and intelligible to the meanest Capacity. Necessary to be had in all Families*, Henry Lintot, London, 1755, Preface. Also John Millar, *The Origin of the Distinction of Ranks; or, An Inquiry into the Circumstances which give Rise to Influence and Authority in the Different Members of Society*, 3rd edn, John Murray, London, 1781, pp. 302, 323–9.

[2] John Taylor, *Elements of the Civil Law*, privately printed, Cambridge, 1767, pp. v, 407–47.

[3] Taylor, *Elements*, p. 413.

[4] Joseph's story was referred to in much godly advice to servants in the early century. Rather than his prophetic abilities or his skill in dream analysis, the dangers of predatory mistresses were emphasised. Thomas Broughton, *Serious Advice and Warning to Servants, More Especially Those of the Nobility and Gentry*, 4th edn, J. Rivington for the SPCK, London, 1743, p. 11. Broughton recommended the Revd Mr Jenks's, *The Glorious Victory of Chastity, in Joseph's Hard Conflict, and His Happy Escape, while he was a Servant unto Potiphar, an Officer of Pharoah's, in Egypt*, W. Rogers, B. Tooke, London, 1707, to young

Figure 1. A shift in gender as well as in status and persona for the baker? Yet all authorities agree that the servant to whom Joseph announces death, *is* a man.

dreamed last night 'that my [Thrale's] eldest Daughter was going to be married to Mr Crutchley, but that Mr Thrale *himself* prevented her. – an odd thing to me, who think Mr Crutchley to be his Son'.[5] Peggy

men pursing the question. They could have read a much more amusing expiation: Henry Fielding, *Joseph Andrews* (1742).

[5] Katharine C. Balderson (ed.), *The Diary of Mrs Hester Lynch Thrale (Later Mrs Piozzi) 1778–1809* (1941), 2 vols., Clarendon Press, Oxford, 1951, vol. 1, p. 515.

Rice's dream certainly got to the heart of Thrale's anxieties about her dis-located, dysfunctional family, about the (first) husband she did not love, and her disastrous relationship with her daughters.[6] The dream was also a measure of how much the servant knew – was forced to know – about the affective and sexual life of her employers, though the incest signalled here belonged to the realm of Thrale's imagination – it was *her* dream work – rather than Margaret Rice's.[7] Sometimes Thrale dreamed about the servants. In 1778 she remembered her sixteen-year-old self living 'at Dean Street with My Father and Mother'. They kept 'two Maids and a Man: a Person whose name was Susan Verity was our under Servant, cleaned the House & cook'd the Victuals, she came from Mr Bird the Ribbon Weaver's, answered her Character perfectly, and had lived with us three Years & been a great favourite'. Young Hester had dreamed about going down to the kitchen to find 'six ill looking Fellows sitting round a Table on which was a bowl of Rum Punch . . . a Brace of Pistols with Bottles Glasses &c: & Susan appearing as their Servant – waiting on them'. She woke up terrified, decided not to go down, turned over, went back to sleep. In the morning she told Susan about the dream; she 'trem-bled and seem'd in great Confusion'. Alarmed that a good maid might think herself under suspicion (all over the country, girls would up and leave at such an imputation) Thrale 'made a Laugh of it, & assured her that I had no such Thoughts in my Head'. Some months later, her dream turned out to have been predictive. Susan's husband was taken as a thief, and 'she confessed to my Mother, that . . . [he] would frequently come to our house when all were a bed; bring his riotous Companions with him & drink themselves drunk . . . they threatened her Life if She did not let them in . . . '. Twenty years on, Thrale concluded 'How providential then was my uncommon dream!'[8] In the generality of stories like this, taken from histories ancient, modern and sacred, the servant's dream work was to alert employers to housebreaking, theft, and general depredation.[9]

---

[6] Carolyn Steedman, 'Servants and their relationship to the unconscious', *Journal of British Studies*, 42 (2003), 316–50.

[7] For the servant's sexual knowledge as legal testimony, Lawrence Stone, *Uncertain Unions: Marriage in England 1660–1753*, Oxford University Press, Oxford, 1992; *Road to Divorce: England 1530–1987*, Oxford University Press, Oxford, 1990.

[8] Balderson, *Thraliana*, vol. 1, p. 339.

[9] John Boswell, *A Method of Study: or, an useful Library. In two Parts. Part I. Contain-ing short Directions and a Catalogue of Books for the Study of several valuable Parts of Learning, viz. Geography, Chronology, History, Classical Learning, Natural Philosophy, &c. Part II. Containing some Directions for the Study of Divinity*, printed for the author, Lon-don, 1738–43, Part II, pp. 272–3; David Simpson, *A Discourse on Dreams and Night Visions, with numerous Examples Ancient and Modern*, Edward Bayley, Macclesfield, 1791, pp. 52–3.

But there is the servant's dream in its other meaning: 'dream' as the endless longing of the underprivileged that history (and life) be different from what it has been, and what it still is. This book will suggest that this kind of dream was more available to eighteenth-century domestic servants than other categories of labouring people, because of the work they did, the material objects on which they exercised their labour and the interpellation of both by a legal system. In the period covered by this book, older dreams were given social and economic substance, and the hope of a future for proletarian men and women was – according to their historians – first itemised as: the possibility of entering the polity, of possessing civil rights and (for men) enfranchisement. Discussing the revolutions in manners, thought and politics (and the social, economic and philosophical revolutions) through which she was living, Hester Thrale (now Piozzi) told a friend that she wanted to rewrite the servant's dream for modern times; for 'if the World does not come to an End, tis at least turned upside down.' Apropos she continued –

Do you remember a Print so called? when you were a child – Kitchens &c with Compartments: in one The Baby beating the Nurse, in another the Fowl roasting the Cook &c. . . . Peasants sitting with their Hats on, and the King bowing before them and pulling off his Crown. Two Footmen riding in a Chariot and the Noblemen stuck up behind.

If I could find that foolish old Thing I'd give a new Edition of it *with proper Comments* – that I would . . . make good Sport out of it these Democratic Days.[10]

These Days were October 1793. Robespierre had entered the Committee of Public Safety in July; the reign of Terror had begun, the *levée en masse* declared and Marie Antoinette guillotined two weeks since (the King of the French had lost his head as well as his crown in January).

Reversals of fortune and the servant's ascendancy were a feature of the social narrative Thrale/Piozzi had told since her girlhood. 'Laura Carter has become a very fine Lady, & very rich, her name is Rush now – I could not guess who the Wench was when She addressed me', she wrote in 1777; 'I kept her in my Nursery & about my Person for Charity a Maid servant thirteen Years ago – & here is Laura the finest of the fine at every Publick Show.'[11] In 1764 she had promised the girl's father to get her a place 'but finding she could neither read, nor write, nor work, nor wash, I found no body would be plagued with her but myself; I took her home therefore – taught her to read myself and taught her

---

[10] Edward A. Bloom and Lillian D. Bloom, *The Piozzi Letters: Correspondence of Hester Lynch Piozzi, 1784–1821 (formerly Mrs Thrale)*, 3 vols., University of Delaware Press, Associated University Press, Cranbery NJ, 1989–93, vol. 2, p. 147.

[11] Balderson, *Thraliana*, vol. 1, p. 682.

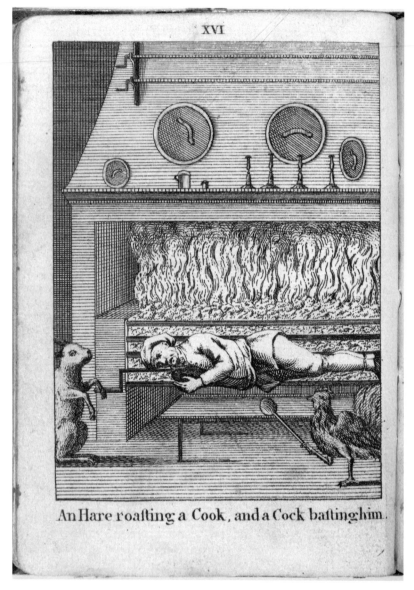

XVI

An Hare roafting a Cook, and a Cock baftinghim.

Figure 2. The Roasted Cook. Not the print Hester Thrale remembered from her childhood, but rather a contemporary image of the world gone topsy-turvy.

her prayers, her Catechisme &c'. She sent her out 'to learn washing – ironing Lacemending, clearstarching and such like, paid a Master to instruct her in Writing & then took her into my Nursery – to complete her Education'. It did not work. Laura 'was encouraged by her Mother... to be saucy'; she insisted on the other servants calling her '*miss* forsooth', would not eat with them, provoked general dislike ('made them all abhor' her).[12] Laura evidently had rather different ideas from Thrale about her social status and the education appropriate for it. These stories, of rise and fall through social space, were the way of the world. 'Ainsi va le Monde', Thrale wrote in March 1798; 'there are Vicissitudes upon this Little Globe among Little Folks – my Handsome Maid that was with me in Italy... came to our Door... this morning a poor Woman asking Charity'.[13]

All Thrale's servant-stories were individualised in this way. She contemplated their personalities, liked some of them ('Grosset is a nice Man' she wrote after recruiting him in 1788), and disparaged others.[14] She spent much time analysing their purported folk-beliefs, once trying to explain to her maid how the Itch (all the servants had what was probably scabies in the winter of 1778) was transmitted, showing her 'the Animal magnified; & told her how it burrowed under the Cuticle, how it was catching as Lice were catching &c'.[15] This educational session with the microscope had no effect at all, she noted ruefully: 'when I had done my harangue – I think however Madam says She that the Girl should have some Physick given her – to *strike it out*. So little could I make myself comprehended'. She needed the servant's obduracy, and her own self-deprecation in the face of it. She could amuse by telling of their little lives. She and her friends exchanged chillingly comic vignettes about their servants' sexual life, the joke always being that they, the servants, did not understand what stock-type they were playing. 'My maid Beckwith is married to our Welsh Gardiner', she reported in 1799. And then, a few days later, 'Mrs Beckwith's Conduct amazes even *me* who am not easily astonished at Proofs of human Depravity. She married... just in Time it seems, and is ready to lye in at 3 Months End. A poor, meek, mortified, unhealthy, unhappy, but completely *ladylike* Person as She appeared to me... but too much Opium, and too many Novels were the Cause...'. And then, recycled, to someone else: 'You are... very comical about the

---

[12] *Ibid.*, pp. 116–17.   [13] Bloom, *Piozzi Letters*, vol. 2, p. 483.
[14] *Ibid.*, vol. 1, p. 277. For disparagement of the cold-hearted Eleanor Allen, see Steedman, 'Servants and... the unconscious'.
[15] Balderson, *Thraliana*, vol. 1, pp. 13, 251, 347.

Gardener; he and his Lady's Conduct seem indeed as if they both had been deep read in Boccacio . . . '.[16]

The servants were constantly on her mind; they were a means to understanding the relationship between her and her husband and children; they provided her with psychological perception. She analysed Mr Thrale thus: 'the easiness of his Temper and slowness to take Offence add greatly to his Value as a domestic Man: yet I think his Servants do not much love him, and I am not sure that his Children feel much Affection for him: low People almost all indeed agree to abhor him, as he has none of that officious & cordial Manner which is universally required by them – nor any Skill to dissemble his dislike of their Coarseness –'.[17] The servants' function – apart from dusting, dinner and dressing Hester Thrale's hair – was to provide the content of her anecdotes and jokes, the shrill laughter of social disdain, and her work of cultural commentary. They were means to celebrate her own perceptiveness, social and psychological. In 1778 she had positively encouraged Sally Bean 'who always nurses me in Lying In' to bring her little boy with her for yet another confinement, for they 'were all so fond of the Child, & I like an Ideot let him come . . . because they said he fretted so at being from his Mother'. It was he who brought scabies to the household – another means to a good story – 'so I suppose we are all to begin & scratch speedily . . . '.[18]

Historians pondering the structural reordering of social relations at the century's end, have dwelled on workers' resistance to 'an ever encroaching capitalism to fuel the development of class consciousness'.[19] Roger Wells says that we should remember the harvest failures and hungers of these war years; we have forgotten the state, its intrusive actions in enforcing, by law, changes in the diet of a people in a condition of famine-induced trauma coming at the end of a long-term decline in living standards for key sections of the working population.[20] Domestic servants are not often included in these assessments, even though E. P. Thompson once noted that 'it is exactly in servant–master relations of dependency, in which personal contacts are frequent and personal injustices are suffered against which protest is futile, that feelings of resentment

---

[16] *Ibid.*, vol. 2, p. 991; Bloom, *Piozzi Letters*, vol. 3, pp. 75, 81.

[17] Balderson, *Thraliana*, vol. 1, p. 53.

[18] Mary Hyde, *The Thrales of Streatham Park*, Harvard University Press, Cambridge MA and London, 1977, p. 207.

[19] John Rule, *The Experience of Labour in Eighteenth-century Industry*, Croom Helm, London, 1981, p. 209.

[20] Roger Wells, *Wretched Faces: Famine in wartime England, 1798–1801*, Alan Sutton, Gloucester, 1988, p. 335.

or of hatred can be most violent and most personal'.[21] He thought that we could do away with 'deference' as a means of understanding these feelings, for they had 'no inwardness'; servants and other employees 'do not love their masters, but in the end . . . must be reconciled to the fact that for the duration of their lives these are likely to remain their masters'. And yet most eighteenth-century service careers were short; they did not last a lifetime. This book will present evidence that young women, doing their time in order to gain a settlement, flitting as soon as a mistress shouted at them, or failed to provide tea to their breakfast, were not at all fatalistic about their future, but rather, with the means available to them in a profoundly inequitable society, expressed their resentments in inventive and sometimes terrifying ways. Thompson found his sites of class feeling among servants in grand establishments like Potiphar's and Hester Thrale's: in the army ('the NCO may despise or hate his officers'), the Oxbridge college, and the great house, where the footman may 'despise those whom he serves'. This book will move out of the big house to restore such feelings, and the waged domestic workers who articulated them, to our social histories of England, 1760–1830, and to accounts of modern social structure more generally, that have been derived from this time and place. It will not assume that there is a fight to be had – following Karl Marx – over who can represent him- or herself, and who must be represented.[22] Eighteenth-century domestic servants represented themselves – spoke their subjectivity, their dreams and desires – to an astonishing degree, and in sophisticated ways. If, by the end, we come to understand what the servant's dream may have been, then we already know that they did dream-*work* for others, who had purchased their energies (including the energies of their imagination) to do what the law said really belonged to them, the employers.

[21] E. P. Thompson, 'The crime of anonymity' in Douglas Hay *et al.* (eds.), *Albion's Fatal Tree*, Allen Lane, London, 1976, pp. 255–344.

[22] Karl Marx, 'The Eighteenth Brumaire of Louis Bonaparte' (1858) in David McLellan (ed.), *Selected Writings*, Oxford University Press, Oxford, 1977, p. 318.

1   Introduction: A new view of society

Sometime in 1796, when he was working on the series of essays that would become *The Enquirer*, William Godwin visited (in imagination only; let us be clear about this) the servants' quarters of a rich man's mansion. He had started to write about servants for educational purposes: he was as much troubled by the question of how parents were to manage the relationship between children and domestics as his lover Mary Wollstonecraft had been ten years before, in her *Thoughts on the Education of Daughters*.[1] Or maybe she was his wife by the time he made his imaginary journey downstairs, and he a prospective father. Wollstonecraft and Godwin married in March 1797 and joined households, to avoid the obloquy of her bearing a second bastard child. Godwin conjured a grand establishment out of Wollstonecraft's much more typical and modest one, which in 1796 consisted of Margeurite the child-maid, Mary in the kitchen, and the Boy (Mary's child and Wollstonecraft's Boy) who had run errands between their separate households during the six months before they married. In neither of these did Godwin experience the kind of domestic labour force that was big enough to provide the 'riot in the kitchen' that he thought so corrupting of small children's manners and morals.[2]

---

[1] Mary Wollstonecraft, *Thoughts on the Education of Daughters: with Reflections on Female Conduct, in the more important Duties of Life*, Joseph Johnson, London, 1787.
[2] Janet Todd, *Mary Wollstonecraft: A revolutionary life*, Weidenfeld and Nicholson, London, 2000, pp. 379–457; Ralph M. Wardle (ed.), *Godwin and Mary: Letters of William Godwin*

'Of Servants' opens with a sustained meditation on the severe difficulties a large establishment of servants presents to parents wishing to
pursue a scheme of home education: what degree of intimacy to allow
between children and servants – who 'initiate . . . low maxims, and coarse
thinking?' and who will surely instruct them in 'cunning and the arts
of deceit?'[3] Godwin is thinking about servants long before he leaves
behind the airy upstairs apartments. In his mind, he connects the spatial
hierarchies of the house with the social hierarchies deposited in modern
society by the historical process. The mansion is 'inhabited by two classes
of being, or, more accurately speaking, by two sets of men drawn from
two distinct stages of barbarism and refinement'.[4] He uses eighteenth-
century social theory and philosophical history to tell himself a domestic
version of modern society risen from former modes of production: sav-
agery, barbarism, pastoralism etc. In modern, polite, commercial society
and in the mansion that represents it, he sees the discarded husks of earlier economic eras.[5] Then 'the fancy strikes [him] of viewing the servants'
offices'. He descends by a narrow way (he will soon observe that whilst
so far he has been describing the household arrangements of the rich,
exactly the same topography of division is to be found in modest middle-
class households). He creeps 'cautiously along passages . . . everywhere
is gloom. The light of day never fully enters the apartments . . . there is
something in the very air that feels musty and stagnant'. Entering a servant's room he notices 'a general air of slovenliness and negligence, that
amply represents to [him] the depression and humiliated state of mind
of its tenant'. The thought of a wealthy man maintaining a household
inhabited by 'two different classes of being' enrages him: 'if we were told

---

and Mary Wollstonecraft, University of Kansas Press, 1967, pp. 42–50; Wollstonecraft,
   Thoughts, pp. 19, 60.
3 William Godwin, 'Of Servants', Essay IV in The Enquirer. Reflections on Education, Manners, and Literature. In a Series of Essays, G. G. and J. Robinson, London, 1797, pp.
   201–11.
4 Godwin, 'Of Servants', p. 205.
5 For conjectural history and the four- (or five-) stage model of the past, see Adam Smith,
   'Lectures on Jurisprudence', Works and Correspondence of Adam Smith, R. L. Meek,
   D. D. Raphael, P. G. Stein (eds.), Clarendon Press, Oxford, 1978, vol. 5, pp. 76–8, 175–
   9; Adam Ferguson, An Essay on the History of Civil Society, Boulter Grierson, Dublin,
   1767; John Millar, The Origin of the Distinction of Ranks; or, An Inquiry into the Circumstances which give Rise to Influence and Authority in the Different Members of Society
   (1771) 3rd edn, J. Murray, London, 1779. Also Robert Wokler, 'Anthropology and
   conjectural history in the enlightenment' in Christopher Fox, Roy Porter and Robert
   Wokler (eds.), Inventing Human Science: Eighteenth-century domains, University of California Press, Berkeley, CA, 1995, pp. 31–52; Keith M. Baker, 'Enlightenment and the
   Institution of Society: Notes for a conceptual history' in Willem Melching and Wyger
   Veleman (eds.), Main Trends in Cultural History, Rodopi, Amsterdam, 1994, pp. 95–120.
   The century's most famous conjectural history was Rousseau's: A Discourse on Inequality
   (1755), Penguin, Harmondsworth, 1984, pp. 118–37.

of a man who appropriated a considerable portion of his house to the habitation of rats, and pole-cats, and serpents and wolves, we certainly should not applaud his taste or judgement'.[6]

The servant's depression – of social being, of mind and spirit – is palpable, even though the inhabitant of the squalid room is nowhere to be seen, and makes no appearance in the text. Godwin broods on the two alternatives available to someone like him: servants must either develop a consciousness of their position as subordinates, of that 'monstrous... union of wealth and poverty', or – this was the more likely – introject their depression:

> Servants... must either cherish a burning envy in their bosoms, an inextinguishable abhorrence against the injustice of society; or, guided by the hopelessness of their condition... must blunt every finer feeling of the mind, and sit down in their obscure retreat, having for the constant habits of their reflections, slavery and contentment. They can scarcely expect to emerge from their depression. They must expect to spend the best years of their existence in a miserable dependence.[7]

A 'monstrous association and union of wealth and poverty together' had produced both the servant's consciousness of social difference and his depression of mind and spirit.

Godwin's mental journey to the servants' quarters was not unusual: novelists, playwrights, and anyone who told one of the truly bad servant-jokes that circulated in the later eighteenth-century, had to imagine kitchens (they rarely got as far as a servant's bedroom) in order to forward the plots of their stories, great and small. His diagnosis of depression – a humiliated and lowered state of mind – may well have been learned from the intense discussion of slave psychology that took place during the 1780s and early 1790s. Comparison between chattel slaves and English domestic servants had been conventionalised in a wide range of social theory for the past twenty years. Godwin concluded 'On Servants' with a reference to slavery, but on a gloomier note than many of his contemporaries, who for the main part considered the voluntary service contract a true mark of English freedom. But Godwin thought otherwise: 'it is the condition under which he exists, not the way he came into it, that constitutes the difference between a freeman and a slave'.[8]

---

[6] Godwin, 'Of Servants', p. 204.

[7] Godwin, 'Of Servants', p. 209. For some acute political and philosophical fun had with Godwin's depressed-servant thesis, see Elizabeth Hamilton, *Memoirs of Modern Philosophers. In three volumes*, G. G. and J. Robinson, Bath and London, 1800, vol. 2, pp. 177–94.

[8] He conceded however that 'the slavery of an English servant has its mitigations, and is, in several intelligible and distinct particulars, preferable to that of a West-Indian Negro': 'Of Servants', p. 211.

There were many modern histories available in which the domestic servant was used to trace the happy effects of the climb to civil society. Godwin was typical in framing his servant-question in this way. He was also typical in his gendering of domestic service as male. The contemporary domestic labour force was at least 75 per cent female; Godwin's own dinner was cooked and his linen washed (and soon, his hugger-mugger household of motherless children, brought up) by women, but Godwin did what all commentators on the service economy did – figured the servant as a man. Contemporary debates about the deleterious effects of 'luxury', of which keeping a liveried footman was a prime example, made it difficult to conceptualise the much greater number of young women labouring in the back kitchens of modest households as 'servants', even if there was not the conventions of a gendered language to make imagined men in powdered wigs stand in for them.[9] The servant taxes, inaugurated in 1777 to extract a payment from employers who displayed their opulence by means of a liveried man-servant, reinforced this gendered linguistic usage. This was one of the many ways in which the eighteenth-century servant and her labour were lost to view. Godwin's account of the domestic servant then, and the social theory and conjectural history he used to imagine him, was only unusual in the suggestion that depressed footmen might be the first among the labouring population to develop 'an inextinguishable abhorrence against the injustice of society', or what would be called by some later historians, class consciousness.

Labours Lost offers not so much a new view of eighteenth-century England, as one that allows us to see and understand what William Godwin saw and understood – and what escaped his view – of the society he inhabited. It offers a view of a social realm that all manner of people – masters, magistrates and maidservants – put in place. Domestic servants were a rich resource for thinking about the social order – particularly so among the man- and maidservants who were themselves so frequently used to tell a story of the English constitution and the making of modern society. Domestic servants were used – more than any other social group – to write histories of the social itself. This was an important aspect of their function, not the same as dusting, boot-cleaning and water-carrying but, rather, an involuntary labour, by which they were employed by all manner of legal theorist and political philosopher, to think (or think-through) the

---

[9] For 'luxury', John Sekora, *Luxury: The Concept in Western thought, Eden to Smollett*, Johns Hopkins University Press, Baltimore, 1977; Christopher Berry, *The Idea of Luxury: A conceptual and historical investigation*, Cambridge University Press, Cambridge, 1994; Maxine Berg and Helen Clifford (eds.), *Consumers and Luxury: Consumer culture in Europe 1650–1850*, Manchester University Press, Manchester, 1999; Maxine Berg, *Luxury and Pleasure in Eighteenth-century Britain*, Oxford University Press, Oxford, 2005.

social and its history. There was the labour process involved in making the master's dinner, and there was also the process by which it was conceptualised, in terms of domestic service. In eighteenth-century terms, the woman in the kitchen cooking the family dinner was a *worker*: she had sold her labour for wages; the labour relationship was managed by law; she belonged to the newly emerging category of 'the employed'. Many twentieth-century histories of this time and place found the origins of English class-structure and class consciousness in its workers' experience of life and labour. Histories can now be rewritten with service labour and a largely female workforce in view.

Our view of the way in which gender was embedded in the institutional dimensions of eighteenth-century society is altered when we recognise that women were conceptualised as workers and that a very large component of the general workforce was made up of domestic servants. The law provided the formal means for both the making and understanding of social relations, personhood and identity. It told masters and mistresses, and men and maids, what was the godly and legal nature of what had passed between them when she had agreed at the hiring to wash the baby's nappies for 2s extra a year and a new gown; and he, to churn butter (but not to milk the cows). The employer's capacity to do these things – the employer's labour – had been handed over to the worker, to exercise on his or her behalf; the grace and favour of the law allowed this to happen; both parties were told this. Identity and personhood were shaped by this legal transaction.

The legal handbooks, and the plays, poetry and jokes that inscribed and interrogated these ideas, were at once representations of the social order and, at the same time, part of that social order, because thoughts, words, language, writing, printed texts are – and were – *things*. Historians do not always like this approach, believing perhaps, that it transgresses the boundaries between hard-won historical facts and the mere representation of those facts (people, things, events, happenings) in some kind of text. But material things – jokes, jests and the well-set jam a maidservant had just produced – were objects and entities, part of the social world or the social order. Material things, men and women – and animals, horses in particular – interact in this book because the material world, as it was experienced, allowed them to be *thought with* by all manner of people. A kind of 'flat social' has recently been urged on historians as a conceptual substitute for the term 'society'.[10] But we cannot abandon the notion of

---

[10] Patrick Joyce, 'The Necessity of social history: Putting the social back in social history', *Past and Present*, forthcoming. See Chapter 12. Also Patrick Joyce, (ed.), *Class*, Oxford University Press, Oxford, 1995, pp. 1–6.

a layered, or hierarchical, or ranked society in the English eighteenth-century, not just because so much strenuous intellectual effort was put into *making* or *writing* it as a description of the present and the past, but because, out of their own resources of theory-construction (maidservants were particularly adept at articulating social theory) ordinary men and women thought about, occasionally wrote about, and sometimes contested a world of division, rank and hierarchy. They believed it was *there*.

The service relationship provided a major means to conceptualise the social. Considering the full range of forms with which this thinking was done – jokes, rude poetry and much ruder skits and satires about servants that employers told in tap rooms to amuse their companions and ladies sent in letters to friends – removes political philosophising and what we now call social theory from the province of society's designated thinkers (High Court judges and the like) and locates it in the everyday world, in kitchens in particular. The invented voice of a servant in a novel; an actually existing maidservant's impolite poem about her employers' literary and culinary taste – these were some of the forms with which the service relationship was articulated and argued about. They were expressions of an interest in, a worrying-away at, 'one of the most important and universal relations in the ordinary affairs of life', as one anonymous compiler of the laws that governed service put it in 1831.[11] The domestic servant was 'good to think [with]' in eighteenth-century England.[12]

For these historical actors the social was an already-existing, ever-present thing. There was nothing outside the social, for High Court judges, political philosophers, and employers and servants arguing about details of a hiring agreement in a provincial justicing room. Histories traced the development of social order and social distinction from the remote past to modern commercial refinement. Adam Ferguson said that his work was written to confirm a proposition of the Baron de Montesquieu, that 'Man is born in society... and there he remains'.[13]

---

[11] Anon., *A Familiar Summary of the Laws Respecting Masters and Servants, Apprentices Journeymen, Artificers and Labourers, by the Author of 'Plain Instructions to Executors and Administrators', 'Plain Advice on Wills...'*, Henry Washbourne, London, 1831; William Blackstone, *Commentaries on the Laws of England. In Four Books* (1765), 6th edn, Company of Booksellers, Dublin, 1775, Book 1, p. 422.

[12] The proposition that groups of people, animals – any entities of the natural world – might be good for cognition as well as their more obvious use (for food, in the case of animals) is derived from Claude Levi-Strauss, *Totemism*, Beacon Press, Boston, 1963, p. 89: 'We can understand, too, that natural species are chosen [as totems] not because they are "good to eat" but because they are "good to think".' The 'with' was added by later commentators and translators.

[13] Ferguson, *Essay on... Civil Society*, p. 31.

There was nowhere else to be. Society always had been the context for the human story, for it had been given by God at the beginning of the world. At the end of the seventeenth century, John Locke had affirmed that the first society had pertained between man and wife – our Great Parents – in the Garden of Eden (though he did say that this first society was not a fully political one).[14] Conjectural history of society, like Locke's and Ferguson's, was a description of God's Creation, a constant present in the *now* of the eighteenth century. The social always *had been* made; it inscribed the very limits of what was, and what could be known about past and present. Within this frame, servants – real and figurative – were a means for articulating this knowledge and the everyday tensions and antagonisms of the differentiated world ordered by the Creator.

Why then, if it is possible to understand eighteenth-century society understanding itself in this way, are there so few domestic servants in our conventional historical accounts of this period? Why are they absent from the tabulations of rank, hierarchy, income distribution and social relations, by which many historians measure out eighteenth-century English society?[15] If it is possible to argue, as this book does, that law, labour, and the meaning of things, were articulated around domestic service, why do servants not have a role in social formation in English modernity? Partly because the plot lines of modern social history have a tenacious grip on us all. Adam Smith's 1776 formulation of the servant's labour as a kind of non-work, or anti-work, and Karl Marx's use of the formulation to analyse the occupational structure of modern (1861) capitalist society, underpins much canonical twentieth-century social history.[16] Edward Thompson's *The Making of the English Working-Class* co-joined political reaction to structural changes in the local and national economy with revolutionary events in France and government repression at home, to show how the English working class *made itself*, through experience of life, labour and counter-revolutionary state action.[17] In this famous and enduring account from 1963, servants may be a social fact (footnotes attest this) but they cannot be a part of the working class that made

---

[14] 'The first society was between man and wife, which gave beginning to that between parents and children, to which, in time, that between master and servant came to be added...': John Locke, *Two Treatise on Government* (1689), Dent, London, 1993, p. 153 (*Second Treatise*, Chapter 7).

[15] See, for example, Douglas Hay and Nicholas Rogers, *Eighteenth-century English Society*, Oxford University Press, Oxford, 1997, pp. 17–36.

[16] Adam Smith, *The Wealth of Nations*, Books I–III (1776), Penguin, London, 1986, pp. 430, 133–40; Karl Marx, *Capital*, vol. I (1867) Penguin, Harmondsworth, 1976, p. 574.

[17] E. P. Thompson, *The Making of the English Working Class* (1963), Penguin, Harmondsworth, 1968.

itself, for they were not really . . . workers.[18] Thompson's account of class and class formation has been scrutinised, adjusted, altered, moved back and forward in time and gendered.[19] Historians have been urged to abandon the notion of class altogether, and to substitute for it, the idea of a 'differentiated sociality'.[20] The 'experience' that Thompson understood as the motor of class formation has been used to put in place many more-complex accounts of the way in which identity has been shaped by individual social actors in vastly different social worlds from that of late eighteenth-century England.[21] A litany of objections, revisions and adjustments have been added to the original story. But neither the original nor the revised versions have much to say about domestic servants.

There is also the weight of a sociological concept – 'status' – hanging about the domestic worker. Having determined that domestic service in a household different from a young man's or woman's natal one was a stage in the life cycle of many from the medieval period onwards, it has been an easy step for their historians to discuss servants in terms of Max Weber's distinction between class and status. 'Class' is an active economic relationship to the market, or the productive realm, in contrast with status, which designates groups segregated by distinct criteria from others within society. Servants have sometimes been thought of as an occupational status group, with a distinct style of life based on what they did, where they lived and how they consumed.[22] The production/consumption distinction has also been useful to historians. As it has been almost impossible

---

[18] Thompson, *Making*, pp. 231, 259, 344.

[19] R. J. Morris, *Class and Class Consciousness in the Industrial Revolution, 1789–1850*, Macmillan, London, 1979; R. S. Neale, *Class in English History, 1680–1850*, Basil Blackwell, Oxford, 1981; John Rule, *The Experience of Labour in Eighteenth-century Industry*, Croom Helm, London, 1981; Eric Hobsbawm, *Worlds of Labour: Further studies in the history of labour*, Weidenfeld and Nicolson, London, 1984; Joan Wallach Scott, 'Women in *The Making of the English Working Class*' in *Gender and the Politics of History*, Columbia University Press, New York and London, 1988, pp. 68–90; William H. Sewell, Jnr, 'How classes are made: Critical reflections on E. P. Thompson's theory of working-class formation' in Harvey J. Kaye and Keith McClelland (eds.), *E. P. Thompson: Critical perspectives*, Polity, Cambridge, 1990, pp. 50–77. Catherine Hall, 'The tale of Samuel and Jemima: Gender and working class culture in nineteenth-century England' in Kaye and McClelland, *E. P. Thompson*, pp. 78–102; Anna Clark, *The Struggle for the Breeches: Gender and the making of the British working class*, University of California Press, Berkeley, Los Angeles, CA, and London, 1995; Joyce, *Class*; Andy Wood, *The Politics of Social Conflict: The Peak Country, 1520–1770*, Cambridge University Press, Cambridge, 1999.

[20] Joyce, *Class*, pp. 183–5; Geoff Eley and Keith Neild, *The Future of Class in History: What's left of the social?*, University of Michigan Press, Ann Arbor, 2007, pp. 1–8.

[21] Eley and Neild, *Future of Class*, pp. 35–40.

[22] Max Weber, 'Class, status and party' (1924) in H. Gerth and C. W. Mills (eds), *From Max Weber: Essays in sociology*, Routledge and Kegan Paul, London, 1991, pp. 180–95; Reinhard Bendix, 'Inequality and social structure: A comparison of Marx and Weber', *American Sociological Review*, 39: 2 (1974), 149–61.

to understand domestic workers as part of an emerging social class, they have been described as one of the first groups of consumers in the new market of fashionable goods and clothing, albeit involuntary ones.[23]

In *Economy and Society* Weber described a 'status contract'; it was the way in which one unrelated person could become the legal dependant of another, by the nature of the agreement between them.[24] In the English eighteenth century, there were powerful Christian narratives to promote the thesis that master and servant were really relations; each part of the other. Religious tract material repeated the injunction that the servant was bound in obedience and subordination to a master who was also a kind of father; it promoted the Biblical texts that carried this message well into the nineteenth century. High Court judges sometimes appeared to aver the principle too, for was not the perfection of the English common law that it embodied the tenets of the reformed faith? But despite all the repeated prescriptions for godly relations within a household, as far as I can discover, the anonymous author of a *Laws Concerning Master and Servants* of 1785 was the last *legal* voice to aver that 'Master and Servants are Relatives'; and in any case, his declaration was accompanied by a brisk affirmation of modern contractual relations: 'And a Servant in the Intendment of our Law seems to be such a one as by Agreement and retainer oweth Duty and Service to another, who therefore is called Master.'[25] Legal voices are not necessarily the most important ones, and they may not express common understandings and perceptions. Naomi Tadmor has argued that in this period the term 'family' was used in everyday life, and in a wide range of literature including legal literature, to describe households of people living together, including servants.[26] But servants *in* a household were not necessarily *of* the family. They were there by legal arrangement (by 'Agreement and retainer'). Even the 1785 proclamation of status from a much older religious and political world

---

[23] John Styles, 'Involuntary consumers? Servants and their clothes in eighteenth-century England', *Textile History*, 33:1 (2002), 9–21.

[24] Max Weber, *Economy and Society: An outline of interpretive sociology* (1925), Guenther Roth and Claus Wittich (eds.), Bedminster Press, New York, 1968, vol. 2, p. 672; Robert J. Steinfeld, *The Invention of Free Labour: The employment relation in English and American law and culture, 1350–1870*, University of North Carolina Press, Chapel Hill and London, 1991, pp. 56–7.

[25] Gentleman of the Inner Temple, *Law Concerning Master and Servants, Viz Clerks to Attornies and Solicitors . . . Apprentices . . . Menial Servants . . . Labourers, Journeymen, Artificers, Handicraftmen and other Workmen*, His Majesty's Law Printer, London, 1785, p. 1, quoting William Sheppard, *A Grand Abridgment of the Common and Statute Law of England alphabetically digested under proper heads . . .* , Richard and Edward Atkyns, London, 1675.

[26] Naomi Tadmor, *Family and Friends in Eighteenth-Century England: Household, Kinship and Patronage*, Cambridge University Press, Cambridge, 2001, pp. 1–35.

confirmed the modern legal commentator's brisk view that 'servitude is nothing else but plain Contract, and to be guided by the Rules and Conditions of that Bargain Invariably'.[27] And linguistic usage ('my family' to include household servants) is no consistent guide to meaning. It depended on circumstances. The formulations of employers protesting to the servant-tax appeal commissioners that their Man was not *really* a servant (not a taxable item) says as much. A grocer's shopman did 'little matters for the use of the family' said his master to the Northamptonshire commissioners in 1778; a Derbyshire landowner said that his stable boy (so called by the tax assessor) *did* go into Derby 'on family errands', but doing that did not make him a servant. These employers were attempting to deny that their servants *were* servants in order to avoid paying tax; but in all the services they did admit to, men and boys were described as doing things *for* a family of which they were *not* a part. If these employers had been asked to reckon up family size, they may well have included their Boys, Men and Maidservants. But in these immediate circumstances linguistic usage reflected social and domestic reality. Their servants were not running their own errands or cleaning their own boots. They served the family unit; they were not part of it.[28]

The most eminent legal theorist of them all, William Blackstone, said that the relationship between employer and servant was 'founded in convenience', when a man is 'directed to call in the assistance of others, when his own skill and labour will not be sufficient to answer the cares incumbent upon him'.[29] There was a strong implication in ensuing legal discussions that the labour 'really' belonged to the employer – was a capacity or attribute of him or her – and that the servant had been employed to perform, or act out, the potential labour of the he or she who had bought the servant's energies and time. This proposition was much pondered in eighteenth-century England; it was articulated across a range of cultural and literary forms; jokes were made about the servant as a kind of extra limb, or prosthesis, of the employer. Much painful fun was had with the idea of the servant as an automata, thing, or non-person.[30] There was very little expression of status in this vast outpouring of legal and cultural

---

[27] John Taylor, *Elements of the Civil Law*, privately printed, Cambridge, 1767, p. 413.

[28] Commissioners of Excise, *Abstract of Cases and Decisions on Appeals Relating to the Tax on Servants*, T. Longman and T. Cadell, London, 1781 (Northamptonshire, 1 Feb. 1779; Derbyshire, 14 Dec. 1778).

[29] Blackstone, *Commentaries*, p. 422.

[30] Carolyn Steedman, 'Servants and their relationship to the unconscious', *Journal of British Studies*, 42 (2003), 316–50. For automata, Anon., *Reflections on the Relative Situations of Master and Servant, Historically and Politically Considered; the Irregularities of Servants; the Employment of Foreigners; and the General Inconveniencies Resulting from the Want of Proper Regulations*, W. Miller, London, 1800, p. 10.

Figure 3. George Woodward, Manservant Wearing Apron.

commentary; very little of the vision that informs much modern sociology and anthropology of waged domestic work. Eighteenth-century employers ordered their servants about, denigrated, sneered and laughed at them; in a violent society they exercised physical violence towards them; servants were called a variety of insulting and demeaning names. One 1800 guide to the management of maidservants told employers that their psychology was shaped by 'the repeated tales [told] to degrade them'.[31] But servants' function and purpose was not *to be* ordered about, denigrated and verbally abused, for example in the manner that Araminta Wright finds to be the case in modern Peru. She observes of service in 1990s Lima that 'All maids are *cholas* and having a maid to order about is key in the ability to *cholear*, a verb created specially for the task of

---

[31] Anon., *Hints to Masters and Mistresses, Respecting Female Servants*, Darnton and Harvey, London, 1800, p. 5.

putting others down. *Yo choleo*, I cuss. *Tu choleas*, you cuss. *El/Ella cholea*, he/she cusses. If you have a *cholo* maid it automatically excludes you from being a *cholo* yourself for it puts you in the class of ordering and not of obeying.'[32] Investigating domestic service in nineteenth-century Brazil, Sandra Graham suggests that a similar relationship of subordination – at least in Rio de Janeiro – arose from absence of legal regulation. Free women and slaves working as domestics counted as 71 per cent of all Rio's working women in the 1870s. There were no public institutions for them to appeal to, to counter the *patrao*'s power; neither was there a slave code to regulate relations between owner and owned; the will of the master was the paramount authority within the household unit for all its workers.[33] The system was strongly inflected by the experience of slavery and racial categorisation (as is the one Wright describes for modern Lima, in the second regard).

There were slaves in eighteenth-century England, for the main part bought by naval captains in the Americas as cheap servants – or so contemporaries believed. Their presence, and their encounters with the common and poor law, provided a rich resource for lawyers and constitutional historians thinking through the service relationship. But there was a notable reluctance to make English slave-servants subjects of the kind of joke, anecdote, satire and sheer rudeness that domestics were subjected to. The *institution* of slavery was important for legal and constitutional historians describing a modern social order coming into being; the slave – the figure of the chattel slave – was a most economical way of depicting the happy position of the meanest he or she in England, who enjoyed self-possession and legal rights in a society that had long abandoned vassalage – a convenient lesson in the gratitude that working people ought to feel at their 'Condition . . . [as] Servants in comparison with that of many others . . . in Other Times and Places, which have been, and are compelled to Slavery'. Maybe, pondering these things, they might do 'their *Work heartily, without grudging*'? 'Have you never heard of Slaves in the Plantations, and how they are used . . . by some who are more savage than the Negroes they call so?'[34] Slavery and slave-servants also figured in the newish genre of literature for children that flourished from

---

[32] Araminta Wright, *Ripped and Torn: Levi's, Latin America and the blue jean dream*, Ebury Press, London, 2006, p. 34. Also Jennifer Clement, *A True Story Based on Lies*, Canongate, Edinburgh, 2001.

[33] Sandra Lauderdale Graham, *House and Street: The domestic world of servants in nineteenth-century Rio de Janeiro*, Cambridge University Press, Cambridge, 1988, pp. 1–13, 123.

[34] Anon., *A Present for Servants, from their Ministers, Masters, or Other Friends*, 10th edn, J. F. and C. Rivington, for the SPCK, London, 1787, pp. 58–9.

the mid-century onwards.[35] Its mission was educational. It was written, and parents of the polite classes bought it, to teach children civility: about kindness to animals, servants and other social inferiors. But slaves in England (though that is not the correct way to describe them; they had no legal existence, and there was no name to call them) were not laughed at, or made into jokes about inferior persons enacting the labour that 'really' belonged to the masters and mistresses. This reluctance had something to do with the mechanism of the jokes that employers made: about whom and what was fit vehicle for sneering and laughing deprecation. Hester Thrale (whose experience with her servants threads its way through this book) made no jokes about her troublesome, rejecting and disdainful daughters (their attitude towards her was a hurt that lay too close for laughter), but scarcely ever paused in the stream of witticisms concerning her domestics. Servant-jokes were *legal* jokes: they examined the anxieties, terrors and profundities of the legal fiction that servants were 'really' the master or mistress, a detached body-part enacting the employer's atrophied – certainly unused – labour power. Not being persons, of any kind or degree, slaves did not substitute for or enact any part of the owner's capacity. Rather, they were labour embodied: labour itself.

The late twentieth-century rise in household service and the development of a global economy of waged domestic work has given rise to a similar kind of commentary. Much of it is written in terms that eighteenth-century employers might recognise, though now novels rather than jest books intertwine histories and sociologies of domestic service to tell a story of how we got to be the way we are. Maggie Gee's *My Cleaner* (2005) reworks the eighteenth-century's most famous servant story. Samuel Richardson's Pamela from 1740 is a servant who *writes*. In fact the fiction – the joke – is that the book you hold in your hands was really penned by a fifteen-year-old Bedfordshire cottager's daughter, servant in a Bedfordshire upper gentry household. What Mary Tendo, the Ugandan 'help' of *My Cleaner* ('I am not your cleaner!') of London-based writer Vanessa Henman turns out to have been doing all along, is producing a novel.[36] Her writing is the source of strange thumping from her bedroom, which 'the Henman', in an excess of cultural sensitivity, has thought to be Ugandan food-preparation – perhaps the movement of a pestle in a mortar? It is in fact the sound of a word-processor in

[35] Mitzi Myers, '"Servants as They are now Educated": Women writers and Georgian pedagogy', *Essays in Literature*, 16 (1989), 51–69; Jan Fergus, *Provincial Readers in Eighteenth-Century England*, Oxford University Press, Oxford, 2006, pp. 118–54; Dorothy Kilner, *The Life and Perambulations of a Mouse*, 2nd edn, John Marshall, London, 1787, pp. 61–2.
[36] Maggie Gee, *My Cleaner*, SAQI, London, 2005.

use. As befits such a profound acknowledgement of *Pamela*, this discussion of the service relationship is conducted with much edgy hilarity, in several voices, and from shifting perspective. Gee's text, like Richardson's, prevents conclusion, the determination of what 'really' happened and whether or not it was really Mary Tendo (or Pamela Andrews) who really (or fictionally) wrote what you have just finished reading. Fay Weldon's *She May Not Leave* (2005) is structured by a series of extended aphorisms about servants and the service relationship; its characters speak a social history of twentieth-century waged domestic work.[37] Agnieska the au pair (the one who doesn't leave) ends up with the husband, the baby, marriage and the house. These were not the eighteenth-century mistress's fears to any great degree (though she may well have read the fairy-tale *Pamela*, in which the humble heroine nets Mr B.). Her fear was that the servant *would* leave, 'run away' to a place that gave her 1s a month more, tea to her breakfast, and a new pair of stays, leaving her frantic, with no cook for the dinner, the house cow unmilked, slut's wool under the beds, and a screaming, dirty baby. The majority of master-and-servant disputes discussed in this book were brought to a local magistrate by employers complaining about servants leaving their place before time.

Modern domestic-service literature like Gee's and Weldon's, hilarious and thought-provoking though it is, works with a narrower range of references than did the eighteenth-century variety. Eighteenth-century writers were able to draw on a rich repertoire of everyday and scholarly thinking about servants, who embodied important propositions about social order, social organisation and relationships within civil society. Writers and the servant-characters they invented knew that they were bound together in systems of difference, antagonism and exasperation within one shared social order. But the use of contemporary history and sociology to plot a novel might well have been recognised. Weldon's *She May Not Leave* and Gee's *My Cleaner* make reference to recent sociological investigation of domestic work. Historians too, have been influenced by this sociology, by one of its central assumptions: that the labour a working woman sold when she went into service comprised her own 'natural' capacities and abilities. What she exchanged for wages was something she would do anyway (scrubbing, scouring, cooking) in her own or her parents' home, but was now taken onto the market place and exchanged for cash (at the end of the year's hiring), for food and living accommodation (and maybe, a new pair of stays). This powerful understanding was articulated

---

[37] Fay Weldon, *She May Not Leave* (2005), Harper, London, 2006, pp. 33, 92, 116–17, 128.

in 1970s sociology of housework and in the Wages for Housework movement.[38] It made significant theoretical advances in understanding housework as labour, but only when performed by a 'housewife', not by a waged worker.[39] The new feminist economics has revived the domestic-labour debate in inventive new ways; but the focus remains women's unpaid housework, not waged domestic workers.[40]

In 1974, sociologist Ann Oakley outlined the way in which girls were and had been inducted into domestic roles. The way in which 'preparation for housewifery [was] intermingled with socialization for the feminine gender role', was a transhistorical process.[41] 1970s and 1980s women's history used this sociology to write a past in which servants were conceptually attached to the housewives who lost autonomy, individuality and independence during England's long transition to industrial capitalism. In these histories, the family economy was eroded; the household was no longer the focus of production; middle-class women were relegated to the home: 'the most enduring consequence of industrialisation has been the emergence of the modern role of housewife as "the dominant mature feminine role"', said Oakley, evoking this history.[42] As alternative analyses of waged domestic work in the past were not available, servants have for the main part continued to occupy the role assigned them by late twentieth-century sociology and social history. Bridget Hill's study of women, work and sexual politics in eighteenth-century England was framed by the imperative to find the origins of modern women's oppression: 'The notion that "housework is women's work" influenced every attempt to train women for future work roles and influenced the

---

[38] Ann Ferguson, 'Feminist perspectives on class and work', *Stanford Encyclopedia of Philosophy*, www.plato.stanford.edu/archives/fall2004/entries/ferguson/; Maria Dalla Costa, *The Power of Women and the Subversion of the Community*, Falling Wall Press, Bristol, 1974; Sylvia Federici, 'Wages against housework' in Ellen Malos (ed.), *The Politics of Housework*, New Clarion Press, New York, 1975, pp. 187–94.

[39] Deborah Fahy Bryceson and Ulla Vuovela, 'Outside the domestic labour debate: Towards a theory of modes of human reproduction', *Review of Radical Political Economies*, 16:2/3 (1984), 137–66; Euston Quah, 'Persistent problems in measuring household production', *American Journal of Economics and Sociology*, 45:2 (1986), 235–46; Leopoldina Fortunati, *The Arcane of Reproduction: Housework, prostitution, labor and capital* (1981), Autonomedia, New York, 1995.

[40] Anne Phillips and Barbara Taylor, 'Sex and skill: Notes towards a feminist economics', *Feminist Review*, 6 (1980), 79–88; Marianne A. Ferber and Julie A. Nelson, *Beyond Economic Man: Feminist theory and economics*, University of Chicago, Chicago, 1993.

[41] Ann Oakley, *The Sociology of Housework* (1974), Basil Blackwell, Oxford, 1985, p. 113. Also Ann Oakley, *Woman's Work: The housewife past and present* (1974), Vintage, New York, 1976, pp. 233–41.

[42] Oakley, *Woman's Work*, pp. 24–43; p. 32, quoting Talcott Parsons, 'The social structure of the family' in Ruth N. Ashen (ed.), *The Family: Its functions and destiny*, Harper, New York, 1949, p. 193.

Figure 4. Maid Sweeping. This is a child. The broom is far too big for her.

way in which their working identities, in whatever occupation, were seen and evaluated.'[43] The origin of this notion was the eighteenth century she said, when a 'blurring of all definition of [women's] working identities' took place; it continued to the present day. It was closely related to 'the recruitment of domestic servants in the second half of the century to do the household tasks dictated by a newly acquired affluence . . . and with it a new gentility that found such tasks distasteful and demeaning'.[44] With this picture in place, it is difficult to find a place for servants as workers, or to see the housework they performed as waged labour.

But eighteenth-century domestic servants were not the type of working woman that the twenty-first century sociological imagination reads out of gender history. They were not interpellated by the reforming imagination, and made – shamefully – to connive in the project of reforming their bodies, their voice, their dress. They were not dirty, disgusting (all terms used in the recent literature on this imagination) social others.[45] They *were* complained about, daily and insistently. They *were* called rude and denigrating names. But James Boswell for example, wondered about

[43] Bridget Hill, *Women, Work and Sexual Politics in Eighteenth-Century England*, Basil Black-well, Oxford, 1989, p. 123.
[44] Hill, *Women, Work . . .* , p. 124.
[45] Beverley Skeggs, 'The making of class through visualising moral subject formation', *Sociology*, 39:5 (2005), 965–82.

sleeping with a cookmaid, as if for all the world she were just another woman (we shall explore the outrage to our modern sensibilities and those of eighteenth-century cooks in a later chapter). Ann Walker pleaded with an imagined audience of maidservants to consider *her* feelings over the startling appearance of one of them in a new gown *like hers:* 'Can you believe any mistress can be pleased . . . no sooner [she] puts on a new thing, than her maid immediately jumps in something as like as she can?' Some have described the maidservant's new gown (and all the new consumer goods she got hold of) as cheap and showy; but Ann Walker did not see it like that. If it were just like hers, it was surely neither of those things.[46]

Recent history and sociology of service has also defined it – covertly or overtly – as a relationship between women, past and present, rather than as a wage relationship, or a legal and social relationship. Modern domestic service may be seen as constitutive of class, ethnic and racial categories in some societies, but those very categories originate in deeply divisive and antagonistic relationships between women: 'until domestic service ends, there will be no possibility of solidarity . . . among women'.[47] (There are few men in modern accounts of waged domestic work. Male servants were a minority of eighteenth-century domestic workers, but they did exist, did housework and childcare, and were used as much as women were to inscribe the contemporary social order and its history; it must be possible to write a gendered history of domestic labour and labour relationships that includes them.) At the end of *The Servant Problem*, an account of waged domestic work in a modern Britain embedded in global economies of labour, Rosie Cox has many practical solutions to offer to those who employ servants – nannies, cleaners, au pairs – as well as those responsible for the 10,000 or so people who currently work in wealthy 'formal households', as 'traditional' domestics.[48] For modern cleaners and carers there is the route of trade union organisation. But the real solution lies with the employer. It is she who should deal with the considerable guilt that feeds into the service relationship, says Cox;

---

[46] Margaret Bailey (ed.), *Boswell's Column. Being his Seventy Contributions to the London Magazine, under the Pseudonym The Hypochondriac from 1777–1783*, p. 99, No. XVII 'On Cookery' (Feb. 1779); Ann Walker, *A Complete Guide for a Servant Maid; or, the Sure Means of Gaining Love and Esteem*, T. Sabine, London, 1787, pp. 20–1; Styles, 'Involuntary consumers'.

[47] Heidi Tinsman, 'The indispensable service of sisters: Considering domestic service in United States and Latin American studies', *Journal of Women's History*, 4:1 (1992), 37–59.

[48] Rosie Cox, *The Servant Problem: Domestic employment in a global economy*, I. B Tauris, London, 2006, pp. 125–46; Alexandra Jones, *Domestics: UK domestic workers and their reluctant employers*, The Work Foundation, London, 2004.

a guilt that prevents her from treating her cleaner as a worker to whom she has ordinary responsibilities. (And men could do more housework; or women could stop worrying about standards of cleanliness and order.) Women's guilt about employing cleaners and carers comes perhaps, says Cox, from not wanting to be the sort of person who employs them in the first place: 'employers of domestic workers have much more complicated feelings about their position than employers in other situations and this tends to stop them wanting to take on that role in a straightforward way'.[49] Solutions to the global inequalities embodied in the domestic-service relationship will come with the employer's recognition that she purchases cheap overseas labour and thus sustains poverty.

Cox's account is not given from the standpoint of the domestic servant, except when a cleaner's or an au pair's experience of exploitation and cruelty is recorded by the researcher. In the 1970s and 1980s the new feminist and labour history worked hard to rescue domestic servants from historical silence, but preferred to hear them tell of physical violence rather than listen to their loud opinions on an inequitable labour regime, or notice their effective and intelligent access of a legal system that this current book records. The historical story of women's oppression deeply inflects much recent sociology of migrant domestic labour. But we can look to the places eighteenth-century domestic workers chose to speak rather than to our own assumptions about their silence and suffering – to Elizabeth Hands's poetry for example. In 1789, with the apparent encouragement of her employers, this Warwickshire maidservant published two extraordinary poems satirising them (as well as exploring the edgy business of doing what she was doing: writing verse about them). Eighteenth-century servants' experience of domestic labour is no more available than that of their twenty-first century counterparts; but there was perhaps more of it recorded, because of the variety of cultural forms in which it could be expressed, and because the law recognised the service relationship and regulated it. Domestic workers in *The Servant Problem* are almost entirely unregulated, working in the informal economy for cash in hand. That is why they constitute a category for Cox's investigations. As she says, there is very great deal of investment on both sides of the relationship, in keeping things that way, 'relatively safe from detection'.[50] In eighteenth-century England on the other hand, the recognition of domestic workers by common and statute law, made the relationship an open one, available for scrutiny and commentary.

In the constant movement between history and sociology in recent accounts of domestic service, the history evoked is foreshortened, or

---

[49] Cox, *Servant Problem*, pp. 54, 133.   [50] *Ibid.*, p. 48.

concentrated in a reference point of the wealthy, hierarchical household of the late Victorian period.[51] (In the UK the 1970s television series 'Upstairs, Downstairs', set in a very grand London establishment at the turn of the twentieth century, has exercised a mighty fascination over the common historical imagination, including that of historians.[52]) But the large household (the sort William Godwin imagined) with ranks of servants designated by name and job-description, was the minority in both eighteenth- and nineteenth-century England. Employers were most likely to rely on one, or at most two, domestics, and a number of bought-in cleaners, scrubbers and washers. And by way of striking contrast with the twenty-first century, the young woman or man who was a permanent servant in the eighteenth-century household was a contracted employee, who possessed rights within the relationship that could be – and sometimes were – upheld by law. The story of nineteenth-century and indeed, twentieth-century domestic service, is to do with those legal rights being substantially lost. The eighteenth-century hired domestic servant's contractual status and legal persona make her or him difficult to compare with unregulated, informal twenty-first century domestics. The cash-in-hand, informal transactions by which the modern service economy operates were also a means of managing the ordinary business of eighteenth-century life. But because casual domestic work was not assessed for tax purposes, there was no point to hiding it from view, as the work of modern cleaners and carers is hidden.

And it is not clear that any eighteenth-century employer of domestic servants saw things in the way of modern history and sociology of service – saw the daughters of the labouring poor as possessing a house-working capacity either 'natural' or the result of socialisation. Few of them, in the elite and middle-class employer's view, had any experience of the work needed to sweep *this* house, scour *these* iron vessels, prepare a joint of veal for roasting, here and now, in this employer's kitchen. Employers complained that the children of the poor lacked the most elementary skills for keeping everyday life in their household going. As far as Hester Thrale was concerned, no household work at all was 'natural' to the teenager Laura Carter.[53]

The dislocation between what the household servant actually did, and what the employer wanted to be done, has been noted by modern investigators, though perhaps inadvertently. In *Servicing the Middle Classes*

---

[51] Deborah Valenze, *The First Industrial Woman*, Oxford University Press, Oxford and New York, 1995, pp. 167–8.
[52] *Upstairs, Downstairs*, dirs. Bill Bain and Derek Bennett, 1971–5.
[53] See Prologue.

(1983) Nicky Gregson and Michelle Lowe report a conversation with a cleaner who more than anything else, hates polishing. Her 'lady' likes her to use a wax polish; she would rather whip round with a can of Pledge.[54] There are elaborate and very different knowledges – about things and labour – articulated in this difference. The employer thinks of her furniture, some of it antique; she knows about the needs of wood – how it needs 'feeding' (it is actually not very good for good furniture to get the multi-surface spray treatment). The cleaner thinks about time and effort and the true drag of trying to raise a shine on a surface wiped with beeswax. Why should she care about the needs of early Victorian rosewood? (It is actually really hard work, polishing with wax. 'Elbow-grease', and 'put some elbow into it' emerged from exactly this kind of labour.) Young women in eighteenth-century England listened amiably to their mistress's instructions for cleaning a stew pan, to warnings just learned from the latest advice literature, about never pickling in copper vessels, and then as soon as she had left the back-kitchen, did it their way. The mute obduracy of the servant, or her loud refusal to do it the way they wanted, was a consistent complaint of employers, in published advice material, and in their private writing.

The categories of domestic work that modern researchers sometimes feel impelled to use sometimes just do not work. Bridget Anderson has noted how the ILO International Standard Classification of Occupations (frequently used in investigations of labour markets, past and present) does not include child care on the list of domestic helpers' and cleaners' tasks.[55] The effect of this is not only omission in recent studies of women and men who do the work of child care as well as housework, but also the neglect of an important historical dimension to studies of the commercialisation of intimate life. Eighteenth-century parents bought care for their children. (So of course did parents in many other times and places.) The extraordinary complexities of the relationships that ensued, the measuring of whatever was the 'love' that had been purchased and the servants' feelings in the matter were expressed in sometimes terrifying ways. The case of fifteen-year-old child-maid Ann Mead (discussed in Chapter 8) who in 1800 killed her employers' baby, can help make plainer the modern agonies of affection bought and sold, as described by Arlie

---

[54] Nicky Gregson and Michelle Lowe, *Servicing the Middle Class: Class, gender and waged domestic labour in contemporary Britain*, Routledge, London, 1994.

[55] Bridget Anderson, *Doing the Dirty Work? The global politics of domestic labour*, Zed Books, London, 2000, pp. 15–16; International Labour Organisation, ISCO 9131, 'Domestic helpers and cleaners', www.ilo.org/.

Hochschild and Barbara Ehrenreich.[56] Hired to bake and brew, wash children and love them, the servant could make a very clear statement about the purchase of love and intimacy.[57]

This book is organised by the idea of possession – many of its chapter headings indicate as much. Who owned the servant's labour and its products? What kind of possession, or property, was the capacity to work? How was it conceptualised and understood? And how did contemporary labour-theory (though it not yet at all certain that we should be calling it that) connect with reformulations of the human subject, by which self and personhood could be conceived of – by ordinary people as well as legal philosophers – as another kind of thing which could be owned? These are the terms in which eighteenth-century people (magistrates in their sessions as well as the maidservant before the bench) thought through these questions, and they are terms to guide any answers there might be to them. The law was an important resource for such thinking, not only because theorists like Sir William Blackstone and a Chief Justice like the Earl of Mansfield said it was, but because the law – its assumptions, principles and practices – was a certain presence in plebeian lives, shaped the course of so many of them, demanded self-narratives (autobiographies) of applicants for poor relief for example and in this way forced self-reflexivity on many people (who may well rather have done without it; got the dole they were asking for; or 6d a week in bread instead).[58] The law was a major means for understanding who and what you were, your relationship to the wider social order and to the polity. In *Annals of the Labouring Poor*, Keith Snell wanted to emphasise 'the effects of the law on the quality of life: on wages and employment, work discipline and, primarily, on the quality of social relationships'. For him, the old poor law provides the key 'to a social understanding of the eighteenth century'.[59] This book builds on that powerful insight, to show how in practice poor law interacted with labour and employment law to affect working lives in yet more pervasive ways.

---

[56] Arlie Russell Hochschild, *The Commercialisation of Intimate Life: Notes from home and work*, University of California Press, Berkeley, Los Angeles, CA, and London, 2003; Barbara Ehrenreich and Arlie Russell Hochschild, *Global Woman: Nannies, maids and sex workers in the new economy*, Granta, London, 2003.

[57] Carolyn Steedman, *Master and Servant: Love and labour in the English industrial age*, Cambridge University Press, Cambridge, 2007, Chapters 9 and 10. See also Julia Wrigley, 'Feminists and domestic workers', *Feminist Studies*, 17:2 (1991), 317–29.

[58] Carolyn Steedman, 'Enforced narratives: Stories of another self' in Tess Cosslett, Celia Lury and Penny Summerfield (eds.), *Feminism and Autobiography: Texts, theories, methods*, Routledge, London, 2000, pp. 25–39.

[59] K. D. M. Snell, *Annals of the Labouring Poor: Social change and agrarian England 1660–1900*, Cambridge University Press, Cambridge, 1985, p. 104.

In this book when the word 'servant' is used, it describes a person, male or female, who performed domestic work for some kind of recompense, unless it is otherwise stated that it is 'servants in husbandry' or servants of a master in trade, craft or manufacturing who are being discussed. 'All those who worked for others for compensation on whatever terms were in some sense "serving" their masters', says Robert Steinfeld. It was not simply a linguistic hangover from Tudor legislation to call labourers, artificers and other workers 'servants'; 'the broader usage of the term "servant" [captured the] common qualities of all versions of labor relationship'.[60] But I intend to be absolutely clear in my use of the term 'servant' here: a servant is, unless labelled otherwise, a waged domestic worker. (Though the question of wages in 'waged domestic work' raises further problems, because as the judges of the Court of King's Bench several times pointed out, it was not necessary for any wages to have been paid to a person hired as a servant for them to gain a settlement under the old poor law. It was the fact of contract that counted, not monies handed over.) Eighteenth-century domestic servants, the majority of them working in single- or two-servant households, did all sorts, in a era when 'housework' did not have the narrow connotations of 'indoors', 'in a house or other dwelling place'. She (sometimes he) mopped the floors, milked the house cow, turned out a bedroom, fed the pigs, hoed in the vegetable garden, washed the baby's nappies, and helped with the hay if the family was growing a cash crop. She was no more bound by the occupational category bestowed on her by later demographers and historians than were the laundresses who were street traders from time to time, or the multitasking farm labourer who spent a lot of time driving the cart into Taunton to take his mistress's library books back to the Book Society. (Chapter 3)

Labours Lost covers the period from about 1760 to about 1830, in this way attempting to fill a gap in existing historical accounts of domestic service in England. There are good histories of early-modern service and service in the first half of the eighteenth century (though they deal mainly with the London labour market).[61] Service in the Victorian period in the UK is well covered, and innovative work on twentieth-century

---

[60] Steinfeld, *Invention of Free Labor*, pp. 18–21, 85–6, 102–5.
[61] Peter Earle, 'The female labour market in London in the late seventeenth and early eighteenth centuries', *Economic History Review*, 42:3 (1989), 328–53; *A City Full of People: Men and women of London, 1650–1750*, Methuen, London, 1994; D. A. Kent, 'Ubiquitous but invisible: Female domestic servants in mid-eighteenth-century London', *History Workshop Journal*, 28 (1989), 111–28; Tim Meldrum, *Domestic Service and Gender, 1660–1750: Life and work in the London household*, Longman, London, 2000.

servants is beginning to emerge.[62] Perhaps gap-filling is a puerile thing –
no justification for a book – but historians do love doing it.[63] More
important to begin with is a modern colonial world put in place in the
1760s: new political and territorial maps were traced over the global
distances laid out by trade, commerce in men and goods, and godly
conquest, over the preceding three hundred years. Law and government
adjusted many arrangements in domestic civil society to the economy
of war. There were interludes of peace between the end of the Seven
Years War in 1763 and the American Wars (and the French Wars, and
Revolutionary Wars), but not many. The ability of the British state to
mobilise its wealth allowed an extraordinarily sustained military effort
over many decades; it allowed an Empire to be made. The administrative
edifice put in place in England at the end of the seventeenth century
extended its reach over many lives. As John Brewer remarks, 'even the
most humble of subjects became part of an economic order whose scope
and complexity rendered it liable to fiscal measurement, and vulnerable
to wartime adjustment'.[64]

This economic order was underpinned and promoted by law. According to Paul Craven and Doug Hay in *Masters, Servants and Magistrates
in Britain and the Empire*, labour law originating in the English fourteenth century was to operate on a global scale in the four centuries
that followed.[65] A restless, unceasing search for 'hands', for embodied
labour – from anyone, from anywhere – that would carry, heave, dig,
shove . . . an economic system into being, is the great historical story
told by the fifteen contributors to their book. They describe the survival and spread of English labour law into (literally) a thousand colonial
settings – and by default perhaps, make the original body of law appear
much more stable and coherent than it ever was in practice. In England,

---

[62] Leonore Davidoff, 'Mastered for life: Servant and wife in Victorian and Edwardian
England', *Journal of Social History*, 7:4 (1974), 406–20; Edward Higgs, 'Domestic servants and households in Victorian England', *Social History*, 8:2 (1983), 201–10; Valenze,
First Industrial Woman; Antoinette Fauve-Chamoux (ed.), *Domestic Service and the Formation of European Identity: Understanding the globalization of domestic work, 16th–21st
Centuries*, Peter Lang, New York and Oxford, 2004; Selina Todd, *Young Women, Work
and Family in England 1918–1950*, Oxford University Press, Oxford, 2005.
[63] 'You know how it is, fellow historians – you look for a little patch not trod too hard
by other footsteps, where maybe, you can grow a few sweetpeas', says John Updike, in
ironic role as historian-narrator of *Memoirs of the Ford Administration* (1993), Penguin,
London, 2007, p. 45.
[64] John Brewer, *The Sinews of Power: War, money and the English state, 1688–1783*, Unwin
Hyman, London, 1989, pp. 42, 183.
[65] Douglas Hay and Paul Craven (eds.), *Masters, Servants and Magistrates in Britain and
the Empire, 1562–1955*, University of North Carolina Press, Chapel Hill and London,
2004.

the complex relationship between poor law and labour law, countless individual decisions by magistrates, masters, and servants to mobilise it – any law to hand to order the ordinary exigencies of life and for personal purposes soon to be forgotten – must make us question its status. The determinations of magistrates did not – could not – make legal precedent; rather, they reflected an unstable system, punctuated by vast areas of not-knowing: magistrates' not knowing what the law was in the first place, how it had been used in the recent or the distant past or for what purposes. In *Masters, Servants and Magistrates*, in whatever social and cultural context, under whatever colonial legal regime, master and servant law is described as 'a marvel of efficiency, coercion and finality'.[66] But 'at home', in its medieval English origins and in its use well into the nineteenth century, it served myriad individual purposes *because* it was inefficient – or rather because it could be accessed from many different perspectives and for so many different purposes, and because no determination or judgment was ever final. It reworked and redefined the relationships of the social order, between employer and all kind of servant and worker, particularly by means of the poor laws (which contemporaries also understood, from time to time, as a system of police, a means of ordering and managing the relationships of civil society, and as labour law). One of the endpoints to this book is the early decades of the new century, for there was peace (or, a formal end to a historical 'period'). And then in 1834 the Poor Law Amendment Act inaugurated radical changes in the legal status and lives of domestic servants (and a great many others).[67] If you consider the experience of working people living through these years, you must focus on the 1790s, as does this book: a decade of harvest failure, hunger and state repression in time of war. The servant's labour, and labouring bodies in general, were rethought under the propulsion of hunger: hunger experienced and hunger anticipated.

A series of chapters is interspersed with shorter essays, to do with topics and themes that expand the main line of inquiry. I stole this form of organisation from Kathryn Hughes after reading her biography of Isabella Beaton – which would not also be the brilliant account it is, of texts as social things, without her 'Interludes'.[68] I hope that this book will be read chronologically, with its interludes, in order to discover eighteenth-century servants, contrary to their historical reputation, as a workforce, and a modern workforce at that, with women establishing its norms. If

---

[66] Hay and Craven, *Masters, Servants and Magistrates*, p. 58.
[67] By ending settlement by service or hiring (4 and 5 Will. IV, c. 76, s. 64).
[68] Kathryn Hughes, *The Short Life and Long Times of Mrs Beeton*, Fourth Estate, London, 2005.

the reader has hope of finding servants to be part of an English working class that made itself during these years, then they can be so found, much of their consciousness of class and social relations expressed – strangely to modern eyes – in poetry. The modern reader may find that game not worth the historical candle, having forgotten the immense efforts of late twentieth-century historians to find class consciousness in the most out of the way places and in the remotest of times.[69] It is probably impossible now, for most of us to understand 'class' as the position of individuals and groups in relationship to a dominant mode of production, that is, in its classic meaning.[70] Now, at the beginning of the twenty-first century, 'class' signals the way in which people experience themselves and the life they live; it is an identity – a way of knowing yourself in the place you have been put by a 'classing gaze'. It is argued that for women in particular, 'class' describes a difficult way of being in the world, and in an individual body. This version of 'class' was shaped by the historical materialism that emerged in British Cultural Studies under the influence of Pierre Bourdieu's sociology of social distinction and embodiment.[71] It owed much unacknowledged theoretical debt to E. P. Thompson's notion of 'experience' (even though his innovation in historical analysis was in dialogue with older, 'classic' versions of class). Thompson once famously described class 'as a relationship . . . not a thing', by which he condemned crudely reductionist, structuralist readings of Marx used to describe the experience of living through a great reordering of society that took place in England between 1780 and 1850.[72] The relationships were between individual members of this class-in-the-making – and between them and the ideologies and repressions promulgated by political elites, owners of land and capital, and their agents of physical force. In this book, the focus is on the relationship between owners and workers (masters and servants) so the reader must expect as many middling-sort employers as domestic servants bearing witness to the relationship, in many kitchens and in the ordinary affairs of life. We shall just all have to deal with the fact that the most available form for articulating this relationship, was the comedic – and that it was thought by means of *things*. They are a constant presence. I have written this so that they press upon the reader: laundry

[69] Mike Savage, 'Class and labour history' in Lex Heerma van Voss and Marcel van der Linden (eds.), *Class and Other Identities: Gender, religion and ethnicity in the writing of European labour history*, Berghahn, New York and Oxford, 2002, pp. 55–72.

[70] Georg Lukács, *History and Class Consciousness: Studies in Marxist dialectics*, Merlin Press, London, 1968.

[71] Lynette Finch, *The Classing Gaze: Sexuality, class and surveillance*, Allen and Unwin, St Leonards NSW, 1993; Beverley Skeggs, *Formations of Class and Gender: Becoming respectable*, Sage, London, 1997; Eley and Nield, *Future of Class*, pp. 139–43.

[72] Thompson, *Making*, pp. 11–12.

and laundry-lists, horses and hay, small coin and candles, manchets and muslin, dripping pans and dusters – the material through which lives were lived, and the furnishings of all the imaginations that reworked and remade a society. (In this book, servants are in possession of imagination as much as their masters – rather more imagination, in fact.) Rather than fitting all these things into one of the narratives that presides over history as a subject ('the industrial revolution'; 'the making of the English working class') this book invites a remaking of the historical story of these years.[73]

Now we must consider the labour exercised on these things, the theories of labour and property that informed these people of the state they were in, and of their relationship one with the other.

---

[73] Giorgio Riello, 'Things that shape history: The material culture of historical narratives' in Karen Harvey (ed.), *Practical Matters: History and material culture*, Routledge, London, 2009 (forthcoming).

2 Servants numberless: Theories of labour and property

There were a lot of servants in the English eighteenth-century; they were *there* – the reason to climb mountains and for social historians to account for them. The service relationship was widely experienced. The imperfect enumeration of eighteenth-century waged domestic workers and their employers can be read to suggest that it was – that it must have been – the most widely and consistently experienced extra-familial relationship in the society. Using contemporary surveys and speculations, Jean Hecht and Bridget Hill concluded that one person in eleven was a domestic servant, perhaps one in five or six in the Metropolis; perhaps forty per cent of the population of eighteenth-century England were servants at some point between early adolescence and marriage.[1] In 1972, Richard Wall estimated that between 1574 and 1821 households with servants were 28.5 per cent. Perhaps a quarter of modest artisan and tradesman households employed some kind of servant.[2] In 1786 in Shrewsbury, Shropshire, where seventy-nine of the town's shopkeepers paid the new shop tax, twenty-seven of them (34 per cent) also paid for an 'official', or taxable, male or female servant.[3] Published appeals against the

[1] J. Jean Hecht, *The Domestic Servant Class in Eighteenth Century England*, Routledge and Kegan Paul, London, 1956, pp. 33–4; Bridget Hill, *Servants: English domestics in the eighteenth century*, Clarendon Press, Oxford, 1996, pp. 15–16.

[2] Peter Laslett (ed. with the assistance of Richard Wall), *Household and Family in Past Time*, Cambridge University Press, Cambridge, 1972, pp. 151–3.

[3] Shropshire Archives (SA), 3365/274, Shrewsbury Borough Records, Taxes (Shops, Servants, Carriages and Horses), 1778–9, 1780 and 1786. For the servant taxes, and why this

servant tax (published means that they had been to the higher courts for the opinion of the judges whose determinations had been printed up as case law) suggests that 59 per cent of employers (*aggrieved* employers) were tradesmen, farmers, shopkeepers, medical men and merchants. Gentlemen and landowning protestors against assessment made on them were sometimes testing the provisions of the legislation regarding their gamekeepers rather than their menial servants, so the proportion of non-elite employers was probably higher than this.[4]

In 1806 Patrick Colquoun speculated about 910,000 servants in England and Wales (in a population of some 9 million) 800,000 of whom were women – an astonishing 10 per cent or so of the general population.[5] Perhaps his figures were produced (or invented) to induce moral panic about habits of 'opulence' in keeping servants.[6] When William Pitt announced the end of the maidservant tax in 1792, he said that in the previous tax year (1790–1) 90,000 'different families . . . the poorer class of householders' had paid the tax on an unspecified number of female servants.[7] If we reckon the general population of England and Wales at 9 million persons, and the average family at 4.5 individuals (as contemporaries often did)[8] then there were perhaps 2 million family/household units, some 4.5 per cent of them paying for one or more 'official' female servant. This is a figure considerably lower than Colquhoun's, even if each head of household had paid for a veritable retinue of maidservants. But domestic service was not universally provided by the kind of live-in domestic the tax assessors netted. Women might go on working in the

---

figure certainly underestimates the number of servant-keeping shopkeepers, see Chapter 7 below, and 'Horses'.

[4] Estimated from the 133 appeal cases sent to the higher courts and discussed in Commissioners of Excise, *Abstract of Cases and Decisions on Appeals Relating to the Tax on Servants*, T. Longman and T. Cadell, London, 1781 and John Smee, *A Complete Collection of Abstracts of Acts of Parliament and Cases with Opinions sought of the Judges upon the following Taxes, viz, upon Houses, Windows, Servants . . .* , 2 vols., J. Butterworth, London, 1797, vol. 2.

[5] Patrick Colquhoun, *A Treatise on Indigence; Exhibiting a General View of the National Resource for Productive Labour . . .* , J. Hatchard, London, 1806, pp. 11, 23. Colquhoun did not count servants at all, in fact; he marked their absence from his other categories: 'labourers in agriculture, manufactures, commerce, navigation, and fisheries, &c, *exclusive* of menial servants' (emphasis added). E. A. Wrigley and R. S. Schofield, *The Population History of England, 1541–1871: A reconstruction*, Cambridge University Press, Cambridge, 1989, pp. 2–4, 571–2 for the earlier estimates with which Colquhoun was in dialogue.

[6] Leonard Schwarz, 'English servants and their employers during the eighteenth and nineteenth centuries', *Economic History Review*, 52:2 (1999), 236–56.

[7] *The Parliamentary History of England*, vol. 29, p. 829 (17 Feb. 1792).

[8] Frederick Morton Eden, *The State of the Poor: or an History of the Labouring Classes in England, from the Conquest to the present Period . . .* 3 vols., J. Davis, London, 1797, vol. 3, p. 847.

house where they had been permanent servants, long after marriage and children, coming in to cook dinner for company, turn out a room, help with the washing; they were paid by the hour or by the day. But if the amount of *waged domestic work* provided by women and men is reckoned, rather than the 'servant' which tax-law defined – which is what Pitt used – then even Colquhoun's inflated numbers may have been close to the mark. We certainly can speak of ubiquity, of paid domestic service as the most common work experience of women in the society.

The Westmorland Census of 1787 gives a snapshot employment picture for one English county – or rather, for part of that county. Only forty-five returns have survived from the four Wards into which the county was divided for administrative purposes. (Perhaps some of them were never made in the first place.) Nevertheless, out of a total Westmorland population of about 40,000 (40,805 in 1801), some 12,500 named individuals were recorded, set in 'their locations, occupations and family units'.[9] Many of the extant returns are incomplete. Pages are missing from some; in some places, the constables who were charged with the task of enumeration only named the head of household and simply recorded the number of others living in it, omitting names, family relationships and occupations (it was no clearer to these men why they had been asked to count local populations than it is to us; the quarter sessions order for the census gave them no instructions apart from 'make out correct Lists in Writing . . . the Names Residences Occupations and Ages of Inhabitants within their . . . Constablewicks').[10]

For the purpose of counting Westmorland servants, thirty-three of the returns are useful. They detail 9,102 people (men, women, children, lodgers, servants, apprentices . . .) whom the constables collecting the data located in 2,039 family/household units. In this odd conglomeration of places from across the county, average household size was very close to what contemporaries assumed it was (4.46 persons, including servants, apprentices and lodgers: everyone recorded by the constables as having their habitation within it). Sixteen per cent (343) of these households employed one or more female servant. We should expect a census like this to capture more than the Tax Office's reckoning of 90,000 householders across the country paying for 'official' maidservants. There were many exemptions and much evasion as far as the female servant taxes were concerned. I have assumed that the Westmorland constables who did the job assigned them, counted every female servant they came across, even though a few months before, in role as tax assessors and collectors

[9] Curwen Archives Texts, *Vital Statistics: The Westmorland 'Census' of 1787*, Curwen Archives Trust, Berwick, 1992, pp. iii–viii.
[10] Curwen Archives Texts, *Vital Statistics*, pp. iv–v.

they had *not* listed exempted maidservants: those in families with two children ... by whom the master and mistress made a living or profit through their knitting or spinning ... a housemaid a yeoman claimed was a *bona fide* dairymaid. (Or that as tax officials, they had ignored the girl sweeping the yard because someone had bought them ale not to 'see' her. Or so it was said. Accusations of corruption and partiality flew thick and fast across the country during the maidservant tax years, 1785–92.) The Westmorland census gives as accurate an account of the female domestic workforce as we are likely to find, albeit a partial one and for a remote rural county (however, these figures include the major part of Kendal, so it was not entirely rural).

In the places where the constables counted everybody they were meant to count, 343 householders or heads of family employed 392 female servants. In the aggregate of these odd and random Westmorland settlements, female servants made up 4 per cent of the general population, though of course, there *is* no general population here, these figures being compiled from a geographically incoherent map. It is more informative to say that in individual places, within the coherence of a parish, or a constablewick (like Hilton, pop. 159, or Kendal, pop. 2,106), male and female servants together could represent anything between 2 per cent and 20 per cent of a local general population. The extraordinary 20 per cent is from Lowther, seat of the Earl of Lonsdale. He employed thirty-nine men and women as servants; the whole of Lowther was in some sense in service to him and the house – the kind of establishment that has exercised much fascination over the popular historical imagination – but which was the only one like it that the Westmorland constables enumerated. In ordinary life, five servants made up a large establishment, and these were rare. Most of Westmorland's 392 enumerated female servants worked alone, as they did in other parts of the country.

Male servants were thin on the ground. To add to the 392 female servants in the complete returns, there were 160 men. The majority of these were servants in husbandry (or at least, they were workers called 'servant man', 'servant' or 'Man-servant' employed by husbandmen, yeoman and farmers; or they were men recorded as 'servants' working for a tradesman). In many small households across the country, men hired as husbandry servants or to shopkeepers or tradesmen, did do domestic work. Their knife cleaning, boot scraping, and water fetching were particularly vexatious activities for local Tax Commissioners and High Court judges. If a man had been hired as a servant in husbandry or to a tradesman and that was the work he actually did, then the employer was exempt from the servant tax, for the man's labour earned him or her a living. But if the man (or the woman) undertook household offices, then he was a domestic servant in law, and his employer liable to the tax. But

Table 2.1 *Work experience of female servants in three towns, 1785–9*

	Shrewsbury 1785–6	Kendal (part) 1786–7	Doncaster 1788–9
No. servants taxed or enumerated	236	91	248
Men servants as % service workforce	34% (60)	13% (14)	17% (43)
Women servants as % service workforce	66% (176)	87% (77)	83% (205)
% women in single-servant households	47% (83)	54% (42)	61% (126)
% women in 2-servant households	14% (25)	18% (14)	21% (45)
% women in 3-servant households	13% (24)	23% (18)	14% (29)
% women in 4-servant households	5% (8)	0	1% (4)
% women in 5-servant households	3% (6)	0	4% (9)
% women in 6+ servant households	17% (30)	6% (5)	(0)

Sources: Shropshire Archives, 3365/274, Shrewsbury Borough Records, Taxes (Shops, Servants, Carriages and Horses)1786; Curwen Archives, *Vital Statistics... 1787*; Doncaster Metropolitan Archives, AB6/8/59, 'An Assessment made upon the Township of Doncaster...for the year 1788 ending Ladyday 1789'.

this kind of domestic work by men was only intermittently undertaken; most of these Westmorland male 'servants' were not domestic workers.

Women servants employed by farmers, tradesmen or weavers, may also have undertaken outdoor work, shop work, manufacturing and home knitting, spinning and weaving for a putter-out: part of the purpose of this book is to describe the catch-all nature of the female servant's work. But only one woman out of the 392 considered here was listed as a 'servant in husbandry' by the constables – in Stainmore, where Isabel Brunskill worked for John Mason Fenton, Curate, Schoolmaster and Clerk. Perhaps she really did do nothing but husbandry work. The household was made up of Fenton's widowed mother (listed as a boarder) and a sister who worked as a sempstress and at 'housekeeping'. But it is highly unlikely that Brunskill never worked in the house; Mr Fenton may have found a way of convincing the constable (in his role as tax assessor) that she wasn't 'really' a domestic servant.

The total of 160 male servants in the returns includes the twenty-eight men employed by the Earl of Lonsdale about his house, cellars, stables and kennels (and – a rare sighting – the Man Cook in his kitchen). Lowther parish, in which the Lonsdale seat was situated, returned twelve male servants employed by gentlemen and gentlewomen (clearly not husbandry workers); another was actually listed as a 'Footman' (apart from the Earl of Lonsdale's there were only two of these in the whole county.) These forty-one men were probably the only male domestic servants – in the official sense – out of the total 552 man and woman servants counted by the constables in all these Westmorland places; so there were about thirteen maidservants here to every male servant.

Most domestic servants were female and they comprised a major section of the workforce, probably the largest after men and women working in the agricultural sector. Adam Smith said that their work was *not work*. In *The Wealth of Nations* (1776) he defined labour in relationship to the production of *things*, remarking that 'the labour of the menial servant . . . does not fix or realise itself in any particular subject or vendible commodity. His services generally perish in the very instant of their performance, and seldom leave any trace or value behind them for which an equal quantity of service could afterwards be procured.'[11] Smith's gendering of the servant as male here is not very surprising; it has more to do with his point of comparison in the service-is-not-work passages – a male worker who produces commodities – than with conventions of writing, or with his own experience as employer of a man-servant.[12] And the male livery servant, the subject of much social theory and taxation policy after the 1760s, was the figure that came to mind whenever domestic workers were discussed. Some servants were in fact acknowledged as female in another of Smith's comparisons, when he argued that like the work of 'players, buffoons, opera-singers, opera dancers &c', the servant's labour did not have the transformative potential to make products out of the goods of the earth, fix living labour in commodities to be sold for money, which might then employ new labour, to create yet another wave of durable, vendible things.[13]

---

[11] Adam Smith, *The Wealth of Nations*, Books I–III (1776), Penguin, London, 1986, pp. 430; see also 133–40.

[12] Ian Simpson Ross, *The Life of Adam Smith*, Clarendon Press, Oxford, 1995, pp. 402, 407. For most of Smith's domestic life, household services were provided by his mother and his cousin, Janet Douglas.

[13] For the opera singers '&c', Neil de Marchi, 'Smith on ingenuity, pleasure and the imitative arts' in Knud Haakonssen (ed.), *The Cambridge Companion to Adam Smith*, Cambridge University Press, Cambridge, 2006, pp. 136–57, esp. pp. 147–8.

Near a century later, Smith's version of 'labour' was used by Karl Marx as he made the theoretical move from understanding 'labour' as a kind of commodity – a thing – to be sold and bought, to labour as an abstract entity, that does not exist until its moment of realisation.[14] Then, and only then, as the man or woman sets to work spinning the greasy mass of combed wool into worsted thread, or starts to draw out the wire in one of the eighteen operations that will result in a fully fashioned pin, does labour (a capacity, or ability) congeal itself, or get crystallised, into a thing; an object.[15] Marx formulated the idea of labour-power (the potentiality to labour) as a conceptual bridge over its absence as a real thing, with shape and form in the world.[16] Despite what many a late eighteenth-century employer and political philosopher had believed, Marx's 'labour' was not a thing. Rather, labour happened, or took shape, in a moment of action, when it was deposited *in* things, or commodities. What determined the value of these made things was 'the labour-time necessary for their production': the worker sold his or her labour-power (*not* his or her labour). The moment work started, it ceased to belong, as labour-power, to the spinner or the pin-maker.[17] Labour may have been the substance and immanent measure of value, but it had no value in itself. Servants (and opera dancers) don't make things; they are not labourers; they do not have the relationship to a mode of production that a pin-maker might have, nor experience of the social relationship between capital and labour (master and men) of a worsted spinner.[18] Marx contemplated statistics from 1861 that showed domestic servants to be (still!) the largest group of employed persons in the society, shook his head in deprecation, then swiftly elided their history and existence with irony (even political scientists have attempted to make jokes out of domestic servants): they were he said, 'domestic slaves . . . an elevating consequence of the capitalistic exploitation of machinery'. Or they were the mere (though massive) legacy of an older, feudal form of society. Overall, he said, 'types of work that are consumed as services and not as products separable from

---

[14] Karl Marx, 'Wage labour and capital' in Karl Marx and Frederick Engels, *Selected Works: In two volumes*, Progress Press, Moscow, 1962, pp. 79–105; Karl Marx, *Capital*, vol. 1 (1867), Penguin, Harmondsworth, 1976, pp. 128–31.

[15] The most famous example of them all, of a concrete, vendible thing. Smith observed the eighteen operations in *The Wealth of Nations*, pp. 109–10.

[16] Karl Marx, *Capital*, vol. 1, pp. 128–31; E. K. Hunt, 'Marx's theory of property and alienation' in Parel and Flanagan (eds.), *Theories of Property*, pp. 283–315, 298.

[17] Marx, *Capital*, vol. 1, p. 675. See Richard Biernacki, *The Fabrication of Labour: Germany and Britain, 1640–1914*, University of California Press, Berkeley, Los Angeles, CA, and London, 1995, pp. 12, 41–92 for an extended discussion of these points.

[18] John Rule, *Experience of Labour in Eighteenth-century Industry*, Croom Helm, London, 1981, pp. 194–213.

the worker and not capable existing as commodities independently from him . . . are of microscopic significance when compared with the mass of capitalist production. They may be entirely neglected, therefore.'[19] Many twentieth-century historians of labour and class took this advice seriously, as permission to quietly pass over domestic servants, who did not 'really' work or make things, and thus could not be conceptualised as working class.[20] Historians used a plot that never could have – certainly never did – contain servants in the first place. This plot is an especial problem for historians now, at the beginning of the twenty-first century, because our own economy is to a great extent a service economy, in which most workers do not produce *vendible objects*, but rather, services.

On the other hand, many eighteenth-century historians and social theorists, unlike Adam Smith, were willing to understand the servant's (though perhaps not the opera dancer's) labour as work. We need to follow arguments about, discussion of, legislation for, and legal adjudication of, the servant question, in its own (eighteenth-century) terms; to contemplate, along with High Court judges sitting in King's Bench, the differences between the labour that produced a well-cooked (or, indeed, an indifferently cooked) dinner, and a row of beans in the kitchen garden, well-hoed and watered and now gathered for household consumption (by your maidservant) and for sale to your neighbours, and the work that produced the packet of pins, or the hank of worsted yarn. Eighteenth-century England, in transition to capitalist modernity, understood labour and property in relation to the very large occupational category that comprised domestic servants. These understandings had practical effects, in tax law, social and family policy and on the actual workers who were the subjects of so much covert and overt theorising. On Mary Cant for example, Nottinghamshire maidservant, who complained to a local magistrate in 1785 that the work of her place was too hard for her; or at least, it was too hard for one person. Hadn't her master promised he would employ another girl to help her? And didn't she know the work of her place? It was hers after all, and she knew where its priorities lay: that there were a great many more things to do than dress a baby at the most pressing time of the domestic day as he had asked her to do (and slapped

---

[19] Marx, *Capital*, vol. 1, p. 1044.
[20] The distinction between productive and non-productive labour was encountered again and again by twentieth-century scholars, notably by Nicos Poulantzas and David Harvey. Nicos Poulantzas, *Classes in Contemporary Capitalism*, New Left Books, London, 1975, pp. 209–23; David Harvey, *The Limits to Capital*, Basil Blackwell, Oxford, 1999. What their reading made plain at least, is that *Capital* is a story about Capital, not Labour; that the productive work that produces surplus value does so for the capitalist (or more strictly, for Capital); that 'the only productive labour is that which is directly consumed in the course of production for the valorization of capital'. Marx, *Capital*, vol. 1, p. 1038.

her round the head when she refused)?[21] Complex theories of domestic labour, its place in the polity and social thought were also expressed when a magistrate like Thomas Netherton Parker (Oswestry, Shropshire) had his clerk record that this day, February 1810, he had heard the complaint of Elizabeth Humphries against Mrs Jennings of Penylan, for wages due. 'She is to return to her service', Mr Justice Parker determined; 'and no deducting for the days which she has been absent from her wages – Mrs Jennings agreed to allow her 1s a week more than her wages for such time as there was not a girl . . . to assist her in the work, to return to her service tomorrow by 12 o'clock'.[22]

This young woman was not in some semi-feudal relationship of dependence and subordination, and both she and Justice Parker knew it. She was a properly hired domestic servant who possessed legal rights in the employment relationship. It was she, who brought the case before the magistrate, not her employer, even though it was she, the servant, who had 'run away' (not as dramatic as it sounds: a technical term for leaving a hiring before its term, or without notice) and the employer had possible redress for this, under the same body of legislation. In employment disputes like this, employer, employee and magistrate would refer to the 'hiring' or the 'hiring agreement', or to 'the contract of hiring'. Though they did not mean by such agreements exactly the same thing as modern contract theorists and legal historians mean by 'contract', it is likely that the most articulated idea of a contractual relationship in the society was developed between servant and master or mistress, in the language and range of references seen above, as Elizabeth Humphries complains that Mrs Jennings had not kept her promise, or her side of the bargain clinched at the hiring, to employ a second servant to help her with her work. With this everyday, taken-for-granted assumption of a formal, legally enforceable agreement to manage the employment relationship, domestic servants constituted a kind of first modern labour force, through the sheer weight of their numbers and the amount of 'contract' spoken by them and about them.

In *The Gifts of Athena* Joel Mokyr proposes the idea of an 'Industrial Enlightenment' as a context to Cant's, Humphries' and Parker's lives. According to Mokyr, instead of an 'industrial revolution', we should see economic progress from about 1700 to 1830 fuelled by a knowledge revolution, with technical information (propositional knowledge, and its how-to-do variant) spread rapidly by a print- and communications

---

[21] Mary Cant is further discussed in Chapter 8.
[22] SA, 1060/168, Justices of the Peace, Justicing Notebook of Thos. N. Parker, 1805–1840 (7 Feb. 1810).

revolution.[23] He remarks on 'our convention of not including housework in our measures of national income', either for this period or any other, a convention that prevents *his* reckoning-up knowledge about household labour (cookery books, manuals that told employers how to tell the servants to wash, scour, clean, pickle and preserve ...). *The Gifts of Athena* has perceptive things to say about housework, and Mokyr is interested in it as work (though not in the circulation of printed information about household work, travelling along the same pathways as all the technical and industrial information he describes). Neither is he concerned that so much of the household work he is interested in was performed as the result of an economic transaction between two parties under a hiring agreement. The historical problematic of his book remains the *industrial* revolution; conventions of writing simply do not permit the labour of domestic servants to be reckoned. We have already observed the iron grip of the plot-line Mokyr uses. However, there may be a way of including housework in measures of later eighteenth-century national income. After 1777 for men, and between 1785 and 1792 for women, the employment of domestic servants was taxed to increase revenue for a war economy. The tax was a levy laid on employers for the use of a particular kind of contracted labour (though that is not how the original promoters of the servant tax saw it). The 1777 Servant Tax and those that followed may give access to contemporary understandings of domestic work as a primary form of waged labour. And perhaps Mokyr also suggests (though this is surely not what he set out to do) that there really is nothing but convention to prevent us from understanding cooking as work, the master's dinner as a form of production by the servant, the knowledge that produced it of the prescriptive kind and the servant's verse about all of this as a form of commodity production.

Who owned all these things and entities? It was quite clear to all manner of eighteenth-century commentator that the master owned his own dinner, though dinner was rarely the example. He had purchased, or laboured to grow, or paid for others to produce, its ingredients; he had provided the maidservant with her tools for its processing (firing, pots and pans, a good sharp knife). He had purchased her time (or leased, rented, or acquired an interest in her time; terms for describing the agreement between them were legion). Or he had purchased her energies, or her labour (another multiplicity of terms for what had happened, legally

[23] Joel Mokyr, *The Gifts of Athena: Historical origins of the knowledge economy*, Princeton University Press, Princeton and Oxford, 2002; Joel Mokyr, 'Accounting for the Industrial Revolution', *The Cambridge Economic History of Modern Britain*, vol. 1, *Industrialisation, 1700–1860*, Roderick Floud and Paul Johnson (eds.), Cambridge University Press, Cambridge, 2004, pp. 1–27.

speaking, between them at the moment of hiring). In the great abundant world made by God, all of His Creatures had the capacity, or the potentiality, to labour. Labour is an attribute, or capacity, of all human beings. If the master were ever to read High Court judgments or the more plain-speaking legal treatises he would be told that the law of the land favoured him, the master, by allowing him to transfer this God-given capacity to the young woman toiling in the back kitchen with pork and parsley and bread-crumbs (she is making a stuffed chine of pork for the family dinner, struggling with a recalcitrant fire and a Boy who hasn't yet brought in the water she needs).[24]

Really, in this philosophy of labour and embodiment, he could have stuffed and pot-roasted his own pork (just like Mary Cant thought her master could have changed his own baby). The capacity to do so had been given him (given to all men and women) at the beginning of things; it is *in* their body, and also in the abstract *persona*, which is their legal body. None of them (neither maidservant nor master) actually own their body; rather, it is held in a kind of trust from God. They may not do away with that body; they may not kill it, or sell it into slavery. Their first responsibility for the body given them by God, is to keep it going: to preserve life. But they may (many of them must) sell, or hire out, its capacities, attributes and energies (though that is an arrangement of civil society, not a godly arrangement).

The young woman in the kitchen, wondering whether the timing is better for broccoli or spinach to go with the pork, may have invested her own labour, energies, capacities and intelligence in the fruits of the earth (pig-meat and parsley; things that are also goods and commodities); but the exercise of her labour did not *make* her own dinner. When she eats her potion of the chine, it is by virtue of the contract she has made with the man. It is his agreement to lodge and board her during the year served to earn the three guineas clinched at the hiring, that produces her dinner. Her piece of stuffed chine with spinach is a meal made in law.

Political and legal philosophy originating in the seventeenth-century underpinned this view of things. When the lawyer John Barry Bird told masters and magistrates in 1799 that really, 'in strictness every body ought to transact his own affairs', that it was only 'by the favour and indulgences of the law that he can delegate the power of acting for him to another', he was reiterating the political philosophy of John Locke, reformulated for a modern commercial world. Lockean formulations explained why 'the acts of servants are in many instances deemed the

---

[24] Elizabeth Raffald, *The Experienced English Housekeeper*, 8th edn, R. Baldwin, London, 1782, p. 112, 'To Stuff a Chine of Pork'.

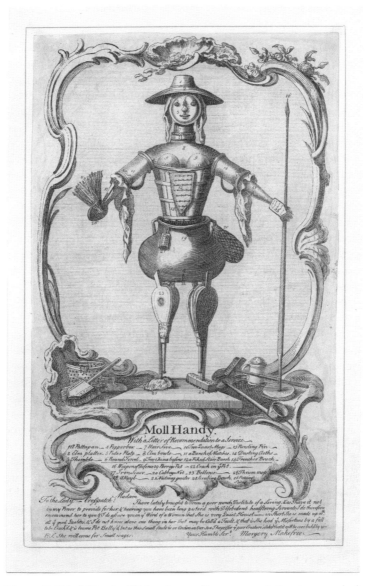

Figure 5. 'Moll Handy. With a letter of recommendation to a service'. The fascination with servants as automata elided the theories of law and property they represented. The caption reads: 'With a Letter of Recommendation to a Service ~ 1 A Pattapan ~ 7 Hair Sive ~ 4 A Pepperbox ~ 10 Two Quart Mugs ~ 13 Rowling Pin ~ 2 Elm Platter ~ 3 Pewter Plate ~ 8 Elm Bowle ~ 11 a Bunch of Matches ~ 14 Dusting Cloths ~ 6 Thimble ~ 6 Round Towel ~ 9 Two China basons ~ 12 a Fixed? Stair Brush ~ 16 Trencher Bruch ~ 16 ~ Weapon of Defence ~ 19 Porrige Pot ~ 22 Crack in ye Pot ~ 17 Iron ~ 20 Cabbage Net ~ 23 Bellows ~ 25 Thrum Mop ~ 18 A Payl ~ 21 Nutmeg grater ~ 24 Scrubing Brush ~ 26 Pudding Sieve'.

acts of the masters'.[25] This was a lesson you taught children in the later century: that servants were there to do what was actually the employer's business. An appallingly behaved child, who has just been extremely rude to her nursemaid, is castigated by her mother in Dorothy Kilner's *Perambulations of a Mouse* (1783): "'And who do you think will do anything for you, if you are not good, and do not speak civilly! Not *I*, I promise you, neither shall nurse or any of the servants, for though *I pay her wages to do my business for me*, I never want them to do anything, unless they are desired in a pretty manner.'"[26] Throughout the eighteenth century the boy cleaning the knives, and the nursemaid dressing a recalcitrant child, were conceived of as aspects of their employer's capacities and abilities.

This story – or legal theory – had an origin. When John Locke wrote about the servant's labour in the *Treatises of Government*, an image occurred to his imagination, and there sprang up a horse and a turf-cutter: 'the grass my horse has bit, the turfs my servant has cut...become my property...The labour that was mine removing them out of the common state they were in, has fixed my property in them.' This is how property is made, by any employer, including John Locke. The labour of the servant and the horse enact that of the owner and employer, and make his property. Perhaps Locke eschewed the table on which he wrote (the most common analogy among philosophers, for describing all kinds of mental and material process), looked up, gazed out of a window, saw a man at work in a field, a horse with panniers on its back quietly standing by, cropping the grass of the field not yet cut.[27] Or perhaps the man and the horse were simply the best examples he could find for the appropriation of property and the circulation of labour in an agricultural market economy. Wherever Locke was when he either conjured or espied the servant at work and described the servant's labour as his own, it was highly unlikely to have been in Somerset, the county of his birth. He owned substantial Somersetshire property, but did not live there permanently after his schooldays.[28] But in the 1680s, as he formulated his philosophy of labour and property, he spent much time answering a barrage of

---

[25] James Barry Bird, *Laws Respecting Masters and Servants, Articled Clerks, Apprentices, Manufacturers, Labourers and Journeymen*, 3rd edn, W. Clarke, London, 1799, p. 6.

[26] Dorothy Kilner, *Life and Perambulations of a Mouse*, John Marshall, London, 1783, p. 31; second emphasis added. Servants hated, above all else, small children ordering them about. See Chapter 9.

[27] For philosophers and tables, see Jacques Derrida, *Spectres of Marx: The state of the debt, the work of mourning, and the new international* (1993), Routledge, London, 1994, pp. 149–51, 203–4.

[28] He was in exile in Holland, perhaps, where peat (from the turf) – so much better for his bronchitis than coal – was burned more than it was in England. Maurice Cranston, *John Locke: A biography*, Longmans, Green, London, 1957, pp. 184–213; Vere Chappell (ed.), *The Cambridge Companion to Locke*, Cambridge University Press, Cambridge, 1999, pp. 14–15. But a real Dutch man in a real Dutch field does not really fit the

questions from the county. The questions suggest that for him, as much as for the eighteenth-century people who were to manage everyday life under the long legal shadow of his philosophy, the modern world was made by dirty clouts and dish pans as much as it was by ideas. Letters from the Vale of Taunton, from his friend Edward Clarke of Chipley and his wife Mary, came thick and fast.[29] The Clarkes' letters sometimes concerned Locke's Somerset property, sometimes their common financial and fiscal schemes to be promoted in Parliament, but many more sought Locke's advice about the care and upbringing of the Clarke children. Locke may not have answered the question he raised by means of the turf-cutter and the horse – about the ownership of the servant's labour and its products – but he answered the Clarkes' questions, regularly and at length. He kept drafts and copies of the child-care and educational letters which, though subsequently lost, were transcribed for *Some Thoughts Concerning Education*.[30] He published this in 1693, three years after the two works of politics and philosophy, *An Essay Concerning Human Understanding* and *Two Treatises of Government* (1689).[31] Locke's educational manual has been described as the how-to-do-version of the philosophical treatise, prescription for doing sensationalist psychology with infants, or (in reference to the *Treatises*) a handbook for producing a property-owning, self-determining citizen out of your boy child (though Locke believed that young Edward Clarke was already that, considering that 'an ordinary Gentleman's Son' like him 'should have different ways of Breeding' from those in other ranks of society).[32] Both the *Thoughts* and the *Essay* assume the political importance of the domestic sphere and the care of children within it. *Thoughts* reproduces almost word for word the strictures of the *Essay Concerning Human Understanding* against servants' telling ghost stories to frighten small children into compliance,

---

composition timetable of the *Two Treatises*. Roger Woolhouse, *Locke. A biography*, Cambridge University Press, Cambridge, 2007, pp. 200, 181–96.

[29] Mary Jepp as was, was a distant cousin of Locke. Trained as a barrister, Clarke was elected MP for Taunton in 1690. Mark Goldie, 'Clarke, Edward (1649 × 51–1710)' in *Oxford Dictionary of National Biography*, Oxford University Press, 2004, www.oxforddnb.com/view/article/37290, accessed 17 Apr. 2007; Sara H. Mendelson, 'Clarke, Mary (d. 1705)' in *Oxford Dictionary of National Biography*, Oxford University Press, 2004, www.oxforddnb.com/view/article/66720, accessed 17 Apr. 2007.

[30] Woolhouse, *Locke*, pp. 203–6, 236–7, 249–50, 325–7.

[31] E. S. De Beer, *The Correspondence of John Locke*, 8 vol., Clarendon Press, Oxford, 1976, vol. 1, Introduction, pp. xxxix–xl for the archival fate of the Clarke–Locke correspondence. There were evidently many more letters exchanged than those presented by De Beer, or transcribed in Benjamin Rand, *The Correspondence of John Locke and Edward Clarke*, Harvard University Press, Cambridge, MA, 1927. See 'The letters on education', in De Beer, p. 624.

[32] John Locke, *Some Thoughts Concerning Education*, A. and J. Churchill, London, 1693, p. 330.

though the two nursery vignettes were for different purposes.[33] These two passages were repeated endlessly in eighteenth-century child-care manuals and books of advice on how to manage servants. A commentator would pause in the middle of a treatise on poverty and taxation systems to declare that domestic servants and their ghost stories produced criminality in the most carefully reared of children.[34] This kind of repetition may be a source for the reputation of the *Thoughts* as a recipe book for putting philosophy into practice (or the prescriptive version of propositional knowledge, in Joel Mokyr's terms).[35] Locke had this advice about servant maids for the Clarkes, and a great deal more besides. To the modern reader they appear anxious parents, but were perhaps not really so; only parents with a sure and prolix source of advice.[36] After the publication of *Some Thoughts* (which Edward Clarke thought embodied a great service to the state and society in general), some readers of the correspondence might find a diminution of Locke's interest in the children's colic, their reading ability, want of facility with a pen and Mary Clarke's swollen legs. The letters become shorter, the advice more perfunctory; Locke takes a long time to answer, and his excuses for silence are more elegantly conventional than they were in the 1680s ('I trespasse, aske pardon, & trespasse agn. Thus the world goes round'). But perhaps his seeming weariness with clouts, wet-nursing and the thorny questions of checking a child's temper, finding it a tutor and teaching it to read, had more to do with the fragmentary nature of the Clarke letter-archive than with having got the book out of the way.[37]

33 In the *Essay* servants' tales demonstrate the psychological principle of the association of ideas ('The *Ideas* of Goblings and *Sprights*, have really no more to do with Darkness, than Light; yet let a foolish Maid inculcate these often upon the Mind of a Child, and raise them there together, possibly he never shall be able to separate them again so long as he lives, but Darkness shall ever afterwards bring with it those frightful *Ideas*'). The *Thoughts* warns parents about servants, 'whose usual Method' is to control children 'by telling them of *Raw-head and Bloody-bones*, and such other Names, as carry with them the Idea's [sic] of something terrible and hurtful'. John Locke, *An Essay Concerning Human Understanding. In four books* (1689), 7th edn, J. Churchill and Samuel Manship, London, 1715–16, vol. 1, p. 367; *Thoughts*, p. 206.
34 William Sabatier, *A Treatise on Poverty, its Consequences and Remedies*, John Stockdale, London, 1797, pp. 73, 100.
35 Mokyr, *Gifts*, pp. 8, 56–76. Locke, *Essay*, vol. 1, p. 367; Locke, *Thoughts*, p. 206.
36 The Clarkes – for certain, Mary Clarke – did not limit queries to their friend. Somerset County Record Office (SCRO), Sanford MSS., 3109; M/1170, Notes on the lives of Edward and Mary Clarke of Chipley, 1679–1705 by Margaret Sherren, 1971. Also Bridget Clarke, 'Huguenot tutors and the family of Edward and Mary Clarke of Chipley, 1687–1710', *Proceedings of the Huguenot Society of Great Britain and Ireland*, 27:4 (2001), 527–42.
37 De Beer, *Correspondence of John Locke*, vol. 4 (1979), Letter 1644 (22 Jul. 1693); Letter 1647 (2 Aug. 1693); SCRO, DD/SF 3304/15/4, Sanford MSS., 3077, Bundle of Clarke

The Clarkes asked Locke many questions about wet nurses. Rickets in childhood was no disadvantage in such a servant, said Locke, and should not affect her milk. It was a disease of the poor, he thought; it did not affect capacity to work, in this or any other way, later in life.[38] In fact, he knew, and approved very much of the woman who had served Mrs Clarke after several of her confinements.[39] He made direct comparisons between the Clarkes' maids, weighing up their capacities, abilities and personalities.[40] His opinions on toilet training, the general care, washing and dressing of children, and their first speech and literacy learning, are better known than his interest in the servants, because the former were transmogrified into *Some Thoughts*. If the Clarkes' advisor on child-care and the servants had been anyone but a renowned political philosopher – and did not the correspondence between the two men demonstrate the warmest and most equal of friendships between two orderly households of the lesser and greater English gentry – then Locke might be seen made a servant himself, by their constant appeals for help in doing their business as parents.[41] For quite a long time, as he philosophised about all of this and evolved the eighteenth-century's most accessed theory of labour, John Locke was in role as servant, to the Clarke family enterprise. He was, to use his own image, his own turf-cutter.

In the *Two Treatises of Government* (1689) there is a man – someone's servant – cutting turf. The servant enacts a legal and a philosophic formula as he wields his spade: he demonstrates how property is made, and how labour may be transferred from one person to another. The tense structure of the passage indicates that the philosopher does not describe an actual event so much as something that must have happened in the remote conjectural past, at the beginning of things. And that is always happening. It happens now, in the late seventeenth-century anthropological present ('thus in the beginning all the world was America'). The man, the horse, the turf, what happens to them and what they do one with the other are an analogy of the constant making and transfer of property in all societies, past and present. Some have also said that despite the scene in the field being set in remote conjectural times, if you understand the

---

Papers, mainly Edward Clarke, 'Touching on the Subject of Betty's writing', Letter from John Locke to Edward Clarke (23 Nov. 1694).

[38] De Beer, *Correspondence of John Locke*, vol. 2 (1976), Letter 683 (16 Feb. 1682), Letter 758 (22 Feb. 1683), Letter 774 (Feb. 1684).

[39] De Beer, *Correspondence of John Locke*, vol. 2, Letter 844 (8 Feb. 1686).

[40] De Beer, *Correspondence of John Locke*, vol. 2, Letter 758 (22 Feb. 1683).

[41] From 1689 onwards, Locke lived 'the orderly life of the lesser English gentry'; De Beer, *Correspondence of John Locke*, vol. 1, p. xvi. For Clarke putting his friend's advice into practice – pasting letters onto wooden bricks for the reading games of the *Thoughts*, see *Correspondence*, vol. 2, Letters 807, 822.

horse as capital, the servant as hired labour and the turf (and ore, which is also mentioned), as resources, it is also a view of Locke's immediate and modern context, where property is capital.[42] Before the turf-cutting scene, Locke had already described an attribute or characteristic of all people: how 'every man has a property in his own person; this nobody has any right to but himself'.[43] The labour of his body, the work of his hands, belong to him, and he has property in them. People may mingle their labour with the fruits of the earth, behave like the Maker who made them, and the natural things with which they mix their labour become theirs.[44] To have property in a product of labour meant something akin to the modern 'rights over', or 'interest in' (but it was also more connected to the idea of possession than are those two terms). It derived from an extension of the maker's or owner's self into the fashioned thing.[45] From this last meaning comes the modern understanding of property as some kind of tangible possession owned by some actual person.

Later, Locke explains how the servant got there; how, and why, it is he who is cutting turf. Locke tells how a man might, of his own will and volition, 'make himself a servant to another, by selling him for a certain time, the service he undertakes to do, in exchange for wages he is to receive'. The hiring gives the master a certain power over the servant, but no more than 'what is contained in the contract between them'.[46] Locke did not discuss domestic or menial servants, though they may be assumed to have fallen within his much more general category of 'my servant'. The general meaning of 'servant', as a he or she who worked for some kind of recompense (sometimes cash wages), is at work in the turf-cutting passage, in the moment when the labour is actually transferred, in the digging, cutting and transporting of the turf. But Locke was concerned with the *employer's* capacities, not the servant's. The servant is a mere cipher (or automaton), as the master uses him and the horse to take grass and turf into his personal possession. In the great cycle of creation

---

42 Herman Lebovics, 'The uses of America in Locke's *Second Treatise of Government*', *Journal of the History of Ideas*, 47:4 (1986), 567–81.

43 Locke, *Two Treatises on Government* (1689), Dent, London, 1993, p. 128. (Book Two, Chapter 5, Section 27.)

44 James Tully, *A Discourse on Property: John Locke and his adversaries*, Cambridge University Press, Cambridge, 1980, pp. 116–24; Robert J. Steinfeld, *The Invention of Free Labour: The employment relation in English and American law and culture, 1350–1870*, University of North Carolina Press, Chapel Hill and London, 1991, pp. 78–81.

45 Tully, *Discourse on Property*, pp. 107–8, 119; J. G. A. Pocock, 'The mobility of property and the rise of eighteenth-century sociology' in Anthony Parel and Thomas Flanagan (eds.), *Theories of Property: Aristotle to the present*, Wilfrid Laurier for the Calgary Institute for the Humanities, Waterloo, Ontario, 1977, pp. 141–66.

46 Locke, *Two Treatises*, p. 156 (Book 2, Chapter 7, Section 85).

established by the Maker of all things, the turf will be used as firing in the production of some other commodity (bread or beer, perhaps); the horse (the horse's labour) will pull the cart full of turfs to the drying shed. The servant is just another pair of hands – in the paradigmatic synecdoche of the English language he is 'a hand'. He exercises the master's capacity to labour rather than his own. Locke's location of labour (as a capacity or potentiality) in the employer rather than the servant doing the work, has been silently passed over in modern commentary, much as it was in the eighteenth century.[47] Elizabeth Cook has remarked that Locke's turf-cutting passages are a justification of property ownership as 'a by-product of the body/subject'; that is to say, just one more result of the immense efforts of political theorists and philosophers from the mid-seventeenth century onwards, to make the singular human body the locus of individuality and personhood. Cook says that Locke described the servant's body as 'simply a kind of prosthesis'.[48]

In all of Locke's writing, man is a maker, and his making makes him a person. People fashion things out of the material of the earth, which is provided by God. Labour transforms the earthly provision into objects of use; those who labour have a property in the product. And yet, in everyday acts of hiring and contract, employers acquired the labour of social inferiors (acquired a property, or interest in it) and bestowed on them their own (unused) capacity to exercise their own energies in labour. The rent or lease of the servant's time and energies, the turfs stacked, the corn threshed (the dinner cooked? the sheets ironed? the room turned out and dusted?) became that of the master or mistress. One of the capacities that made people possessive individuals, in law and polity, was exercised on a daily basis by people who were not persons at all, in the way that 'person' was coming to be defined during the seventeenth and eighteenth centuries.[49]

[47] Margaret Jane Radin, 'Property and personhood', *Stanford Law Review*, 34 (1981–2), 957–1015; Alan Ryan, *Property and Political Theory*, Basil Blackwell, Oxford, 1984, pp. 14–48; Carol Pateman, *The Sexual Contract*, Polity, Cambridge, 1988, pp. 142–3, 149–51; Thomas A. Horne, *Property Rights and Poverty: Political argument in Britain, 1605–1834*, University of North Carolina Press, Chapel Hill and London, 1990, pp. 48–65; Daniela Gobetti, *Private and Public: Individuals households and body politic in Locke and Hutcheson*, Routledge, London, 1992; Matthew H. Kramer, *John Locke and the Origins of Private Property: Philosophical explorations of individualism, community and equality*, Cambridge University Press, Cambridge, 1997, pp. 132–5. But see Keith Tribe, *Land, Labour and Economic Discourse*, Routledge and Kegan Paul, London, 1978, pp. 49–51.

[48] Elizabeth Heckendorn Cook, *Epistolary Bodies: Gender and genre in the eighteenth-century republic of letters*, University of California Press, Stanford, CA, 1991, pp. 162–3.

[49] C. B. MacPherson famously remarked that in the seventeenth century, the employed labour force (including servants in husbandry, domestic servants and day-labourers) were not really persons, in legal and political understanding. 'Servants and labourers in

Locke's scene in the field was about labour relations in general, and all kinds of worker (including domestic-servants), who had agreed to perform certain tasks for some kind of compensation. His propositions were to do with the conditions of early capitalism and a very wide variety of occupational categories. Within the broad legal and economic category of 'servant', domestics were a large minority. But it was the weight of their presence as a type of worker, and the domestic-service relationship as one of the most widely experienced in the society, that underlay the assertion of Sir William Blackstone that the contract between employer and servant embodied the first of the 'three great relations of private life' in which the law must be interested. According to Blackstone, the others – between husband and wife, and parent and child (or guardian and ward) – were founded on this first and primary one.[50]

There have been fervent arguments among political philosophers over what Locke *really meant* in the turf-cutting passages. Perhaps his overall purpose was to create individuals who would be 'habituated to labour and docility'? Perhaps his 'state of nature' in which all people are free to make property out of the common gift of God by labouring on it, did (or did not) actually exhibit many features of the capitalist economy of the later seventeenth century? There are many charges of anachronism to be made about these arguments: Locke has been read with modern (mid nineteenth-century) concerns over the alienation of property and individual autonomy in mind. The way in which all of Locke's work was informed by a broadly religious agenda has been largely ignored.[51] Despite what he bequeathed to eighteenth-century thinkers ('this is almost incalculable', says John Pocock) Locke was not writing as a theorist of property in the *Treatises*; and anyway, as Lord Chief Justice Mansfield was later to tell everyone, all questions of property and property transfer were completely imponderable: 'no common person has the smallest idea of any difference between giving a person a horse and a quantity of land. Common sense alone would never teach a man the difference.'[52] Thomas Horne says that Locke's 'mixing' argument – that

seventeenth-century England' in *Democratic Theory: Essays in retrieval*, Clarendon Press, Oxford, 1973, pp. 207–33.

[50] Blackstone, *Commentaries*, p. 425.

[51] Jeremy Waldron, "'The Turfs My Servant Has Cut'", *Locke Newsletter*, 13 (1982), 1–20; W. M. Spellman, *John Locke*, Macmillan, Basingstoke and London, 1997, pp. 54, 83; Tully, *Discourse*, p. 137; C. B. MacPherson, 'Servants and labourers in seventeenth-century England'; David Lieberman, 'Property, commerce, and the common law: Attitudes to legal change in the eighteenth century' in John Brewer and Susan Staves (eds.), *Early Modern Conceptions of Property*, Routledge, London, 1995, pp. 144–58; 146.

[52] J. G. A. Pocock, 'The myth of John Locke and the obsession with liberalism' in J. G. A. Pocock and Richard Ashcraft (eds.), *John Locke: Papers read at a Clark Library Seminar*,

property is created by mixing human labour with the stuff of material world – was rejected by virtually every eighteenth-century thinker who considered it. He finds only one commentator worried by the implications of the servant – the hired hand – actually doing the mixing and acquiring property in the things he produces, and that was a worry about tenant farmers making (their own) property by working a landowner's earth.[53] Yet Horne concedes that Blackstone's description of the process by which moveable property became subject to exclusive rights in terms of 'bodily labour' had long-lasting political effects, particularly in North America. Blackstone indeed said that bodily labour processes gave men 'the fairest and most reasonable title to exclusive property therein'.[54] In his quotidian manifestation as High Court judge, he also promulgated the thesis in the practical world of the case reports, discussing property ownership conferred by mental as well as bodily labour.[55]

Political scientists must explain to their readers the structure of particular philosophies – how theories work now, in the present time of their readers; they must explain them *as ideas*.[56] They are allowed for example, a preoccupation with the absence of women from Locke's thesis ('And yet are not women as able to labour as men? Why ought they not to have a right to the products of their labour, and to that with which they have mixed their labour?').[57] What we need, on the other hand, is to understand how Locke's ideas and propositions had practical effects in the century that followed, in the everyday life of magistrates, maidservants and turf-cutters; and of course, in the minds and writing of philosophers of various kinds. On the occasions when the question of a female servant's labour came before King's Bench, the judges had no trouble at all in conceiving of her as a worker, as someone with entitlement to the

10 December 1977, William Andrews Clark Memorial Library, University of California, Los Angeles, 1980, pp. 3–24; Mansfield quoted by Lieberman, 'Property', p. 152.

[53] Thomas Rutherford, *Institutes of Natural Law, being the Substance of a Course of Lectures on Grotius de Jure Belli et Pacis*, 2 vols., J. Bentham, Cambridge, 1754–6, vol. 1, pp. 50–62, cited by Horne, *Property Rights*, p. 125.

[54] Horne, *Property Rights*, pp. 128–9; William Blackstone, *Commentaries on the Laws of England. Book the First*, 3rd edn, 4 vols., John Exshaw etc., Dublin, 1769, vol. 2, pp. 4–6.

[55] William Blackstone, *Reports of Cases determined in the several Courts of Westminster-Hall, from 1746 to 1779. Taken and compiled by the Honourable Sir William Blackstone*, 2 vols., His Majesty's Law Printers for W. Strahan, T. Cadell, London, 1781, Vol. 1, pp. 321–2. See below, Chapter 5.

[56] Kramer, *John Locke*, pp. 93–150.

[57] Lorenne M. G. Clark, 'Women and John Locke; or, Who Owns the Apples in the Garden of Eden', *Canadian Journal of Philosophy*, 7 (1977), 699–724. Daniela Gobetti, *Private and Public*, pp. 80–4 argues that Eve owned them, and continues to do so in the modern world, through the exercise of her labour. See also Carole Pateman, *The Sexual Contract*, Polity, Cambridge, 1988.

fruits of her labour. In poor-law settlement cases sent on appeal from county quarter sessions, what was in dispute was a woman's (or a man's) right to settlement and consequent relief in a particular place, by virtue of having been in service there for a calendar year. The determination was never that women had no such right, only that this particular one did not have it. Sometimes in disagreement with the Chief Justice, the other judges used the language of rights and entitlement to this reward of labour, on one occasion speaking of a London maidservant's settlement as 'her only one, which she deserves so well'; 'Justice as well as reason of the thing are here with the Settlement', they said.[58] Even when the case of the slave-servant Charlotte Howe (to be discussed in Chapter 4) who had no legal identity or persona at all, came before the Judges in 1783, attorneys urged the 'great hardship and inconvenience' of her situation on the judges, and the unfairness of things 'if, after many years of service, a negro could not obtain that asylum and relief' afforded to other servants, that is, a parish settlement.[59]

'Contract' framed the understanding and determinations of magistrates across the country when they heard employment disputes between employers and servants. Shropshire magistrate Thomas Netherton Parker kept careful records of his work as JP between 1805 and 1842, noting 653 items of magisterial business, of which 194 (29 per cent) were employment cases, broadly conceived, concerning all sorts of worker, including domestic servants.[60] The law directed the magistrate's attention to what had been agreed between the two parties, and the administration of that agreement; that was what Parker believed he was bound to deal with. April 1805 in Parker's notebook: three canal labourers complain against the canal-company surveyor; *contra* the agreement, they have lost time and wages; moreover, no one has been paid for measuring and valuing the work they have completed. (Parker determines that the men are due half the wages they are claiming.) Later that month he hears 'Matthew Wilding against John Ellis for not completing his engagement to saw boards'. Ellis agrees to return to his work this day and to stay for a week; he'll then go back on 10th

---

[58] Lincoln's Inn Library, Dampier Manuscripts, A. P. B, 19, Easter Term, 1778. Thomas Caldecott, *Reports of Cases relative to the duty and office of a Justice of the Peace, from Michaelmas Term 1776, inclusive, to Trinity Term 1785, inclusive*, Strahan, London, 1785, pp. 48–51.

[59] For 'entitlement' see W. M. Spellman, *John Locke*, p. 115; Horne, *Property Rights*, pp. 130–1, 141, 201–3; Lynn Hollen Lees, *The Solidarities of Strangers: The English poor laws and the people, 1700–1948*, Cambridge University Press, Cambridge, 1998, pp. 7–22, 29–33, 177; James Stephan Taylor, *Poverty, Migration and Settlement in the Industrial Revolution: Sojourners' narratives*, Society for the Promotion of Science and Scholarship, Palo Alto CA, 1989, pp. 18–19, 42.

[60] Shropshire Archives (SA), 1060/168–171, Justices of the Peace, Justicing Notebooks of Thos. N. Parker, 1805–1840. See Chapter 6.

July and stay until the job is completed. For a servant in husbandry or a domestic servant, a year's hiring was what had been almost universally agreed, and what had been breached. 19 May 1806: 'Thomas Davies Farmer of Plas yn y Coer Township of Duddliston Parish of Ellesmere v. Thomas Jones his Servant Boy, running from his service'. 'Ordered the Boy to return to his Place' noted Parker; ' – & recommended that if Mr Davies approve of his conduct during the remainder of the Year he do not deduct the Expenses of proceeding.' It was a very simple matter in most cases as far as Parker was concerned: one party to the agreement had not done what he or she had undertaken to do: 'Heard complaint Ricd Edwards . . . v Thos Edwards for neglecting to come to his service according to his hiring.' Elizabeth Griffiths, servant to Samuel Jackson clearly thought her master had failed to deliver what he had promised at the hiring and Parker agreed with her. She must keep her side of the bargain too: 'Heard her complaint for wages – she was hired from 17 May till Christmas at the rate of £5 a year – She is to return to her service this eve'g . . . and to have 5 days deducted for wages . . .'. Parker might make adjustments to an agreement, but that hiring agreement was what he must constantly have in mind.[61]

The servant's labour – what he or she did in the way of work – was important, but only insofar as it was the subject of a legally binding agreement between two parties. To whom it belonged (the servant or the master), whether or not it produced value and for whom it produced value were not questions within these myriad daily discussions. It was the same with tax law after the inauguration of the servant tax in 1777. Again, all over the country (but with much less frequency than magistrates' contemplation of employment questions) the servant's labour was discussed at hundreds of appeal meetings (until 1937 in the case of male servants, but only between 1785 and 1792 in the case of maidservants). When employers discussed the work their Man or their Maid did before the appeal commissioners, it was in order to demonstrate that their servant *wasn't really* a domestic servant, so that they might avoid paying the tax. When surveyors, assessors, collectors and appeal commissioners discussed the servants' labour, it was in order to determine whether the Man *was* a domestic servant 'within the meaning of the act'. (He brought in the hay harvest, said his master; he did a bit of ploughing; yes: once in a blue moon he donned some silk knee breeches and served at table when they had company to dine, but . . . *really* he was a servant in husbandry.)[62] An employer whose servant's labour enabled him to earn a living was exempted from the tax, so a man or woman kept for the

[61] SA, 1060/168 (9, 25 May 1805; 19 May, 22 Jul. 1806; 21 May 1807; 30 Jul. 1808).
[62] See Carolyn Steedman, 'The servant's labour: The business of life, England 1760–1820', *Social History*, 29:1 (2004), 1–29.

purposes of husbandry, manufacture or trade was an important thing to conjure before the commissioners. In September 1778 George Geree Elwick appealed to the Kent commissioners against the assessment made on his servant William Lucas. (Lucas had been assessed as a 'foot boy and gardener'.) Elwick had 16 acres he said, which he worked himself. Lucas ploughed and harrowed for him, looked after the cows, churned the butter, and did some other, unspecified 'husbandry matters'. He never wore the livery of an indoor servant, claimed his master. He didn't wait at table; he cleaned no knives and forks in the kitchen. He did, on the other hand, clean boots and shoes; he went on errands and messages for the family; he looked after their riding horse, which was also plough and cart horse from time to time. The family employed others to look after the garden; Lucas only worked there when 'he has time'. In what was often a clincher with commissioners (or what employers, with a keen eye for the wording of the Servant Tax Act, thought would be a clincher) Elwick said that Lucas was only there because of the 'husbandry business', to enable Elwick to make a living. He wanted the judges' opinion on the case, which the Act provided for. But when the case was forwarded to King's Bench, he was disappointed. The judges determined that William *was* 'a servant by him retained ... in some or other of the capacities mentioned in the act, jointly with the husbandry business', and that Elwick was liable to the tax.[63]

The everyday administration of common, statute and tax law did not provide an arena in which labour and its products were discussed as property; they did not need to be so discussed. A magistrate going about his daily business might refer to one of the many legal handbooks available which repeated the legal philosophers on the question of property in labour. At the very end of the century, John Bird took 'Domestic, Usually Stiled Menial servants' as his first topic in his legal handbook, explaining 'the Interest a Master has in the Time and Attendance of his Servant', and the 'reason and foundation upon which all this doctrine is built'. He cited Blackstone, and *his* explanation that what underpinned it 'seems to be the property which every man has in his domestics, acquired by the contract

---

[63] John Smee, *A Complete Collection of Acts of Parliament and Cases with opinions of the Judges upon the following Taxes, viz. Upon Windows, Servants, Horses, Carriages and Dogs; the Duties upon Hair-powder Certificates . . .* , 2 vols., J. Butterworth, London, 1797, vol. 2, pp. 513–50; Kent, Bredegar, 2 Sep. 1778. This contains 131 appeal cases, in which judges' decisions were published as case law. The rough and ready compilation, Commissioners of Excise, *Abstract of Cases and Decisions on Appeals Relating to the Tax on Servants*, T. Longman and T. Cadell, London, 1781, covered the years 1778 to 1780 and 114 local cases that went through to appeal. John Smee's 1797 collection repeated many of these, but also added more judgments from the period 1781 to 1796.

of hiring, and purchased by giving them wages'.[64] Labour mattered as an aspect of a contractual arrangement; the political philosophy of the thing was not at stake.

Slavery as a social institution did however, provide one of the spaces and places in which the servant's labour – the Boy churning butter, the maidservant making the beds – might be discussed as a form of property.[65] What the law said about persons as property and property in persons framed the pamphlet war between the pro-slavery lobby and the abolitionists in the 1770s and 1780s. One hard-line apologist for slavery suggested that all philosophical anxieties of his contemporaries would simply disappear if slaves were renamed: remove 'the odious name "slave",' said Samuel Estwick in 1777, and call them 'property', plain and simple; that was the solution. 'They are vested as goods and chattels', he said; 'that is their nature'.[66] If this point of nomenclature applied to Africans used for labour in the Americas, then it applied as well to those residing in England, for where was the law that said otherwise? 'I mean to conclude generally that the right and property . . . of every subject of great Britain in his Negroe or Negroes is . . . founded in him by the law of this land.'[67] Questions of involuntary and voluntary servitude were thought-through in terms of law; there was no other way of doing this thinking. The principles of Christianity and the law of God that abolitionists said were violated by slavery and slave ownership were subsumed under a larger question of law and legality.[68] Slavery was opposed to the law of God and the law of nature, said the Reverend James Ramsay from the abolitionist side. Certainly civil law had given and secured to everyone 'the rights adapted to his particular station in society'. But the relationship of master and slave was 'artificial, or unnatural', for it transferred law out of the commonweal and made every slave owner 'his own legislator'.[69] As former rector of St Kitt's, he knew what he was talking about, he told his readers, though he needed the usual recourse to constitutional and legal history to explain his argument: 'In every independent state, whether monarchy or republic, that has got beyond the first steps

---

[64] Bird, *Laws Respecting Masters and Servants*, pp. 4–6.
[65] Tim Meldrum, *Domestic Service and Gender, 1660–1750: Life and work in the London household*, Pearson, Harlow, 2000, pp. 25–7.
[66] West Indian (Samuel Estwick LL.D), *Considerations on the Negroe Cause, Commonly so Called. Addressed to the Right Honourable Lord Mansfield. Lord Chief Justice of the Court of the King's Bench, &c. By a West Indian*, J. Dodsley, London, 1772, pp. 7–12.
[67] West Indian, *Considerations*, pp. 24–5.
[68] Granville Sharp, *Serious Reflections on the Slave Trade. Wrote in March 1797*, W. Calvert, London, 1785.
[69] James Ramsay, *An Essay on the Treatment and Conversion of African Slaves in the British Sugar Colonies*, James Phillips, London, 1784, p. 3

of civilization, the people, or citizens, naturally divide into sovereign and subject, master and family, employer and employed; all other ranks being arbitrary or artificial.' This was the rule of law, universal in its application. It was the same with the householder as it was with the community at large. To be sure, the ordinary employer of servants and labourers in England had 'a kind of property, either continued or temporary, in all under his roof'; but the agreement between master and servant was a voluntary one, and should be considered for what it was, as an employment relationship. This ordinary employment relationship might appear to be reciprocal, but it was not really so, for 'custom has universally affixed to property the idea of superiority over personal ability, or labour'. If a person owned materials, 'or a subject to be improved for use by the skill or labour of another' then the owner had a right to dictate how the skill was to be exercised.[70] This is what you told the workers – the servants themselves – albeit in a different register: they had liberty and property, ready recourse to a concerned magistracy, and the poor laws, the Reverend Chubbe told them in 1793; 'the greatest Lord amongst you, offending in a like manner, is subject to ... the same punishment'. They might be in an '*inferior* station', but they could not be deprived of their wages 'by the tyranny or injustice of [their] Masters'. But were they to act on the words of radicals with a Levelling agenda, it might well be their '*future* lot to work *without wages* ... In other words, you may be SLAVES.'[71]

The institution and practice of slavery provided a rhetorical space for a discussion of John Locke's unspoken question from the 1680s, concerning the servant's labour. Slavery allowed many interlocutors to focus on property: property in persons, labour as a form of property and employers' and workers' rights in regard to this property. It introduced employers (certainly the employer of servants to be discussed in the next chapter) to a vocabulary and a conceptual framework for considering labour itself – what kind of thing it was that they had contracted and paid for. These shifts in understanding did not just take place at the philosophic and textual level, but had real effects in the social realm and in actual employment relationships. Ways of writing about the experience – the assumed experience – of servitude, emerged in this literature in antislavery publications. The depression and hopelessness attributed as a state of mind to the English domestic servant in the 1790s was first articulated in the discourse on slavery, which also introduced the modern language of 'employer' and 'employee' to lawyers and magistrates and

---

[70] Ramsay, *An Essay*, pp. 5–9.
[71] William Chubbe, *A Few Words to the Labourers of Great-Britain*, R. Loder, Woodbridge, 1793, pp. 4–7.

masters and servants – the last being told that they were servants, not slaves, because of the nature of contract in English society;[72] and also of course, because of its history. It was history itself that produced the happy circumstance of the English servant, domestic or otherwise. Philosophers had long been writing histories in which all had risen from a condition of general servitude akin to slavery, to an ordered and ranked civil society. From the 1770s onwards the lessons of history were inflected by the slavery debate; history lessons were given to workers with New World chattel slaves as examples.

John Vancouver's *Enquiry into the Causes and Production of Poverty* (1796) was a response to the current poor-law crisis. The old poor law was under severe strain in 1790s, not least because of war, blockade and a series of poor grain harvests. As a solution Vancouver proposed a detailed 'General Subscription Plan', a form of state-managed unemployment insurance, with contributions to be paid by employer and worker.[73] He thought his scheme offered distinct advantages over current poor-law assessment through local rates, for he proposed something very like a tax on labour, that is an employer would pay a higher contribution the more employed he engaged (rather than assessment being based on rental value of the employer's property, as with the current system).[74] His plan was also to net those who currently did not pay poor rates: 'manufacturers and ship-owners; single women, bachelors, and others, not housekeepers, but who are in the habit of employing servants'.[75] For clarity of proposal he said, he must separate the whole community into two 'societies' or 'grand divisions': into 'the society of the *employers*, and the society of the *employed*'.[76] This second category had to be further divided for the purposes of analysis, into the 'employed' and the 'poor'.[77] Domestic

---

[72] Ruth Paley, 'After Somerset: Mansfield, slavery and the law in England 1772–1830' in Norma Landau (ed.) *Law, Crime and English Society 1660–1830*, Cambridge University Press, Cambridge, 2002, pp. 165–84.

[73] John Vancouver, *An Enquiry into the Causes and Production of Poverty, and the State of the Poor: together with the proposed Means for their Effectual Relief*, R. Edwards, London, 1796; 'General Subscription Plan', pp. 111–48.

[74] Vancouver, *Enquiry*, pp. 46–7.

[75] Vancouver, *Enquiry*, p. 81. He anticipated their response to this alarming innovation: '– start not ye to whom Heaven hath thus given the means of employment; nor think the meditated attack upon your wealth is of that nature, to cause you a shadow of inconvenience'.

[76] Vancouver, *Enquiry*, p. 3.

[77] Vancouver, *Enquiry*, p. 5. Other commentators used the terms 'employers' and 'employed' in this new way. See Granville Sharp, *Short Sketch of Temporary Regulations (until better shall be proposed) for the intended Settlement on the Grain Coast of Africa, near Sierra Leona*, H. Baldwin, London, 1786, where the term 'employed' is used for all 'hired labour'. Also Edmund Poulter, *Address and Report on the Enquiry into the General State of the Poor. Instituted by Order of the last Epiphany General Quarter Session for the*

servants were unambiguously included in his category of 'the *employed*' – they were workers, just like the shepherds who provided his main example.

Preliminary to all his proposals was the question, 'what is property?', with Vancouver answering that 'That property can ultimately be resolved into no principle but labour, will not be denied.' The unfortunate thing was that in late eighteenth-century England, neither the common law nor statute law recognised this fundamental principle; it was only interested in property as a moveable commodity that could be exchanged or bartered for.[78] In Vancouver's social vision, the property of employers originated in the bodies of the workers: the 'property of the employers arises from the reserved *transferable* proportion, which they contract for, out of the productive labour and ingenuity of the employed'. The employed may not have much real or personal property; but they have 'each one's individual talent of labour or ingenuity'. This was 'their *untransferable* stock of productive labour, whether of a corporeal, or mental quality'.[79] Employers had been protected against poverty by their own stockpile of surplus property, an accumulation which could be traced back to the beginning of things: 'this capital had its commencement on the first division of the community, and hath been gradually encreasing ever since. It is in constant circulation within the society to which it belongs.' No one ever gave it up for nothing. Employed men and women, on the other hand, were unable to preserve their 'surplus property of productive labour'.[80]

Vancouver thought hard about what kind of thing labour was, advancing upon the discourse on slave labour in the Sugar Islands, which had conceptualised slaves as labour itself. He answered John Locke's implied question, about who owned the servant's labour. The employed in England – the workers – *possessed* property; they were not property themselves, as was the slave. Their property was their labour. But it was a peculiar kind of property. It belonged to the worker, but it couldn't be transferred. When in health and strength, the labourer possessed it, but if he or she fell ill, it was completely lost. The worker could not put his or her own price on it, 'for the employers alone assume, and exercise the sole right of determining on the value of the property purchased of the employed'. Vancouver's example was the shepherd. 'His personal

---

County of Hampshire, Robbins, Winchester, 1795, pp. 3, 15, 28. Thomas Ruggles, *The History of the Poor; their Rights, Duties, and the Laws respecting Them*, 2 vols., J. Deighton, London, 1793, retains a distinction between 'employers and employed' and 'masters and servants'.

[78] Vancouver, *Enquiry*, pp. 17–18.
[79] Vancouver, *Enquiry*, pp. 4–6.
[80] Vancouver, *Enquiry*, p. 14.

attendance on his flock, and the application of his ability, i.e. his care and judgement' constituted his property-in-labour. But only by 'continual exertion' could he gain any benefit from it. The shepherd – the worker – who ceased to labour became poor (a member of the 'society of the poor') and joined those already there by reasons of 'weakness, imbecility, illness, old age, [and] infancy'.[81] It was this point about the dispersal and disappearance of labour that struck the *Gentleman's Magazine* reviewer so forcefully: that a form of property might simply disperse itself – be no more – in the instant a labourer fell ill, or died.[82]

It was this very great peculiarity of labour as a form of property that necessitated the interest of state and government in insuring the employed against the disaster of sickness and their families against the disaster of their death, said Vancouver. His summary was trenchant, delivered as a series of aphorisms. It reached a conclusion that may go some way to explain the muted response to his scheme: 'time out of mind' workers had not received full compensation for their property; 'the price of their labour hath not been equal to the demand of their wants'. Moreover, poverty was 'of physical origin', not moral; everyone who laboured was liable to it.[83] Vancouver's insurance scheme seems strikingly modern; it is strange that it has received no attention in histories of national insurance in Britain.[84] It was well reviewed at time of publication, and there were approving references to it in the works of other philosophers of poverty; but after Patrick Colquhoun listed Vancouver as one of the ablest writers on the poor 'whom the country has produced', it appears quite lost to view.[85]

---

[81] Vancouver, *Enquiry*, pp. 3–7, 17–24.

[82] *Gentleman's Magazine*, 67 (Jan.–Jun. 1797), 134–5.

[83] Vancouver, *Enquiry*, pp. 33–5.

[84] It is mentioned in biographies of his more famous brother, Captain George Vancouver (1757–98), as something else he did with his life besides editing and completing the dead George's *A Voyage of Discovery to the North Pacific Ocean, and round the World*, (John Vancouver (ed.)), 3 vols., G. G. and J. Robinson, London, 1798; Sir James Watt, 'The voyage of Captain George Vancouver 1791–95: The interplay of physical and psychological pressures', *CBMH/BCHM*, 4 (1987), 31–51; *Dictionary of Canadian Biography OnLine*, 'Vancouver, George', www.biographi.ca/index-e.html, accessed 10 Oct. 2006. But *The Enquiry* was completed and published before John undertook this task; he showed much concern for the welfare and relief of sailors. Like domestic servants, he included them in 'the society of the employed'.

[85] Sir Frederic Morton Eden, *The State of the Poor: or, an History of the Labouring Classes in England, from the Conquest to the Present Period;... together with Parochial Reports... In three volumes*, B. and J. White; G. G. and J. Robinson; T. Payne and others, London, 1797, Vol. 1, p. 472; John Mason Good, *Dissertation on the best Means of Maintaining and Employing the Poor in Parish Work-houses. Published at the Request of the Society for the Encouragement of Arts, Manufactures, and Commerce: having obtained the Premium offered by the Society for the best Treatise on this Subject*, Cadell and Davis and Morton, London,

His were new propositions, given in the form of a very old story. Vancouver used the same kind of conjectural history that John Locke had used, in his much briefer discussion of property in labour a century before. The story had been much elaborated by philosophic historians of the mid-century. Like all of them, Vancouver started at the beginning of things, with 'the first introduction of labour . . . [when] it was soon found, that, by combining the powers of several men together', work went better and faster. Here was the first accumulation of property among 'a certain portion of . . . that community', which by 'extraordinary exertions' produced more food than they could eat and so bartered it for cattle and other moveables: 'This was the first creation of transferable property.' Then 'these industrious possessors' got cultivating. In the remote past when 'occupancy alone . . . was necessary to secure a title to a landed estate . . . a part of the surface which had been fertilized, by the superior ability and endeavours of this class, was lent, or let, to neighbours of the other division'. Vancouver was unusual in writing history this way, postulating the first labour contract as a service contract emerging in pastoralism; but it was also the implication of the more extended versions of Adam Ferguson and John Millar. Vancouver's owner and possessor 'knew precisely the quantity of labour expended on the spot in question, [and] would not part with it to another . . . without exacting, in the service contracted for, some additional labour'.[86] And so it went on; it was the story of how the modern world came to be what it was, as owners increased their demands for borrowers' services on improved and more valuable land.

Following the trajectory of forgotten social policy is a mere antiquarian exercise unless the claim for its importance was that someone *was able to think this*, in specific historical circumstances, and that others were able to read and make sense of it. From those acts of reading and appropriation, ideas become active in social worlds, as we shall see in the next chapter, where the social theory read by one Somerset employer of the later eighteenth century allows access to the way in which she managed her own property and profit and the labour she employed to make that profit.

1798, p. 75; Patrick Colquhoun, *A Treatise on Indigence; Exhibiting a General View of the National Resource for Productive Labour . . .*, J. Hatchard, London, 1806, p. 13.
[86] Vancouver, *Enquiry*, pp. 29–32.

3   Frances Hamilton's labour

Frances Hamilton (1742–1802) lived in Somerset in the century after Locke's friends, the Clarkes, wrote their busy letters to him. Her questions, about the organisation of life and labour on her 60-acre farm, and in the wider world, were not put directly to a political philosopher (though she did own Locke's major works) but rather, to books. This chapter is concerned with the ideas that informed her daily life, the management of her property and profit, and with the circulation of social and political theory more generally. It is specifically concerned with the theories of labour, profit, and accumulation that Hamilton encountered in the 1780s, when she read intensely and widely on the topic of slavery, and with the experiences – in life and with the book – that made her the kind of employer she was. Her father had been a Taunton attorney; her marriage to Thomas Hamilton, a Bath medical man, was brief ('My dear Mr Hamilton [died] 7th June 1779 . . . Married 5 Years & five Weeks,' she brooded in her diary). She returned as widow to the small family estate at Bishops Lydeard (about 7 miles from Taunton) which she farmed up until her death.[1]

Hamilton kept detailed records of everything she owned, spent and borrowed. Every farthing that left her purse had its passage recorded.

[1] Margaret Allen, 'Frances Hamilton of Bishops Lydeard', *Notes and Queries for Somerset and Dorset*, 31 (1983), 259–72. Somerset County Record Office (SCRO), DD/FS 5/4, Estate and farm account book kept by Frances Coles [Hamilton], reusing her arithmetic exercise book 1767, 1765–77. She had evidently been involved in farming it before her departure for Bath.

Once, in 1796, she could not recall exactly how much she had paid her washerwoman at 6d a day ('Catherine paid her abt 2s'), but that was one of her few falterings in twenty years of reckoning up her profits and losses.[2] Anyway, she often lent Catherine money, and their meetings to settle accounts always involved complicated calculations on both sides. On this occasion Hamilton remembered that she had lent her 2s after a previous wash, as well as paying her. These were highly useful accounts as far as Hamilton was concerned, and they have been called meticulous.[3] She moved with evident ease between old prescription books of her husband containing builders' bills and indoor servants' wages, and an old volume of inventories where she recorded payment to her casual workers. Borrowings from the Taunton Book Society were listed next to her washerwomen's accounts. When she kept a diary – what she called a 'Day Book' – it was in an old ledger of lawyer's bills, probably her father's.[4] She used all these volumes regularly, to transfer records from her day-book to her housekeeping or farm accounts and, quarterly, to compile a statement of farm outgoings and income. She owned under 100 acres and was perhaps unusual in keeping such detailed records; it is said that the practice was more likely among 'men or women with a larger than average holding, making . . . complex sales and purchases and employing a labour force sufficiently large to require a written record'.[5]

The model of writing and recording at work in the seventeen or so volumes that survive was modern and secular. She did not use her notebooks and ledgers as an aid to worship in the way that Michael Mascuch has described for other eighteenth-century diary-writers.[6] Hamilton sat through many a sermon at Bishops Lydeard, but made notes on not one of them. Each year on her birthday she inscribed a prayer asking that she might be granted an increase in goodness over the coming year, but she

[2] SCRO, DD/FS 5/8 (26 Dec. 1786).   [3] Allen, 'Frances Hamilton,' pp. 259–72.

[4] SCRO, DD/FS 7/1, General account book kept by Frances Hamilton, reusing a doctor's prescription book (1776–9); DD/FS 7/4, Wage book (1801–2) kept by Frances Hamilton, reusing a volume of inventories (1779–1802); DD/FS 5/8, Household and farm account book kept by Frances Hamilton with valuations (1791–9); DD/ FS 7/2, Farm and general diary, partly indexed, kept by Frances Hamilton, reusing a lawyer's bill book (1787–8). Nicola Verdon, '"A Much Neglected Historical Source": The uses and limitations of farm account books to historians of rural women's work', *Women's History Notebook*, 8 (2001), 5–12.

[5] M. E Turner, J. V. Beckett and B. Afton, 'Taking stock: Farmers, farm records, and agricultural output in England, 1700–1850', *Agricultural History Review*, 44 (1996), 21–34, 27, 29.

[6] Michael Mascuch, *Origins of the Individual Self: Autobiography and self-identity in England, 1591–1791*, Cambridge University Press, Cambridge, 1997, pp. 82–6. See also Carolyn Steedman, *Master and Servant: Love and labour in the English industrial age*, Cambridge University Press, Cambridge, 2007, pp. 59–65.

did not write in daily conversation with God, as some of her contemporaries did.[7] She did not often copy out from her reading aphorisms or extended passages that had struck her; rather, when she made a comment it was brief and succinct – an expression of her opinion on the matter. Compared with some of her more godly contemporaries, her relationship with texts that furnished her religious and political imagination was one of some independence. When she read, she was a woman who not only knew her own mind but also how it had been cultivated. Her note of Dugald Stewart's *Philosophy* ('Edin prof of Moral Philosophy The University of Edinburgh. a Book I have a high opinion of') was initialled 'FH'.[8] This indicates a sense of an audience for her writing, even if the audience was just herself. But writing '1 pound Mackaroons', '1 pound of Sausages', 'Oisters 1/2 C', 'Worsted for my Apprentices', 'Straw', '[paid] Spiller Haberdasher in full', '[paid] Dinham shoemaker in full', was not done for an imagined audience in the same way. It was done so that she knew how much money she had spent, and though she might read these entries again (and again) she had no intention of communicating something by them. There were dozens of entries for lemons, butter, barm, pigeons, treacle, mace, anchovies, blue for washing, 'candles, one pound' – the result of every marketing trip to Taunton was exhaustively recorded, for over twenty years. She had read several contemporary guides to keeping accounts and knew the section on 'Book-Keeping' in the *Encyclopaedia Britannica*, which, from 1777 onwards, told its commercial and trade readers that, for proper account keeping, they should always keep going a Waste Book, a Journal, and a Ledger, at the same time. The Waste or Day Book was to be 'an exact register of all occurrences' as they took place. Later, in the Journal, a fair copy should be made of all transactions in the Waste Book, in the same order but in a more technical style. Then on regular basis, all this material was to be collected together in the Ledger 'under proper titles' with expenditure and income on opposite pages, and items divided into Personal and Real Accounts.[9] The advice from *Britannica* was a counsel of perfection. What an actual late eighteenth-century account-keeper like Frances Hamilton did, was leave out the middle stage, that is the Journal. She made the attempt at

---

[7] SCRO, DD/FS 7/1 (14 Oct. 1787).
[8] Duguld Stewart, *Elements of the Philosophy of the Human Mind*, 3 vols,. A. Strahan and T. Cadell, London and W. Creech, Edinburgh, 1792–1827 (vol. 1, 1792), pp. 1, 19, 526; SCRO, DD/FS 6/3, Household and farm account book kept by Frances Hamilton, using book kept as administrator to her husband, 1779–85. (12 Apr. 1795).
[9] 'Book-Keeping', *Encyclopaedia Britannica; or, a Dictionary of Arts and Sciences, Compiled Upon a New Plan*, Edinburgh, 1771. Hamilton took '7 Dictionarys of Art & Sciences' to Bath and her marriage in 1775; SCRO, DD/FS 6/1.

double-entry just a few times a year, and then only for the farm accounts. If this was the model of writing and recording that Hamilton used, it makes sense of the pig killings and works of political philosophy that brush up against each other, and helps make a pathway through the labyrinthine records of muffins bought and social theory read. A memory or observation, that (some time earlier) 'NB. I bought a hank & a shirt [for Edward her apprentice] which I did not let him have for disobedience', is next to the real-time note, '1 pocket hank 1s 2d', so knowledge of the model she was using can restore time and chronology to the everyday life that a list makes abstract.[10]

By way of contrast with the journal-keeping of another gentleman's daughter of the same period, the Lancastrian Elizabeth Shackleton, Hamilton's focus was on production rather than consumption, on the men and women, their labour and their wages for labour, that allowed her to wrest a living from her own 60 acres.[11] She certainly recorded her behaviour as a consumer, but for the main part a consumer of everyday items (butchers' meat, lighting, tools for house cleaning and hedging, hair trimming and shoe mending) rather than the luxury items that have focused recent attention on the eighteenth-century consumer revolution.

In 1797, twenty years into her farming career and widowhood and five years before her death, Hamilton made her own assessment of what she spent on labour. She recorded a wages bill as part of a calculation of her land and real estate holdings and the profit she made by renting out some of her fields.[12] She listed together payments for outdoor work ('Labourers work done on the Farm') and annual wages of £7 7s to one 'servant for the Farm' (a servant in husbandry on an annual hiring). She reckoned that in the preceding year she had spent some £13 on this kind of farm labour. She counted up indoor wages in different volumes; but George Shattock shows how permeable was the boundary between house and farm. She first recorded paying him as a ploughboy in January 1796, at 3d day. 'The price of labour, throughout the whole district, is nearly the same', said John Billngsley in his survey of the Vale of Taunton in 1795. 'Men, through the year, one shilling per day

---

[10] SCRO, DD/FS 5/8 (15 Jul. 1796).

[11] Amanda Vickery, 'Women and the world of goods. A Lancashire consumer and her possessions, 1751–81' in John Brewer and Roy Porter (eds), *Consumption and the World of Goods: Consumption and society in the seventeenth and eighteenth centuries*, Routledge, London, 1993, pp. 274–301; Amanda Vickery, *The Gentleman's Daughter: Women's lives in Georgian England*, Yale University Press, New Haven, 1998, pp. 165–72, 183–93. Elizabeth Shackleton does also appear here as a producer, but it is her minor role; see pp. 154–5, 390–3.

[12] SCRO, DD/FS 5/8. For 1797 she reckoned 30 acres farmed by her own labour (labourers), and a rental income of £11 3s 6d on three further parcels of land.

and beer; women, for weeding and common work, six-pence per day.'[13] Hamilton gave the occasional cash present to her farm workers, and she sometimes substituted a penny or so for liquor; but these were the wages she paid throughout her time at Bishops Lydeard: the bottom of the scale that Billingsley recorded for the area. George Shattock was very young. Threepence a day was what she paid the children to weed and help with the hay harvest. Paying Shattock for his time as ploughboy cost her £1 11s 7½d between January and May 1796 (not including the 1½d she gave him for drink in March and 1s 2d as a present in May). Then George got his first domestic service contract, Hamilton noting on 12 June 1796 'Geo Shattock. . . plow boy. . . commencing this day my Footman & is to have Cloaths meat washing and Lodging during [my] pleasure & to return his Cloaths to me if he turns out untoward.'[14] He was given cash for odd jobs around the house and outbuildings, for making matches at ½d a score (he got 3d) and catching rats (he earned 6d). He was not paid a wage. When she dismissed him in January 1797, she noted that she had 'expended on him about £4'.[15] In fact, if George is tracked through her various account books, it turns out to be more than that – closer to £5: money spent on a failed experiment that she may have been reluctant to contemplate. By the autumn of 1796 he was well kitted-out with 'a Thick set Coat & Waistcoat', two shirts, three pairs of stockings and a pair of shoes, clothes more likely to be worn for outdoor work than by a putative footman. Then there was lining for his breeches, shoe- and clothes-mending, and more hose. He did not get a pair of slippers for indoor wear until October 1796, three months after her man-servant Jonathan Hembrow had left 'to go for a shoemaker'.[16] Hembrow had come to her service in June 1793, though she had not noted terms until the following year: '27 June [1795] Jonathan in full for one Years service £1 1s. 0d NB. Jonathan if he lives with me to June 1796 is to have £2 2s 0d.'[17] He had no wage in his first year, but got his clothes, his hair

---

[13] John Billingsley, *General View of the Agriculture of the County of Somerset, with Observations on the Means of Its Improvement, drawn up in the year 1795, for the Consideration of the Board of Agriculture . . .*, 3rd edn, R. Cruttwell, Bath, 1798, p. 294; Nicola Verdon, *Rural Women Workers in Nineteenth-century England: Gender, work and wages*, Boydell Press, Woodbridge, 2003, pp. 48–9.

[14] SCRO, DD/FS 5/8 (12 Jun. 1796).   [15] SCRO, DD/ FS 5/3 (12 Jan. 1797).

[16] SCRO, DD/FS 5/2 (9 Jun. 1796). Hembrow was one of many eighteenth-century embodiments of Richard Brown's 1982 discussion of 'the work history' and the pitfalls for sociologists (and historians) using the idea of the occupational category for describing how people earned a living over a working life. Richard Brown, 'Work histories, career strategies and the class structure' in Anthony Giddens and Gavin MacKensie (eds.), *Social Class and the Division of Labour*, Cambridge University Press, Cambridge, 1982, pp. 119–36.

[17] SCRO, DD/ FS 5/8 (27 Jun. 1795).

trimmed and some pocket money. He was rat-catcher too from time to time, earning an extra 1s 6d this way in January 1796 (three times what George Shattock made at the same task). He stayed the full three years and Hamilton gave him 'for serving me . . . to this day over & above his wages 6s'. He also got his capsule wardrobe and at least one pair of shoes. Immediately after this entry, George Shattock the ploughboy became a footman – for just six months.[18]

She remembered the bargain she had made with Hembrow when she took on another boy, Raymond Williams, in March 1798: 'Raymond & mother came here & I made a bargain for Two years at the same Rate that I paid Jonathan . . . One Guinea the second year & Two guineas the third Year if I recollect right but I will look in my Book & be certain.'[19] Raymond was also paid for many outside jobs about the garden and fields at the same rate as George Shattock had been – $1\frac{1}{2}$d a day. In July 1796 she had paid the hairpowder tax, so Jonathan Hembrow spent some of his time in full dining-room gear, including a powdered wig.[20] She had not paid the male servant tax since 1782,[21] which suggests that both she and the local assessor were able to categorise Jonathan, George, Raymond (and the other boys she employed) as something other than the footmen she called them in her diaries. (She paid the maidservant tax for the seven years the legislation was in force.) The crown surveyor for Somerset and his tax assessors and collectors do not appear to have been very vigorous. No cases went to King's Bench from the county on the request of an employer appealing against the assessment of his Boy as a footman – whilst all he did, the master swore, was catch rats and run errands. In Woodbridge, Suffolk, in the late 1770s, the Reverend Mr Humphryes had been assessed for John Stephenson, a foot-boy. But! – he was only 'twelve years of age', said Humphryes; 'was fatherless, and taken by him out of charity'. He got no wages, only clothes and board. The boy wore no livery and did not wait at table. However, for 'two or three times when his master had been at a public dinner, the boy had then waited on his master'. It was stated that 'the boy only went on errands, cleaned his shoes, sharpened knives, swept the garden, lighted the fire, and did other occasional business in the house'. All to no avail. The Appeal Commissioners and the judges of the King's Bench declared that John Stevenson 'came under the description of a male servant, acting in the capacity of a footman'. He was a servant and his employer was liable

---

[18] SCRO, DD/ FS 5/8 (9 and 12 Jun. 1796).
[19] SCRO, DD/FS 5/3 (26 and 27 Mar. 1798).   [20] SCRO, DD /FS 5/8 (8 Sep. 1796).
[21] SCRO, DD/FS 6/3 (21 May 1782).

to the tax.[22] But Frances Hamilton appears to have got away with half a dozen John Stephensons between 1778 and her death in 1802. Boys like Shattock and Williams lived in her house and were fed and maintained by her. She clearly had the intention of employing them as house servants. George Shattock made an unsatisfactory transition from field to dining room if the briefness of his stay is anything to go by, but by June 1797 he was plough boy no more. She did not attempt the same with girls and young women, who in her account books also move between kitchen and field, as did Jane Philpot. In February 1797 she 'came here to work'. In July, whilst 'The Women this week make Hay and . . . Weed Potatoes in ye Quarry Field & . . . Jane Philpot weed in the Garden & gathers Fruit'. In January 1798 'Jane Philpot [was to] pick up sticks & stones.' She was often ill; she was sent home from helping in the kitchen in July 1797 and on 3 January 1799 Frances Hamilton 'Discharged Jane Philpot on acc of illness'. She was back again during Frances Hamilton's final illness, one of the many village women Frances Hamilton paid to sit up with her at night.[23]

In 1797 (the year in view) her account of household labour shows a makeshift set of arrangements. Her so-called footman, the ploughboy George Shattock was dismissed in January; but already in November 1796 she had had to buy in Richard Huckleburgh (or Huckleborough) for '1 day waiting at table 2s 6d . . . 15 days in ye Garden 17s 6d'.[24] Who was he? Possibly related to the woman from whom she had bought more labour than any other, Betty Huckleburgh, who first appeared in Frances Hamilton's diary, 'here mending my Stays', in December 1787.[25] Frances Hamilton called her 'Huckleburgh Betty Mantua maker' in 1792.[26] But she also worked for Hamilton in the kitchen when Jane Philpot was ill and in 1798 she came in for half a day's work every day for two weeks.[27] She slept at the house during Hamilton's last illnesses, in January 1799 once going 'Home to breakfast & work for herself: [then] came at night'.

---

[22] John Smee, *A Complete Collection of Abstracts of Acts of Parliament and Cases with Opinions of the Judges upon the following Taxes Viz, upon Houses, Windows, Servants . . .* , 2 vols., J. Butterworth, London, 1797, vol. 1, pp. 513–50; Commissioners of Excise, *Abstract of Cases and Decisions on Appeals Relating to the Tax on Servants*, T. Longman and T. Cadell, London, 1781; Richard Burn, *The Justice of the Peace and Parish Officer . . . In Four Volumes*, 15th edn, A. Strahan and W. Woodfall, London, 1785, vol. 2, pp. 131–2.

[23] SCRO, DD/FS 5/3 (19 Feb., 9 Jul., 22 Jul., 1798; 1 Jan. 1798, 3 Jan. 1799); DD/FS 5/9: '4 April Jane Philpot sat up wt me . . . three nights'. DD/ FS 7/4: '5th – to Jane Philpot this night included at 6d, 1s 6d'; also DD/FS 5/8; DD/FS 7/4. Illness did not stop Frances Hamilton's usual book-keeping practices.

[24] SCRO, DD/FS 5/8 (21 Nov. 1796).

[25] SCRO, DD/FS 7/2 (6 Dec. 1787). A week later she had 'finished my stays & begin a Gown' (10 Dec. 1787).

[26] SCRO, DD/FS 5/7 (7 May 1790).   [27] SCRO, DD/FS 5/3 (17–28 Jun. 1798).

On the 19th January she came for 'breakfast and sweep my room'. Then two days later Hamilton took her into service: 'Betty came here. Months warning or Months Wages. £6.6.0'.[28] The Richard Huckleburgh who did the work of a footman by piece-work was very likely related to her. The 'Betty Huck:' of the ledgers and accounts books was provided for in Hamilton's will, to the tune of a 'Dwellinghouse and Outhouses with twelve feet of Garden Ground next adjoining the same and free access to the necessary' (the significance of rights to a privy will be discussed later) and 'for her Life . . . one clear annuity of seven pounds'.[29]

Life-style advice telling employers to use their maidservant in the capacity of a footman as a cheap and efficient method of household management was not as available as it was to be in the early nineteenth century, and Hamilton clearly believed that you needed a Man when there was company to dine – even if the Man were really a Boy, called in from the field, washed and brushed up and told to put on his stockings and slippers.[30] From the time she returned to Bishops Lydeard in 1779, she bought in labour like this, and frequently used her parish apprentices as footmen for the occasion. In October 1787 when 'Parson Slocombe, Mr Davey & Mr Chester dined here: Thos waited at table.' (Thomas Vosey – or Vasey – was put on her by the parish, an apprentice in husbandry; he was with her from 1780 to 1792.) His more usual work was cutting and sawing wood, cleaning the cider-making equipment, working in the kitchen garden, and sometimes accompanying her into Taunton on shopping trips.[31] When she had him actually perform husbandry work – mowing the clover grass in August 1789, for example – she deducted the price of his labour from the payment to the mower she employed for the occasion ('3 Acres Clover grass at 1s 3d deduct for Thomas 9d. Mowing also 7 Acres . . . deduct for Thomas . . . ').[32]

In January 1793 her apprentice Edward Williams's contribution to her guests' dinner was considerable: he was to 'heat the Oven cleav wood & wait at Table'. He had been washing turnips, beating cow dung for manure, cleaning the pig stye and mixing the ordure with coal ash to put round the raspberry bushes since 1788; this was the first time he waited at table. Frances Hamilton bought him presents of books and

[28] SCRO, DD/FS 5/3 (Jan. 1799).
[29] SCRO, DD/CH Bx 16, Copy of the Will and Codicils of Mrs Frances Hamilton.
[30] John Trusler, *The Way to be Rich and Respectable, addressed to Men of small Fortune,* 6th edn, privately printed, London, 1787; *Trusler's Domestic Management, or the Art of Conducting a Family, with Economy Frugality & Method,* J. Souter, London, 1819, pp. 96–116.
[31] SCRO, DD/FS 7/2 (22, 26, 30 Oct.; 1 Nov. 1787).
[32] SCRO, DD/FS 5/7 (30 Aug. 1789).

handkerchiefs, but he was an unreliable boy. In April 1793 'he behaved so ill that I was obliged to place him out of my House', though he was back ten days later, setting potatoes with one of her regular female field hands.[33] (It was not that easy to get rid of an apprentice placed on you by the parish.) In 1799 she had to pay for the services of a temporary footman again, when Bob Nott waited at table. That year Nott also worked seventy-seven days for her, making hay (in June), planting some trees in the orchard, and stacking up the hay (in July). He accompanied her into Taunton several times. In September he was employed to clean the knives in the kitchen; the next day he was outside again to take up the onions. He worked in the kitchen garden setting cabbages in October. The day he performed as footman he had already done half a day in the garden. He (or a relative) was in the bakery line in the village, in some way. Ten years before, in 1789, she had paid a Bob Nott for wood ashes (for use as a fertiliser) and settled an account with him for baking.[34] Nott waited at table again, at the same rate, at Christmas-time 1799.[35]

These domestic-service arrangements, put together at the last minute for particular social occasions and using what labour there was to hand, had always been a feature of her housekeeping, but were particularly important in 1797 when she had only her boy servant Raymond and just one maid in the house. Molly Evans, who had been with her since 1783, left in April 1796. She had earned £3 3s when she started; this had risen to £4 4s in 1787 but no further.[36] Betty Shearn Evans (a relative?) had joined her in 1795 at the rate of £5 5s a year; but she too left, in January 1797.[37] (Two years later, she was back as casual household help: 'Betty Shearn in House . . . '; 'Betty Shearn digging Potatoes'; 'Betty Shearn in House & sit up all Night with me'.[38]) Now, in January 1797, as Betty Evans left, Betty Murch came: '8 January Elizabeth Murch made a bargain to live with me after the Rate of Five pounds a year – a month's warning or a month's Wages at any time : if either Chuse to part.' Sometime in the autumn of 1798 she went back to her note of the hiring agreement to add that 'Betty Murch lived with me one year & three quarters & I believe she is honest & can be a very good Servt. but a more impertinent one was never in being.'[39] There was not much waged domestic labour in Bishops Lydeard House for Frances Hamilton to deploy in 1797: only Raymond Williams and the impertinent

[33] SCRO, DD/FS 5/2 (3 Jan., 26 Apr., 8 May 1793).
[34] SCRO, DD/FS 5/7 (24 and 28 Dec. 1789).
[35] SCRO, DD/FS 5/3 (Jun. to Dec. 1799).   [36] SCRO, DD/FS 5/7, 5/8, 6/3, 7/1.
[37] SCRO, DD/FS 5/3, 5/8.   [38] SCRO, DD/FS 5/3 (11, 12 Sep., 28–30 Oct. 1799).
[39] Ibid. (8 Jan. 1797; 9 Jan. 1798).

Betty Murch, supplemented by bought-in waiting at table. There was an apprentice girl put on her by the parish, but she lived out, Frances Hamilton paying her father a guinea out of the money she had received for taking her, so that the child could board at home.[40] Frances Hamilton's wage bill for the two household servants came to £6 0s 9d (Raymond was in his second year, now earning 21s; she was sure to have reckoned 15s 9d for the nine months from the bargain, which was dated 27 March). 1797 was unusual in the number of servants who left Frances Hamilton's employ – though her various stratagems in smuggling ploughboys into the house as footmen were common among employers all around the country.

Hamilton's employment strategy had changed since she first came home from Bath. She had returned to Bishops Lydeard in 1779 fully accoutred with a man-servant, then employed Abraham Cavell as one in 1783 at the rate of £6 6s a year, and, when he left in 1784, Edward Manley at 7 guineas.[41] Cavell had been much more finely kitted out than were her later Boys, with 'a suit of fashion Cloathes coat & waistcoat & a pair of Buckskin Breeches & a hat. If I chuse to keep him one year he is intitled to carry with him his suit. But is not intitled to great coat or Boots which he wears of mine. If I should not chuse to keep him a year upon a provocation that may be esteemed just then he is not to have his cloathes...'. She was not to pay at the rate of 7 guineas a year again, relying instead on poor and village boys who, if taken on as servants, worked their first year for food, lodging and clothes ('everything found') and were only formally hired at its end, when wages were about to commence. It was evidently more efficient to run a household this way, and certainly cheaper.

Hamilton's bids and stratagems for cheap male household labour were not a reflection of uncertain or decreasing income. She believed what her account books told her, that her income from the farm rose steadily over twenty years. But she could get more and more varied household labour out of a boy like Raymond Williams, or an apprentice like Edward Williams who also worked the land, for 'house' encompassed dwelling place and its kitchen, kitchen garden and garden, myrtle house (conservatory), orchard, pig pen, poultry house, cow byre, barns, bee hives, stable – the list goes on. It was men and boys who moved between these

---

[40] SCRO, DD/FS 7/3 (15 Jun. 1796, 13 Aug. 1797): 'Michael Nation gave him £1.1.0 to maintain his Daughter [Betty] my Apprentice. Three years from this Day & to pay for her Funeral if she dies within Three Year To maintain her everything included'. Hamilton was paying for 'Betty Nation Tapping Shoes all over 1s 8d', in 1801: DD/FS 5/8 (12 Sep. 1801).

[41] SCRO, DD/FS 6/3 (Mar. 1783).

household spaces and places and the types of work they implied, indoors and out. Frances Hamilton never – at least not on paper – asked a maid-servant to work at the hay, put down the peas and beans, or shovel out the necessary house. But husbandrymen – her outdoor workers – went shopping for her, carried her library books into Taunton, and occasionally put on a powdered wig to act as footman for the day. We end up knowing more about what the men did as work, because they moved between types of labour, played a variety of roles, and Frances Hamilton had to record these transitions so that she could tell them what to do and work out what to pay them. The maidservant knew what to do – what to scrub and bleach, peel and boil – and no daily reckoning of her labour was necessary, for women like Molly Evans were paid annually. Or perhaps more to the point, Hamilton understood what they did on a daily basis and did not have to write down instructions for household work in the way she did for farm work.

In 1789 there had been two maidservants in the house, Hannah Burston and Molly Evans. Evans, with Hamilton since 1783, was now at £4 4s; Hannah Burston with Hamilton since 1787, was at £6 6s a year. Edward Williams and Thomas Vosey, her parish apprentices, had been taken on in the early 1780s. This core of permanent staff was supplemented on a daily or weekly basis by at least eight women, men and children who worked about the house, garden and yard and sometimes the farm, adding some £7 13s 11½d to her domestic wages bill.[42] She actually spent more on her casual workers than that, making presents to the women of cash (about 4s in total in 1789), buying linsey and lining for two gowns (about 14s), and allowing Bet Gard her rent. Edward Williams was an apprentice, so no payment to him, though she expended 16s 10½d on his clothes, shoes and pocket money. In 1789 then, she spent just over £20 on domestic and household work, her permanent maids' wages accounting for half the bill.

Three years later in 1792 the permanent staff was the same, and some six women and children (same surnames, different first names) were bought in, and her total wages bill was £24 4s. If she had totalled up the hat and linsey she bought for Bet Gard, the £1. 19s 3d spent on the apprentices (a hat for Edward, breeches mending, shoe tapping...), the extra payments to Thomas Vosey for netting the fishpond, the

---

[42] In these calculations I have been consistent in adding a worker like Abraham Mullins to the list, because though he occasionally did field work, most of what she paid him for was work in the kitchen and flower garden. Equally, Bet Gard worked at the hay in summer, but did much more laundry, garden work and household waste disposal on a regular basis. These calculations do not involve the men and women who did farm work as their main job.

Table 3.1 *Frances Hamilton's expenditure on domestic labour, 1789, 1792, 1796, 1801*

	Household servants	Casual domestic workers	Presents, gratuities etc.	Total
1789	£10 10s	£7 14s	18s	£19 2s
1792	£10 10s	£12 18s	£2 14s 7d	£26 18s 7d
1796	£14 8s 8d	£10 18s	£21 8s 11½d	£46 15 s7½d
1801		£19 5s 8½d		£19 5s 8½d

presents . . . , then she would have reckoned her domestic labour expenses at £26 18 7d. Bought-in labour now accounted for much more than half the total. This trend continued. In 1796 there were more resident servants and apprentices to pay (or to pay for, in the case of the apprentices) but they cost less. It was a year of resignations and new hirings. Six casual workers were paid regularly over the year, with the same family names as in 1792. Molly Evans left in April, leaving Sally and Betty Shean and Sarah Hicks as resident maids (very briefly then, Hamilton had employed four maids at one time). Raymond Williams (on no pay for this his first year) arrived in March. George Shattock began his metamorphosis in June, after Jonathan Hembrow had departed. Edward Williams was still apprentice. The wages bill for these permanent workers was only £14 8s 8d, because of the extraordinarily economical arrangements she had put in place with Williams and Shattock. She spent £10 18s 0d on bought-in labour in and about the house and gardens, making a total household labour bill of £25 6s 8d. She made presents of money, clothes, trinkets and medicine to her casual workers, totalling £2 6s 2d. She spent £18 15s on clothing, shoes, mending, pocket money and treats for the apprentices and the boys and maids. This included Edward Williams' lodgings; he was now living out; perhaps he had always been boarded in the village. Together she spent £46 7s 10d on all the workers who serviced the house and gardens, near double what she had expended three years before. The maidservants had made a different though comparable move into modern labour arrangements: by way of contrast with 1792, Hamilton recorded buying 'Tea for the servts' on six occasions in 1796. She thought about the cost of feeding them, as we shall see. But this current accounting does not include the servants' or the casual domestic workers' food.

By 1801 she had come to rely on bought-in labour for running the house. In February 1800 she had hired 'Mrs Marriett/Cook – Six guineas a year . . . a months Wages or a months warning'.[43] Her first cook – designated cook – may still have been around in 1801, but there is no record of her being paid. Hamilton had charge of another parish apprentice – Sarah Pike – to add to Betty Nation. (She seems to have got but one pair of shoes, value 2s 9d, out of the arrangement – which after all was not her deal, but the parish's.[44]) Frances Hamilton was ill for much of 1801; she spent four months in Sidmouth attempting recuperation, and took other breaks away from Bishops Lydeard. For the Sidmouth trip she noted that she took four servants with her, but it is not clear who they were. Perhaps they were all like Betty Huckleburgh, paid at the rate of 6d a day to accompany her – one of the small army of familiar women who had spent the 1790s washing, weeding, brewing and cooking for her, at the rate of 6d a day.[45] For these helpers, the daily rate had not risen to 8d a day, as it had for female field workers. On this band of 'helpers' she expended all her domestic labour budget. She also started to keep her accounts in a new way, no longer scattering housemaids, apprentices, weeders and washerwomen across several volumes, but now putting them all together with her farm labourers in a 'Wage Book'. She had new categories of labour as well: 'Indoor Women & sitting up at Night with me'. Betty Shean Evans (once a regular live-in domestic servant) got £4 11s 0d during the course of the year, for night nursing, for washing and brewing, and what Frances Hamilton just called 'Service'. She expended nearly £20 on domestic work by the day or the piece (£19 5s 8½d) performed by six women over the year. Hannah Clemens earned just 3s of this total for sitting up at 6d a night, but another £3 4s 9d at field labour, paid at 8d per day. But perhaps some of her labour was in the house: some of it came at the sixpenny rate, and should be added to the £20 bill. Hamilton bought these women no presents: no hats or gowns or buckles as she had done for twenty years past. In her time, Catherine Vickery the washerwoman had got a fair number of hats and linsey gowns. Not any more. And the labyrinthine state of debt between her and Frances Hamilton had ended. No longer did every four days washing involve Mrs Vickery's handing back 2s she owed, and being lend another 2s. Hamilton was ill of course, and unable to shop for lengths of cloth, ribbons, tape and thread, but that does not explain the move into the modern terms of labour reflected in her account books. She paid for more domestic work by the hour and the piece than she had ten years before; the gift-giving that had sustained the relationship with her female casual workers had

---

[43] SCRO, DD/FS 5/3 (24 Feb. 1800).   [44] SCRO, DD/FS 5/8 (21 Jul. 1801).

[45] Joyce Burnette, 'The wages and employment of female day-labourers in English agriculture, 1740–1850', *Economic History Review*, 57:4 (2004), 664–90.

diminished. Hamilton's behaviour as an employer of domestic and other workers was perhaps part of a more general response to the financial exigencies of these crisis years, but more certainly the result of an individual and determined financial intelligence organising everyday life in the cheapest and most convenient way for Frances Hamilton.

In 1797, Hamilton reckoned that she spent £13 5s 4½d on 'Labourers work done on the Farm'. The annual wage to William Coombs, her hired farm servant, added another £7 7s. In running accounts it is not easy to tell whether 'Apprentice to the Farm £1 11s 6d' was reckoned by her as income and expenditure; but she had given a guinea of this parish payment to Betty Nation's father to maintain her so it is likely that she thought of the total sum as a form of income. In 1797 then, her total recorded expenditure on farm labour was just over £20. The year before, she had done her reckoning in February, the month she paid Coombs' annual wage; she recorded a total outdoor wages bill of £32 7s 9½d for the previous calendar year.[46] In another ledger she recorded all that she had spent on the farming business in 1796 ('Outgoings of the Farm') reckoning it up at £140 7s 5d. She listed 92 hogshead of lime fertilizer (paid for now, in 1796, but actually spread in 1795), a pig, seed, gloves for hedging, nails, the price paid for threshing and thatching, and the wages of William Coombs. The bills for labour amounted to £21 13s 11d, or about 15 per cent of her total outgoings. In a different account book she named the plough boys and the weeders who had worked for her at 3d a day during 1796, thus adding another £3 1s 4½d to the bill and increasing her expenditure on labour to 17 per cent of her outgoings in the farming business.[47] By her reckoning she made a profit of £40 7s 8d during the year from the sale of wheat, barley, cider, potatoes, nuts, beeswax, orchard produce . . . .[48] In 1801, a year in which household labour cost her about £20, she paid the husbandry men and women £35 7s 4d – but this is not easy to calculate. This sum includes work in the flower garden, for example, and payment for looking after the bees; and it is really not possible to tell on occasions when a woman was being paid to weed or being paid to wash.[49] The figures in her account books made the same movements between house, garden and field as her actual workers did.

[46] SCRO, DD/FS 5/8.   [47] *Ibid.*

[48] SCRO, DD/FS 5/1, Farm account book kept by Frances Hamilton (1792–1801). This was not her only source of income. She rented out several of her fields, owned at least two other rental properties in the neighbourhood, several cottages in Bishops Lydeard rented by some of her workpeople, and had income from an annuity bequeathed her by Thomas Hamilton.

[49] SCRO, DD/FS 5/6; 7/4.

Table 3.2 *Frances Hamilton's total expenditure, 1796*

	Household, farm & domestic labour	Food and household goods	Farm equipment, supplies, maintenance	General expenses	Total
1796	£78 17s 11d	£92 0s 4½d	£108 5s 1½d	£252 15 10½d	£532 19s 3½d

This small mixed farm did not provide for self-sufficiency. Bread was baked from Hamilton's own wheat, beer and cider brewed from her barley and apples, meat provided by a series of pigs; she kept cattle and poultry. But the household and its workers consumed large quantities of shop- or market-bought produce. The road to Taunton and its market and shops was travelled about every two weeks to procure non-native products – oranges and lemons, tea, sugar, spices, almonds and raisins; and also household cleaning and laundry products, lighting and cooking oil, fish and shellfish, very large quantities of butchers' meat (smaller quantities of poultry and game) and many bakery products, including cakes, muffins and manchets (a fine wheaten flour bun, rather like *brioche*). Early vegetables – forced asparagus for example – and barm for home baking were also purchased. In 1796, a year in which it is possible to bring all her various account books together in one reckoning, some £532 19s 3½d flowed out of her purse – on everything.

'Everything' is not a calculation she ever appears to have made for herself, though she did, as we have seen, reckon up the cost of the labour that falls within this total. It is not possible to be certain of Frances Hamilton's annual income, but it is possible to say that she had £500 to spend on the business of living, in this calendar year.

Her outgoings on 'Housekeeping' (that was how she headed these sections of her accounts) amounted to £92 0s 4½d, so food and household goods accounted for less than a quarter of her total expenditure. The three account books that cover 1796 distinguish in this way between spending on food and cleaning materials and other purchases that were clearly for household use – paper and dipping pens for example; the mending of kitchenware; flower seeds; clothes for herself, her apprentices and work women; the hire of a piano. When she listed '2 mopps' and 'earthenware' under non-housekeeping, this could either mean that she was an account keeper with the most fastidious sense of indoor and outdoor – that the mops were reserved for cleaning the outhouses, the earthenware for use in the dairy, perhaps – or that she used the book she had to hand to record expenditure 'to the moment'.[50] General expenses, that is non-housekeeping expenditure, also covered transport (the price of a trip to Taunton including the turnpike charge, a hostler paid for looking after the horse, drink for the Bishops Lydeard man driving the cart) though a different kind of accountant from Frances Hamilton might have reckoned them as part of the total expenses of the shopping trip. She also reckoned work done in the house by sweeps, glaziers, carpenters and all her washerwomen, as general expenses, along with hairdressing (for herself) and hair trimming (for the apprentices), postage, carriage of wine from Exeter, her Book Society subscription and books bought (Count Rumford's *Essays* telling how to feed the poor in this difficult year), and the charity she doled out (to the poor of Milverton parish where she held property, to a woman begging) as general expenses. Labour, indoor and out, cost her in wages, payment in kind, clothes, presents and trinkets, £78 17 11d of her total expenditure of £532 19s 3½d – less than she spent on food and housekeeping (17 per cent). She complained about the price of many things ('N.B The first time I ever paid 2s 8d a hundred for sawing Elm'), caught the butcher out in his calculations, and thought all lawyers' bills outrageous, but she always appears to have paid up. In 1796 she spent a lot on presents and gratuities for her workers. This may have been her adjustment of the wage economy of Bishops Lydeard's House to the wider food crisis that followed the harvest failure of 1795: '29 Jan 1796 NB The market price [of wheat] is 10s a bushel' she noted; 'I sell to the work people for 7s.'[51]

Thomas Cooper of New Place Farm, Guestling in East Sussex kept his accounts between 1788 and 1824. His were less complex than Frances Hamilton's (what have survived are household accounts; they do not show the constant movement between indoors and out, house and farm of Hamilton's). Moreover, he reckoned once a year, presumably from the same innumerable bits of paper that Hamilton used to record her daily – sometime hourly – expenditure. Perhaps he had never read the *Encyclopaedia Britannica*. He did his tidy accounting in March, always usefully reckoning up 'The Familly this Year' as well as what they had

---

[50] Samuel Richardson believed he had invented a new form of writing in *Pamela* (1740) – 'to the moment'. It was an extraordinary attempt to dissolve the boundaries between reality and representation, to heal the rupture that was to distress Rousseau, between warm, living speech, and its cold, dead, representation in writing. But if we look for 'writing to the moment', we find it, not in the novel, or in diary-writing, but in innumerable account books like Frances Hamilton's. Samuel Richardson, *Selected Letters*, ed. and intro. by John Carroll, Clarendon Press, Oxford, 1964, Letter 14 Feb. 1754 to Lady Bradshaigh; Jean-Jacques Rousseau, *A Discourse on Inequality* (1758), Penguin, Harmondsworth, 1984, pp. 118–37.

[51] SCRO, DD/FS 5/2.

cost, which in 1795–6 consisted of himself, his wife, five children, a young woman who was either a governess or relative acting as one, and 'Cook . . . Housemaid . . . Childs Maid . . . Footman'. 'Gardener & Gardening' he reckoned 'the same as last year', that is, as a household expense, and though bought-in, to be added to the servants' wages bill. He recorded a total expenditure of £410 8s 5d for this year (this total does not cover the farm equipment, supplies, and wages, that contributed to Hamilton's total outgoings). He spent half of it on food and drink (£207 16 8d) and 10 per cent of it on servants' wages (£45 1s 9¼d). The muffins and manchets, mole candles, hartshorn for bleach, oranges and lemons, mops and brushes and so on that Frances Hamilton so carefully recorded suggest what Thomas Cooper's efficatory and efficient 'Shop Things: £96.6.2' actually comprised. His efficiency in this regard may simply reflect the fact that he did not personally go shopping for lengths of lawn and lamp oil – that he worked from a heap of receipts provided by those who did. This accounting method provides a persona for Cooper as a consumer rather than a producer. The Coopers bought in help for washing, and gave generous allowances in terms of gowns, guineas and holidays to the cook maids who would agree to wash the baby's dirty nappies.[52] In the aggregate, this family/household spent roughly the same proportion of its total outgoings on household and garden labour as did Frances Hamilton (the £46 7s 10d calculated in her case amounts to 8 per cent of her total outgoings).

Things were simpler in the advice books. Neither of these householders went about buying goods and services in the recommended manner. In 1781 'The Economist' demonstrated 'in a variety of estimates' how households possessed of £80 a year or more might 'live with Frugality for a little money'. If, on the other hand, there was £400 a year in income, then there were many ways of living comfortably, as man, wife and four children. They could employ one maid and a man (the man to deal with the shop and go on errands, if this were a tradesman's family) their wages costing £11 4 0d, or 3 per cent of a total expenditure of £320. Employ a second maid, and the householder must work out what she cost to keep as well (which was £18 plus £6 in wages). Now, household labour cost him £30, or 9 per cent of his total outgoings. Possibly, the family could manage a man-servant – out of livery of course – and get rid of the dogsbody who shut up shop. Now the domestic service bill will be £57 a year, or 17 per cent of total outgoings. The 'Gentleman of Experience' taught that a private gentleman (not in trade) could live well with his wife, four children, two maidservants and a Man, spending £613

---

[52] See Chapter 8.

a year of which a mere 5 per cent (£34) went on servants' wages. But maidservants and men must eat, and wear out clothes, as they did in more vulgar households. The Gentleman of Experience should have added £18 for the keep and maintenance of them, making a total domestic labour bill of £70, or an 11 per cent of total expenditure on waged domestic work.[53]

In 1787 the Reverend Trusler plagiarised and updated the Gentleman of Experience's calculations, when he showed how to be rich and respectable on a mere £104 a year.[54] According to Trusler a man and his wife might live 'comfortably and genteely' on that in the country with two servants, paying £5 for a maidservant, 2s 6d for the tax on her, and £7 16s a year to 'a sturdy girl, not boarded nor lodged, but attending only in the daytime, 3s *per* week'. Waged domestic work would cost about 12 per cent of total expenditure. (Another £2 should be added for looking after the garden over the year – worth it for the vegetables got from that outlay). Did the indoor maid not eat? Trusler did not reckon her food separately, but rather calculated 'Bread for three persons a week . . . butter 2 lb a week'. If the maid consumed a third of all foodstuffs brought into the house, her maintenance would have cost the pair £18 8s 3d, a figure that bears remarkable comparison with the Gentleman of Experience's account of what a female servant cost to maintain.

Trusler's maidservant may have been taxed, but she appears not to have needed her stays mending, nor a new petticoat, nor the heels of her shoes tapping. No one comes in for an afternoon to clean out the water closet in the yard, or for a bout of general charring, but that may be because, in this book, all of Hamilton's real-life helpers are concentrated in the figurative 'sturdy girl' who did all the rough. Frances Hamilton's accounts show the economic and budgeting realities of a prescribed system of household organisation. What looking at the prescription and the reality side by side allows us to say is that those who paid for any kind of household labour in the later eighteenth century were likely to expend between 10 and 20 per cent of their total outgoings on it.

All the payments that Frances Hamilton made for indoor and outdoor labour were initially recorded in the real-time household account books

---

[53] A Gentleman of Experience, *The Economist. Shewing, in a variety of Estimates, from Fourscore Pounds a Year to upwards of £800, how comfortably and genteely a Family may live with Frugality for a little Money*, 15th edn, privately printed, London, 1781, pp. 4–20.

[54] Trusler, *Way to be Rich*. 'Experience' was first published in 1774, Trusler in 1776. This kind of advice had long been purveyed to women. Mary Johnson's *The Young Woman's Companion; or the Servant Maid's Assistant* (1753) became *Madam Johnson's Present: or every Young Woman's Companion, in Useful and Universal Knowledge*, 4th edn, W. Nicholl, London, 1776, with a substantial 'Estimate of the Expences of a Family in the middling Station of Life', including the servants.

kept in three volumes, which she used to note daily expenditure on housekeeping as well as the farm.[55] (Only a couple of the thousands of little scraps of paper – receipts for 'Forster Horse Doctor 7s', 'fish', 'tea for Molly', 'Cress 10 at 9d', 'Straw 10s', 'Turnpike to Taunton 2d', 'lamp Oil', 'lemons & Oranges 3 doz 6s', 'bread 2d baking 4d' – survive; usually they were thrown away the moment the item was entered in the ledger.[56]) They show, not the relatively tidy divisions between farm and house that her quarry and quarterly accounting sessions put in place on the page, but the permeability of boundaries between types of worker and types of work. We have already seen this for 1797: a livelihood held in place by a small number of permanent workers (William Coombs for the farm, just one maid and one Boy in the house for most of the year) supplemented by up to a dozen casual workers. This may have been Hamilton's conceptualisation of management as well. The farm labourers who worked for her throughout the year were not casual in the same way as the washers, scrubbers, sweepers and needlewomen who were paid by the day or part day. They worked much more regularly, their tasks being allocated by the day or the week. Hamilton recorded payment to them as those payments were made: every two days, or at the end of the week. In 1796 John Mere worked consistently on the farm, throughout the year, at a shilling a day. She paid him for 114 days' labour this year (reckoning up all the quarter and half days) and for one job by the piece, for which he charged 8s 6d. His wife – it was almost certainly his wife – Bet Mere was paid 8s 6d for work on the wheat crop in June, and then, at the rate of 6d a day, worked for Hamilton for a further 57½ days that year. (She also got a present of a shilling in June.) This year Hamilton paid a girl from the Shattock family to clear the January snow. She settled her washerwoman's account – with Catherine Vickery accepting potatoes to the value of 2s 6d in part payment – in July. She had washed at the rate of 6d a day, every month, sometimes twice a month, often spending three days at it.

In 1788 Hamilton's written instructions made it very clear what work these men and women did. Departing for a month's holiday she wrote several pages of 'Directions in my absence', which included:

Meer to go to Taunton for coal and take the Coal Book & have the last he brought wrote down in the Book.

Tho. to drive the wood into the Court & pile it away & Cut up the rest of it.

Drive in some coal Ashes upon the rasbery plants & place abroad the dung when the weather admits of it. Not to take up any of the plants only break off the dry bark . . .

---

[55] SCRO, DD/FS 5/8; 5/9; 7/1.   [56] SCRO, DD/FS/ 5/8; 7/1 (Jan. 1792).

To beat up the earth together & the little dung that is thrown up in the piggs court. & a few Coal Ashes together & place it up against the cellar Wall

To remember to put some Coal Ashes on the Raspberry plants in the little garden... To throw out the pigg Stye... To mend the wall that is Broke down in the place where the Cattle are to drink in the Barton.[57]

'Above all' neither Thomas nor anyone else was 'to leave the... Cow without Clean Water, that Water in the Barton [Yard] is not wholsome'. To keep it as clean as possible, Thomas was to make sure he threw up 'the dung away from the Water'. 'When the Glazier comes to put up the ladder & Glaze the Window in the East side of the House' someone must tell him that 'there are 2/ Quarrels broken'. The cold must be kept 'out of the Window of the Myrtle House [conservatory] putting a little Straw – but not to hinder the Sun'. Thomas Vosey was also 'to remember in severe weather to put something into the mouth of the Bee-but'. On a wet day he was 'To wash the bottles... but not to mix them with those already washed and numbered'. Also he could 'thoroughly clean the Stable on a wet day – and clean the tacking'. Thomas should remember that if he 'behaves well, he will find Advantage from it. If bad, He shall meet with a punishment sooner or later.' There were instructions for Edward Williams. He was to work with John Mere, 'to part the Turnip field & have home the remainder of the Stubbs from the Horsery. And the Tyle as it may serve to mend with.' Mere was to continue Edward's instruction in husbandry work: 'Meer to put the Cattle into the Turnip field & Edward to drive them up, & down, & Meer to observe that he drives them properly.' Together they were 'to Stake the Apple Tree, remove the Apple Tree that is too near the Horsery. To get furze for to put round the Stems... To set some Turnips for Seed And Bank the ground where the Turnips now are – Not to plant the Turnips for seed in the same bed'. Any spare moment for Edward could be filled by stone picking 'when the weather admits of it: And to make a heap so that I may see how many he picks up'. Mere was to take out the more advanced apprentice Thomas if things came to lambing in her absence: 'Meer & Thos to take care of the Ewes observe when they have lamb'. There were labour agreements already in place, and these should be adhered to: 'Westcott says he will work by the ffoot and not by the day.' The servants and workers needed to know this, not because anyone was going to pay him until she returned home, but to understand his comings and goings,

[57] But the Bath and West of England Agricultural Society thought that 'ashes are but little used as a manure in the Western Counties'. Bath and West of England Society for the Encouragement of Agriculture, Arts, Manufacture and Commerce, *Letters and Papers on Agriculture, Planting, &c*, 6 vols., The Society, Bath, 1792–3, vol. 2, pp. 70–5 (orig. pub. 1783).

for 'if Westcott helps to spin the dressing then he is to have liquor'. The network of reciprocity that helped maintain the household was to be kept going: Hannah was 'to have home the peaches from Mr Troy, in the box sent for that purpose'. And if anyone brought grape vines to the house, then 'plant one upon the Terras in the little Garden & the other in the border near the Chinese Gate near the apricot tree', she wrote, in direct instruction. Molly was to take particular care to 'bolt the Stair case door & lock it also', every night. These instructions – there were many more – were to maintain a household and farm enterprise during a month's absence of its mistress. She handed over her account book to the workers, and left for Wells.

At this point in the farming year, things were kept going by the employment of one labourer, the two apprentices, and one job by the piece. Their labour was added to by the task of responding to these instructions, in writing. It is not clear whether they had been asked to do this, but respond they did. There is an entry for every day, reporting for example that '4th John Meer went to taunton with the box & broght home same of Coal Westcot didge Stones & Meer in the afternoon . . . 16th Thos Finished dressing the midle feild & Bigan the upperfield brought home Turnips for the Cow . . . .' On the 25th 'the yow [was] brought to Lambs'. The day before Frances Hamilton returned home, Edward Williams finally got round to 'Clean[ing] Coart'. These entries were most likely made by John Mere and the apprentices dictating to a house servant – to Hannah Burston, who could write; in the entry for 30 January the 'we' is crossed out in: '[we] Jon meer Jon westcott fish [finished] the ground up in the orchard & we beat up the ground'.[58] The servants and labourers knew their own mind, or rather, knew what needed to be done over and above the instructions left them, doing much work including fetching stone from the quarry that they had not been instructed to fetch. This was because William Hill, Frances Hamilton's builder, whose remodelling of the dining room had been arranged before she left ('Will Hill came and measured the Parlour and drank a cup of Cyder and went away again'), arrived with his men, in the arbitrary-seeming way of all builders, asking for stone to be conveyed to the house.[59]

Hamilton's day book – or writing itself – acted as a form of surveillance in her absence. Her own daily surveillance recorded much exasperation over the years she employed John Mere. She came home from Wells in February 1788 to a spring of intense reading on slavery – books borrowed from the Taunton Book Society. She lifted her eye from the page one day

[58] See Chapters 9 and 11.
[59] SCRO, DD/FS 7/2, 31 Jan. 1787–1 Feb. 1788; 10 Dec. 1787 for Hill's visits.

in June to observe (from the window?) 'John Meer from 6 to 8 o'clock attending the Cattle. Then he took the Stones from under the Lime Trees & put them down again a little higher up: this is literally true.'[60] Margaret Allen has noted other run-ins with John Mere: he had done 'a very bad job for one day and 2 hours' spreading coal ashes; 'Meer went and tacked the horses and got into the field at 7 o'clock to work – *a very great shame* not to be at work sooner'; 'Meer in the higher orchard. He was very angry that I sent up and did not find him there.'[61] Things came to an unprecedented pitch in 1795 when 'Jno Mere insolently left my service, because I told him to go up for saw-dust and chips – The Saw dust I wanted to have dry – the chips ought to be brought home.'[62] But he was back in January 1796, repairing one of the hedges with Jonathan the man-servant. She laughed – or at least wrote wryly – about the irritation she knew she brought on herself with decisions concerning charity and responsibility, such as that relating to John Hooper for example, 'a poor old man [who] cannot do anything' whom she employed at the rate of 8d a day. She reflected on the fruits of responsibility every time he 'wasted away the day', or she saw him 'doing very little', or paid his rent, or the apothecary's bill for attending him. Yet she never got rid of him.[63] Abraham Mullins was a different proposition. He had worked for her since at least 1788, mostly in her flower garden. She liked him; he was kind and attentive to her and she noted this in her diary: 'Abraham came here at 12 o clock – brought me a present of Watercresses & Eggs – which to my mind is soothing, and Attentive'. He brought her more eggs, later in the month.[64]

The exasperation with John Mere came from her knowing what he was doing, and why he was wasting his – or rather, her – time. Like many an eighteenth-century mistress, she wrote the truncated diary-ese in which, with pronouns either abandoned or restricted to the first person plural, mistress merges with her servant in the performance of tasks. Amanda Vickery has remarked that we really cannot be sure if Elizabeth Shackleton ever washed the china with her servant, put on a pinny, got her hands wet, as signalled by the 'we' in 'we washed the china in the closet'.[65] With pronouns missing, it is quite impossible to work out who

---

[60] SCRO, DD/FS 7/2 (7 Jun. 1788). I think she found Mere's movements with the stones – like Hill's mysterious coming and goings – amusing, as well as maddening. She wrote of them both with the kind of self-mocking exasperation of any middle-class person who has ever had the builders in: 'Wm Hill was here this whole day: wonderful!'; 'Wm Hill came & looked at the work, worked a little, then went away'; 'Wm Hill came abt 12 o clock & went to sleep' (26 May, 4, 16 Jun. 1794).

[61] Allan, 'Frances Hamilton', p. 265.   [62] SCRO, DD/FS 5/2 (17 Dec. 1795).

[63] *Ibid.* (25 Oct. 1792).   [64] *Ibid.* (2 Jan. 1793).

[65] Vickery, *Gentleman's Daughter*, pp. 146–7.

did what by way of household task. This was a convention of writing that inadvertently supported the legal fiction that master and man and mistress and maid were one person. The presence of a pronoun might efface a servant actually present. 'I carried 7 more loads of Hay from the Clay Pit Close', the Reverend Cole recorded in July 1766, though there was clearly 'help' present, driving the cart and forking the hay, just as there was in his more descriptively accurate 'Had my Raspberry Jam & Currant Jelly made'.[66] The typical formulation of Frances Hamilton was: 'made hedge. I had company', meaning that someone else, one of her workers, made a hedge and she had company to dine.[67] We cannot tell if Frances Hamilton ever dug in coal ash around the raspberry bushes. And yet there is one entry in her twenty years' worth of diaries, day books and accounts, that suggests that she might have done so. On October 15 1794 she wrote that 'In the garden I worked hard.' I believe that she did work in her garden here (and possibly on many other occasions); that she put on a pair of stout shoes, kirtled up her skirts, and did some early autumn tidying and pruning, leaf sweeping, turning over, and put in some double hyacinth bulbs, perhaps, as recommended by James Maddock in the *Florist's Directory* which she had borrowed from the Book Society the previous year. Or tulips (though it was a bit early for tulips, according to Maddock), or moved the auricula to 'their winter habitation', which here was the myrtle house.[68] Frances Hamilton 'worked', which is what fully possessed, autonomous individuals do, mixing their bodily capacities and strength with the earth, and bringing forth from it that which is theirs, by virtue of their labour. In fact, Frances Hamilton who we may assume had put down a library book or her pen to take up her spade (which is, admittedly, conjectural, whilst the pen is not), was the perfect encapsulation of the proposition that Judge Blackstone had recorded in 1781, that property 'may with equal Reason be acquired by *mental,* as *bodily* Labour... [by] the Exertion of the *animal* Faculties... common both to Us and the Brute Creation, in their Nests, Caves &c... and the Exertion of the *rational* Powers, by which we are denominated Men'.[69] Or on this case, Woman. Thus was one Lockean moment inscribed: a day spent (preparing for) a bringing forth of the fruits of the earth

---

[66] Francis Griffin Stokes (ed.), *The Blecheley Diary of the Reverend William Cole, MA, FSA, 1765–67*, Constable, London, 1931, pp. 71, 243.

[67] SCRO, DD/FS 5/2 (Jan. 25 1791).

[68] James Maddock, *The Florist's Directory; or a Treatise on the Culture of Flowers: to which is added A supplementary Dissertation on Soils, Manures etc*, privately printed, London, 1792, pp. 31, 54, 130–1. SCRO, DD/FS 6/3 for Hamilton reading Maddock.

[69] William Blackstone, *Reports of Cases determined in the several Courts of Westminster-Hall, from 1746 to 1779. Taken and compiled by the Honourable Sir William Blackstone*, 2 vols., His Majesty's Law Printers for W. Strahan, T. Cadell, London, 1781, vol. 1, pp. 321–2.

and property, without the irritating, maddening, intermediary of 'my Servant' or 'my Horse'. (Abraham Mullins had not been at all maddening in the garden; by way of contrast, John Mere was rarely set to work there, unless it was to do some hard digging.) But in the usual run of events, Frances Hamilton's labour was exercised by the servants and other workers. The products of their labour (the wheat, the barley, the apples, the vegetables and flowers) belonged to her, because of contract, and 'the favour and indulgence of the law', in allowing the existence of such arrangements, and the transfer of energies, strength, and capacity, from one person to another. It is unlikely that Hamilton worked in her own kitchen, although twenty years of precise and incisive accounting for, amongst other things, lemons, cucumber, 'A Crab', 'Salad', '3 pd flower', 'Mace', 'Anchovies', 'Leg of Veal', '3 Couple of Chicken'... make it possible to compile a shopping list for cooking your way through Elizabeth Raffald's *Experienced English Housekeeper* – the one cookery book Hamilton possessed and had taken into her married state in 1775 – by following the lists of ingredients purchased.[70] But she does not actually have to have boiled the crab, dressed it and made a salad for this food preparation to be Lockean; in the realm of political and legal philosophy the servant doing so *was* Frances Hamilton in this moment (or for the good two hours it would take to process the crab and get it to the table with accompaniments).

What did Frances Hamilton understand of a day spent gardening, in comparison with all of Mullins's labouring in the same spot, with John Mere's exercise of his own self-possession, as he turned up late, did what *he* thought should be done with the stones in the cow pasture, said it was too cold to work, lost his temper – for more than fifteen years? All of Hamilton's relationships with her servants and workers express the paradox and impossibility of the labour relationship, whatever form it takes, the 'unfortunate necessity' that it inscribed: if they could do it themselves, they would do it better, whether it be spreading coal ashes, fetching sawdust, dusting, or shelling a crab. Or: if only they knew how to do it, *then* they would. *They* would not answer back, as did the insolent Elizabeth Murch. It's just that there are insurmountable reasons for not doing it themselves: reasons of gender, class, rank and station. Being a gentleman, or a gentleman's daughter means that it has never – possibly never could have – crossed their mind that they might. And yet: it is *their* work, because *their* capacity to labour is being exercised by the servant, so very badly, right now.

---

[70] Elizabeth Raffald, *The Experienced English Housekeeper, for the Use and Ease of Ladies, Housekeepers, Cooks, &c*, 2nd edn, R. Baldwin for the author, London, 1771.

Much knowledge was brought to bear on Hamilton's direction of all the labour she employed over these twenty years. She knew how a field should be ploughed (though not from direct experience); she was forced to reflect on all the activities that kept house and farm going, as she made her daily (sometimes hourly) records in her journal. She had owned guides to the management of this kind of life since her girlhood.[71] She kept up with recent developments in soil chemistry and agricultural innovation in general, mainly through the publications of the West Country Societies for the Encouragement of Agriculture. Labour – the feeding and maintenance of it – was a preoccupation of their publications in the 1790s. She thought of herself as a farmer (though she would scarcely have *called* herself that) reflecting on her abilities in running an agricultural enterprise: 'Killed a pig weighed 12 score 16 pounds', she wrote in March 1796. 'To my shame be it spoken I had a Man to kill my pigg and suffered Wm & Edward to assist him – *good management.*'[72] (She gained 4s 6d from the sale of the pork in Taunton market, paying the anonymous Man 6d for his labour – Edward's and William's cost her nothing: a profit by the labour of three others of 4s.) She thought about these relationships of labour, property and persons throughout her

---

[71] SCRO, DD/FS 5/4, Estate and farm account book kept by Frances Coles [Hamilton], reusing her arithmetic exercise book 1767, 1765–77. R. Bradley, *A General Treatise of Husbandry and Gardening; containing a new System of Vegetation: illustrated with many Observations and Experiments. In two Volumes. Formerly publish'd monthly, and now methodiz'd and digested under proper heads, with additions and great alterations. In four parts.... Adorn'd with cuts*, T. Woodward and J. Peele, London, 1726; Nathan Bailey, *Dictionarium Domesticum, being a new and compleat household Dictionary. For the use both of City and Country*, C. Hitch, C. Davis and S. Austen, London, 1736; Richard Hayes, *Interest at one View, calculated to a Farthing: at 2^1/$_2$, 3, 3^1/$_2$, 4, 5, 6, 7, and 8 per cent. For 1000£. to 1£. for 1 day to 96 days; ... The fifteenth edition, with additions. Carefully calculated and examined from the press by Richard Hayes. To which is added a concise table, whereby to cast up salaries*, James Potts, Dublin, 1772.

[72] SCRO, DD/FS 7/1 (13 Mar. 1796); DD/FS 5/8 (11 Apr. 1796). For 'good management' in all sorts of eighteenth-century sense, Paul Langford, 'The management of the eighteenth-century state: Perceptions and implications', *Journal of Historical Sociology*, 15:1 (2002), 102–6: 'Management was a favourite eighteenth-century term'. Hamilton's shame – it is ironic I think – probably came from Elizabeth Raffald's recipe for roast pork: 'To roast a Pig. Stick your pig just above the breast bone, run your knife to the heart...'. Raffald, *Experienced English Housekeeper*, p. 55. Raffald produced culinary terror across the country: 'I understand you are quit set up in the Cookery way by a volume of the new addision', wrote Elizabeth Ramsden to Elizabeth Shackleton in Aug. 1774. 'I hear it contains half as much again as the other did so your Ladyship will out shine all your Neighbourhood in the Eligants of your Table. and if the author should paid you a viset you need not put yourself in a pannice as you can entertain Her in Her own way.' Raffald lived in Manchester at the time; perhaps a visit to Brownsholme really was in the offing. Lancashire Country Record Office, DDB/72/ 188–298. Parker of Brownsholme, Correspondence, Letter 279, Elizabeth Ramsden to Elizabeth Shackleton (7 Nov. 1776).

Figure 6. The Maidservant's Book of Hours. Frances Hamilton first acquired Bailey's book when she was a girl.

recorded life. She was widely read in contemporary politics and political theory. She managed the enterprise of her life at the intersection of experience and book-knowledge.[73]

After her return from Wells, between February and May 1788 Hamilton undertook a programme of reading on slavery, the majority of it abolitionist. (Her book lists and inventories recorded nearly twenty on the topic, borrowed or acquired between 1775 and her death.) She had inherited Mr Hamilton's copy of *Considerations of the State of the Sugar Islands*, but that had been about British financial policy in regard to the Caribbean.[74] Now, in the spring of 1788 she borrowed works that urged the offence against Christianity of slavery as an institution and that demonstrated its injustice and impolicy. They explored the legal question of property in persons and self-possession, so dramatically raised by commerce in the human species.[75] Thomas Clarkson's argument was framed by a history of mankind 'from their first situation to a state of government', in order to demonstrate that all 'were originally free, and . . . possessed an equal right to the soil and produce of the earth'. Nature had made 'every man's body and mind *his own*; it is evident that no just man can be justly consigned to *slavery* without his own consent', or be counted 'as lands, goods or houses, among *possessions*'. And how, asked Clarkson 'does the *slave* differ from his *master*, but by *chance*?'[76] Next there was Joseph Priestley's condemnation of the trade,

---

[73] See 'France Hamilton's library books: An eighteenth-century employer reads social theory', forthcoming for further discussion of this point.

[74] SCRO, DD/FS 6/3. West-India Planter, *Considerations on the State of the Sugar Islands, and on the Policy of enabling Foreigners to lend Money on real Securities in those Colonies. In a Letter addressed to the Right Hon. Lord North; by a West-India Planter*, S. Bladon, London, 1773.

[75] SCRO, DD/FS 6/3 shows her borrowing from the Taunton Book Society: Thomas Clarkson, *An Essay on the Slavery and Commerce of the Human Species, particularly the African, translated from a Latin Dissertation, which was honoured with the first Prize in the University of Cambridge, for the year 1785*, T. Cadell and J. Phillips, London, 1786; William Roscoe, *A General View of the African Slave-trade, demonstrating its Injustice and Impolicy: with Hints towards a Bill for its Abolition*, R. Faulder, London, 1788; Joseph Priestley, *A Sermon on the Subject of the Slave Trade; delivered to a Society of Protestant Dissenters, at the New Meeting, in Birmingham; and published at their Request*, Pearson and Rollason, Birmingham, 1788; Thomas Cooper, *Letters on the Slave Trade: first published in Wheeler's Manchester Chronicle; and since re-printed with additions and alterations*, C. Wheeler, Manchester, 1787; William Hughes, *A Discourse in Favour of the Abolition of Slavery in the British West Indies. Preached on the first Sunday in Lent, in the Parish Church of Ware, Herts.*, T. Cadell, London, 1788; Robert Robinson, *Slavery Inconsistent with the Spirit of Christianity. A Sermon preached at Cambridge, on Sunday, Feb. 10, 1788*, Robbinson, Bowtell and Cowper, Cambridge; Dilly, London, 1788.

[76] Clarkson, *Essay*, pp. 50–5. For a recent account of Clarkson, see Simon Schama, *Rough Crossings: Britain, the slaves and the American Revolution*, BBC Publications, 2006, passim; pp. 207–8 for the *Essay*.

which made the same references as Clarkson to systems of rank and hierarchy in the modern social world; as Christians, his readers should 'consider all distinctions among men as temporary'. Certainly, social inequality and subordination *must be*: they were calculated for the benefit of all, 'for the interest of the lowest orders, as well as the highest'.[77] But the very existence of subordination should persuade all Christians to respect their servants and to think of all mankind as brethren. He did not know 'whether it can be proved that these principles necessarily lead to the emancipation of the slaves or not (any more than they lead to take away all inequalities among men, those of rich and poor, masters & servants, &c)'; but they would certainly provide the conditions for the self-improvement of all.[78] As for pro-slavery arguments that dwelt on commercial considerations and slavery as a source of profit, Priestley argued that abolishing the trade would increase demand for English goods; but more important – the English had not always consumed sugar, and they could do without it again: 'Let everything for the use of man be raised by men who shall be paid the full price of their labour, and let those who cannot pay that price go without it . . . '.[79] (These arguments did not persuade Frances Hamilton to give up shopping for sugar.)

These questions of property and profit in slave systems were given extensive treatment by James Ramsay in his *Essay on the Treatment and Conversion of African Slaves*, which Hamilton borrowed in April 1788.[80] Ramsay remembered his own domestic attempts to raise his St Kitt's house slaves to rationality and dignity. They did improve, he reported, but 'the necessity of following them up in every step of duty imposed on them, and of keeping the fear of punishment suspended over them; in short, the apparent uneasiness on one side, and the indispensable mistrust on the other, plainly proved that they had no solid enjoyment of themselves'. It had been exhausting. He had returned home to a land where he could exercise benevolence 'without regret'.[81] He was an insightful commentator on the politics and impossibilities of the domestic labour relationship, whether the labour be enslaved or not; Hamilton used the same wry voice when writing of the impossible John Meer [Mere], and the insolent Elizabeth Murch. Like Priestley, but at greater

---

[77] Priestley, *Sermon*, p. vii.   [78] Priestley, *Sermon*, p. 15.   [79] *Ibid.*, pp. 25, 27–8.

[80] James Ramsay, *An Essay on the Treatment and Conversion of African Slaves in the British Sugar Colonies*, James Phillips, London, 1784. See Schama, *Rough Crossings*, pp. 201–9, and passim. Also Folarin Olawale Shyllon, *James Ramsay: The unknown abolitionist*, Canongate, Edinburgh, 1977; Anne Stott, *Hannah More: The first Victorian*, Oxford University Press, Oxford, 2003, p. 87; J. Watt, 'Ramsay, James (1733–1789)' in *Oxford Dictionary of National Biography*, Oxford University Press, Sep. 2004, online edn, May 2006, www.oxforddnb.com/view/article/23086, accessed 16 Mar. 2007.

[81] Ramsay, *Essay*, pp. 173, 177

length, Ramsay emphasised the psychological consequences of being the personal property of another, in particular the lack of any sense of a future. Like Priestley, he wrote of the slave's depression of mind and spirit.[82]

Ramsay's book stood out from Hamilton's other Book Society borrowings for the connections it made between slavery and servitude, and the detail it provided of slave-labour-systems economics. The religious and ethical arguments for abolition he took for granted: he would 'not insult the reader's understanding, by an attempt to demonstrate it to be an object of importance, to gain to society, to reason and religion, half a million of our kind, equally with us adapted for advancing themselves in every art and science ... equally with us made capable of looking forward to and enjoying futurity'. His central economic thesis was that 'the people [slaves], whose improvement is here proposed, toil for the British state'.[83] He described in detail the labour regime of a typical sugar plantation and calculated the profit of slave labour ('the several articles that a slave had annually returned to [a master] out of his labour') over one year (1774) at £1 6s 0d.[84] Slaves in the Sugar Colonies 'exceeded not the fortieth part of the inhabitants of the empire' but 'they contributed, in that neglected state, perhaps nearly a sixth part of its ... revenue'; he demonstrated this in four pages of tables. His conclusion anticipated much more recent Black Atlantic arguments: the Sugar Islands should be thought of 'as manufactures established in convenient distant places, that draw all their utensils from, and send all their produce to, the mother country'.[85] He described human energy in labour (enslaved and free) as a mechanical effect, in order to compare the output of a labourer who worked 'diligently eight hours a day' with the slave who 'drawls out in languid exertions fourteen hours'.[86]

In order to place slavery within the realm of the social, as something that might be discussed – Ramsay presented a history 'Of the Various Ranks in Social Life' as the first chapter of his *Essay*. In Ramsay's view, slavery stood outside the social: it 'could never have been intended for the social state'.[87] God secured to everyone the rights adapted to their particular station in society; in opposition to this schema stood 'the

---

[82] Priestley, *Sermon*, pp. 18–19: '[slaves] have little reflexion on the past, or anticipation of the future ... Through agony of mind, great numbers of Negroes put an end to their own lives.'

[83] Ramsay, *Essay*, pp. iv–v.   [84] *Ibid.*, pp. 69–90; 85.

[85] *Ibid.*, pp. 109–12. Robin Blackburn, *The Making of New World Slavery: From the Baroque to the Modern, 1492–1800*, Verso, London and New York, 1997, pp. 371–580.

[86] Ramsay, *Essay*, pp. 132–49. For further discussion of Ramsay's account of labour mechanics and the feeding of labour, see 'Horses' and Chapter 9.

[87] Ramsay, *Essay*, p. 173.

artificial, or unnatural relation of master and slave; where ... every man becomes his own legislator'. Society was *about* law; its 'prime design ... is the extension of the operation of the law, and the equal treatment and protection of the citizens. Slavery, therefore, being the negation of law, cannot arise from law, or be compatible with it.'[88] Service was a different matter; the agreement between master and servant was voluntary; it could be looked upon as an employment relationship (though not of course an equal relationship).[89] Ramsay pondered the very great freedoms that contract bestowed on employer and employed. You could call this relationship 'social servitude, which must take place in the freest state', he said; it existed because of the natural and universal division into rank and hierarchy. Slavery on the other hand was 'artificial servitude'.[90] Frances Hamilton read a great deal more on slavery over the coming months, but this was the only sustained argument about slave labour wedded to a general theory of labour that she encountered in all her immense reading in political economy and social policy.[91] Robinson's sermon, *Slavery Inconsistent with the Spirit of Christianity* (borrowed by Hamilton in May 1788) reinforced Ramsay's trenchant economic analysis: 'Many plausible arguments have been used to defend this traffick ... but, to say the truth, they are all reducible to one, that is the *gain* of it.'[92]

Hamilton borrowed apologies for the trade later in 1788, including the extraordinary *Scriptural Researches on the Licitness of the Slave-trade*, which was a far less elegant piece of Biblical scholarship than she was used to.[93] In the autumn she read the Reverend Stanhope Smith's *Essay on the Causes of the Variety of Complexion and Figure in the Human Species* – perhaps an enlightened, anthropological context to all she had read over the past months. It was a powerfully monist account of human kind.[94]

---

[88] *Ibid.*, pp. 18–19.   [89] *Ibid.*, p. 5, 9.   [90] *Ibid.*, p. 17.

[91] She borrowed Thomas Cooper's *Letters on the Slave Trade* at the same time as Ramsay's book. He offered a history and statistical survey of slavery, and went into some detail on the villeinage question. (Could slavery exist in England? How was villeinage related to slavery?) *Letters on the Slave Trade*, p. 22.

[92] Robinson, *Slavery Inconsistent*, p. 20.

[93] Raymund Harris, *Scriptural Researches on the Licitness of the Slave-trade, shewing its Conformity with the Principles of Natural and Revealed Religion, delineated in the Sacred Writings of the Word of God*, John Stockdale, London, 1788; SCRO, DD/FS 6/3. A tawdry and shallow piece of work, thought the Revd Hughes, with a 'very extraordinary title'; *An Answer to the Rev. Mr Harris's 'Scriptural Researches ....'*, T. Cadell, London, 1788. Hamilton did not read this, but borrowed his *Discourse in Favour of the Abolition of Slavery* in May. She also borrowed West-India Planter, *Considerations*.

[94] Samuel Stanhope Smith, *An Essay on the Causes of the Variety of Complexion and Figure in the Human Species. To which are Added, Strictures on Lord Kames's Discourse on the original Diversity of Mankind. A new edition. With some additional Notes, by a gentleman of the University of Edinburgh*, C. Elliot, Philadelphia and Edinburgh, and C. Elliot and T. Kay, London, 1788, pp. 165, 167. SCRO, DD/FS 6/3 (8 Dec. 1788).

Sprung from the same parents, we are all the same as one another; social convention and child rearing practices are what make cultural differences. The appearance of the English lower orders was environmental, like that of the enslaved African, said Smith: 'coarse and meagre food is ever accompanied in mankind with hard features and a dark complexion', though happily 'if, in England, there exists less difference between the figure and appearance of persons in the higher and lower classes, than is seen in many other countries of Europe, it is because a more general diffusion of liberty and wealth has reduced the different ranks more nearly to another'.[95]

In the Vale of Taunton, in the spring and summer of 1788, we must assume that no silence fell around the dinner table when the gentlemen of the Book Society visited Bishops Lydeard House and the topic of slavery was raised.[96] Hamilton's understanding of pro-and anti-slavery arguments (on the page and round the table) was achieved as intellectual and citizen (perhaps also as an active seeker after Christian truth). Did she also understand the slavery question *as a woman*? 'Describing women as slaves... was an ancient trope, rooted in the classical citizen/slave antimony', notes Barbara Taylor of Mary Wollstonecraft's writing.[97] The analogy had had its most recent airing in 'the radical attack on government-sponsored religious intolerance' of the 1780s (Hamilton encountered this in many books she borrowed on the Test and Corporation Acts).[98] Ancient and modern versions of the citizen/slave opposition framed Wollstonecraft's novel *Maria* (1798).[99] But unlike Mary Wollstonecraft (or the fictional Maria, who embodies the political arguments of *The Vindication of the Rights of Woman*) Frances Hamilton *was* a citizen – or as much of a citizen as a woman could be in late eighteenth-century England. She was a property-owner, and as a widow she had full direction of her property in law. She was a legal person. She worked her own land (in the Lockean sense of taking the fruits of her own earth into possession through the activities of her labourers with spade and plough, and her maids with chopping board and knife). She paid her own taxes and tithes. During the invasion scares of the 1790s, her horses were requisitioned by the military.[100] The parish put apprentices out on her, just

---

[95] Smith, *Essay*, 87–8.

[96] Edward Said, *Culture and Imperialism*, Chatto and Windus, London, 1993, pp. 95–116; Jane Austen, *Mansfield Park* (1814), Penguin, Harmondsworth, 1986, pp. 212–13.

[97] Barbara Taylor, *Mary Wollstonecraft and the Feminist Imagination*, Cambridge University Press, Cambridge, 2003, p. 240.

[98] Taylor, *Mary Wollstonecraft*, p. 226.

[99] Mary Wollstonecraft, *Mary, and The Wrongs of Woman; or Maria* (1798), Oxford University Press, 1976; Taylor, *Mary Wollstonecraft*, pp. 240–5.

[100] SCRO, DD/FS 5/3.

Figure 7. Richard Bradley, *The Country Housewife and Lady's Director, in the Management of a House, and the Delights and Profits of a Farm* (1732). The later edition owned by Frances Hamilton, did not contain this image of rural plenitude.

as it did on any gentleman farmer. She had no husband now to compare to a West Indian slaveholder – even had Mr Hamilton ever behaved like the obnoxious and tyrannical Venables of *Maria*. Given *what* she read during these months, and her social and legal position as a reader and a person, it is not very likely that she made connection with anti-slavery arguments, as 'a Woman'.[101]

We can know, then, something of the arguments and images that furnished her political and social imagination, as she looked out of the window and contemplated John Mere purposelessly moving stones in the orchard, or recorded '$\frac{1}{2}$ pound of Tea for Molly'.[102] What she had read conceptualised labour in terms of strength and work-capacity, and the relationship of food input to output of energy. The works she borrowed were not solely concerned with chattel slaves' souls and their lack of freedom to choose between salvation and sin, as Boyd Hilton has suggested of abolitionist literature of the later century.[103] In what Hamilton read, there was extended attention to the bodies of slave-workers in the Americas, and a fully worked-out theory of labour as physiological and mechanical phenomenon. She borrowed *The Connexion between Industry and Property*, which proposed a system of family allowances to English labourers so that bodily needs and wants might be met.[104] The locus of this discussion, like John Vancouver's (which she does not appear to have read) was the human body in labour.[105] Much of this material was

---

[101] She pressed on with the slavery question in her later reading career, borrowing Gilbert Imlay, *A Topographical Description of the Western Territory of North America: containing a succinct Account of its Soil, Climate, Natural History, Population, Agriculture, Manners, Customs...* 2nd edn, J. Debrett, London, 1793; SCRO, DD/FS 6/3 (11 Mar. 1794) and John Matthews, *A Voyage to the River Sierra-Leone on the Coast of Africa... With an Additional Letter on the Subject of the Slave Trade*, White, London, 1791. SCRO, DD FS/6/3 (23 Jan. 1795). Imlay's strong anti-slavery opinions were well-known. Janet Todd, *Mary Wollstonecraft: A revolutionary life*, Weidenfeld and Nicholson, London, 2000, pp. 232–3. She read a more traditional account in Thomas Gisborne's 'On Slavery' in *The Principles of Moral Philosophy Investigated, and briefly applied to the Constitution of Civil Society: together with Remarks...*, *The second edition*, B. White, London, 1790, pp. 95–8; it was untouched by the recent anti-slavery debate. SCRO, DD/FS 6/3 (16 May 1791).

[102] SCRO, DD/FS 7/1 (28 Jul. 1789)

[103] Boyd Hilton, *A Mad, Bad, and Dangerous People? England 1783–1846*, Oxford University Press, Oxford, 2006, pp. 184–8.

[104] Anon., *The Connexion between Industry and Property; or a Proposal to make a fixed and permanent Allowance to Labourers for the Maintenance of their Children. Addressed to the Society for bettering the Condition and increasing the Comforts of the Poor*, Trewman, Exeter, 1798. SCRO DD/FS 6/3.

[105] Hamilton's favourite philosopher, on the other hand, asked her to contemplate the individual body contrasted with the 'wonders of combined and... persevering industry'. It was not the single arm of a Theseus or a Hercules that raised the Pyramids, but 'the hands of such men as ourselves'. Stewart, *Elements*, vol. 1, 1792, p. 268.

circulated by the West of England Society, in its promotion of research into the nutritional values of foodstuffs, especially the potato.[106] In what Hamilton read discussion of labour was conducted around the needs of labouring bodies.

Hamilton expressed her own practical philosophy of labour in 1796, in the middle of her farm account book. She paused in the middle of listing her farm stock ('3 Cows 5 Horses . . . 3 piggs . . . ') to note '1 Apprentice' and then, thinking of him, of Edward Williams whom she had now fed and clothed for eleven years, wrote

1 Maidservant earns double her Meat & drink
2 Maidservant each half their Wages & Maintenance
1 Lad earns his living
1 Man Good.[107]

The Man – the day-labourer – was the best deal, for she did not have to maintain him. The boy (bought-in at 3d a day, from time to time) was good in the same way. The maidservant did most for the money, but having two of them doubled the cost of the labour she bought, because what they ate and drank did not produce double the labour.

Good deal the single maidservant may have been, but Frances Hamilton did not – could not – ask her to clean out the necessary house, which was a labour of great importance in the ordinary affairs of life, and to which we now turn.

---

[106] Bath and West of England Society, *Letters and Papers on Agriculture* vol. 6, pp. 210–58 for promotion of *The Connexion between Industry and Property* and other insurance schemes. For promotion of the potato as a food for labouring bodies, see Chapter 9.
[107] SCRO, DD/ FS 5/1 (1 Feb. 1796).

Necessity

The processes of waste disposal were not unmentionable in eighteenth-century England; they could be spoken of in a sentimental novel by a lady, for the ladies – and in Bishops Lydeard House.[108] Architectural plans for the grander kind of dwelling and farmhouse included design details and costings of water closets and necessary houses.[109] There was a philosophy of the privy: a *Dialogue concerning Decency* (1751) was a powerful argument for enclosed and secluded necessaries, *with doors*, as private places that promote domestic and social civility in the individual. The argument is conducted by Philoprepon and Entrapelus, two visitors from the philosophical realm of classical antiquity to the country house of the modern English gentleman who is its author (and who suffers dreadfully from the gripe – 'Oh these horrid gripes!... they plague me every day of my life. I wish I was now at home; that I might ease myself in the neat apartment I have lately made in my garden; for I hate to do such things in publick').[110] Natural and cultural histories of the necessary house also provoked philosophy.[111] One frosty morning

108 Mary Julia Young, *The Family Party. In three volumes*, Minerva Press for William Lane, London, 1791, vol. 3, p. 159.
109 John Crunden, *Convenient and Ornamental Architecture, consisting of Original Design, for Plans, Elevations and Sections; beginning with the Farm House, and regularly ascending to the grand and magnificent Villa...*, Henry Webley, London, 1767; *The Builder's Magazine: or Monthly Companion for Architects, Carpenters, Masons, Bricklayers, &c...*, F. Newbery, London, 1774; William Pain, *Pain's British Palladio: or the Builder's General Assistant...*, William and James Pain, London, 1788; Board of Agriculture, *Communications to the Board of Agriculture; on Subjects Relative to the Husbandry and Internal Improvement of the Country*, W. Bulmer, London, 1797, vol. 1, pp. 66–71 and Plans.
110 Samuel Rolleston, *A Philosophical Dialogue concerning Decency. To which is added a critical and historical Dissertation on Places of Retirement for necessary Occasions... By the Author of the Dissertation on Barley Wine*, James Fletcher, Oxford, London, 1751. 'Eutrapelia' means something like 'ready wit, liveliness', a cultured insolence; 'Philoprepon' probably signalled 'fond of propriety or decorum'. I am grateful to William and Peter Mack for providing me with this information.
111 Jean Rodolphe d'Arnay, *The Private Life of the Romans. Translated from the French of M. D'Arnay*, printed for the translator, Edinburgh, 1761.

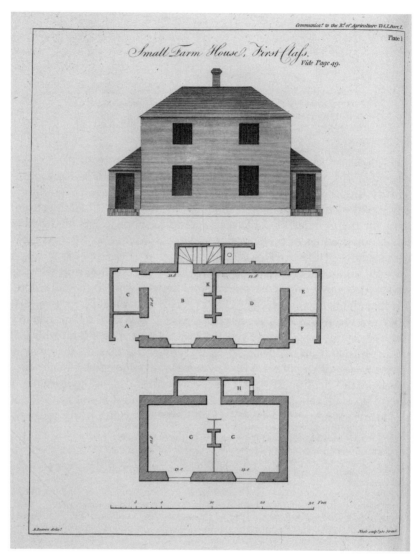

Figure 8. On the plan, H indicates the 'pigeon house over the necessary.'

sometime in the early 1780s, a gentleman naturalist sat in a necessary in a country place, watching entranced 'a charming and elegant representation' of 'Landscapes, with Groves of Trees' formed by the spiders' webs spun across the glass windows. The effect was produced, he supposed,

by the 'additional Intermixture of animal Salts' in such a place.[112] Genus
of insects were classified according to their habitations, and the necessary house had a fly all of its own.[113] In another country and in the earliest version of *Wilhelm Meister*, Johann von Goethe wrote about the
places of unclean necessity where thwarted lovers were forced to meet.[114]
No matter that this work was not available in English until the early
twentieth century; a local literature, high and low, furnished many examples of lovers compelled to meet therein.[115] Necessary houses were where
maidservants deposited the corpses of their bastard babes (low literature
made this a particularly well-known social fact) and where criminals
concealed decaying bodies and their swag, across the long eighteenth
century.[116]

A great part of the servant's labour involved the disposal of household
waste. *A Modern Dissertation on a certain Necessary Piece of household Furniture* (1752) thought the maidservant always to blame when a drunken
gentleman woke in the night, could not find his chamber pot, and performed the comic set-piece of contemplating the vase on the chimney
piece, the closet, his boots . . . as a receptacle.[117] The emptying of chamber pots and other containers, the carrying of buckets and pails – to a
cess-pit, to a necessary house, to (in very modern dwellings under strong
Continental influence) a water closet or slop-sink; the carting by a man-
servant of shit to the town fields – is probably what the mid-century
guides to domestic service meant when they warned servants about the

[112] Henry Baker, *Of Microscopes, and the Discoveries made thereby. Illustrated with many
Copper Plates. In Two Volumes*, J. Dodsley, London, 1785, vol. 2, pp. 223–4.
[113] Anon., *The Natural History of Insects, compiled from Swammerdam, Brookes, Goldsmith,
&c. Embellished with copper-plates*, Morison, Perth, G. Mudie, Edinburgh, W. Coke,
Leith, 1792, p. 140.
[114] Johann Wolfgang von Goethe, *Wilhelm Meister's Theatrical Mission*, trans. Gregory A.
Page, Heinemann, London, 1913, p. 12.
[115] Andrew Bayntun-Rolt, *The Trial of the Right Honourable Lady Maria Bayntun . . . in the
Arches Court at Doctors Commons, for committing the Crime of Adultery, To which is added,
a very pathetic and affecting Letter, from Lady Maria to her Husband*, printed for the
editor, London, 1781, p. 8.
[116] Mark Jackson, *New-Born Child Murder: Women, illegitimacy and the courts and eighteenth-
century England*, Manchester University Press, Manchester and New York, 1996; Joseph
Blake alias Blueskin, Foot-pad, and John Sheppard, *The History of the Lives and Actions
of Jonathan Wild, Thief-taker . . . Housebreaker*, Edward Midwinter, London, 1725,
p. 106; James Caulfield, *Blackguardiana: or, a Dictionary of Rogues, Bawds, Pimps,
Whores, Pickpockets, Shoplifters . . . Illustrated with eighteen Portraits of the most remarkable
Professors in every Species of Villainy. Interspersed with many Curious Anecdotes, Cant Terms,
Flash Songs, &c. The Whole intended to put Society on their Guard against Depredators*,
printed for the author, Bagshot, 1793.
[117] Anon., *A Modern Dissertation on a Certain Necessary Piece of Household Furniture*, H.
Kent, London, 1752, p. 6.

many little menial tasks they would have to perform in the course of their work.[118]

Over the years, Frances Hamilton had her workers deal with at least three necessary houses dotted about her gardens and grounds, and others which belonged to her tenants and neighbours. In May 1788 she spent 1s on anonymous labour for 'cleaning 3 Necessary Houses'.[119] She regularly bought in labour for the job. In 1794 'Jno Bray came here & washed the little House wth the remainder of the whitewash ~ I bottled port Wine.'[120] (Perhaps a second example of Frances Hamilton rolling up her sleeves and taking the barrel of port into her own possession by mingling her energies with it.) She had her own little house – not the one the servants and other workers used. In 1792 Bray earned £3 13s for 'day work repairing my House'.[121] In May 1795 it took two days to prepare it for the summer months ('25th White Washed my House'; '26th finished Whitewashing the House').[122] She made no distinction by gender of the workers who were to do the digging out and whitewashing: in 1792 'Bet gard & Hooper taking up the House-Dung'.[123] (Hooper was the old 'useless' man for whom she kept jobs – out of charity, she believed.) There was a hierarchy of labour at work here. She did not use the household servants for these sanitary tasks, though sometimes involved her apprentice boys. She bought in workers who, like Bet Gard and John Hooper, were either past it, or who undertook almost any task for 6d or 8d a day.

When a new necessary was made she used bought-in and household labour for its construction 'Tom Bodger dig a pit for a little House . . . 29th Edw Vickery beat house dung & Cow Dung' – or if not household labour for the processing of the collected waste, a boy closely connected to Catherine Vickery, her washerwoman.[124] She had long known how to direct workers in the making of a dung heap for later use as fertilizer. Instructions were available in the husbandry guides she owned and from many other sources.[125] In June 1793 'Edward [her apprentice]

---

[118] For eighteenth-century household waste disposal, see Frank Latham, *The Sanitation of Domestic Buildings*, Sanitary Publishing Company, London, 1898, pp. 2–7, 96; Elizabeth Burton, *The Georgians at Home, 1741–1830*, Longman, London, 1967; Joe Heslop, *According to Local Custom: Waste disposal in Hull from the middle ages to the end of the eighteenth century*, Local History Archives, College of Further Education, Hull, 1990, p. 118; Susanna Whatman, *The Housekeeping Book of Susanna Whatman, 1776–1800*, intro. Christina Hardyment, National Trust, London, 2000, pp. 24–5, 37–8.

[119] SCRO, DD/FS 5/7 (11 May 1788).   [120] SCRO, DD/FS 5/2 (29 Apr. 1794).

[121] SCRO, DD/FS 5/8 (6 Mar. 1792).   [122] SCRO, DD/FS 5/2 (25, 26 May 1795).

[123] *Ibid*. (29 Oct. 1792).   [124] *Ibid*. (27, 29 Dec. 1792).

[125] Arthur Young's essay 'On the Farm-Yard Management of Dung' did not provide a recipe for adding house-dung to the produce of the yard. Bath and West of England

& Hooper make a dunghill under the hedge . . . Hooper cleaned the little House.'[126] Rights in a necessary house were an important aspect of community and neighbourly relations. In February 1793, in an unusually extended entry in her account book, she described how George Knight had 'walled the Hole of the late Mrs Winters little Necessary House – which I permitted to be opened to oblige Mrs Winter who was Subject to disorders in her Mind or I should not have indulged her to have it opened: NB I never permitted her servants to Clean it but always my Servants removed it'.[127] This house on Hamilton's land with access from Mrs Winter's garden was subject of a long-standing dispute with a family history. A collection of little necessary houses like this meant often having the Brays in, to 'build up' (point) the walls and limewash inside. Hamilton's will suggests how very important were sanitary arrangements for choice (if choice there were) of dwelling house in the first place. She was very clear that a substantial part of the legacy to her former household servants was good lavatory arrangements. Molly Evans got the 'Dwellinghouse and Buildings in Bishops Lydeard . . . called Shattocks with twelve feet of Garden Ground next adjoining the same for her Life with free access to the Necessary' and Betty Huckleburgh (here called 'Hucklebridge') the house and garden next door to Evans, with the same access to the necessary.[128]

This important aspect of servants' everyday work has not been much noted by historians, not even by those who take seriously the experience of labour in the past. Or, if it is noted, understanding is massively mediated by the Victorian *belle-lettriste* and pornographer of working-class women's dirt, Arthur Munby.[129] He attributed to Hannah Cullwick his maidservant lover, a positive desire for dirt and filth. Hannah, her day's labour increased by Munby's instruction that she write down and record every chimney swept, midden shovelled, and filthy task performed, wrote with a pen finely attuned to what he wanted, and what he desired in her. Certainly she loved Munby (and perhaps God), and wanted to

---

Society for the Encouragement of Agriculture, Arts, Manufacture and Commerce, *Letters and Papers on Agriculture, Planting, &c Selected from the Correspondence of the Society*, The Society, Bath, 1792–3, vol. 3, pp. 1–28; but see the guide Hamilton possessed, William Ellis, *The Modern Husbandman, complete in eight volumes*, published for the author, London, 1750, vol. 8, p. 399.

[126] SCRO, DD/FS 5/2 (1 Jun. 1793).   [127] *Ibid.* (23 Feb. 1793).

[128] SCRO, DD/CH Bx 16, Copy of the Will and Codicils of Mrs Frances Hamilton.

[129] Derek Hudson, *Munby, Man of Two Worlds: The life and diaries of Arthur J. Munby, 1828–1910*, John Murray, London, 1972; Hannah Cullwick, *The Diaries of Hannah Cullwick*, ed. and intro. by Liz Stanley, Virago, London, 1984; Barry Reay, *Watching Hannah: Sexuality, horror and bodily de-formation in Victorian England*, Reaktion, London, 2002.

perform the desirable, filthy self he wanted. But there are other ways of understanding workers' attitude to the filth they were charged with removing: Emma Christopher's discussion of working conditions among slave-ship crews breaks the barriers of silence that historians have built around the sanitary question. She describes the common sailor's complicated and desperate feelings about the task of cleansing his human cargo and their quarters (if quarters they can be called).[130] Removing human effluent (literally, shit-work) was a job for servants as well as sailors. We shall come to the psychological effects on workers of having to deal with human excrement (especially in conditions of intense heat and social anxiety) later in this book. What we have for the moment is the comedy – low comedy and philosophical comedy – that veiled as effectively as any historian's silence, servants' attitude to the dirt produced by the persons employing them.

[130] Emma Christopher, *Slave Ship Sailors and Their Captive Cargoes, 1730–1807*, Cambridge University Press, Cambridge, 2006, pp. 167–87.

4   Lord Mansfield's Women

Lord Mansfield's Women were seven female servants who never actually encountered the Chief Justice in person. He – and later his replacement, Lloyd Kenyon – encountered them through paperwork forwarded to the court of Kings Bench by a county quarter sessions unable to settle the differences between two parishes disputing their responsibilities under the old poor law. 'Lord Mansfield's Women' are a quasi-legal category (or a heuristic device) devised to show how eighteenth-century labour law operated in conjunction with the poor laws to affect many working lives in eighteenth-century England. By means of these women's cases (and many others) the Chief Justice and the judges revised and adjusted the law to be used by provincial magistrates in the lower courts, in their management of local domestic labour relations.[1]

One of these seven women servants was a slave (or a slave-servant – really, there was nothing appropriate to call Charlotte Howe: in a society without slave law, she had no legal identity).[2] Yet her case was an important reference point for lawyers and legal theorists reformulating the terms of labour for a late eighteenth-century market economy. Other, better-known cases brought before the English courts in the mid-eighteenth century involved the terms of freedom and the master's property right in his slave – his right to remove a slave from England for

---

[1] See Chapter 7.
[2] Seymour Drescher, 'Manumission in a society without slave law', *Slavery and Abolition*, 10 (1989), 92–3.

example, as in the famous Somerset case of 1772. But Howe's case focused on her labour. It was important because she was a woman who had worked as a domestic servant. The work she had done – when, where and how she had exercised her labour – was emphasised by the parishes who profoundly did not want responsibility for her. The haphazard amalgam of poor law and employment law that allowed them to contest the case in the first place, forced this perspective. Howe – and all of Lord Mansfield's Women – had much to say to these questions of labour, ownership of labour, and legal entitlement, from their position as domestic servants. They were women workers who believed that domestic work *was* work; that their energies (which earned them sometimes money, sometimes clothes and keep, sometimes a settlement) was exercised in something called labour, which arose out of the job in hand. They all believed that they were entitled to the major benefit that domestic service brought – that is, settlement, inaugurated by Act of Parliament in 1662.[3] The two of them who were mothers may also have known what differences illegitimacy made to the legal ability of their children to inherit a settlement. And all of them show what their historians have only recently understood: that the Law of Settlement was 'in fact, the most important branch of law, if judged by the number of lives affected and lawyers' hours expended'.[4]

Under the complex of sixteenth- and seventeenth-century legislation that set the old poor law in place, a dominant mode of operation emerged: a poor or indigent person claiming relief from a local authority was required to demonstrate his or her 'settlement', that is, that they 'belonged' to a place, and were among its settled poor.[5] Settlement could be acquired in a variety of ways but 'earning' it by service was the common route for women – it certainly produced the most litigation. A man or a woman fulfilling the agreement to serve for a year had an important claim to relief. Settlement by service was something that a woman could gain by her own labour, and in certain circumstances, pass on to her children. Female domestic servants forced legal questions about settlement as a form of possession, or property, and about the permeable boundaries between the laws of settlement and the laws of service. Confronted with

---

[3] The amending acts of 13 and 14 Charles II, c. 12, and 3 William III, c. 11 were actually more important to all these women, establishing the rule of hiring for 365 days.

[4] James Stephen Taylor, *Poverty, Migration and Settlement in the Industrial Revolution: Sojourners' narratives*, Society for the Promotion of Science and Scholarship, Palo Alto, CA, 1989, pp. 18–19.

[5] For settlement and belonging, Keith Snell, *Parish and Belonging: Community, identity and welfare in England and Wales, 1700–1950*, Cambridge University Press, Cambridge, 2006, pp. 81–161.

women like Mansfield's seven, High Court judges and local magistrates had to move between two categories of law, using one as if it were the other, in order for the law to give some kind of answer to the problems the women presented. In these encounters, poor law became labour law, and labour law, settlement law; bodies of law were used together because of the particular kinds of body the judges encountered.[6] Above all, the cases of Lord Mansfield's Women raised questions of people's property in their own labour.

William Murray, 1st Earl of Mansfield (1705–93) was Chief Justice of the court of King's Bench from 1756 to 1788. His historical reputation is heavily marked by his strict interpretation of seditious libel law and riot law, and the unpopularity gained thereby – and by Charles Dickens's Mansfield-narrative in *Barnaby Rudge* (1841). The scenes in which the Gordon Riot mob fires Mansfield's Bloomsbury mansion have underpinned historians' much later assessments of Mansfield and his judgments as the very epitome of state repression during long years of counter-revolution.[7] An account of him as appeal court judge in interaction with his Women restores some of the eighteenth-century significance of the Chief Justice as social policymaker, by his intervention in poor – law administration.[8]

There were more of Lord Mansfield's Women than these seven female servants; we can add the women of his family and household. Mansfield was surrounded by women, their complicated legal personae making a bridge between his domestic life and the questions of bastardy, illegitimacy and slavery that he adjudicated in poor law appeals, not just as a lawyer, but as a person. The personal and the domestic were political (the personal was legalistic), even for a man; even for the most eminent jurist of the mid-eighteenth century; even for the Chief Justice himself.

---

[6] Simon Deakin and Frank Wilkinson, *The Law of the Labour Market: Industrialization, employment and legal evolution*, Oxford University Press, Oxford, 2005, pp. 110–99 for the way in which the poor law established the legal status and conditions of all those who were dependent on wages for subsistence.

[7] Charles Dickens, *Barnaby Rudge* (1841), Penguin, London, 1973, chapter 66 where Mansfield escapes fire and mob 'by the back way', playing the part assigned him by historians: an elusive symbol of a justice that is not to be had. See Ian Gilmour, *Riot, Rising and Revolution: Governance and violence in eighteenth-century England*, Pimlico, London, 1992, pp. 260, 307, 316–17, 337–9, 342–70; John Stevenson, *Popular Disturbance in England, 1700–1832*, 2nd edn, Longman, London, 1992, pp. 94–110. E. P. Thompson confronted the Chief Justice in *Whigs and Hunters: The origins of the Black Act*, Allen Lane, London, 1975, pp. 251–5. See also Sir William Holdsworth, *A History of the English Law*, 17 vols. Methuen, London, 1936–72, vol. 10, pp. 676–96.

[8] For the judges as policymakers when on circuit, see Joanna Innes, 'Parliament and the shaping of eighteenth-century social policy', *Transactions of the Royal Historical Society*, 5th ser., 40 (1990), 67, 73–4.

So 'Lord Mansfield's Women' is a dual category, including, in a minor key, the Countess of Mansfield, whose life of blameless sociability ended in 1784, and the several young women, all of them nieces of one sort or another, who lived as companions to the aging earl after Lady Betty's death. After Mansfield retired there was much nursing for them to do as well. *The Times*, having waged a relentless campaign for him to go during the early months of 1788, reported that once he departed the bench, he entered 'his second state of childhood'.[9] Caring for him were the daughters of Mansfield's brother, 6th Viscount Stormont, Anne and Marjory Murray, and his great-niece, Lady Elizabeth Murray, who was daughter to his nephew and heir, David, the 7th Viscount. These three were all cousin in some way or other to Dido Elizabeth Belle, 'the black girl at Kenwood', whose existence has been long known to historians of the black presence in Britain.[10] She was the illegitimate daughter of another of Mansfield's nephews on his sister's side, Sir John Lindsay and a slave woman; she arrived at Kenwood House (Mansfield's summer retreat in rural Hampstead) shortly after her birth in 1763.[11] She lived there until her great-uncle's death in 1793, as a kind of companion and personal attendant to her half-cousin Lady Elizabeth Murray.[12] Mansfield was by all accounts, both fond of and reliant on the services of his illegitimate great-niece, and left her well provided-for after his death.[13] In drawing up his will in 1783, Mansfield confirmed Dido Elizabeth Belle's (more properly Elizabeth Lindsay's) freedom, indicating that 'he had already bestowed it upon her sometime earlier in life'. It has been suggested that

---

[9] *The Times*, 9, 12, 14, 19 Jan., 7 Aug., 10 Oct. 1788.

[10] Edmund Heward, *Lord Mansfield*, Rose, Chichester and London, 1979, pp. 90–2; Gene Adams, 'Dido Elizabeth Belle: A black girl at Kenwood. An account of a protegée of the 1st Lord Mansfield', *Camden History Review*, 12 (1984), 10–14; Peter Fryer, *Staying Power: The history of black people in Britain*, Pluto, London, 1984, 120, 518, n. 15. *Le tout Londres* knew about Dido after *The Times*, reporting on her father's death in 1788, wrote of her as his 'natural daughter, a Mulatto . . . whose amiable disposition and accomplishments have gained her the highest respect from all [Lord Mansfield's] relations and visitants', *The Times*, 10 Jun. 1788.

[11] For Lindsay, *Gentleman's Magazine*, 58, Part 1 (1788), 564; *The Times*, 10 Jun. 1788; *London Chronicle*, 7–10 Jun. 1788. Also Hugh Thomas, *The Slave Trade: The history of the Atlantic slave trade 1440–1870*, Picador, London, 1997, p. 469; Heward, *Mansfield*, pp. 161–2.

[12] The household evidently understood who and what Dido was, but visitors were sometimes confused about her role and status. See Peter O. Hutchinson, *The Diary and Letters of Thomas Hutchinson: Compiled from the original documents*, Sampson and Low, 2 vols., London, 1883–6, vol. 2, pp. 276–7.

[13] Sometime in 1793 or 1794, Dido got married and left Kenwood for good. C. Hoare and Co., Bankers, Customers Ledgers, 46/303 (16, 17 Apr.; 14, 31 May; 29, 30 Jun.; 2 Aug.; 19 Oct.; 14 Nov. 1793). After these months of activity (deposits of £700, investments of £457 13s 4d, and withdrawals) 'Miss Dido Elizabeth Belle'/'Mrs Davinier' disappear from her bankers' accounts.

this was done to make doubly certain that 'once his personal protection was ended, she should not be at the mercy of strangers or unscrupulous people'.[14] In his last years then, Mansfield was surrounded by these vibrant and elegant young women (and all the maidservants who performed the practicalities of their tender care).[15]

In London, in King's Bench, the Chief Justice had been a severe critic of the law he had to exercise in poor law appeal cases. He frequently lambasted 'the litigious zeal of public bodies', eager to see disputed settlement cases 'travel through every stage which the law allow[ed]'. In disputes like these, where parish ratepayers were responsible for the relief and maintenance of the poor, the collective financial resources of a county often led them to discount the considerable outlay of county funds involved in briefing attorneys for a dispute between two quarter sessions, and the even greater expense involved in preparing a case for the higher courts. 'The litigation of the poor laws . . . are . . . a disgrace to the country', said Mansfield. He thought them 'a dropsey . . . swollen to monstrous proportions' by 'the invitation offered to each parish to cast its burden upon its neighbours'.[16] 'There ought to be no litigations at all in the settlement of the poor', wrote an equally exasperated Thomas Ruggles in 1793; '"le jeu ne vaut pas la chandelle;" there should be no attornies' bills on overseers' accounts; it is cheaper to relieve . . . than to remove a family . . . which, if the overseers are peculiarly astute in watching over the interests of their parishes, or in other words, are tenacious in their opinions, will go into the King's Bench'.[17]

---

[14] Adams, 'Dido Elizabeth Belle', p. 14; Heward, *Mansfield*, pp. 161–2; *London Chronicle*, 7–10 Jun. 1788; Douglas A. Lorimer, 'Black slaves and English liberty: A re-examination of racial slavery in England', *Immigrants and Minorities*, 3 (1984), 144, n. 17; Scone Palace (SP), Murray Family Papers, Earls of Mansfield, NRA(S) 0776, Second Series, Bundle 2346, Incl. attested copies (1793) of will and codicils of William, Earl of Mansfield.

[15] Joyce Hemlow (ed.), *The Journals and Letters of Fanny Burney (Madame d'Arblay)*, vol. 1, 1791–92, Oxford University Press, Oxford, 1972, pp. 203–4; *The Life of William Russell Birch, Enamel Painter, Written by Himself*, privately printed, Philadelphia, 1927, pp. 18–24. For the elegance of these young women, see the Zoffany portrait of Dido and Elizabeth Murray, reproduced in Adams, 'Dido Elizabeth Belle'.

[16] Cecil Fifoot, *Lord Mansfield*, Clarendon Press, Oxford, 1936, pp. 206–7, citing Rex v. Inhabitants of Newington, 1786; SP, Murray Family Papers. Earls of Mansfield, NRA(S) 0776, Box 68, King's Bench Papers, 1782–5; James Oldham, *The Mansfield Manuscripts and the Growth of the English Law in the Eighteenth Century*, 2 vols., University of North Carolina Press, Chapel Hill, NC, and London, 1992, vol. 1, p. 108.

[17] Thomas Ruggles, *The History of the Poor; their Rights, Duties, and the Laws Respecting Them*, 2 vols., J. Deighton, London, 1793, vol. 2, p. 91; also Anon. [H. C. Jennings], *A Free Inquiry into the Enormous Increase of Attornies, with Some Reflections on the Abuse of our Laws. By an Unfeigned Admirer of Genuine British Jurisprudence*, W. Clacher, Chelmsford, 1785; Richard Burn, *The History of the Poor Laws: With Observations* (1764), Augustus M. Kelly, Clifton, NJ, 1973, pp. 211–12; Henry Zouch, *Hints Respecting the Public Police*,

There were no reporters regularly at work in any of the trial courts before the end of the eighteenth century. But individual judges like Mansfield made notes, and these might become the source for printed case reports, which in turn informed magistrates and other readers about recent changes in the law.[18] Joseph Burchell's digest of cases adjudged between 1756 and 1794, reported on more than a hundred disputed settlements. Over a third of them involved questions of settlement by service.[19] Other means of gaining settlement (by birth, residence, apprenticeship, marriage, office-holding, purchase or paying rates) did not give rise to anything like as much litigation. The 1793 revision of Bott's standard *Decisions of the King's Bench* devoted most space to the question of 'Settlement by Hiring and Service', in that 'late and most active period' in the making of 'law positive' (statute law) and legal judgment, the 1770s and 1780s.[20] James Taylor used 985 settlement examinations to produce his 1989 account of poverty and migration during the early Industrial Revolution; 679 of them involved a disputed service hiring as the basis for settlement.[21] These were cases settled locally, some of them not even forwarded from parishes to quarter sessions for adjudication; had they gone on appeal to King's Bench, he would not have found them in the local records. It was through local settlement disputes, and the judges' adjustment of them into case law in the higher courts, that the poor laws affected so many late eighteenth-century lives.[22]

A Victorian commentator might deprecate former days when 'an imagined, but mistaken analogy between a settlement and a right of property' had preoccupied both claimants and High Court judges; a

---

Published at the Request of the Court of Quarter Sessions held at Pontefract, April 24, 1786, John Stockdale, London, 1786, p. 8; Anon., *A View of Real Grievances, with the Remedies Proposed for Redressing them, printed for the author,* London, 1772, pp. 45–7, 53–7; John Scott, *Observations on the Present State of the Parochial and Vagrant Poor,* Dilly, London, 1773, p. 79.

[18] Out of the three common law High Courts able to hear local cases on appeal, the Court of King's Bench saw by far the largest amount of business in the second half of the eighteenth century. There were technical and procedural reasons for the limited sitting of the Court of Common Pleas. Oldham, *Mansfield Manuscripts,* vol. 1, pp. 164–8; for unreported cases, see pp. 183–5.

[19] Joseph Burchell, *Arrangement and Digest of the Law in Cases Adjudged in the King's Bench and Common Pleas from the Year 1756 to 1794, inclusive,* T. Jones, London, 1796.

[20] Francis Const, *Decisions of the Court of the King's Bench, Upon the Laws Relating to the Poor, Originally Published by Edmund Bott Esq. of the Inner Temple, Barrister at Law. Revised . . . by Francis Cost Esq. of the Middle Temple,* 3rd edn, 2 vols., Whieldon and Butterworth, London, 1793, vol. 2, pp. 315–541. The remark about legal activity in the second half of the eighteenth century is Joseph Burchell's in his *Arrangement and Digest,* Preface. See *The Parliamentary History of England from the earliest period to the year 1803,* vol. 19, Preface. See also Holdsworth, *History of the English Law,* vol. 10, p. 100; and Oldham, *Mansfield Manuscripts,* vol. 1, p. 163.

[21] Taylor, *Poverty,* p. 188. n. 2.   [22] Taylor, *Poverty,* p. 190, n. 13.

once-upon-a-time when 'as it appears in the [eighteenth-century] Law Reports . . . judges used to speak of a settlement as a thing to be favoured in the law, and when, they seemed to consider it . . . as a peculiar privilege of the poor'; but modern historians have emphasised that perspective.[23] Pamela Sharpe says that 'the settlement can be seen as a property right for the poor'.[24] Both she and Keith Snell (who refers to some thousand settlement examinations in *Annals of the Labouring Poor*) chart typical eighteenth-century working lives by outlining the many bids and stratagems poor people made to obtain one.[25] Women could gain their own settlement in exactly the same way as men, by a series of annual hirings. For women, just as for men, the service contract was practically the only way of doing this. Indeed, it is likely that more women than men sought settlement by service in the period 1750–90; certainly more disputed women's cases reached King's Bench. The difference between men and women was that on marriage a woman took her husband's settlement, and there were difficulties in proving it for women or children 'needing to show a "derivative" settlement from husband and parents', and for married women claiming relief for whatever reason, on their 'maiden settlement', as in the case of Tabitha Reynolds.[26]

She is the first of Lord Mansfield's Women, even though her struggles of the late 1760s never went further than Doncaster Quarter Sessions and her case was resolved without any appeal to King's Bench. Reynolds and her three youngest children (Sarah, John and Mary, aged five, three and one year respectively) were removed to Leeds on the order of two West Riding justices at the very end of December 1767 and the family was received by the Leeds overseers.[27] The removal order followed on the life story Reynolds had told the magistrates – a story largely

---

[23] Robert Pashley, *Pauperism and Poor Laws*, Longman Brown Green and Longman, London, 1852, p. 269; Snell, *Annals*, pp. 71–4; Pamela Sharpe, '"The Bowels of Compation": A labouring family and the law, c.1790–1834' in Tim Hitchcock, Peter King and Pamela Sharpe (eds.), *Chronicling Poverty: The voices and strategies of the English poor, 1640–1840*, Macmillan, Basingstoke, 1997, pp. 87–108; Taylor, *Poverty*, p. 42, calls settlement 'an important patrimony of any poor child, for good or ill'. Also Thomas A. Horne, *Property Rights and Poverty: Political arguments in Britain, 1605–1834*, University of North Carolina Press, Chapel Hill, NC, and London, 1990, p. 141; Lynn Hollen Lees, *The Solidarities of Strangers: The English poor laws and the people, 1700–1948*, Cambridge University Press, Cambridge, 1998, pp. 29–33.

[24] Pamela Sharpe, *Adapting to Capitalism: Working women in the English economy, 1700–1850*, Macmillan, Basingstoke, 1996, p. 34.

[25] Snell, *Annals*, p. 73, 105–8; pp. 17–18 for legislation affecting settlement; and Sharpe, *Adapting*, pp. 109–21; Paul Slack, *The English Poor Law, 1531–1782*, Cambridge University Press, Cambridge, 1996, pp. 51–6.

[26] Sharpe, *Adapting*, pp. 118–20, and Notes; Burn, *History*, pp. 283–4

[27] West Yorkshire Archives (WYAS), Wakefield District, West Riding of Yorkshire Quarter Sessions, Doncaster Sessions, Jan. 1768, Quarter Sessions Rolls, QS1/107/3–7, Orders;

to do with her unfortunate choice in men. Before she married she had gained her own settlement by hiring herself for a year to William Pookett of Methley (in the triangle between Leeds, Castleford, and Wakefield): 'about 1742, when she was a Spinster, *she was hired for* a year ... *& served such year Service* & consequently was then legally settled there', ran the brief prepared by Leeds solicitors for the Doncaster Sessions. Seven or so years later she married Joseph Turner of Garforth (some five miles north of Methley) and had one or two children by him (her memory, or more likely, the solicitor's clerk recording her story, was uncertain on this point). When Turner left her in 1752 and she applied for parish relief, it was on her husband's settlement. But where Turner's 'legal Settlement was she never knew for a Certainty, or otherwise than as she has heard him say yt it was at Hepelstone or some such like Place in Staffordshire'; and that was where she was removed. This could have been Eccleshall, or Mucklestone, or any one of a dozen places; but there is no Hepelstone in Staffordshire. In 1752 she had not known where she was going, which scarcely mattered, because 'the Officers of the Place, to which she had been so removed agreed with the Officer who conducted her tither, to bring her [back] to Methley, which he did accordingly'. (In 1767 solicitors were alarmed to find that 'This Order seems not to have been appealed from – We have applied to the Officers of Garforth & endeavoured to possess our selves of this Order but in vain – Indeed they alledge there was no such Order, but the Pauper says otherways, & will acquaint the Court, if proper to touch upon this Matter.')

Sometime after her turn-around journey to Staffordshire (or maybe, not Staffordshire at all: her journey to somewhere, someplace), Tabitha Turner heard that her husband was dead. In June 1755, believing herself to be a widow, she married Jonathan Reynolds of Leeds, boatman and porter, by whom she had the three children named above, all of them born in the township of Leeds. Nine years after his disappearance, not dead at all, Joseph Turner turned up in Leeds '& findg. the Pauper in the Possession of Reynolds as his Wife, demanded her of him, but at last Turner & Reynold came to an Agreement touching her whereby the former pretended to sell, and the latter to buy her, & so Reynolds still continued in Poss[ess]ion, till he ran away & left her some 20 or 30 Weeks ago', that is in the summer of 1767.[28]

Order of Removal for Tabitha Reynolds ... from Doncaster to Leeds Wedon, 26 Dec. 1767.

[28] Pamela Sharpe, 'Bigamy among the labouring poor in Essex, 1754–1857', *Local Historian*, 24 (1994), 139–44.

There were strenuous attempts made by Bridges, Solicitors, to trace Turner and Reynolds, and, more to the point, to discover whether either of them 'did any Act whereby to gain a Settlement at Leeds'. They discovered that as a young man, Reynolds had hired himself to a miller at Castleford Mills and served for a year; indeed 'tis said, Reynolds served . . . for sevl. years successively as his hired Servt for a year', in which case, the townships of Castleford or Ollerton would have been responsible for Tabitha and the children. But very soon into preparation of the case, Tabitha Reynold's own marital and settlement status became the point at issue, for 'As it appears, ye Woman has acquired a Settlement at Methley in her own Right, & the Settlement of her real Husband cannot be ascertained & the 3 children mentd in the order are Bastards.' None of the adults in the case had their settlement at Leeds, neither Turner, nor Tabitha nor Jonathan Reynolds; 'and altho' the Children . . . may, possibly, be Bastards, & the Place of their legal Settlement may be [at Leeds] as being the Place of their Birth', they had not in fact, been removed to Leeds on those grounds. Until they were bastardised by a justices' order, they had to be assumed legitimate. But thinking through the technicalities of the case, the solicitors thought that 'even admitting them Bastards, for Argument sake', was not to the point, for they were supposed in law 'to be inseparable from their Mother, being all Nurse Children under the Age of 7 years, & ought to have been removed with her to her Place of Settlement, as a necessary Appendage of hers, & not she with them'. In other words, Tabitha Reynolds and her children ought to have been removed to Methley.[29]

When it came to court, Leeds' lawyers argued that the proper place of settlement for Tabitha Reynolds and her children was in Castleford Township (where her second husband had gained a settlement) or 'at Methley in her own Right' – though where mattered less than its not being at Leeds, but somewhere else. The West Riding magistrates found for the appellants at their Doncaster meeting on 20 January, and the next day the children were sent for by the Doncaster overseers, to be transported by waggon from the Leeds Workhouse. The solicitors' bill, the flurry of paperwork in Leeds (the letters sent vainly seeking removal orders twenty-odd years old, and persuading former employers to appear as witnesses), the maintenance of the children in Leeds Workhouse, and the price of legal opinion and representation, cost something between

---

[29] WYAS, Bradford District, 16D86/1150, Sharp Bridges Accounts, 'Brief To Doncaster Sessions 20 Janry 1768'. For the ways in which a woman's settlement might apply to her children and grandchildren, Edmund Bott, *Digest of the Laws Relating to the Poor, by Francis Const*, 3 vols., Strahan, London, 1800, vol. 2, pp. 161–2, 164–6.

£3 and £4.[30] It is not clear whose settlement removed Tabitha Reynolds and her children from the responsibility of Leeds, her own or that of her common-law husband, Jonathan. It seems likely though, that it was her maiden settlement rather than her derivative one that determined the next place to which she was sent off in the waggoner's cart, as the evidence to support Jonathan Reynolds' settlement at Castleford was not very compelling.

Women's complicated legal personae are exemplified by Tabitha Reynolds, in her relationship to a body of law (the poor law, and the Law of Settlement) in which it mattered very much what kind of body *she* possessed, in all its dramatic mutability. The legal status of Tabitha Reynolds rested on her body, which was in succession, a pregnant body, a parturient body, a lactating body; a body she exercised in labour (in both its meanings); and on the connection of that body to men, whether in the married relation or not. Accounts of women and property (of women as property, and as possessors of it) that emphasise their effacement by *coverture*, simply will not do in the deciphering of her as a legal person, for she was perpetually being covered and uncovered.

One of the tendencies of ratepayers, satirised by magistrate Richard Burn and scandalised everywhere, was that 'if they will hire servants . . . for a year, [they] then to endeavour to pick a quarrel with them before the year's end, and . . . get rid of them'.[31] But magistrates also had to deal with the question of the master's or mistress's right to dismiss. This was bound up with their general authority over a female servant, and how it was to be exercised under a complex and antique body of service law. For example, magistrates had long been instructed that 'if a woman who is a *Servant* shall *marry*, yet she must serve out her Time and her Husband cannot take her out of her Master's Service' – that the law of service overrode marriage law in this regard.[32] A servant hired according to 5 Eliz. c. 4 was not to leave his or her service, unless allowed to do so by a magistrate. There was a similar jurisdiction exercised by magistrates as far as the employer's dismissal of a servant before time was

---

[30] WYAS, Wakefield District, QS 1/107/3–8, West Riding of Yorkshire Quarter Sessions, Quarter Sessions Rolls, Doncaster Sessions Jan. 1768, Miscellaneous. 'Expences of the Maintenance of Tabitha Reynolds and her Three Children in Leeds Workhouse . . . 3 Weeks'; QS 10/25, Quarter Sessions Order Books, 1767–9 (20 Jan. 1768).

[31] Burn, *History*, p. 211; Snell, *Annals*, pp. 75–77.

[32] Michael Dalton, *The Country Justice. Containing the Practice, Duty and Power of the Justices of the Peace, as well as in as out of their Sessions*, Henry Lintot, London, 1742, p. 139; Samuel Clapham, *A Collection of Several Points of Sessions Law, Alphabetically Arranged*, 2 vols., Butterworth and Clarke, London, 1818, vol. 2, pp. 83–6; Anon., *A Familiar Summary of the Laws respecting Masters, Servants, Apprentices, Artificers and Labourers*, Henry Washbourne, London, 1831, p. 4.

concerned.[33] But did any of this legislation apply to *domestic* servants? Did the original legislation intend husbandry servants only, or did 'servants' mean household ones as well? In 1793, Richard Burn could only advise his fellow magistrates that the question was entirely unresolved.[34] But as Chapter 6 will show, county justices *did* act as if they had jurisdiction over many aspects of the domestic service relationship. Many lawyers thought that even though the original legislation related only to artificers and servants in husbandry, nevertheless 'it may well be construed to give justices a general jurisdiction over servants of every description, and such jurisdiction is in fact exercised by them'.[35] They thought that this is what had actually happened, throughout the long eighteenth century.[36] Part of the legal irresolution was to do with the work female servants did. The work itself – the servant's labour – effectively rendered useless the legal distinction between husbandry work and domestic work – *when performed by a woman*. Debating the maidservant tax in 1785, MPs recognised how many women servants were kept 'for the double purpose of doing the work of . . . house and . . . farm'.[37] In 1824 Richard Stileman JP of Winchelsea in Sussex, recorded in his notebook 'the complaint of Mercy Lacy of the Parish of Beckley . . . hired by Mrs Stonham . . . to serve her as an *Indoor Servant and Dairymaid* . . . and tht . . . John Stonham & his Wife neglect & refuse to pay her . . . her Wages . . . '.[38] The Court of King's Bench discussed an employment arrangement like this in

---

[33] Anon., *Laws Relating*, p. 40. The key legislation here was 5 Eliz. c. 4, 'An Act containing Divers Orders for Artificers, Labourers, Servants of Husbandry and Apprentices' (1562); and 20 Geo. 2 c. 19, 'An Act for the Better Adjusting and more easy Recovery of Wages of certain Servants and for better Regulation of such Servants' (1747). See also Clapham, *Sessions Law*, p. 5.

[34] Richard Burn, *The Justice of the Peace and Parish Officer. Continued to the Present Time by John Burn, Esq. his Son*, 17th edn, 4 vols., A. Strahan and W. Woodfall, London, 1793, vol. 4, p. 147. See also Gentleman of the Inner Temple, *Laws Concerning Masters and Servants*, His Majesty's Law Printer, London, 1785, p. 40.

[35] James Barry Bird, *The Laws Respecting Masters and Servants, Articled Clerks, Apprentices, Manufacturers, Labourers and Journeymen*, W. Clarke, London, 1799, p. 3.

[36] Thomas Walter Williams, *The Whole Law Relative to the Duty and Office of a Justice of the Peace*, 4 vols., John Stockdale, London, 1812, vol. 3, pp. 887–93. Also Richard Burn, *A New Law Dictionary. Intended for General use, as well as for Gentlemen of the Profession, Continued to the Present Time by his Son, John Burn*, 2 vols., Strahan and Woodfall, London, 1792, vol. 2, pp. 325–8; Ruggles, *History*, vol. 2, p. 255. Two published servants certainly thought this the case: Samuel and Sarah Adams, *The Complete Servant; Being a Practical Guide to the Peculiar Duties and Business of all Descriptions of Servants from the Housekeeper to the Servant of All-Work, and from the Land Steward to the Footboy; with Useful Receipts and Tables*, Knight and Lacy, London, 1825. See their 'Laws', in the Appendix, pp. 9–14.

[37] *Parliamentary History*, 25 (1785–6), 559–60 (9 May 1785).

[38] East Sussex County Record Office (ESCRO), AMA 6192/1, Notebook of Richard Stileman of Winchelsea, JP, 1819–27, pp. 115–116 (3 Jun. 1824).

1795 in relationship to a disputed settlement case. (No matter that Mansfield is dead, replaced by Lord Kenyon; Elizabeth Lamb embodied – and experienced – the arbitrary, inconsistent workings of settlement law as labour law, just as much as did Tabitha Reynolds.) At Michaelmas 1793, Lamb had been hired by Joseph Scrivener of Potterspury, Northamptonshire, 'to work in the Dairy, but not to milk the cows'. She worked until May 1794, 'when becoming insane her Master took her before . . . one of His Majesty's Justices of the Peace'. The magistrate declared her unfit for service, discharged her from the hiring, and she was removed to the village where she had gained a prior settlement. The removal was disputed, and her case went to quarter sessions, where it was decided that she was indeed a servant in husbandry who could be discharged by a magistrate. The order of removal was confirmed. The appeal case hung on the question of whether or not the order of a justice removing someone like Elizabeth Lamb had to state, *in writing*, that she was a servant in husbandry, as the Northamptonshire justice had failed to do. In King's Bench, Eliz. c. 4 s. 6 was pondered yet again: the wording of the Act was general, it was declared; it specified 'no person, who shall retain *any* servants'. The judges had doubts about what kind of servant Elizabeth Lamb was. In the manuscript notes of the hearing the phrase 'but not to milk the cows' is underlined, as if that might be the dividing line between domestic and farm work.[39] Their decision was that the order of removal was void 'because it did not appear on the order itself to be a case within the jurisdiction of a magistrate . . . [so] the order of Sessions must be quashed', thus leaving the distinction between farm and domestic work for women as unclear as it had been for the past century.[40] Elizabeth Lamb's case is the one Doug Hay cites as effectively taking from domestic servants the summary wage remedies available to them.[41] This is an odd way of putting things, for domestic servants had

[39] Lincoln's Inn Library (LIL), Dampier Manuscripts, L.P.B, 104, 'The King agst. the Inhabitants of Hulcott, argued on Wednesday 10 June 1795'; Charles Durnford and Edward Hyde East, *Term Reports in the Court of the King's Bench*, vol. 7 (1794–6), Butterworth and Cooke, London and Dublin, 1817, pp. 583–7. This was the kind of case that Samuel Glasse used to urge his magistrate readers to secretarial caution; A County Magistrate, *The Magistrate's Assistant; or, a Summary of those Laws which immediately respect the Conduct of a Justice of the Peace*, R. Raikes, Gloucester and London, 1788, pp. xii-xiii. See Chapter 6, Note 12.

[40] See Michael Roberts, 'Wages and Wage-earners in England: The evidence of wage assessments, 1563–1725', DPhil, University of Oxford 1982, pp. 168–76 for the heterogeneous work performed by women servants in households in the later seventeenth century.

[41] Douglas Hay, 'England, 1562–1875: The law and its uses' in Paul Craven and Douglas Hay (eds.), *Masters, Servants and Magistrates in Britain and the Empire, 1562–1955*, University of North Carolina Press, Chapel Hill, NC, 2004, p. 89 and Note 110.

simultaneously never had those remedies *in law*, and hundreds of magistrates had behaved as if they did have them. Whether Lamb was a domestic servant, a farm servant or just 'a servant', was not what determined the outcome of her case. A careless magistrate had forgotten to use the correct form of words on his removal order; that was why the judges were able to void it.[42] Wages had not been a question (though they probably were for Elizabeth Lamb, insane or not).

In February 1777 Lord Mansfield and his fellow judges had heard the case of Rex v. the Inhabitants of Brampton, Derbyshire. It involved Hannah Wright, who had gone to service in the village of Eyam, and worked under agreement there until just three weeks short of the year, when 'her master discovering her to be with child, turned her away, and paid her year's wages, and half a crown over; whereupon she went home to her father's'.[43] She was swiftly carted off from there, not to Eyam, but to another parish where she had gained her own settlement. What came to King's Bench was a dispute between two parishes over responsibility for her and the baby she was expecting. Hannah Wright's thoughts on the matter were that she 'was willing to have staid her year out, if she might; but . . . it was not material to her whether she staid or went, as she had received her whole year's wages; and that she was not half gone with her child when she left her service; and hoped that she could have done the work of her place to the end of the year'. At Derbyshire Quarter Sessions, when the parishes of Ashover and Brampton slugged it out, questions had been to do with whether or not the agreement between her and her master had been dissolved before the end of the contract year, and whether or not he had acted 'either arbitrarily or fraudulently' in dismissing her. An employer surely had a right to dismiss his servant if he had 'just and reasonable cause'? There could be no doubt 'but that a criminal conduct like [hers] amounts to a reasonable cause'. Yes, there was earlier case law to say that 'a maid-servant, got with child' couldn't be dismissed, but that surely meant, could not be removed *by the parish*

---

[42] Hay quotes the editor of a posthumous edition of Blackstone's *Commentaries* on the question of the removal of wage remedies from domestic servants in this case. William Blackstone, *Commentaries on the Laws of England*, 12th edn, Edward Christian (ed.), 4 vols., T. Cadell, London, 1793–95 (1796), vol. 1, p. 425. But Christian did not mention the Lamb case here, remarking only, as so many lawyers had, that 'it is not clear whether justices of the peace have any jurisdiction over servants'. See also Richard Burn, *The Justice of the Peace and Parish Officer*, 19th edn, 4 vols., T. Cadell, W. Davies, J. Butterworth, 1800, vol. 3, pp. 369–70.

[43] Derbyshire County Record Office (DCRO), Quarter Sessions Records, Q/SO 1/9, Translation Sessions, 1776, 'Ashover v. Walton' [Brampton]; TNA, KB 16/18/1, Records of Orders Files, 17 Geo. III, 1776–1777. The Order – 'the Writt' – demanding the production of local documents is dated 23 Feb. 1777.

officers before the contract was dissolved? In this case, Hannah Wright's misconduct was a very good reason for her master to dissolve contract. There were those who said that a magistrate should have been applied to; 'but in the first place, this [was] not the case of a servant in husbandry, and therefore a justice of the peace had no jurisdiction . . . or if he had, it was in this case unnecessary, as the servant consented [to her own dismissal]', for had she not said that she really wasn't *very* pregnant and could easily have worked out her time? The question of wages was important: did her master give her her full wages (and that extra half-a-crown) because he assumed that the contract was to last until the end of the year? No, because it has been 'again and again . . . determined that a deduction of wages does not prove a contract *dissolved* within the year'. Yet 'all the authorities say, that when dismission of a servant is accompanied . . . with the payment of the whole wages, it shall be considered as a . . . constructive continuance of it to the end of the year'. If you argued it this way, you denied her consent to the dissolution of the contract, and saw the extra 2s 6d as a substitute for her board and lodging. And if you followed that train of thought, then 'the only object of the master was to defeat . . . [her] settlement . . . in his parish'.[44]

In King's Bench, Lord Mansfield moved with lightning speed into the role identified by his first biographer, that of '*custos morum* of the people'.[45] He thought that Wright's saying she could have worked out her time, was not to the point: 'it is not her ability but her criminal conduct that must be the test; or otherwise a master might be obliged to keep a woman in the house for many months, though he were a clergyman, or had a wife and daughters'.[46] His colleagues pointed out that by getting pregnant, Hannah Wright had committed no crime: that 'an unmarried woman by being with child is not guilty of any crime, or even misdemeanour at common law'. The Chief Justice then moved to the question of hiring, and referred to 8 & 9 Will. 3 c. 30 (1697) to say that 'there must be a hiring for a year, and a continuance for a year in that service, to gain a settlement'.[47] Service, by its very nature, 'admits often of questions upon the circumstances' he said; 'but these questions have always been brought to this point. Whether the contract was put an end to within the year.' A servant could not of course, be dismissed without good cause; the solution here, to the problem of Hannah Wright, rested

---

[44] Caldecott, *Reports*, pp. 11–14.
[45] John Holliday, *The Life of William Late Earl of Mansfield*, P. Elmsly and D. Bremner, London, 1797, p. 214.
[46] Caldecott, *Reports*, pp. 11–14.
[47] 'An Act for Supplying some Defects in the Laws for the Relief of the Poor'. Mansfield's comments here are taken from Bott, *Digest*, 1793, pp. 516–18.

on asking a different question: 'Has the master done right or wrong in discharging his servant for this cause?' Mansfield thought not. 'I think he did not do wrong', he said. Certainly, if an employer agreed under these circumstances to the continuance of contract (agreed to keep on a pregnant servant) 'the overseers it is true, shall not take her away, because she is with child'.[48] But did this then mean, pursued Mansfield, that 'the master therefore be bound to keep her in his house'? To do this 'would be contra *bonos mores*; and in a family where there are young persons, both scandalous and dangerous'. His fellow judges agreed that 'if the master had daughters, it would not be fit that he should keep such a servant'.[49] The removal orders were affirmed.

It was now February 1777, and matters had proceeded apace in Derbyshire. Hannah's daughter Mary had been born, and baptised in July 1776 at Ashover, her grandfather's parish.[50] Wright's case was cited as late as 1812 for the benefit of justices of the peace to show that 'a master may of his own authority, and without the intervention of a magistrate, dismiss [a] servant for moral turpitude; even though it be not such for which the servant may be prosecuted at common law'.[51] Hannah Wright's insouciant and marvellous resistance of Lord Mansfield's disapproval (though she probably never heard of it, and had shown her amazing confidence in her own capacities before he uttered it) was spoken between the lines of a judgment that convinced servants and their employers for the next fifty years that pregnancy in a maidservant was grounds for lawful dismissal. Commenting on the likelihood of dismissal for a pregnant servant before the Mansfield judgment and after it (and on the contingent, but clearly likely 'new born child murder' in which he is interested), Mark Jackson points out that servants were 'in theory protected by law from summary dismissal'.[52] But such protection

---

[48] Keith Snell, 'Pauper settlements and the right to relief in England and Wales', *Continuity and Change*, 6 (1991), 384; Norma Landau, 'Going local: The social history of Stuart and Hanoverian England', *Journal of British Studies*, 24 (1985), 279; 'Laws of Settlement and the surveillance of immigration in eighteenth-century Kent', *Continuity and Change*, 3 (1988), 391–420; 'The eighteenth-century context of the Laws of Settlement', *Continuity and Change*, 6 (1991), 417–39.

[49] Williams, *Whole Law*, vol. 3, pp. 902–3.

[50] DCRO, M77 vol. 2, Parish Records, Ashover Parish Register, 'Christenings at Ashover 1776 July . . . Mary Base Dr of Hannah Wright'. Three years later her second 'Base Dr' was baptised, baby Sarah's father being named; Mary's had not. M77 vol. 2, Ashover Parish Register (4 Jul. 1779); Quarter Sessions Records, Q/SO 1/9, Order Books, 1774–80, Easter Sessions 1779.

[51] Williams, *Whole Law*, vol. 3, pp. 902–3.

[52] Mark Jackson, *New-Born Child Murder: Women, illegitimacy and the courts and eighteenth-century England*, Manchester University Press, Manchester and New York, 1996, pp. 48–9.

afforded under 5 Eliz. c. 4 extended only to servants in husbandry, and as a legal fiction cuts both ways (it is a fiction, after all) many a pregnant woman who worked outdoors and in, found herself called a household servant, who might be dismissed after Mansfield's judgment in the case of Hannah Wright.[53]

The judges behaved quite differently a year later when, in the case of Ursula Owens of St Bartholomew's by the Exchange, London, they confirmed the settlement of a servant seven days short of her year's service (but then, Owens was not pregnant). Her employer had gone to Manchester to buy a factory, telling his servants on his return that he would soon be moving there, 'but he did not mention any time & that they might look out for other services if they chuse and might stay with him till he went to Manchester'. Then one evening in June 1777 he abruptly paid Owens the whole of her wages and half a guinea over, and left for the North. She found a new job in another parish, but things did not work out, and a year later found herself removed back to St Bartholomew's. Mansfield's fellow judges spoke of Owens's loss of settlement, 'her only one, which she deserves so well'; they said that 'Justice as well as reason of the thing are here with the Settlement'. The notes on the back of the case say: 'Service wanted 7 days of a Year but whole years wages pd gains a Settlement.'[54] But not for Hannah Wright.

The case of Hannah Phillips demonstrated that even when a year's service was not mentioned at the hiring, even when the concept of hiring was imperfectly understood by the parties involved, then the law would assume that it was a 'general hiring' for a year: a true hiring, that brought with it settlement rights. Phillips's chequered service career in Bridgenorth, Shropshire, lasted for seven years, until sometime in 1792 she was removed to Worfield where her father was legally settled. The Bridgenorth overseers attempted to make her claim relief on this derivative settlement in her natal village. For Shropshire Quarter Sessions – the case was forwarded to King's Bench from the 1793 April Sessions – it raised the question of whether payment of wages at all, never mind for a year, was necessary for settlement.[55] In 1789 (or thereabouts; she was uncertain about dates) Phillips had gone to live with the Smith

---

[53] You did not *have* to dismiss a pregnant servant. See Carolyn Steedman, *Master and Servant: Love and labour in the English industrial age*, Cambridge University Press, Cambridge, 2007.

[54] LIL, Dampier Manuscripts, A.P.B, 19, Easter Term, 1778; Caldecott, *Reports of Cases*, pp. 48–51.

[55] Shropshire Archives (SA), *Orders of Shropshire Quarter Sessions*, vol. III, Sir Ofsey Wakeman and R. Lloyd Kenyon (eds.), 'April Sessions, 1793, Worfield v. St Leonard Bridgenorth. Adjourned; the opinion of the Court of the King's Bench to be taken'.

family in St Leonards, Bridgenorth 'and served . . . near a year, but was not hired . . . as she knows of'. Some time later she was approached by a Mr John Jones who asked her if she had hired herself again to Mr Smith for the coming year. When she said no, Jones invited her to come and live with his family 'and take care of his child, to which she consented', arriving at Christmas-time 1790. A few days into her new place, Mr Jones asked her if it would be all right to pay her in kind – to 'find her meat, drink and clothes' – and she agreed. In her statement to quarter sessions she said that Jones had been willing to pay her in cash, but 'it was better for her to have clothes, as she was connected with bad friends, who would take her money'.[56] She stayed for two and a half years under these terms, leaving in May 1792, when her mistress told her that 'the child was old enough not to require any further attendance, and dismissed her'. Quarter sessions concentrated on the hiring contract: had she ever actually been hired for a year? A very long argument, and much quoting of precedent on behalf of the two parishes in dispute, was cut through in Westminster Hall by Chief Justice Kenyon (Mansfield had retired his post in 1788; this makes Hannah Phillips no less one of Mansfield's Women; she is a legal category, embodying the strategies and principles so far outlined). Kenyon said that 'it has been so long settled, that a general hiring is for a year, that it ought not to be controverted. In my opinion in this case there was a hiring for a year . . . '. His fellow judges agreed: 'clothed by the master the day after she went into the service, could it have been the intention of the parties that she might have left the service immediately [?] . . . both parties meant that the service should be permanent'. The order was quashed, and Hannah Phillips gained her Bridgenorth settlement, the judges confirming that neither wages nor service for a full 365 days were always needed for a woman to gain her own settlement.[57]

Charlotte Howe, the last of Lord Mansfield's Women, had been brought to England in 1781 when very young, by naval Captain Tyringham Howe, who then settled in Thames Ditton with his wife.[58] She had been purchased in America as 'a negro slave', perhaps out of the maelstrom of war, in which slaves, the goods and moveable property of the

[56] Durnford and Hyde East, *Term Reports*, vol. 5, pp. 224–6.

[57] For the reception of this judgment, SA, QS/3/1, Quarter Sessions Records, 1708–1800, Sessions Minutes, Jul. 1793. For its continued importance, County Magistrate, *A Letter addressed to the Agriculturalists in general, and to the Magistrates and Clergy in particular throughout the Kingdom, on the Subjects of Hiring, Service and Character*, Longman and Whittaker, London, 1821, p. 7.

[58] Sylvester Douglas, *Report of Cases Argued and Determined in the Court of the King's Bench, Volume 4 (1784–1785)*, Sweet and Stevens, London, Milliken, Dublin, 1831, pp. 301–2.

rebels, were stolen back and forth by both sides, and the British could not make up their mind about a half-hearted, and never official, policy or strategy of subverting the rebels by recruiting their slaves as soldiers, or simply as runaways.[59] Howe's ship *The Thames* was at anchor off Sewell's Point, Virginia in January 1781 when 'Came on board Several Negroes who had made their escape from the rebels', and she may have been among them; but it is more likely that the young woman (or child, perhaps) was acquired in one of the slave markets of the North, where Captain Howe was on sick leave from his ship from February to June 1781.[60] Having been transported across the Atlantic, she continued in the Howes' service in Surrey until the death of Howe in June 1783.[61] It brought about a change in the household's perception of its circumstances – as the death of a master often did – for Charlotte (or perhaps her mistress arranged it) got herself baptised in December of that year, the Thames Ditton churchwarden recording in the parish register that she was 'Charlotte, an african servant to Mrs How'.[62] Sometime in the new year, Mrs Howe moved to Chelsea, London, taking her black servant with her. In June, Charlotte Howe walked out (we cannot tell whether this was done with encouragement), thus perhaps making herself free, which Douglas Lorimer has suggested was the major route to the end of slavery in Britain, brought about by the actions of slave-servants themselves rather than by the more conventionally evoked abolition inaugurated by legislation.[63]

This young woman may have freed herself (and certainly, no one went after her), but she was without means of subsistence; in the late summer of 1784 she applied to St Luke's (Chelsea) parish officials for relief

[59] Sylvia R. Frey, *Water from the Rock: Black resistance in a revolutionary age*, Princeton University Press, Princeton, NJ, 1991, pp. 64, 95, 134; James A. Rawley, *The Transatlantic Slave Trade: A history*, Norton, New York, 1981, pp. 385–418.

[60] TNA, ADM 51/982, Captains' Logs, Part 10, pp. 20, 22, 38, 42. Howe departed for New York on 7 Feb. on board HMS *Charles Town*. Parties of slaves had got on board *The Thames* before. National Maritime Museum (NMM), ADM. L/T84, Lieutenants' Logs, HMS *Thames*, 10 Sep. 1780–20 Nov. 1780, Montagu Blackwell, 1st Lieutenant (22 Nov. 1780).

[61] It is not possible to trace Charlotte Howe's passage across the Atlantic. The Admiralty records allow pursuit of Howe's ship and the supply ships he escorted, to the giddy limit of recording, but a young black female is not mentioned anywhere. This young woman was a personal possession of Captain Howe, not to be mustered, listed, or accounted for. She was not mentioned as either property or person in Tyringham Howe's will, TNA, PROB 11/1106.

[62] Surrey History Centre (SHC), 2568, Thames Ditton Parish Records, Baptisms (17 Dec. 1783). See Taylor, *Poverty*, pp. 67–8 for the case of the black servant Ann Clossen.

[63] Lorimer, 'Black slaves', pp. 121–50. But see Norma Myers,'Servant, sailor, soldier, beggarman: Black survival in white society, 1780–1830', *Immigrants and Minorities*, 12 (1993), 47–74.

(she does not appear to have been examined by the magistrates as to the state of her settlement) But then, without any official recording of events, she turned up in Thames Ditton, from whence in October, she was removed back to St Luke's (this was on the order of two magistrates) and was placed in the parish workhouse.[64] The Chelsea parish won its appeal against Surrey, and in January 1785, Charlotte Howe was carted back to Thames Ditton. At the end of the month, the vestrymen determined to seek the opinion of King's Bench, a decision that was to cost them over £50, and which brought no one much satisfaction, for what churchwarden and magistrates learned from Lord Mansfield and his fellow judges was that their attempts to deal with Charlotte Howe in terms of her settlement, or lack of it, had been completely erroneous. It was argued most eloquently at quarter sessions and again in King's Bench that she had 'lived as a servant from year to year, and therefore is to be considered a servant as far as the laws of England will permit', and that 'it would be hard if a person of this description should not be maintained and taken notice of by the law'.[65] She had *acted* as a servant said the attorneys; she had shown a clear understanding of the nature of her obligation, for 'she never thought of quitting the service of the family till her master's death: [and] that to deprive her of her settlement, the court must hold that she might have gone away at any time'.[66] But Mansfield cut briskly through the narration of her circumstances with the observation that 'it cannot be contended that this was a voluntary hiring, and [is] therefore not a service'.[67] Whether she had been paid wages or not was irrelevant, for wages were not necessary to make a settlement (as the case of Hannah Phillips was to emphasise a few years later); indeed, there was no entitlement to wages anyway, whether cash was handed over or not, 'because there never was a contract for wages'. All of this was irrelevant, he said; and so were clever arguments by the lawyers from Chelsea and Surrey that the English legal system recognised the condition of slavery, or at least serfdom, and should thus recognise Charlotte Howe.[68] None of this would do, for although the poor law was a 'subsisting positive law, enforced by statutes which began to be made about the time of Queen Elizabeth, when villeinage was not abolished, and villeins...[might]...in point

---

[64] TNA, KB 16/19/5, Records of Orders Files, 25 Geo. III, 1784–5.
[65] Douglas, *Reports*, p. 301.   [66] Caldecott, *Report of Cases*, pp. 515–20.
[67] Douglas, *Reports*, p. 301.
[68] Granville Sharp, *A Representation of the Injustice and Dangerous Tendency of Tolerating Slavery; or of Admitting the Least Claim of Private Property in the Persons of Men, in England. In four parts*, Benjamin White and Robert, London, 1769, pp. 108–11, suggested these arguments were well known among lawyers.

of law . . . subsist to this day', nevertheless 'the statutes do not relate to them, nor had they them in contemplation'. The point was rather that for Charlotte Howe to 'bring herself under a positive law, she must answer the description it requires'. Further, 'her colour or [her] being a slave, or [her] having become such will not affect the question'. Her case was indeed, 'very plain': 'the statute says there must be a hiring, and here there was no hiring at all. She does not come within the description'; or, as another transcription has it, 'There is nothing in it.' As the notes on the back of the King's Bench papers tersely summarise: 'Easter term 25th Geo: 3d a black who was purchased abroad and continues to live with Mar [Master] or his Exectr for years in England without any Hiring does not gain a *Settlement*'.[69] The case of Charlotte Howe became no case at all: neither Thames Ditton nor Chelsea was responsible for her; she disappears from the records leaving behind fragments of a story made for her by the legal system. The Thames Ditton authorities paid St Luke's for its three months keep of her, settling the bill in January 1785, though the 1s 5d expended was vastly less than monies paid to the local attorney, briefed to attend Surrey Quarter Sessions, and the immense sum that preparation for the King's Bench appeal was later to cost.[70]

Charlotte Howe's former mistress made her will in December 1785, some months after her slave-servant's case was settled in King's Bench – or probably, not *her* slave; Charlotte had belonged to her late husband, not to her. Charlotte had been a kind of servant to her, for whom there was no name, and no legal existence. Looking to the hour of her death, attempting to ensure that she should not spend it alone, Mrs Howe bequeathed to her maidservant Elizabeth Chaddon several luxury goods, the furniture in her bedroom, and the sum of thirty pounds, all on the familiar condition that Chaddon should be living with her when she died,

[69] LIL, Dampier Manuscripts, B. P.B., 377, 'Surrey. The King agt the Inhabitants of Thames Ditton'.

[70] SHC, Thames Ditton Parish Records, 2568/8/4, Overseers Accounts, 1773–1805 (10 Dec. 1784, 2 Apr. 1785 and undated entries 1786); 2568/7/4, Poor Rate Assessment and Vestry Minutes, 1778–96 (31 Jan. 1785); Surrey Quarter Sessions Order Books, QS2/6/. LMA, St Luke's Chelsea, P74/LUK/111, Workhouse and Discharge Register, Jan. 1782–Dec. 1800 (25 Oct. 1784, 20 Jan. 1785). Charlotte Howe's name is the only one listed with '20' beside it, signalling not that she was younger than the age of majority ('21' recorded a legal adult, not an actual age) but that she had the status of a child, or some other minor, and was certainly not a full legal subject. But she was probably in her teens when she arrived in England in 1781. Candidus, *A Letter to Philo Africanus upon Slavery, in Answer to his of the 22nd November in the General Evening Post; together with the Opinions of Sir John Strange, and other Lawyers upon the Subject, with the Sentence of Lord Mansfield in the Case of Somerset and Knowles* . . . , W. Brown, London, 1788, pp. 38–9 called her 'a negroe girl' and 'this girl'.

and stay in the house in Sloan Street for three months afterwards. There was twenty pounds a year for 'the poor of the Parish of Thames Ditton' to be laid out in 'Good Household Bread'. There was nothing in it for Charlotte Howe.[71]

The Times reported on this 'curious case', engaging its readers' attention through the strangeness of conjunction between 'slave' and 'parish': can 'a negro slave obtain settlement in a parish?'[72] Its account of the arguments heard in Westminster Yard (which were to be repeated in the Law Reports for the next fifty years) is important for being the most immediate, and the more revelatory of the understandings at work in court that Tuesday morning than, for example, the tired repetition of them in the 1831 edition of Douglas's *Reports*. (Anyway, three years on from then, settlement-by-service case law, the very purpose for telling again and again, the narrative of Charlotte Howe, would be rendered quite redundant by the Poor Law Amendment Act.) It had been said in court that 'she had gained a settlement under the rule of law that, all general hiring is hiring for a year'. It had been claimed that although 'having been a slave in America, [she] became on her arrival here to a certain degree free'. She was called 'the pauper' in court (as if for all the world she really was what that meant: a poor person claiming her rightful relief, and actually getting what Tabitha Reynolds and Hannah Wright got, which was a lot of time on the road in parish carts). The 'great hardship and inconvenience' of the case had been urged upon the judges, the reporter said; and so had the unfairness of things 'if, after many years of service, a negro could not obtain that asylum and relief afforded to others'. 'Asylum', 'relief', 'entitlement', were at work in the court's language-in-common.[73] Lord Mansfield had made his point, so often noted, about statute law, and having to bring yourself within its terms if seeking its application. But then, using a vocabulary nowhere else recorded, *The Times* writer said that 'the poor law [is] a system of positive law established by several acts of Parliament... whoever comes to *claim benefit* under them must exactly answer the description given in them, that of being hired and serving for a year... in this case there was no hiring at all'. [italics added]. Later on, other reporters noted this

---

71 TNA, PROB B11/1142; SHC, 2568/8/4, Thames Ditton Parish Records, Overseers' Accounts, 1773–1805 (18 Sep. 1786, 12 Jul. 1790); 2568/7/4, Poor Rate Assessment Book, containing Vestry Minutes, 1778–96, (25 Feb. 1790). Five years later churchwardens had not received these monies from Elizabeth Howe's executors.

72 'Law Report', *The Times*, 29 Apr. 1785, p. 2.

73 For entitlement, W. M. Spellman, *John Locke*, Macmillan, Basingstoke, 1997, p. 115; Horne, *Property Rights*, pp. 130–1, 141, 201–3; Lees, *Solidarities*, pp. 7–22, 29–33, 177; Taylor, *Poverty*, pp. 18–19, 42.

language of entitlement and benefit. In 1800 Thomas Caldecott quoted one of the barristers (presumably for St Luke's) saying that 'where a party is in a condition to perform and bound also to perform in the parish where his master lives, he seems to be directly an object of these acts; and if he performs such service, justly entitled to the benefits they hold out'. Furthermore, the words 'deprive her of her settlement' were also used that day, according to Caldecott.[74]

'Benefits', 'right', 'justly intitled', '*her* settlement'.... These reported words were probably not Mansfield's (perhaps we can only be clear that they were the words of a court reporter in 1785, and Thomas Caldecott fifteen years on). The interest of the case for the Lord Chief Justice (or rather, the interest attributed to him by generations of commentators) was the clarification it allowed him of the judgment he had made in the famous Somerset slavery case of 1772.[75] That judgment, that a master had no right to remove a slave from England against his or her will, had allowed Mansfield to expiate on the 'odious' condition of slavery, so disgusting that it could not be inferred from, or be taken to be supported by either natural law or common law principle. Indeed, it was so horrible a condition that it could only be upheld by statute (positive) law. Abolitionists of the time and Mansfield's historians judged him kindly over his judgment in this case, pointing to the courage with which he implicitly found against the West Indian and commercial pro-slavery lobbies. But on 29 April 1785, faced with Charlotte Howe, Mansfield made his famous Somerset judgment seem a very small thing indeed. It is his qualification that will echo through the law reports, down to the 1830s: all he had done fourteen years before, he said, in the case of James Somerset the slave, was to 'go no further than to establish, that the master had no power to take the slave by force out of the Kingdom'.

Just as manumission was a difficult thing in a society without slave law, so is any legal procedure that needs knowledge of legal bodies standing there, in a court of law. Charlotte Howe's problem in King's Bench (as it had been in all the lesser tribunals considering her) was that there was no legal category for her condition of existence. Perhaps *The Times* reporter understood the perfect *uselessness* of the terms of the debate since 1772. Did slavery exist in England? Could it? Was William Blackstone correct, that a slave was free the moment he or she breathed Albion's

---

[74] Caldecott, *Reports*, vol. 3, pp. 517–20.

[75] Lorimer, 'Black slaves', pp. 121–50; Drescher, 'Manumission', pp. 92–3; Oldham, *Mansfield Manuscripts*, vol. 2, pp. 1221–38; James Oldham, 'New light on Mansfield and slavery', *Journal of British Studies*, 27 (1988), 45–68; James Walvin, *The Trader, The Owner, The Slave*, Vintage, London, 2008, pp. 226–7.

air?[76] He (the anonymous reporter) devised his own contradictory and socially accurate category to describe Charlotte Howe: she 'became on her arrival here to a certain degree free'. Felicitous and accurate; and as perfectly useless to Howe as everything else that was said in King's Bench that day.

Six weeks later, Mansfield made (yet another) codicil to his will: 'Besides the annuity I give Dido the sum of Two hundred pounds to set out with'. The timing is probably quite coincidental: he was always upping the Kenwood girls' inheritance, and had started having serious financial conversations with his nephew and heir, the girls' father, 7th Viscount Stormont.[77] And yet some (I certainly) will want to see a connection made, in some recess of Mansfield's consciousness, between two young black women, from vastly different social circumstances, in that frisson of anxiety, that uncertainty of future, in the words 'to set out with'.

According to the 'Gentleman of the Inner Temple', who published his *Law Concerning Master and Servants* later that year, the problem with young people like Charlotte Howe was that having been brought to England as cheap servants, 'they put themselves on a Footing with other servants, [became] intoxicated with Liberty . . . and either by Persuasion of others, or from their own Inclinations, begin to expect Wages according to their own Opinion of their Merits'. They would deliberately get themselves dismissed (never mind the legal impossibility of that); then they would 'enter into Societies, and make their Business to corrupt and dissatisfy every fresh black Servant that comes to England'. They would persuade new arrivals to get themselves baptized, or married, 'which they inform them makes them free', insolently ignoring what 'England's most able lawyers' told them: that such an act altered a master's property in them not one jot. They did it because it got 'the Mob on their side'.[78] There is only fragmentary evidence of these support groups existing among the eighteenth-century black poor; but it is pleasant to think

---

[76] For the origin of the much quoted formulation, see William Blackstone, *Commentaries on the Laws of England. In Four Books* [1765], 6th edn, (Dublin, 1775), vol. 1, pp. 424–5.

[77] SP, NRA(S) 0776, Murray Family Papers, Earls of Mansfield, Second Series, Bundle 2346, 'Incl. attested copies . . . of will and codicils of William, Earl of Mansfield'; Second Series, Bundle 54, Accounts and Vouchers 1774–8 [in error for 1798], 'Important Notes respecting the state of Lord Mansfield's affairs . . . '; 'Notes respecting the state of Lord Mansfield's affairs . . . '. Elizabeth Lindsay was well set up. Her father also left money for another illegitimate child about whom nothing is known. TNA PROB 11/1167: 'I further give and bequeath unto my dearest Wife Mary Lindsay One Thousand pounds in Trust to be disposed by her for the benefit of John and Elizabeth Lindsay my reputed Son and Daughter in such Manner as she thinks proper' (29 Sep. 1783).

[78] Gentleman, *Law*, pp. 28–30.

of Charlotte Howe, who was without a settlement, who had nothing to set out with, in connection with something like this.[79]

The interest of Charlotte Howe for the lawyers was not to be what her story said about slavery, within England, or without. For Michael Nolan, writing his careful scrutiny of the poor laws twenty years later, her case showed the elevation of statute and contract law above common law and customary practice. He told his readers there was 'a presumption which might have arisen from [Charlotte Howe's] service', from her relationship with Captain and Mrs Howe and from its 'reciprocal acts of service and maintenance', that is the presumption that she had obtained settlement through the relationship and the actions and deeds (living the life) it involved. But in this case 'the situation of the woman, previous to her arrival in England, negatived the presumption'. She had been 'in the condition of a slave in America'; she had worked without reference to a contract; there *was* no – *could not be* a – contract for service in a case like hers.[80] No hiring, no settlement.

They had argued in King's Bench that the law should take note of Charlotte Howe, and it did, despite the manifold impossibilities of so doing as outlined by Lord Mansfield. This is the paradox that all his Women demonstrate: the law admitted them – to consideration and to discourse – even though it said it didn't. And because it did admit them, the state came face to face with the poor law as labour law, saw how it worked and what kind of thing it was, through its effect on women in far provincial places, those effects described in written words, and heard in London through the appeal system. These marvellous girls – Lord Mansfield's Women – spoke out: 'not half gone with child – could have done her work . . . to the end of the year – better to have clothes . . . connected with bad friends – the Pauper says otherways & will acquaint the Court' – knowing what and who they were, as women, workers and as legal persons. But not Charlotte Howe – of course. It is not possible to retrieve her spoken voice from the court transcripts. Through the fifty years that her story is repeated, it is always written in a way that makes it impossible to recover the first person singular.

[79] Walvin, *The Trader*, pp. 243–55.
[80] Michael Nolan, *A Treatise of the Laws for the Settlement of the Poor*, 2 vols, J. Butterworth, London, 1805, vol. 1, pp. 191–2.

5 In a free state

All politicians debating the servant taxes agreed with, first, Lord North and, later, William Pitt, that they embodied the first principle of enlightened taxation policy, which was to 'throw the weight as much as possible upon the opulent... to tax property instead of labour' (that is, not to tax labouring people). A tax like the one North proposed in May 1777 (calculated to bring in £105,000 from employers of an estimated 10,000 male servants) was, MPs agreed, a tax on life's 'elegant conveniencies', ever 'true objects of taxation in every well regulated state'.[1] The irony was pointed out, that in the attempt to maintain the dignity of the nation in the face of the North American rebellion, 10,000 men were to be reduced to 'the humiliating level of salt, soap, and candles'.[2] But as they also said, this was clearly to be a tax on luxury, not one that would affect merchant or manufacturer, or that would be 'felt by the community, either in raising the price of raw materials, or falling heavy upon articles of daily and necessary consumption', as would increased excise duties.[3] So too said

---

[1] *The Parliamentary History of England from the earliest period to the year 1803*, vol. 19 (29 Jan. 1777–4 Dec. 1778), R. Bagshaw, London, 1814. pp. 243–4, 251 (14 May 1777).

[2] *Ibid.*, pp. 288–9 (26 May 1777).

[3] *Ibid.*, pp. 243–4 (14 May 1777). For the inflation of both excise and assessed taxes to fund the American and the French Wars, William Kennedy, *English Taxation, 1640–1799: An essay on policy and opinion*, Bell, London, 1913, pp. 61–78; Clive Emsley, *British Society and the French Wars*, Macmillan, Basingstoke, 1979, pp. 38–42, 49, 53, 67, 99–123; John Brewer, *The Sinews of Power: War, money and the English state, 1688–1783*, Unwin Hyman, 1989, pp. 67–8, 100–1, and passim; P. K. O'Brien, 'Public finance and the wars with

William Pitt eight years later, when he proposed additional taxes on serving men – the more kept, the higher the rate – and a new one on females. A maidservant tax would fall upon the rich, just like the one on manservants, he argued; it would be 'more upon unnecessary extravagance than upon industry'. Moreover, the tax would be 'open and perceptible to those who were to pay it' and its produce 'nearly ascertainable'. To be sure, there was the usual trouble with counting female servants: although it would be a universal tax its calculation could not be as accurate as it was for male servants.[4]

This kind of enlightened thinking on taxation was expressed outside government circles as well. Hare-brained schemes for increasing war revenue sent into the Tax Office by private citizens were often accompanied by the assurance that 'if adopted [they] wou'd . . . raise large Sums for the State & not affect the lower Class of people'; a lady might report herself a good deal 'discombobulate[d]' by the watch tax, but would hasten to tell her correspondent that she knew it fell harder 'upon servants and tradesmen, who really wear them for use, not ornament'. Sentiments like these were approbation of those who were useful to the state – those who laboured and traded. Elite protestors against the male-servant tax used similar arguments, clergy and military men presenting themselves as employers who had done the state some service and whose own servants ought to come tax free.[5]

Historians have agreed for the main part with North's and Pitt's judgement on their own tax policies. Patrick O'Brien has calculated that during the twenty-two years of war with France, from 1793 to 1815, 'something like 63% of the extra taxation required [for] combat . . . emanated from

---

France, 1793–1815' in H. T. Dickinson (ed.), *Britain and the French Revolution, 1789–1815*, Macmillan, Basingstoke, 1989, pp. 165–87; J. V. Beckett, 'Land Tax or Excise: The levying of taxation in seventeenth- and eighteenth-century England', *English Historical Review*, 100 (1985), 285–308; J. V. Beckett and Michael Turner, 'Taxation and economic growth in eighteenth-century England', *Economic History Review*, 43:3 (1990), 377–403.

[4] *Parliamentary History*, 25, pp. 551, 552–3 (9 May 1785).

[5] Jane H. Adeane, *The Early Married Life of Maria Josepha Lady Stanley, with extracts from Sir John Stanley's 'Praeterita'. Edited by one of their Grandchildren*, Longman, Green, London, New York, Bombay, 1899, p. 133 (10 Jul. 1797). Between 1777 and 1781 clergymen and army officers together made 27% of elite employer appeals against the tax. See Chapter 2. TNA T 1/577/200, To Lords Commissioners of the Treasury . . . respecting the duties on Chocolate and also . . . the duty on male servants (15 Mar. 1782); T1 609/36–37, taxes, proposal to put a tax akin to rates on houses and a tax on furniture; T1 609/111–112, suggestions regarding taxes; T1 609/395–399, Proposal for increasing the tax on servants; T1 610/404–426, Various proposals upon the new tax on hats; T1 624/397–398, Letter from William Pratt regarding his suggestions on tax and hoping for reward; T1 7000/45–48, Suggestions concerning a tax on bakers.

taxes falling upon the incomes and consumptions of the rich'.[6] But in the last revision of his *History of the Public Revenue of the British Empire*, Sir John Sinclair – 'maverick backbencher', 'agricultural improver', 'codifier of useful knowledge' – pondered the other 37 per cent of revenue that did not come from opulence, luxury, or the elegant conveniency of a liveried footman.[7] In principle he thought it correct that revenue should be derived from modest housekeepers, for 'a total exemption from taxes in favour of the poor, is a system impracticable in a country so loaded . . . ; and in a free state, perhaps would be unjust: for there the poor have rights to which they are entitled as well as the rich; and they ought to pay for the privileges they enjoy'.[8] For twentieth-century economic historians Sinclair's proposition – that the poor had rights and responsibilities that made them fit subjects for taxation – rang false. In 1913 William Kennedy reminded his readers that in the eighteenth-century the poor man 'tended to be conceived as a different kind of being from the taxable citizen of means, and much more like a beast of burden or a mere factor of production . . . to live rather for the benefit of others than for the enjoyment of rights of his own'.[9] Even exempting necessities had not been a tax doctrine favouring labour, argued Kennedy, so much as general social policy benefiting those for whom they laboured. 'And so it remained in essence' throughout the eighteenth century he thought, an 'assertion against the theory of tax-paying citizenship of a not well-defined feeling that the poor man did not properly fit into that conception of society'.[10]

Sinclair conceded that opulence was useful to a well regulated state – was 'not a little favourable to an increase of revenue' – for where 'private economy reigns, no productive impost can be laid, but on property

[6] Patrick K. O'Brien, 'The political economy of British taxation, 1660–1815', *Economic History Review* (2nd Ser.) 41 (1988), 1–32; W. R. Ward, *The English Land Tax in the Eighteenth Century*, Oxford University Press, London, 1953.

[7] John Sinclair, *The History of the Public Revenue of the British Empire*, P. Byrne, Dublin, 1785; third part added in 1789 (W. and A. Strahan, London); reissued as *The History of the Public Revenue of the British Empire. Containing an Account of the Public Income and Expenditure from the remotest Periods recorded in History, to Michaelmas 1802. With a Review of the Financial Administration of the Right Honourable William Pitt*, A. Strahan, London, 1803–4. Sinclair's account of taxation policy and history has earned the approbation of modern economic historians. See Rosalind Mitchison, 'Sinclair, Sir John, first baronet (1754–1835)' in *Oxford Dictionary of National Biography*, Oxford University Press, 2004, www.oxforddnb.com/view/article/25627, accessed 1 Jan. 2007. Boyd Hilton, *A Mad, Bad and Dangerous People? England 1783–1846*, Oxford University Press, Oxford, 2006, pp. 93, 135, 261–2 for his maverick qualities and policy differences between him and Pitt, particularly over the role of government in promoting economic growth by taxation strategy. Also Martin Daunton, *Trusting Leviathan: The politics of taxation in Britain, 1799–1914*, Cambridge University Press, Cambridge, 2001, pp. 32–57.

[8] Sinclair, *History of Public Revenue* (1803–4), vol. 2, pp. 30–6.

[9] Kennedy, *English Taxation*, p. 110.   [10] *Ibid.*, p. 78.

alone . . . but in luxurious ages, a considerable revenue may be raised, without hurting the feelings of the people'. For example, the consumer was usually unaware of the extent to which excise duties raised the purchase price of goods and thus 'furnishe[d], without reluctance, to the treasury, a sum, which by any other means could hardly have been exacted'.[11] He was writing about the period 1760–85, when 'such sums of money were paid into the public treasury, as no former statesman would have believed, that this country could have furnished'.[12] As Boyd Hilton remarks, the British state 'expanded fiscally to a degree that made it quantatively different from anything it had been before'. He points out that 60 per cent of the cost of the French Wars was met from taxation, compared with 20 per cent of the cost of the American War.[13]

The servant taxes – male and female – did not contribute greatly to these war revenues. In the fiscal year 1785–6, just before the female-servant tax was inaugurated, male servants brought in £26,803, compared with the £56,829 obtained from horses and waggons, and the £59,231 that the government garnered from two- and four-wheeled carriages.[14] In this year, taxing male servants accounted for about 7 per cent of assessed-taxes income (these totals do not include what was derived from excise). Five years later, when Pitt proposed the repeal of the maidservant tax, he suggested that the trifling sum it brought it (far less than he had estimated back in 1785) made the game of pursuing it as policy in the face of a barrage of complaints and petitions against it, scarcely worth the candle of keeping it going.[15] So it is not because of their fiscal importance that the servant taxes should be paid attention, but because of their oddness and anomalous nature, and for the policy they inaugurated and revealed, at the legislative stage and in operation. They provide an example of financial expediency become policy, a way of understanding the policing of eighteenth-century society in contemporary terms, and some insight into elite understandings of labour – in both senses: Lord North's meaning of 1777 as 'those who labour; the labouring population', and the abstract Lockean (or Marxist) sense of an abstract quantity of energy or work, exercised upon the material world.

---

[11] Sinclair, *History of Public Revenue* (1803–4), vol. 2, pp. 5–6.

[12] *Ibid.*, pp. 30–36; Hilton, *Mad, Bad and Dangerous*, pp. 113–24.

[13] Hilton, *Mad, Bad and Dangerous*, p. 118.

[14] *Parliamentary History*, vol. 29, pp. 452–87 (10 May 1791), 'Report from the Select Committee on Public Income and Expenditure, since 1786'.

[15] *Ibid.*, p. 828 (17 Feb. 1792); Patrick Karl O'Brien, 'The triumph and denouement of the British fiscal state: Taxation for the wars against Revolutionary and Napoleonic France, 1793–1815', Working Paper No. 99/07, London School of Economics, 2007 (tables calculate income from all taxes, not just the assessed taxes), www.lse.ac.uk/collections/economicHistory/pdf/WP99.pdf.

They have been seen by some as an attempt to exclude domestic workers from the categories of industriousness and productive labour and to code household work as female.[16] William Kennedy thought that eighteenth-century tax policy was a neglected means for discovering 'social attitude or . . . the practical political theories of the period'.[17] A century later, during which time our knowledge of fiscal systems has been vastly expanded, Boyd Hilton believes that the spreading of the fiscal net, especially in the last quarter of the century, can explain why the 'society became more politicized'.[18]

The servant taxes uncover 'practical political theories' at work. The state intruded in domestic arrangements, judged whether the purchase of hair-powder revealed a household harbouring a footman in disguise as a plough-boy, determined whether planting beans in the kitchen garden by a household servant, some of them later intended for sale, actually made him or her one, in the law's meaning. This intrusion had perceptible effect on how households were organised, from making sure that a servant in husbandry was never seen leading the horse out of the stable (for that would make him a 'stable boy' – a servant 'within the meaning of the act'), to judges of the King's Bench and Tax Office officials solemnly deliberating the question of 'Labourers or Husbandmen . . . Cleaning Boots'.[19] A shopkeeper might want to see to it that the maidservant did very little kitchen business, stayed visibly in the shop, for the first labour rendered the employer liable (between 1785 and 1792) to the tax, and her assistance behind the counter did not for, by her labour there, the shopkeeper earned an income exempted by law.[20] The servant-tax legislation forced changes in management of daily life, as it did for Ann Linton of Dutchworth in Hertfordshire in February 1816. She had moved in with her brother-in-law, kept a four-wheeled carriage and a horse, had no servant and borrowed one of the family's men. He looked after her horse and carriage; her brother-in-law paid the tax on him; he was not *her* servant. The appeal-meeting commissioners agreed with her, but the crown surveyor said that this was contrary to the meaning of the Act – she should pay for the man as well – and he wanted her case stated for

[16] Susan E. Brown, 'Assessing men and maids: The female servant tax and meanings of productive labour in late-eighteenth-century Britain', *Left History*, 12:2 (2008), 11–32.

[17] Kennedy, *English Taxation*, p. 4.   [18] Hilton, *Mad, Bad and Dangerous*, p. 118.

[19] TNA, IR 70/3 'Assessed Taxes and Inhabited Houses Duties. Judges Opinions, 1805–1830', vol. 3, Feb. 1810–Jun. 1813; 'No. 609 – Labourers or Husbandmen as Grooms or Cleaning Boots'.

[20] TNA, IR 83/131, Appeals before Commissioners, 1770–85, 'Hastings Rape Sussex to wit Appeals heard Determined at Meeting of the Commissioners held at the George Inn Battel on Tuesday the 21st day of January 1785'.

the opinion of the judges.[21] The politicization that the servant taxes provoked came from the rethinking and articulation of the social relations
on which they levied duties. Practical political theories were forced into
being in a lot of kitchens and cow-byres, in contemplation of the work
that took place in them and the people who performed it.

There was overt principle and policy in the proposals to tax the employment of male servants, and it had been around for a very long time. Lord
North did not get the idea from reading *The Wealth of Nations*, as some
contemporaries and nineteenth-century historians thought; proposals for
taxes on luxurious commodities had been made as early as 1718.[22] The
severe test of the Seven Years War brought forth many suggestions for
taxing the wealth that escaped direct taxation. They came from the only
source at the government's disposal, said W. R. Ward, 'from below the
political level', that is, from civil servants in the revenue departments,
who suggested doing inventive things with the window tax, bringing
the poll tax back from the mists of history, taxing shopkeepers and other
traders who occupied houses above a certain rent; or taxing householders
keeping livery servants and pleasure horses; or perhaps a tax on dogs and
hounds would 'catch the hunting gentry'. Long before the American War
broke out, 'fresh thought on fiscal questions was already demanded'.[23]
All these schemes were adopted by later governments: North's taxes
on carriages, cards, dice, newspapers – and male servants – closely followed the drift of policy papers produced in the 1750s and 1760s.[24]
George Rose, first Secretary to the Board of Taxes and then to the Treasury between 1776 and 1801, from whose assistants and colleagues so
many of these ideas had emanated, thought their result gratifying. He
contemplated 'a country powerful in exertion . . . flourishing in revenue,
commerce and manufacture'. As he saw it, tax revenue was not only the
produce but also 'the criterion of national wealth; especially as much of
it is raised on articles of convenience and even luxury; which shows in

---

[21] TNA, IR 70/5, 'Assessed Taxes and Inhabited Houses Duties, Judges Opinions, 1805–
1830', vol. 5, Mar. 1817–Dec. 1819, 'No. 1182 – Occasional Servants 52 Geo. 3rd'.
The judges determined that the commissioners were wrong: she should pay up. 52 Geo.
III, c. 93 (1812) was one of many legislative adjustments to the male servant tax. Ann
Linton had two years to make up her mind about what to do – or to carry on as usual.
The Herts. commissioners met on 9 Feb. 1816; the judges issued their opinion on
23 Feb. 1818. There were complaints about the slowness of the appeal system.

[22] Kennedy, *English Taxation*, pp. 133–5, 142, 156–7; Ian Simpson Ross, *The Life of Adam
Smith*, Clarendon Press, Oxford, 1995, pp. 121, 222; Sir Lewis Namier and John Brooke,
Charles Townshend, Macmillan, London, 1964, pp. 146–86; Adam Smith, *The Correspon-
dence of Adam Smith*, Ernest Campbell Mossner and Ian Simpson Ross (eds.), Clarendon
Press, Oxford, 1977, pp. 328–34; 332.

[23] Ward, *English Land Tax*, pp. 81–4.   [24] Ward, *English Land Tax*, p. 124.

a most satisfactory manner, as well what the people enjoy as what they contribute'.[25]

The notion of a tax on livery servants was part of a common conversation about the police and management of the nation, from the 1760s onwards.[26] Continental models were frequently referred to. Sinclair (who vastly disapproved of the tax on female servants) told his readers that in the Netherlands, by way of contrast with Britain, employers paid tax on the servants they kept for business purposes, but not on their domestic or family servants. This kind of comparison had been available since the middle years of the century.[27] British residents in France in the 1750s and 1760s complained that the servants they had taken with them had been fingered for the capitation tax – it 'renders every British Subject who is a servant liable to . . . payment'.[28] Continental practice like this may be the source of the misapprehensions that Pitt met with in the House of Commons when he proposed the maidservant tax. As a way of laughing at Pitt's 'dirty little maidservant tax', MPs purported to believe that poor girls were going to have to pay the tax themselves.[29] The same sneering jocularity came from those who claimed that they had done extensive research on comparative taxation policy and combed the works of M. Necker and Madame d'Eon Beaumont, only to find no 'such idea as a tax upon women'. They claimed they had looked to Holland, and found, 'in a Dutch library', the works of Mynheer Vander Vanfrow from which

[25] George Rose, *A Brief Examination into the Increase of the revenue, Commerce and Navigation of Great Britain, from 1792 to 1799*, Graisberry and Campbell, Dublin, 1799, pp. 6, 31; Leverson Vernon Harcourt, *The Diaries and Correspondence of the Right Hon. George Rose. Containing Original Letters of the most distinguished Statesmen of his Day. In Two Volumes*, Richard Bentley, London, 1860; Hilton, *Mad, Bad and Dangerous*, pp. 321–233. Also Roland Thorne, 'Rose, George (1744–1818)' in *Oxford Dictionary of National Biography*, Oxford University Press, 2004, www.oxforddnb.com/view/article/24088, accessed 22 Aug. 2007.

[26] John Powell, *A View of Real Grievances: or a Dissertation Upon the State of the Poor in this Kingdom, Shewing by what Means the Poor Rates have grown to such enormous Heights, with Remedies proposed for redressing them*, 2nd edn, W. Whittingham, London, 1786, p. 357; Anon., *An Essay on Trade and Commerce: Containing Observations on Taxes, As they are supposed to affect the Price of Labour in our Manufactures: Together with some interesting Reflections on the Importance of Our Trade to America. To which is added the Outlines, or Sketch, of a Scheme for the Maintenance and Employment of the Poor, the Prevention of Vagrancy, and the Decrease of the Poor Rates. By the Author of Considerations on Taxes*, S. Hooper, London, 1770, pp. 152–3, 169 and passim.

[27] Sinclair, *History of Public Revenue* (1803–4), vol. 3, Appendix; Anon., *Essay on Trade and Commerce*, p. 169.

[28] TNA SP 78/273, 276, 296, Letters from Paris dated 16 Sep. 1767, 14 Dec. 1768, 28 Jun. 1775.

[29] Jonathan Thompson, *The Commutation Act candidly considered, in its Principles and Operations. To which is annexed, an Address to the Freeholders of Northumberland, assembled in the Town-Hall, in Morpeth, January 21 1789 . . . addressed to Gawen Aynsley, Esq.*, T. Reynolds, London, 1800, pp. 2–4 for Pitt's 'dirty little female servants tax'.

might be gleaned the information that there was such a tax in existence in the Netherlands, and that 'when a female servant is out of bread in Holland, the state is obliged to provide for her' – quite the opposite to what Pitt proposed, they said, in sending dozens of girls to street-walking.[30] The maidservant tax was to be a case in point for all manner of fiscal reformer, until the day it was repealed – and after it was repealed. Thomas Paine believed that Pitt had lifted his proposal to abandon it from *The Rights of Man*, the first part of which he completed in January 1792. Reducing the national debt by taxing the interest on it, Paine argued, would allow the steady removal of some particularly objectionable taxes born by the public, for example the levy on waggons and female servants.[31] Paine's difficulties in getting his work published are well known. He believed that his first publisher abandoned it in the face of repeated visits by government agents; a copy had found its way to Pitt via a Tax Office spy. When *The Rights of Man* finally came out, he claimed that Pitt's proposals to repeal or lower taxes on carts, candles and maidservants were 'every one . . . part of a plan contained in [my] work'.[32] Paine's was only a very high-profile version of the dozens of schemes for reducing, increasing or abandoning the assessed taxes, or making the servant tax part of a system of police and registration. They poured into the Tax Office from lawyers, provincial tax officials, magistrates and concerned citizens.

It was difficult to collect the servant taxes; widespread evasion was reported; there was a constant harrying of surveyors and collectors by the Tax Office. Officials complained about how much new work there would be now they had the male-servant tax business laid upon them. They asked for an increase in salary, which they got.[33] Weighty volumes of legal opinions (the opinions of the judges on cases forwarded on appeal by local commissioners) were written up for reference. A whole series of George Rose's complaints to local commissioners about 'the very great Inconvenience resulting to the Public from those Taxes not being

---

[30] *Parliamentary History*, 25, pp. 817–19 (8 Jun. 1785). Van der Vanfrow was a stock figure of Dutch fiscal efficiency. For the cross-dressing d'Eon Beaumont, Anna Clark, 'The Chevalier d'Eon and Wilkes: Masculinity and politics in the eighteenth century', *Eighteenth-Century Studies*, 32.1 (1998), 19–48; Dror Wahrman, 'Percy's prologue: From gender play to gender panic in eighteenth-century England', *Past and Present*, 159 (1998), 113–60; *The Making of the Modern Self: Identity and culture in eighteenth-century England*, Yale University Press, New Haven and London, 2004, pp. 29–36. Jacques Necker was French minister of finance.

[31] Thomas Paine, *The Rights of Man* [1792], *Common Sense and Other Political Writings*, Mark Philp (ed.), Oxford University Press, Oxford, 1995, p. 317.

[32] Paine, *Rights of Man*, Appendix, pp. 327–31. See John Keane, *Tom Paine: A political life*, Bloomsbury, London, 1995, pp. 304–5.

[33] TNA T1 542/191–196, Letters from Tax Office.

collected more easily and more regularly . . . the Inconvenience resulting from the Delay of the money finding its way to the Exchequer', were also preserved.[34] The Office started a system of incentive payments to particularly diligent surveyors, and received many complaints from private citizens about that diligence in action.[35] It discussed with surveyors the legal niceties of how, for example, to distrain against those who refused to pay the tax on their male servants, the trouble most of them had with their collectors and allegations of their accepting bribes. The surveyor for Essex wrote in July 1780 with a complicated question about what kind of warrant he should obtain to act against those who refuse to pay, telling how 'a great many persons this year have refused to enter their Gardeners, and declare if they shall be surcharged for them they will not pay'. The Tax Office heard how humble – and troublesome – collectors were threatened with prosecution by 'persons of property'.[36] They could also have learned a very great deal about the ways and means by which private citizens managed the business of every-day life under the exigencies of the new system. The volumes of judges' opinions contained detailed discussion of domestic labour in middling-sort households. The Reverend John Simpson was master of a local school in Worcestershire; he employed a married man at weekly wages who ate and drank, but did not sleep at his house. The man was 'occupied in cleaning the shoes of himself and scholars, knives and forks for the same persons, breaking coals for the Family, and occasionally draws Beer for them'; he waited on the Boarders at supper; he also swept the courts and yards and went on errands 'but never works in the gardins'. Simpson had a small field 'the hedges of which are repaired by this Man'.[37] Another cleric described very similar household arrangements. The Reverend Mr Nott, Curate of Droxford and Rector of Wyke, occupied 100 acres of land; 'he appealed against a charge for a Male Servant – He stated that he employed a Man chiefly in Husbandry . . . also in cleaning Knives Boots and shoes in his garden and in saddling his horse but in no other domestic occupation. He paid him after the rate of 1/6d pr day and considered himself at liberty to discharge him at the end of any day. Mr Nott contended that this person . . . [was] chiefly employed in husbandry . . . the Surveyor contended

[34] TNA E 102/70, 'Land Tax, Property Tax, Assessed Taxes' Letter Book, 1777–1805, pp. 218–19, 298–9, 304–5.
[35] TNA E 102/70, pp. 502–3 (list of payments to surveyors, 28 Sep. 1790).
[36] TNA IR 71/2, Board of Taxes, Miscellaneous, Entry Book of Law Opinions, 1780–1823, pp. 6–8.
[37] TNA IR 70/5, Assessed Taxes and Inhabited Houses Duties, Judges Opinions, 1805–30, vol. 5, Mar. 1817–Dec. 1819, 'No. 1320 – Servants – General Questions 52 Geo 33 c. 93'. The Worcester City tax commissioners allowed the appeal; the judges thought them wrong. The man was a servant.

that the Servant being employed on domestic concerns, the appellant was liable to the . . . duty'.[38] In 1819 in Great Yarmouth, Richard Ferrier, woollen draper, appealed against a charge made on one of his two shopmen. The second one was his uncle, who lived with him and paid his nephew for his board. Uncle attended 'constantly' in the shop, served customers, took orders; 'but all this he does for his own amusement, and receives no wages or emolument for his services whatsoever'. Uncle was 'not employed by him' and so he was 'not liable to be assessed for his service', or so he thought.[39]

News about what transpired at local appeal meetings was transmitted rapidly around the country. Readers of the Devonshire press for example, heard a mere ten days later the Cambridge local appeal commissioners' views on what constituted the proper domestic workforce for an innkeeper; how the master of the Rose Inn in that city would be expected in private life to keep one maidservant, and so would be assessed accordingly for one of the four females he employed to work in the inn.[40] The Tax Office bought advertising space in provincial newspapers to explain the new legislation to those who had for whatever reason, 'omitted to enter . . . their Horses used for Riding, and likewise their Female Servants'.[41] A tax on a work animal controverted the principle of the male-and female-servant taxes that made them half-way acceptable: that of not paying for labour by which the employer earned a living. The fiscal principal that a male servant was a taxable item because he was a luxury item, was not questioned by correspondents to the Tax Office, nor in Parliament and the wider public sphere. Rather, energies were devoted to producing abundant evidence that they *were* necessary items of ordinary life and commerce. The appeal system dictated the wisdom of playing down the involvement of men in domestic labour, though much involvement was actually recorded. What the Tax Office saw as evasion was also a means of continuing household arrangements and the employment of domestic labour in familiar ways.

There is practically no way of discovering what effects the male-servant tax had on their employment. Outraged citizens might write to local

[38] TNA IR 70/5, Assessed Taxes and Inhabited Houses Duties . . . , vol. 5, Mar. 1817–Dec. 1819, 'No. 1609 – Labourers Employed as Grooms'. The commissioners confirmed the charge; Nott demanded a case for the opinion of the judges, who confirmed that the man was a servant.

[39] TNA IR 70/6, Assessed Taxes and Inhabited Houses Duties . . . , vol. 6, Dec. 1819 – Jul. 1822, 'No. 1723 – Shopmen – Relations'. The judges agreed with the local commissioners in relieving Ferrier.

[40] *Western Flying Post; or Sherbourne and Yeovill Mercury*, 16 Jan. 1786, 'Country News, Cambridge Jan. 6'.

[41] *Western Flying Post*, 9, 16 Jan. 1786, 'Office for Taxes, London, 15 December 1785'.

surveyors asking 'the reason I am assessed for a Horse as I have not
kept one for three years', or telling them that they had ceased to use
hairpowder ages ago and were fed up with having notices of assessment
served on them;[42] but there are no traces of households who made an
obvious decision to give up keeping male servants after the 1777 Act. In
the parish of Cuckney, Nottinghamshire, one male servant was returned,
assessed to the Reverend Mr Oller for the tax year 1777–8. Four years
later, Mr Oller still employed the parish's only formally defined servant,
though not the same man. A new household in the parish increased the
number of male servants to six in 1788. There were still six in 1791–2,
and five in 1792–3. By 1801–2 the employment of taxable male servants
had dropped back to a mere two. In the parish of Edwinstowe, a place of
much larger establishments, the decrease of male servants from thirteen
to twelve between 1778 and 1779 was accounted for by the Duchess
of Kingston's getting rid of a gardener from among the seven servants
she paid tax for. She tried further retrenchment the following year, but
was employing six servants again in 1785–6. In 1790–1 there were ten
men in Edwinstowe for whom duty was paid (and eight 'official' female
servants).

The point here is not the shadow population of servants in both these
parishes – ploughboys in borrowed wigs waiting at table, husbandry men
cleaning the master's boots, girls under fourteen and women over sixty
(neither of them taxable items), the nursemaids in families with babies
and small children (families with children were exempted), the Boy
playing with the children before feeding the pigs, all the charwomen
and 'char-men' of Cuckney – but rather the suggestion that in these
tiny places at least, during the first twenty years of the male-servant tax,
employment of them actually increased.

In a different and much larger place, in Doncaster, in the tax year
1779–80, fifty-one employers paid for fifty-five male servants (557 tax-
paying inhabitants were listed). A year later the collectors' lists show
forty-one employers of forty-three male servants. These fragmentary
records show a decrease of taxable male servants in the town in the
early years of the 1777 Act's operation. Nine years later, nothing much
had changed: forty employers paid tax for forty-three men between them.
And in 1792–3 (the last year for which records were preserved) forty-one
employers coughed up for fifty-eight male servants. Numerous personal

---

[42] Cheshire and Chester Archives (CCA), P 88/13/3, Macclesfield Parish, Macclesfield
Forest with Wildboar Clough, Letter dated 19 Mar. 1798; West Yorkshire Archives
(WYAS), Bradford District, 16D86/temp. 0440, Francis Sharp Bridges of Horton Old
Hall, Bradford, Account Book with Payments for Domestic Duties and Wages, 1802–43
(letter dated 28 Jan. 1825).

Table 5.1 *Employment of taxed male servants in three places, 1777–97, available years*

	Cuckney, Notts	Edwinstowe, Notts	Doncaster
1777–8	1	13	
1778–9		12	
1779–80		12	55
1780–1			43
1785–6	1	9	
1786–7	1		
1788–9	6		43
1789–90	6	10	41
1790–1	4	10	41
1791–2			58
1792–3	5		
1794–5	3		
1796–7	3		

Source: Nottinghamshire Archives, PR 2728, DD 871/1, PR 2731, PR 2131; Doncaster Metropolitan Archives, AB 6/8/56, AB 6/8/57, AB6/8/59, AB 6/8/62, AB 6/8/60, AB 6/8/62, AB 6/8/63.

decisions about the organisation of everyday life in Doncaster lie behind these unalarming fluctuations. One householder gave up his man-servant, another employed one for the first time. Men left their place to look for a new job. The increase in number of Doncaster male servants between 1791 and 1793 was mainly accounted for by a new and opulent establishment in the town, which employed five male servants – and four taxed females.

This relatively un-noisy adjustment to state intrusion into ordinary (and elite) lives was not the case with the maidservant tax, which was the subject of vociferous debate from the moment it was first proposed in the House of Commons. Sir Cecil Wray (another maverick back-bencher) was never allowed to forget his proposal of 1783, to replace the receipt tax with 'ten shillings . . . annually laid on all servant maids kept for domestic use. This raised a loud laugh . . . '. The public prints started the rumour that maids themselves were to be taxed: cartoons depicted them 'striking him with their brooms and denouncing him as a niggardly brute'.[43] Wray was 'treated with ridicule by all parts of

---

[43] *Parliamentary History*, vol. 24, pp. 98–9 (4 Dec. 1783). David Wilkinson, 'Wray, Sir Cecil, thirteenth baronet (1734–1805)' in *Oxford Dictionary of National Biography*, online edn, Oxford University Press, Oct. 2006, www.oxforddnb.com/view/article/30013, accessed 3 Jan. 2007. See also 'An Epigram Written at the time Sir Cecil Wray

the House'; his proposal had 'kept the baronet an object of ridicule without doors ever since'.[44] Loud laughter continued in the house, for nine years. The habit of MPs to sarcastically correct themselves when they used the term 'maid' instead of 'female', and the display of social theory – simple in the extreme – that had every dismissed maidservant turn prostitute, was inaugurated in 1783, two years before Pitt revisited the idea.[45] In 1785 he was joined to Wray in the comedic imagination of the political elite. Any fiscal innovations embodied in his tax proposals were quite elided by the sheer vulgarity of taxing maidservants' labour. Satirising the proposal was also a way of casting light on Pitt's somewhat opaque sexuality.[46] 'On the female servants tax there can be but one opinion', Northumberland voters were told in January 1789; 'such a tax would never have entered the head of a generous statesman. But Mr Pitt, gentleman, knew the exact value of half a crown in his dealings with a servant wench, not having ever dared to look up to my lady's maid, at hap hazard he sets her down at double the price . . . *this degrading valuation of the sex* . . . has filled our streets with prostitutes, our hospitals with deseased [sic], our poor houses with paupers. Blessed effects of Mr Pitt's administration'.[47] Sir John Sinclair wrote that 'it is a tax which cannot yet be justified by the necessities of the country . . . every friend to the female sex . . . ought to unite in compelling the impost of so obnoxious, cruel, unmanlike, and unproductive'.[48] Richard Brinsley Sheridan thought that Pitt's proposal was going to 'occasion more ridicule than all [his] . . . cheerfulness . . . would be able to cope with'.[49]

Reading these debates is to enter the elite social and sexual imagination that Samuel Richardson wrote *Pamela* to condemn. Pamela is called rude, denigrating names (to which she mightily objects) for simply *being there*: being a maidservant with a pretty face and a nubile figure.[50] Her sexual availability is assumed by this language. MPs knew this sexual script very well indeed, dragged out tired and puerile comparisons between dairymaids, wet-nurses and cows, and smiled knowingly when the Earl of Surrey said that domestic servitude was 'the only means these

proposed a tax upon maid servants', Anthony Pasquin, *Poems: by Anthony Pasquin*, 2 vols., J. Strahan, London, W. Creech, Edinburgh; J. Exshaw, Dublin, 1789, vol. 1, p. 152.

[44] *Parliamentary History*, vol. 25, p. 567 (9 May 1785).
[45] *Ibid.*, vol. 24, pp. 97–111.
[46] Hilton, *Mad, Bad and Dangerous*, pp. 53–4, 191.
[47] Thompson, *Commutation Act*, pp. 2–4.
[48] Sinclair, *History of Public Revenue* (1789), vol. 3, pp. 146–7.
[49] *Parliamentary History*, vol. 24, pp. 563–4 (9 May 1795).
[50] Samuel Richardson, *Pamela* (1740), Penguin, Harmondsworth, 1985, pp. 59–75.

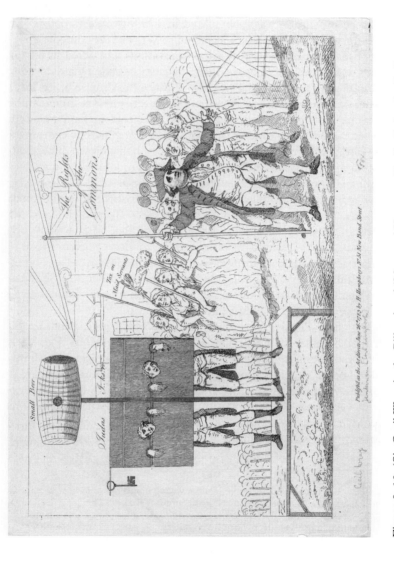

Figure 9–10. 'Sir Cecil Wray in the Pillory' and 'Mars and Venus, or Sir Cecil chastised'. Concentrate on the marching maidservants, and this becomes an early image of industrial protest by the workers.

Figure 10. (*cont.*)

female had of earning a livelihood'.[51] Every turn of phrase must have produced a snigger (Pitt 'had laid his hand on maidservants') though these are not recorded. They knew what they were doing. One of them remarked that it was shameful 'to bring forward these poor unfortunate females as a subject of speculation and merriment' (probably meaning quite the opposite).[52] One Devonshire newspaper editor campaigned against the maidservant tax, 'not because we think it so very oppressive . . . but because it affords an opportunity for the writers of ribaldly to raise inflammatory censure on the minister'.[53] But the same newspaper published a highly amusing lamentation (in the Biblical manner) on Pitt's policy: 'And it came to pass in the days of Georgius, that a stripling of the house of Chatham, found favour in the king's sight . . . He turned his

[51] *Parliamentary History*, vol. 25, p. 568 (10 May 1785). For a script of voluntary sexual availability, see Anon., 'Qualifications of a Modern Maidservant', *The Wit's Magazine* . . . , 2 vols., London, 1784–5, vol. 2 (Dec. 1784), p. 466, where 'Dorothy Redfist' lists nine of them: 'Fifthly. If my master should come home late, and in liquor, I can help him up to bed; and in case my mistrus is out of town, supposing he should be incapable of undressing himself, I can pull off his cloaths; and, if required, can go to bed to him as well as my mistrus.'

[52] *Parliamentary History*, vol. 25, pp. 559–60 (9 May 1785).

[53] *Trewman's Exeter Flying Post; or Plymouth and Cornish Advertiser*, 19 May 1785, 'Retrospective of Politics'.

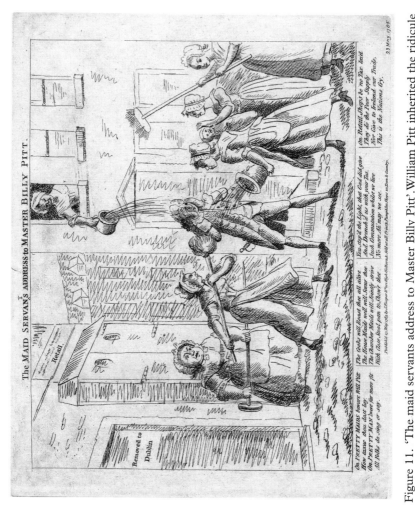

Figure 11. 'The maid servants address to Master Billy Pitt'. William Pitt inherited the ridicule that had been directed at Sir Cecil Wray when he proposed a maidservant tax in 1783.

back upon the people . . . And he taxed them with heavy taxes . . . Then a woman named Mary, who was a sojourner in the great city, lifted up her voice and said unto him . . . Therefore will I trundle my mop into thy face, and blind thee with the waters of impurity. Moreover, the napkin shall be far from thee, that the filth may remain upon thy countenance; for thou hast dealt wickedly unto me.'[54] More seriously, had Pitt gone mad? Was he dealing with the Irish question with 'money squeezed out of the shops of the poor tradesmen, and out of the hard-earned wages of the poor servant maids!'?[55]

Demonstrations were held, organised by the national committee protesting against the shop tax, which Pitt proposed as part of the same budget package as the one on maidservants.[56] In Norwich, in July 1785, posters were displayed proclaiming 'No Pitt! No Shop Tax! No Servant Tax!' Late in the afternoon, an effigy of Pitt on horseback entered the city by the London road, 'attended by six executioners with white wands, a female servant in mourning rode behind him with a whip, and at intervals severely scourged him, repeatedly exclaiming "There, curse you, that's for turning me out of my place by your villainous servant's tax!"'[57] Provincial newspapers reprinted the *London Gazette*'s 'Advertisement Extraordinary': 'To be sold by public cant, several thousand *brushes*, the property of English *maidservants*, and very proper for exportation. N.B. Several of them want handles.'[58] A lady entered her writing closet to produce a tirade of a novel about 'the fatal day that passed the mortifying government tax into law'.[59] The eponymous Widow of Kent is most concerned that 'every family must now send in the names and employment of the people about them . . . there is more tyranny and ill-mindedness in it, than in the inquisition itself'. It was an invasion of domestic privacy that alarmed Mrs Rowley most (though she discussed the public drama of prostitution with some frankness; this was a melodrama known in private houses as well as the House of Commons).[60] And

[54] *Trewman's Exeter Flying Post*, 21 Jul. 1785, 'The Contrast, Or 1784 and 1785 compared'.
[55] *Trewman's Exeter Flying Post*, 14 Jul. 1785, 'The Retrospector'; Hilton, *Mad, Bad and Dangerous*, pp. 188–9.
[56] Ian Mitchell, 'Pitt's shop tax in the history of retailing', *Local Historian*, 14:6 (1981), 348–51.
[57] *Western Flying Post*, 18 Jul. 1785, 'London, July 12. Extract of a Letter from Norwich, July 6'. Similar protests in Bath and Bristol were also reported this day.
[58] *Trewman's Exeter Flying Post*, 19 May 1785.
[59] Renata Lana, 'Women and the Foxite strategy in the election of 1784', *Eighteenth-Century Life*, 26:1 (2002), 46–69 for the maidservant tax as a woman's issue.
[60] Anon., *The Widow of Kent; or, the History of Mrs Rowley. A Novel in Two Volumes*, F. Noble, London, 1788, vol. 2, 137–9: '"From what point has this calamity reached me?" – "From the new tax bill . . . upon female servants, which passed this morning . . . every family must now send in the names and employment of the people about them . . . What

indeed, the Tax Office did have plans to compile a register of all those keeping servants, horses and carriages, to print and publish it in alphabetical form 'in order facilitate a Discovery of Frauds in the . . . Duties'. It publicised its intentions in notices to all tax districts and in the newspapers, and actually paid for the list to be compiled, though it appears never to have seen the light of day.[61]

Pitt had said that the sum of £413,000 had to be raised 'by new and additional burdens upon the people'; he thought a tax on maidservants would contribute £35,000 of it. He knew the proposal would encounter 'jocular ideas and merry witticisms', but he wanted MPs to understand that it was part of a rethinking of the 'indiscriminate . . . very partial' male-servant tax, which he now proposed should be increased 'to the proportional number of the servants, and that the portion of the higher incomes should contribute accordingly'. As the servants the wealthy kept were more for vanity than for real use he said, the tax for them in future, 'would be more . . . upon unnecessary extravagance than upon either industry or servitude'.[62] In these debates maidservants represented the very opposite of luxury and opulence. Charles Fox thought that in general, a tax upon male servants was 'very well founded. There could not be easily pointed out any set of men who were more useless subjects in a state than men servants . . . They . . . were kept for parade, and as the instruments of vanity, idleness, and ostentation.'[63] Maidservants on the other hand 'were always employed in works of industry and management. The former were retained by the rich, and the latter by the

---

will become of thousands of . . . young girls . . . ? . . . The streets of London must swarm with them, and the bad houses overflow with unhappy victims".'

[61] Devon Record Office (DRO), 818A/PZ 44, 'Office for Taxes, Sept. 17, 1785, Notice showing rates of rewards payable to informers about houses, windows, servants, horses, carriages, etc', 1785; *Trewman's Exeter Flying Post*, 6 Oct., 3 Nov., 1785. There certainly was such a list, now lost. TNA E 102/70, 'Land Tax, Property Tax, Assessed Taxes', Letter Book, 1777–1805, pp. 322–3: 'To: paid for making an alphabetical list of Persons keeping Servants, Horses and Carriages throughout England, pursuant to a Treasury Order of 17th October 1787 – £483.11.6'. Accounts were for the year ending 5 Jan. 1788. This is a sad thing for historians wanting to count (taxed) female servants: no one can do what Leonard Schwarz has done with the male servant returns from 1780: 'English servants and their employers during the eighteenth- and nineteenth-centuries', *Economic History Review*, 52 (1999), 236–56.

[62] *Parliamentary History*, vol. 25, pp. 551–3 (9 May 1785).

[63] The common-sense view from the provinces too: 'The tax on men servants meets with universal approbation. The servants belonging to the nobility, are a species of men the most useless, idle and insignificant, and are as fair an object of taxation as *Perigord pies* or any luxury we can do without. But nobility cannot do without them – Very well – Then nobility can afford to pay for them.' All the aristocracy did anyway, was breed horses and support luxury, was the opinion of *Trewman's Exeter Flying Post*, 19 May 1785, 'Retrospective of Politics'.

poor... this tax... pressed most on those who were least able to bear it'.[64]

Once past the cat-calling, sexual innuendo and lascivious puerility of MPs, their heavy-handed classical and historical references to the misty times when other chancellors had tried taxing 'female commodities' (and the dire consequences of so doing), these debates constitute the first serious – the first – discussion of female labour and employment to be held in the House of Commons.[65] Such discussions were not to be had again for a hundred years. And what would later be called family policy was at work here. The very least they reveal is how some political members of the ruling elite conceptualised the social order they inhabited and its social, domestic, sexual, and productive relations. Taxing female servants would create 'universal odium' and 'general unpopularity', said Fox; it would affect 'a great body of the people'; it would fall most heavily on 'persons of large families' and 'the increase of their offspring would become particularly distressing... it would become a tax upon infants, not a tax upon luxury or extravagance'. He was thinking, he said, of 'the middling class of people, who kept servants only in proportion to their children'.[66] It was 'a tax on families, and would be considered as having a tendency to accumulate the oppressions to which domestic life in this country was already subjected'; abandon it, he said, and instead put 'a tax on all ladies who were married and put out their children to nurse'. It did not follow that if you kept a couple of maidservants, you were opulent – 'In many cases where three or four female servants were kept, the sole reason was the great number of children the family had...'.[67] It was going to fall particularly hard on 'many farmers who kept a number of women servants for the double purpose of doing the work of their house and their farm'.[68] Sheridan thought that among people like these the only

[64] *Parliamentary History*, vol. 25, pp. 569–70 (10 May 1785).
[65] *Ibid.*, pp. 571–4: (10 May 1785). 'It was a tax imposed upon women' said MP John Courtenay, 'a measure... directed to that commodity at which no other Chancellor ever publically presumed to point', except one from the realm of myth and fable. He mentioned Jacob Bryant, *A New System, or, an Analysis of Ancient Mythology: where in an Attempt is made to divest Tradition of Fable; and to reduce the Truth to its original Purity*, 2nd edn, 2 vols., T. Payne, P. Elmsly, B. White, and J. Walter, London, 1775, vol. 2, pp. 133–40, and turned Orpheus into a Chancellor of the Exchequer 'not indulgent to the ladies'. This was a long shot of interpretation, figuring Pitt as a social and sexual isolate soon to be torn to pieces by enraged women. A modern Chancellor ought to be 'tender of meddling with the sex', said Coutenay; 'their enmity was fatal... An attempt of this kind terminated once before in the reign of Richard II. The idea... was... started of taxing female commodities...' The result had been Watt Tyler's rebellion.
[66] *Parliamentary History*, vol. 25, p. 557 (9 May 1785).
[67] *The Parliamentary Register*, vol. 27, pp. 205–31, 239–49, 483–92 (9, 10 May, 8 Jun. 1785).
[68] *Parliamentary History*, vol. 25, p. 557, p. 561 (9 May 1785).

reason for keeping servants 'was the great number of children the family had'. He thought any maidservant tax ought to be balanced by a tax on single men, 'who certainly were a description of persons less useful to the community than men who were married and had families . . . the tax on female servants could be considered in no other light than as a bounty to bachelors and a penalty upon propagation'. (Pitt remarked that it was not necessary to resort to alliteration to make the point that all taxes falling on consumer goods had this effect; Lord Mahon said that families with a certain number of children could be exempted – and you could not do this with consumer goods.) No one objected to individual women being degraded to the level of salt, soap and candles, as they had regarding men in 1777.[69] And analogies were not with everyday goods subject to excise duty, but to those subject to the principle of the stamp duty: why not tax the wearing of silk stockings instead, asked the earl of Surrey, 'with every unmarried person paying an addition for [a] . . . licence, more than a person with a family'? (Occasion for more guffaws, possibly, when Pitt responded that a tax on stocking would have to rely on a system of informers to be effective.[70])

Objections to useless, non-productive bachelors getting away with paying the same tax as men with families were heeded.[71] The revised bill allowed one tax-free female servant to a family with children, the shortfall to be made up by every single man keeping one male servant paying 25s extra.[72] Bachelors would pay at twice the rate for a female servant compared with employers with children, who might also engage any number of girls under fourteen or women over sixty, tax free.[73] Fox thought that sliding scales and exemptions would actually encourage the employment of maidservants: as with the revised tax on men, its rates should be 'proportionately higher according to the number kept, for the most fit objects of taxation were single persons who would afford to keep a number of servants'.[74]

---

[69] *Ibid.*, pp. 559–566.   [70] *Ibid.*, pp. 812–20 (8 Jun. 1785).

[71] *Ibid.*, pp. 563–4 (9 May 1785); Brown, 'Assessing men and maids', pp. 22–3. Wild (perhaps satiric) rumours reached Devon in December when *Trewman's Exeter Flying Post* reported 'London Intelligence' of a tax to be laid on all bachelors in lieu of the shop tax – headline news (as much as there was such a thing in eighteenth-century newspapers, but this item was on the front page). 'Noblemen to pay £20, day labourers, 2s, per annum – Remedy at hand, *Marry*'; 29 Dec. 1785. Or perhaps this was a skit for the holiday season.

[72] *Parliamentary History*, vol. 25, p. 812 (8 Jun. 1785).

[73] 25 Geo. III c. 43, 'An Act to repeal the Duties on Male Servants; and for granting new Duties on Male and Female Servants'; s. 5 for the female servant exemptions.

[74] *Parliamentary History*, vol. 25, pp. 816–17 (8 Jun. 1785).

ALADIES MAID PURCHASING A LEEK.

Figure 12. 'A lady's maid purchasing a leek'. Parliamentary debates on the maidservant tax were part of the social comedy of denigrating maidservants. For why would she? (A lady's maid purchase a leek?) Or have to make the choice between a drooping leek and an upright carrot? ('Mr Pitt, gentleman, knew the exact value of half a crown in his dealings with a servant wench, not having ever dared to look up to my lady's maid, at hap hazard he sets her down at double the price . . . ').

It is difficult for the modern reader to concede that the discourse on prostitution threading its way through these debates was an aspect of social and fiscal theory brought to bear by parliamentarians on the question of female employment in a modern state; but barely suppressed sniggering and the universal assumption that every housemaid was an easy lay apart, that is what it was. The last flourish before the bill passed (it became operative on 5 July 1785) was from John Courtenay, MP for Tamworth ('ever keen to make the members laugh with his sharp wit' notes his *DNB* entry), who said it was useless Pitt's declaring that this was a tax on employers, not on employees; it would be like a tax on dogs which the master was to pay, but which the dogs would feel, for they would be 'hung up, to avoid the expense of keeping them'. In fact, 'this impost on their servitude, would be the means of numbers [of women] losing their bread, their honest, industrious means of livelihood, and, in the end, being driven to the necessity of prostitution'. He wanted the House to spare a thought for these 'persons of no property', who had 'no protector but man'. He gave them a literary source for doing so: the unhappy girl turned out of doors in Goldsmith's *Deserted Village* – a nice example of the high-cultural references available for thinking this aspect of the social, after a month's debate characterised by the low and lewd.[75]

Perhaps they were not so dense as to believe that women were to experience the effects of the tax in the manner of hanged puppies. There was no precedent at all, for taxing women, of any description, or by whatever method, and maidservants were 'that part of the sex who were least able to bear any burthen of the state'. It was thought that in a free state, female servants were not in 'the same predicament with male servants, who might continue or not in that state of servitude'. Men 'could alter when they pleased, as they might go into the navy, or the army, or even to some branch of manufacture or mechanics; but females in that low condition, were condemned to continue where they were. In their case it was not voluntary but necessary slavery; and were they to be punished for what was their misfortune, not their crime . . . ?'. Moreover, said MPs, many of the trades formerly exercised by women, such as stay- and mantua-making, had been taken over by men. Instead of women, 'men-milliners, barbers, stay-makers, and every effeminate

---

[75] Roland Thorne, 'Courtenay, John (1738–1816)' in *Oxford Dictionary of National Biography*, Oxford University Press, 2004, www.oxforddnb.com/view/article/6453, accessed 5 Jan. 2007. The tax provoked truly bad poetry: 'Who thought of taxing woman kind!/Tax wealth with judgment, but take care,/Would you succeed, the sex to spare!/Tax Luxury and Dissipation . . . '. *Nottingham Journal*, 25 May 1785, 'Lines on the Tax upon Female Servants' by 'Sancho', who wrote by analogy with the most famous literary servant of them all.

person throughout the kingdom ought to be severely taxed'. Maidservants were an 'order of individuals intitled to the most humane usage, to
whom society had many obligations, and by whom the evils of humanity
were considerably alleviated: this was consequently making them a poor
return for all their labours and attentions' – tax male mantua-makers,
tax 'all the effeminate in the kingdom' instead.[76] (If there was a gender
crisis in the 1790s, then these debates foreshadow it, in the contemplation of dissolving boundaries between work fit and proper for men and
women of the poorer sort.[77]) MPs can have had no more evidence that
prostitution was increased by the female-servant tax than their historians
can find. Street-walking by dismissed maidservants was a cultural text,
not a sociological observation. Anyway, as Pitt said, everyone believed
that prostitution 'appeared to be in so forward a state that to countenance
it any further would be needless'.[78] In Parliament at least, prostitution
was not discussed as part of a makeshift economy of the poor as some
recent historians have had it, of poor women using petty crime to supple-
ment uncertain incomes in the agricultural and textile sectors. In these
elite accounts of working lives, prostitution was not noted because it came
under the heading of 'minor criminal activity'. Neither did MPs employ
sentimental narratives that charted the servant's route from seduction to
street walking. They presented a limited set of labour-market opportunities for women to be sure – dressmaking and related trades, domestic
service, prostitution – but nevertheless waged domestic work was conceptualised as a form of labour and employment. Domestic servants
constituted a female workforce; forced to leave service, women would
turn to other, less formal, sectors of the economy.

There is no evidence that employers, faced with an impost of 2s 6d
on their maidservant, threw her out onto the streets. How could they?
Frances Hamilton did not stop paying Molly Evans her four guineas a
year between 1785 and 1786, for that was the wage they had contracted
for. The maidservant tax may have determined Hamilton in maintaining
wages at £4 4s until Evans left her service in 1796, but that calculation,

---

[76] *Parliamentary History*, vol. 25, pp. 558–60 (9 May 1785).
[77] Wahrman, 'Percy's prologues'; *Making of the Modern Self*; Jane Humphries, with Sara
Horrell, 'Women's labour force participation and the transition to the male breadwinner
family, 1790–1865', *Economic History Review*, 98 (1995), 89–117.
[78] *Parliamentary History*, vol. 25, p. 574 (10 May 1785). For the discourse on prostitution
in the later century see Laura J. Rosenthal, *Infamous Commerce: Prostitution in eighteenth-
century British literature and culture*, Cornell University Press, Ithaca and London, 2006;
Penelope Lane, 'Work on the margins: Poor women and the informal economy of
eighteenth and early nineteenth-century Leicestershire', *Midland History*, 22 (1997),
88–99; Sarah Lloyd, '"Pleasure's Golden Bait": Prostitution, poverty and the Magdelen
Hospital in eighteenth-century London', *History Workshop Journal*, 41 (1996), 50–70.

were it made, is unavailable to us. The tax may have meant that some employers paid for stay-mending less regularly, decided the girl could do without a new pair of shoes, that she didn't really need tea to her breakfast, and that reducing her dinner would do no harm; but these tiny acts of domestic economy in the face of fiscal policy are equally lost. After 1785, John Trusler and other lifestyle advisers simply added the new tax to their recommended calculations for householders employing female servants, as in 'Wages of a maid-servant and tax'.[79] This may have been the way in which many householders saw this new drain on their income. An alternative route to economy was suggested by Trusler's additional budget example of 'a sturdy girl, not boarded or lodged, but attending only in the daytime'; the calculation that they would not need to pay tax on such a worker may well have occurred to many. There was widespread and vociferous opposition to the tax; but according to William Pitt, 90,000 householders did pay up in the fiscal year 1791–2, most of them paying for one assessed woman, so in relatively modest households.

Something of the effects of the tax can be retrieved from those places that preserved their records for the period 1785 to 1792 as Doncaster did. A run of four years (1788–9, 1789–90, 1790–1, 1791–2) does not allow consideration of the immediate impact of the maidservant tax (if there was one), but the schedules do reveal many individual household decisions about the employment of domestic labour (though the reasoning behind them remains opaque) and some insight into the work experience of men and women employed as servants. In 1788–9 the returns listed 509 taxpayers and a further 153 'poor'. These were not paupers or those in receipt of aid under the poor law, but rather townsmen and women who paid no taxes: no poor rate, no church rates, no assessed tax: no taxes of any sort. Out of 509 taxpayers, 180 employed servants, male and female; 35 per cent of those who paid taxes paid the servant taxes. Forty employers paid for a total of forty-three male servants; 176 paid for employing 205 female servants. Women made up 83 per cent of the taxed domestic workforce. Nineteen per cent of employers paid tax on a mixed domestic workforce; men (taxed men) were much more likely to work with a companion than were women: only 9 per cent of the male servant workforce was returned from a single-servant household, whilst 61 per cent of women were returned as working alone. (We cannot know

---

[79] John Trusler, *The Way to be Rich and Respectable, addressed to Men of Small Fortune*, 6th edn, privately printed, London, 1787, p. 55; see in comparison with 5th edn, R. Baldwin, London, 1781.

Table 5.2 *Taxed Doncaster servants, 1788–92*

	Male servants	% of service workforce	Female servants	% of service workforce
1788–9	43	17%	205	83%
1789–90	41	16%	214	84%
1790–1	45	17%	216	83%
1791–2	42	16%	219	84%

Source: Doncaster Metropolitan Archives, AB6/8/59, AB6/8/60, AB 6/8/62, AB6/8/63

how many charwomen, pubescent girls and women over sixty were also employed in these officially single-servant households.[80])

In the last year maidservant numbers had to be returned to the Tax Office, 1791–2, the total number of servant-employing taxpayers had increased, very slightly: 38 per cent of those who paid taxes, paid for servants. Women accounted for 84 per cent of the official domestic labour force. The numbers of men and women working as single servants had not changed. Working alone was the most common experience for maidservants across the country.[81]

Probably, the numbers of taxable servants in Doncaster, their work situations and the gender balance of the domestic workforce, remained steady over the five years that the maidservant tax was in operation. The number of returned male servants in Doncaster certainly dropped from the fifty-five recorded in 1779–80 (see Table 5:2) – a relatively rapid change; but to discover employers ridding themselves of a man-servant or a maidservant *because* there was now a tax levied on their services, would need a different kind of record. Andrew Warde of Hooton Pagnell near Doncaster preserved a series of references for men he considered employing, but appears not to have given a moment's thought to replacing a man with a maid in his substantial establishment. He was not a taxpayer in the town (Hooton is some 6 miles from Doncaster), the county tax returns are not extant and some of the knowledge he gained of prospective employees came long after the male-servant tax could be called new; but the servant taxes do not seem to have entered into his

---

[80] These figures are comparable with Roger Bellingham's findings for Selby where in 1788, 53 people paid tax on 58 female servants. R. A. Bellingham, 'Demographic, economic and social change in the later eighteenth and early nineteenth centuries: Some conclusions from a study of four small towns in Yorkshire from circa 1750 to circa 1830', PhD, University of Leicester, 2000.

[81] See Chapter 2, Table 2:1

judgement of William Craven, for example. He considered Craven as potential butler in 1791, was told that though the man was *very honest and civil* he was 'not... able to withstand liquor... not a quality for a Butler'.[82] He heard of Richard Jackson that he was 'perfectly sober honest' had been useful in the family and understood 'all the business of a butler'. As for the skills of *coiffeur* that Warde had asked about, Jackson's former master could not say, as his 'hair-dressing was of very little consequence... [and] I did not often trust him in that way'.[83] Warde pursued the hairdressing question, to be told that there was not much to say about him, in that or any other regard. He had 'left of his own accord without assigning any other reason than that of disliking his situation'. He wasn't a bad hairdresser: 'I thought him well qualified beyond what one usually finds in such as are not valets' – quick enough with the comb and the hairpowder 'though remarkably slow in every other department. I can say nothing in favour of his temper which I verily believe to be odd indeed, though I myself never experienced the smallest incivility from him...'.[84] In 1792 William Lambert was recommended with the not very compelling 'has taken good care of his horses and carriage... he thinks he has too much work... likely to make you a good servant he is rather slow and requires speaking to now and then'.[85] Six years later, when the male-servant tax had been in operation for twenty years and was simply part of the landscape of elite household domestic economy, Warde heard of William Gibbs that he was 'accustomed to dress my hair and I may venture to say, No man can wait or set dishes upon a Table more readily than he can, or have their plate and sideboard in nicer order. With regard to his brewing, I can say little about it, not having employed him in that capacity more than twice and that sufficiently satisfied me.' The problem was that although he had 'behaved himself vastly well' six months ago his master '*discovered* too great a *familiarity* between him and my House-keeper on which account solely it was, that he quitted my Place... He would have answered very well had he continued my servant ...'.[86] In a household like Warde's there were assumptions about gender and work that did not pertain in more modest ones. He and his correspondents assumed that brewing was man's work, not an assumption you could make if you employed one or two maidservants and no

---

[82] DMA, HP/27/4, Records of the Warde Family of Hooton Pagnell, letter to Andrew Warde (23 Nov. 1791).
[83] DMA, HP/27/4, letter to Andrew Warde (29 Dec. 1791).
[84] *Ibid.*, letter to Andrew Warde (31 Dec. 1791).
[85] *Ibid.*, letter to Andrew Warde (20 Apr. 1792).
[86] *Ibid.*, letter to Andrew Warde (27 Dec. 1797).

man. The servant taxes do not appear to have altered one jot any of these assumptions.

There is some suggestion that in the households of the Doncaster middling sort, male servants were replaced by women in the years after 1777, but no indication at all of a similar reduction in tax-paying employers of female servants. From 1779 to 1792, there was a decrease in male service in the town, and a probable increase in female service. The calculation here is easy to reconstruct: maidservants were cheaper items. In 1789–90 for example, Mr Bower, Surgeon, paid £1 5s tax for his male servant, and a mere 2s 6d for his maid. Even at the higher rate for two maids, the levy on their labour was still cheaper than that of a man: Mr Alderman Heeton paid £1 5s for his man-servant, and a total of 10s tax for his two maids. Even for a bachelor, penalised by the fiscal state for his 'perfect uselessness', the maidservant still came cheaper than the man: Mr John Danser, attorney, paid 5s for his maidservant (double the rate he would have paid were he married) and a thumping £2 10s in tax for his man-servant. Perhaps he compared himself as bearer of the burdens of the state with one of his neighbours in High Street East, Richard Hattersly, grocer and married man, who paid the shop tax certainly, the inhabited houses tax, the window tax, and 10s for a horse (as did Mr Danser), but ran his household with just one female servant taxed at 2s 6d, half the rate Danser paid.[87]

The numerical steady state of the female servant workforce elides numerous household decisions made by employers. Between 1789 and 1790 Mrs Arthur replaced her two male servants with a man and a woman; a Mrs Kelk, presumably living alone, or at least paying her own taxes, reduced her number of maids and cut her servant tax bill from 10s to half a crown. Against the trend, William Walker, gentleman, replaced his female servant with a man; a barber employed a maidservant for the first time (a *taxable* maidservant, that is), a surgeon got rid of his; a female grocer appeared in the tax records for the first time, adding one maidservant to the total in the town. By the end of the tax year 1790–1, Abraham Elston, gunsmith, was no longer paying for a female servant; perhaps he found a thirteen- or a sixty-year-old to take her place. John Crossley, bachelor and collar-maker, appears to have done the same. Robert Naylor, married blacksmith, also stopped paying the female-servant tax. So too did an innholder; but he kept his taxable horse. Most movement in the maidservant market came from tradesman and artisan households like this, that had formerly paid for a single servant. There were other decisions about household outgoings that were more clearly related to

---

[87] DMA, AB6/8/60, 'Doncaster &c Window Duty 1789'.

the assessed-taxes system: substantial householders might stop keeping a carriage, as had the mercer Mr William Heaton by the end of 1791 (he continued to pay tax for a man-servant, two maids, two horses and two carts). They could reduce the number of their windows, as did Mrs Glew, from thirteen to nine (she paid for no servants, nor any other of the assessed taxes). Mrs Shepley did not block up hers, but must have found a cheaper way of obtaining domestic service, for her maidservant disappeared from the records over this year. Thomas Ainley, a bricklayer in the Fish Shambles evidently made the decision to retrench by giving up his horse.

There are minute traces of household economies at work in this kind of cutting back, and similar traces of households doing well, or at least acquiring more servants: a merchant got himself a man-servant to add to his maid; a waggoner did the same, adding to his three existing maid-servants; a Mrs Smith got another female servant, bringing her total to two; a substantial innkeeper found himself a man-servant; John Thorpe, bricklayer, acquired the title of 'Mr' and a maidservant; Miss King the milliner paid the female-servant tax for the first time (or perhaps the girl had reached her fourteenth birthday). Mr Foster, Exciseman living in the town, got himself a wife and a maidservant. Over this year the number of taxable servants in Doncaster was increased by the establishment by Mrs Fenton of a substantial household in the town (two man-servants, three maids, a four-wheel carriage, two horses – and twenty-six windows). At the other end of the scale of female employers, when a lady lodger left a house, so too did a female servant disappear from the records. The death of an employer might remove five servants from the assessed-tax schedules. And the administration of the system caused some of the shifts on the lists of returnable servants: Stephen Wakefield, glazier, suddenly *became* a bachelor, paying 5s for his maid instead of 2s 6d; the assessors had not noted his marital status the year before. A gentleman got married, and paid less for his female servant. The processes of household decision-making can sometimes be traced over the years. As a bachelor in 1789, William Bulay, farmer of Marshgate, had a maidservant; he got rid of her in 1791 before he married in 1792, when he also acquired a horse. Daniel Jarret, a turner, payed the tax on one horse between 1789 and 91, replacing it with a maidservant in the tax year 1791–2. William Morris, grocer, paid for a horse and a maidservant from 1789–91, and added another maid to his list in the tax year 1791–2. Mr James Peat, the town's perfumer, employed one maidservant from 1789 until 1791, when he was returned as employing none.

In 1788–9 there were 205 taxed female servants in Doncaster; by 1791–2, there were 216 of them. In regard to this place at least, MPs were wrong in their speculations of 1785, that the tax would see many women turned out of doors – but only in the aggregate, because they were correct in surmising that many modest householders might decide that a horse was a necessity whilst a maidservant was not, replacing her with a sturdy girl by the day. But that attribution of motive is also highly speculative; we can only see that some decisions were made, not why they were made. Nor can we know what happened, for example, to the Doncaster perfumer's maidservant in 1792. Given the small (but certain) increase of taxable women in the town, we can speculate that she found another place, perhaps with Daniel Jarrett, turner of Frenchgate, who acquired a maidservant for the first time that year. Or perhaps Mr and Mrs Peat had a second baby (a James Peat was christened in Doncaster on 15 April 1792, parents James and Ann Peat) and she became, perforce and according to the legislation, a non-taxable item for her master and mistress, did not leave at all, and had clout-washing and child-care added to her duties.[88] Perhaps nobody got rid of a maidservant, but used the tax as an incentive to procreation. No wonder, given the myriad household arrangements and stratagems that the state provoked, the Treasury and William Pitt were disappointed at its outcome. Pitt had hopes of £140,000 per annum from it, but it scarce brought in a quarter of that. Writing in 1789, Sir John Sinclair thought that as its 'produce decreases, it is a sign that the apprehensions entertained that the tax would have a tendency to diminish the numbers of female servants were too well founded'. It evidently did nothing of the sort. It only reduced the number of returned, taxable female servants, employers finding many ways through its labyrinthine system of exemptions of not paying it at all. In the year before it was abandoned, it produced just £31,000.[89]

There was a ready-made system onto which to graft the servant taxes when they were inaugurated. Management was given to the commissioners of duties on windows and houses; they appointed assessors to count the number of male servants living locally and to issue pro forma to employers for their enumeration. Professional crown surveyors were appointed by the Tax Office to manage the local system. This addition to existing assessed taxes forced the updating of justices' handbooks and other guides to the administration of local law.[90] There was an

---

[88] For servants and nappy-washing, see Chapter 9.
[89] Sinclair, *History of Public Revenue* (1789), vol. 3, pp. 146–7; *Parliamentary History*, vol. 25, p. 568 (10 May 1785); *Parliamentary History*, vol. 29, p. 829 (17 Feb. 1792); 'Report from the Select Committee on Public Income and Expenditure, since 1786', pp. 452–87 (10 May 1791).
[90] Brewer, *Sinews of Power*, pp. 226–7, 249. The taxes produced a whole new line in ready-reckoners for the assessed taxes: Anon., (Mrs Newbery), *The Housekeeper's Accompt-Book*

important right of appeal to the higher courts. (Common Pleas and Exchequer were mentioned in the Act, but by far the greater number went to King's Bench.) A fiscal bureaucracy, seemingly superimposed upon a system of parish and local law, was, in fact, integrated into the legal system as a whole by this right of appeal.[91] Lord North's servant tax was operated in this way from July 1777 until May 1781. Then, for the next four years, the management of the business was removed from local commissioners (usually, though not invariably, also local magistrates) to the Excise Office.[92] Employers then became (briefly) responsible for making lists of their own servants, and taking them to the nearest excise officer (21 Geo. III, c. 31).

For five years then, appeal to King's Bench and the other higher courts, was abandoned. Employers with grievances about assessments made on them must now appeal to the Commissioners of Excise if they lived in London and if in the provinces to the county quarter sessions. Then in July 1785, the former system was restored (by 25 Geo. III c 43). There had been very great anxieties about the way in which Excise collection of 'inland duties' cut across the common-law right of appeal.[93] What employers noted, and what the provincial press kept them fully informed about in 1785, was that they had already paid the male-servant tax for the year under the now-abandoned Excise regime. The Excise Office in London inserted a series of notices in the provincial press, telling employers that on the production of a receipt they could get their monies back at local offices, on designated days. The repayment timetable stretched well into 1786. If employers read a newspaper in the 1780s, new, confusing and bothersome tax

---

for the Year 1782; or an Easy, Concise, and Clear Method of Keeping an Exact Account of every Article Made Use of in Every Family throughout the Year, R. Cruttwell, London, and W. Taylor, Bath, 1782. Anon., The Housekeeper's Account Book for the Year 1820, Cruttwell, Longman, Hurst, Rees, Orme and Brown, Bath and London, 1820. With the maidservant tax in 1785, local newspapers undertook the public service of informing their readers about the new duties on servants, coaches, chaises, landaux, carriages, wains, carts, horses and on retail shops, pawnbrokers, coach makers, hawkers and pedlars and on gloves. See Trewman's Exeter Flying Post, 7 Jul. 1785, for a large print full-page spread on 'New Taxes for 1785'; Nottingham Journal, 18 Jun. 1785, 'A List of all the TAXES laid upon the People during the present Session of Parliament'. Also 20 Aug., 3 Sep. 1785. This was modern, public-service journalism. Editors puffed new-written guides, as 'useful companion[s] for gentlemen, farmers, tradesmen &c'. Western Flying Post, 5 Sep., 3, 27 Nov., 11 Dec. 1785.

[91] See Brewer, Sinews of Power, pp. 62–8, 91–5.

[92] For a 'sense of trust between taxpayers and in the central state' because of its embedding in local systems of power and authority, see Daunton, Trusting Leviathan, p. 41 and passim.

[93] Parliamentary History, vol. 25 pp. 795–812 (3 Jun. 1788), 'Debate on the Excise Jurisdiction Bill'.

arrangements were constantly brought to their notice.[94] The same newspapers informed their readers that there had been a mistake in the June drafting of the maidservant legislation – to do with the number of children that brought householders tax relief. The Act had to be repealed, 'for every two children' substituted for 'two children', and the whole business of the Lords' and royal assent gone through again – front page news for the *Exeter Flying Post*.[95] The collection of duties on horses, carriages and other forms of transport had been returned to the local commissioner system before the servant taxes.[96] So by the time female servants were taxed, between 1785 and 1792, the system was a local one again, with right of appeal to the higher courts.

This is how the system worked: a Northamptonshire grocer for example, had a tax notice served on him for his 'Boy'. The boy lived out, and was hired and paid by the day. He delivered groceries to customers, ran errands for his master, and also 'did other little matters for the use of [his] family', such as cleaning shoes and table knives. In the grocer's opinion he was not a servant at all, and not a taxable item. The grocer attended the appeal meeting held by the commissioners for assessed taxes, and protested his case. The commissioners pondered, and agreed with him: the boy was not a servant 'within the meaning of the Act'. But the crown surveyor insisted that the case be stated for the opinion of the High Court judges. At a regular meeting of the court of King's Bench, the grocer's and the commissioners' understanding was confirmed (by ten judges, including Lord Chief Justice Mansfield and William Blackstone): the boy was not a servant, despite the shoes and the knives.[97]

The assessment notice had been served on the grocer out of a list put together by men like Roger Oldham and William Tudsbury, assessor and collector (and also constables) for the parish of Edwinstone, Nottinghamshire, who trudged round its man-servant employing households, recording them, and later, collecting twelve guineas for the twelve men

---

[94] *Trewman's Exeter Flying Post*, 6 Oct., 3 Nov., 1, 8, 15 Dec. 1785, 'Excise Office, London'; *Nottingham Journal*, 10, 22 Oct., 12, 19, 26 Nov., 2 Dec. 1785; *Leicester and Nottingham Journal*, 5 Nov. 1785.

[95] *Trewman's Exeter Flying Post*, 4 Aug. 1785; *Western Flying Post*, 1 Aug. 1785.

[96] 25 Geo. III, c. 47 (1785), 'An Act for transferring the receipt and management of certain duties from the commissioners of excise . . . to the commissioners for the affairs of taxes'.

[97] Commissioners of Excise, *Cases Relating to the Tax on Servants*, T. Cadell and T. Longman, London, 1781, Commissioners Appeal Meeting Northampton, 1 Jul. 1777; King's Bench Meeting, 1 Feb. 1779. Richard Burn, *The Justice of the Peace and Parish Officer. To which is added an Appendix, including the Statutes of the last Session of Parliament (24 G. 3) and some adjudged cases*, 15th edn, 4 vols., A. Strahan and W. Woodfall, London, 1785, vol. 1, pp. 128–31.

of the parish defined by taxation law as servants.[98] The Reverend John Murgatroyd of Lingards near Huddersfield, first learned that his servant Phoebe Beatson was a taxable item in July 1791, when 'Mr Wilkingson, ye Window looker counted our Windows . . . & charged for ym – & our servt. – & left me a printed Paper – ye first payment will be about old Michaelmas'.[99] The administrative state appears to have moved slowly in West Yorkshire, even in the dynamic Colne Valley. Phoebe Beatson had been in his service since 1785. The London Office for the Affairs of Taxes attempted to deal with slowness, forgetfulness and up-front evasion by offering substantial rewards to those willing to inform on their neighbours for keeping undeclared carriages, horses and servants. The prize for spotting a clandestine horse or maidservant was ten shillings – in her case, four times what an employer was attempting to get away with by not declaring her. (For a man-servant, the reward was £1 5s, much closer to the actual tax rate for him.)[100] This was a noisy system, its administration, changes of direction, the sheer weight of public and personal arrangements that it inaugurated, constantly brought to the attention of householders and horse keepers.

Appeal meetings were noisy too. Gentlemen loudly spoke their probity and honour; they employed attorneys to protest their honesty in declaring their footman a husbandry man, their stable empty of a horse these three years past. Surveyors felt themselves hard done-by, *their* honour and integrity under attack by local taxpayers who accused them of partiality, of letting a neighbour's servant through the net or ignoring the number of horses another kept. Antagonism towards men who were characterised as agents of an interfering central state *and* social inferiors, continued long after the 1770s, and after the maidservant tax had been and gone. The Tax Office kept records of conflicts like this. A letter from Barnsley in 1802, from Mr Carr, surveyor for Doncaster district quivered with the rage he felt at having been accused of allowing several local gentlemen 'knowingly thro' favour' get away with calling a gardener (a servant within the meaning of the Act) a jobbing labourer (not a taxable item). It was 'the most gross false wicked & malicious' accusation; 'an unwarranted

---

[98] Burn, *Justice of the Peace*, vol. 1, pp. 239–44. Brewer, *Sinews of Power*, pp. 114, 126–9. Nottinghamshire Archives (NA), PR 2131, Edwinstowe Account Book, 1778–1817, 'A Duplicate of the servants retained in the Parish of Edwinstowe from the 25th March at £1.1, each Servant'.

[99] West Yorkshire Archives (WYAS), Kirklees District, KC 242/1, Reverend John Murgatroyd, Diary (7 Jul. 1791).

[100] DRO, 818A/PZ 44, Notice showing rates of rewards payable to informers. 'West Alvington Part', wrote the crown surveyor for the district on the back of the printed notice; 'Assessors to fix this at the Church Door . . . '.

Figure 13. 'The Horse turned Groom'.

attack...upon my character'.[101] Really, it was all about horses. Carr had assessed these gentlemen as keeping more horses than they wished to declare; they wanted recovery of the £50 penalty for withholding information. The gardener business was a way of getting back at Carr,

---

[101] 'The Commissioners of the Affairs of Taxes received the following Letter from Mr Carr Surveyor of Taxes for the upper & lower divisions of the Wapentake of Strafford and Tickhill in the County of York....'. TNA IR 71/2, Board of Taxes, Miscellaneous, Entry Book of Law Opinions, 1780–1823.

Figure 14. 'How to Avoid the Horse Duty'.

'an attack . . . in consequence of his having surcharged [one of them] for a Gardener', wrote the Tax Office to the judges, asking for an opinion on 'filing an information *ex officio* against [the gentleman concerned] for a libel'. It was pointed out Carr had the full support of the local commissioners.[102]

Patrick O'Brien and Philip Hunt say that fiscal states come into being when private individuals as well as county and city authorities undertake and finance activities which serve the broad interests of the Crown.[103] The assessed taxes were used in this way during the American and French Wars, when more and more individual interests, in horses and hairpowder, in the lighting and heating and provisioning of households, were yoked to the state by the taxing of them.[104] O'Brien and Hunt point

---

[102] The view of the Attorney-General was not very encouraging to Mr Carr. Spencer Perceval thought it best to do nothing; but everyone – in the Tax Office and up near Doncaster – should remember that the power of surcharge 'is given for the benefit of the Revue', not for those of 'private pique or revenge'. TNA IR 71/2, '(Copy Opinion) . . . May 15 1802'.

[103] Patrick O'Brien and Phillip Hunt, 'The rise of the fiscal state in England, 1485–1815', *Historical Research*, (1993), 66–176.

[104] Beckett, 'Land Tax or Excise'.

out that in modern fiscal states, the total revenues of the Crown may understate the scale of 'state' activity, a point well taken in regard to the maidservant tax, for it probably had more effect on the ways in which those who paid it (and evaded it) organised daily life than any other tax besides the one on horses.[105] Departments of government, Parliament and the higher courts of justice were all forced to take notice of these arrangements, or at least to become cognisant of the organisation of work on a family smallholding for example, how shopkeepers managed the interaction between house place and counter by means of their female servant, how many men cleaned knives in kitchens all over the country and what multiplicities of arrangements there were for milking cows and feeding pigs. The Tax Office had to explain, in yet another series of notices and newspaper advertisements, exactly what the Acts of Parliament said and what they meant: that not returning a female servant 'who may have the milking of a cow or two' was an evasion of the tax. *Bona fide* dairymaids *were* exempted (they were servants in husbandry, by whose labour the employer made a living) but a maidservant's nipping out before breakfast to get some milk did not make her a dairymaid, and if employers failed to pay for her they were practising tax evasion.[106] Between the lines of this inadvertent knowledge, policy came into being. A punitive tax rate for unmarried men keeping servants and the generous concessions to families with children are early stirrings of much later tax relief for married persons with children. The domestic life – the ordinary household arrangements – of the people was not to be a target for state intervention, or entered into in this manner again, for a very long time indeed. It has been said that public objections to the tax on women servants resisted the definition of domestic work as unproductive labour.[107] But no servant, male or female, was as good for conceptualising labour as the horse. It is to horses that we now turn.

[105] O'Brien and Hunt, 'Rise of the fiscal state', p. 135.
[106] *Western Flying Post*, 9, 16 Jan. 1786.
[107] Brown, 'Assessing men and maids', p. 27.

Horses

Working men and women and horses were bound together in the deep structure of political thinking about the servant taxes, and labour and the social order. Those who drafted the early servant tax legislation learned their lessons rather slowly from the much longer-standing taxes on varieties of horse and vehicle. It was not until 1785 that a point about what servants *did* as opposed to how they were *named,* was underscored in an Act of Parliament. Then for the first time, towards the end of the long list of servants and their implied tasks, was added the severe warning that they were to be taxed 'whatever name or names, male servants really acting in the said capacities shall be called'. You could call him what you liked, but if he exercised himself in the labour of servant, then servant was what he was, and his employer was to be taxed. That owners and employers tended to believe, Adam-like, that in naming something so, it *was* so, could have been learned from the very first imposition of rates and duties on coaches and carriages. All ensuing legislation for the taxation of transport was careful to repeat the original stricture of 1747, that the intention was to tax carriages 'by whatever name such carriage is now or hereafter may be called or known'.[108] Horses had a narrower potential vocabulary attached to them, but the same point applied to the duties on those kept for the purpose of riding and for drawing types of vehicle (whatever they might be called).[109]

There were few jokes about the 1785 horse tax, whilst the tax on maidservants proved irresistible to all sorts of comedian, high and low. There *is* a horse joke to be found in the Devonshire press, where it was reported that 'Since the taxes laid on horses the country people

---

[108] By 20 Geo. II c. 10; repeated in 16 Geo. III c. 34, 19 Geo. III c. 25, 21 Geo. III c. 17, 22 Geo. III c. 66, 23 Geo. III c. 66, and crucially, for the administration of the servant tax, by 24 Geo. III c. 31.

[109] John Smee, *A Complete Collection of Abstracts of Acts of Parliament and Cases with Opinions sought of the Judges upon the following Taxes, viz, upon Houses, Windows, Servants . . . . ,* 2 vol., Butterworth, London, 1797, vol. 2, pp. 553–77, 'Cases on the Duties upon Horses and Carriages'.

in . . . Warwick, Chester, Derby and Stafford are . . . frequently seen on the roads mounted on oxen, cows, and sometimes bulls, which are in hundreds of instances, equally as tractable as horses' – but this was a dig at the odd habits of Northerners, not a horse-tax joke, or a report of anyone actually riding a bull to market.[110] No jokes; but there was protest, direct and to the point. No introduction, no preface nor preamble to Thomas Day's *Dialogue between a Justice of the Peace and a Farmer* (1785). Day plunged the reader into an outrage experienced across the country:

> *Justice:* I am exceedingly sorry for your situation; but the act is so clear, that you are incontestably subject to the penalty.
>
> *Farmer:* So, then, I am subject to a penalty of twenty pounds, merely because I rode Old Ball, the blind mare, along with a sack of bran, from the mill.
>
> *Justice:* Indubitably. You ought to have entered her within twenty days. The clause is clear, 'All persons, &c.'
>
> *Far:* So, then, I am not to be severely punished, because I did not understand all the quirks of the law as well as our attorney or his clerk; and yet this is a land of liberty![111]

An assessed-taxes appeal meeting in Tavistock, Devon, in December 1785 broke up in tumult. Mr Whitchurch, one of the crown surveyors for Devon, dashed off a note to the Tax Office about 'riotous Proceedings at the Appeals in my Division'. He had been 'obliged to let them (the Mob) have my Book of the Acts of Parliament, and they demolished them' in front of him; he needed another copy, and fast. And this had not been the first disturbance: 'A similar Riot to what I have informed [you] . . . happened here on Wednesday last, which totally put a stop to the proceedings of the Commissioners who were obliged to skulk off at a back door to save their lives.'[112] Did the Mob (farmers, tradesmen and gentlemen, if other appeal meetings are anything to go by) tear up the most potent symbol of an active and interfering fiscal state, the statutes at large declaring the horses taxes, or proclaiming the tax on maidservants?[113] Or perhaps they resented the return of power to the

---

[110] *Trewman's Exeter Flying Post*, 8 Dec. 1785.

[111] Thomas Day, *Day's Dialogue between a Justice of the Peace and a Farmer*, 2nd edn, John Stockdale, London, 1785.

[112] TNA T 1/624/118–121, 'Tavistock 17 December 1785'. For surveyors, see Great Britain, Parliament, House of Commons, *Select Committee on Finance. First [-twenty-second] Report from the Select Committee on Finance*, 2 vols., 1797, vol. 2, p. 19.

[113] Mr Whitchurch might have been asking for George Waller's *Abstract of the several Acts of Parliament passed in this Kingdom from the 33d of His late Majesty King George the 2d. for the better regulating the Collection of the Revenue, and for preventing of Frauds therein,*

commissioners (most of them local magistrates) and the loss of servant-smuggling opportunities that making up their own lists for the Excise had provided? Which tax drove Tavistock taxpayers to direct action? The maidservant tax had come into operation on 5 July; riding horses had been taxed for the first time from 29 September 1784 (24 Geo. III c. 31); and those used to draw certain kinds of carriage in 1785. Assessors started to count 'Horses, Wagons and Carts' from 10 October 1785. In November, owners, occupiers and employers were served assessment notices for three quarters of the year (5 July 1785 to 5 April 1786) for female servants, and for half a year for horses (5 July 1785 to 5 April 1786). November was the month in which all the tax pigeons came home to roost. Though it is impossible to discover the immediate cause of the Tavistock riot, it is more likely to have been the tax on transport rather than the one on female servants.[114] A female servant cost 2s 6d a year in tax; a horse, 10s. A horse was the major means of transport, and a major source of labour, not just in this rural area, but everywhere; moreover it was possible – easy – to find alternative sources of domestic labour should you resent payment of half a crown to the degree of getting rid of your maidservant.

Discussing domestic service in London before 1750, Tim Meldrum found 'horsework', the involvement of male servants with horses and transport of all kinds, to be an indicator of the sociability available to men as opposed to women servants. The care of horses got them out of the house, to inns, stables, blacksmiths' and hostlers' yards, and into wider social networks of conviviality and culture than were available to women. 'Horsework' is taken as a measure of the gender stratification inherent in waged domestic labour.[115] However, not all, nor even a majority of male servants worked with horses. In Doncaster, in the tax year 1779–80, out of fifty-five male servants named in the schedules, eleven were designated as working with horses, as grooms, stable boys or postillions, exactly the same number who were returned as 'menial servants', suggesting, with the last, very close ties to house and kitchen, and few opportunities to hang out at the hostler's. The others were ubiquitous 'footmen'. If Frances Hamilton's deployment of labour is anything to go by, Doncaster

George Grierson, Dublin, 1784; or for Gentleman of the Inner Temple, *A Concise Abstract of the most important Clauses in the following interesting acts of Parliament, passed in the Session of 1785*, J. Walker, London, 1785.

[114] It is not mentioned in the local press. It was faster to circulate news from London (a stage coach a day to Exeter) than from Tavistock, where no newsman or woman was based. For this to have become an item in either the Exeter or Sherbourne papers, someone would have had to travel or write in with the news.

[115] Tim Meldrum, *Domestic Service and Gender, 1660–1750: Life and work in the London household*, Longman, Harlow, 2000, pp. 174–82.

'footmen' may well have driven carts or waggons from time to time; but there were probably greater limits on their social life than there were for grooms and postillions. And some women did ride horses as part of their everyday working life and contracted duties.[116] In 1815, Joseph Woolley, framework knitter of Clifton, Nottinghamshire, and an excellent source of gossip and information about many cases noted by local magistrate Sir Gervase Clifton (to be encountered in the next chapter) described a local 'servant... rideing to the pasture a milking with William Hoe behind her upon the poney'.[117]

I once thought that John Locke's example of labour and labour value in the late seventeenth-century – servant and horse at work – was a mere accident of theory-construction and writing.[118] But the man and the horse were connected in ways far beyond the metaphorical. For eighteenth-century theorists, legislators and farmers, the horse was the immanent measure of labour-power and labour-time. A horse was a measure of labour itself. There were perhaps a million horses in England and Wales in the late eighteenth century, about half of them workhorses in farming. Their contribution by manure to cereal crop yield, is attested by economic and agricultural historians.[119] Horses indicate the role of chance – or at least contingency – in the British industrial revolution: the ability of the nation, by and large, to feed an increased population out of its own natural resources and sources of labour power, compared with

---

[116] But one of John Trusler's major moans about them was a sense of job demarcation so rigid that they would refuse even to bolt the stable door when asked, saying pertly 'I don't understand horses'; *Domestic Management; or the Art of Conducting a Family with Economy, Frugality and Method*, J. Souter, London, 1819, p. 38. He may have been ready 'to brain the fool', but the maidservant was not his invention; she was plagiarised from Jonas Hanway's admonitions to servants in 1774, in *Virtue in Humble Life; containing Reflections on the Reciprocal Duties of the Wealthy and the Indigent, the Master and the Servant: Thoughts on the various Situations, Passions, Prejudices, and Virtues of Mankind, drawn from real Characters: Fables applicable to the Subjects: Anecdotes of the Living and the Dead: the Result of long Experience and Observation. In a Dialogue between a Father and his Daughter, in rural Scenes. A Manual of Devotion, comprehending Extracts from Eminent Poets. In two Volumes*, J. Dodley, Brotherton and Sewell, London, 1774, vol. 1, p. 360.

[117] Nottinghamshire Archives (NA), 311/6 (1815), Diary of Joseph Woolley, framework knitter.

[118] John Locke, *Two Treatises of Government* (1690), Cambridge University Press, Cambridge, 1970, pp. 288–9. (Book Two, Chapter 5, Sections 26–8.) See Chapter 2.

[119] E. A. Wrigley, *Continuity, Chance and Change: The character of the Industrial Revolution in England*, Cambridge University Press, Cambridge, 1988, pp. 35–46; Dorian Gerhold, 'Packhorses and wheeled vehicles in England, 1550–1800', *Journal of Transport History*, 14:1 (1993), 1–26; Michael Turner, 'Counting sheep: Waking up to new estimates of livestock numbers in England c. 1800', *Agricultural History Review*, 46:2 (1998), 142–61.

other European countries in the period 1660–1820.[120] The historical role
of the horse in the agricultural sector, in output and productivity seems
assured, though this was not always the view of contemporary economists
who, in the face of the harvest failures of the 1790s and on-going crises
of dearth, complained of *too many* horses, and the vast expenditure of
grain and labour in foddering and caring for them.[121]

The energy output of a human being is very similar to that of a horse
per unit of calorific intake, though the eighteenth century did not know
that, the calorie not being available as a unit of measurement until the
1820s.[122] It did however, know and inscribe a very similar knowledge in
relation to men and horses, first by the use of Newtonian mechanics and,
later in the century, by means of modern physiology and chemistry. This
knowledge was widely available. The assumption that modern 'scientific'
propositions were mere descriptive clothing for a divinely ordained system of labour and productivity decreased towards the end of the century,
but it was still a potent factor in reading men and women – and horses –
as embodied labour. If the indolent worker would 'only stand still and
reflect upon the frame and structure of his own body' a clergyman told
his congregation in 1751 – in a figuratively contradictory passage – 'to
his shame he would find that it was originally intended and made for
action . . . His bones, sinews, muscles and nerves, disposed to move with
ease . . . His own hand by nature peculiarly fitted for work, and the dex-
terity of which is much increased by use and habit.' Forty year's later,
Edmund Burke's thoughts on scarcity made reference to the same god-
given bodily organisation, though his actual analogies were the classical
divisions of the social order into the *instrumentum vocale* (human labour),
the *semivocale* (working animals), and the *instrumentum mutum* (agricultural tools and implements). They were evoked to promote the thesis that
the interests of farmers and their workers were 'always the same . . . It
is the interest of the farmer, that his work should be done with effect and
celerity: and that cannot be, unless the labourer is well fed, and otherwise
found with such necessaries of animal life, according to its habitudes, as

---

[120] E. A. Wrigley, *Poverty, Progress and Population*, Cambridge University Press, Cambridge, 2004, pp. 44–67.

[121] Nick Crafts, 'British economic growth, 1700–1831: A review of the evidence', *Economic
History Review*, 2nd ser., 36 (1983), 177–99; William Brooke, *The True Cause of our
Present Distress for Provisions; with a natural, easy, and effectual Plan for the future Prevention
of so great a Calamity. With some Hints respecting the absolute Necessity of an encreased
Population*, H. D. Symonds etc., London, 1800, pp. 1–34.

[122] Fred Cottrell, *Energy and Society: The relations between energy, social change and economic
development*, McGraw Hill, New York, Toronto, London, 1955, vii–viii; also James
L. Hargrove, 'History of the calorie in nutrition', *Journal of Nutrition*, 136 (2006),
2957–61.

may keep the body in full force, and the mind gay and cheerful.'[123] Concentration on singular labouring bodies in mechanics, physiology and chemistry added a psychology of labour to the input-output equation. The question of the slave-labourer's productivity raised by the abolitionist debates of the 1770s and 1780s accessed the same science. If in this period 'labour' came to be conceptualised as more than 'the number of industrious poor', but also as a constitutive activity, then dissemination of information about human and animal energy had discernable effects on the development of an idea.[124] A 'man of ordinary strength', the contemporary unit of calculation for work output, was defined in relationship to the horse: 'the strength of one good horse is equal to that of five men . . . and he will carry for from 240 lb to 270 lb '; 'a man can draw but about 70 or 80 lb horizontally, for he can but apply half his weight'.[125] This knowledge was disseminated through dictionaries and encyclopaedias, and through the periodical publications of the agricultural societies of England. The new physiology, that described the relationship between food intake and the ability to exercise strength in labour, proceeded by analogy with the horse. In order to comprehend an axiom that '*the living power or energy of an organ is in proportion to the quantity of arterial blood that circulates through it*', readers had to 'attend to the manner in which horses are fed and worked', wrote Joseph Townsend in 1796.[126] James Ramsay used mechanics to discuss labour extraction from slaves in the British Sugar islands, and to draw attention to irrational labour regimes. A 'labourer of ordinary strength' ('having spirits and inclination

---

[123] John Mickleborough, *The Great Duty of Labour and Work, and the Necessity there is at present for agreeing and fixing upon some Plan for a general Workhouse for the Poor of this Place; Urged and Illustrated in a Sermon before the Corporation of Cambridge in the Parish Church of St. Andrew the Great January 27 AD 1751*, J. Bentham, Cambridge, 1751, p. 13; Edmund Burke, *Thoughts and Details on Scarcity, Originally presented to the Right. Hon. William Pitt, in the Month of November, 1795*, J. F. and C. Rivington, London, 1800, p. 10.

[124] Mitchell Dean, *The Constitution of Poverty: Towards a genealogy of liberal governance*, Routledge, London, 1991, pp. 18–34, 48–50.

[125] William Emerson, *The Doctrine of Motion*, J. Nourse, London, 1769; Erasmus Middleton, *The New Complete Dictionary of Arts and Sciences*, 2 vols., privately printed, London, 1778, vol. 2, 'Machines'; John Anderson, *Institutes of Physics*, 3rd edn, 3 vols., Robert Chapman, Glasgow, 1777, vol. 3, pp. 41–2; 4th edn, 1786, vol. 3, p. 281; James Ferguson, 'Useful projects' in *Annual Register, or a View of the History . . . for the year 1771*, 4th edn, J. Dodsley, London, 1786, pp. 126–7, where this comparison between horse and man is tabulated, and *Lectures on select Subjects in Mechanics, Hydrostatics, Hydraulics, Pneumatics, and Optics*, 8th edn, T. Longman etc., London, 1793, pp. 121; *The Principles of Mechanics. Explaining and demonstrating the general Laws of Motion . . . A work very necessary to be had by all gentlemen . . . and extremely useful to all sorts of articers [sic]*, 5th edn, G. Robinson, London, 1800, p. 177.

[126] Joseph Townsend, *A Guide to Health; being Cautions and Directions in the Treatment of Diseases*, Cox, London, 1795, p. 317.

to work') might have accomplished in half the time what a party of thirty slaves did in digging and preparing 50 square feet of ground. The free 'man of ordinary strength' had his conceptual origin in the horse. Ramsay's argument was given more point by his characterisation of planters' refusal to purchase any implements (let alone horses) for cultivation. He characterised their refusal as irrational, whilst simultaneously describing the economic rationality of employing nothing but the body- and hand-power of slaves. He had watched the 'languid exertions' of St Kitts' slave workforce, over twenty years and many fourteen-hour days; he knew the connection between food intake and energy output before medical physiology and agricultural chemistry theorised the relationship.[127] For him, strength, or bodily power, were the means for assessing labour and labour regimes.

In Locke's seventeenth-century scene in the field, the horse was easier to theorise than the man, for its labour was the more transparent in changing the gifts of God into the master's property (labour a crystallised, vendible thing). For what is it that the master acquires through Dobbin's cropping? Not only a load of turfs, for home consumption and for sale (for firing that will, in its turn, make some other kind of thing out of the goods of the earth, like bread or beer), but rather labour itself (the potentiality to labour, *and* the labour realised): the ability of the horse, through ingestion, *to carry on carrying* loads from field to house. The confusion of horse and man continued in the nineteenth-century political science that found its origins in Locke's tableau. Early twentieth-century commentators on eighteenth-century law and social policy knew that what historians ought to be doing was tracing the aetiology of 'practical political theories'.[128] Horses help us do that. The horse is present for example, in Marx's theory of labour. For Marx, labour-power was to be distinguished from the actual expenditure of labour, or its realisation: it was the capacity *to* work, or *potential* labour. Labour power is actualised in the performance of work, and it becomes embodied in a commodity. Richard Bernacki asked: where does Marx's labour power *come from?*[129] One answer might be that it comes from the horse.[130]

---

[127] James Ramsay, *An Essay on the Treatment and Conversion of African Slaves in the British Sugar Colonies*, James Phillips, London, 1784. See also Philo-Africanus, *A Letter to Wm. Wilberforce*, J. Debrett, London, 1790, p. 38.

[128] William Kennedy, *English Taxation, 1640–1799: An essay on policy and opinion*, Bell, London, 1913, p. 4.

[129] Richard Biernacki, *The Fabrication of labour: Germany and Britain, 1640–1914*, University of California Press Berkeley, Los Angeles, CA, and London, 1995, p. 42.

[130] Karl Marx, 'Wage labour and Capital' in Karl Marx and Frederick Engels, *Selected Works: In two volumes*, Foreign Language Publishing House, Moscow, 1962, vol. 1, pp. 66–97; p. 83 for the ox.

Or at least, it came from the horse in 1847, long before Marx made the theoretical move from 'labour' to 'labour-power'. The horse is 'the ox' in 'Wage Labour and Capital', when Marx still believed that labour was a thing ('this peculiar commodity . . . [which] has no other repository than human flesh and blood'), which the worker sold to the capitalist, but which the ox could not sell. That is why the turf-cutter remained a problem – he has always been both more than a horse, and at the same time, the mere metaphor (the synecdoche, to be precise) for some unexercised capacity of his master or mistress. But in the later eighteenth century, the law asserted the servant's personhood, and his capacities. Eighteenth-century tax law named him a luxury item, but at the same time, minutely considered what he (and she) *did*, and what kind of labour was cleaning the knives and chopping wood for firing. In the Lockean servant, the skills and capacities are the master's: they do not exist in the man or the woman doing the work. All the deliberations that accompanied the servant tax, on the other hand, located them *in* the man or the woman performing certain acts and tasks. The servant's capacities and skills were recognised obliquely by the law, and that recognition, made him a legal person.

Labouring men and women were slowly and conceptually detached from the horse that had provided the measure of their labour capacity. In the ways in which they could be thought, valued and assessed, they were to become individual labouring bodies, with mind and spirit. The discourse on slavery forced some kind of consideration of strength and energy as made and contingent things. And by the repeated depiction of languid, listless slaves moving across landscapes of spiritual desolation in the Sugar Colonies and in many kinds of text, a psychology of labour was first evolved, and depression of mind in the worker related not only to inadequate diet and consequent lowering of the animal system, but also to their own apprehension of hopeless circumstances and absence of futurity. This was the understanding of William Godwin and many other observers, when they wrote of the domestic servant's depression. The depression was a measure of how far the worker – the servant – had been detached from the horse, at least in the political imagination of the late eighteenth century.

6   The law of everyday life

The operation of law in the English eighteenth century – common law and tax law – inscribed servants as individuals and legal persons. To determine what might reasonably be required of a hired servant, wrote Edward Spike in 1839, you now looked not only to the law itself, not only to the 'nominal rank or class of servant' (what he or she was called), 'but also [to] his real and acknowledged station in society as an individual'.[1] Simon Deakin and Frank Wilkinson suggest that legal concepts, the abstract categories and formulations that make up the building blocks of legal discourse, provide an epistemological frame of reference, 'a "cognitive map" of social and economic relationships'. In *The Law of the Labour Market* they argue that changes in legal form over time provide an important source of knowledge about the historical changes that accompanied the emergence of modern labour markets.[2] This chapter considers a related proposition: that examining legal *practice* in regard to domestic servants reveals the making of a modern labour force.[3]

But for an employer wanting redress for maidservant's absconding (or desperate for her to return to work), for a servant wanting her unpaid

[1] Edward Spike, *The Law of Master and Servant in regard to Domestic Servants and Clerks. Chiefly Designed for the Use of Families*, Shaw, London, 1839, Preface.
[2] Simon Deakin and Frank Wilkinson, *The Law of the Labour Market. Industrialization, Employment and Legal Evolution*, Oxford University Press, Oxford, 2005, p. 3.
[3] Peter Karsten, *Between Law and Custom. 'High' and 'Low' Legal Cultures in the Lands of the British Diaspora – The United States, Canada, Australia, and New Zealand, 1600–1900*, Cambridge University Press, Cambridge, 2002, pp. 298–360.

wages and for a magistrate willing to take notice of them both, then it was important to quietly avoid nominative legal forms and what existing labour law actually *said*. Doug Hay has noted the laconic observation of a judge in 1714, that despite the Statute of Artificers giving magistrates no authority in the case of menial servants, 'they do it everyday'.[4] This chapter will add the practice of local law to Hay's important account of legal evolution and labour law in England, by considering the ways in which magistrates operated within the interstices and ambiguities of 'high' law, to produce conclusions that employers and servants before the bench (sometimes) found satisfactory.

One early twentieth-century investigator of the everyday regulation of the domestic service relationship thought it only possible to do this by collecting 'the results of a considerable number of decisions of the courts' regarding servants, over a very long period of time.[5] Only in this way could he discover who was defined as a domestic servant in the first place. J. D. Casswell wanted the easiest possible management of domestic labour disputes in the courts, and spotting a (legally defined) domestic servant in 1913 was a much more straightforward thing than it had been a century and a half before: a domestic servant was interpellated by a much narrower range of laws than her counterpart of a century before; her employers were not so interested in denying that she was one (or loudly proclaiming that she was one type of servant than another) in order to get one branch of law or other activated to cover their particular case. By 1913 whole bodies of law governing this ordinary affair of life had disappeared.

In late eighteenth-century England magistrates were the key regulators and managers of the service relationship. Labour, or employment law (anachronistically so-called), was used and administered by a magistrate sitting alone, accompanied only by a clerk – often *his* own personal servant – transcribing and filing for him. The justicing room set aside in his own private house, *was* a court, in the narrowest and most technical meaning of the word, and was sometimes called that by contemporaries, but it was not furnished with the paraphernalia and personnel of the Victorian magistrates' or post-1846 petty-sessional court. There were such courts in the late eighteenth century – two or more magistrates meeting together to administer the statute law that required more than

---

[4] Douglas Hay, 'England, 1562–1875: The law and its uses' in Douglas Hay and Paul Craven (eds), *Masters, Servants and Magistrates in Britain and the Empire, 1562–1955*, University of North Carolina Press, Chapel Hill, NC, and London, 2004, pp. 59–116, p. 87.

[5] J. D. Casswell, *The Law of Domestic Servants: With a chapter on the National Insurance Act, 1911*, Jordan, London, 1913, p. 2.

one of them to be present – but most of the activity discussed below was by magistrates acting alone.[6] This constituted a social problem as far as Thomas Gisborne was concerned. He thought of the magistrate's responsibilities, and of the fact that his 'jurisdiction was extremely extensive'. It comprised a 'multitude of persons and cases'; the people he saw were 'almost universally his inferiors; and commonly in the lowest ranks of society'. Moreover, he saw most of them 'in his own house, before few spectators, and those in general indigent and illiterate'. These were the factors that could make him 'dictatorial, brow-beating, consequential, and ill-humoured; domineering in his inclinations, dogmatical in his opinions and arbitrary in his decisions'.[7]

Magistrates determined in all sorts of cases; but they did not *make* law; they administered it. (Indeed, Ralph Heathcote thought that most of the cases brought before them were 'hardly reduced to, or determined, by any rule of law'.[8]) When for example in June 1747, Wiltshire magistrate William Hunt determined that William Giddings, yeoman of Bishops Canning should pay Thomas Drew his full wages for farm service, this decision did not pass into the law books to be referred to as precedent, as did the King's Bench judges' decision in the cases of Hannah Wright and Hannah Phillips. There, law was made. Moreover, the outcome Hunt brought about was not a 'decision', either in the everyday or the legal meaning of the term, for Hunt merely granted Drew a summons (which he paid for), and Giddings obeyed it. Hearing Drew make his complaint in front of the magistrate, the yeoman came to his own decision and agreed to pay up in full.[9] Or at least, that is how Hunt recorded the incident. Parliament *made* law; and so too did the higher courts *make* law. The decisions in law that the judges made were written up in the

---

[6] For the development of petty sessions and magistrates welding together an administrative machine, Norma Landau, *The Justices of the Peace, 1679–1760*, University of California Press, Berkeley CA, 1985, pp. 220–2; see also J. M. Beattie, *Crime and the Courts in England, 1660–1800*, Clarendon Press, Oxford, 1986, pp. 59–67. See Elizabeth Crittall on the notebook kept by the Wiltshire justice William Hunt between 1744–1749, and the considerable administrative machine of special sessions for the administration of the poor laws, highways, and licenced premises. Yet Hunt did most of his work alone. Elizabeth Crittall (ed.), *The Justicing Notebook of William Hunt, 1744–1749*, Wiltshire Record Society, vol. 37, Devizes, 1982, pp. 6–11.

[7] Thomas Gisborne, *An Inquiry into the Duties of Men in the Higher and Middle Classes of Society in Great Britain, Resulting from their Respective Stations, Professions and Employments*, 2nd edn, 2 vols., B. and J. White, London, 1795, vol. 1, p. 410.

[8] Ralph Heathcote, *The Irenach: or, Justice of the Peace's Manual. II Miscellaneous Reflections upon Laws, Policy, Manners &etc &etc. In a Dedication to William Lord Mansfield. III An Assize Sermon Preached at Leicester, 12 Aug. 1756*, privately printed, London, 1781, p. 188.

[9] Crittall, *Justicing Notebook*, p. 64; Peter King, 'The summary courts and social relations in eighteenth-century England', *Past and Present*, 183 (2004), 125–72.

law books, and described in the manuals, handbooks and guides for the better management of the system – by magistrates.[10]

These handbooks, manuals and case reports were plentifully in supply (Burn's *Justice of the Peace and Parish Officer* went through fifteen editions between 1756 and 1785), though 'A Country Magistrate' (Samuel Glasse) thought that his brethren could always do with another one, they were so badly in need of 'some more *obvious* direction . . . to dispatch the business which presents itself, with expedition, safety and satisfaction'.[11] Glasse's book was for those men who were willing to act as justices, but 'frightened of making a mistake' – 'well-meaning but timorous Magistrates', without legal training, who dreaded the censure that might follow on their errors.[12] His *Assistant* included a fold-out table or 'Abstract of various Laws for the bettering order of Society', a nice example of the bold innovations in presentation and printing that authors of these guides inaugurated.[13]

The variety of law that could be brought to bear on the service relationship was very great, such as the poor law, settlement law, the statute of

---

[10] Lynn Hollen Lees is surely correct in saying that for several hundred years the Poor Laws 'provided daily occasions for the reexamination of social duties and social rights by both the haves and the have-nots'; but 'decisions of justices of the peace and their administrative practices' were not 'codified in handbooks for magistrates'. Rather, these handbooks codified old and new law that emanated from the higher courts and Parliament, and commended a course of behaviour to magistrates. *The Solidarities of Strangers: The English poor laws and the people, 1700–1948*, Cambridge University Press, Cambridge, 1998, pp. 11, 117.

[11] But even with his new one, they would need Dr Burn's 'always at hand'. A Country Magistrate (Samuel Glasse), *The Magistrate's Assistant; or, a Summary of Those Laws which immediately respect the Conduct of a Justice of the Peace: to the end of the Fifth Session of the Sixteenth Parliament of Great-Britain, viz., to July 12, 1788*, 2nd edn, R. Raikes, Gloucester, 1788, pp. ix-xx. The Webbs listed many eighteenth-century handbooks published between 1699 and 1818. Sidney and Beatrice Webb, *English Local Government*, vol. 1, *The Parish and the County* (1906), Cass, London, 1963, pp. 321–55.

[12] Actually, Glasse cannot have allayed their fears very much, emphasising as he did that 'Dr Burn enumerates not less than *twenty* instances, in which an Order of Removal has been, or is liable to be, quashed, on account of some apparently insignificant error in the mere matter of form . . . '. Glasse, *Magistrate's Assistant*, Preface. See the case of Elizabeth Lamb discussed in Chapter 4.

[13] The range of these annotated, indexed and tabulated guides for magistrates was enormous. Some of them included tear-out or fold-out pro forma. They constitute a true development in the history of print and of the book. Burn produced his own *Blank Precedents Relating to the Office of Justice of the Peace, Settled by Doctor Burn, and printed for by the King's Law-Printers . . .* , T. Cadell, London, 1787. See Attorney at Law, *The Attorney's Complete Pocket Book*, 3rd edn, Henry Lintot, London, 1751, Preface, on the want of them in the first half of the century. For networking among magistrates for the better policing of society through effective use of the law to hand, see Joanna Innes, 'Origins of the Factory Acts: The Health and Morals of Apprentices Act 1802' in Norma Landau (ed.), *Law, Crime and English Society, 1660–1830*, Cambridge University Press, 2002, pp. 203–55.

artificers and tax law.[14] The legislation (statute law, or 'law positive') that obliged magistrates to act in disputed employment relations was ancient law. The central state had interested itself in the regulation and policing of labour from the mid-thirteenth century onwards, and re-codified its concerns with wage rates, the management of workers' time, their movement from place to place, their productive capacity and status, in the English Statute of Artificers (1562).

Settlement law was also used as labour law in the local cases brought into King's Bench, as in the example of Lord Mansfield's Women. A timorous magistrate faced with a servant complaining that she had been turned away before her time, that her wages were due; or faced with an employer, perhaps with an eye to the poor rate, who evidently did not want her back to complete the full 365 days... might thumb through his Burn's *Justice* and find 'Servants'. He already knew that 'Under this title are also comprehended labourers, journeymen, artificers, and other workmen', 'Who may be compelled to serve, and for what term. Rating of wages... Time of Working for Labourers... Leaving Work Unfinished... Servant Fleeing into another Hire'; but the magistrate must turn to another section of the guide for the settlement question: 'Concerning the settlement of servants, see title Poor'.[15] In the developing industrial society of eighteenth-century England, says Simon Deakin, 'it was the "poor law" which established... the legal status and condition of those who were dependent on wages for subsistence'.[16] Settlement was key here. Settlement emphasised the place of *contracted* domestic service in achieving it, or 'earning' it, as Lord Chief Justice Mansfield made abundantly clear in 1785, in the case of Charlotte Howe, the slave-servant of Thames Ditton. Settlement acquired through service depended on the hiring, on the verbal or written contract, to work for a year in one place. Being a slave (or *having been* a slave – no one was very clear about what she was), Howe had never been in a position to make a hiring agreement.

Settlement law as employment law preoccupied one Gloucestershire justice, who kept a journal between 1714 and 1756.[17] Francis Welles

---

[14] Hay, 'England, 1562–1875', pp. 59–116.

[15] Richard Burn, *The Justice of the Peace and Parish Officer*, A. Millar, London, 1756, pp. 622–43. This was the first edition; but in the 1790s readers still had to move between sections to find out how they should deal with servants.

[16] Deakin and Wilkinson, *Law of the Labour Market*, p. 47.

[17] It has not been seen since 1861, when an interested local lawyer wrote it up for the *Law Magazine*. Anon., 'The Journal of a Gloucestershire Justice, A. D. 1715–1756. Journal of the Rev. Francis Welles, Vicar of Presbury, Gloucestershire, and Justice of the Peace for the County of Gloucester, A. D. 1715 to 1756. Folio. MS', *The Law Magazine and Law Review or Quarterly Journal of Jurisprudence*, 11 (1861), 125–42; 12 (1861), 99–126; 13 (1862), 247–91. Hereafter Welles, 'Journal'.

wrote it up as a record after quarter sessions (the log of business he transacted as single justice was evidently kept in another, lost notebook). These delayed entries reveal the thinking of his fellow magistrates, as they moved seamlessly between the bodies of law that governed the life of the poor. Welles wrote at greatest length about the settlement cases he heard at quarter sessions, hinting perhaps, at his weariness with the topic with 'There was a Settlement try'd which I think had something new in it.'[18] But was this *really* a settlement, he mused: 'The major part of the Bench was against it being [so] . . . For though a Justice of the Peace might authoritatively dissolve . . . [a] Contract [this one] did not seem much to exert that authority but rather to try to end it amicably between them. And 'twas plain the master did not abide by the determination of the Justice'. He pondered cases in detail:

A maid was hired at Midsummer to Michaelmas, and served that quarter. Then her master treated with her for a year, but they could not agree upon wages; the maid would have fourty shillings, the master would give her but thirty-five shillings. So they parted; but the master told her that iff she could not mend herself [i.e better herself], she might come again upon those terms. She went and hired herself for another year at another place, but staid but eight or nine days, (and received, I think, nothing there,) and came back to her former place, and without making any other bargain than that what was made at Michaelmas, or so much as mentioning anything about their bargain, staid up the year to Michaelmas, and received her year's wages, that is, the thirty-five shillings. The Bench was much divided upon this case . . . But there being a hiring between, and eight or nine days' service upon that hiring, the majority of the Bench was against it being a settlement . . . For all the hiring that the maid had was at Michaelmas, and though she went away and hired herself afterwards, yet she had her master's leave to return again, and so she did. And he, without the least scruple, paid her all her wages as iff she had never went away.

'I am very doubtful how it would go if it were to be removed into the King's Bench', he concluded.[19] The justices' notebooks discussed in this chapter do not show Welles's detail of reasoning, but they all bear witness to an admixture of labour and poor law in magistrates' minds.

Anxieties among lawyers and legislators over the question of whether the Statute of Artificers *really* extended to domestic servants, were of long-standing and on-going. Had magistrates the ability to act when domestic servants, as opposed to servants in husbandry, ran off or complained about their work conditions? There were constant pleas for the Elizabethan legislation regulating service in general to be extended to domestic servants, even into the new century, when more modern and

---

[18] Welles, 'Journal', vol. 12, pp. 111–12 (5 Oct. 1736).
[19] *Ibid.*, Vol. 11, pp. 247–8.

innovative systems of police and regulation had been proposed.[20] Many good authorities believed that a careful reading of the statutes was a way round the problem of regulating the domestic-service relationship; to be sure, 'this Statute 5 Eliz. cap. 4 extended not to *Serving Men*, but to Servants in Husbandry, and Handicrafts: And yet where the Words of any Statute be *Servant* in general, there it seems to extend to all.'[21] Blackstone said that the wages of domestic servants were not within the purview of magistrates because it was impossible for 'any magistrate to be a judge of the employment of menial servants, or ... to assess their wages', but there were many others to say otherwise, and this caution did not stop Shropshire JP Thomas Netherton Parker doing so, right into the 1830s, as this chapter relates. Nineteenth-century legal commentators thought that most eighteenth-century magistrates had behaved like Parker: had assumed, if not believed, the legal fiction that all servants come before them were servants in husbandry and thus exercised jurisdiction over the domestic-service relationship when requested to do so by either party.[22]

Naming a servant as one thing or another – 'menial servant', 'servant in husbandry' – depended on the tribunal in which master and servant were disputing, and on what the parties concerned were after from the law. Decisions about the status of domestic servants only *appear* clearer in King's Bench. The judges made their decisions as they acknowledged the dislocation between the wording of the statutes, and the real, modern,

---

[20] Anon., *Public Nuisances considered under the Several Heads of Bad Pavements, Butchers, infesting the Streets, the Inconveniences to the Publick occasioned by the present Method of Billetting the Foot-guards, and the Insolence of Household Servants ... by a Gentleman of the Temple*, E. Withers, London, 1754; Gentleman of the Inner Temple, *Laws Concerning Master and Servants, Viz Clerks to Attornies and Solicitors ... Apprentices ... Menial Servants ... Labourers, Journeymen, Artificers, Handicraftmen and other Workmen*, His Majesty's Law Printer, London, 1785, p. 241; Thomas Ruggles, *The History of the Poor; their Rights, Duties, and the Laws respecting Them*, 2 vols, J. Deighton, London, 1793, vol. 2, p. 292; Anon., *Reflections on the Relative Situations of Master and Servant, Historically and Politically Considered; the Irregularities of Servants; the Employment of Foreigners; and the General Inconveniencies Resulting from the Want of Proper Regulations*, W. Miller, London, 1800, pp. 1–3, 25.

[21] Michael Dalton, *The Country Justice: Containing the Practice, Duty and Power of the Justices of the Peace, As well in as out of their Sessions*, Henry Lintot, London, 1742, p. 139; Richard Burn, *The History of the Poor Laws. With Observations* (1764), Augustus M. Kelly Press, Clifton NJ, 1973, Postscript; Gentleman, *Laws Concerning Masters and Servants*, p. 2; Richard Burn, *A New Law Dictionary: Intended for General Use, as well as for Gentlemen of the Profession ... Continued to the Present Time, by John Burn, his Son*, 2 vols., Strahan and Woodfall, London, 1792, vol. 2, pp. 325–8.

[22] James Barry Bird, *The Laws Respecting Masters and Servants, Articled Clerks, Apprentices, Manufacturers, Labourers and Journeymen*, W. Clarke, London, 1799, p. 3; Thomas Walter Williams, *The Whole Law Relative to the Duty and Office of a Justice of the Peace. Comprising also the Authority of Parish Officers*, 3rd edn, 4 vols., John Stockdale, London, 1812, vol. 3, p. 893.

social world in which a maidservant worked indoors and out, and was, in her own person, domestic and husbandry servant combined. Employers might decide that calling their servant a husbandryman or woman was the quickest way to make the law operative in their particular case. Doug Hay describes 'a master dealing with a recalcitrant coachman' trying to convince King's Bench that the man was 'really' a servant in husbandry. The master was a Middlesex magistrate, who with one of his colleagues had committed Thomas Brown his livery servant under the legislation that gave 'a jurisdiction to two Magistrates to take into consideration the disputes between master and servants in certain trades and in husbandry'. Brown had walked out after being abused by Mr Reid. Wages were owing and he employed an attorney to bring an action against his former master. His apprehension, incarceration, and flogging was response to this, and constituted a 'gross abuse of the Justices of the County', said his barrister, in a new case. Magistrates Reid and Hyde asserted that they were permitted to act as they did, because Brown was *really* a servant in husbandry who thus fell under 20 Geo. II, c. 19 (1746), employed to work on a toy farm (which may not have actually existed). Brown was quite clear that he had been hired as 'a Coachman, and occasionally to wait at table, and to clean knives and forks'. Brown's improper behaviour in sleeping with a fellow servant was produced as evidence by the defendants in order to claim conspiracy between him and the cook in swearing that he was a household servant.[23]

Appealing against servant-tax assessments brought a different set of definitions and desires – the employers' desire not to be taxed – into play; for were their servant a man or (between 1785 and 1792) a woman by whose labour a living or a profit was earned, then they were exempted. Something was at stake in having a servant named a husbandry servant, though that label might bear little relationship to what he or she actually did, most of the time, by way of work. The Reverend Mr Cutting of Wyke Regis in Dorset appealed against being charged for his servant Robert Pritched. Cutting said he hired the man as a servant in husbandry to take care of his glebe and look after his tithe crops. Pritched *had* occasionally worked in the garden, to be sure; and had looked after Cutting's horse, but had never been employed 'in waiting at table, or other domestic affairs'. The man had been hired by the week since 1774, paid 4s, 'and lodged and dieted' at the appellant's house. If he didn't need a husbandman to

---

[23] Hay and Craven, *Masters and Servants*, p. 89, on the case of Rex v. Reid and Hyde, Esqs; 'Law Report. Court of King's Bench, Nov. 15, Criminal Information, The King, v. Reid and Hyde, Esqrs. Justices of the Peace', *The Times*, 16 Nov. 1796; 'The King, v. Reid and Hyde, Esqrs. Justices of the Peace', 25 Jan. 1797.

look after his glebe, said Cutting, he would not employ him. The local commissioners did not admit this appeal (to them, the man had every appearance of a domestic servant) but Cutting wanted a case stated for the Judges, who were of the opinion that the commissioners were right, that is that Cutting was employing a household servant – a horse-man, a footman, a gardener – in the guise of a servant in husbandry. What was at issue here was Cutting's guinea in tax for the employment of such labour. Had he and Pritched come to words, or Pritched gone off and found another job leaving the work on the glebe land unfinished, and had either of them complained before a magistrate, there would have also been some quite different legal point in calling Pritched a servant in husbandry, had the magistrate in question been particularly timorous in interpreting 5 Eliz. c. 4 (or 20 Geo. II, c.19) and unwilling to deal with a domestic servant or gardener. But the evidence is that Pritched would have been dealt with as the vague, all-encompassing 'servant' that he actually was. In most of the situations discussed in this chapter, 'informal law' ('customs and popular norms of conduct') actually happened in the formal site of the provincial magistrate's justicing room and in the magistrate's mind, as much as they happened in the minds of 'ordinary folk', which is where Peter Karsten has said low law was manifested in the British diaspora between 1600 and 1900.[24]

The first modern Master and Servant legislation was enacted in 1747 – 'modern' in the nineteenth- and twentieth-century use of 'Master and Servant' – to describe a whole complex of laws to regulate the employment relationship, and to provide criminal sanctions against workers (not against employers) for failing to perform what had been agreed at the hiring. An Act of 1758 extended jurisdiction to servants in husbandry hired for less than a year (31 Geo. II c. 11). In 1776 there was legislation making it an offence for a servant to quit before the end of an agreed term. In 1823 (4 Geo. IV c. 90) came new crimes: absconding from work, and refusing to start work that had been agreed between two parties.[25] This legislation was, as Deakin and Wilkinson observe, for the management of labour in an industrialising society – 'the master and servant model was the product of industrialisation' – and it served an industrial society until the 1870s.[26] Enacted for the management of workers in a wide variety of trades, it was used – not always properly or accurately – by masters and magistrates to serve the needs of everyday life. Simply, there were

---

[24] Karsten, *Between Law and Custom*, pp. 14–17.
[25] Deakin and Wilkinson, *Law of the Labour Market*, pp. 62–3, 106.
[26] *Ibid.*, p. 62. See also Stephen Caunce, 'Farm servants and the development of capitalism in English agriculture', *Agricultural History Review*, 45 (1997), 49–60.

more domestic workers than there were textile workers or metal workers. For them and their employers, appeal to law was a necessity; magistrates (some of them) responded, and used legislation that did not in point of law, apply to domestic servants at all. That is why 'the superior authority of King's Bench over master and servant . . . seems hardly to have mattered in many parts of the country',[27] and why a social history of the use of law is more relevant to our purposes than is legal history, useful though that is.[28] Stephen Caunce observes that the tradition of radical social history assumes that legal processes have never had much to offer the poor.[29] But the justices' notebooks discussed below show that in an imperfect world, and under an inequitable legal regime, many of the poor actually did find something useful – occasionally got something – out of legal process. And of course it was an inequitable labour regime. Labour regimes *were* inequitable – that was their characteristic – for all sorts of eighteenth-century thinker. ('Thinker' includes the philosophers of law and labour cited here, *and* the maidservant who was girlfriend to the coachman mentioned above, who, when she was found in his room by their master undressing for bed, remarked that 'as Thomas and she did his business to his satisfaction, she thought it very hard they were not allowed to sleep where they pleased'.[30])

Doug Hay examined sixteen magistrates' notebooks – the kind of record that Samuel Glass urged them to maintain – kept between 1608 and 1850, in order to determine the number of master and servant cases heard by them.[31] One set was kept by Sir Gervase Clifton, bart. (1744–1815) of Clifton Hall in Nottinghamshire; it forms the basis of the following discussion, along with those of Thomas Netherton Parker (d.1848) of Sweeney Hall, two miles south-west of Oswestry in Shropshire. Clifton kept his records between 1772 and 1812; Parker his between 1805 and 1840.[32] Clifton's was a much more haphazard record than Parker's (the latter was a tidy-minded man), filled in by different hands, odd sheets and pages from one notebook bound in the other, random, incomplete

27 Hay, 'England', p. 91.
28 Susan Staves, *Married Women's Separate Property in England, 1660–1833*, Harvard University Press, Cambridge, MA, and London, 1990, p. 10.
29 Caunce, 'Farm servants', p. 56.   30 'Law Report', 26 Jan. 1797.
31 Hay tabulates records of the London Chamberlain's Courts for apprentices (1823–59), and from a mid-nineteenth-century police court and petty sessions. The focus here is the single justice, so these have not been counted in the following discussion. Hay, 'England', pp. 71–9.
32 Nottinghamshire Archives (NA), M 8050, M8051, Notebooks of Sir Gervase Clifton JP, 1772–1812; M 8050 (1772–1812), M 8051 (1805–10); Shropshire Records (SR), 1060/168–171, Justices of the Peace, Justicing Notebook of Thos. N. Parker, 1805–40. Volume 168 ends 23 Jul. 1813; its continuation is 171.

entries, and containing much verbatim evidence from Clifton's own pen. I do not think he was a particularly timorous man or magistrate, but long before Samuel Glass told justices to do so, he had cut out and pasted in sets of blank precedent forms showing eighty forms of procedure, which he attempted to use as an index to the notebook, and a list of warrants that might be executed by the constables. At the beginning of his career he clearly found Burn's *pro forma* useful: there is a list of his 'Blank Precedents' copied out in a hand other than his own. He listed a variety of oaths, and the 'Oath for him who craves the Peace' (as so many Clifton people did; he heard accusations of minor assault, slander, theft and about neighbours from hell, on a regular basis). He prepared himself then, for his role as justice of the peace. He did not start to consistently record his decisions until about 1784; but his notebooks offer a racy read, with a fine line in verbal transcription, especially in cases of domestic violence and sexual assault.[33] Netherton's two notebooks are more organised, date order is reliable, and for the main part they appear to have been filled in by an assistant – a clerk or a secretary – Parker initialling – 'T.N.P' – at the end of a day or a week.

Over the period 1608–1850, Hay found that master and servant cases constituted between 3 per cent and 80 percent of the business transacted before the sixteen justices whose notebooks he consulted. Norma Landau found that in late seventeenth-century Kent, 19 per cent of one rural justice's business involved such disputes.[34] Labour relations preoccupied some magistrates a great deal of the time, some not at all. The published deposition book that Richard Wyatt JP kept in Surrey between 1767 and 1776, contains 317 complete statements (examinations, informations and depositions) contributing to 224 cases. Only six of them were to do with the regulation of service (wage disputes, quitting before time . . .) four of them clearly involving husbandry servants, one a domestic and one indeterminable.[35] Thomas Horner of Mells in Somerset, noted an equally tiny number of master and servant cases between 1770 and 1777 – just four in seven years, out of some two hundred.[36] Between 1819 and 1827 Richard Stileman's (Winchelsea, East Sussex) notebooks show wage disputes and servants' absconding occupying between 8 per cent

---

[33] Some of these are noted by Anne Bloomington, *The Clifton Dynasty: A chronicle of the Cliftons of Clifton Hall, Nottinghamshire*, Authorhouse, Bloomington, IA, 2005, pp. 35–42.

[34] Landau, *Justices*, p. 178.

[35] Elizabeth Silverthorne, *The Deposition Book of Richard Wyatt, JP, 1767–1776*, Surrey Record Society, vol. 30, Guildford, 1978.

[36] Michael McGarvie (ed.), *The King's Peace: The justice's notebook of Thomas Horner, of Mells, 1770–1777*, Frome Society for Local Study, Frome, 1997. The laws of settlement and labour law interacted constantly in Horner's mind and his notebook.

and 68 per cent of his business in any one year (which in any case, were never more than the twenty-eight items he noted in 1824).[37] These tiny figures show minute tremors in local labour markets and in perceived breaches of monetary and moral economies – and also in the nature of a magistrate's business, according to agreements with colleagues about what kind of case to hear, an individual justice's absence from home and employers' and workers' decisions about whether it was worth going to see him. This may have depended on whether or not he had a reputation for being 'ill-humoured; . . . arbitrary in his decisions'. And perhaps, if there was the luxury of this, how well he was understood to know the law.

For current purposes, the thing to be retrieved from these notebooks is magistrates' involvement in domestic employment relationships, so my enumeration of Sir Gervase Clifton's business as a magistrate has been different from Doug Hay's. He was interested in master and servant cases heard by a justice of the peace; I am interested in the regulation of, and intervention, in employment relationships outside the confines of the statutes as well as within them, and in Clifton's (and Nettleton's) adjudication of disputes concerning domestic servants in particular. Over the years covered by Clifton's notebooks, he transacted 195 items of business – as far as it is possible to tell – including the administrative business of being a justice of the peace (swearing in constables, for example). Of these 195 items, 24 were employment cases (13 per cent of Clifton's business) broadly defined. (I have not counted two apprenticeship settlement cases, where the dispute was between the overseers and a master.) Hay reckons Clifton's master and servant cases at 9 per cent; these two percentages are not incompatible, though some might argue that I ought to include some, or all, settlement cases in my category, especially if you accept that the poor laws constituted a form of labour law. But I have not done so, restricting myself to cases in which there was some kind of argument within the employment relationship, between employer and worker. For example, if an employer beat up, assaulted or otherwise ill-treated his servant, or a servant claimed she was not getting food to her liking in her place, I have counted it as something gone wrong, from the perspective of both parties within the relationship and, in the case of domestic servants, within a household. I shall call these cases (and Parker's 194) 'employment cases' from now on; part of the point is to understand domestic service in the context of employment relationships more generally and to see whether or not Clifton and Parker treated domestic workers differently from other categories of labour.

---

[37] East Sussex County Record Office (ESCRO), AMA 6192/1, Notebook of Richard Stileman of Winchelsea, JP, 1819–27.

Half of the employment cases coming before Clifton were inaugurated by masters and half by workers, including domestic servants. Other complaints by servants were heard by Clifton, but not as issues arising from the employment situation. For example, in June 1772, 'Mary Barring of Clifton servant maid to Mrs Lambert [made] complaint . . . that some shepherd lads and a male servant at her place made jest with her as she came from milking & attempt to take her to the [place] where they clip their sheep'. Clifton then noted a serious assault taking place. In October 1788 a serving maid complained of being abused by a serving man near the house where they worked. No names, no outcome: many of Clifton's entries simply record the complaint; somehow, in some way, things were settled, but not by him *as* justice of the peace, though the mere fact of going before him and telling the story must have brought about a result for some of these complainants.[38] One October Tuesday in 1809, Ann Brown, servant to a Barton husbandman, took the harvest men's dinner to the fields, and there 'Everard Whitlock servant man he came up to her he got the Cart whip and beat her over the shoulders kicked her and threw her down and much abused her saying that if she spoke another word he would kill her upon the spot.' What personal histories and antagonisms culminated in this assault were probably as opaque to Sir Gervase as they must be to us. Nothing happened – at least not in his notebook; he merely recorded the complaint. Perhaps the point for Ann Brown was to say what had happened, in a public forum, before a justice. These cases were not to do with the employment relationship. Brown and Barring complained as individuals, not as employees.

In the twenty-four employment cases that Clifton noted, he never, on my reading, found unambiguously for the employee (masters' and servants' unambiguous 'success rate' is the category Hay used for calculation). In three of them the worker got *something* out of it all (*some* wages, a dissolution of contract that he or she evidently wanted), but workers were still liable for costs, and never got the full sums they asked for. On the other hand, Clifton did find unambiguously for the employer in three occasions, and the balance of his determinations went to employers slightly more often than it went to employees. Over half of

---

[38] The diaries of Joseph Woolley, framework knitter of Clifton, provide a mirror to Sir Gervase's account of these cases, in the years when their dairy-keeping coincides (1801, 1803, 1804 and 1809). Woolley's account of goings-on among the poorer sort of Clifton is heavily inflected by the language of the law. He must have spent time in Clifton's justicing room, listening. His reporting of cases like this suggests that making a public statement of a wrong done before a magistrate, was all that some complainants wanted, in bringing the offending party to heel. NA, DD 311/1–6, Diaries of Joseph Woolley, framework knitter. See Carolyn Steedman, 'How to frame everyday life: A framework knitter and the law, 1800–1815', forthcoming.

these employment disputes had no outcome recorded (though much bad behaviour, resentment and ill-treatment was detailed), so it is difficult to come to conclusions about Clifton's behaviour as a magistrate. However, the position of the person complaining may have made a difference to the outcome. In the twelve cases brought by an employer, Clifton determined unambiguously or partially for him or her in six of them. The other six have no recorded outcome.

For workers, things fell out in a different way. In the twelve cases they brought before Clifton, he found partially for only three of them. There were no unambiguous decisions for workers. If they got some of their wages, they might still be responsible for the cost of a summons, or a warrant. Whoever brought the case, employer or worker, was more likely to have a decision in his or her favour, but the evidence of the fragmentary entries in Clifton's notebooks, is that the system was weighted towards the employer. And 'success' (or not) is not a useful category for understanding what Clifton was actually doing here. Both he and Parker attempted a kind of arbitration – they read the wishes and desires of the disputing before them, looked to the law – perhaps – as well, and made a decision that attempted to satisfy both parties. There was not an objective and certain set of rules by which one or other party could win or lose. It was not a game, which is what the term 'success rate' implies it may have been.

Five of Clifton's twenty-four employment cases clearly involved *domestic* servants (though many of the others were called 'servant'). Four of them were brought by the servant. The balance of Clifton's determination went to the employer in one; the other four were not determined or not recorded. This is a small proportion of the employment cases he heard (only 20 per cent), but they are revelatory of the uses of the law in household and working life. In April 1773 Elizabeth Clayton complained about her master turning her away from her service before the end of her time, and for not paying wages due. It had fallen out like this, according to Clifton's transcription: she had been scalded whilst working for the Cheethams (she had been there since the previous November). Her mistress had proffered various remedies 'but she would not take anything when Mrs Cheetham would have had her. and therefore was Disabled the whole time . . . Excepting one month'. Mr Cheetham said he had not *dismissed* her; rather, Clayton had asked him a few days before to send the Boy to fetch her father to take her home, but he hadn't turned up. The Cheethams sent further messages the next day, asking him either to get his daughter some medical treatment, or take her back to Nottingham. She had been hired at £3 a year, they said, and had worked hard when she had been able, but that had been for just one month of the five she

Table 6.1 *Employment disputes before two magistrates, Nottinghamshire and Shropshire, 1772–1840*

	Total items of business	Employment cases	Brought by employer	Brought by worker	Found for employer	Partially for employer	Found for worker	Partially for worker	No outcome
Clifton 1772–1812	195	24 (12%)	12 (50%)	12 (50%)	3 (12.5%)	4 (16%)	0 (0%)	3 (12.5%)	14 (58%)
Parker 1805–40	653	194 (29%)	54 (27%)	140 (73%)	52 (26%)	21 (11%).	50 (25%)	65 (33%)	6 (4%)

Source: Nottinghamshire Archives (NA), M 8050, M 8051, Notebooks of Sir Gervase Clifton JP, 1772–1812, 1805–10; Shropshire Archives (SA), Shrewsbury, 1060/168–71, Justices of the Peace, Justicing Notebooks of Thos. N. Parker, 1805–40.

had spent in their house. Clifton decided for the Cheetham's, noting the sum of £1 4s 6d. Perhaps he worked this out, or it may have been Clayton's calculation. At £3 a year she was earning the equivalent of 1s 1¾d a week; she had been in the house for twenty-three weeks. Was she asking for the full amount for these weeks, which would have amounted to £1 6s 4¼d? Had Clifton decided that she was owed only for the month she'd worked, it would have still amounted to more than 3s 10¼d, which is the difference between the two sums. In his deciding for the employers, we can assume that Clayton got the lower sum.[39] The balance of Clifton's decision favoured Mr and Mrs Cheetham, and they did not have to take her back. Clayton got some of her wages. It is not possible to say that either the Cheethams or Clayton were unambiguously 'successful' here.

This all happened thirty years before Chief Justice Lord Kenyon reminded magistrates and employers that 'a master took a servant for better and for worse; that if a servant, conducting himself properly in the service of his master, and discharging his duty with fidelity, fell sick, the master was bound to pay for medical assistance, and for other necessaries, till he recovered'; but Clifton had Burn and Blackstone in 1777 to indicate that the Cheethams had clearly failed to provide their maid with medical care.[40] Lord Mansfield would say the same in 1785, but with more ambiguity than Kenyon, when a Cambridgeshire settlement case was brought to King's Bench. A young yearly farm servant had suffered severe agricultural injury and his leg had been amputated. The original action was brought by parish officers against the master in an attempt to cover the cost of medical treatment and maintenance for the boy during the time he had been unable to work. Mansfield declared that personally, and in general, he thought that 'a master ought to take care of servants in sickness. Upon every principle of humanity he ought; but the question here [was], Where is the law?'. To which a response might have been, that it was not in remote and uncertainly interpreted statutes, but in the folds and interstices of everyday life and the ordinary operation of the

---

[39] Perhaps Clifton or the Cheethams had to hand the extraordinarily useful *Madam Johnson's Present*, which included 'A Table to cast up Expences, or Wages', or Clifton one of many, more manly ready-reckoners available. Mary Johnson, *Madam Johnson's Present, or every Young Woman's Companion, in Useful and Universal Knowledge*, 4th edn, W. Nicholl, London, 1766, p. 190. You could (and can!) calculate to the farthing using this table; but any servant, earning a wage in which farthings really mattered might have been alarmed to read that 'fractional Parts of a Farthing... are added or omitted, as they exceed or are under Half that Coin'; and also perhaps that months were computed at 28 days.

[40] 'Obligations of Masters Towards their Servants in Sickness', *The Times*, 6 Feb. 1800, p. 3.

law by magistrates and masters.[41] And perhaps in the deeper recesses of Mansfield's legal memory. For back in 1760 Mansfield had himself affirmed that if a servant were 'taken *ill*, by the Visitation of God, It is a Condition incident to Humanity, and is *implied* in all Contracts. Therefor the Master is *bound* to provide for and take Care of the servant so taken ill in his Service . . . '. He had delivered his usual lambastation of the poor laws; he was forced to work with most inadequate law; but the rights and obligations put into train by the hiring could not be circumnavigated: 'I see no Difference between such an Accident of *Sickness* happening in the *Middle*, or . . . at the *End* of the Year: it is equally an Act of God, and without any Fault of the Servant.' This case was reproduced in the law books into the 1800s, long after Mansfield had asked where the law had gone, and Clifton had politely ignored the Cheetham's evasion of it.[42]

In July 1777, John Osborn of Sutton Bonnington, husbandman, appeared before Clifton to make a complaint about his servant girl Ann Townsend. He had a long list. She had got up after the family had gone to bed, 'and let a man into the House and they sat up all night and moreover Mrs Osborn says she lost a petticoat and Sarah Wolley [the other] servant Girl says one morning she and Ann Townsend were dressing thems . . . [she] asked her how she came by the petticoat and she said her Mistress lent it her upon that she said no more of it till her mistress found it in a cradle in the passage and asked her who had been wearing it as it was dirty . . . she then bated with her having wore it she owned she had and said she never would do so again'. There was more. Mrs Osborn said that the week before she had sent Townsend to the baker's to pay for some baking. The charge was 'three pence halfpenny and out of the Sixpence she gave her Mistress two pence and when the servants were ill she went for treacle and mostly kept the change again she said she sent her last Wednesday Sennight to take Butters she said one of her customers had not paid her for the Butters but she took care before last Wednesday to give another sarvant the Butter money lest she should be

---

[41] Edmund Bott, *The Laws relating to the Poor*, 5th edn, 3 vols., London, 1807, vol. 1, pp. 409–20. In fact, by focusing on the poor law – there was nothing to show that any parish had a remedy against a master in a case like this – rather than master and servant law, Mansfield obviated the need for any such question.

[42] James Burrow, *Reports of Cases adjudged in the Court of King's Bench, since the Death of Lord Raymond, in March 1732, to June 1776, inclusive, during which Time Lord Hardwick, Dudley Ryder, and Lord Mansfield presided . . .* , 2nd edn, 5 vols., London, 1790, vol. 2, p. 948–9, summarised at No. 158 in the 'Table of Principle Matters'. Also (Edmund Bott), *The Laws relating to the Poor in which the Statutes and Cases to Easter Term 1807, are arranged under their respective Heads; and the whole System of the Poor's Laws, including the Collections originally made by E. Bott . . .* , 3 vols., J. Butterworth, London, 1807, vol. 1, p. 784–5.

found out . . . '. Here Clifton's clerk made a rapid series of dashes – a recording outwith language – as (presumably) Mrs Osborn paused for breath; and then she was off again:

and she says she has frequently cheated her in the price of Butter by selling her Mistress['s] butter at 10d and accounted to her mistress for eightpence——and Mr & Mrs Osborn says she used to send her to suckle the calves and she has thrown down the milk and shut up the calves without their meals and Joseph Hopwell servant man to Mr Osborn has seen her frequently throw it away and shut them and then saw her beat them with a stick which he said he would tell his Master and he told him it was no business of his and bid him mind his own business.

Clifton recorded no outcome here, but the Osborns certainly had their day in court. Fragments of cases brought by servants, perhaps abandoned after the narration was given, were also without outcome, as in June 1783 when Clifton scrawled 'Mary Yeomans of Wysay servant Girl sixteen years of Age has been in service about three years – was hired at Costock Statutes – was to do anything they [had to do] Burnt at home . . . none'. We have already encountered Mary Cant telling her master when he told her to dress the baby 'that he might dress it himself for she was busy'. She complained to Sir Gervase because he had then thwacked her round the head, and aired her grievance about his failing to employ a second girl to help her, as he had promised at the hiring. No outcome was recorded. Isabba Sharp of Gotham also complained of her working conditions in January 1795 when she explained why she had left her place after only five days: 'the reason was she was to have some body to help her in the place but there was nobody but a wet nurse who did not offer to assist her and the place was too hard for her by herself'. No outcome was recorded by Clifton in this case of a domestic servant 'running off' from a house with a newborn baby in it. Another Gotham maidservant had her say in July 1800 when she complained about her mistress, Mrs Wheatley. The son of the house had sent her out to look for the servant man 'who was gone into the town'. She couldn't find him. Upon return home 'she met her Mrs who said what the Devil are you doing you Nasty Whore and gave her a push into the passage which pushed her down broke her Knuckles and sent her to bed'. No recorded outcome here either, but a good deal of information about Elizabeth Pollard's working conditions and what she felt about them; about the division of authority in this household between mother and son; about her objection to Mrs Wheatley's verbal as well as physical abuse of her.

It is not clear that any of the parties in these disputes expected Clifton to do anything about the conflicts they related (though they may have had their hopes); rather they believed that one of his purposes was to hear them out. Visiting Clifton Hall and stating what had happened before him, might bring into play other, informal systems of disapprobation, censure and punishment. Most of these were not the cases that John Bird and Thomas Williams had in mind when they described how eighteenth-century magistrates would assume that all servants were husbandry servants in order to act in domestic cases, for Clifton did not *act* in the majority of them.[43] He listened to people; he wrote down what they said. Perhaps magistrates, servants and locals understood the justicing system as a forum in which the tensions and tragedies of domestic life could be discussed.

Thomas Netherton Parker was a magistrate of different generation from Clifton, though his situation in the Morda Valley was similar in many ways to Clifton's in the industrialising villages that skirted Nottingham, a jurisdiction in which the problems of many establishing industrial enterprises pressed their labour conflicts upon him. It was by farming that the majority of the local population earned its living, but many mining ventures established themselves here from the 1790s onwards; mills were thrown up along the banks of the Morda for calico printing and for woollen. Supplies of pauper children from Lancashire were delivered to the calico manufacturers in Weston from 1803 onwards. There was an important mill for wool here, a fulling mill at Llanforda by 1797, and corn mills at Maesbury, all employing the labour, some of it migratory, that gave rise to the disputes that Parker heard during his time as a magistrate. Many of the wage cases he heard were complicated matters arising from the systems of subcontracting in coal mines and lime works, and from the internal contracting that the largest calico printers operated.[44] There was modern, infrastructural support for Parker's management of the labour-supply system, that did not pertain in Clifton in late eighteenth-century Nottinghamshire. Oswestry district had professionalised the management of its poor in an unstable labour market. The Oswestry Society for Bettering the Condition of the Poor was founded in 1811; Parker had been subscribing to the London-based society since 1798. He became President of the local branch in 1815. A House of Industry was opened in 1792, conveniently located near Henry Warren's calico printers on the Morda.[45] It was here that apprentice calico workers

---

[43] See note 22.

[44] R. D. Thomas, *Industries of the Morda Valley: Life and labour in the 19th century*, Woodhall, Minshall and Thomas, Oswestry, 1939.

[45] Anon., *The History of Oswestry, From the Earliest Period; its Antiquities and Customs: With a Short Account of the Neighbourhood*, William Price, Oswestry, 1815, p. 118.

were lodged and from which they sometimes ran away, though in the one industrial apprenticeship case brought before Parker, it was the employers who complained to him. In his first month as magistrate in September 1805, Messrs Roberts and Co. complained against 'Mary Evans apprentice for quitting her service'; Parker 'ordered her to return to her work tomorrow morn:g at 6 o'clock, and expenses to be deducted from her wages at . . . the rate of 6d week until the whole is discharged'. The costs had been paid by Mr Roberts; Evans's repayment of 6s included them, and 2s for being two weeks absent.[46]

Parker was a modern magistrate, a proto-Victorian professional, sewn into the administrative structure of the county. He had been appointed deputy lieutenant of Shropshire in 1803, before joining the commission of the peace.[47] He thought about these things, of himself as a practical man, and the disorganised – chaotic – lives and labour arrangements that were recounted to him in the justicing room. He was moved to write a treatise on gates before he became a magistrate, so irritated was he by straying livestock, people trespassing after cattle and pounds left open or easily broken into. Gates were not a topic to set the heart racing, he admitted: among readers of the 'more abstruse researches of art and science . . . economy and convenience in things of daily necessity is less regarded and slow of improvement'; but his book 'actually involve[d] consequences of considerable moment'.[48] It was a highly practical treatise; but it did no good; he spent thirty years in what looks like high irritation at the steady stream of cases caused by badly hung and inadequately fastened gates.

Between 1805 and 1843, Parker recorded dealing with 653 pieces of magistrate's business (see Table 6:1). They should be called this, as in Nottinghamshire, rather than 'cases'. If we remove the swearing in of constables, militia business, and the inspection of poor-law accounts, then 609 items of business passed through his notebooks. But this brief assessment of his work is made with the total of magisterial business in mind: 194 employment cases, broadly conceived. More workers brought

---

[46] For the Society see John Riddoch Poynter, *Society and Pauperism*, Routledge and Kegan Paul, London, 1969, pp. 91–8; Joanna Innes, 'Politics and morals: The late eighteenth-century reformation of manners' in E. Hellmuth (ed.), *The Transformation of Political Culture. Late Eighteenth-century England and Germany*, Oxford University Press for the German Historical Institute, Oxford, 1990, pp. 57–118; Innes, 'Origins of the Factory Acts'.

[47] For county elites' self-identity through philanthropy and local government work, Richard H. Trainor, *Black Country Elites: The exercise of authority in an industrialised area 1830–1900*, Clarendon Press, Oxford, 1993, pp. 354–93.

[48] Thomas N. Parker, *An Essay on the Construction, Hanging and Fastening of Gates*, 2nd edn, Lackington, Allen, London, 1804.

complaints to Parker than they did to Clifton in Nottinghamshire. Many categories of worker, often new to Morda Valley, turned to the local magistrate in pursuit of their wages. This was a much more heterogenous workforce than Clifton dealt with, and Parker saw many more of them than Clifton ever did. Of these 140 workers, only 5 were unambiguously domestic servants (3 per cent). But the notebook recorded the vocabulary of 'service', 'hiring', 'return to her service' in a further fifty-one cases; many of these workers may have been domestic servants. (These five domestic workers will be shortly discussed, along with another five who were almost certainly so.) About 60 per cent of complaints were bought by employees for whom there is practically no information, only that they had been labouring at the limekilns, or were a waggoner just wanting to get paid for a morning's carting. On my reading of the notebooks, Parker only found unambiguously for the employee in a quarter of these cases, that is 25 per cent of workers got their full wages, did not have to pay costs, or got away from a work situation that they evidently wanted to leave (which was however, a much better outcome for them than it was for Clifton workers). And Parker only found unambiguously for the employer in a quarter of cases (26 per cent) as well. Of the remaining ninety-two cases, six were undetermined (4 per cent) – they were referred to another magistrate, or a really complicated new wages arrangement was agreed before Parker.

Of the remaining eighty-six items of employment business, the balance of Parker's determination went to the master on only twenty-one occasions (11 per cent). It could be argued that Parker's judgments favoured employees, if getting tiny wages but having to pay all or most of the costs, shows favour to the worker. Or going back to a place a servant has left because his master broke his arm, but getting a better wages agreement on so doing, as a 'favour' to the employee, and all arranged before Parker. As for the question of determination in relation to which party brought the case, things went on much as they had done in Clifton's Nottinghamshire jurisdiction: whichever party brought the case, they were more likely to have an outcome in their favour, but the system was weighted towards the employer.

As far as domestic servants were concerned, Parker made decisions inverse to those he made for farm and industrial workers. There were ten of these (possibly far more), four brought by employers and six by servants. Parker found for employers (entirely, or mostly) in 30 per cent of cases; for the servant in 70 per cent. Domestic servants, in the Oswestry district under Parker's jurisdiction, had more favourable decisions made for them than the generality of workers (though 'favourable' and 'better' can scarcely be how they saw it). It is so difficult to determine who was actually a domestic servant that discussion here certainly underestimates their number.

As a single justice, Parker was permitted by 6 Geo. III c. 25 (1766) to send to the House of Correction any servants who absented themselves before their term was up. Parker used this sanction – or the threat of it – three times during his early years on the bench. In September 1805 he heard the complaint of 'Messrs Roberts & Co. against Edward Jones, a hired servant for a year, at the Factory'. He had been absent for three months. Parker ordered Jones to return to his work by next Monday morning and to pay costs; he noted that 'This being the 2nd offence I pledged my hnor to Edw Jones that I would commit him to the house of correction if he were guilty of the like again'. In July 1806 he actually committed a husbandry servant for a month. One insistent girl avoided committal in August 1813. Probably another husbandry servant (as far as the title applied to female servants), Jane Jones complained against Mrs John Marlow for her wages. Parker released her from her service, 'and fined her a quarter's wages, as she would not go back to her service and was very obstinate'. Unusually, he recorded the thinking behind his decision: 'Jane Jones was only 19 years of age, and I therefore objected to send her to the House of Correction . . .'. Obstinate, determined and vocal young women could have some small effect on the operation of the law, as Clifton's notebook also shows.

In the very first employment case he heard, Parker operated with very old law, and very old assumptions indeed. Three months into office in July 1805, he heard 'the business Edward Minshall . . . against Mary Hughes for quitting his service, being hired from 1st May last as Dairy maid for one year'. She had been gone two weeks and the constable had been out for three days in search of her at some considerable cost. Minshall really wanted her back. Netherton's ability to proceed with a complaint like this was in no doubt. A dairymaid (though all the evidence was that she did a great many other things besides milking and butter making) was easy to conceptualise as a servant in husbandry (tax law had done so also). He 'ordered that she return to Mr Minshall's service tomorrow . . . No wages to be paid for the fortnight's service by Mr Minshall'. The employer paid the costs, which amounted to 9s 6d; he was 'to deduct the same out of Mary Hughes's wages, who is to serve him from 31st July 1805 to 1 May 1806'. But in 1808, by no stretch of the magisterial imagination could Jane Evans, servant to Mr Owen of Wiggington, be thought of as a servant in husbandry, for Parker ordered her to return to her service which was 'to take care of the children, make the beds, and milk . . . [and] to do such work as may be reasonable'. (Young women like her had been called farm servants for the occasion, for at least the century past.) She

Table 6.2 *Decisions made for domestic servants by two magistrates, Nottingham and Shropshire, 1772–1840*

	Total employment cases	Involving domestic servants	Brought by employer	Brought by servant	Partially for employer	Partially for servant	No outcome
Clifton 1772–1812	24	5 (20%)	4 (80%)	1 (20%)	1 (20%)	(0) (0%)	4 (80%)
Parker 1805–40	194	10 (5%)	4 (40%)	6 (60%)	3 (30%)	7 (70%)	

Source: Nottinghamshire Archives (NA), M 8050, M 8051, Notebooks of Sir Gervase Clifton JP, 1772– 1812, 1805–10; Shropshire Archives (SA), Shrewsbury, 1060/168–71, Justices of the Peace, Justicing Notebooks of Thos. N. Parker, 1805–40.

had left because she found the work too much for one woman. Parker noted that her wages were to be two guineas a year up to Christmas (it was now July), and that Mr Owen intended 'to keep another servant'. Costs were 6s, which though he paid them now, Owen was to deduct from Evans's wages.

Local domestic servants were clear about what constituted a reasonable workload and reasonable wages, and what work conditions ought to be like. In July 1806, Elizabeth Griffiths servant to Samuel Jackson complained for her wages, 'She was hired from 17 May till Christmas at the rate of £5 a year', noted Parker; 'She is to return to her service this eve'g... and to have 5 days deducted for wages – Wm Jackson agreed to accept six weeks warning from this 22 July when Eliz Griffiths should be at her liberty to quit her service'. The trouble had been the food: 'Mr Jackson promised that she should have a sufficient quantity of bread and common vegetables, the want of which was the ground of her complaint... [she] admitted that her master allowed her plenty of good butchers meat'. Elizabeth Humphreys also came to Parker in February 1810 to get her wages out of Mrs Jennings of Penylan. 'She is to return to her service... tomorrow by 12 o'clock' he decided, 'and no deducting for the days which she has been absent from her wages.' Moreover, 'Mrs Jennings agreed to allow her 1s a week more... for such time as there was not a girl under her to assist her in the work...'. His jurisdiction over the employment relationship and the life of households – servants' households as well as employers' – was considerable. A few months later, in June, he heard from Mary Hughes, hired to serve Mr John Hopkins of Woolstone 'as a kitchen maid and to feed the pigs etc' at 5 guineas a year. She was ill and had gone home. She should be allowed to stay with her mother till she was fit to return to her service, Parker recorded; she should give Mr Hopkins a week's notice when she was well enough to go back to work 'during the present year till 1st May 1811, and offer herself to him if he chuse to receive her and pay the due proportion of her wages till 1st May next'. Moreover 'she should be allowed to go out to work at her needle or otherwise during her illness, without such employment being considered as evasion of this agreement with Mr Hopkins'. How else was a young woman to get her living? She was to be responsible for costs. In July 1811, another maidservant complained to him for her wages. She had been turned away on suspicion of being pregnant. The employer was 'to take the girl again if she is not with child and pay expenses – if she is with child she is to leave [his]... service and to pay expenses'. (Perhaps Hannah Wright from 1770s Derbyshire occupied his legal imagination here; her case was available in the justices' manuals.) Nettleton made his usual minute calculations, reckoning up a gown she had from her master worth 13s 6d. Sometimes his notes show a concern with how servants were actually to get their money. In December 1840, he recorded that Mrs Thomas Davies undertook to leave the 4s 4¾d due her former servant 'at John Vaughans of the Pants before the 1st Jany'. Parker's grasp of the wage relationship was practical and minute, but parties were not bound by his calculations. In November 1815 he heard 'Elen Williams v Mr Bickerton of Dandford for wages'. She was to return to her service, and to conduct herself obediently, he determined; no wages were to be deducted for the few days she had been absent. Sometime later the pair appeared before him again – perhaps immediately after they had both aired their grievance – and he heard that they had come to another kind of arrangement: 'that she should have £1 as 2 months wages, instead of notice, and £3 for her half years wages, and she was discharged from her service and the money was paid'. They would have had to come back to the justicing room, so that Parker could formally discharge her.

Parker had an informal notion of workplace injury and compensation. In August 1817, Elizabeth Evans pressed for her wages from Mr Radcliffe 'she having scalded her feet in his service – ordered her half a year's wages £2 2s 6d and discharged her'. This was indeed cheaper for Radcliffe than having a maidservant lie up at his house for six months and having to pay the doctors' bills (bills that had at least crossed the Nottinghamshire Cheethams' mind in 1773). Mr Radcliffe appears not to have contemplated medical treatment at all, and to have thought that he need not pay his servant wages due. How much everyday, deliberate violence domestic servants accepted as part of the job, is not known, but the evidence is – not much. William Evans, servant boy to Mr Davies of Kinnerley complained that his master had struck him 'with his fist on his chin for misbehaviour' in January 1814. Parker's brief note suggests that all three of them, master, servant and magistrate knew when a line had been crossed, for 'Mr Davis gave the boy 2s 6d'. In 1841, when a boy complained of his master's beating him, he saw to it that 'Mr Holditch of Freflach gave him 5s'.

Parker operated a more rigid, 'criminalised' labour regime, at least during the latter half of his time as magistrate, than had Clifton in Nottinghamshire, not as a result of legislation but because of changing social practice in relation to the civil law.[49] Writing 'a history of the middle and working classes' in 1833 (on the very eve of the Poor Law Amendment Act), John Wade thought that these changes were related to the poor law,

[49] Hay, 'England', p. 106.

not to labour law. In the case of servants in husbandry, he said 'the practice of *hiring for a year*, by which the master became bound to maintain his
servant for a twelvemonth, in sickness or in health' was not so common as
formerly. To evade settlement, Wade said, employers made sure that there
never was a hiring in the first place, or that it was for less than a year.[50]
The employment of domestic workers by the hour, day, or week, that
Frances Hamilton undertook towards the new century, may have been
the result of very similar calculations. In a changing social situation, in
which masters managed their employment arrangements in new ways,
the kind of decision that was required of Parker served to bring about the
'new' picture that someone like Wade was able to provide a history for,
in 1833. But Parker did not in fact, change his practice very much over
the years. His last 'sickness' case was in 1833. In April Charles Paddock
(probably a household servant) complained to him for his wages. He had
gone sick in January, left his place with an inflamation of the lungs. He
had served since July 1832. The agreement had been 30s 'till may' – that
is less than a year. 'Mrs Humphreys sent him no assistance during his illness', noted Parker. He worked out exactly what was owing to Paddock –
in one of the entries where the outcome is entirely unclear. Technically
legal handbooks might tell him that he should not do this, for Paddock's
was not a yearly hiring; but he did so. There is no telling if Paddock
got his money or not. Charles Paddock, forever in the historical limbo
of *our* not knowing whether he got his wages or not is an appropriate
conclusion to this account of the way in which working people used the
law to navigate the exigencies of life. So too did magistrates use what law
there was – work with an uncertain set of legal promulgations – to further
the interests of some of the parties who sought their aid. We could call
this 'informal law', or even see English magistrates operating the kind of
customary law that is supposed to have emerged in the wider societies of
the British diaspora in the face of promulgated 'high law'.[51] Yet Thomas
Parker *was* a magistrate, and he worked within the framework of formal
law but by using its gaps, spaces and ambiguities as much as its prescriptive statements. He had no power to enforce his decisions, neither in the
abstract by the statutes, nor by the practical agency of a police force.[52]

---

[50] John Wade, *History of the Middle and Working Classes: with a popular Exposition of the
economical and political Principles which have influenced the past and present Condition of the
Industrious Orders*, E. Wilson, London, 1833, p. 391.
[51] Karsten, *Between Law and Custom*, pp. 498–540.
[52] Lord Mansfield was perpetually irritated at JPs administering law solely in regard to the
local case before them without recourse to general principle. This 'amounted to saying
there was no Rule at all': 'It is Important in most Cases that the Law shou'd be certain

Nevertheless, it was with the category 'servant' that profound thinking about the policing of society was undertaken (that is the topic of the next chapter). Some of this thinking underlay systems of police that were to emerge in the nineteenth century.

than what the Law is.' Scone Palace (SP), Murray Family Papers, Earls of Mansfield, NRA(S)0776, Box 68, King's Bench Papers. He was discussing the poor law here, but his irritation held good for many categories of magistrates' business.

7   Policing society

'Policing' meant – and means here – the internal good ordering and management of society. In contemplating the defective state of police in eighteenth-century England, the agencies to accomplish its amelioration – police forces – were as yet only dimly imagined by legislators, magistrates and social commentators. But domestic servants – such a large group of workers, so noticeable, already within the purview of the law, sometimes counted, listed and registered – *were* conceived of as a possible means to order and management. A first strategy was to police them, as a means towards the policing of society.

A Proposal for the Amendment of Servants of 1752 concluded on a comparative note, looking to arrangements across Europe, suggesting that 'those Countries will bid most fair for Happiness, where the best Regulations are made, or (if you like that Phrase better) where the best *Police* is established'.[1] Here was a scheme for the policing of domestic life by which private citizens (employers) would be brought together for a public purpose – to manage the domestic service sector 'without the Terrors or Fetters of the Law'.[2] In essence, the proposal concerned a savings and banking system for London servants. There would also be a subscription fund for employers, the monies to be dispensed as prizes to servants who had 'lived long in a place'. It was open to 'all Sorts of Servants, of

---

[1] Anon., *A Proposal for the Amendment and Encouragement of Servants*, J. Shuckburgh, London, 1752, p. 33.
[2] Anon., *Proposal*, p. 15.

both Sexes', provided they were domestics and had lived with the same family for some time. They were to pay in their money but not to apply for it until they had served three years (though graded *ex gratia* rewards were available for those who managed to make it to the end of just one). Servants could let their money accumulate for longer if they wished, and they were permitted to will it. The gentlemen managing the system would call themselves the Society for the Encouragement of Honest and Industrious Servants. The committee would meet every Thursday; it would manage by a variety of means, not just by holding servants' monies. Servants would manage their own employment record, marshalling it into a kind of autobiography, or testimonial: 'a Narrative, of Information, containing an Account of his or her Service' (when, where, how long, with whom – 'in what Quality'); this must be underwritten 'by two substantial Persons'. It must be in writing – this was important. Servants must register themselves on 'the Books of the Society', giving notice of each new situation. There would be a small fee for registration. It really did not matter that beginnings were so modest, nor that the scheme was constructed on such a slender actuarial base; 'the very Name of such a Society would have a good Effect and bind [servants], as it were, to their good Behaviour'.[3] And why confine this system to the Metropolis? Why not try it in the major provincial cities? Indeed, there were existing schemes like this around the country, 'as at Canterbury, Oxford and some other Places', but small-scale ones indeed, being the experiments of benevolent local notables. In their proposals the gentlemen of the Society said that they had only 'very lightly touched, any Arguments drawn from that . . . Charity, or Compassion (call it what name you please) which is due to Persons in inferior Status, from those who are blessed with more easy Fortunes'; what induced them to make their proposals was not 'a Tenderness for Persons in low Life . . . [more] the great Utility we foresee in such a Design to the Publick'.[4] But they had some insight into the servant's position. Society members knew that 'Service is No Inheritance', that is to say, that wages did not tend to increase from year to year, and that it was difficult to accrue savings in boxes and stockings kept under beds in unsecured rooms.

The system was designed to encourage the type of servant employers wanted; but theirs was not the apoplectic rant about the 'public nuisance' of servants published two years later. In this second pamphlet, all servants lived the life of Riley and had 'really nothing but a very easy Duty, to perform'. But could you get them to 'behave with Humility and Obedience

---

[3] Anon., *Proposal*, p. 15.   [4] Anon., *Proposal*, p. 29.

to their Superior as becomes their Station'? No. You could not.[5] There were summary laws for when a servant had a problem, said the pamphleteer, but absolutely none for 'Breaches of Duty and Respect towards the Master'. These offences were 'not Breaches of the publick Peace, properly so called yet they are great Offences against the Government and Peace of a Family, and therefore ought likewise to be provided for and punished in a proper and summary Way'. The author was not the first and would not be the last to propose a legal solution: he made yet another plea for the extension to domestics of the Elizabethan Acts regarding husbandry servants. This would 'produce in the Household Servant, what it does in the Husbandry Servant, a suitable Humility and Observance of their Duty towards those they serve and keep good Order in the Master towards them'.[6] Legal men might remind private gentlemen that law cannot operate on 'Manners' (on culture), but for the main part, private gentlemen took no notice.[7] In 1692, John Locke's friend, Somerset MP Edward Clarke had annotated in great detail a proposal for a 'Publick Office for Registering Servants'. Clarke knew about the possibility of extending 5 Eliz. to domestic servants, but had in mind an altogether more considered and sophisticated plan than the anonymous pamphleteer was to propose in 1754.[8] Registration was a constant feature of these schemes. If only, said another complainant in 1785 – he had been considering the extension of 5 Eliz. by 20 Geo. 2 c.19 and 31 Geo. 2 c.11 – 'If instead of Servants in Husbandry . . . it had been said servants in general, it would have extended the Law to all Domestic servants whatever, and have subjected them as well as their Masters and Mistresses, to have their Misconduct and Misbehaviour and Disputes about Wages, etc. to be inquired into. The Body of Domestic Servants is very large, and at present without any Regulation . . . '.[9] Country gentlemen and magistrates continued

---

5 Anon., *Public Nuisances considered under the Several Heads of Bad Pavements, Butchers, infesting the Streets, the Inconveniences to the Publick occasioned by the present Method of Billetting the Foot-guards, and the Insolence of Household Servants . . . by a Gentleman of the Temple*, E. Withers, London, 1754, p. 40.

6 Anon., *Public Nuisances*, pp. 40–42.

7 Ralph Heathcote, DD, *The Irenach: or, Justice of the Peace's Manual. II Miscellaneous Reflections upon Laws, Policy, Manners &etc &etc. In a Dedication to William Lord Mansfield. III An Assize Sermon Preached at Leicester, 12 Aug. 1756*, privately printed, London, 1781, p. 118.

8 Somerset County Record Office (SCRO), DD/SF 1678 (22), Parliamentary papers and pamphlets of Edward Clarke, MP for Taunton, 'The Usefulness of, and Reasons for a Publick Office for Registering Servants' (handbill, printed notice, annotated by EC 1692).

9 Gentleman of the Inner Temple, *Laws Concerning Master and Servants, Viz Clerks to Attorneys and Solicitors . . . Apprentices . . . Menial Servants . . . Labourers, Journeymen, Artificers, Handicraftmen and other Workmen. By a Gentleman of the Inner Temple*, His Majesty's

to look for legislative opportunities to extend husbandry-servant provisions to domestic servants. When Thomas Gilbert's poor-law bill was before Parliament in 1786, the recorder of Derby, JP Sir William Fitzherbert, inquired whether this might not be an opportunity to 'subject menial servants to the same Law as Servants in Husbandry'?[10] No, was the opinion of the Home Secretary, and 'here the attempt must end'.[11] But it did not.

The poor laws *were* a system of police, present and potential, as far as many provincial magistrates were concerned. In his *History of the Poor* one of Thomas Ruggles's intentions was to 'throw out some observations and offer a few strictures on the duties and conduct for the domestic menial servants of this kingdom'. His police plans would not involve servants in husbandry, trade or manufacture – these were already regulated by act of Parliament – only those who were necessary to 'the arrangements of domestic economy'. The only attempts to legislate for their regulation had been in 1529 and 1792 (the last with legislation making the issuing of false references an offence), he said. He evoked the farce *High Life Below Stairs*. No one had ever disputed its 'exactness of... representation'. It showed exactly what he meant by 'arrangements of domestic economy': in life as on the stage any 'master in the rank of private life must submit to similar depredations, or clean his own shoes'. Maidservants might be policed by some method analogous to the female servant tax, Ruggles

Law Printer, London, 1785, p. 241; John Fielding, *A Plan of the Universal Register-Office, Opposite Cecil-Street in the Strand & of That in Bishops Gate-Street the Corner of Cornhill. Both by the Same Proprietors*, privately printed, London, 1752. See Miles Ogborn, *Spaces of Modernity: London's geographies, 1680–1780*, Guilford Press, New York, London, 1998, pp. 201–38.

10 Thomas Gilbert, *A Bill, intended to be Offered to Parliament, for the better Relief and Employment of the Poor, and for the Improvement of the Police of this Country*, Harrop, Manchester, 1787; Derbyshire County Record Office (DCRO), D239, M/0134, Sir William Fitzherbert, JP, Recorder of Derby, letter from Thomas Coltman, 17 Feb. 1787. Doug Hay reports Home Secretary Lord Sydney saying that 'the Lords would never suffer such a power to be given as might subject them to be summoned by a Servant.... such a controul would have very good consequences but the objections of the Lords is not to be removed'. 'England, 1652–1875', Douglas Hay and Paul Craven, *Masters, Servants and Magistrates in Britain and the Empire, 1562–1955*, University of North Carolina Press, Chapel Hill and London, 2004, p. 90.

11 Gilbert's many proposals for management of the poor, were all conceived as schemes of police. Thomas Gilbert, *A Plan of Police: exhibiting the Causes of the present Increase of the Poor, and proposing a Mode for their future more effectual Relief and Support*, privately printed, London, 1781, (2nd edn 1787). Richard S. Tompson, Gilbert, Thomas (bap. 1720, d. 1798) in *Oxford Dictionary of National Biography*, Oxford University Press, 2004, www.oxforddnb.com/view/article/10703, accessed 31 Jan. 2007. Poor law *as* police was a common perception. See R. Potter, *Observations on the Poor Laws, on the Present State of the Poor, and on Houses of Industry*, J. Wilkie, London, 1775, pp. 30–1 on the poor laws as a 'civil police', and 'starving, naked, unshelter'd miserable Poor' as a disgrace to 'our interior police'.

thought. That actual legislation had certainly not been productive nor popular; but a percentage charged on both male and female servants could be held by employers, and the monies forfeited if he or she left before time.[12] The attempt to extend husbandry servant regulations to domestic servants continued. In 1800, there existed still 'the necessity for establishing some more coercive system of police for domestic servants'. 'It [was] a wonderful thing', said another anonymous pamphleteer, that 'our stupendous pile of statutes does not contain one article of regulation for servants, except some antiquated statutes before the reformation'. What was wrong with applying 'the whole of that excellent statute [5 Eliz.] and that of 20 Geo III to our menial servants'?[13] Of course, that might give magistrates – many of them of inferior status – 'a power to interfere in families'; but needs must. Here the regulatory imagination did not extend beyond the expansion of existing legislation.

In the very large number of schemes produced for the management of domestics from 1770 onwards, local magistrates were the nodal point of imagined systems, just as they were of existing ones. They constituted a police in themselves, in their daily operation of (inadequate) poor and labour law. This understanding of government and good ordering was to endure well into the nineteenth century and after the establishment of paid, professional police forces in the English provinces. Most eighteenth-century 'improvers' were themselves magistrates, practised in the policing of local communities with the law they had to hand (or none at all).[14]

It is not clear whether or not the Society for the Encouragement of... Servants transmogrified, forty years later, into the Society for the Encrease and Encouragement of Good Servants (founded in 1792) nor whether London's servants had deposited their savings, registered their employment details, and received gratuities for sheer-staying power, for these forty years. It rather looks as if the 1752 Society went the way of many similar small-scale, provincial police experiments of the

---

[12] Thomas Ruggles, *The History of the Poor; their Rights, Duties, and the Laws respecting Them*, 2 vols., J. Deighton, London, 1793, vol. 2, pp. 246–55.

[13] Anon., *Reflections on the Relative Situations of Master and Servant, Historically and Politically Considered; the Irregularities of Servants; the Employment of Foreigners; and the General Inconveniencies Resulting from the Want of Proper Regulations*, W. Miller, London, 1800, p. 25.

[14] John Scott, *Observations on the Present State of the Parochial and Vagrant Poor*, Edward and Charles Dilly, London, 1773; Henry Zouch, *Hints Respecting the Public Police, Published at the Request of the Court of Quarter Sessions held at Pontefract, April 24, 1786*, John Stockdale, London, 1786, p. 10; William Man Godschall, *A General Plan of Parochial and Provincial Police*, T. Payne, London, 1787, pp. 7–9; Ruggles, *History of the Poor* (1793); Carolyn Steedman, *Policing the Victorian Community*.

Figure 15. 'Hiring a Servant' The gentlemen of the Society for the Encrease of Servants (1792) intended to professionalise the recruitment of domestics. (And perhaps diminish this kind of innuendo.)

earlier century. The new Society of 1792 used a similar banking system and prize-giving for long-serving men and women; its office was kept open at regular hours for servants to register themselves; but it did not undertake to keep servants' savings. It was a professional, and professionally organised body: its secretary John Huntingford said that he had done 'deep researches' at the planning stage; he provided a history of service in England from before the Conquest as introduction to the scheme.[15] It was not a benevolent society, but rather a superior kind of employment agency – and a system of police. Huntingford said that 'a settled form of the certificate of a servant's character' was the most important aspect of the scheme. The servant's reference would be written by the employer on a form provided by the Society; only servants with properly completed forms might register. 'Long and approved service in the family of a subscriber, or of two or more subscribers successively', would entitle a servant to relief, if by 'sickness, accidents or infirmities of old age' he or she became unfit for work.[16] Ladies, in relationship to their female servants, were targeted. 'Public societies' were not generally open to gentlewomen, for they only 'extended to objects which cannot with propriety fall within the reach of female patronage'; but here was a fine way for them to contribute a 'share to the common stock, for the encouragement of . . . female servants'.[17]

Another Huntingford (it is not known if the two were related) had acted for one of the several provincial agricultural societies attempting to police labour and service by prize-giving during the 1780s. James Huntingford was secretary to the Society for the Encouragement of Agriculture and Industry, at Odiham in Hampshire, which was formed in 1783.[18] During its first years of operation, it had devoted most of its energies to agricultural production, to ploughing in particular, and producing better

[15] John Huntingford, *The Laws of Masters and Servants Considered; with Observations on a Bill intended to be offered to Parliament, to prevent the forging and counterfeiting of Certificates of Servants [sic] Characters. To which is added an Account of a Society formed for the Encrease and Encouragement of Good Servants*, privately printed, London, 1792, p. iv.

[16] Huntingford, *Laws of Masters and Servants*, p. 109–122.

[17] Huntingford, *Laws of Masters and Servants*, p. 116.

[18] James Huntingford, *An Account of the Proceedings, Intentions, Rules, & Orders of the Society for the Encouragement of Agriculture and Industry, instituted at Odiham in Hampshire. To which is added, A List of the Society's Premiums, the Society's Queries, and the Names of Servants that have obtained Certificates of Good Characters . . .* , Frys and Couchman, London, 1785 (1786); Barry Stapleton, 'Inherited poverty and life-cycle poverty: Odiham, Hampshire, 1650–1850', *Social History*, 18:3 (1993), 339–55. For James Huntingford, Anon., *Browne's General Law-list; for the year 1779*, 3rd edn, privately printed, London, 1778, p. 187; also Reynold Gideon Bouyer, *An Account of the Origin, Proceedings, and Intentions of the Society for the Promotion of Industry, in the Southern District of the Parts of Lindsey, in the County of Lincoln. . . . The third edition. . . . To this edition is also added, a report of the Board of Trade to the Lords Justices, . . . by Mr. John Locke*, privately printed, Louth, 1789.

and more skilful ploughmen by distributing prizes and exciting – so the gentlemen of the Society believed – a spirit of 'industry, attention and emulation' among them. But part of their aim was also to encourage 'diligence and honesty' in servants of both sexes, not just those employed in husbandry. They advertised in the *Reading Mercury*, asking employers to issue their deserving servants with certificates of good behaviour. The Society published the names of the ninety-eight servants recommended in this way. Exactly half of them were domestics, the other forty-nine being made up of ploughmen, carters, threshers, labourers etc. The domestic forty-nine were listed as 'housekeepers' (six of these), male and female 'upper servants', cooks and dairymaids (one woman combined the two functions), one nursemaid, one kitchen maid, a groom, a coachman, five footmen (one was also a gardener), and twenty housemaids, by far the largest category of certificated domestic servants. Length of service among these last twenty women ranged from one year to twenty-one years, the most usual length of service being three. It is the assumptions and wishes of employers across the Odiham-Basingstoke district we should look to here, rather to those of their servants. A certificate of good behaviour may have been a pleasant thing to possess, and certainly useful on the labour market; but the labour market was precisely the place that employers did not want their servants to go, in bestowing on them such praise; they wanted their maidservant to stay put, for twenty-one years if possible. Servants got nothing, really, out of the Odiham reward system – not, for example, the guinea that the girl 'under fourteen . . . who in the space of four weeks . . . earne[ed] the most in spinning worsted yarn', nor even one of the smaller premiums for less-productive spinners, let alone the three guineas that the best ploughman received. Henry Fielding (whose magistrate brother knew much about rewards to servants) had Deborah Wilkins, the housekeeper in *Tom Jones*, brood on the question of what is the best 'Encouragement to Servants to be Honest'; it is certainly not the likes of a certificate; it is money that does it.[19] Individual gentlemen – who were also magistrates – tried prize-giving and gratuities on their own estates, reporting varying results.[20]

---

[19] See note 9. Henry Fielding, *The History of Tom Jones, a Foundling. In three volumes*, John Smith, Dublin, 1749, vol. 1, p. 241.

[20] Thomas Ruggles, *The History of the Poor; their Rights, Duties, and the Laws Respecting Them. A New Edition Corrected, and continued to the present Time*, W. Richardson, 2 vols., London, 1797, vol. 1, pp. 94–100, vol. 2, pp. 35, 161, 232–44. Ruggles mentioned other schemes from around the country, but they were box-clubs or friendly societies – insurance systems – and did not offer *ex gratia* financial rewards. Thomas Haweis, *Hints Respecting the Poor: submitted to the Consideration of the Humane and Intelligent*, C. Dilly, London, 1788.

The 1792 London Society promoted legislation to regulate the writing of references – 'characters' – for servants. Its first publication included 'observations on a Bill intended to be offered to Parliament, to prevent the forging and counterfeiting of Certificates of Servants', which Charles James Fox introduced in March 1791, along with a petition from the householders of London and Westminster, concerned about robberies committed by servants with forged characters.[21] This was substantially what became law in the following year.[22] Concerns here were shady and dodgy registry offices – well-organised thieves' kitchens, as far as some London householders were concerned – though the first conviction under the new legislation actually occurred in Liverpool, 'where a woman being detected in an attempt to put off a false certificate was fined £20, but not being able to pay it was committed to prison for six months'.[23] Register offices had been housebreakers' employment agencies in the dramatic imagination for a very long time indeed.[24] But 'the only good I ever saw in [the] statute', said the author of *Reflections on . . . Masters and Servants* in 1800, was that 'it sanctioned the word *character*, a technical term well understood in families, but heretofore unknown in law'. He thought that by now, in 1800, a 'character' had been made into a kind of worker's possession, something he or she owned.[25] Meanwhile, provincial register offices, the few we know of, got quietly on with the business of finding cooks for frantic mistresses, operating a low-key system of registration and police, as they had done for many years. An efficient Woodstock office (not all of its business was servant-business) operated in Broadway, in Oxford, up through Charlbury, Chipping Norton, Banbury, Stratford, Warwickshire and into Northamptonshire. 'Bank and Public Office for General Purposes of Agency, Registry, Intelligence,' said the flyers. People wrote in on the back of these; the proprietor drafted a response. He also used them for writing drafts of mayorial letters (he *was* the mayor of Woodstock). By 1806 he was not doing much in the servant line; the newspapers were taking over the business; he was sent

[21] 'House of Commons Friday March 5', *The Times*, 12 Mar. 1791, p. 2, 'Offices for Hiring Servants'.

[22] 32 Geo. 3 c. 56, 'An Act for Preventing the Counterfeiting of Certificates of the Characters of Servants'.

[23] *The Times*, 24 Oct. 1794, p. 4. For accommodation offices as 'nest[s] of housebreakers', 'Parliamentary Intelligence, House of Commons', *The Times*, 11 May 1791, p. 2, 19 May 19 1791, p. 2, 17 Mar. 1792, 6 Jun. 1792, p. 2, 19 Oct. 1792, p. 3.

[24] J. Reed, *The Register-Office: A Farce in Two Acts Acted at the Theatre Royal in Drury Lane*, H. Saunders, Dublin, 1761.

[25] Anon., *Reflections on . . . Master and Servant*, p. 31.

notices of their advertising rates.[26] In the Metropolis, gentlemen went on proposing more and more elaborate systems for policing servants, as if no one had ever had the thought of them before. The author of *Reflections* (1800) believed himself unique in proposing a public register of menial servants in London and a five-mile radius of other great towns, each servant's name, county of domicile, height and description to be recorded, alphabetically; each to carry with him a certificate (an early form of identity card) 'on a long slip of parchment, to be endorsed by every master when a servant left his employ'. This would only cost the man a shilling. A typical entry in the register might read '"A. B, a thin man, five feet eight inches high, in his shoes, native of London, with dark hair, hazel eyes, low forehead, long nose, and small chin, entered his name this — day of — in the year — "...'. Apart from all the obvious advantages, the register would provide a census of able bodied men 'for government', that is for the militia and the army. The writer's thinking was strongly inflected by the current crises of war, dearth, and counter-revolution: he was the commentator who believed that every coachman in London was agent of the French revolutionary government, fomenting rebellion among his brethren. That was why 'all clubs of servants in and out of place, consisting of more than seven [should] be declared illegal'.[27]

There may have been philosophic and legal doubts about the owner-ship of the servant's labour; but 'character' was very clearly understood to belong to the domestic servant. Or so the story went. For later eighteenth-century servants and employers, 'character' meant both the honour and good reputation that all in civil society might hope to possess;[28] and also the innumerable scrappy bits of paper that litter the county records offices of England, shoved into the back of household account books by an employer two centuries ago, as in 'Shotswell October 18 – 1800 Madam Sharah Hunt She his a verey in Drust gurl And honst Sarvent and Verey well licked at Shotswell'.[29] Or more elegantly (and perhaps more legally sensitive) as in 'Exeter Octr 19 1771 The bearer, Biddy Page lived in the character of an upper servant with me, about a year & five Months: & I believe her to be strictly honest, sober, & well Disposed

---

[26] Berkshire Record Office (BRO), D/ESv(M) B19–21, Stevens Papers, Correspondence of a servants' agency at Woodstock. Papers survive for 1804–6. For one frantic mis-tress searching for replacement servants, Amanda Vickery, *The Gentleman's Daughter: Women's lives in Georgian England*, Yale University Press, New Haven, 1998, pp. 142–6.

[27] Anon., *Reflections on... Master and Servant*, pp. 43–5.

[28] Margot Finn, *The Character of Credit: Personal debt in English culture, 1740–1914*, Cambridge University Press, Cambridge, 2003, pp. 18–20.

[29] Warwickshire County Record Office (WCRO), CR 656/36, Holbech of Farnborough, Volume containing cuttings from newspapers... printed ephemera and... letters or copies of letters.

witness my hand...'.[30] What Orlando Patterson described in *Slavery and Social Death* as 'the game of honour' (which the slave stood outside, by having 'no power and no independent existence... no public worth') was available to servants as well as to their masters and mistresses, albeit on vastly unequal terms: perhaps 'honesty' rather than 'honour' was all that plebeian men and women might hope to posses.[31] Some magistrates thought it a first duty of gentlemen *not* to provide 'a written [one], since it may be used very improperly by [the servant], or be transferred to some other person... [for] various purposes of deceit'. Thomas Ruggles thought that nothing short of making the issue of false ones a felony would 'stop the contagion'.[32] But as late as 1821 a JP went into print to point out that 'where complaints have been presented before a Magistrate of the misconduct of a servant, the master has generally been so imprudent as to have hired that servant without requiring a written, or indeed any, character from his last master'. Some thought that there were psychological benefits to servants from the character system: 'a character is the only property which many people can call their own; and when untarnished, is the most valuable that any man can possess'.[33] But nothing really worked in regulating the recruitment of domestic servants. A most agitated and *moving* footnote to the Reverend Samuel Clapham's severely unemotional *Several Points of Sessions' Law* of 1818 witnesses the eruption of domestic life into this handbook of legal advice:

Would every master be prevailed with to give a fair and just character of every servant, exactly what his behaviour entitles him to – would nothing extenuate through compassion, nor aught set down in malice through resentment – this description of persons would be rendered abundantly more happy in themselves than they now are, and would cease to introduce into very many families the vexations and troubles which perpetually agitate them.[34]

---

[30] Somerset County Record Office (SCRO), DD/SF, 2918, Testimonial from B. Limbry, Exeter for Biddy Page a servant (19 Oct. 1771).

[31] Orlando Patterson, *Slavery and Social Death: A comparative study*, Harvard University Press, Cambridge, MA and London, 1982, pp. 10–11. On the relationship of elite 'honour' to plebeian 'honesty', Michael McKeown, *The Origins of the English Novel, 1600–1740*, Johns Hopkins University Press, Baltimore, 1987, pp. 131–75.

[32] Ruggles, *History of the Poor* (1793), vol. 2, pp. 250–1.

[33] Thomas Gisborne, *An Inquiry into the Duties of Men in the Higher and Middle Classes of Society in Great Britain, Resulting from their Respective Stations, Professions and Employments*, 2nd edn, 2 vols., B. and J. White, London, 1795, vol. 2, pp. 453–7; County Magistrate, *A Letter Addressed to the Agriculturalists in General, and to the Magistrates and Clergy in Particular throughout the Kingdom, on the Subjects of Hiring, Service and Character, to which are added Printed Forms of Contract between the Master and Servant, designed to be filled up by the contracting parties, and calculated to prevent disputes about wages, and lessen the number of appeals...*, Longman and Whittaker, London, 1821, pp. 7–9.

[34] Samuel Clapham, *A Collection of the Several Points of Sessions Law, Alphabetically Arranged, contained in Burns and Williams on the office of a Justice, Blackstone's*

The game of honour was stacked against the domestic servant because their character was a means of survival in modern commercial society: 'A good Character is valuable to everyone, but especially Servants, for it is their Bread; and without it they cannot be admitted into any respectable Family.'[35] In his cut-and-paste advice to employers, culled from a half-century of legal and household guides, John Trusler said that servants should not be disparaged in the testimonial, for 'a character is all a servant has to depend on; it is his bread; and if a good character was received with such servant it never should be withheld'.[36] Here 'character' meant labour potential. Servants made the same point. In 1747 an anonymous London footman proposed the full sanctions of the criminal law against employers to a 'Club-meeting of the Cloath' should they keep 'from a Servant any Part of the Good Character he justly deserves'. In doing so, they were 'guilty of the greatest of crimes. A servant's good Name is his Life; it is all he has to live upon: His Character is his Property; to which he has as good a Right as to his wages. It is therefore Murder, Theft, Perjury and Ingratitude to keep from a Servant his good Character, or any Part thereof'.[37]

A very grand household, like that of the earls of Ailesbury, at Savernake in Wiltshire, might establish a filing system, holding testimonials of servants over many years, a useful form of domestic police exercised over several domiciles and large establishments. The family preserved over a hundred letters from and about servants from the period 1714–1829, many of them testimonials ('he speaks confidently of understanding his Business particularly the cleaning of Plate . . . has a civil and humble appearance'), but also many letters from sacked servants asking: *'Why did you dismiss me?* It is only justice to tell me what my fault was.' 'My lord', wrote one young woman from Marlborough in November 1819, 'iham sorry to inform you iwas discharged from your serveas on the 4 of April by mrs daws your houskeeper after being in your serveas five

---

Commentaries, East and Hawkins on Crown Law, Addington's Penal Statutes and Const and Nolan on the Poor Laws; Designed to assist Magistrates to refer to these several Authorities; to supply the Clergy with professional Information; and to enable Vestries to transact the Business of their Respective Parishes. The Statutes continued to 57 Geo. III 1817, Inclusive, 2 vols., Butterworth and Clarke, London, 1818, vol. 2, p. 9. Richard Sharp, Clapham, Samuel (1757–1830) in *Oxford Dictionary of National Biography,* Oxford University Press, 2004, www.oxforddnb.com/view/article/5432, accessed 5 Feb. 2007.

[35] David Barclay, *Advice to Servants,* privately printed, London, 1800?.

[36] John Trusler, *Trusler's Domestic Management, or the Art of Conducting a Family, with Economy, Frugality and Method,* J. Souter, London, 1819, p. xii.

[37] J. B., Brother of the Cloath, *The Footmans Looking-glass; or, Proposals to the Livery Servants of London and Westminster, . . . for bettering their Situations in Life, and securing their Credit in the World. To which is added, an humble Representation to Masters and Mistresses,* M. Cooper, London, 1747, p. 26.

years and eight months and not gilty of any thing but being sent from hous like adog my lord and worse'. This very long complaint detailed the depredations of the housekeeper: 'if your lordshipwill ask of her to know if iver idid aney thingamis the ole time she was there . . . '. In Jane Dedman's view it was 'avery hard thing to take apore girls bread away from her in sush abad way . . . I have onley my hands to get my lives ican't get me another plase without sending to mrs daws and she says she will keep me from ever having another plias without ican get afrind buy someone else'.[38] Letters like these may also have been an archive of social comedy for the Ailesburys, preserved for the purposes of laughter. Recording the malapropisms, rusticisms and uncertain spelling of domestics was one of the many categories of degrading story that could be told about them, for the purposes of amusement and for the policing of many barriers of personhood in civil society. Besides being a ready catalogue of servants available in the locality, a volume with carefully pasted-in, or patiently transcribed (down to the last misplaced letter) letters from servants stretching back over many years, served purposes other than housekeeping. A Warwickshire gentry family kept many 'Letters from Servants wanting a placing': 'Warwick October 1st 1808 Madam I Being in formed you Wanted too Servants for House maids & we take This oportunity of Troubling your Ladyship, with these Lines to aquaint you: that Sarah Smallwood . . . & Ann Rolings . . . flater ouer Selves Caparble of your Ladyships place . . . we can Bring our caracters with us . . . '.[39]

The higher courts, should she even dream of going there, were not of much use to a young woman like Jane Dedman, though in the earlier century one at least had threatened her employer with the judges, and followed through on it. In 1766, a maidservant brought an action against her former mistress for saying to a potential employer enquiring about her character 'that she was saucy and impertinent, and often lay out of her own bed; but was a clean girl, and could do her work well'. The young woman (only ever referred to as A in the law books), may have 'proved that she was by this means prevented from getting a place'; but Lord Mansfield determined that this was not to be considered as an action for defamation 'by words . . . it was a confidential declaration, and ought not to have been disclosed' to be sure; but no ground for action. If calling her these names had been groundless, he said, and the intention purely to defame, then a false character would have been given and it would have been a proper ground for an action; but that was not the case

---

[38] Wiltshire Record Office (WRO), 9/35/62, Ailesbury of Savernake, About 100 letters on the employment and dismissal of employees, 1714–1829.
[39] WCRO, CR 656/36, Holbech of Farnborough.

here. The 1766 case was first written up and printed in 1772; it received sustained attention after 1792 and the new legislation concerning the issuing of characters for servants.[40] To maintain an action against an employer for words spoken or written by him or her, the servant had to prove the malice as well as the falsehood of the charge, said Thomas Williams in 1812. A tested the general belief that an employer was obliged to provide a reference at a very high level indeed. By her mistress's refusal to provide one, 'she had been damnified', said A. In 1800 Lord Chief Justice Kenyon determined that 'notwithstanding the feelings which he might entertain on the subject ... a man is not bound by law to give any character at all, although if he do, he must take care to give a true one'.[41]

Perhaps, after 1792, employers were more careful in their use of language when discussing servants, wary of giving a 'false character'. But they had always policed their own language in regard to the recommendation in this way, as did Thomas Woodford of Chertsey in 1749, telling Robert Lee that 'My ... Coachman was I think very honest & sober as far as I ever saw. & I esteemed him to be a good Coachman & to look well & carefully after my horses'. Lee should take him, but should make it a condition that he promise not to 'go out without leave'. He added 'this condition you need not say you had hinted at by me ... I told him I would give him a good Character, and therefore I would not willingly Tack anything to it but as it is here found, you have a little hint ...'. They were both magistrates, attuned to the question of defamation.[42] Masters and servants had to find a way of buying and selling labour within the boundaries of the law – or whatever they understood that law to be. Sometimes the ordinary business of life was best effected by circumnavigating the strict truth of the matter, as in July 1766 in Buckinghamshire, when the Reverend Coles received a letter 'from Mr Tho: Collett of Hendon to enquire the Character of Tom Watts, as having lived with me, and his Capacity for a Carter & under Gardener'. Tom Watts had never been his household servant, though 'He denied his having told Mr Collett that he lived with me; [he] only said, that he lived in the Parish, & that I could speak for him: I wrote, that, did I want such a sort of Servant, I knew none I would take sooner, having known him

[40] Francis Buller, *An Introduction to the Law relative to Trials at nisi prius. The sixth edition, corrected*, R. Pheney, London, 1793, p. 8.

[41] Thomas Walter Williams, *The Whole Law Relative to the Duty and Office of a Justice of the Peace. Comprising also the Authority of Parish Officers*, 3rd edn, 4 vols., John Stockdale, London, 1812, vol. 2, pp. 880–1.

[42] BRO, D/ED/033, Letters of Thomas Woodford (of Chertsey?) to Robert Lee, a fellow justice (24 Mar. 1749).

from a Child, he being one of the first I carried to the Bp to be confirmed, tho' not absolutely of the Parish'.[43]

Thomas Ruggles, John Huntingford – all the legal gentlemen discussed above who were so exercised by the good ordering and management of domestic service – discussed the law of character (its defects, and their proposals for its amelioration) as a form of policing. In 1800, Lord Chief Justice Kenyon appears to have concurred with this view, remarking that 'it was near two centuries ago . . . [that] the law had provided that another class of servants, those employed in agriculture, who were a labourious, industrious, and innocent set of people . . . [be placed] under the controul of the magistrates. And the want of such a jurisdiction over servants in livery, his Lordship considered as a defect in our police.'[44] In March, Daniel Parker Cole, MP for Nottingham, introduced a bill for the better settling of disputes between masters and servants, quoting Kenyon's remarks, and the Statute of Artificers.[45] Evidently in his other life as Nottingham JP, Coke had never behaved as contemporary legal commentators believed most eighteenth-century magistrates behaved, namely that they used what law came to hand when confronted with a service dispute, and treated domestics as husbandry workers. Rather, he said 'on application to him . . . when he was informed that the parties were menial servants, he was obliged to inform them, that he had no jurisdiction over them, but that they must have recourse to an action at law'.[46] As Doug Hay observes, Coke's bill would have provided for summary determination before a magistrate of domestic service disputes to do with wages, the retention of clothing, leaving the employment before time, and unfair dismissal. Closely modelled on the statutes for other workers of the earlier century, the main point about it was, as Hay also observes, that it was never enacted.[47] Justices of the peace were perfectly incompetent in domestic cases, was one MP's objection to the bill. Magistrates might be 'sufficiently good judges of whether a ploughman took proper care of his horses, and did his work properly in the field; but to

---

[43] Francis Griffin Stokes (ed.), *The Blecheley Diary of the Reverend William Cole, M.A. F.S.A. 1765–67*, Constable, London, 1931, p. 76.

[44] 'Law Report. Court of King's Bench, 13 February. Sittings before Lord Kenyon', *The Times*, 17 Feb. 1800, p. 3.

[45] 'House of Commons, Tuesday March 4', *The Times*, 5 Mar. 1800, p. 2; *Parliamentary Register*, 11, 1800, pp. 4–5; *The Senator; or, Parliamentary Chronicle*, vol. 25, J. Stratford, London, 1799–1800, pp. 6–7. Mark Pottle, 'Coke, Daniel Parker (1745–1825)' in *Oxford Dictionary of National Biography*, Oxford University Press, 2004, www.oxforddnb.com/view/article/5825, accessed 5 Feb. 2007.

[46] 'House of Commons, Monday April 22', *The Times*, 23 Apr. 1800, p. 2; 'House of Commons, Monday May 26', *The Times*, 27 May 1800, p. 2.

[47] Hay, 'England, 1652–1875', pp. 89–90. Thomas Ruggles had proposed the essentials of Coke's Bill in 1793. Ruggles, *History of the Poor* (1793), p. 255.

determine disputes between a mistress and her maid, whether the dairy was properly attended, or whether the kitchen and *other utensils* were kept clean, it would be necessary to summon a jury of matrons'. (This bill did not give the House the same opportunity to perform the comedy of bathos that the maidservant tax bill had provided, back in 1785; but the joke of bringing colanders and cheese-cloth into the purview of high law was evidently still much appreciated.) The chief objection to Coke's bill however, was that it encroached on trial by jury, and would thus change 'the mode of administering justice in the country'. And what was wrong with present arrangements, asked Richard Brinsley Sheridan. Currently, either party might give warning; you could get rid of a servant by paying a month's wages; a servant might give up the month's wages and depart when he pleased. 'Masters already had sufficient controul over the behaviour of their servants, as by refusing them a character they might deprive them of their bread'. Perhaps he was displaying his wit here, his 'sense of fun and mockery of sentiment'.[48] Or he may have made reference to the Biblical proposition, understood as the foundation of the poor laws and of all law regulating labour from the medieval period onwards, and – some said – of the common law itself, that 'if any would not work, neither should he eat' (II Thessalonians, 3, 10). This was very old social theory, as well as ancient religious prescription.[49] It was social theory that Jane Dedman wrote against in 1819 Wiltshire, complaining that the housekeeper would not provide her with a character: 'avery hard thing to take apore girls bread away from her . . . ican't get me another plase without'.[50]

A month later Daniel Coke brought a petition to the House of Commons from the Journeymen Workmen of Nottingham 'praying for the repeal of the Workmen Combination Acts'.[51] The Acts had provided against the 'combining' of two or more persons for the purposes of obtaining wage increase, or better working conditions. This second of

---

[48] *Parliamentary Register*, vol. 12, pp. 108–9 (11 Jun. 1800). A. Norman Jeffares, 'Sheridan, Richard Brinsley (1751–1816)' in *Oxford Dictionary of National Biography*, Oxford University Press, 2004, www.oxforddnb.com/view/article/25367, accessed 7 Feb. 2007; Boyd Hilton, *A Mad, Bad and Dangerous People? England 1783–1846*, Oxford University Press, Oxford, 2006, pp. 62–3, 103–4 and passim. Sheridan had just had a theatrical success (his first for many years) with a tragedy of colonialism, *Pizzaro*. John Loftis, 'Whig oratory on stage: Sheridan's *Pizzaro*', *Eighteenth-Century Studies*, 8:4 (1975), 454–72; Hilton, *Mad, Bad and Dangerous*, p. 104. Latin America was the setting for all sorts of dramas of British state, society and servitude was; see John Witherspoon, *The History of a Corporation of Servants. Discovered a few Years ago in the interior parts of South America*, John Gilmour, Glasgow, 1765.

[49] For mercantilist theories of labour, see Chapter 9.

[50] WRO, 9/35/62, Ailesbury of Savernake.

[51] 'House of Commons, Monday June 30', *The Times*, 1 Jul. 1800, p. 2.

them (1800) had been passed in very great haste, the bill read first on 18 June, committed on 19, passed on 1 July, and with an equal haste in the House of Lords. Sheridan called it a 'foul and oppressive' piece of legislation, whilst William Pitt disingenuously claimed its virtue as enabling workers to get all disputes between themselves and their masters settled in a summary way; it saved them 'the circuitous process of a suit at law'. But as Sheridan remarked, all the power was in the hands of the master; under the Act, he summonsed the journeyman, but the journeyman could not summons him. Now he objected to a legal arrangement that he had appeared to condone earlier in the year when he dismissed Coke's proposals regarding menial servants. These had indeed, suggested rather different penalties and remedies for masters and servants, but at least they would have been able to summons each other.[52]

In his account of the massive and persistent presence of the domestic servant in between the lines of nineteenth-century fiction, Bruce Robbins writes of 'character' as 'the mask the people were expected to don in the face of power'. He finds it no coincidence that from the early eighteenth century, as his own line of work, literary criticism, established itself, 'a "character" was a statement in which one employer described to another employer the habits and qualities of a servant, vouching for and thus controlling such key traits as honesty, chastity, sobriety, and industriousness'.[53] Thus for the literary critic, emerges modern fictional realism's fixation on 'character' as the key term for reading, understanding and assessing all kind of literary production. Jane Dedman certainly wrote to, and in, the face of social power when she asked her aristocratic addressee to tell her why she had been dismissed, even though her direct complaint was about the housekeeper. Was Jane Dedman's self-characterisation as 'apore girl . . . [with] . . . onley my hands to get my lives', a mask donned for the occasion? We could look to other structural factors enforcing self-characterisation among the poorer sort of eighteenth-century England. The poor laws in general and the settlement examination in particular, produced massive amounts of compulsory autobiographical activity, delivered (or at least recorded) in a set form; the chronological narration of a working life was demanded by law and

---

[52] Hilton, *Mad, Bad and Dangerous*, pp. 65–74; John V. Orth, 'English Combination Acts of the eighteenth century', *Law and History Review*, 5:1 (1987), 175–211; John Batt, '"United to Support But Not Combined to Injure": Public order, trade unions and the repeal of the Combination Acts of 1799–1800', *International Review of Social History*, 31:2 (1986), 185–203; E. P. Thompson, *The Making of the English Working Class* (1963), Penguin, Harmondsworth, 1968, pp. 199, 262–4, 546–65.
[53] Bruce Robbins, *The Servant's Hand: English fiction from below* (1986), Duke University Press, Durham SC and London, 1993, pp. 35.

by the magistrate operating that law.[54] When the magistrate wrote in his notebook (or got his clerk to write) of a woman asking for poor relief that 'she is poor and impotent and unable to find work', or 'poor and impotent and unable to provide for her child', he used a formula extracted from the legislation, perhaps known to and uttered by the woman herself, but only certainly used by those recording the interview.[55] We cannot know if these descriptions were items of self-definition or personal identity, briefly donned to make something happen in the world: an order to the overseers for relief, a reference and a job, in the case of Jane Dedman. A list of attributes – keeps a nice washhouse, her own room kept very clean, industrious, honest, likeable – was what Dedman needed to operate in the labour market, and get her bread.[56]

We cannot read personality, or individual identity, out of 'character', but *persona* was the century's own useful term for understanding it as a form of policing. In 1767, the legal theorist John Taylor had contemplated these questions of character and identity, under the heading of 'servitude'. His topic was Roman Law, but the point applied equally to eighteenth-century England, he said.[57] The 'Persona . . . or Character, of a Magistrate, Guardian, etc.' was different from that of father and son, for example. For the public official in social life, a persona was analogous to a stage performance, 'a character to put on and off; a convenient Method of Considering, an useful Way of Conceiving, such or such a Citizen, in order to carry on the Business of the Public more advantageously'. But that persona did 'not enter into the Legal Notion of his Real Circumstances or Condition' and had nothing to do with it. On the other hand, between father and son, or 'between being a Slave, and *not* being a Slave, is something intrinsic in regard to the Circumstance and Operation of the Law'.[58] Taylor did not here mention domestic servants (though he had much to say about them elsewhere) perhaps because they complicate

---

[54] Carolyn Steedman, 'Enforced narratives: Stories of another self' in Tess Cosslett, Celia Lury and Penny Summerfield (eds.), *Feminism and Autobiography: Texts, theories, methods*, Routledge, 2000, pp. 25–39.

[55] Nottinghamshire Archives (NA), M 8050, Notebook of Sir Gervase Clifton JP, 1772–1812 (13 Jul. 1777; 14 Oct. 1785).

[56] Anne Taylor, *The Present of a Mother to a Young Servant: Consisting of Friendly Advice and Real Histories*, 2nd edn, Taylor and Hessey, London, 1816, p. 102, thought that the wash house and her own bedroom the best demonstrations of a girl's character. For her advice to young women to construct a serving persona, see Carolyn Steedman, *Master and Servant: Love and labour in the English industrial age*, Cambridge University Press, Cambridge, 2007, pp. 131–51.

[57] The third and last relationship of civil life 'in regard to Persons, is Servitude; or with the Ancients, Slavery': John Taylor, *Elements of the Civil Law*, 3rd edn, Charles Bathurst, London, 1769, p. 407.

[58] Taylor, *Elements of the Civil Law*, p. 408.

and blur the distinctions of his argument. They were not public officials of course, but their character was a mask, and their character could be put on or off (and lost, refused, forged, and stolen). They could live as, or play the part, of servant, as Mrs Limbry implied of Biddy Page. Their condition – their being a servant – was then something intrinsic to them, and to the law that recognised and regulated them. But that condition was not derived from familial relationship or from ownership, as in Taylor's two other examples. It was always contingent, depended on the intentions, promises, and agreements expressed in the contract of hiring. We could say that despite its difficulties and complications, many employers had found a satisfactory method of governing the relationship, with what law there was to hand. Or we could agree with Doug Hay, that elite men of the political class who refused the domestic servant rights to claim for wages under summary jurisdiction as Daniel Coke proposed, simply could not countenance the idea of being summonsed themselves.[59] Domestic servants may not have been *able* to claim for wages within the form of the law, but we have abundant evidence that they *did* so claim, before many magistrates (and sometimes even got those wages). From a much later perspective, they may constitute an idiosyncratic and anomalous workforce, but it was a very large eighteenth-century one. Being a servant – a waged domestic worker – meant being interpellated by the law in many ways; the character was a most useful way of policing service. These were some of the factors that obviated the need for other forms of police and more consistent legislation regarding domestic servants, for such a very long time.

[59] See Note 10.

Servant-stories

Stories about servants circulated freely in eighteenth-century England. The dominant one from 1740, about the servant who writes, and tells abroad the story of the family within doors – Samuel Richardson's *Pamela* – was a major reference point, and has been much discussed by modern historians.[60] Its most important lesson as far as employers were concerned, went on being taught into the new century: 'Never tell the affairs of the family you belong to; for that is a sort of treachery... but kept their secrets and have none of your own'; 'A tale-bearing servant is always an unfaithful servant.'[61] Hester Thrale had her own domestic example of the treacherous, literate, letter-writing servant in Joseph Baretti (a very grand servant indeed, whom her first husband had appointed steward). He published three articles satirising her mothering in the *European Magazine*. (The world was interested in an 'audacious Libel' on Thrale; *she* believed that his 'astonishing performance' had been dictated by her eldest daughter working with Old Nurse Tibson.) He followed up these cruel and demeaning satires on her parenting skills and child psychology with a play script entitled 'The Sentimental Mother', in which she was portrayed as Lady Fantasma Tunskull.[62] Even nice,

---

[60] Samuel Richardson, *Pamela, or, Virtue Rewarded* (1740), Penguin, Harmondsworth, 1985; Judith Laurence-Anderson, 'Changing affective life in eighteenth century England and Samuel Richardson's *Pamela*', *Studies in Eighteenth Century Culture*, 10 (1981), 445–56; Naomi Tadmor, '"Family" and "Friend" in Pamela: A case-study in the history of the family in eighteenth-century England', *Social History*, 14:3 (1989), 289–306; M. G. Spencer, 'Pursuing Pamela, 1740–1750', *Eighteenth Century Life*, 26:2 (2002), 96–100; Margot Finn, *The Character of Credit: Personal debt in English culture, 1740–1914*, Cambridge University Press, Cambridge, 2003, pp. 26–34.

[61] Charles Jones, *The History of Charles Jones, the Footman. Written by Himself*, J. Marshall, London, 1796, pp. 4–5 (I have very severe doubts about this being written by Himself.); Anon., *Domestic Management, or the Art of Conducting a Family with Instructions to Servants in general, Addressed to Young Housekeepers*, H. D. Symonds at the Literary Press, London, 1800, p. 92; 'This is the servant's original sin: the making known outside the dialogue of what goes on within it', says Robbins, *The Servants Hand*, p. 83.

[62] Mary Hyde, *The Thrales of Streatham Park*, Harvard University Press, Cambridge, MA and London, 1977, p. 256; Balderson (ed.), *Thraliana*, vol. 2, pp. 680, 719; Joseph

genteel girls, who in the textual realm at least, have been reduced to the condition of domestic servant from some other place in the social hierarchy, might be watching, subjecting a mistress to scrutiny, and finding her wanting, in sentiment, civility, and good taste in china.[63]

Thrale/Piozzi herself was the author and editor of many servant-stories. A constant of her diary-writing and correspondence, they were vehicle for celebratory display of her own self-knowledge, understanding of the social order she inhabited, and the psychology of social inferiors. Many of the jokes Thrale collected (as opposed to the jokes she made) were of the 'stupid' variety: a modern version would be 'How many servants does it take to change a light-bulb?' Much hilarity was engendered by recounting servants' malapropisms, and incorrect use of English.[64] Thrale also used her servants as repositories of family history, and as commentators on it – as a kind of chorus (though a chorus only activated by her own writing of it) often recounting painful and fractured family relationships by means of their prescient observations (the prescience was hers of course; they were mere conduits of her perspicacity). In 1784 she wrote to her eldest daughter about 'Foolish Jemmy [who] says to me this morning – "Your Daughters will come back in half a Year . . . " What do you think half a year means Jemmy? "Six months my Lady; 12 months makes a year, I know that tho' I am a Fool"'.[65] Any reader of her letters to her daughters, the ones written after they abandoned their newly wed mother in an excess of embarrassment and social disdain (at her choice of husband, his rank, status and nationality – and her age at marriage) will notice that the only way in which she was able to get off her high horse of rejection and hurt, indeed, the only way in which she could communicate with them, was by telling the girls stories of the servants they had known since their childhood. She used the servants as paper intermediaries. They stood in for her in her letters, said what she could not write.

Baretti, 'On Signora Piozzi's Publication of Dr. Johnson's Letters. Stricture the First', *European Magazine and London Review*, 13 (May 1788), 313–17, '. . . Stricture the Second', *European Magazine*, 14 (Jun. 1788), 393–9; '. . . the Third', 14 (Aug. 1788), 89–99; *The Sentimental Mother. A Comedy in Five Acts; the Legacy of an Old Friend, and his Last Moral Lesson to Mrs Hester Lynch Thrale, now Mrs Hester Lynch Piozzi*, James Ridgeway, London, 1788.

63 Anon., 'No. 79. Saturday August 5. 1786', *The Lounger. A Periodical Paper published at Edinburgh in the Year 1785 and 1786*, 3 vols., Strahan and Cadell, London, William Creed, Edinburgh, 1786, vol. 3, pp. 96–110.

64 Balderson, *Thraliana*, Vol. 1, p. 57; Janet Thaddeus, 'Swift's directions to servants', *Studies in Eighteenth-Century Culture*, 16 (1986), 107–23.

65 Edward A. Bloom and Lillian D. Bloom, *The Piozza Letters: Correspondence of Hester Lynch Piozza, 1784–1821 (formerly Mrs Thrale)*, 3 vols., University of Delaware Press: Associated University Press, Cranbery, NJ, 1989–1993, vol. 1, pp. 110–11.

These ways of representing and of writing servants were formalised in one eighteenth-century novel, which Thrale read in her girlhood and remembered in 1786. She consciously used Charlotte Lennox's *The Female Quixote* (1752) to construct a good story about her and James Boswell's separate biographies of Samuel Johnson.[66] She dwelt on Lucy, maidservant to the Female Quixote – who is Arabella, heroine of a satire that has her solipsistically interpret every single thing that happens to her in her remote rural life, and every person she encounters, according to the old-fashioned chivalric romances she has read throughout her childhood. Indeed, Arabella is still busy reading, for the house (the proto-gothic castle) is stuffed with them: a mother's legacy to an orphaned daughter. Arabella observes that each and every heroine she reads about possesses one attribute and prize possession, which is a story of herself, related by a faithful servant. She calls Lucy into her closet, and informs her that she has been chosen 'to relate her History'. Lucy's first objection is that she is no story-teller: 'It is not such simple Girls as I can tell Histories'. Nonsense! is Arabella's response. Would Lucy *be* her maid, if she wasn't clever enough? And anyway, 'There is no Occasion... for you to *make* [emphasis added] a History', for 'There are accidents enough in my Life to afford Matter for a long one: All you have to do is relate them as exactly as possible.' Telling the mistress's life-story is 'Part of [her] Duty'; and anyway, 'Did you ever hear of any Woman that refused to relate her Lady's Story, when desir'd?' The orders are detailed and explicit: Lucy must recount all her mistress's 'Words and Actions', every incident and thought ('however instantaneous'), every 'Change of my Countenance... Smiles, Half-smiles, Blushes... the Rise and Falling of my Voice; every Motion of my Eyes; and every Gesture which I have used these Ten Years past'. Remembering the novel, Thrale had some sympathy for the fictional maid; she had just performed the same labour of biography in writing her *Anecdotes of the Late Samuel Johnson*. Lucy is 'excessively astonished' at Arabella's instructions: 'Lord bless me!', she exclaims. 'I never, till this Moment, it seems, knew the hundred Part of what you expected from me: I am sure, if I had, I would never have gone

---

[66] Bloom, *Piozzi Letters*, vol. 1, p. 191; Charlotte Lennox, *The Female Quixote, or, the Adventures of Arabella* (1752), Oxford University Press, Oxford, 1989. This discussion is based on vol. 1, Book 3, Ch. 5. Adam Sisman, *Boswell's Presumptuous Task: Writing the life of Dr Johnson*, Penguin, London, 2001; James Boswell, *Life of Samuel Johnson, LL.D, comprehending an account of his studies and numerous works, ... In two volumes*, Charles Dilly, London, 1791; Hester Lynch Piozzi, *Anecdotes of the Late Samuel Johnson, LL.D during the last Twenty years of his Life*, Moncrieffe, White, Byrne, Cash, W. Porter and others, Dublin, 1786.

to service; for I might well know I was not fit for such Slavery'. (Even servants in texts will remind mistresses that they are not slaves.)

In a different modality and genres, compilers of domestic manuals, magistrates' handbooks and guides to the law, traced England's constitutional past by writing histories of 'the connexion between Master and Servant', tracing a development from barbarism to a state of modern refinement in which the majority had escaped conditions of enslavement and vassalage. In these texts, a maidservant like Lucy would have been the emblem of History, rather than the mouthpiece of her mistress's biography. Adam Smith, Adam Ferguson (1767) and John Millar (1771) wrote histories of civil society in which the historical account was inextricably connected to the way in which modern subjects were described, as legal and social beings. Their distinction and rank, their place in the great ordering of the world, was not just an external description, but an item of their identity.[67] These were 'natural histories' of humankind.[68] Ferguson and Millar focused on the transition from one mode of production to another; on the inauguration of private property; on 'the woman question' (on the treatment of women as a measure of civility and refinement); and above all else, on the question of subordination and servitude. The history of the world was a history of the diminution of servitude. We were all servants once, in vassalage and fealty to some lord, during the pastoral and agricultural stages of human history; civilisation is a state of society in which we have risen from that state.

Formal historical statements about servitude as social condition were translated into popular histories of nation formation, again by means of the servant's story.[69] The servant told of 'our ancient constitution', and of ourselves: of how we got to be the way we were. The conjectural past of the philosophic historians was joined with the Fall that had inaugurated the division of ranks and the regime of subordination, though the biblical version was often modified in these amalgamations. In the first, lost realm of community when there were no masters and no servants,

---

[67] Adam Smith, *Lectures on Jurisprudence. Glasgow Edition of the Works and Correspondence of Adam Smith*, R. L. Meek, D. D. Raphael, P. G. Stein (eds), Clarendon Press, Oxford, 1978, vol. 5, pp. 76–8, 175–9; Adam Ferguson, *An Essay on the History of Civil Society* (1767), University of Edinburgh Press, Edinburgh, 1966; John Millar, *The Origin of the Distinction of Ranks; or, An Inquiry into the Circumstances which give Rise to Influence and Authority in the Different Members of Society* (1771), 3rd edn, J. Murray, London, 1779.

[68] Robert Wokler, 'Anthropology and conjectural history in the Enlightenment', Christopher Fox, Roy Porter and Robert Wokler (eds), *Inventing Human Science: Eighteenth-century domains*, University of California Press, Berkeley, 1995, pp. 31–52.

[69] Anon., *The Laws Relating to Masters and Servants. With Brief Notes and Explanations to Render them Easy and Intelligible to the meanest Capacity. Necessary to be had in all Families*, Henry Lintot, London, 1755, Preface.

we may have been all on a foot with each other, but 'that Community of goods which we read of, *Acts* iv, 34, was extraordinary and lasted but a little while'.[70] Anonymous footman 'B. J.' told his fellow workers in 1747 that every master should remember 'that had it not been for some accidental Circumstances, he might perhaps have been in his [servant's] condition', that is, 'without Estate' and 'undergoing the temporal Punishment inflicted upon them for Sin, and in the mean Time, serving others, as Servants'.[71] Connections between the two Biblical and the historical-philosophical versions of the servants' story provoked the uneasy sense, discernible in other varieties of eighteenth-century history-writing, that the people – the mob – were a repository of the true history of English society.[72]

A social order, its divisions, inequities and conflicts were written about in relationship to the domestic servant, whether he or she was figured in a novel, or complained about in a parliamentarian's pamphlet. A society was constantly being worked over, brought into being, and expressed. It was of course, *already there*, in order for regulatory clauses in acts of parliament to be drafted and jokes to be told. Thinking the social by means of the servant was a bourgeois and elite strategy; the employing class – certainly Hester Thrale – knew that servants were there to think with, as well as to cook their dinner and buckle their shoes. Knowing this was an important component of her self-consciousness and identity.

Many servant-stories dwelt on their venality, low-cunning and dishonesty; or on the comedy provided by their foolishness, gullibility and imperfect grasp of language, literature and general workings of the world. In these jokes, anecdotes and fictions, the master or mistress is not so much the victim of the servant, as the exasperated unfortunate who suffers from their ministrations and mistakes. The joke – or the really good anecdote – hinged on the employer *knowing* this, and thus turning the joke back on the servant, and making him (most usually him) or her the butt of it. Story-structure was thus derived from social knowledge wielded as privilege. But the laughable, self-deprecating (and only ever temporary) victimisation of the employer was reversed in a series of well-known

---

[70] Anon., *A Present for Servants, from their Ministers, Masters, or other Friends*, 8th edn, John Rivington for the SPCK, London, 1768, pp. 14–15. This was reprinted for the last time in 1787.

[71] B. J., *The Footman's Looking Glass:, or Proposals to the Livery Servants of London and Westminster for bettering their Situation in Life, and securing their Credit in the World. To which is added, An Humble Representation to Masters and Mistresses. By J. B. a Brother of the Claoth*, M. Cooper, London, 1747, pp. 5–6.

[72] Matthew Adams, 'Imagining Britain: The formation of British national identity during the eighteenth century', PhD, University of Warwick, 2002.

stories that circulated from the mid-century onwards in which the servant was the victim.

The best known of these originated in the late 1730s and was remembered well into the 1790s.[73] Elizabeth Branch and her daughter Mary stood trial at Taunton Assizes in March 1740 for the murder of their servant Jane Buttersworth. Mrs Branch, the high and proud widow of a gentleman worth £300 a year (that is how the story goes) had driven him to the grave by perverse disposition and repeated cruelties and barbarities. Once in possession of his estate, nothing could stop her: 'the Moroseness, Pride and Insolence she harbour'd in her Mind before, now became altogether intolerable'. Slavery was specifically referenced: Mrs Branch had always had trouble with staff, 'imagining that Servants were Vassals or Slaves'. Some had stayed because of her husband; once he was dead, none would live with her, and she was 'oblig'd to put up with unhappy Orphans, &c from the Parish, on whom she exercised her cruel Temper, well-knowing they had no Body to complain to but the Churchwardens, Overseers, and Committee Men, who seldom listen to their Complaints'.[74] There was testimony to this from other servants. 'A Brief Account of the Lives of Mrs Branch and her Daughter, and the many Cruelties they were guilty of' was inserted in the pamphlet trial report, occupying the pages between the verdict and execution; here she was made a monster from her infancy, and described as quite insane.[75] Over forty years, in the scandal sheets, pamphlets and case-books that repeated all of this, there was much discussion of Betty Branch's social status and origins: she was *in fact* the daughter of a farmer, who brought £1,000 on marriage to Mr Branch, who had used this substantial sum in the improvement of his lands; or she was *really* the daughter of a gentleman of small fortune at Philips Norton, Somerset, where she had tortured animals and flies from the cradle and, when she was grown, her father's servants.[76] She had quietened down on the advice of family,

---

[73] Anon., *The Trial of Mrs. Branch, and her Daughter, for the Murder of Jane Buttersworth, before the Hon. Mr. Justice Chapple, at Somerset Assizes, March 31, 1740. . . . To which are added, true Copies of some very material Informations, . . . With a just Account of the Prisoners behaviour at their Trial; . . . and at the Place of Execution*, James Leake, Bath, 1740; Anon., *The Cruel Mistress; being, the genuine Trial of Elizabeth Branch, and her own Daughter; for the murder of Jane Buttersworth, their Servant Maid: who were executed on Saturday, May 3. 1740. . . . Together with an Account of their Lives*, C. Simpson, London, 1740; William Jackson, *The New and complete Newgate Calendar; or, Villany displayed in all its Branches. . . . containing the most faithful Narratives ever yet published of the various Executions, and other exemplary punishments, . . . from the year 1700, to the end of the Year 1795*, 6 vols., Alexander Hogg, London, 1795, vols. 3 and 4.

[74] Anon, *Cruel Mistress*, p. 7.   [75] Anon, *Cruel Mistress*, pp. 31–4.

[76] This was an acknowledged activity for Somerset children, to which county sixty years before, John Locke had sent his advice about not letting children torture flies, in case they

in order to get a husband, but a month into marriage was at it again, her husband paying off the servants and buying their silence. In widowhood she was 'oblig'd to take up with Strangers, Strollers . . . any poor Person's Child she could light of [as servants], for she was so infamous for her Cruelties and Barbarities'. All the contemporary trial reports made much of Mrs Branch forcing a parish Boy to eat his own excrement after he had soiled himself in terror of her. They said that the execution was ordered for dawn, otherwise in all likelihood the local people would have pulled the mother and daughter to pieces. All accounts of the Branchs' murder offer a sustained meditation on £300 a year, the type of person come to occupy such rank and station in modern commercial society, and their fitness (or lack of it) to employ servants. The other point of the trial narrative, which also echoed for a very long time, was – as one of the council for the prosecution was reported as saying – 'the Laws of England are as careful, and tenacious of the Life of the poorest Person as of the richest'.[77] Mrs Branch was given this expression of legal history, principle, and sentiment in her (almost certainly spurious) 'Last Dying Words', addressing herself from the gallows to 'Masters and Mistresses of Families' and saying 'never harbour Cruel, base and mean Thoughts of your Servants, as that they are your Slaves and Drudges, and that any Sort of Usage be it never so bad, is good enough for them. These and such like were the Thoughts that led me to use my Servants as Slaves . . . '.

Then there was 'Mrs Brownrigg the Murderer' who abused and killed an apprentice girl in 1767. Thirty years later when Hester Piozzi contemplated her crime (she had just read a new account of Brownrigg's oft-repeated story) she made the same points of national and class approbation that characterise the Branch story.[78] 'How very strangely Conscience

grew up just like . . . Betty Branch. Killing animals 'will, by degrees harden [children's] Minds towards Men; and they delight who in the Suffering and Destruction of inferior Creatures will not be apt to be very compassionate or benign towards those of their own kind'. John Locke, *Some Thoughts concerning Education*, 10th edn, George Risk and others, Dublin, 1737, pp. 130–131. See Chapter 2.

[77] Anon, *Cruel Mistress*, p. 8.

[78] Balderson (ed.), *Thraliana*, Vol. 2, pp. 936–7. Anon., *Cries of the Afflicted . . . Being a faithful Account of the Sufferings of Mary Mitchell, Mary Jones and Mary Clifford, Apprentices to Mrs Elizabeth Brownrigg, a Painter's Wife in Fetter Lane, Fleet Street*, London, 1795. John Wingrave, *A Narrative of the many horrid Cruelties inflicted by Elizabeth Brownrigg upon the Body of Mary Clifford, deceased; and for which the said Elizabeth received Sentence of Death, on Saturday the 12th of September 1767*, privately printed, London, 1767; Anon., *An Appeal to Humanity, in an Account of the Life and cruel Actions of Elizabeth Brownrigg. Who was tried at the Old Bailey on the 12th of September 1767, . . . To which is added the Trial of Elizabeth Branch and her Daughter*, Harrison and Ward, London, 1767; Anon., *The Tyburn Chronicle: or, Villainy display'd in all its Branches. Containing an authentic Account of the Lives, Adventures, Tryals, . . . of the most notorious Malefactors. . . . From the year 1700, to the present Time*, J. Cooke, London, 1768.

forbore to operate!' she wrote of Brownrigg. 'When sentence of Condemnation was pass'd on her for whipping her wretched Apprentice to Death – the Council heard her exclaim with Admiration; *All this for a Parish Girl!* – as if it were no matter whether a Parish Girl was killed or not. Aristocratic Maxims more horrible & dangerous, could not be promulgated in Turkey sure'. By the 1790s Brownrigg was the most notorious of the century's apprentice-murdering mistresses. The Branch and Brownrigg stories were often joined to a third, that of Sarah Metyard who in 1762, again with a daughter, had murdered and then concealed in a common privy the body of her apprentice Ann Nailor.[79]

In these reports, the children and young women who suffered cruelty, abuse and death at the hands of mistresses were presented as marginalised people; they were usually very young, with few ties to a local community – the kind of 'poor Person's Child' – employed by Elizabeth Branch. They were not servants at all, in the estimation of someone like Mrs Piozzi, contemplating her properly contracted, hired, and uppity household. Or they were apprentices (again, not domestic servants) ignored by the parish who put them out, or lost to view in a great city. 'Your objections to Parish indentures of Apprenticeship is too well founded', wrote Lincolnshire magistrate Thomas Coltman to the Recorder of Derby in 1787 after yet another apprenticeship scandal.[80] 'There is scarcely any human precaution to prevent many of the evils of them.' The case they were discussing 'happened in this County, aggravated by Cruelties almost incredible, and too horrible to relate. The Monster lived in this neighbourhood (Hagnaby)', and the only charitable (and comforting) way of

---

[79] Sarah Metyard, *The Last dying Speech (and last Farewell to the World) of Sarah Metyard, and her own Daughter Sarah Morgan Metyard*, n.i, London, 1762; *The Annual Register, or a View of the History, Politicks, and Literature, of the Year 1762*, R. and J. Dodsley, London, 1763, 1767, 1780, 1787; *Remarkable Trials and interesting Memoirs, of the most noted Criminals, who have been convicted at the Assizes, the King's-Bench Bar, Guildhall, &c. . . . From the year 1740, to 1764. . . . In two volumes. . . .* , vol. 1, W. Nicoll, 1765; John Villette, *The Annals of Newgate; or, Malefactors Register. Containing a particular and circumstantial Account of the Lives, Transactions, and Trials of the . . .* , 4 vols., J. Wenman, London, 1776, vol. 4; *The Malefactor's Register; or, the Newgate and Tyburn Calendar. Containing the authentic Lives, Trials, Accounts of Executions, and dying Speeches, of the most notorious Violators of the Laws of their Country; . . . from the Year 1700 to Lady-Day 1779. . . . Embellished with a most elegant and superb set of copper plates*, 5 vols., Alexander Hogg, London, 1779, vol. 3; Thomas Dogherty, *The Crown Circuit Assistant: being a Collection of Precedents of Indictments, Informations, . . . in criminal and penal Proceedings*, London, 1787; James Montagu, *The Old Bailey Chronicle; containing a circumstantial Account of the Lives, Trials, and Confessions of the most notorious Offenders*, 4 vols., London, 1788, vol. 3.

[80] Derbyshire County Record Office (DCRO), D239, M/0134, Sir William Fitzherbert JP, Recorder of Derby, Letter from Thomas Coltman, 17 Feb. 1787.

Figure 16. *The Cruel Mistress*; The century's most enduring image of employer cruelty.

accounting for it, was that 'he was insane'.[81] In these widely-circulating stories about physical violence, abuse and murder, it was not servants who were the victims, but rather apprentices. The only solution that magistrates could see to the apprenticeship problem was their own better management of the system, in the display of some administrative will to police the putting-out system with which they were charged. They recognised their role in these narratives of cruelty, neglect and abuse. However, a century that devised a multiplicity of servant-stories did not have one for a child-murdering maidservant, as the case of Ann Mead now demonstrates.

[81] DCRO, D239, M/0138, Letter from Thomas Coltman to Sir William Fitzherbert, 18 Jul. 1787; N. V. Gagen, *Hanged at Lincoln, 1716–1961*, privately printed, Welton, Lincoln, 1998, pp. 66–7; *The Date Book for Lincoln, and Neighbourhood, from the Earliest Time to the Present; collected with Care and from the most authentic Sources*, R. E. Leary, Lincoln, 1866, entry for 6 Mar. 1787 records that William Rawby, a farmer from Dogdike was 'executed at Lincoln for the murder of Ann Leary, aged 13, a parish apprentice. The girl's death was caused by ill-usage: her mistress also had beaten her severely.' Rawby was tried at the Lincoln Lent Assizes (12 Mar. 1787). Eighteenth-century crime sheets usually described the kind of abuse perpetrated by Rawby and his wife as 'unspeakable'. Certainly the Rawbys' treatment of the child was very horrible. The exhumed body showed burn marks around her waist and a deep hole in her side; her feet had been badly burned; 'All the way to the place of execution [Rawby] seemed to be much agitated.' The papers of the Midland Assize Circuit do not survive for this date. I am grateful for the help of Adrian Wilkinson, Lincolnshire Archives, in helping me track down this case.

8   Servants and child care: Ann Mead's murder

'I hate the sight of the girl, she is such a proud little minx'... 'If Miss
Mary was my girl, and chose to behave rude... to the servants, if I was
her papa I would order them all to refuse to do anything for her. I would
soon humble her pride I warrant you...'
> Dorothy Kilner, *Life and Perambulations of a Mouse* (1787)

'Why don't you keep that baby quiet?' said the Man.
> Katherine Mansfield, 'The Child-Who-Was-Tired' (1911)

Discussing the sheer hard work that made up the servant's labour, Pamela
Sambrook speculates that 'there must have been compensations' for it
in the relationship with little children, in their capacity to break down
'barriers of status, albeit temporarily'.[1] This may have been the case in
the elite households she deals with, in the long careers of nursemaids
kept on to serve generations of children, and in affections and obligations expressed by families by pensions and care into old age.[2] But none
of this says anything about the servant's feelings in the matter: for the
generality of servants, working for smaller families and in much more
modest households, a good place was a place without children.

[1] Pamela A. Sambrook, *The Country House Servant*, Sutton in association with the National
Trust, Stroud, 1999, p. 102.
[2] This kind of long-service nursemaid is to be found working for the Stanley family of
Alderley, Cheshire, briefly discussed below; Cheshire and Chester Archives and Local
Studies Service (CCA), DSA 59, Stanley of Alderley, Maria Josepha Stanley, Letters to
Moomie, 1808–50; DSA 60, Stanley of Alderley, Letters from Moomie, 1811, 1828,
1829.

In June 1760, Thomas Hutton wrote on behalf of his brother, button-maker and historian of Birmingham, to persuade Patt King to return to his family's service. There was the inducement of £3 5s a year, he said; and 'if you please, you may drink tea to your breakfast'. Though brother William and his wife intended 'to keep but one servant', the excellent news was that they meant 'to lesson [sic] the work of the house till one maid shall be able to do the work without slaving herself'. There was reassurance on this point, for as Patty 'must know bro: has buri'd one of his little boys about a fortnight ago'. The very next day, Mrs Hutton had been brought to bed of another son, but the new baby's uncle sup-posed that they intended to put him out to nurse, as well as 'such of the household business as will best suit them, untill they have reduc'd work to one woman's employment only'. This would not be a hard place; death had removed one of its children.[3]

Of course Patt King ended up looking after – and cleaning up after – children. She was typical of the vast majority of domestic servants, a jobbing girl who did everything in the household way. Lifestyle advice to the emergent commercial bourgeoisie was that they could manage it: with four children, in a trade that brought in 'but £200 a year', the father of a family should be able to afford one maidservant at £5 per annum.[4] Young women were counselled about the catch-all nature of their work. Under the ominous heading 'Carelessness of Children', Ann Walker told the lone housemaid that 'if you happen to live in a family where the mistress either suckles, or brings an infant up by hand, part of the duty of a nurse will fall to your share'.[5]

Employers like the Huttons knew how little servants liked places with children. The anonymous and hilarious *Letter from Betty to Sally* of 1781 was an elaborate exploration of the employing class's own pleasure of knowing what the servants are like and how they feel about child care in particular, working in a two-servant household for a master with an annual income of £300.[6] In the servant-voice adopted by its author,

---

[3] Birmingham Central Library Archives, Hutton 16, Hutton Family, Letters and papers, Thomas Hutton to Patt King, Jun 1760.

[4] Gentleman of Experience, *The Economist. Shewing, in a Variety of Estimates . . . how Comfortably and Genteelly a Family may live with Frugality for a little Money*, 15th edn, privately printed, London, 1781, pp. 14–20.

[5] Ann Walker, *A Complete Guide for a Servant Maid; or, the Sure Means of Gaining Love and Esteem*, 5th edn, T. Sabine, London, 1787, pp. 14–16.

[6] Anon., *A Letter from Betty to Sally, with the Answer; a New Year's Gift. Recommended to be learnt by every Servant in the Three Kingdoms. Read once by every Mistress of a Family, in the Hearing of every Master, whose Fortune does not exceed Three Hundred a Year*, Fielding and Walker, London, 1781. This poem was in some kind of intertextual exchange with the Gentleman of Experience's careful budgets. See note 4 above.

Betty has left her place, and 'gone into the Country to be Married'. She writes to her former companion Sally, giving her the news, and insouciantly enquiring (really *not* enquiring) after the children, high on her own good fortune: 'The children too I hope are better /But shou'd they die, 'tis no great matter;/Another's coming, I'm away,/Thank God, nurse it who may,/I do not care, 'tis not my lot,/I'm better off, a man I've got...'. This was the rumbustious and Swiftian (after Swift's looking-glass instructions to servants of 1745) version of the domestic servant.[7] Speaking in her voice like this, inventing her psychology, affirms the employer as someone who *can do* the work of imagining social others, although the hyperbolic solution to the maid's problems in the death of her charges (and her cheerful carelessness at the idea of it) suggests that the 'insufferable insolence' and 'arrogant compassion' that William Godwin attributed to all employers of servants, were the motor of any imaginative sympathy expressed. Godwin thought that the domestic servant's depression originated in relationships with children in employing households.[8] Parents would caution children 'against the intercourse of menials and explicitly tell them that the company of servants is by no means a suitable relaxation for the children of a family'. The practice outraged him:

It is a lesson of the most insufferable insolence and magisterial aristocracy, that it is possible for language to convey. We teach them that they are themselves a precious species of creatures, that must not be touched too rudely... Come not near me! In the exuberance of our humanity perhaps, we inform our children, that these creatures are to be tenderly treated, that we neither scratch nor bite them, and that, poisonous and degraded as they are, we must rather soothe than aggravate their calamity. We may shake our heads in arrogant compassion of their lot; but we must think of them as the puppy-dog in the hall, who is not to be touched because he has got the mange. – This lesson of separation, mixing with the unformed notions of childhood, will almost necessarily produce the most injurious effects.[9]

---

[7] Swift's *Directions* had a long run right through to the nineteenth century. See Janet Thaddeus, 'Swift's Directions to Servants', *Studies in Eighteenth-Century Culture*, 16 (1986), 107–23. A 1780s version emphasised Swift's inverted instructions to the nurse-maid: 'if you happen to let the child fall, and lame it, be sure never to confess; and if it dies, all is safe'. Jonathan Swift, *Polite Conversation, consisting of smart, witty, droll, and whimsical Sayings collected for his Amusement, and made into a regular Dialogue*, Joseph Wenman, London, 1783, p. 185.

[8] William Godwin, *The Enquirer. Reflections on Education, Manners, and Literature. In a Series of Essays*, G. G. and J. Robinson, London, 1797, Essay IV, 'Of Servants', pp. 201–11.

[9] Godwin, 'Of Servants', p. 203.

Insufferable haughtiness of tone, an arrogance of superiority uttered in baby lisping, was the manservant's consistent complaint. 'How cruel it is to encourage a young Child to reign over a poor Footman', said 'B. J'. in what he described as an oration to a club-meeting of his fellow London workers in 1747.[10] The anonymous footman-author of *Directions to Lords and Ladies, Masters and Mistresses* (itself a riposte to Swift's 'impertinent directions' to him) believed that John Locke's venerable advice to parents was the source of his fellow workers' problems with rude and overbearing children. He did not name *Some Thoughts Concerning Education* (1693) but many of its strictures are criticised in his book. Haughtiness of manner had been recommended by Locke to gentry fathers of small boys, as a method for eradicating 'sheepish bashfulness' and inculcating in the elite child a proper sense of his own worth and status.[11] In the 1766 footman's *Directions*, Locke's ends are to be achieved by the Swiftian method of sarcastic inversion. Parents should begin in the nursery and as they mean to go on: 'As soon as he can understand, let him be taught to look upon himself as a Species quite exalted above the rest of his fellow-Creatures; that the World was made absolutely for his Pleasure and Conveniencey; but above all, let him be thoroughly informed that he is a Man of Quality at Birth, his Will is not to be controuled in any Particular . . . '.[12] The hated voice of confident authority was actively inculcated in some small upper-class boys. Catherine Stanley of Aldeney certainly read her Locke as she supervised the care of her children in early nineteenth-century Cheshire, and she took his lessons to heart. She worried a good deal about the oldest boy's passions and tempers, his timidity and shyness (his babyishness), as well as brooding in her journal on his slowness in learning to read and his imperfect understanding of the Creator, or indeed, of a First Cause. There were also the extreme

[10] B. J., *The Footman's Looking Glass: or, Proposals to the Livery Servants of London and Westminster for Bettering their Situations in Life, and securing their Credit in the World. To which is added, An Humble Representation to Masters and Mistresses, by B. J. A Brother of the Cloath*, M. Cooper, London, 1747, p. 21.

[11] John Locke, *Some Thoughts Concerning Education*, A. and J. Churchill, London, 1693, pp. 199–200; Anon., *Directions to Lords, and Ladies, Masters and Mistresses, for the Improvement of their Conduct to servants and Tenants, Tradesmen and humble Friends and Cousins. Design'd as a Return for their Impertinent Directions to Servants*, M. Cooper, London, 1766. Young Edward Clarke, the target of Locke's advice in the 1680s and 1690s, did not turn out very well. Roger Woolhouse, *Locke: A biography*, Cambridge University Press, Cambridge, 2007, pp. 416–17.

[12] Anon., *Directions to Lords and Ladies*, p. 9. 'Many readers [would] cry out . . . with some degree of indignation, *What! does this presumptuous Brass-button'd Fellow dare to instruct his Betters?*'; but Anon *knew* he was as good as them. He had been told by a college principal when at Oxford 'with a young nobleman' that 'there was no Difference between [him] . . . and me as Academicks, but that he wore a Gown, I a Livery' (p. 4).

difficulties a home-educator like her experienced in getting a toddler to draw the line between 'the lawful and unlawful play of imagination'.[13] But a couple of months past little Owen's fourth birthday she was pleased to note that all babyishness disappeared when he was 'amongst servants & people where he knows his influence'; then his manner became 'quite self sufficient & important'.[14]

It was all very well for the guidebooks to advise that 'a child should never imagine that it is in his power to ruffle the temper of those about him', but ruffle and provoke servants these children certainly did.[15] The nurse, child-maid (and the benighted general servant of 1780s Nottinghamshire) was more likely to complain to her employer than to write a pamphlet about the problem, if the evidence of a burgeoning literature for children and home-educators produced by Georgian literary ladies is anything to go by. Many texts reproduced the servant's complaint in fictional dialogue with small children.[16] The type of 'proud little Minx' of Dorothy Kilner's *Life and Perambulations of a Mouse* was the target for improvement. A fictional nursemaid speaks her mind to an extremely ill-behaved child, as Nimble the mouse listens and takes notes:

'It does not signify, Miss', said the woman who I found to be the children's nurse. 'I never will put up with such behaviour; you know I always do everything for you when you speak *prettily*; but to be *ordered* to dress you in such a manner is what I never will submit to; and you will go *undressed* all day before I will dress you unless you will ask me as you *ought* to do . . . Aye! You may cry and sob as much as you please . . . I shall not dress you for *crying* and *roaring*, but for being good, and speaking with civility'.[17]

She turns to the child's mother and asks, '"Ma'am, is it by your desire that Miss *Nancy* behaves so rudely and bids me dress her directly, and

---

[13] CCA, DSA 75, Stanley of Alderley; Catherine Stanley, 'My Mother's Journal of her Four Children', 1812–20, p. 37 and passim.

[14] CCA, DSA 75, Stanley 'My Mother's Journal', p. 42 (18 Aug. 1815).

[15] Anon., *Directions to Servants; particularly those who have the Care of Children*, G. Kearsley, E. and C. Dodd, London, 1779, pp. 16–17.

[16] Mitzi Myers, '"Servants as They Are Now Educated": Women writers and Georgian pedagogy', *Essays in Literature*, 16 (1989), 51–69. Mrs William Parkes thought it the main job of a woman's life to listen to 'all their little complaints', alerting her readers to their propensity for claiming a sickie: 'There is not a class of people more fanciful, or inclined to imagine themselves more indisposed than they really are.' Mrs William Parkes, *Domestic Duties; or, Instructions to Young Married Ladies, on the Management of their Households, and the Regulation of their Conduct in the Various Relations and Duties of Married Life*, Longman, Hurst, Rees, Orme, Brown and Green, London, 1825, pp. 118–19.

[17] Dorothy Kilner, *The Life and Perambulations of a Mouse*, John Marshall, London, 1784, pp. 18–19, 28–32, 68. What the servants gathered in the kitchen want is for the children to speak nicely to them, say '"yes, if you *please*, Miss Sally, or no *thank* you Mr Bob; or I should be so obliged to you . . . Mrs Nelly".'

change the buckles on her shoe, or else she will slap my face? Indeed, she did give me a slap upon my hand... really Ma'am, I thought you would not wish me to do it, while she behaved so... "'. In a highly satisfying textual move, the mother supports the maidservant, from the same impulse as Kilner's we may presume, and that prompted Mary Wollstonecraft to write dialogues to teach a three-year-old that she was but 'a little girl... assisted because she is weak' and inferior in years and experience to her nursemaid.[18] The child's dependence on servants is a lesson of all Wollstonecraft's pedagogic writing, and it was for the mother to teach it.[19] Her own education in civility and social sympathy were part of the point, for a woman's 'temper depends very much on her behaviour to [servants]. Servants in general are, ignorant and cunning; we must consider their characters, if we would treat them properly, and continually practice regard to them.'[20] (When she wrote this, Wollstonecraft had not encountered Godwin to tell her sarcastically what this 'exuberance of [her] humanity' really meant, nor yet employed a nursemaid or general servant herself.)

Middle-class and gentry wives worried much about the questions of authority hinted at by Kilner and Wollstonecraft. Having delegated the physical care and management of their children to subordinates, it was a nice question whom the child should obey. Or rather, if it were to be made to do as it was told, who should do the telling and the slapping? Young wife and experienced wife debate these questions in Mrs William Parkes's *Domestic Duties* of 1825. Mrs L. asks Mrs B. whether she would 'allow a servant to correct the children whom she has under her charge?' The answer was unequivocal: 'I would on *no account* permit even the most unexceptionable servant to inflict on children correction... The power of a nurse ought to extend no further than to enforce... wishes and orders of the parent'.[21]

Mothers found many ways of negotiating the boundaries of authority and subordination in the nursery. Catherine Stanley showed a true interest in nursemaid Sally's reports of little Owen's speech development, though it is clear that the young woman had been told to listen and observe for the purposes of her mistress's baby-journal. She was

---

[18] Mary Wollstonecraft, *The Works of Mary Wollstonecraft*, Janet Todd and Marilyn Butler (eds), 7 vols., Pickering, London, 1989, vol. 6, p. 472.
[19] These are the lessons of *Elements of Morality* (1790), *Original Stories from Real Life* (1788); and the posthumous *Letters* (1798). Wollstonecraft, *Works*, vol. 2, pp. 412–13; vol. 4, p. 142; vol. 6, p. 472.
[20] This is the opinion of *Thoughts on the Education of Daughters* (1787): Wollstonecraft, *Works*, vol. 4, pp. 38–9.
[21] Parkes, *Domestic Duties*, p. 163.

sceptical however, about Sally's forays into child psychology, noting in January 1813, that when Owen came running to her 'with a high colour & much agitation...shuddering' because he had pulled the top off a pencil case she had given him to play with, Sally suggested that 'perhaps it put him in mind of his [toy] blacksmith whose head he had pulled off & wh. had alarmed him very much'. His mother thought it impossible to determine 'whether this was the case, or whether he caught the idea from hearing her say so'.[22] She certainly thought that she could deal better with his temper than did the servants: in April 1814 she found him 'in a great passion with the Maids about leaving his Drum behind'. She addressed the two-year-old 'calmly and directly'; he stopped his roaring immediately and 'said not a word more about it'.[23] Stanley's extreme plainness of language with Owen was evidently part of an educational strategy; it was by way of marked contrast with the world of speech play and fantasy that Sally created in the nursery: 'Sally said...he cannot catch sleep...Owen jumped up & said "Sleep run away, Owen can't catch it"...Sally told him there was a *nice good* fire to warm him –"Does the fire never cry Sally?"...Sally told him the wind whistled – "Has the wind got a face? has it got a mouth to whistle?"..."I never saw anything like you you will drink the sea dry" – "then what will become of the ships?"'.

Writers of journals, advice manuals, and fiction for parents and children, all repeated John Locke's strictures against the ghost stories told by servants to quiet children into obedience. Stanley's beliefs about proper and improper fantasy in language may have made reference to Locke, but her linguistic theory also derived from Rousseau, from whose work she copied copiously. In 1790s Staffordshire, Josiah Wedgewood II pursued a distinctly Rousseau-istic programme with his children, and probably interpreted the nursemaid's verbal play with them as the 'harmful habit' he had observed often in 'servants & other persons with little judgement...of pleasing themselves by setting their wits against that of a child'.[24] It was certainly difficult to be a governess (let alone a laundry maid) in this liberal and progressive household. Miss W. (who appears to be the addressee of his home-made instruction manual entitled 'Hints on the Management of the Children') simply could not get it right, what with her 'mistaken conception of our opinions', and her persistence in thinking that 'we have meant the children to be *obeyed*. Persons should

[22] CCA, DSA 75, 'My Mother's Journal', p. 6 (Jan. 1813).
[23] CCA, DSA 75, 'My Mother's Journal', p. 30 (20 Apr. 1814).
[24] Keele University (KU), Special Collections and Archives, W/M 1116, Josiah Wedgewood II, 'Hints on the Management of the Children', 1797–8, p. 24.

pursue their occupations & not appear so evidently to be *mere* attendants on the children.'[25] But this was difficult indeed under the injunction that 'We must not have [the children's] activity diminished and their pleasures checked by a frequent admonition not to dirty a frock. A little washing more or less is of no consequence, but we cannot begin too early to give unbounded scope to the activity & exertions of children.'[26] The governess's dilemma, which coincided with the servant's in this regard, has been brilliantly dealt with by Kathryn Hughes in *The Victorian Governess*, and of course, by Anne Brontë in *Agnes Grey* (1847).[27] But no governess had to deal with the material fall-out of the Wedgewood educational project as the nursery- and laundry-maids perforce had to do.

It appears that Stanley had found herself the kind of 'sensible woman' to be later recommended by Mrs Parkes; Sally's voice (strongly inflected by her Cheshire dialect) emerges clearly from beneath several layers of reportage; her mistress had no need of the advice delivered to mothers less certain of their social and parental position than she. *The Present of a Mother to a Young Servant* of 1816 advised parents to let the nursemaid play with the children, telling the girl herself that 'all young things are playful . . . those who love infants, will be amused by playing with them; those who do not, are unfit to be nursemaids'.[28] The addition of play to the list of the servant's duties was a relatively new one, an important part of the civilising mission of the middle-class household in offering patterns of behaviour and attitude to the daughters of the poor. So perhaps was Mrs Taylor's strategy of asking the servant to remember her own childhood in order to understand her charges by the exercise of imaginative sympathy: 'they should never be terrified with nonsensical stories of ghosts, and old men, and witches' she said, 'unless you wish to render them as unhappy about such things as you may have been, and perhaps still are, when alone in the dark'.[29] In 1787 Ann Walker had told her intended readers – maids of all work, to whom the 'duty of a nurse' had also fallen – that 'it was by diligence and tenderness that you yourselves were reared to what you are; and it is by the same disposition you will bring up your own children when you have them'. But this was care for the body rather than the infant mind.[30]

[25] KU, W/M 1116, Wedgewood, 'Hints', pp. 33, 42.   [26] Wedgewood, 'Hints', p. 14.

[27] Kathryn Hughes, *The Victorian Governess*, Hambledon, London, 1993. See also Mary Poovey, *Uneven Developments: The ideological work of gender in mid-Victorian England*, University of Chicago Press, Chicago, 1988.

[28] Ann Taylor, *The Present of a Mother to a Young Servant: Consisting of Friendly Advice and real Histories*, 2nd edn, Taylor and Hessey, London, 1816, p. 116.

[29] Taylor, *Present of a Mother*, pp. 117, 118.   [30] Walker, *Complete Guide*, pp. 14–16.

In Soham, Cambridgeshire in 1779, John Peach, surgeon and apothecary, employed two servants – or rather, was assessed for two, under the servant tax legislation. But Peach thought that twelve-year-old James Bye, an orphan he had taken in out of charity, was nothing of the sort. James did not wait at table he said; he cleaned no knives, he wore no livery. What he did do was work in the shop, run errands, and play with and generally look after the two children. But to the assessed tax commissioners gathered at the appeal meeting, the Boy was plainly a servant: in their view playing with the children constituted *waiting upon* or *serving* them.[31] This was exactly the kind of household arrangement that Patt King wanted to avoid in 1760s Birmingham (even though she was to have wages for it). She had better reason for avoiding such a place than James Bye who (we may suppose – this is the way the story is set up) was grateful for being taken in in his orphan state, for no one – as far as we know – ever asked a Boy or Man to wash the children's clouts.

On the clout question, we can return to a household like John Peach's, a Nottinghamshire one, in 1785. John Butler employs Mary Cant as general servant, not as nursemaid, for she has many other things to do. He tells her to dress the child, which suggests she has dressed it on other occasions, but more importantly, that right now it is undressed, and that it is either early morning or evening, and the child has been washed, as the most modern and up-to-date advice suggested it should be, or that at least its soiled napkin has been removed and it has been cleaned.[32] (The counsel of perfection by the turn of the century, was washing by immersing the child in water *at least twice a day*.[33]) In Mary Cant's world, it is not impossible that a man should know what to do with a baby, but her retort, that he should dress it himself, provokes him into hitting her.[34] Advice manuals of the late eighteenth century

---

[31] Commissioners of Excise, *Abstract of Cases and Decisions on Appeals Relating to the Tax on Servants*, T. Longman and T. Cadell, London, 1781.

[32] John Theobald, MD, *The Young Wife's Guide, in the Management of her Children*, W. Griffin and G. Kearsley, London, 1764, pp. 6, 10, 29; Anne Barker, *The Complete Servant Maid: or Young Woman's Best Companion*, 6th edn, J. Cooke, Dublin, 1770, pp. 29–33; Sarah Brown, *Letter to a Lady on the Management of the Infant*, Baker and Galabin, London, 1779, p. 8; Hugh Smith, *Letters to Married Women, on Nursing and the Management of Children*, 6th ed, C. and G. Kearsley, London, 1792; Hugh Moss, *Essay on the Management, Nursing and Diseases of Children*, 2nd edn, C. Boult, London, 1794.

[33] Mrs Wright, Midwife, *An Essay to Instruct Women how to Protect themselves in a State of Pregnancy . . . Also, Some Observations on the Treatment of Children, which, if attended to, may ward off Dangerous Disease, and prevent future Evils*, privately printed, London, 1798, pp. 25–6.

[34] Nottinghamshire Archives (NA), M 8050, Notebooks of Sir Gervase Clifton JP, 1772–1812, p. 124. It would have taken some time to dress the child in a shirt with strings, short loose roller, blanket, little gown, and cap that Brown recommended, *Letter to a*

were quiet on the topic of what had probably just been removed from Baby Butler: a nappy, also called a clout, diaper cloth, or napkin; though they were eloquent on the cleaning, powdering and dressing of infants.[35] Societies of philanthropic ladies provided napkins (and what look to be something very like nappy liners) on loan for poor women during their confinement.[36] One Sussex gentleman farmer paid extra to a succession of his cookmaids 'to wash the child's Clouts', for dirty nappies could not be stored up against the monthly (or quarterly, in some old-fashioned households) wash.[37] There is some evidence that the laundry-maid's task became more difficult in the later century, as diaper-weave cotton replaced linen clouts, rags, and especially cut squares like the ladies of Hertlingford produced for their settled poor.[38] Linen is amenable to stain removal by soaking in lye or in stale urine, whilst cotton cloth requires rubbing, scrubbing, and best of all, boiling, to loosen stains to the same degree.[39] If the laundry-maid's task was made harder by new fabrics and the washing techniques they implied, then so was that of young women like Mary Cant, who were child-maid, house-maid and laundry-maid in one person. 'A little washing more or less' *was* of consequence, because new and more labour-intensive laundry techniques were required of a general servant in a household with children.

We have seen that the process of human-waste disposal could be discussed in this society, sometimes at the highest philosophical level, and that a great part of the servant's labour was taken up with it. That babies produced copious amounts of waste was discussed by some

Lady, p. 6. The long stay was optional, and no need for a belly band after the naval string was off. But we do not know how old Baby Butler was.

[35] Brown, *Letter to a Lady*, pp. 6, 16, 23. Sarah Brown thought that starch was better for powdering than the white lead powder that Mrs Wright suggested! Wright, *Essay*, pp. 25–6. Wright did however counsel mothers to see that the nursemaid did not let it get into the child's food.

[36] Anon., *Instructions for Cutting Out Apparel for the Poor; principally intended for the Assistance of Patronesses of Sunday Schools . . . But Useful in all Families . . . Published for the Benefit of the Sunday School Children at Hertingfordbury in the County of Hertford*, J. Walter, London, 1789, pp. 73–85, 'Child-bed Linen for the Use of the Poor'. '24 squares of double Diaper' were included in the loaned layette and 'One yard and three quarters of white baize . . . This being very necessary and useful to the poor women, it is not to be returned with the Childbed linnen'.

[37] East Sussex County Record Office (ESCRO), AMS 6191, Household account book of Thomas Cooper of New Place Farm in Guestling, 1788–1824 (14 Mar. 1795, 21 Jan. 1790, 29 Dec. 1792, 30 Dec. 1803).

[38] Anon., *Instructions for Cutting Out Apparel*, p. 82

[39] Susanna Whatman, *The Housekeeping Book of Susanna Whatman, 1776–1800*, Intro. Christina Hardyment, National Trust, London, 2000, p. 29. William Watson, *Textile Design: Colour, elementary weaves and figured fabric*, Longman, Green, London, 1912, pp. 47–62, 146 for diaper weave. I owe much to the Textiles Department of the Victoria and Albert Museum for information on diaper weave and varieties of diaper cloth.

female advice-book writers of the late century ('young children frequently soil themselves up to the top of the stays', Sarah Brown warned her lady readers in 1779), but the laundering of their dirty clothing was not mentioned.[40] A servant (nurse, child-maid, nurserymaid, Girl) was expected to be involved with the child's excretions from the word go.[41] It was assumed in all this literature that babies did wear some form of nappy, and that it would in all cases be handled by the servant.[42] But nappies, or clouts, are hard to track down. Tobias Smollett referred to nappy washing, but he only noticed it because he was in Nîmes, watching the crystal water of the Roman bath in the town square being polluted by a group of washerwomen pounding away at children's clouts and raising a great stink.[43] His sarcastic comments here on French notions of cleanliness may have been based on knowledge that at home, the same job was done by some lone girl at the back-kitchen sink, or in a pail in the back yard. A spurious continuation of *Tristram Shandy* contains a learned debate between Mr Shandy and Dr Slop over the parturient, supine (though not un-vocal) body of Tristram's mother, about the thing most necessary for the child being 'a continual succession of clean clouts'. The point is some heavy-handed satire against every doctor 'that has wrote about women and children'.[44] Commentators and dispensers of advice were eloquent on maidservants' insane prejudice against changing children's linen, attributing to them all sorts of quasi-medical folk beliefs about the dangers of so doing (they 'entertain a strange opinion about changing the linen and keeping the child clean; they imagine clean things draw away and rob them of their nourishment'), but never mentioned the laundry work attendant on the instruction that the child's linen 'cannot be changed too often'.[45] The labour of the servant's laundry work did not escape the observation of Dorothy Kilner's alter ego and anthropologist in the nursery, Nimble the Mouse, who overhears two horrid boys describe the great fun of cutting a washing line just as the servants have finished their mammoth task, thus obliging them 'to wash every rag over

[40] Brown, *Letter to a Lady*, p. 23.

[41] Immediately after birth the nursemaid should check 'whether there is a stoppage in the passages . . . by administering the corner of the child's napkin, dipped in a little warm water, sweet oil or pomatum'. Brown, *Letter*, p. 6.

[42] Brown, *Letter*, p. 23: 'There is another thing that particularly demands your attention; that is, not to suffer the nurse-maid to lift the child's legs too high, when she puts on a napkin'.

[43] Tobias Smollett, *The Miscellaneous Works of Tobias Smollett, M. D. with Memoirs of his Life and Writings*, 2nd edn, Robert Anderson (ed.), 6 vols., Mundell, Edinburgh, 1800, vol. 5, pp. 314–15. (*Travels in France and Italy*, 1766.)

[44] John Carr, *The Life and Opinions of Tristram Shandy, Gentleman*, privately printed, London, 1760, pp. 214–15.

[45] Brown, *Letter*, pp. 20–21.

Figure 17. The Servant's Labour now increased, as observed by Nimble the Mouse.

again'. Susan the housemaid actually cries, and no wonder; and then Nimble becomes Kilner again, to ask the boys (and her many types of reader) how they would feel if it happened to them – 'and even that would not be half so bad for you, as it was for the maids . . . washing is very hard labour, and tires people sadly'.[46]

If we had always and conventionally described this society by means of anthropological concepts of pollution and danger, understood it in terms of traditional hierarchical divisions, each group or caste with assigned tasks that rigidly maintained a system of social stratification and morality, then eighteenth-century domestic servants' role would be seen as the removal and disposal of polluting (or at least dirty) matter from the vicinity of their betters.[47] But eighteenth-century English society was not a caste society. Domestic servants were contracted workers with – as we have seen – a very nice sense of what the job should and should not entail

[46] Kilner, *Mouse*, pp. 69–70.
[47] Nineteenth-century Brazil was not a caste society either, but Sandra Graham assesses the servant's social role by her relationship to human waste, and changes in sanitation and sewage systems. Sandra Lauderdale Graham, *House and Street: The domestic world of servants in nineteenth-century Rio de Janeiro*, Cambridge University Press, Cambridge, 1988, pp. 41, 55–67.

and of their rights within the employment relationship; they appear to have been more willing than other workers to take complaints about it to a magistrate, at least in country places. The law itself, and the vast amount of legislative attention to eighteenth-century domestic servants was one of the factors that promoted their convictions about the rights and wrongs of work situations. How many of them knew William Blackstone on *The Laws of England* is not an entirely foolish question to ask, for whilst few may have whiled away a leisure hour with the *Commentaries*, his assertion that the relation between master and servant was the first great relation of private life, underpinned the everyday legal understanding and practice of provincial justices and was thus at work in the kind of law that domestics were most likely to encounter. But not in the case of Ann Mead, a servant girl sentenced to death by Lord Chief Justice Kenyon (she encountered the criminal law in his person; we encounter it for the first time in this book) in July 1800, for the murder of her employers' child. Questions of social hierarchy, class feeling, the experience of a particular kind of labour (and the dirty clouts) can illuminate one short, sad, lost story from Royston, at the turn of the nineteenth century.

She cannot have encountered the Lord Chief Justice for very long – a distant, unknowable figure in a wig (he and Sir Nash Grose) across the small but infinitely divided space of the courtroom.[48] Most trials for capital offences were over in a matter of minutes. Hertfordshire Assizes opened on Monday 28 July, the first of the summer Home Circuit. By Wednesday the judges were on the road for Chelmsford, where in role as 'chief moral censor in the market place', Kenyon delivered his charge to the Grand Jury of Essex, denouncing the practices of regrating and engrossing, both in legal principle and in the context of these hot and hungry summer months.[49] He had in target the Kentish hop-dealer Samuel Waddington, whose contracts with local growers for standing crops and the concomitant raising and fixing of prices, focused the ominous question of what would happen if the practice were extended to the staple wheat crop. The country was already in a severe crisis of dearth.[50] The Chief Justice had already remarked that if supporters of Waddington and

---

[48] V. A. C. Gatrell, *The Hanging Tree: Execution and the English people, 1770–1868*, Oxford University Press, Oxford, 1994, pp. 466–8, 532–3, and passim; for the judges –'furred homicides, sable bigots' – pp. 497–514. Also James Beattie, *Crime and the Courts in England, 1660–1800*, Oxford University Press, Oxford, 1986, pp. 314–99.

[49] Doug Hay, 'The state and the market in 1800: Lord Kenyon and Mr Waddington', *Past and Present*, 162 (1999), 100–62, 129; Roger Wells, *Wretched Faces: Famine in wartime England, 1798–1801*, Alan Sutton, Gloucester, 1988, pp. 37–8, 77–9 for the weather; pp. 85–89, 323 for Waddington and Kenyon, and trials for regrating held all over the country in 1800–1.

[50] See Chapter 9; Wells, *Wretched Faces*, pp. 35–52.

a free market in grain and other commodities had done as he had, gone 200 miles from London and observed 'people at every avenue of a country town, buying up *butter, cheese and all the necessaries of life* . . . in order to prevent them coming to market', then they might be of his opinion, that playing the market in foodstuffs and thus starving the poor was immoral. As Doug Hay says, he had long shown himself to be a judge of 'robust and unfashionable notions'.[51] These notions were in fact shared by his fellow common-law judges who had worked hard in the previous months to reinstate engrossing, forestalling and regrating as offences at common law, though the statutory penalties against them had been repealed in 1772.[52] Kenyon had also recently reinforced traditional labour relations embodied in the service contract when, in February 1800, he reminded all employers of their legal obligations towards their servants in sickness: that they took a servant 'for better and for worse'.[53]

The first conviction of Waddington was achieved at Worcester City Assizes whilst the Chief Justice was sitting at Chelmsford. The news was brought to him by express and Kenyon was able to tell the Essex grand jury that Waddington had been found guilty on every count. Had the news from Worcester come a couple of days earlier, then Hertford might have been the theatre for Kenyon's denunciations; but the caravan of London reporters had moved on, leaving only a local correspondent to write that there had been twenty-three prisoners at trial, 'an unusual number for this county'. (There were high numbers at trial across the southern and midlands circuits during this very hard year.) Among the Hertford twenty-three was Ann Mead, 'a young woman only 16 years old, convicted of the willful murder of Charles Proctor, an infant not 18 months old'.[54] Six had been condemned to death by Kenyon and Grose. Two sheep stealers and three highway robbers had their sentences commuted to terms in the house of correction and transportation, respectively. Mead went down with one other of the condemned, James alias 'Shock' Oliver for a shooting at Dudley in Worcestershire. By the time Kenyon charged the Essex Grand Jury, Ann Mead was hanged.

'Thursday 31st July 1800 – Was Hanged at Hartford Ann Mead about 14 years of Age for poyseing one of the Proctors Children about $1\frac{1}{2}$

---

[51] Hay, 'State and market', pp. 118–19. For Kenyon, also Douglas Hay, 'Kenyon, Lloyd, first Baron Kenyon (1732–1802)' in *Oxford Dictionary of National Biography*, Oxford University Press, 2004, www.oxforddnb.com/view/article/15431, accessed 6 Apr. 2007.

[52] Hay, 'State and market', pp. 118–119; *London Chronicle*, 29 Jul.–3 Aug. 1800.

[53] Hay, 'State and market', pp. 120–1 (citing *Summary Trial of the King v. S. F. Waddington* . . . , Crosby and Letterman, London, 1800, p. 125); 'Obligations of masters', *The Times*, 6 Feb. 1800.

[54] *Courier and Evening Gazette* (London), 31 Jul. 1800; *The Times*, 29 Jul. 1800.

old, of Royston', noted the tax collector from Bramfield, whose journey
to the county town was on this occasion not for the usual purpose of
depositing the assessed tax money in the bank, but because as constable
for the Liberty of St Albans, he was obliged to give in his presentments
to the court of quarter sessions which sat at the same time as the assize
court. 'She lived with them as Servant Girll' Carrington continued, '&
her Mistress & she had words so she took revenge on the Child.'[55] In his
account of judicial hanging between 1770 and 1868, Vic Gatrell notes
that 70–80 per cent of executions took place not at the notorious venues
of Tyburn and Newgate (and other London sites) but in assize towns
like Hertford, where they were 'a focal event in the country calendar'.[56]
He also notes how very rare hangings were in some places. But earlier
in 1800, Hertford had been the scene of a botched execution that, in
the reporting of it at least, reached terrible depths of comic horror.[57] If
memories of the April farce lasted until June, they do not surface in the
annals of the death of Ann Mead. This was reported in the Cambridge
and London press, and made a small item in some Midlands' papers,
but there was no account of the execution itself, nor of the demeanour of
the crowd, nor its size. It is not even clear that tax collector Carrington
stayed to witness it, for his diary entry is word for word what he could
have read in the newspapers.

Ann Mead's time in court must have been very short. She had already
confessed the crime at the inquest held in Royston a month before, where
after initial loud denials, she admitted to administering half a teaspoonful
of arsenic to the child on 16 June. Charles Proctor had lingered a few
hours, to die the next day. The charge against Mead was murder, not
murder and petty treason as it was for a servant like Thomas Armstrong,
who in Gloucester in 1777, administered arsenic to his employer's wife,
unable to stand her bad temper any longer. Women who killed their

---

[55] W. Branch-Johnson, *The Carrington Diary, 1797–1810*, Christopher Johnson, London,
1956, pp. 50, 144–5, 152–3. Hertfordshire County Record Office (HCRO), D/EX3/3,
Diaries of John Carrington Snr, vol. 3, May–Dec. 1800. Beattie, *Crime and the Courts*,
pp. 35–73. Royston is on the border of Hertfordshire and Cambridgeshire; the parish was
in both counties for poor-law purposes. The Mead family lived in the Cambridgeshire
part, but the crime had been committed in the Hertfordshire part where the Proctors
lived and Ann Mead was servant; after the coroner's inquest she was committed to
Hertfordshire Assizes. This explains the early interest of the Cambridge press in her
case. Hertfordshire had no county newspaper. There are no extant issues for 1800 of
the *County Chronicle for and Weekly Advertiser for Essex, Hertfordshire, Kent etc* (essentially
the Home Circuit counties); it may well have carried reports. The murder made first
news in June 1800, in the *Cambridgeshire Chronicle* and the *Cambridge Intelligencer*. Their
reports were used by the London press.
[56] Gatrell, *Hanging Tree*, p. 57. Beattie, *Crime and the Courts*, pp. 316–17.
[57] Gatrell, *Hanging Tree*, pp. 99–100; *Cambridge Chronicle*, 15 Mar. 5 Apr. 1800.

husbands and servants their employers were the only categories to whom the charge might apply; killing an employer's child did not constitute petty treason.[58] The Royston inquisition and indictment of Mead did not cite motive as the newspapers did: 'her mistress had called her a dirty slut and she was resolved to spite her'. Lord Kenyon, maddeningly and unusually for him, kept no notes, perhaps because it was so clear a case of willful murder, a crime already confessed (though he made notes on equally uncontroversial cases at Hertford in the following year, and all across the Home Circuit in 1800).[59] Ann Mead spent five weeks in Hertford Goal awaiting assizes, and then four nights awaiting execution.[60]

Poisoning maidservants were – or in a few years would become – figures of great public interest and note. Fifteen years later the case of Elizabeth Fenning was a reference point for deep interest in the arsenic question (Fenning was hanged for attempting to murder the entire household by putting it in the dinner dumplings).[61] A maid who put arsenic in the stew or in the gruel showed the permeable boundaries between poison and

---

[58] TNA, ASSI 94/1497, English Assize Records, 1559–1971, Criminal Trial Records, Herts. Indictments, Summer Assizes 40 Geo. III 1800, Hertfordshire, Felony File. There was a report of her apprehension and the inquest on the body of Charles Proctor in the *Gentleman's Magazine*, vol. 69, 20 Jun. 1800; *Lloyd's Evening Post and British Chronicle* (London), 20 Jun. 1800; *Cambridge Chronicle and Journal*, 21, 28 Jun. 1800; *Cambridge Intelligencer*, 21 Jun. 1880; *Observer*, 22 Jun. 1800; *Northampton Mercury*, 28 Jun. 1800. For the Armstrong case see Wiltshire Record Office (WRO), 635/152, Murder of Catherine Pierce Ashe A'Court (Gloucester) by a family servant, 1776. TNA (PRO), ASSI 5 97/4, English Assize Records, 1559–1971, Criminal Trial Records, Gloucestershire Indictments, Lent 1777.

[59] Lancashire Record Office (LRO), DDKE. acc 7840, Lloyd Kenyon, 1st Baron Kenyon, Diaries, 1767 to 1802: 'Sunday 27 July Set out for the Home Circuit . . . Dined at the Marquis of Salisbury's in Hatfield . . . Monday 28 July To Hertford. Wednesday 30 July To Chelmsford'. Correspondence in quarto boxes, 1–26 (1753–1802), box 23, 1800; Folio boxes, 'Briefs Cases Opinions 1783–1800'. Sir Nash Grose appears not to have kept trial notes. Information from Isle of Wight Record Office.

[60] James Neild visited Hertford Goal in August 1801: *Account of the Rise Progress, and Present State of the Society for the Discharge and Relief of Persons Imprisoned for Small Debts throughout England*, privately printed, London, 1802, pp. 151–2; his report allows some reconstruction of Mead's last days. See also James Neild, *State of the Prisons in England, Scotland and Wales . . . not for the Debtor only, but for Felons also . . .*, J. Nichols, London, 1812, pp. 270–3.

[61] Gatrell, *Hanging Tree*, pp. 339–70; John Marshall, *Five Cases of Recovery from the Effects of Arsenic . . .*, privately printed, London, 1815; *Remarks on Arsenic, considered as a Poison and a Medicine . . .*, Callow, London, 1817; John Watkins, *The Important Results of an Elabourate Investigation . . .*, William Hone, London, 1815. Cases like these were routinely given to coroners as guides for the detection of arsenic poisoning. John Impey, *The Practice of the Office of Sherrif . . . also The Practice of the Office of Coroner . . . with a Copious Appendix of Useful Precedents*, 5th edn, J. and W. T. Clarke, London, 1822. Ian A. Burney, *Poison, Detection and the Victorian Imagination*, Manchester University Press, Manchester, 2007.

foodstuffs and the role of domestic servants in holding (or not holding) the line between the two.[62] In 1800 many foodstuffs, bread in particular, were strange in texture and taste because of the use of substitutes for the failed wheat crop.[63] Reports of domestic poisoning cases – the poisoning of masters and mistresses by servants, of maidservants by masters (attempting the abortion of the child got on her) – focused on the preparation of food, on the ratsbane rolled into little pellets with putrid meat to look exactly like oatmeal, and left unlabelled on a kitchen window sill, as it was to be in the Fenning case.[64] This kind of case – certainly in 1800 – was reported alongside the accounts of domestic violence and murder that assizes always produced for public consumption.[65] In 1815 the Fenning *cause célèbre* would also be about a deep interest in her person, her demeanour, her alluring bosom, the little lilac boots she wore on the scaffold. Vic Gatrell has described this reaction to her person and her story (and what was clearly her unsafe conviction) as 'the beatification of Eliza Fenning'. A kind of beatification (or more accurately, sentimentalisation) also took place early in 1800, when the resolutely proletarian and unchaste Sarah Lloyd, servant of Bury St Edmunds, who wrote no letters from prison (unlike Fenning) and who was extremely difficult to appropriate to the chivalric imagination, was hanged for robbing her mistress. Yet she was so appropriated, and made at least in iconographic terms, the true trope of 'virtue in distress'.[66] None of this literary and sexual interest attended the death of Ann Mead, who was too young, too unimportant and who had on her own confession committed

[62] A. Fothergill, *Cautions to the Heads of Families, in three Essays: I. On Cyder-Wine, prepared in Copper Vessels; with Hints for the Improvement of Cyder, Perry, and other Fruit Liquors. II. On the Poison of Lead – Method of Detecting it in various Liquors, Foods, Medicines, Cosmetiks &c. with general Indications of Cure. III. On the Poison of Copper – How it may be discovered though in very minute Quantity – Methods of Cure*, R. Cruttwell, Bath, 1790, pp. 74–6; Hannah Glasse, *A Servant's Directory, or House-keeper's Companion Wherein the Duties of Chamber-maid, House-maid, Laundry-maid, Scullion or Under-cook, Are fully and distinctly explained. To which is annexed a Diary, or House-keeper's Pocket Book for the Whole Year with Directions for keeping Accounts with Tradesmen, and many other Particulars, fit to be known by the Mistress of a Family*, W. Johnson, London, 1760, pp. 53–5. Dr Fothergill was alarmingly amusing on verdigris poisoning: 'If our pickles must absolutely look green to please the eye at the expence of health, or even life, why [do those] . . . who preside over all culinary operations . . . mince the matter? Why not steep the pickles at once in a strong solution of verdigris?'

[63] See Chapter 9.   [64] Marshall, *Five Cases*; Watkins, *Important Results*.

[65] In the summer of 1800 the London papers made much of the Medhurst wife-murder case heard at York Assizes. See, for example, *London Chronicle*, 28 Jun.–1 Jul. 1800; it was everywhere in the provincial press, reported in great detail.

[66] Gatrell, *Hanging Tree*, pp. 340–53; R. F. Brissenden, *Virtue in Distress: Studies in the novel of sentiment from Richardson to de Sade*, Macmillan, London, 1974.

a horrible crime that had no generic conventions by which it might be related.[67]

The evidence was powerfully against Ann Mead, but she only admitted giving the child arsenic when the results of the autopsy were presented to the coroner's court, showing that traces had been found in the stomach. Further evidence was given a month later at Assizes, that she had been to a Royston grocer's shop and purchased the poison herself.[68] It was now, five weeks after she had taken her revenge for being called a dirty slut, that attribution of motive was deepened: she had been called so not on account of her morals, but because 'her mistress . . . had found fault with her for not keeping the child so clean as she might have done'.[69]

Royston, along with other Hertfordshire and south-eastern parishes, had been inventive in getting its poor girls off ratepayers' hands in these years of dearth and distress.[70] Indeed, the Hertfordshire side of Royston parish had advertised in the London press that it had 'Cheap Servants' available as early as 1786.[71] By the 1790s there was a smoothly running system for getting workhouse girls and other parish poor, places in north London, where they worked not as apprentices to housewifery (a traditional way of getting pauper girls domestic work) but as contracted domestic servants (albeit on very low wages).[72] The system produced

---

[67] Infanticide, on the other hand, possessed the most resonant repertoire of narrative devices; Josephine McDonagh, *Child Murder and British Culture, 1720–1900*, Cambridge University Press, Cambridge, 2003, passim and pp. 71–2, describes a plethora of plots, tropes and narratives for writing and telling a parent's crime; but there is not one mention of the murdering maidservant. In English law, infanticide could – and can still – only be committed by the biological mother of a child less than one year old. There are currently discussions underway about extending the legal category 'infanticide' to carers other than the natural mother – perhaps a belated recognition by the state of the clout question discussed here.

[68] At Worcester Assizes in March 1800, fourteen-year-old William Winwood stood trial for poisoning his mistress. Arsenic had been found mixed in her basin of morning gruel, 'but the fact of its being bought or administered by the prisoner was not substantiated by the evidence', and he was acquitted. *Whitehall Evening Post*, 15–18 Mar. 1800, 'Lent Assizes'.

[69] *Courier and Evening Gazette*, 31 Jul. 1800, 'Hertford – July 29'.

[70] Roger A. E. Wells, 'The development of the English rural proletariat and social protest, 1700–1850' in Mick Reed and Roger Wells (eds.), *Class, Conflict and Protest in the English Countryside, 1700–1880*, Frank Cass, London, 1990, pp. 36–7; Roger Wells, 'Social protest, class, conflict and consciousness, in the English countryside 1700–1880', in Reed and Wells (eds.), *Class, Conflict and Consciousness*, pp. 142–3.

[71] HCRO, D/P/18/1, Royston Parish Records, Correspondence concerning placing of paupers as apprentices and servants and notebook containing addresses to which servants were sent, 1784–1804; also 'Notice to put out Boys and Girls, Royston 21st March 1786'.

[72] Keith Snell, 'The apprenticeship system in British history: The fragmentation of a cultural institution', *History of Education*, 25 (1996), 303–21.

some gratifying success stories. 'I Licke your Girl very well', wrote Sarah Clapham from London to the girl's mother;

and she likes hir plase very well and I will Give hir after the Rate of 40 shillings a year I never hire one by the Munth but wen a Servant wants to go away from me I Never want Them to stop I like Girl very well but I Can't keep her without yo send them which I rote for your Daughter will be very Glad to be of use of you when yo Come up I don't think it proper to let so young a Girl come Down by hir self.[73]

But Ann Mead was not a girl like this: not a pauper or parish child. As far as can be discovered she was the daughter (or grand-daughter) of a family in a position to pay the Royston poor rate and to rent farm buildings from the parish. A Simeon Mead (father or grandfather) served briefly as overseer for the Cambridgeshire part of the parish. Both her parents signed when they married in 1777.[74] She was however, very young to be put in charge of a small child. The north London recipients of Royston's cheap servants thought that a girl should be older than this if she were to have care of children, and of amiable disposition. Here they were calculating physical as well as emotional maturity: a fourteen-year-old did not have the strength to undertake many household tasks.[75] Ann Mead was hanged sixteen years almost to the day from when she had been baptized, so she had been fifteen when she killed baby Proctor. It is not known how long she had been looking after him, but the Proctors were new arrivals in Royston, appearing in parish rate books from 1799 onwards when Charles (evidently not their only child) was born.[76] If they followed the timetable of the advice books, they would have taken her into service sometime in the summer of 1799, but it really is impossible to tell when she joined the household.[77] The Proctors stayed on in Royston after the death of their child; Sarah and Simeon Mead and their other four children disappear from the records. Ann was the youngest of five,

[73] HCRO, D/P/18/1, Sarah Clapham to Mrs Jacob of Roiston, 17 May 1804. For apprenticeship, Joan Lane, *Apprenticeship in England, 1600–1914*, UCL Press, London 1996.

[74] Cambridgeshire Record Office (CRO), P 135/12, Royston Parish Records, Accounts, 'Account of Rents for the several Houses Belonging to the Parish of Royston', with details of receipts and payments. HCRO, D/P87/1/22, Royston Parish Records, Register of Marriages, 4 Feb. 1777.

[75] HCRO, D/P 87/18/1, John Bower to Mr William Sparks, Overseer, Royston, 27 Aug. 1794: 'I should like to take one not younger than 15/as we have three children'; William Jagg to same, 28 Aug. 1794, 'a Girl not less than 18 of a good Disposition (her Business being chiefly to look after Children) . . . Attentive, willing & Industrious'; William Sadler to William Locket Royston, 28 Aug. 1794: 'a strong girl . . . one about sixteen or seventeen strong girl . . . I have got a wife and 3 children'.

[76] HCRO, D/P87/11/2 and 3, Poor Rate Assessments, 1793–1803.

[77] The Proctors do not appear in Royston baptism, marriage or burial registers. They may well have been dissenters.

but it would be a far step from that to assume that she thus had little experience of small children and their dirty clouts.[78]

It was keeping the child clean that was the problem, and being called a dirty slut that enraged her. She did not like this at all; in a profound and terrible way, she knew who and what she was. She was (in political and psychological terms) self-possessed. In a determined and calculated way she purchased her means of revenge. She knew that arsenic could be procured at a grocer's shop (knew what arsenic was, and its effects); she had money to spend on it. Her administration of the poison was calculated: half a teaspoonful, not a full one, out of the ounce she purchased. She cared not one whit for the child, whom we may assume was the mere source of hard, dirty and stinking work; she rather understood baby Proctor as a prize possession of her mistress, the best target for what the newspapers called her malice. She certainly left an evidential trail, but this was not reported as the frenzied and hopeless act of the century's other child-murdering maidservant of forty years before, fifteen-year-old Elizabeth Morton who, in the high summer of 1762 strangled one child and twisted the neck so violently of another that blood issued from its ears and nose, because, she said, 'they cry'd and were troublesome'.[79] (But who, at this distance of time and telling, can know what frenzy or calculation was?) When hanged in Nottingham in 1763 Morton was 'attended to the place of execution by a prodigious concourse of people'; eye-witnesses were interested in her demeanour on the scaffold, her relationship to her God and with the two ministers who accompanied her, the prayers she stuttered, the state of her soul. From the changing generic conventions of gallows literature – from flash, criminal and bawdy ballads, through the execution sheet, to Eliza Fenning's letters *de profundis* – we should not expect a similar reaction to Ann Mead's hanging.[80] It was not so much that tastes in the lessons of the noose had changed between 1760 and 1800 (though they had) but because this was a case from which absolutely no lessons could be drawn except the one impossible to entertain, that it was best not to employ (as you did, the moment you had 1s a week to spare) a truculent teenage girl to look after the baby. There are no direct accounts of her execution, the newspapers only noting (as they did of all death sentences pronounced at assizes) that it had been duly carried out. She had no textual afterlife; her ghost did not walk to tell of a broken rope and social injustice as

[78] HCRO, D/P87/1/1, Royston Parish Records, Register of Baptisms.
[79] *Leicester and Nottingham Journal*, 26 Mar. 1763, 8 May 1763.
[80] Gatrell, *Hanging Tree*, pp. 109–96.

did the servant Mary Nicholson's, after her murder of her mistress in 1799.[81]

Morton and Mead killed small, dirty, smelly children in high summer (in 1800, a hot and hungry one, with prolonged drought, 'aridity and relentless heat nationwide' throughout June, July and the first half of August).[82] The effect of prolonged drought on the water supply is not mentioned either by contemporaries or their historians, so it is speculation that it might be particularly hard-felt in the swift-draining chalk land in which Royston is situated.[83] Everything and everybody smelled. A correspondent to the London *Observer* wondered why the 'lower and labourious orders of society' could not be induced to observe the rules of cleanliness ('at all times essential to health' but 'indispensably necessary' in this torrid heat). Perhaps some measures could be devised to get them to change their linen more often?[84] In Mead's case, the dirt and the stink were what her mistress blamed her for. In Bermondsey, London, on 18 June, two days after Ann Mead administered her careful dose of arsenic, Ann Vines (or Vine) killed a toddler in her care because the child had soiled herself. She was charged with feloniously killing and slaying the child Esther Dandy by immersing her in a copper full of boiling water.[85]

There was a visiting grandmother on the scene; Esther's mother was upstairs, brought to bed of another child. Vines brings the child into the kitchen having collected her from a neighbour's, saying to grandmother Marshall that Esther is 'a nasty little creature, the child having dirtied itself'. Then Mrs Marshall directs Vines to put the child to bed, and goes upstairs to her daughter. (Put to bed in punishment? Because it was time for bed? Vines to wash the child first?) The child says: 'I won't go to bed'. The copper bubbles away ominously ready for the wash that is now increased. Then Mrs Marshall hears screams from downstairs and calls out 'Nanny, what are you doing with the child?', to which Vines answers 'Nothing'. Vines comes running up with Esther wrapped in an apron, or the skirt of her frock (the witness cannot recall which); or in

---

[81] *A Full and Particular Account, of the Wonderful Apparition of Mary Nicholson which appeared to two Men her intimate Friends and Acquaintance, at a Village near Durham, during the late ahunder [sic] Storm; and an account of her meditations after the Rope Broke*, n.i, Durham 1799. For ghosts as a claim for social justice, see Sasha Handley, '"Visions of an Unseen World": The production and consumption of English ghost stories, c. 1660–1800', PhD thesis, University of Warwick, 2005.

[82] Wells, *Wretched Faces*, pp. 77–9.

[83] *A General View of the Agriculture of Hertfordshire, Drawn up for the Consideration of the Board of Agriculture and General Improvement, by the Secretary of the Board*, B. McMillan, London, 1804, p. 7, and maps.

[84] *Observer*, 22 Jun. 1800.

[85] *Courier and Evening Gazette* (London), 15 Aug. 1800; *The Times*, 16 Aug. 1800, 'Guildford Assizes, August 13'.

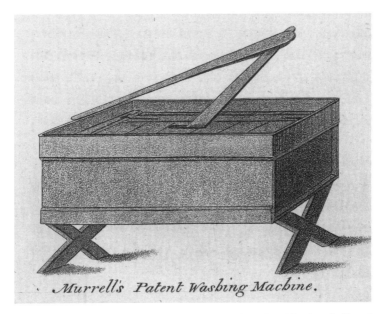

Murrell's Patent Washing Machine.

Figure 18–19. The Gentleman of the West of England Society believed that 'a stout lad' was needed to operate this machine, whilst a girl could operate Beetham's Royal Patent Washing Mill (at least in the realm of advertising). Neither Ann Mead nor Ann Vines had access to this kind of domestic appliance.

another report, Mrs Marshall runs down to the kitchen where the child says 'Oh, grandma! Nanny has put me in the copper.' 'Oh you jade,' says Mrs Marshall, 'you have dipped the child in the copper', to which Vine replies 'No ma'am, I ha'nt, I will tell you.' Vines insists that the child climbed into the copper when her back was turned (although injuries were consistent with her having been held under the arms and dipped in). She calls a witness to her good character and sense of humanity. The surgeon testifies that had he been fetched earlier he would have saved the child; as it was, rank cooking oil had been most improperly applied to Esther's legs and thighs, and she had been suffered to linger overnight wrapped up in her mother's bed, dying the next day.

The children in these cases were at the stage of being mobile, verbal, and still incontinent, factors which Vines's sentence appears to take into account; though Sir Nash Grose (it was he, hot from Hertford and the hanging of Ann Mead) merely directed as the law dictated. He told the jurymen that they must determine whether Esther Dandy's death was accidental, or caused by the negligence of the prisoner. If the first, then

Figure 19 (*cont.*).

they must acquit, if the second, must find Vines guilty of manslaughter. They did the latter, and Vines was fined the modest sum of one shilling and sentenced to six months imprisonment, suggesting perhaps that, at some level in that courtroom, the story of what had actually happened could be read by the symbols of the boiling copper and the dirty clouts.[86] Perhaps legal gentlemen and jurymen remembered the widely circulated adage – and psychological insight – that 'cleanliness may be said to be the foster-mother of love'; how difficult it is to love the dirty and the unclean.[87]

But there were in fact, no narrative forms for telling Mead's and Vines's stories (perhaps there still are none). In the early twentieth century Katherine Mansfield devised one for 'The Child-Who-Was-Tired', whose entire consciousness is made up of orders to light the fire, dress the children, peel the potatoes, and above all to keep the baby quiet, issued by the gigantic and ogre-like figures the Woman and the Man. She learns that there is another on the way:

'Another baby! Hasn't she finished having them *yet!*' thought the Child. 'Two babies getting eye teeth – two babies to get up for in the night – two babies to carry about and wash their piggy little clothes!' She looked with horror at the one in her arms, who, seeming to understand the contemptuous loathing of her tired glance, doubled his fists, stiffened his body, and began violently screaming....

Then, later, the Child-Who-Was-Tired claps her hands and laughs at 'the beautiful, marvellous idea' that occurs to her after the final commandment of the day, to shut the baby up. Smiling, tiptoeing gently, she brings a bolster and presses it down on its face.[88] But in 1763 and 1800, there was no structure of narrative explanation like this for Morton's and Mead's murderous acts, nor for an Ann Vines at the end of her tether at the sight and smell of piggy little clothes. By the 1840s in the textual realm (not in the social world) you could be a servant and kill the child in your care with impunity if you were: a maidservant of a superior kind;

---

[86] TNA, ASSI 31/18 folio 280, 'Crown Minute Book for the Home and South Eastern Circuit, for the Summer Assizes in 1800'.

[87] *The Spectator*, 8 vols., Edinburgh, 1776, vol. 8, p. 308. This was not the poet John Clare's view regarding smelly little babies; but then he was writing about a mother's love for her own child 'all beshat', not the love purchased at a hiring. Jenny Uglow, *Nature's Engraver: A life of Thomas Bewick*, Faber and Faber, London, 2006, p. 431, n. 315, citing Jonathan Bate, *John Clare*, Picador, London, 2003, p. 279.

[88] Katherine Mansfield, 'The-Child-Who-Was-Tired', *In a German Pension* (1911), Penguin, Harmondsworth, 1964, pp. 77–86. This story was recognised after Mansfield's death as having a very strong resemblance to Chekhov's 'Spat Kochetsia' translated into English as 'Sleepy' or 'Sleepy-Eye' in 1903. The charge of plagiarism was first made in Jeffery Meyer, *Katherine Mansfield: A biography*, Hamish Hamilton, London, 1978. I am grateful to Mary Joannou for pointing this out.

Figure 20. Yet another fatal carer for infant life. The nursemaid is observed by the great anthropologist of the nursery, Nimble the Mouse. The servant is alone with the baby, attempting to stop it crying, and doing something quite dangerous with a candle.

if you have already been ruined (in Brussels, by the aristocratic father of the pretty boy to whom you now are nurse); if you have a dead bastard child of your own in the background; and if dropping a four-year-old off a balcony in full view of the county and its father, your seducer, is an act of implacable revenge by one of those fictional women who helped shape the outlines of Lady Audley and her secret.[89] In Erskine Neale's story from 1847, Reza has gone down for poisoning her master with arsenic; child murder is not something with which she is charged. She bears a guilt about which there is absolutely nothing to be done. Prison chaplains preaching the condemned sermon in the later eighteenth century did sometimes offer a hope of salvation, and sometimes forgiveness.[90]

---

[89] Erskine Neale, 'The Revenge of an Unrelenting Woman', *Experiences of a Gaol Chaplain; comprising Recollections of Ministerial Intercourse with Criminals of Various Classes, with their Confessions*, 3 vols., Richard Bentley, London, 1847, vol. 1, pp. 121–56.

[90] But the condemned sermon was the most difficult task of oratory; it was almost impossible to devise a rhetoric that interpellated both those who were about to die and those who were to live (even the Biblical Joseph did not manage this. See Prologue). Gatrell, *Hanging Tree*, pp. 377–83 for ministry to the condemned. James Neild reported that divine service at Hertford Gaol was a disorganised affair, frequently interrupted by

What – a hysterical? catatonic? – Ann Mead heard in her last days, gathered with the other prisoners around her open coffin (and Shock Oliver's coffin too) is not known. The only record of her time in Hertford Gaol is of her receipt of the extra half pound of bread allowed to all prisoners on order of the magistrates: 'Ann Mead – 14 days – 7 lbs – 5s 3d'.[91]

Were hers and Ann Vines's everyday acts of resistance and rebellion, with arsenic and boiling water used as the terrifying weapons of the weak? These are not the weapons we know. The boiling water and the arsenic are different from the insult shouted at the fat farmer on his way home from market,[92] the rude song, the mute insubordination of the kitchen in never getting the rice bread quite right, or the more eloquent appearance of a maid in a new and startlingly fashionable frock. Perhaps we should see Mead's act as arson has been seen by historians of rural protest. In the post-lucifer-match-era rural workers had the technology to fire a rick in resentment (or from whatever other motive) in a fast and efficient manner. Roger Wells is willing to add rural incendiarism to the list of acts which expressed class consciousness and class feeling, though in his view the matches made arson an expression of individual rather than collective resentment and revenge (the food riot, on the other hand, is always represented by its historians as a collective, dignified and political act). Or perhaps Ann Mead's murder should be explored as a criminal act *tout court* and she as a hyperbolic variant of those muggers and pickpockets who attended every crowd protesting a moral economy to magistrates and grain traders.[93] Or perhaps we should go even further down the scale of dignity and say that the murders of Morton and Mead, the cruelty of Ann Vines, were desperate, crazed reactions to a condition of labour and a class relationship, by immature young women driven beyond endurance during a social crisis in which not quite so desperate acts of anger and protest have been accorded significance and their perpetrators respect by their twentieth-century historians. To suggest that these child murders were at least expressive of the 'burning

---

prisoners, the chapel as dirty as the rest of the prison. Neild, *Account of the Rise...*, p. 151–2; *State of the Prisons*, p. 272. It is not known if James Moore, chaplain from 1787–1820, preached the condemned sermon in July 1800. The gaol was run by Charlotte Wilson, widow of the former keeper. In 1801 she pulled in a salary of £204, but does not appear to have provided her charges (in the gaol and the bridewell) with a very good time of it.

[91] HCRO, QSR/48, Quarter Sessions Rolls 1779–1802, Accounts, 145. Hertford Gaol does not appear to have had a condemned cell, and there was no one in Ann Mead's life able to pay for one of the furnished rooms made available by Charlotte William. See note 90, above. Neild, *Account of the Rise, Progress...*, pp. 151–2.

[92] Wells, *Wretched Faces*, p. 94.

[93] Roger Wells, 'Social protest', pp. 172–3; Wells, *Wretched Faces*, pp. 176–7.

and envy . . . (and) inextinguishable abhorrence against the injustice of society' that, according to William Godwin, domestic servants were the most likely of the labouring population to develop, is not – this has to be said – to recommend dipping children in boiling water and giving them arsenic as courses of action. They were the acts of deranged and desperate – and lonely – young women. They are the footnote to Godwin's thesis, for whilst he thought a terrible psychological loneliness and depression of mind was attendant on the very condition of servitude, he did not have the means to detail the conditions of labour – small children and their shit – around which those feelings developed and upon which these young women have been presented here as acting. Perhaps we should also remember the unwritten baseline to the story that has just been told: Lord Kenyon had come to Hertford fresh from the trial of the traitor (and madman, they said comfortingly) John Hadfield, who in May had made an attempt on the life of the King.[94] We have learned from Lynne Hunt how the murder (attempted murder) of the Father affects all manner of people in civil society.[95]

This book has emphasised the deep theoretical structure of existing historical accounts of lives like Morton's and Mead's and Vines's; particular attention has been paid to accounts derived from, or making some attenuated reference to, Marx's contemplation of class formation in the mid-nineteenth century and his refusal of entry to the largest section of the labouring population, waged domestic workers. Perhaps, as Stephen Caunce remarks of this enduring plot-line, historians' problems with the idea of farm and domestic servants as working-class 'stems from the definition of the proletarian rather than the nature of service'.[96] We have now the means to understand service labour as work, and service labourers as part of a working class, and Mead's and Vines's cases may make some small contribution to the rewriting the history of class and class formation, at least as far as England is concerned. As it has been told here, entry is sought for these young women and their actions, to the classic version of class and class formation, because – as it has been told – their actions were articulated around the experienced and felt conditions of their labour; around the care of small children, and their piggy little clouts.

[94] G. W. Keeton, *Guilty but Insane*, Macdonald, London, 1961. LCRO, DDKE. acc. 7840, Lloyd Kenyon, 1st Baron Kenyon, Correspondence in quarto boxes, 1–2 (1753–1802), box 23.

[95] Lynne Hunt, *The Family Romance of the French Revolution*, Routledge, London, 1992.

[96] Stephen Caunce, 'Farm servants and the development of capitalism', *Agricultural History Review*, 45 (1997), 49–68.

By 1800 the country was already in a severe crisis of dearth, though not to know that these were worse times than the hyper-crisis of 1795 until two weeks of torrential rain in late August ruined an already uncertain wheat harvest. Fields had been too sodden to sow in the preceding autumn of 1799; the anticipated 1800 harvest had been spring sown across many parts of the country.[1] Food prices had risen steadily through spring and early summer; there were large and violent food riots.[2] In the context of this social crisis, MP Richard Brinsley Sheridan – playwright and politician, enthusiast for the French Revolution (in its early days), friend of Charles Fox – suggested that domestic labour relations could be perfectly well managed under existing arrangements. By refusing to provide a character, he said in June 1800, you might deprive servants of their bread.[3] Bread – the want of it, the distribution of scant supplies, substitutes for it – was much in the news in 1800, as it had been during the preceding decade. Domestic servants and other workers occupied

---

[1] For details of the dearth of 1795 and the greater one of 1800–1, see Roger A. E. Wells, 'The development of the English rural proletariat and social protest, 1700–1850' in Mick Reed and Roger Wells (eds.), *Class, Conflict and Protest in the English Countryside, 1700–1880*, Cass, London, 1990, pp. 29–53; Roger Wells, 'Social protest, class, conflict and consciousness, in the English countryside 1700–1880' in Reed and Wells (eds.), *Class, Conflict and Protest*, pp. 121–214; Roger Wells, *Wretched Faces: Famine in wartime England, 1798–1801*, Alan Sutton, Gloucester, 1988, pp. 35–52.

[2] Douglas Hay, 'The state and the market in 1800: Lord Kenyon and Mr Waddington', *Past and Present*, 162 (1999), 140.

[3] Chapter 7, note 48.

the political imagination of the late eighteenth century elite because of hunger. But Sheridan's was a throwaway remark, not a proposition in legal theory; it was vastly revealing in its amused callousness, but probably not made in reference to the hunger anticipated in this oppressively hot summer. If there was any referent at all in Sheridan's solution to the servant problem, it was to the Biblical proposition, understood as the foundation of the poor laws, of all law regulating labour from the medieval period onwards, and – some said – of the common law itself: that 'if any would not work, neither should he eat' (II Thessalonians, 3, 10). In what was still a relatively common educational experience, every child in the society was meant to repeat at least once (in practice more frequently) that 'my duty . . . is to learn and labour truly to get my own living'.[4] This was very old social theory, as well as ancient religious prescription. The connection (between working and eating – and starving) was firmly established by the Author of Nature as well as by historical precedent, said John Mickleborough in 1751, under the title *The Great Duty of Labour*. The rich obeyed the injunction differently from the poor: *they* 'must sometimes have recourse to Abstinence, which is a voluntary fasting, or to exercise, which is but voluntary labour, for their health's sake'; but the poor fulfilled their duty 'through their necessities'.[5]

A complex of social and economic theory stressing the relationship between national resources and balance of trade has been labelled 'mercantilism' since the nineteenth century – so called because as theory it served the interests of trade and commerce.[6] A mercantilist theory of labour also emerged, as in a typical formulation from 1735, that 'by the numbers of People, Labour must necessarily increase, and Labour is the great principle of all Riches'. Wealth derived from the number of inhabitants of a nation; the more populous a country, the more prosperous it was.[7] The poverty of many was not incompatible with national wealth.

---

[4] 'A Catechism, that is to say, An Instruction to be Learned of every Person', *Book of Common Prayer*. See Carolyn Steedman, *Master and Servant: Love and labour in the English industrial age*, Cambridge University Press, Cambridge, 2007, pp. 110–30.

[5] John Mickleborough, *The Great Duty of Labour and Work, and the Necessity there is at present for agreeing and fixing upon some Plan for a general Workhouse for the Poor of this Place; Urged and Illustrated in a Sermon before the Corporation of Cambridge in the Parish Church of St. Andrew the Great January 27 AD 1751*, J. Bentham, Cambridge, 1751, p. 15.

[6] W. E. Kuhn, *The Evolution of Economic Thought*, South Western Publishing, Cincinnati, 1963; Isaac Ilych Rubin, *A History of Economic Thought* (1929), Ink Links, London, 1979, pp. 130–9; Lars Magnusson, *Mercantilism: The shaping of an economic language*, Routledge, New York, 1994.

[7] John Hatcher, 'Labour, leisure and economic thought before the nineteenth century', *Past and Present*, 160 (1998), 64–118; Anon. (William Hay), *Remarks on the Laws Relating to the Poor with Proposals for their better Relief and Employment. By a Member of Parliament*, J. Stagg, London, 1735, pp. 21–3.

Some mercantilist writers believed that 'the majority must be kept in poverty that the whole might be rich'. The economic value of the working population was measured by the increase of exported commodities, made out of their labour expended upon raw materials.[8] The utility-of-poverty thesis was promoted, says John Hatcher, as a contemporary solution to a 'truth recognised in all ages', that the many would not labour for the privileged few unless coerced or enticed. The dilemma of the privileged was 'how to devise and operate effective means of ensuring that the poor did labour assiduously'.[9]

Deprivation in general, and the high price of bread in particular, were some of the means by which a supply of labour might be ensured; low wages promoted industriousness, kept production costs low, and made English commodities attractive in the international markets; or so it was proposed. High wages on the other hand, bred a palpable laziness: it was an observable fact that 'in good times the labouring and artisan masses in the seventeenth and eighteenth centuries refused to take on all the work that was on offer'.[10] 'Labouring *less*, and not *cheaper*, has been the consequence of a low price of provisions... when provisions are dear... labour is always plenty, and, of course, is always cheap', said an anonymous pamphleteer in 1765.[11] From the seventeenth century to the middle years of the eighteenth, the labour of the English poor, including the labour of domestic servants, was not fully conceptualised as something that a worker possessed, to be bought and sold, but rather as 'a substance or resource to be appropriated in the national interest'.[12] Many mercantilist ideas were at work in poor law and police proposals

---

[8] Edgar S. Furniss, *The Position of the Laborer in a System of Nationalism: A study in the labor theory of the later English mercantilists* (1920), Augustus M. Kelly, New York, 1965, p. 8.

[9] Frances Hamilton encountered the theory in one of the first books she borrowed from the Taunton Book Society: John M'Farlan, *Inquiries concerning the Poor*, T. Longman, London, J. Dickson, Edinburgh, 1782. See also Jonathan White, 'Luxury and labour: Ideas of labouring class consumption in eighteenth-century England', PhD thesis, University of Warwick, 2001, pp. 51–67.

[10] Hatcher, 'Labour, leisure', p. 85.

[11] Anon., *Considerations on Taxes, As they are supposed to affect the Price of Labour in our Manufactures: Also, some Reflections on the General behaviour and Dispositions of the Manufacturing Populace of this Kingdom; shewing, by Arguments drawn from Experience, that Nothing but Necessity will enforce Labour; and that no state ever did, or ever can, make any considerable Figure in Trade, where the Necessaries of Life are at a low Price. In a Letter to a Friend*, 2nd edn, J. Johnson, London, 1765, pp. 6–7.

[12] Hatcher, 'Labour, leisure', p. 85; also Mitchell Dean, *The Constitution of Poverty: Towards a genealogy of liberal governance*, Routledge, London, 1991, pp. 18–34, where 'labour' in eighteenth-century social thought is described as not a kind of constitutive activity, 'but merely the number of industrious poor'. William Kennedy's account of the social theory derived from this economic assumption, in *English Taxation, 1640–1799: An essay on policy and opinion*, Bell, London, 1913, is discussed in Chapter 7.

in the 1780s. John Powell's 1787 dissertation on the poor rates opened with the conventional assertion that 'the Riches, Strengths and Power of every Nation are proportionate to the Number, Labour, and moral behaviour of those valuable members of society', the poor.[13] This rhetoric continued to be used throughout the hungry 1790s; Sheridan's comment in the House of Commons in 1800 was only a succinct – and unkind – expression of the utility-of-poverty thesis.

Mercantilist labour theorists made very little distinction between domestic servant and other kinds of worker.[14] They were all 'labour', or increasingly, according to some historians of political thought, they were all 'the poor': those who got their bread by labouring for it.[15] And eighteenth-century social theorists thought in terms of numbers: domestic servant were so 'very numerous', their numbers so large, so palpably present as 'the poor' and as 'labour', that they could not be ignored. Most schemes of poor relief, plans for the reform of settlement and for general police, treated domestic servants as part of an even larger population of labouring poor, sometimes as a subdivision of that category, but in essence, as those who must labour for their bread, and who equally, might be denied that bread. And the law, as social project and social practice, treated all workers as labour to be coerced, enticed, and rewarded – or denied their demands. Workers were labour embodied to be sure, but the body was a free body. Clergymen and magistrates were keen to have labourers and servants acknowledge the advantage of this system of law and police. By the 1790s, they taught their lessons in the context of a globalised economy of labour – slavery – and in the face of international political turmoil.[16]

Bread is a direct route to understanding these developments in social theory, because in the 1790s, bread was wanting.[17] And because bread was wanting, commentators began to conceptualise a labouring body as a body in want of (in both senses, of needing and desiring) food, and food of a particular sort. In the 1780s and 1790s, understandings of physical labour were still largely derived from Newtonian mechanics: labour was

[13] John Powell, *A View of Real Grievances: or a Dissertation Upon the State of the Poor in this Kingdom, Shewing by what Means the Poor Rates have grown to such enormous Heights, with Remedies proposed for redressing them*, 2nd edn, W. Whittingham, Lynnridge, 1786.

[14] In attacking mercantilist labour theory in *The Wealth of Nations*, Adam Smith was unusual in separating domestic servants off from the general labouring population. Hatcher, 'Labour, leisure', p. 96.

[15] Dean, *Constitution of Poverty*, pp. 18–34, 142–3, 211.

[16] William Chubbe, *A Few Words to the Labourers of Great-Britain*, R. Loder, Woodbridge, 1793, pp. 4–7.

[17] Christian Petersen, *Bread and the British Economy, c. 1770–1870*, Scolar, Aldershot, 1995.

calculated in terms of the ability to lift a weight, by 'a man of average strength' (or by a horse.)[18] At the same time, the literature on slavery produced in such quantity by abolitionists and apologists alike, provided a detailed description of labour (slave labour) in terms of food intake and energy expenditure. Comparisons were made between the work-output of the European peasant, the English agricultural labourer, and the slave.[19] James Ramsay described the idiocy of his former slave-owning St Kitt's parishioners in his 1784 *Essay on . . . African Slaves*.[20] Planters were a stupid set of men, he said; bloated with profit, incapable of understanding the physiological principles that produced their wealth. They did not know what labour *was*. He told of one who every year sold £10,000 to £15,000 worth of sugar and rum, 'the produce of his slaves [sic] labour, in number above 500'. He did understand that they needed food. 'Indeed', said Ramsay, 'such was this man's original prejudice against feeding his negroes, and so unable were they, without feeding, to exist in a state capable of labour, that greatly to the lessening of his income, it was his custom to keep on making sugar, almost throughout the whole year, in a lifeless inactive manner, in order that his slaves might have some subsistence from the cane juice'. Only very slowly did it dawn on him that 'his slaves must be fed, if work was to be expected from them'.[21] Frances Hamilton's diaries and account books show her reading authorities like Ramsay in a time of hunger, and social theory articulated around hunger. Her first and only run-in with a worker and a servant over the food supply occurred in 1794 when Hannah Burston (with her for six years at 6 guineas, and literate) hung onto the coat tails of someone else's theft and depredation. On 15 June 'A peck of wheat [was] stolen from me & deposited under Hay in the Stable'. The suspect (one of her casual workers) was interrogated by the magistrate, Hamilton noting that 'I could have had him committed' (though she did not). Two weeks later she 'discharged Hannah Burston from my House: She having concealed a peck of Wheat found in ye Stables returning it in to the Hutch with an intent not to acquaint me with the transaction'.[22]

There had been periodic scarcity of wheat throughout the 1790s, import of unfamiliar grains and pulses, and a barrage of government and

---

[18] See Chapters 2, 3 and 'Horses'.

[19] James Ramsay, *An Essay on the Treatment and Conversion of African Slaves in the British Sugar Colonies*, James Phillips, London, 1784, p. 120.

[20] Ramsay, *Essay*, pp. 132–49.   [21] *Ibid.*, pp. 94–5.

[22] It is not clear whether Burston expected it to be 'found' by someone else, or was in connivance with the thief, and attempting to cover his tracks. Hamilton dismissed her without recourse to a magistrate. Somerset County Record Office (SCRO), DD/FS 5/2 (15, 17, 18, 19, 29 Jun. 1794).

public advice about ways of cooking substitutes for the usual staple. The newspapers published recipes for rice bread and gentry wives swapped them by post, wondering why their cooks could not produce a good loaf from rice . . . perhaps they hadn't understood the advice to use the whole grain, and not ground rice?[23] Concerned citizens wrote to the Tax Office suggesting ways in which government might encourage bakers to provide (and the people to eat) bread made from unfamiliar grains.[24] Medical men and political philosophers pondered the dietary conservatism of English labourers. Why would the English not use the variety of grains in use in continental Europe? Why were they so in thrall to the wheaten loaf? What about the huge varieties of 'hasty pudding' they might live on: *polenta* for example? Or maize porridge? Oatmeal porridge, indeed? Or soup . . . ?[25] William Buchan thought of 'the late scarcity' (of 1795) when 'many labouring men and even artificers, could not earn enough money to keep their families in . . . bread only. It is certain however, that on a different plan, such families might have lived very comfortably.'[26] The problem, as far as Buchan could see it, was that the English labourer lived chiefly on bread'; it was bread combined with salt food that made him thirsty – 'his perpetual cry is for drink'. The real problem with tea-drinking was that it caused excessive bread consumption: habits and manners dictated that it must be accompanied by bread and butter, or so the people believed.[27] And bread substituted for cooking, for it was easy to carry around – it was a fast-food.[28] When Buchan recommended soups to the poor, he was often told that they had no time to make them, that soup-making was expensive. They could however, he observed 'find fuel twice a-day to boil a tea-kettle, and time to make the tea, which is a more tedious operation, by far, than making a mess of hasty-pudding. For a great part of the year even the poorest person must have a little

---

[23] Jane H. Adeane, *The Early Married Life of Maria Josepha Lady Stanley, with Extracts from Sir John Stanley's 'Praeterita': Edited by one of their grandchildren*, Longman, Green, London, New York and Bombay, 1899, p. 209 for discussion between Lady Stanley and her sister on making rice bread. *Northampton Mercury*, 28 Jun. 1800, for recipes for rice bread and potato yeast, warning against using ground rice.

[24] TNA T1/7000/45–8, Tax office and suggestions concerning a tax on bakers, Thos Stone to Tax Office, 12 Feb. 1791.

[25] William Buchan, *Observations concerning the Diet of the Common People, recommending a Method of Living less Expensive and more conducive to Health than the Present*, A. Strahan and T. Cadell, London, 1797.

[26] Buchan, *Observations*, p. 17. Wells, *Wretched Faces*, pp. 212–19 for sustained government efforts to alter the diet of the people, and for the Brown Bread Act operative between November 1800 and April 1801.

[27] For the discourse on proletarian tea-drinking – a veritable tea-scare of 1770s – see White, 'Luxury and labour'.

[28] Buchan, *Observations*, pp. 18–20.

fire; and it would require no more to make a comfortable mess of soup, which is always best when made with a slow fire.'[29]

Above all other substitutes for wheat, rice was the most recommended to the poor during these years, though its import was always an emergency measure and even in 1796, when 407,000 hundredweight was brought in, a third was re-exported.[30] For a foodstuff so little consumed, even in emergency, it was massively promoted. Having analysed the harvest returns for 1799 ('in six counties, the return favourable. In ten unfavourable. In five doubtful') the secretary to the Board of Agriculture, Arthur Young, proposed that all parochial relief in foodstuffs should be restricted to rice, potatoes and soup. Agriculturalists would turn to 'a vast culture of potatoes' as the food culture of the poor changed: they would become habituated to rice, and to 'a cheaper way of satisfying their hunger'. The dietary habits and preferences of 2 million people could be changed in this way. Right now, rice was cheap, and cheaper still if importers turned to India rather than the Carolinas, from whence the bulk still came: 'of what consequence would the present scarcity be, if we had now enough for one or two month's consumption?'[31] Rice was a great favourite of the self-promoting philanthropist Count Rumford (whose schemes for bettering the condition of the poor were so widely publicised and so highly thought of, that they were ripped off at the highest level).[32] However, although rice was 'universally allowed to be very nourishing', perhaps Indian corn (maize) was an even better option? Rumford acquainted his readers with plantation dietaries from North America and the Caribbean, taking his evidence (at second hand)

---

[29] Buchan, *Observations*, p. 41.

[30] James Adair, *An Essay on Regimen, for the Preservation of Health, especially for the Indolent, Studious, Delicate and Invalid*, J. Wilson for the author, London, 1799, p. 27; James Burnett Monboddo, *Antient Metaphysics. Volume Fifth. Containing the History of Man in the Civilized State*, Bell and Bradfute, Edinburgh, T. Cadell and W. Davies, London, 1797, p. 288; John Holroyd, Earl of Sheffield, *Remarks on the Deficiency of Grain, occasioned by the bad Harvest of 1799; on the Means of present Relief, and of future Plenty. With an Appendix...*, 2 vols., J. Debrett, London, 1800–1, vol. 1, pp. 36–7.

[31] Arthur Young, *The Question of Scarcity plainly stated, and Remedies Considered with Observations on permanent Measures to keep Wheat at a more regular Price*, Richardson, London, 1800, pp. 17–80; Appendix III, 'The price of rice in India', pp. 91–2.

[32] David Knight, 'Thompson, Sir Benjamin, Count Rumford in the nobility of the Holy Roman empire (1753–1814)' in *Oxford Dictionary of National Biography*, Oxford University Press, 2004, www.oxforddnb.com/view/article/27255, accessed 9 Feb. 2007. What they said about William Pitt's Poor Law Bill of 1797 was that he had lifted it directly from Rumford's description of the institutions he had directed at Munich. I. Wood, *A Letter to Sir William Pulteney Bart... containing some Observations on the Bill... presented to the House of Commons by the Right Honourable William Pitt*, privately printed, Shrewsbury, 1797; William Belsham, *Remarks on the Bill for the better Support and Maintenance of the Poor, now depending in the House of Commons*, G. G. and J. Robinson, London, 1797.

from slaves themselves, who, having a choice between the two, invariably took the maize: 'the reasons they give for their preference they express in strong, though not very delicate terms', he reported. 'They say that *"Rice turns to water in their bellies*, and runs off;" – but "Indian Corn *stays with them, and makes strong to work"*.'[33] The apogee of proffering a plantation diet to the English working class was probably reached in 1812 with Richard Pearson's *Salt Fish*, which proposed a cuisine for the workers consisting entirely of rice, the odd boiled potato, and much fish powder made from pounded salt cod.[34]

Diet doctors like Pearson and Buchan were well aware of the constraints of fuel and firing, kitchen equipment, and the length of the working day on working-class cookery. The idea of an ancient village dam running a kind of take-away *charcuterie* service for working families occurred to several practical philanthropists.[35] The Society for Bettering the Condition of the Poor promoted rice by recipe ('a little morsel of strong Cheshire cheese . . . grated in . . . will greatly improve its flavour') and by exhortation: 'Rice is the chief food of half the world. It is peculiarly calculated to diminish the evils of a scanty harvest; . . . it comes from a part of the world where provisions are cheap and abundant'; it was light 'and easy of carriage'; it kept well; it did not, contrary to rumour, make you go blind.[36] Provincial branches of the Society provided recipes for dishes that could be cooked slowly during a working day's absence, and on a very low and meagre fire. They paid attention to the problem of

[33] This information had been communicated to him 'by two respectable planters', one from Georgia, the other from Jamaica. Benjamin, Count of Rumford, *Essays, Political, Economical and Philosophical*, vol. 1, T. Cadell, London, 1796, Essay III 'Of Food and particularly of Feeding the Poor', pp. 249–50. This was the volume bought by Frances Hamilton in October 1796. 'Plantation nutrition' as discussed in Kenneth F. Kiple's *The Caribbean Slave: A biological history*, Cambridge University Press, Cambridge, 1984, pp. 76–88 was known in late eighteenth-century, though not in the terms used here, drawn from modern nutritional science. See Harmke Kamminga and Andrew Cunningham, *The Science and Culture of Nutrition, 1840–1940*, Rodopi, Amsterdam and Atlanta GA, 1995; also Ted A. Rathbun and Richard H. Steckel, 'The health of slaves and free Blacks in the East' in Richard H. Steckel, and Jerome C. Rose (eds.), *The Backbone of History: Health and nutrition in the Western Hemisphere*, Cambridge University Press, Cambridge, 2002, pp. 208–25.

[34] Richard Pearson, *An Account of a particular Preparation of Salted Fish to be used with Boiled Rice, or Potatoes, for the purpose of lessening the Consumption of Wheaten Bread*, Rivington, Reading, 1812. See also William Brooke, *The True Cause of our Present Distress for Provisions; with a natural, easy, and effectual Plan for the future Prevention of so great a Calamity. With some Hints respecting the absolute Necessity of an increased Population*, H. D. Symonds and others, London, 1800, pp. 36–40 for salt and fresh cod recipes for cottage cookery.

[35] Society for Bettering the Condition of the Poor, *Information for Cottagers, Collected from the Reports of the Society . . .* , privately printed, London, 1800, pp. 32–3.

[36] Society for Bettering . . . , *Information for Cottagers*, pp. 36–8, 'Of rice'.

cookery equipment, pots in particular, and offered solutions.[37] Gentlemen of the Society, meanwhile, produced elaborate schema for preserving potatoes as a staple food for the people, using equipment that moved beyond the domestic to the industrial scale.[38] The Board of Agriculture had encouraged experimentation with the potato from the early 1790s to determine its 'nutritive matter'. It received extensive reports from Ireland, paid attention to working-class modes of cooking, and considered the whole practical philosophy of the tuber, in its 'Application as Food for Man'.[39]

Beyond the domestic realm, some advocated the organisation of the rice supply in county depots, with all parish provision to be given as rice. When sold on the open market, it should cost no more than 3d per lb, losses to be made up by central government, said John Symmons. His was not the cry against forestalling discussed as one of the contexts to Ann Mead's murder. Legislate against those market crimes and the middleman, said Symmons, and producers would take the profits to be made: 'go round to all your markets and see whether the farmer, or original producer, does not demand as high a price of the consumer, who deals with him *at first hand*, as the middleman is able to obtain at the same market'. His own servants had reported to him on this.[40]

Pamphleteers and dietary commentators described food fit for labouring people using the term 'nutritive', though not in the sense established by nutritional science after the 1840s.[41] Meanings were often multiple within the same text. In his *Essay on Regimen*, James Adair described tea an 'unnutritive beverage', meaning 'not providing nourishment for an animal body'. But he also used the term to mean 'food' – too much food, or too little food. If, said Adair, his project were the same as Count Rumford's, to provide a dietary regimen for the poor, then he would pay

[37] Oswestry Society for Bettering the Condition and Increasing the Comforts of the Poor, *The Family Receipt Book, or, the Cottager's Cook, Doctor, and Friend*, privately printed, Oswestry, 1817, pp. 9–12.

[38] Society for Bettering . . . (Langford Millington), . . . *Letter, suggesting a Mode of Preserving Potatoes for a Long Time . . .* , privately printed, London, 1800.

[39] Board of Agriculture, *Report of the Committee of the Board . . . Appointed to extract Information from the County Reports and other Authorities concerning the Culture and Use of the Potato*, George Nicol, London, 1795, pp. 70–95. The Bath and West of England Society promoted the potato as a food for the poor (and animals) throughout the 1780s. *Letters and Papers on Agriculture, Planting &c. Selected from the Correspondence of the Society*, 6 vols., The Society, Bath, 1792–3, vol. 1, pp. 26–35; vol. 2, pp. 68–70, 244–6, 356–7, vol. 3, pp. 102–9, 114–16, 273–9, 288–304, vol. 4, pp. 7–107, vol. 5, pp. 27–42, 64–6, 230–6, vol. 6, pp. 206–7, 339–94.

[40] John Symmons, *Thoughts on the Present Price of Provisions, their Causes and Remedies; addressed to all ranks of people. By an Independent Gentleman*, T. Reynolds, London, 1800, pp. 38–39.

[41] Kamminga and Cunningham, *Science and Culture of Nutrition*, pp. 1–14.

more regard to 'nutrition' as opposed to 'digestibility' (that which was agreeable to the stomach, pleasant to eat, stimulating). But *his* readers would have no need of advice about quantity of food: 'my readers will not be of that class'; for them 'nutrition is so far from being an object of important consideration, that many evils proceed from us swallowing too much nutrition'.[42] (Adair was rather against meat: 'even the strong and laborious' could not bear 'two full meals of animal food in one day'.) Different foodstuffs were considered to have particular properties, that affected the human body in particular ways.[43] Without notions of calorific intake, or of protein, or of the functions of the major food groups, the qualities and functions of foods were perceived and formulated, often with evidence taken (at second- or third-hand) from workers (and slaves) themselves. Labouring bodies were observed, with increasing pace from the 1780s onwards, and the relationship between food intake and strength in labour was theorised. The category 'animal food' did some of the conceptual work that 'protein' would do a century later. In a new edition of Brown's *Elements of Medicine*, Thomas Beddoes asserted that too much 'vegetable food' in conjunction with a sparing use of animal food 'constantly weakens, and thereby produces asthenic diathesis through all its degrees. Hence arises that remarkable imbecility both of body and mind, which distinguishes the Gentoos, who follow the brahminical ceremonial of religion. Hence the diseases of the poor everywhere.' A meat diet 'needs only a little support of tension from a moderate quantity of bread', but bread alone could not produce strength in labour. Beddoes thought this was evident 'of the poor labouring people in Scotland, who chiefly live on vegetable matter . . . . it would take three to go through the work that one Yorkshire[man], nourished by bolting pork fat, can easily execute. And among the Gentoo servants, a dozen is not able to perform

---

[42] Adair, *Essay on Regimen*, pp. 26–7.

[43] A Gentleman of the Faculty, *Concise Observations on the Nature of our Common Food, so far as it tends to promote or injure Health*, W. Stanes, W. Justin, London, 1787; Robert Wallace Johnson, *Some Friendly Cautions to the Heads of Families and Others, Very Necessary to be observed, in order to preserve Health and long Life . . .* , 3rd edn, privately printed, Brentford, 1793; William Falconer, *An Essay on the Preservation of the Health of Persons employed in Agriculture, and on the Cure of Diseases incident to that Way of Life*, Cruttwell, Bath, 1789 (Falconer was Physician to the Bath Hospital; the material here was originally published by the Bath and West of England Society, *Letters and Papers*, vol. 4, pp. 347–440); Joseph Townsend, *A Guide to Health; being Cautions and Directions in the Treatment of Diseases. Designed chiefly for the Use of Students*, Cox, London, 1795; A. F. M. Willich, *Lectures on Diet and Regimen: being a systematic Inquiry into the most rational Means of preserving Health and prolonging Life: together with Physiological and Chemical Explanations . . . calculated chiefly for the use of Families*, 2nd edn, Longman and Rees, London, 1799; Buchan, *Diet of the Common People*, pp. 20–21.

as much work as a single English servant.'[44] It was perfectly possible to *perceive* the effects of protein deficiency, without a later science and language for describing it. The Reverend Stanhope Smith's work of cultural anthropology (which Frances Hamilton read with such alacrity when it was published in 1788) included an account of a child put on him by the parish some time in the early 1780s, now one of his household servants. Ten years old when she arrived, she had been very small, extremely thin and sallow, 'her hair frittered and worn away to . . . little more than two inches'. Now, four years later, having lived and eaten like his own children, you could scarcely tell them apart.[45]

Yet food played a small role in medical and chemical descriptions of the human body. It was a stimulus in some schema, or an 'exciting power', which along with other sensory input, set the system in motion, the body being understood as a rather elaborate fire-grate, or furnace, the fuel of which must be constantly renewed to produce excitability. Animal bodies died if deprived of food (fuel) and air, to be sure, but the food itself merely fuelled the body by 'the same principle that the oil affords to the lamp'.[46] For these observers, the adult body was an existing entity to be nourished, or set in motion, or given strength, by food intake.[47]

'Hunger' was not a word much used in this vast conglomeration of texts, debates, arguments and private writing, even during the severe crises of 1795–6 and 1800–1. An imagined labourer might have 'hungry children clamouring for bread' – his labour could not provide sustenance for them – but that was the only common usage of the term in all of this literature. 'Famine' *was* used: what was happening would be 'called

---

[44] John Brown, *The Elements of Medicine of John Brown, MD. Translated from the Latin, with comments and illustrations, by the Author. A New Edition, revised and corrected, with a Biographical Preface, by Thomas Beddoes, MD*, 2 vols., J. Johnson, London, 1795, vol. 1, pp. 110–11.

[45] Samuel Stanhope Smith, *An Essay on the Causes of the Variety of Complexion and Figure in the Human Species. To which are added, Strictures on Lord Kames Discourse on the Orginal Diversity of Mankind. A new edn with some additional notes by a Gentleman of the University*, C. Elliot and T. Kay, London, 1788, p. 87. He thought the fritted hair a result of lying in the 'ashes and dirt of [a] miserable hut', not the vitamin B deficiency attendant on protein deprivation. Now her complexion was clear and rosy, 'her hair is long and flowing, and she is not badly made in her person'. Roderick Floud, Kenneth Wachter and Annabel Gregory, *Height, Health and History. Nutritional Status in the United Kingdom, 1750–1980*, Cambridge University Press, Cambridge, 1990, pp. 227–8, 233, 272–4.

[46] A. Crawford, *Experiments and Observations on Animal Heat and the Inflammation of Combustible Bodies*, 2nd edn, J. Johnson, London, 1788; E. Peart, *The Generation of Animal Heat, Investigated*, J. Edwards, London, C. Elliot, Edinburgh, 1788, p. 38; Thomas Garnett, *A Lecture on the Preservation of Health*, J. M'Creery, Liverpool, 1797; Thomas Garnett, *Popular Lectures on Zoonomia, or the Laws of Animal Life in Health and Disease*, Royal Institution of Great Britain, 1804.

[47] J. M. Tanner, *A History of the Study of Human Growth*, Cambridge University Press, Cambridge, 1981, pp. 66–121.

famine in any land but this', they said. Gentlemen (and lady) pamphleteers were familiar enough with a national history punctuated by famines – remote to be sure; 865 AD saw a particularly severe one – but available as a term to conceptualise what was happening now, winter of 1795, summer of 1800 and so on.[48] A new language emerged, for describing the psychological effects of hunger and dearth, on individual men and women of the poorer sort. Roger Wells' title to his account of these years – *Wretched Faces* – is a powerful summary of such a language of the social, of social divisions and of social relationships themselves. Wretchedness, loss of any sense of futurity, and *depression* of the spirit were observed as the effects of dearth. The means to imagine the workers – their thoughts, beliefs, and attitudes – was formalised in these hungry years. In a variety of texts, a working-class psychology was inscribed and a language created for its expression. Thomas Beddoes, Bristol physician, chemist, and political radical, praised contemporary efforts to determine the situation of the poor, but thought that all previous investigators had all asked the wrong questions. The right approach was to look for the 'effect of... privation, on the living system'.[49] He had asked the right questions in 1792, by fictionalising himself as Mr Langford, a medical doctor, and by asking his questions in the highly specific locale of Ludlow in Shropshire. With the famines of the decade yet to come, Beddoes set his tale in that 'terrible time, the latter end of the year 1783', when we now know that the eruption of the Icelandic volcano Laki produced highly abnormal weather conditions across Europe well into 1784, when harvests failed in sequence, and 'what was to become

[48]   Anon., *A compendious History of England, from the Invasion by the Romans, to the present time. Adorned with a map of Great Britain and Ireland*, J. Newbery, London, 1758; Anon., *The British Chronologist; comprehending every material Occurrence, ecclesiastical, civil, or military, relative to England and Wales, from the invasion of the Romans to the present time... in three volumes*, G. Kearsley, London, 1775, vol. 1, p. 27; James Pettit Andrews, *The History of Great Britain, connected with the Chronology of Europe*, T. Cadell, London, 1794, p. 57; Charles Alfred Ashburton, *A New and Complete History of England, from the first Settlement of Brutus, upwards of one thousand Years before Julius Cæsar, to the year 1795*, W. and J. Stratford, London, 1795. Educated elite women may have been more familiar with this history than their brothers. National history was considered particularly appropriate for girls.

[49]   Thomas Beddoes, *A Lecture Introductory to a Course of Popular Instruction on the Constitution and Management of the Human Body*, Joseph Johnson, London, Joseph Cottle, Bristol, 1797, p. 69; Michael Neve, 'Beddoes, Thomas (1760–1808)' in *Oxford Dictionary of National Biography*, Oxford University Press, 2004, www.oxforddnb.com/view/article/1919, accessed 12 Feb 2007. Beddoes longed for a conjunction between 'a reformed (chemical) medicine and a reformed social order', says his biographer. The five editions of *Isaac Jenkins* are expression of this longing. The first one, used here, does not contain the Preface dealing with contemporary revolutionary politics that is a notable feature of later ones.

of the poor ... it was bad already with them and a worse look-out'.[50]
The fictional doctor rides through a village 'at the foot of the Titterstone
Clee-Hill', where is the cottage of a 'poor labouring man', Isaac Jenkins,
his wife Sarah and their three surviving children 'as small as they well
could be'. ('If you ever went that way, you will remember [it] ... close
by the Ludlow road as you come upon the Common at the bottom of
the hill.') The whole family has been laid low by a fever; the middle
child lies for dead; Sarah stammers out her story to the passing doctor.
Langford/Beddoes hears how the two shillings Sarah got from the parish
has been spent by her husband at The Horseshoe, a stone's throw away.
The doctor prescribes a remedy for the child; Sarah feels 'higher and
stronger' (less depressed) all of a sudden, now that she knows what to
do. She begs and borrows the means to make up the prescription. There
are pages of plebeian speech presented and much motive ascribed to the
characters in the tale, even when Mr Langford is not present. He visits
often, and on his last call, itemises the Jenkins's *batterie de cuisine* ('an old
pot, some porringers without handles, a few cracked trenchers, two or
three pewter spoons'). He notes what miracles Sarah has wrought with
these in nursing her children.[51] The problem is actually Isaac – and the
proximity of The Horseshoe – though Isaac was a 'good deal to be pitied
as well as blamed. He was not bad at bottom.' When 'in service he was
sober and thoughtful and saving'.[52] The death of the eldest boy in a mining accident the year before had plunged him into a deep melancholy;
he had taken to drink. Isaac meets the doctor for the first time after
the children are restored to health (he was always at work before, during
Langford's visits and conversations with the increasingly enterprising and
engaging Sarah), and takes part in a twenty-page dialogue on good parenting and human physiology with the doctor. Langford carefully draws
out what Isaac knows about care of livestock and animal nutrition. '"No
doubt", says he, "you think bread and cheese and potatoes and meat to be
the same to us, as hay and straw and oats are to dumb creatures ... Must
not weakness bring disorders upon us as well as upon animals and make
us more liable to fall prey to any distemper?"'[53] Isaac is 'quite staggered'
when he realises the connection between his own behaviour and the condition of his children: '"Mammy mammy, what's the matter with Daddy?
He looks for all the world as Stephy used to do, when we had no bread nor

[50] J. P. Grattan and M. B. Brayshay, '"An Amazing and Portentous Summer": Environ-
mental and social responses in Britain to the 1783 eruption of an Iceland volcano',
Geographical Journal, 161: 2 (1995), 125–34; Thomas Beddoes, *The History of Isaac
Jenkins and of the Sickness of Sarah his Wife, and their three Children*, privately printed,
Madeley, 1792, p. 2.
[51] Beddoes, *Isaac Jenkins*, p. 13.   [52] *Ibid.*, p. 18.   [53] *Ibid.*, pp. 18–26.

potatoes today".' The child attempts to feed his daddy with a spoonful of milk and potatoes that Sarah, in these retrieved times, has set beside the fire to cook. This is entirely too much for Isaac, who abruptly goes to the window and buries his head in his hands. And then to the kindly but relentless Mr Langford who goes on for several pages on child psychology in relation to early experience: the child who has not been cared for and well-fed will have 'no pleasure in himself'; a child raving with hunger will steal food like a beast ('though, poor thing, he knows no more than a dog what a sin it is to steal'). Moreover, Isaac has been denying them their chance on the labour market, for 'who will have anything to do with boys and girls kept ragged, and dirty, and idle... Why, people will be afraid to take them into their houses; or if they happen to hire them... will still look upon them with an evil eye.'[54]

Beddoes's point was not only to deliver these lessons in physiology and psychology to those who did good works among the poor, but to make the political point that 'there would be little misery in the world if there was no distress... Vice always begins among the poor from misery.' In later editions, he made his political project plain: 'that unless the people be humanized by education and the full enjoyment of their rights, no place or person can be at any time secure from the effects of popular fury'.[55] This engaging, compelling tract went into eleven editions, the last in 1860, so some found it useful (and perhaps compelling). Beddoes thought that the poor themselves had found it 'intelligible and interesting' (several thousand copies were distributed to them in the early 1790s, he said), but there is no evidence that any but the concerned, liberal, and philanthropic sort ever read it.[56]

Modern nutritional science has its origins in agricultural chemistry – in the number of experiments on the properties of foodstuffs undertaken in these years, and in England, supported by the Agricultural Societies. Sir Humphrey Davy, one of the most eminent chemists, worked briefly with Beddoes in Bristol, at the end of the old century. After he removed to London in 1802, he lectured on 'the Organisation of Plants', demonstrating the 'quantities of soluble or nutritive Matters afforded by 1000

---

[54] *Ibid.*, pp. 29–30.

[55] The actual political example he had in mind was revolutionary France, but in the 1793 edition it was expedient to disguise it as 'Turkey' – 'Mobs are nowhere more outrageous than in Turkey...'. Thomas Beddoes, *The History of Isaac Jenkins and Sarah his Wife, and their three Children*, 2nd edn, J. Murray and J. Johnson, London, 1793, p. iv. See Hester Piozzi on the Turkey/France formulation, Prologue.

[56] Beddoes, *Isaac Jenkins* (1793), p. iv. Not a discussion for this book – but it was an important development in the history of social realism in the novel, in the social history of class language and the graphic representation of child language. It invites further investigation as a landmark text in the writing of social and class relations.

Parts of different vegetable Substances'. This was practical chemistry he said, 'conducted with a view to a knowledge of the general nature and quantity of the products, and not of their intimate chemical composition'. Knowledge so far allowed him to say which substances were more or less 'nutritive'. He, too, took second-hand oral evidence from those who did the eating (or who experienced hunger) in these years, remarking that he had 'been informed by Sir Joseph Banks, that the Derbyshire miners in winter, prefer oat cakes to wheaten bread; finding that this kind of nourishment enables them to support their strength and perform their labour better. In summer, they say oat cake heats them, and they then consume the finest wheaten bread they can procure.'[57]

Proposals for bettering the diet of the poor during these years of food crises turned gentlemen commentators into roving reporters, lamenting the demise of the cottager's fat hog, collecting information on the decline in milk production, declaiming against the neglect of orcharding, lauding the agricultural output of the Chinese, and tracing all the difficulties of the 1790s back to the close of the Seven Years War when the French got the Atlantic grain trade. One of them stopped off at an inn in Oxfordshire in 1795 to hear a working-class couple debate what they would spend their money on that Saturday morning, in a dialogue to be vividly remembered five years later: 'John, I want some money to go to the grocer's for some tea, sugar, butter, and Heaven knows what.' In 1800 it was written up to demonstrate the point that 'all the sustenance the whole family was likely to receive from the ten shillings, was one peck of wheat, for I count the tea and the other trash to a poor family as worth nothing'.[58]

Many commentators of the 1790s believed like Beddoes, that want of food produced psychological depression. We cannot say that any labourer at dusk, contemplating the half-cooked mess of rice that had been put on the embers of the morning fire (twelve hours ago) *felt* depressed, only that his betters thought he might, and developed a language for describing it. The bodies and minds of the labouring poor were connected; their philanthropic betters allowed them to feel (fictional) resentment at their own earnest interference. (Beddoes allows Isaac Jenkins to – almost – walk out in fury at Langford's lecture.) Commentators focused on plebeian

---

[57] Humphry Davy, *Elements of Agricultural Chemistry, in a Course of Lectures for the Board of Agriculture*, Longman, Hurst, Rees, Orme and Brown, London, 1813, pp. 49–133; David Knight, 'Davy, Sir Humphry, baronet (1778–1829)' in *Oxford Dictionary of National Biography*, Oxford University Press, 2004, www.oxforddnb.com/view/article/7314, accessed 12 Feb 2007; John Gascoigne, 'Banks, Sir Joseph, baronet (1743–1820)' in *Oxford Dictionary of National Biography*, Oxford University Press, www.oxforddnb.com/view/article/1300, accessed 12 Feb 2007.

[58] Brooke, *Distress for Provisions*, pp. 29–30.

women not in order to demonstrate their abjection and hopelessness, but to point up the vigour of their language, their robust state of mind, and their resourcefulness. In *The Family Receipt Book, or, the Cottager's Cook, Doctor, and Friend* which was produced by the Oswestry Society for Bettering the Condition of the Poor (Thomas Netherton Parker's local society), you may find the very first '2Cs in a K' of the 1980s advertising industry, which is no accolade of course, but interesting to those who have learned about working-class female abjection from twentieth-century sociology. Everything we know about the philanthropic endeavours of the better sort in this period tells us to be astonished by Nancy and Rose, the two central characters of this text. Cottage women, field-labourers and charwomen on occasion, they engage in long, intelligent, resourceful discussion about procuring a sheep's head (one of the recipes), borrowing the pot to cook it in and lifting the garden vegetables to put with it. Nancy feels 'so light and happy' once she has this recipe under her belt; feels she can do anything.[59] Hunger may have been unnamed but, around it, it was possible to *think* two plebeian women of intelligence and resource, who were both labouring bodies and psychological subjects. In their self-determination, Nancy and Rose were fictional echoes of the actually existing young women telling a master to change his own baby's nappy in 1780s Nottinghamshire, or just refusing to go back to a place she disliked in 1813 Oswestry. We may surmise that something like them had been met with by Shropshire ladies producing their cookery tract for the poor. The ladies too, appear to have possessed a resourcefulness and eclecticism that allowed them to determine two of the twelve Golden Rules for the poor as loving God and keeping the stewpan lid on tight.

The relationship between food intake and labour output was expressed in terms of anthropological others: New World chattel slaves, feeble Hindu labourers, downhearted Scottish peasants. The experience of these very severe years, of the actual effect of a reduced diet on physical labour, was not formulated as physiological principle until well into the new century. 'They cannot work well, unless they have food enough', wrote Mrs Parkes of domestic servants in 1825, advising her sisters of the commercial and industrial bourgeoisie of the deleterious effects of paying board wages, where they had no control over the diet of their

---

[59] Oswestry Society, *Family Receipt Book*, pp. 11–14. Rose and Nancy actually originate in Ireland, in Mary Leadbeater's *Cottage Dialogues* of 1811. There are as yet no historical or critical means for engaging the history of Irish service with England's. Useful will be Jonathan Swift's *Instruction to Servants* (and his exasperated, affectionate relationship with his Irish servant Patrick), and Maria Edgeworth's *Castle Rackrent* (1800), which features the most opaque servant narrator of them all, Thoady.

household servants.[60] In 1826 one anonymous Shropshire commentator looked back over the past thirty years of 'recommending cheap substitutes to the Poor in place of their ordinary diet', to all the rice and potatoes that had been urged on them in place of 'expensive . . . bread and malt liquor'. But, he concluded, 'hard labour cannot be well sustained upon the slender fare . . . recommended. Men, who are expected to toil from six o'clock in the morning to six o'clock at night . . . must live upon a nutritious diet; they must be supplied with the means of recruiting their exhausted strength.' He thought, like Mrs Parkes, that it was best to feed your own servants and labourers; in Shropshire many farmers did this; experience had taught them 'how much more work will be done by the same men on better food'. Over these years they had learned 'what food is necessary for labouring people': a 'potato diet . . . is . . . totally unfit to maintain a man in full vigour of body for active and laborious exertion'.[61]

The diet of household servants was not much discussed, in this vast conglomeration of proposals and recommendations produced from the 1790s onwards. They were generally assumed to be reasonably well fed, and whilst it is clear that much of domestic work was (and is) gruelling, there were fewer opportunities for observing the effects of a reduced diet on a lone maid feeding the pigs, looking after the children and making the beds, than there were for regretting the lost strength of a field of hay-makers, symbol now of the decline of a golden age English peasantry.[62] To put it anachronistically, domestic servants were believed to be dieted with sufficient protein, and indeed one young Shropshire woman complained to the local magistrate that she was being fed too much butchers' meat at her place, at the expense of vegetables and bread.[63]

Reporting on the state of English agricultural labourers in 1795, on their earnings, diet and housing, the Reverend David Davies did not make personal enquiries of Somerset. Rather, he reproduced the communications of a local gentleman concerning the expenses of two

[60] Mrs William Parkes, *Domestic Duties; or, Instructions to Young Married Ladies, on the Management of their Households, and the Regulation of their Conduct in the Various Relations and Duties of Married Life*, Longman, Hurst, Rees, Orme, Brown and Green, London, 1825, p. 117. Patrick Calhoun conceptualised the relationship when he wrote about 'sufficient food' needed to produce 'extra labour' across the working population. *A Treatise on Indigence; Exhibiting a General View of the National Resources for Productive Labour*, J. Hatchard, London, 1806, pp. 159–61.

[61] Anon., *Remarks on the Present State of the Poor*, privately printed, Oswestry, 1826, pp. 6–9.

[62] Carole Shammas, 'The domestic environment in early modern England and America', *Journal of Social History*, 14:1 (1980), 3–24 for gruelling domestic work.

[63] Kenneth J. Carpenter, *Protein and Energy: A study of changing ideas in nutrition*, Cambridge University Press, Cambridge, 1994. Chapter 6 for the Shropshire maid-servant who wanted more veg and bread to her dinner.

labouring families for the year 1789.[64] One family of seven had spent 1s 6d on bacon and meat out of a week's budget of 11s 11$\frac{1}{2}$d, the second with eight family members, only 7d on animal protein, out of a budget of 6s 8d. Seven pence would perhaps, in 1789 in Holwell parish – in the north of the county – have brought this second family 2 lbs of meat (less if they purchased bacon). If we reckon that there was a child at the breast and a toddler – on six adult mouths to feed – each might have obtained 5 oz of meat a week. (This family did not say it purchased milk, but did spend 4d on 'cheese and salt', the coupling suggesting that they were both used as flavourings for other foodstuffs.)[65] These are calculations that might be thought worse than useless for considering Frances Hamilton's expenditure on household food in 1796. Holwell is in the same county, but did not belong to the same rural marketing economy as Bishops Lydeard, and that is only the first objection. But Davis's reports do allow a relatively local comparison between different protein consumptions for working people, albeit across a space of six years. In 1796 Frances Hamilton's Lydeard household consisted of herself and four maidservants (counted as three – Molly Evans left her employ in April), a man-servant, the ploughboy in transition to a footman from June onwards), her hired servant in husbandry and two apprentice boys, one of them joining the household in March. Also fed, from time to time, were the people who worked her garden, who washed and charred for her, and who did occasional table-waiting. Over the year, there were seven mouths to feed on a daily basis. Contemplating her butcher's bill in 1800, Hamilton herself noted 'when 7 in Family about 4 lb & $\frac{1}{4}$ each person'.[66] In 1796 she spent a total of £49 17s 10d on what she described as 'butchers meat', or 9 per cent of her total expenditure in the year, and 54 per cent of her outlay on 'housekeeping'. I have not counted in this total a bill paid to a Taunton butcher covering the previous year; it was for £6 10s and perhaps brought – it is not clear when she obtained the meat – a few more pounds of it into the Lydeard kitchen in the spring of 1796. Neither have I counted her expenditure on butcher-made brawn and other pork products, on poultry, ducks, pheasants, and other game. Fish (she had her own fishpond as well as purchasing it) has not been

---

[64] David Davies, *The Case of Labourers in Husbandry Stated and Considered in three Parts*, G. G. and J. Robinson, London, 1795, pp. 178–9.

[65] See the calculations for protein intake among the rural poor, 1787–96, drawing on all the contemporary household budgets available, in Gregory Clark, Michael Huberman and Peter H. Lindert, 'A British food puzzle, 1770–1850', *Economic History Review*, 48:2 (1995), 215–37, 223.

[66] SCRO, DD/FS/ 5/8 (30 Mar. 1800). We are urged to consider the food of the middle and upper classes as well as the poor in order to discover the relationship of food supply to consumption. Clark, Huberman and Lindert, 'British food puzzle'.

reckoned either, which also provided protein for Hamilton, and perhaps for her maids. Neither does this total say anything about the pigs killed during the year. She sold the meat at 4d per lb, but also had bacon made for the household; she purchased the saltpetre needed for pork preservation. So this calculation restricts itself to the beef, veal, mutton, and lamb bought from local farmers, and from Taunton butchers. It is not possible to say how many pounds of meat this expenditure of near £50 brought her, for whilst she frequently made an entry like 'Neck Mutton 6 pd ¾ at 4d', there are an equal number that read 'Leg of Veal 5s', or 'forequarter of Lamb 4s'. The highest price she paid for meat was 6d per pound, the lowest 3d; taking all entries like this, the average she paid was 4d a pound. At this average her £49 17s 10d would have bought her 2,493 lbs of meat, or 356 lbs per person, including herself, or just under 1lb a day for all. Even making the most generous allowance for the huge quantities she bought in for a harvest feast, and the number of extra-domestic workers fed at her kitchen table, even halving that quantity (but remembering that Hamilton herself had game, poultry, fish and shell fish to eat, and the servants perhaps, some of the hundred weights of oysters she purchased and the odd duck wing) this is still a generous amount of protein, well within modern recommended daily allowances for a meat source of it. There was also milk, almost all of it provided by the farm cows, and so not entered in the housekeeping book, and cheese purchased from Taunton market. Bishop Lydeard House servants were well fed, and it is reasonable to assume that from the huge quantities of food that passed through their hands and into the pot, they received a share adequate in protein, indispensable amino acids and the fats that carry some of the major vitamin groups.[67] It is not possible to extrapolate from these calculations some general account of household servants' diets across the country during these crisis years. But manual writers and lifestyle advisors thought that these were the quantities needed if housekeepers wanted to keep a servant, even on a much lower income than Hamilton's.[68]

Were they unhinged, these lady and gentlemen pamphleteers and cookery book writers, who told the poor how to avert food crisis by eating more fish, for example? First catch it, said Henry Brooke in 1800, discussing 'distress for provisions'. Don't use expensive recipes with cream and butter(!) Cook your cod with potatoes, add a little milk; or fry fish and potatoes with a little fat hog meat. Or they might make pickled fish salad

---

[67] Ministry of Agriculture, Fisheries and Food, *Manual of Nutrition*, 10th edn, HMSO, London, 1995.
[68] Chapter 3, notes 53 and 54.

Figure 21. Three maidservants processing food, one of them –
probably – using an instruction manual.

like Europeans. In fact, it would be much to the good if the English poor became altogether more like the French: made soup and stews with scraps of meat, instead of baking and roasting it.[69] 'Employ the pot', was his summary advice.[70] Pamphleteers addressed the servants in the kitchen directly as they had been doing for years; the literary form dictated that writers do so, in the teeth of their knowledge that their pamphlets would not be read by many of them.[71] They invented dialogues between cottage women in order to provide recipes for savoury rice and a good but impractical 'Receipt to Make a Stew of an Ox's Head' (which took a full ten hours on a low fire. The fuel would cost 6d – so not only impractical but expensive too).[72] These pamphleteers were not disordered in their mind. Cottagers and household servants may have been the addressees of their texts, but few can have thought that the poor would read them. Women immensely grateful for a hint about an ox head were figures with which the philanthropic sort did their thinking and theorising about the most pressing need of human creation, which was food, and its first duty, which was to labour – especially during these crisis years. And it was in the processing of food, in kitchens, that servants themselves did most thinking about life and labour or, more certainly, from where the most recorded of their thinking emerged, as the next chapter relates.

---

[69] No xenophobic depiction of vegetable-eating Frenchmen here. See Gerald Newman, *The Rise of English Nationalism: A cultural history 1740–1830*, Macmillan, Basingstoke, 1997.

[70] Brooke, *Distress for Provisions*, p. 36.

[71] Taylor, *The Present of a Mother to a Young Servant: Consisting of Friendly Advice and Real Histories*, 2nd edn, Taylor and Hessey, London, 1816, pp. 69–77.

[72] Society for Bettering..., *Information for Cottagers*, pp. 32–3.

10 An Ode on a Dishclout

Now, a kitchen is nobody's premises; a kitchen is not a ware-house, nor a wash-house, a brew-house, nor a bake-house, nor an inn-house, nor an out-house, nor a dwelling-house; no, my Lord, 'tis absolutely and *bona fide* neither more nor less than a kitchen, or as the law more classically expresses, a kitchen is, *camera necessaria pro usus cookare; cum sauce-pannis, stew-pannis, scullero, dressero, coal-holo, stovis, smoak-jacko, pro roastandum, boilandum, fryandum, et plum-pudding mixandum, pro turtle soupos, calve's-headhahibus, cum calipee et calipashibus*... But we shall not avail ourselves of an *alibi*, but admit of the existence of a cookmaid: now my Lord, we shall take it upon a *new* ground...

George Alexander Stevens, *A Lecture on Heads*, 1795, pp. 29–30.

A household with two or more servants might designate one of them cookmaid, though it was unlikely that her work be confined to the kitchen and to cooking. Frances Hamilton did not employ a woman she called a cook until 1800; her maids (usually two, occasionally three) all worked in the kitchen, to a greater or lesser degree. In 1788, from a much larger establishment than Hamilton's, Hester Piozzi (seven servants mentioned by name this year, probably double that number at work in the Streatham household) wrote to a friend about what she wanted in a new cook: she 'should go to Market and take Care of all Kitchen Matters... not be affronted neither if I sometimes go to Market myself; nor insist on other privileges than having a Girl under her... One should like a notable Woman who could do little French Dishes for my Master prettily... Now I don't want a fine 20£ or 30£ a year Cook... *they* do nothing as ever I see

276

but spend . . . '.[1] Here in the Piozzi household, duties were strictly demar-
cated, for there was 'a sort of nominal Housekeeper' to look after the table
linen. There are many letters like this in collections of family papers, some
to employment agents, some to acquaintances who had provided the current cook: 'Could you recommend me a good cook? I shall most likely
part with Betty Byford tomorrow. The poor girl is . . . so ill in mind . . . that
she is quite incapable of any business . . . I am really much concerned on
her account; and not a little on my own for she is a quiet servant and
pleased me much as a cook . . . I have a good deal of company coming to
dinner to day and Betty's total incapacity rather unhinges us . . . '.[2]

What was usually wanted was a wide range of skills, including kitchen
business. 'One that is not very Young' said Mrs Cooke of Doncaster;
'clean ready & handy in doing her family business'. Can she 'Wash & get
up Linning well & sow plain work well'? Does she know 'how to Clean
rooms well'? Could her current employer oblige by giving 'her leave to
be as much in the Kitching as she can . . . & . . . your Housekeeper . . .
instruct her to make different kinds of Pastry &c'?[3] Servants were moved
about between households, sometimes unclear that it was cooks they were
about to become: 'Dear Kitty This comes to desire you to acquaint Sally
Killingley that my maid Alice goes away this Day fortnight and I would
have Sally come that week that the other Leaves me I think the best way
for her to come will be with the carrier she understands I suppose that it
is a cooke maid I want my Place is not a hard Place for two far from it'.[4]
Employers got maids (and sometimes men) to be cooks by many devices,
but found much work for them to do outside the kitchen once they had
made the bargain: all servants in modest households were multitasking
young women and men.

There was a subcategory of the servant-joke – the ritualised complaining about servants, thinly disguised by the employer's self-deprecation –
that can be called the 'cookmaid joke'. Much depends on dinner, and

---

[1] Edward A. and Lilian D. Bloom (eds.), *The Piozzi Letters. Correspondence of Hester Lynch
   Piozzi, 1784–1821*, Delaware University Press, London and Toronto, 1989, vol. 1, pp.
   277, 280, 284, 285 (1, 10 Sep., 7, 21 Oct. 1788).
[2] Norfolk County Record Office (NCRO), BOL 2/113, 2/15, Bolingbroke Collection,
   Leathes Family Papers, Letter . . . re getting Mr Bowness's cook into the Bethel Hospital.
   Revd Bowness thought that Betty's was love-trouble: 'Matrimony she has had in her head
   for some time and I believe her swain, who is a decent young man, is kind and faithful; but
   the apothecary . . . think[s] that there is something more that disturbs her . . . he advises
   that I should suffer her to go to her mother . . . '.
[3] Doncaster Metropolitan Archives (DMA), DD.DC/H7/1/1, Davies-Cooke of Ouston,
   Mrs Mary Cooke, Copy letter book, 1 Vol. 1763–67 (Dec. 1766).
[4] Birmingham Central Library Archives (BCLA), Hutton 12, Hutton Family, Letters and
   papers, Letter from a daughter of Ambrose Rusdell's to Catherine Perkins re . . . the
   employment of Sally Killingley as maid (22 Apr. 1754).

the sudden absence of a cook (committed to bedlam, gone home to mother, in bed with the ague, or just 'Gone') forced contemplation of cooks (or general servants in their aspect as cook), far more than was the case for other categories of domestic servant – particularly among the men of a household. They figured in the anxious and lubricious imagination of several eighteenth-century gentlemen. (I propose that the anxiety was mostly to do with the absence of dinner, not with sexual anxiety, though there are schools of thought that suggest we should always consider these two absences – lacks – together.) There was no reason for James Boswell to imagine making love to a cook; yet he did, musing that 'there is something I think particularly indelicate and disgusting in the idea of a cook-maid. Imagination can easily cherish a fondness for a pretty chambermaid or dairymaid, but one is revolted by the greasiness and scorching connected with the wench who toils in the kitchen...'.[5] Cookmaids were called nastier and more demeaning names than anything the fictional Pamela and many actually existing servants had to put up with – Pamela, so neat and pretty, so very unscorched and unblistered.[6] 'Dish clout' is the most unpleasant name for a cook that I have encountered – no first name, no last name, no appellation; just 'dishclout' – from *The Lecture on Heads* that provides the epigraph to this chapter.[7] As jesting masters and mistresses congratulated themselves on seeing through their servants, being up to the mark with all their wily little depredations, the cook could stand in for the whole lying, cheating race of them. 'Dorothy Redfist' writes to the *Wit's Magazine* on her qualifications as a modern maidservant: 'Eighthly. If there is a crust of bread harder than ordinary, I always carry it to my master's table... Ninethly. If there is any kind of greens for dinner... I always take care to send the outside leaves... and detach the best part in a cullender, over some hot

---

[5] Margaret Bailey (ed.), *Boswell's Column. Being his Seventy Contributions to the London Magazine, under the Pseudonym The Hypochondriac from 1777–1783*, William Kimber, London, 1951, p. 99, No. XVII, 'On Cookery' (Feb. 1779).

[6] Richardson discusses the possible effects of the kitchen on Pamela's pretty person when he has her try – and give up trying – to scour a pewter plate snatched off Rachel the kitchen maid. She is testing herself, to see if she can bear to go home to work in her parents' humble cot. Samuel Richardson, *Pamela, or, Virtue Rewarded* (1740), Penguin, Harmondsworth, 1985, p. 109.

[7] George Alexander Stevens, *A Lecture on Heads with Additions by Mr. Pilon; as delivered by Mr. Charles Lee Lewis... To which is added An Essay on Satire*, William Lane, London, 1795, pp. 28–9. This is literally a series of essays, play-prologues, comic routines, dramatic monologues etc., delivered by and concerning the human head. Perhaps Alan Bennett once encountered it. Dugald Stewart, Frances Hamilton's favourite philosopher said that even the great Montaigne called his servants by their office rather than name. But he was discussing memory-loss here, not verbal disparagement. *Elements of the Philosophy of the Human Mind* (3 vols., 1792–1827), A. Strahan and T. Cadell, London, Creech, Edinburgh, vol. 1 (1792), p. 467.

water, till they have done: for why should not sarvants know what's good as well as their masters and mistresses?'[8] 'Betty' writes to 'Sally', her former companion in the three-servant London household she has left to get married:

> When mutton chops or steaks are drest,
> Mind, for yourselves, to keep the best;
> If th' sweet-bread from the veal does fall,
> Roast it well, and eat it all;
> Green peas, when scarce, and few are bought,
> Eat up the half, tho' but a quart;
> Then make complaint, Lord! How they shrunk;
> The pidgeon pye it really stunk;
> We threw it ev'ry bit away . . .

And on, and on . . . .[9] In this sort of comic literature, the category 'cook' emerges in the 1780s ('cook' as opposed to 'servant who cooks'), but only in fictional London houses (all this literature emanated from the Metropolis). The cook has a range of specific skills acquired at the hiring, and this genre of literature mocks them – those who sell them and those who buy them – as in the anonymous *Trial of Betty the Cook-maid* of 1795. Betty was hired by the plaintiff's 'loving and virtuous lady, to serve in the rank, degree, or situation of a cook maid, when in consideration of the annual sum of seven pounds, she then [sic] prisoner undertook to roast, boil, hash, mince and broil for me and all my family, to scower my brass and pewter, with all the dishes of my scullery, and do and perform all . . . the duties and services appurtenant or appendant to a Cook-maid . . . '.[10] What is the point of this little squib of two folded pages? Perhaps the way in which the law of service operated here to everybody's satisfaction. Its hyperbole is engaging: the huge weight and majesty of the law is brought to bear on the not very important household of the plaintiff (this is the way that the inconclusive trial of 'dish-clout' works – some dispute about a dripping pan is brought into the higher courts). What is mocked is the pretentious, jumped up, middling sort, who assign so many offices to a girl who after all, just chops carrots and keeps the kitchen fire going, as if for all the world they were running an

---

[8] 'Qualifications of a Modern Maidservant', *The Wit's Magazine* . . . , 2 vols., London, 1784–5, vol 2 (Dec. 1784), p. 466.

[9] Anon., *A Letter from Betty to Sally, with the Answer; A New Year's Gift. Recommended to be Learnt by Every Servant in the Three Kingdoms, Read Once by Every Mistress of a Family, in the Hearing of Every Master, whose Fortune does not exceed Three Hundred a Year*, Fielding and Walker and J. Stockdale, London, 1781, p. 8.

[10] Anon., *The Trial Of Betty the Cook-maid, Before the Worshipful Justice Feeler, for Laying a Bed in the Morning*, 'printed and sold in London', 1795, p. 2.

establishment like Hester Thrale's at Streatham Park. Betty the cookmaid does a nice line in Mollspeak, and there was evidently a market for reading the invented voices of servants, even when inverted culinary advice was delivered in the brisker, more elegant, and versified tones of the fictional maids in *A Letter from Betty to Sally*.[11]

Employers wrote about servants, and invented fictional ones in order to complain about them. And from the other side of the kitchen door, cooks – and maidservants who cooked – complained and wrote back. Or just wrote, as part of the job. In discussing the twentieth-century development of recording and writing systems among the Vai people of Liberia, the anthropologist Jack Goody observed that 'in principle a system of graphic representations capable of recording objects or names is not difficult to construct', and he notes in passing that several of the Vai records he consulted had been compiled by men who had worked as cooks and thus become familiar with elementary book keeping during their working life.[12] Christian Tousey's folded and hand-sewn 'Book' was probably put together in the kitchen out of some kind of wrapping paper; it contains undated lists of spending on foodstuffs. On the front cover is written 'Mrs Christian Tousey Hir Book', and then, 'Christian Tousey his My Naime and England his My Naishan/and Solsbury my Dwelling plas and Christ His My Salvaton'.[13] A similar though much larger one – bound with a sago paper wrapper – was kept by Philip Slott of Duntsbourn Abbots in Gloucestershire. Either a servant who cooked or actual designated man cook of Sir Mark Stuart Pleydell, it records in detail spending on kitchen supplies.[14] We can assume that many cooks kept these home-made, ongoing records. In eighteenth-century England if you wanted writing abilities ('graphic-linguistic abilities', in Goody's terms) that *had some use* in a household servant, then it was in the cook you wanted them. In modest households, in a cash-short economy, it was

[11] 'Mollspeak', after Daniel Defoe's *Moll Flanders* (1722) is Janet Taddeus's brilliant label for the eighteenth-century attempt to render plebeian speech by modified orthography; 'Swift's Directions to Servants', *Studies in Eighteenth Century Culture*, 16 (1986), 107–23. Also Carey McIntosh, *Common and Courtly Language. The Stylistics of Social Class in Eighteenth-century British Literature*, University of Pennsylvania Press, Philadelphia, 1986.

[12] Jack Goody, *The Interface Between the Written and the Oral*, Cambridge University Press, Cambridge, 1987, p. 212.

[13] Wiltshire County Record Office (WRO), 776/922A, Household account book, kept by Christian Tousey of Salisbury, a cook or housekeeper.

[14] BCRO, D/EPb A5, Account book of Philip Slott of Duntsbourn (Abbots) Glos. 1768. Slott devised a table at the back of the book, on which he recorded outdoor work done by other staff, so perhaps he was more than cook.

the kitchen door that was the egress for most small coin; it needed to be accounted for on a daily basis.[15]

Mrs Tousey's book was compiled by two hands, the second most likely to have been the mistress's (or the master's) detailing payment to unspecified others (probably charwomen, or bought-in work-boys) and to washerwomen. The way in which a single-servant household was managed and maintained by the employment of a supplementary stream of casual domestic workers or 'helpers', the calculations necessary for paying them, as well as records of daily marketing, meant that an account book like Tousey's was likely to come under regular scrutiny by the employer, even if, as was the case in some households, the live-in domestic made her own arrangements out of her own wages for a work woman to scrub the front step or to do some other 'rough' work like washing down the yard.[16] Someone else besides Christian Tousey had access to her book; but she called it her own. With it, she placed herself within a history of literacy and within many accounts of the social and psychological consequences of writing. She knew what a book was and how organised, with cover, title and epigraph. Her inscription suggests the form of schooling she may have experienced: limited though it may have been, it was in all likelihood conducted in a parochial school, where first steps in reading were to do with the God-given identity that the catechism inquires into ('What is your name?'; 'Who gave you this name?'). This inferred experience suggests that she could read simple literature of the faith, but probably a great deal more besides. Tousey had most likely been taught to read by the syllabic method; the internal evidence of her brief verse is that this was the case.[17] The syllabic method of reading-teaching may have allowed the poetical cooks discussed in this chapter direct access to the rhythmic structure of English, allowing them to play about with its sound system – as babies do in babbling – from their early days of schooling. The method has to be assumed for the main part, from printed instructional and extremely fragmentary autobiographical material. But by whatever method Tousey had been taught to read, she had been enabled to make

---

[15] For shortage of coin, Deborah Valenze, *The Social Life of Money in the English Past*, Cambridge University Press, Cambridge, 2006.

[16] Live-in domestic servants were routinely warned against their own use of charwomen. See Ann Walker, *A Complete Guide for a Servant Maid; or, the Sure Means of Gaining Love and Esteem*, 5th edn, T. Sabine, London, 1787, pp. 26–7; John Trusler, *Trusler's Domestic Management, or, the Art of Conducting a Family, with Economy, Frugality and Method*, J. Souter, London, 1819, pp. 88.

[17] For literacy instruction by the syllabic method, see Ian Michael, *The Teaching of English from the Sixteenth Century to the Present Day*, Cambridge University Press, Cambridge, 1987, pp. 72–130; Carolyn Steedman, 'Poetical maids and cooks who wrote', *Eighteenth-Century Studies*, 39:1 (2005), 1–27.

the discovery that letters, syllables and words represent the sounds of spoken language; she had been given the resources to spell some of the words she used ('his' for 'is', 'Solsbury' for 'Salisbury') from speech, as well as from (sometimes imperfect) visual recall of the words written on page or slate. Her verse inscribes a geography and a cosmology as well. The writer knows that Salisbury is smaller than England. She knows that both of them exist in a much vaster order of things. Anthropologists and psycho-linguists suggest (or until very recently suggested) that she would not have known these things in the way she did, had she not been literate.[18] The inscription also registers a particular form of Protestant Christianity; many histories of its educational project from the sixteenth century onwards tell of social and religious subjects shaped by access to the written word.[19] And the inscription is in doggerel, a rhyme form which no child is or ever has been *taught* in school, but which the exercise books of even modern school children show is acquired there.

Maids who wrote poetry were fashionable in the second half of the eighteenth century. Their popularity is sometimes attributed to proto-Romantic taste for humble genius – for plebeian literary creativity – and to the edifying consequences of contemplating talents that might, with-out a charitable donation to the subscription list of a Mary Leapor or an Ann Yearsley, be doomed to disperse themselves upon the desart air of a provincial village or a gentleman's back kitchen.[20] Some have more unkindly said that 'natural poets' made 'splendid household pets who could fawn in words', usually having in mind the long half-career of the thresher poet Stephen Duck (1705–56) whose talents flourished in

[18] For developments in theories of literacy and cognition, past and present, see David R. Olson, *The World on Paper: The conceptual and cognitive implications of writing and reading*, Cambridge University Press, Cambridge, 1994, pp. 20–44; Goody, *Interface Between the Written and the Oral*, pp. 191–5, 209–57; David Vincent, *The Rise of Mass Literacy: Reading and writing in modern Europe*, Polity, Cambridge, 2000, pp. 20–5; Harvey J. Graff, *The Legacies of Literacy: Continuities and contradictions in Western culture*, Indiana University Press, Bloomington and Indianapolis, 1987.

[19] Paul Delaney, *British Autobiography in the Seventeenth Century*, Routledge and Kegan Paul, London, 1969; Dean Ebne, *Autobiography in the Seventeenth Century*, Mouton, The Hague, 1971; Margaret P. Hannay (ed.), *Silent But for the Word: Tudor women as patrons, translators and writers of religious works*, Kent State University Press, Ohio, 1985; Elspeth Graham *et al.*, *Her Own Life: Autobiographical writings by seventeenth-century English women*, Routledge, London, 1989; Felicity Nussbaum, *The Autobiographical Subject*, Johns Hopkins University Press, Baltimore, 1989.

[20] William J. Christmas, *The Lab'ring Muse: Work, writing and the social order in English plebeian poetry, 1730–1830*, University of Delaware Press, Newark, 2001 for the market in 'rustic' poetry and 'unlettered Muses'. The writing of some female domestic servants is discussed here, for example the 'appalling working conditions' and exploitative labour relationships in Mary Collier's *The Woman's Labour* (1739). See Chapter 12 below for Collier.

inverse proportion to his climb up the ladder of patronage.[21] The cook and poet Mary Leapor (1722–46) served in at least two Northampton-shire gentry families during her brief life, producing there a corpus of work which was first published posthumously in 1748, and then in a crit-ical edition some 250 years later.[22] The relationship between Leapor and her patroness Bridget Fremantle has been particularly well described by her editors, leaving room for modern scholars to imagine the recognition by a rector's daughter of true poetic talent in a subordinate, and the devel-opment of an Enlightenment friendship around the making of poetry – as well as the tensions and impossibilities of a relationship forged across such vast social differences. It is for those impossibilities that the relationship between the philanthropist Hannah More and Ann Yearsley ('Lactilla', 'The Milkwoman of Bristol') is now largely discussed. Yearsley was not More's servant though she had much to do with More's cook and kitchen. The record of her creative independence and More's anxieties about it are particularly well preserved.[23] But even in More's fraught correspondence with friends about Yearsley's insistence on writing the poetry she wanted to write, reaping the financial rewards of its publication, and spending the money on what *she* wanted, not on what More thought proper for a milk woman, More's acknowledgement of Lactilla's talents and abilities is discernible.

Ann Yearsley's poetry came into More's life through the kitchen door. Collecting kitchen waste for her pigs from More's cook, Yearsley showed the woman her poetry, who showed it to her mistress.[24] The pigswill was in fact the most difficult and perplexing factor in the relationship between poet and patron, for Lactilla had an arrangement for it with the cook. More attempted to override what Yearsley called a 'contract' at the high point of one of their quarrels about the subscription money, and as a way of punishing Yearsley for her ingratitude and insubordination. Both

---

[21] Betty Rizzo, 'The patron as poet maker: The politics of benefaction', *Studies in Eighteenth-century Culture*, 20 (1990), 241–66; 242. Actually, Stephen Duck was rather better thought of by his fellow workers than by his fellow poets and modern critics. He had the reputation of being a bit of a wag with a nice line in the edgy hilarity of class relations. See Peter Cunningham, *Peter Cunningham's New Jest Book; or, Modern High Life Below Stairs*, Funny Joe, London, 1785, p. 43.

[22] Mary Leapor, *Poems on Several Occasions* (orig. pub. in two volumes, 1748–51), *The Works of Mary Leapor*, Richard Greene and Ann Messenger (eds.), Oxford University Press, Oxford, 2003.

[23] Madeleine Kahn, 'Hannah More and Ann Yearsley: A collaboration across the class divide', *Studies in Eighteenth-century Culture*, 25 (1996), 203–23. Anne Stott, *Hannah More: The first Victorian*, Oxford University Press, Oxford, 2003, pp. 73–4; Charles Howard Ford, *Hannah More: A critical biography*, Peter Lang, New York, 1996, pp. 71–100.

[24] Kahn, 'Hannah More', p. 204, for discussion of 'the hogwash episode'.

cook and milk woman knew that in doing so More had transgressed the boundaries of custom and customary practice. As Yearsley pointed out at length, and in print, More had no grounds on which to be offended by the kitchen-door arrangement, for the pigswill was the perquisite of the cook, and everyone knew it.[25]

Mary Leapor *was* a cook among a household retinue of servants (or a 'menial Train', as she put it[26]); not a jobbing girl in a single-servant household turning her hand to everything but, rather, hired in the capacity of a cook to a gentry family, and in no other. In 'Crumble Hall' the servant-poet wanders the corridors, chambers and grounds of the country house (at sunup it seems, truly the servant's hour) for the purposes of nostalgia (its 'hospitable Door/Has fed the Stranger, and reliev'd the Poor') and for the purposes of aesthetic judgement, for the grounds are being cleared for a new landscape garden, ancient oaks uprooted 'to clear the Way for Slopes and modern Whims'.[27] The poet spends longest in the kitchen, visiting it twice in the course of her tour. She describes its larder stores of 'good old *English* Fare' sketches out a recipe (for cheese cakes), admires the skill (her own) that went into the 'soft Jellies' and gives the menu for the servants' dinner (boiled beef and cabbage). Jeannie Dalporto has said how disconcerting it might be for a member of the employing classes to see depicted 'servants who have lost sight of their servitude', behaving as if their place in the big house is assured by affective relationships – not by contract or hiring agreement, or by the system of capital and agricultural investment the country estate represented.[28] But there is more to the affront than this. The servants behave and carry on their complex lives as if the family of the house simply does not exist; the affective relationships are between them, not between servant and employer. The kitchen is a social universe presented as completely independent of the economic structures actually inscribed in 'Crumble Hall'. In this poem, labour and the objects of labour, belong entirely to the workers. The ploughman resting by the kitchen fire dreams of '*his* Oxen', and when rain threatens worries for '*his* new-mown Hay'. Urs'la the kitchen maid, in love with the unresponsive Roger, works entirely for him, not for the Family on the other side of the door. 'For you *my* Pigs

[25] Kahn, 'Hannah More and Ann Yearsley', p. 216; Ann Yearsley, 'Narrative', *Poems on Various Subject. A second Book of Poems... by Ann Yearsley*, G. G. J. and J. Robinson, London, 1787.

[26] Leapor, 'Crumble Hall', pp. 206–11, l.110.   [27] Leapor, 'Crumble Hall', l.176.

[28] Jeannie Dalporto, 'Landscape, labor and the ideology of improvement in Mary Leapor's "Crumble Hall"', *The Eighteenth Century. Theory and Interpretation*, 42:3 (2001), 228–44, 239.

resign their morning due', she cries to his snoring form slumped across
the kitchen table:

> My hungry Chickens lose their Meat for you:
> And was it not, Ah! Was it not for thee,
> No goodly Pottage would be dress'd by me.
> For thee these Hands wind up the whirling Jack,
> Or place the Spit across the sloping Rack.
> I baste the Mutton with a chearful Heart,
> Because I know my *Roger* will have a part.

Rhetorically at least, the Crumble Hall servants reject the Lockean conception of the servant's labour as belonging to the master, and claim his
property as their own: the product of *their* labour. To employ a poetical
maid might be a fashionable thing to do and literacy in a cook certainly
a useful commodity; but perhaps these factors did not outweigh the discomfort of realising that the servants might live an autonomous life in
your kitchen, quite independent of what law and legal theory said they
were: mere aspects of your personality, exercising your own (unused)
capacity to turn spits and collect eggs, as kinds of proxy. Perhaps the
kitchen really was 'nobody's premises'.

In smaller, far more modest households than the ones Leapor cooked
in, a mistress might welcome a literary – or at least a literate – servant.
Writing skills were particularly useful in a cook maid, for the purposes
of reckoning and accounting, as already mentioned, but also because
they were a means by which – when she left, as she surely would – you
could get to keep some of the skills and abilities you had acquired at
the hiring.[29] Or a writing maid might be able to exercise the employer's
skills of farm and labour management during her absence, as Hannah
Burston did for Frances Hamilton during her holiday in Wells in 1788.[30]
Employing a cookmaid and being a cook involved a more complex set of
negotiations than this, again undertaken in writing, but on a societal as

---

[29] Cooks could leave these skills behind them, as in the very long recipe for cheese cakes
written out by the 'most Humbol tho unworthy Sarvants James and Mary Williams'
for their mistress: 'Madam the Season for making Bambory Chess is from Lamos to all
Holontids and Let your veats [?] be A bout A inch & a hf Dress and Scald with whay
and water mixed . . . '. SCRO, DD/GB, 148–9, Gore Family Papers, 1521–1814, vol.
1 DD/GB/148, p. 264. Writing matters in the world system of cookery that Michael
Symons describes in *A History of Cooks and Cooking*, Prospect Books, Totnes, 2001,
but it does not figure in the section 'What Do Cooks Do?', pp. 27–188. Jack Goody,
Cooking, Cuisine and Class: A study in comparative sociology, Cambridge University Press,
Cambridge, 1982, p. 99 on the development of 'practical literacy' in connection with
cooking. But the emphasis here is on diet rather than the preservation and transmission
of cooking techniques.

[30] See Chapter 3.

well as a household scale. In examining styles of cookery Gilly Lehmann has noted how women dominated as producers of recipe books and cooking manuals from the mid-eighteenth century onwards.[31] The writers she discusses were or had been cooks themselves and they wrote for other cooks (and says Lehmann, for mistresses eager to retreat to the drawing room). Ann Peckham (for forty years a noted cook in the best families 'in and about Leeds') targeted her *Complete English Cook* at 'such mistresses as think it a burden to be continually dangling after their maids in the kitchen'.[32] Her instructions might also be read by cook maids out of the heat of the kitchen she said, 'with coolness and deliberation at a leisure hour . . . [and] more easily retained in the memory than those of the most respectable mistress'. (She herself was 'almost worn out in the service of the kitchen'.)[33] Like Elizabeth Raffald whose work is better known, she was concerned that every word of her book should be 'easy and intelligible to the meanest capacity'.[34] Elizabeth Raffald's own 'plainess of . . . style' she said, was developed for the kind of 'common servant' she had encountered during her fifteen years' service in 'great and worthy families'. She included two foldout diagrams in her *Experienced English Housekeeper* because she had never been able 'to express [herself] to be understood by young housekeepers, in placing the dishes upon the table. I am very unwilling to leave even the meanest capacity in the dark . . . '.[35]

[31]   Gilly Lehmann, 'Women's cookery in eighteenth-century England: Authors, attitudes, culinary styles', *Studies on Voltaire and the Eighteenth Century*, 305 (1992), 1737–9.

[32]   And to 'the middling and lower ranks' eager to learn how 'to set off before their friends' their cooking. Ann Peckham, *The Complete English Cook; or, Prudent Housewife*, 2nd edn, Griffith Wright for the author, Leeds, 1771, Preface.

[33]   There is a record of Midlands servants' reading between 1746 and 1784 in books purchased from the Warwick bookseller Clay. Jan Fergus, 'Provincial servants' reading in the late eighteenth century' in James Raven, Helen Small and Naomi Tadmor (eds.), *The Practice and Representation of Reading in England*, Cambridge University Press, Cambridge, 1996, pp. 202–25. Books full of prescriptive knowledge were the largest category of servants' orders; the only named cookery books ('2 cookery books, 4s total') being purchased by a manservant. Two maids purchased Anne Barker's *The Complete Servant Maid, or, Young Woman's Best Companion*, J. Cooke, London, 1770 which had a substantial recipe section, and an early edition of Susannah Carter's *The Frugal Housewife, or, Complete Woman Cook. Wherein the art of dressing all sorts of viands with cleanliness, decency and elegance, is explained in five hundred approved receipts . . . To which are added twelve new prints, exhibiting a proper arrangement of dinners, two courses for every month in the year*, E. Newbery, London, 1795.

[34]   Peckham, *Complete English Cook*, Preface.

[35]   Elizabeth Raffald, *The Experienced English Housekeeper, for the Use and Ease of Ladies, Housekeepers, Cooks, &c*, 2nd edn, R. Baldwin for the author, London, 1771. This second edition included a technical drawing of 'a curious new-invented stove' fired with coal rather than charcoal (which she had always found expensive as well as 'pernicious to the cook'). It involved an extraction system by means of a series of chimneys. Incidentally when Mokyr discusses factories and workshops as sites of learning, providing access to know-how knowledge, he forgets the lesson of the kitchen expressed by Elizabeth

Raffald's, like Peckham's, are plain instructions: both writing cooks explain why the kitchen maid is doing what she's doing as she follows their instructions, as well as alerting her to the aesthetics of the job in hand. Almond soup for example, might be garnished with French rolls stuck with slivered nuts (get the right size: too large a roll will take up too much soup); 'these rolls look like a hedge-hog; some French cooks give this the name of hedge-hog soup'. And with onion soup, 'a few heads of asparagus or stewed spinage both make it eat well and look very pretty'.[36] These writing cooks were concerned with their manuals *as books*, not only with how clarity of style might make their meaning plainer, with cross heads, and the lay out of an index, but also with their own integrity as authors. Mary Coles (who had served in a very grand family indeed) stood upon her own originality, saying of Mrs Raffald and others that 'if all writers upon cookery had acknowledged from whence they took their receipts, as I do, they would have acted with more candour to the public. Their vanity to pass for Authors, instead of compilers has not added to their reputation.'[37]

It is not known whether or not the poet and servant Elizabeth Hands worked as a cook, only that before her marriage and the birth of her daughter in 1785 she was maid in at least one Warwickshire family, in the north-eastern part of the county between Coventry and Rugby.[38] Her most notable publication was 'The Death of Amnon' (in a volume of the same title), which appeared in 1789, accompanied by the maidservant's

Raffald: that the efficacy of saying and listening as techniques of instruction depends on the skills of the instructor as well as the abilities of the learner. Joel Mokyr, *The Gifts of Athena: Historical origins of the knowledge economy*, Princeton University Press, Princeton and Oxford, 2002, pp. 146–7, 292.

[36] Raffald, *Experienced English Housekeeper*, pp. 7–8. The language of possession, used for all sorts of household labour, is used by these cooks: 'your meat', 'it will make your meat a better colour', 'your pan'. See Chapter 12.

[37] Mary Cole, *The Lady's Complete Guide; or Cookery and Confectionary in all their Branches*, G. Kearsley, London, 1789, p. vi.

[38] W. K. Riland Bedford, *Three Hundred Years of a Family Living: Being a history of the Rilands of Sutton Coldfield*, Cornish, Birmingham, 1889, pp. 112–14. A letter reproduced here (4 Nov. 1789) from the father of Hands's major sponsor, Philip Bracebridge Homer, is the source of most biographical information concerning Hands. See also Tim Burke (ed.), *Eighteenth-Century Labouring Class Poets*, vol. III, 1700–1800, Pickering and Chatto, London, 2003, pp. 153–5; Cynthia Dereli, 'In search of a poet: The life and work of Elizabeth Hands', *Women's Writing*, 8 (2001), 169–82; Caroline Franklin (ed.), *The Romantics: Women poets 1770–1830*, Routledge, London, 1996, pp. i–xiii; Donna Landry, *The Muses of Resistance: Labouring class women's poetry in Britain, 1739–1796*, Cambridge University Press, Cambridge, 1990, pp. 186–209; Fergus, 'Provincial servants' reading', pp. 223–5. Hands achieved an entry in the *Dictionary of National Biography* in 2004: Cynthia Dereli, 'Hands, Elizabeth (bap. 1746, d. 1815)' in *Oxford Dictionary of National Biography*, Oxford University Press, 2004, www.oxforddnb.com/view/article/45851, accessed 15 Feb. 2007.

pre-emptive strike, entitled 'A Poem on the Supposition of an Advertisement Appearing in a Morning Paper, of the Publication of a Volume
of Poems, by a Servant Maid' ('Supposition I').[39] Hands opens with a
comfortable scene of genteel provincial life: 'The tea-kettle bubbled, the
tea-things were set,/The candles were lighted, the ladies were met'. The
topic is set immediately by the lady of the house, 'a volume of *Poems* . . .
produced by the pen of a poor servant-maid'. There is an immediate
exclamation in response:

> 'A servant write verses!' says Madame du Bloom
> 'Pray what is the subject – a Mop or a Broom?'
> 'He, he, he', says Miss Flounce: 'I suppose we shall see
> An Ode on a Dishclout – what else can it be?'

They move on to contemplate their own household servants, their irritation smoothed by long usage; one of them remembers her own 'poetical
maid' who 'wrote on a wedding some very good lines'. All agree that:

> 'Had she wrote a receipt, to've instructed how
> To warm a cold breast of veal, like a ragout,
> Or make cowslip wine, that would pass for Champagne.
> It would have been useful, again and again'.

Hands hammered home her point in 'A Poem on the Supposition of the
Book having been Published and Read' ('Supposition II'), that talent
is not confined by class, and that genius may be found in the most
obscure of circumstances. The ladies and gentlemen twitter and sneer
their way through some pedestrian literary criticism; and Hands then
firmly closes the drawing room door on them, having most effectively
prevented anyone doing the same to her own verse.[40]

Hands's reading of the professional cookery manuals is inscribed in
her 'Supposition I', with the ability to make 'a ragout' that a local lady
thinks might represent really useful knowledge in a maid. An assertion
of plain English taste has been discerned in the work of authorial women
cooks of this period, an endorsement of simple, clear flavours, and of
cookbooks 'not stuffed with a nauseous hodge-podge of French kick-
shaws', as Ann Peckham assured her readers hers was not.[41] As English
cooking style moved away from debased versions of court cuisine to an
attempt to produce the French sort *à la mode* and on the cheap, many

---

[39] Elizabeth Hands, *The Death of Amnon. A Poem with an Appendix: containing Pastoral and Other Poetical Pieces*, N. Rollason, Coventry, 1789.

[40] Not that it stopped them of course. Landry, *Muses*, pp. 186–9.

[41] Peckham, *Complete English Cook*, Preface.

cooks (the shock-troops of culinary change) contemplated the *ragout*.[42] Martha Bradley, like Ann Peckham, thought that it typified the French way of mixing together so many ingredients that purity of flavour was lost. And yet she had several recipes for ragoux; perhaps her 'To Ragoo a Breast of Veal' had penetrated the poetic imagination, if not the kitchens, of central Warwickshire. Bradley gave detailed instructions for 'ragooing' a fresh cut of veal, a recipe written in the teeth of her opinion that 'the French, who never know when to stop, serve up a Capon [for example] . . . with a rich Raggoo about it, but this is a Confusion, and the Taste of one Thing destroys another'.[43]

It is economical domestic cooking that the fictional Mrs Domestic is after, the using-up of leftovers and the making of ersatz champagne, not fully Frenchified dishes, and Elizabeth Hands makes sure you know this. She also makes sure the reader knows that the servant 'who wrote on a Wedding some very good lines' is herself, for six verses 'On a Wedding' are to be found some thirty pages on, in the real volume – *The Death of Amnon* – that the ladies and gentlemen in the drawing room have just seen advertised (in the real *Coventry Mercury*), and that you, now, hold in your hands.[44] And Hands knows that the reader will know that the bean dish on which Mrs Domestic is complimented ('Your haricots, ma'am, are the best I e'er eat . . . may I venture to beg a receipt?') were actually cooked by her maid; she does not need to labour the point. ('Supposition II', l.60–71).

It is Hands's knowingness, and her control of it for fashioning into a good joke, that astonishes. Modern critics have scarce got the measure of the insubordination – the barefaced cheek, the nerve of it – that the two 'Suppositions' imply (at least to social historians whose understanding of female domestic service in this period is framed by the pathos and melodrama – the knowledge of gender and labour exploitation – taught us by the last half century of labour and women's history). There is simply not a way of concluding that these two poems were 'offensive to none'; they are – surely – intentionally offensive, and wonderfully so.[45] Hands appears to have got away with a sustained satire on bourgeois and gentry manners and to have laughed heartily at their pretensions to literary

[42] For changing culinary style see Lehmann, 'Women's cookery'; Martha Bradley, *The British Housewife: or, the Cook, Housekeeper's and Gardiner's Companion* (1756), Prospect Books, Totnes, 1996, Intro. Gilly Lehmann.

[43] Bradley, *British Housewife*, pp. 55–6 for the veal recipe; pp. 37–9 for her throwing up her hands at the French fashion for 'ragoo-ing' everything.

[44] Hands, *Death of Amnon*, p. 85, 'On a Wedding'.

[45] Dereli, 'In search', pp. 169–82; 180. That they are 'amusing . . . enough' also seems an inadequate critical response; Fergus, 'Provincial servants' reading', p. 224.

taste as well as at the mean-mindedness of their cuisine. The maidservant watching them *knows* more than they do. Part of the hilarity (and its edginess) comes from her placing herself within the scene she observes from her place by the wainscot. Roger Lonsdale, who first brought Hands to modern critical attention by including the 'Death of Amnon' and other pieces from her eponymous volume in his *Eighteenth-Century Women Poets* (1989) remarked that Hands expected 'Amnon' to disconcert her social superiors.[46] Of the two much more discomforting 'Suppositions', Clifford Siskin – he also calls them 'extraordinary' – has convincingly argued that the sublime trick of the second ('on . . . the Book Having Been Published and Read') works precisely because they were *not* read. Hands shows the gentlemen and ladies discussing at length 'precisely those books – from the Bible to "Poems" by a "poor servant maid"' which 'they have never read' and never will read.[47] Hands's textual control appeared to extend to her reviewers and Richard Clough in the *Gentleman's Magazine* opened his by recalling 'A Wag of our acquaintance' who, 'coming into a bookseller's shop in the country, where subscriptions were taken in for the benefit of this poetess, burst out [with] . . . "'The Death of Ammon'! Who the devil is this Ammon? Hah! I have read a great many books, but never met with the 'Death of Ammon' before"'.[48] 'Amnon' is spelled incorrectly in the review header as well, a gloriously inadvertent joke by the compositor, probably. Hands did indeed give her reviewers most of their lines. 'Let Mrs Hands be the judge in her own cause' said the *Monthly Review*; 'in the words of Miss Rhymer and the honest old Rector . . . "There are various subjects indeed:/With some little pleasure I read all the rest,/But the Murder of Amnon's the longest and best".'[49]

It was reviewed not so much for the novelty of the servant's writing, but because a woman – a working woman – treated of a subject so portentous and elevated (and on 'a delicate theme', observes Captain Bonair in 'Supposition II'). ''Tis a Scripture tale, ma'am – he's the son of King David', explains the old Rector.

[46] Roger Lonsdale (ed.), *Eighteenth-Century Women Poets*, Oxford University Press, Oxford, 1990, pp. 422–9.

[47] Clifford Siskin, *The Work of Writing: Literature and social change in Britain, 1700–1830*, Johns Hopkins University Press, Baltimore and London, 1998, p. 221. Donna Landry notes of the two 'Suppositions' that 'not since Swift have we seen comical satirical verse of such calibre', *Muses of Resistance*, pp. 186, 188–9.

[48] 'Review of New Publications. *The Death of Ammon* [sic] *A Poem; with an Appendix, containing Pastorals and other Poetical Pieces*. By Elizabeth Hands', *Gentleman's Magazine*, 60: June (1790), 540.

[49] 'Monthly Catalogue for November 1790', *Monthly Review*, 179, 345–6; also reviewed as 'Article 43', *The Analytical Review, or, History of Literature, Domestic or Foreign*, 6: Jan.–Apr. (1790), 98.

> Quoth Madam, 'I have it;
> A Scripture tale? – ay – I remember it true;
> Pray, is it i' th' Old Testament or the New?
> If I thought I could readily find it, I'd borrow
> My housekeeper's Bible, and read it tomorrow'.
> ''Tis in Samuel, ma'am', says the Rector: – Miss Gaiety
> Bowed, and the Reverend blushed for the laity.

Hands's sponsors were somewhat nervous about her reworking of 2 Samuel, 13, for she dealt with the topic of incestuous rape ('albeit in a biblical context' notes Roger Lonsdale). It shows Hands to be interested in the psychological effect of guilt on perpetrator and victim after a brother–sister rape; but even more interested in questions of family authority and the manipulation of the servants' fealty and loyalty in the royal household where the incest takes place. Absalom, seeking revenge by murder for the violation of his sister by their older brother, instructs his servants to perform the act ('I have servants, they shall give the blow'). 'Why tremble ye?' he asks them. ''Tis I command you – all the deed is mine'. Later, he urges them on with the observation that 'Ye are but instruments within my grasp'. Well might a servant of the 1780s be interested in this question, as the weight of advice about her liability was in the process of shifting from Blackstone's reassuring summary of 1765 that 'as for those things which a servant may do on behalf of his master . . . the master is answerable for the act of his servant, if done by his command, either expressly given, or applied', to the terser advice of the early nineteenth century: 'servant committing a crime, by master's command, liable to prosecution'.[50]

Hands transmuted Amnon's violation of Tamar, and his consequent death at the hands of their vengeful half-brother Absalom, into blank verse, considered to be the noblest of metrical forms by contemporary literary theorists.[51] Her theme was important (as well as delicate): 169 of her 1,200 subscribers were clerical gentlemen including members of Oxford and Cambridge colleges and two bishops, though this high proportion may have had more to do with the networking skills of Hands's sponsor, Philip Bracebridge Homer, than with their interest. (Yet Hands anticipated interest, in the shape of her 'Reverend old Rector'.) Homer

---

[50] Blackstone, *Commentaries*, Book 1, 6th edn, Company of Booksellers, Dublin, 1775, pp. 429–30, 432. Samuel Clapham, *A Collection of Several Points of Sessions Law, Alphabetically Arranged*, 2 vols., Butterworth and Clarke, London, 1818, vol. 2, p. 21.

[51] Franklin, *The Romantics*, p. ix; *Encyclopaedia Britannica; or, a Dictionary of Arts and Sciences, Compiled Upon a New Plan*, Edinburgh, 1771, 'Poetry'; Anne Janowitz, *Lyric and Labour in the Romantic Tradition*, Cambridge University Press, Cambridge, 1998, p. 7.

was classics master at Rugby school, had studied at Oxford, and maintained an extensive clerical and literary acquaintance – 'a community of
interest' in John Brewer's terms.[52] To subscribe to a publishing enterprise
like this was a charitable act: the *Gentleman's Magazine* hoped that monetary homage to the poetical talents of a blacksmith's wife might 'make the
remainder of her life comfortable to herself and family'. This was indeed
how Elizabeth Hands had first been presented to the reading public, as a
deserving – and talented – case.[53] Character and merit in Mrs Hands –
this was evident to all reviewers – were measured by an 'uncommonly
numerous list of subscribers', and the 'extraordinary patronage' of 'persons of rank and consideration' that it showed.[54] Thirty-one members
of the nobility subscribed (including the former Chief Justice, William
Earl of Mansfield and his family of legitimate and illegitimate nieces at
Kenwood); seven members of parliament, including Edmund Burke and
Charles James Fox; bishops as already enumerated (plus the Dean of
Canterbury); the Poet Laureate; the President of the Royal Society; and
the Swan of Lichfield, Anna Seward. Over 400 subscribers came from
Warwickshire (about 600 from Midlands counties including its major
towns and cities), but it sold in London as well (90 subscribers) and
extraordinarily well in Oxford and Cambridge. It was popular in Norfolk, and got as far north as Leeds. It is not very likely that Edmund Burke
or Lord Mansfield read the volume when it was sent out in September
1789.[55] The Newdigates of Arbury, Warwickshire (Sir Roger and his

[52] Birmingham University Library (BUL), Special Collections, 1956/V27–27A, Philip
Bracebridge Homer, Letters, papers, copy of *The Garland* etc. BCLA, Homer 425,
'Accounts of the . . . Children of the Rd. Henry Sacheverell Homer, Rector of Birdingbury, & Vicar of Willoughby, Warwickshire'. Homer may also have been a member of the
Rugy and/or Coleshill book societies. The Rugby Book Club subscribed to *The Death
of Amnon* and some members of the Coleshill society as individuals. Eric Benjamin
Branwell, *The Ludford Journals of Ansley Hall*, privately printed, no place of publication,
1988, pp. 78–85. Books clubs in Lutterworth and Repton were also subscribers. Nearly
a hundred of Hands's subscribers were former customers of the Clays of Warwick,
Booksellers. Fergus, 'Provincial servants' reading', pp. 223; John Brewer, *Pleasures of
the Imagination: English culture in the eighteenth century*, Harper Collins, London, 1997,
pp. 182–3.

[53] 'Had the poetical Fancy derived any Assistance from Education, She would probably
have stood high in the Rank of female Writing . . . but She has had no opportunities of
Improvement, except for the careful Perusal of Books, which she was permitted to make
Use of in the Families to which she was a Servant, and from the gradual Purchase of
a Few, as her Finances could afford it.' 'Proposals for printing by Subscription for the
Benefit of the Author', *Jopson's Coventry Mercury*, 24 Nov. 1788, p. 3.

[54] For subscription, see Rizzo, 'The patron as poet maker'. Also Anne Stott, *Hannah More*,
p. 73; Jonathan Bate in *John Clare: A biography*, Pan Macmillan, Basingstoke, 2004,
pp. 143–92 and passim, but for a later period, when subscription was actually on the
wane. Also Fergus, 'Provincial servants' reading', pp. 223–4.

[55] *Jopson's Coventry Mercury*, 14 Sep. 1789, 3.

wife sent in 5s for the larger, superior version) kept a log of their library during these years, recording books as they came in, and those lent out to friends; *The Death of Amnon* does not appear in Sir Richard Newdigate's lists.[56] They had merely received the object by which they supported a deserving case of 'elevated genius' in a 'poor serving maid'.[57]

Homer had told the *Gentleman's Magazine* reviewer (he was assiduous in getting Hands noticed as well as recruiting subscribers) that there was 'no woman poet, in this age, from whom he [had] received so much entertainment', and he certainly had read it.[58] He was a poet himself and keenly interested in prosody. But in his own published work and private poetic musings he never attempted the heroic, Miltonic metre that Hands employed in 'Amnon', and produced no blank verse on topics tragic and elevated. But he *cared* about poetry and spent much time translating Latin verse into English and composing his own. We should at least entertain the notion that he knew that Elizabeth Hands could do something that he could not do himself; that he recognised poetic talent where he saw it.[59] The *Gentleman's Magazine* thought him generous in precisely this way, 'not jealous or envious of any who aim to attend the Heliconian hill, and particularly attentive to female merit'. Bertie Greatheed, to whom *The Death of Amnon* was dedicated, may have promoted Hands for the same reasons, certainly among his very grand family. His mother was a daughter of the Duke of Ancaster, his wife an Ancaster niece. He wrote plays and poetry and the family had promoted talent in the serving class before. In the 1770s a very young Sarah Siddons (Sally Kemble as was) had been his mother's serving maid and continued to visit the Guy's Cliffe estate just outside Warwick and the Greatheed family well into the nineteenth century.[60] Dramatic and poetic talent might exist in a plebeian woman as far as he was concerned. And beauty; for a cook might be ornamental as well as useful: 'Rebecca Barker came to our service at

[56] WCRO, Newdigate of Arbury, CR 136/A [565]. Notebook of books received and sent out from Arbury; CR 136/A [621], Appointment and memorandum diaries.

[57] *Jopson's Coventry Mercury*, 23 Nov. 1788.

[58] But one wonders about how much space and opportunity there was for Elizabeth Hands to slip off to the *Mercury* offices and have material inserted that Homer had not seen. We simply do not know how far his editorial grasp reached.

[59] BUL, 1956/V27–27A, Philip Bracebridge Homer, letters, papers etc. Philip Bracebridge Homer, *The Garland; A Collection of Poems*, C. S. Rann, Oxford, n.d (1783).

[60] He worried about meeting the great actress playing the lead female role in his play *The Regent* in 1792 for 'as a boy I had been accustomed to her in so different a station'. But social anxieties were dispersed by an 'impressive' encounter. WCRO, CR1707, Heber-Percy of Guys Cliffe, 1759–1826, Diaries of Bertie Greatheed. For Sarah Siddons, CR 1707/116 (10 Sep. 1805); CR 1707/122 (14, 17 Jul., 17 Nov. 1818).

25 Guineas a year', he noted in October 1819. 'I hope she may prove as good a cook as she is a beautiful woman' – a far cry from 'dish-clout'.[61]

Why might a woman like Elizabeth Hands choose to write poetry rather than prose narrative? Our assumption as historians still is that someone like her would more likely first inscribe an 'I' upon the page, telling the story of a hard-won individuality by reference to a range of available religious models for a life-story.[62] 'Why poetry?' is not a question asked about the plebeian and working-class writers whose work continues to be discovered. Modern scholars acknowledge the compulsion to write poetry. Donna Landry says that Mary Leapor wrote not because she *could* make verses but because 'she could not *not* write verse'.[63] But even Jonathan Bate's recent biography of John Clare, extraordinary testament to the extraordinary difficulties that faced a working man who wanted to write, does not ask 'why write poetry?' For Clare there was lack of time, of space, of a surface on which to rest a scrap of paper, of the paper itself, and of writing implements. An unannounced call from an interested reader (and social superior) eager to discuss the lyric form had to be attended, and might cost him a day's wages. Clare wrote when and where he could, in fields, resting by roadsides, and on what he could find; before he entered his madhouse years, paper was much harder for him to come by than it was in Elizabeth Hands's or Christian Tousey's kitchens.

Verse is *short* and semantically self-contained; its form is much less socially ramified than the novel – though for the later eighteenth century the novel cannot be our point of comparison. Neo-literates might have held a chapbook almanac or fortune teller, a Protestant conversion narrative, a ghost-story, a *Trial* of Betty Branch, in their hands, but not a triple-decker proto-gothic novel, which in any case, operated by social and textual conventions that were probably incomprehensible to uncertain early readers. Poetry usually inscribes smaller and more independent units of thought than does fictional prose narrative. This point applies to six lines from – or indeed the whole twelve books of – *Paradise Lost* (or to a Canto of *The Death of Amnon*) as much as it does to 'The Death of Cock Robin': rhyme, metre, assonance and figurative devices hold groups of lines together, as units of perception and understanding. Above all rhyme (to a lesser extent alliteration and assonance) provide a

---

[61] WCRO, CR 1707/122 (2 Oct. 1819).

[62] Michael Mascuch, *Origins of the Individual Self: Autobiography and self-identity in England, 1591–1791*, Cambridge University Press, Cambridge, 1997.

[63] Donna Landry, 'The labouring class women poets: "Hard Labour we most chearfully pursue"' in Sarah Prescott and David E. Shuttleton (eds.), *Women and Poetry, 1660–1750*, Palgrave Macmillan, Basingstoke, 2003, pp. 223–43.

powerful regularity to support the good guessing by which any young (or inexperienced) reader proceeds.

But it is highly unlikely that John Clare, or Christian Tousey, or Mary Leapor – that any eighteenth-century child – was formally instructed in reading by means of poetry. Rather, what we know about reading acquisition much later on in English society alerts us to the resource a child may have found in the mass circulation of verse in the eighteenth century. After the printed sermon-collection, poetry was the most widely available genre of writing.[64] For those who held a volume or sheet of it in their hands, it was a bridge between the world of the book and a resonant oral culture in which newly invented poetry, oral and written, served to celebrate and affirm many social occasions and cultural connections ('she wrote on a Wedding some very good lines').[65] Many a recently discovered plebeian poet of the eighteenth century was a *really useful* social item, in the way of Elizabeth Hands's writing a carillon for a wedding. Christopher Jones the woolcomber, the announcement of whose *Miscellaneous Attempts* (1782) in *Jopson's Coventry Mercury* may have set Elizabeth Hands a-thinking about how she might make some money (or simply, that she could do it too) produced verse on national events (war, naval victories, responses to 'Parliamentary Intelligence' in the press) and local ones, 'On the Death of . . . ' many a provincial notable, productions that must in their own way have been 'useful again and again', for they were what was required at a wake and the funeral bard's metrical blueprint was infinitely reusable.[66] Poetry was a form of language available to the literate, the non-literate and the vastly complex set of abilities between the two that pertained in any English village or community.[67] For children and other literacy learners it provided an immediate form to work with, in the written language.

A working-class poet, writing at the very end of the eighteenth-century, answered the question: 'Why poetry?' The answer was detailed, dealing with the poetic form, the metre and the rhyme-scheme Robert Bloomfield (1766–1823) chose, as well as reasons for that choice. He described a spell of shoemaking in London in the 1790s, away from his Suffolk home

[64] Brewer, *Pleasures of the Imagination*, p. 172.
[65] Vincent, *Rise of Mass Literacy*, pp. 92–4.
[66] Charles Jones, *The Miscellaneous Poetic Attempts of C. Jones. An Uneducated Journeyman-Woolcomber*, printed for the author by R. Trewman, London, 1781, was announced in *Jopson's Coventry Mercury*, 25 Aug. 1783, p. 3. He is discussed in Bridget Keegan (ed.), *Eighteenth-Century Labouring Class Poets, 1700–1800*, vol. II 1740–1780, Pickering and Chatto, London, 2003, pp. 303–32.
[67] Alexander Pope, who was only really cruel about Stephen Duck on one occasion (when Queen Caroline had proposed him as Laureate) said that his verse was only what you could find in any country village. Rizzo, 'Patron', p. 245.

and family. In May 1796 he started to compose what would be published as *The Farmer's Boy* whilst he worked at his bench, completing it in November 1797.[68] He composed all of it and committed it to memory, before writing it down. The final version was dated 22 April 1798.[69] Why poetry? Why rhyming couplets in fact, of mainly iambic pentameters? 'Nine tenths of it was put together as I sat at work', he wrote in September 1798, 'where there were usually six of us.'

No one in the house has any knowledge of what I have employed my thoughts about when I did not talk. I chose to do it in rhime for this reason; because I found allways that when I put two or three lines together in blank verse, or something that sounded like it, it was a great chance if it stood right when it came to be wrote down, for blank verse has ten-syllables in a line, and this particular I could not adjust nor bear in memory as I could rhimes.[70]

Bloomfield concentrated on rhyme; he valued it because it allowed him to remember what he had composed, in a way that blank verse (unrhymed iambic pentameters) did not.[71] It evidently never occurred to him to compose prose narrative. For an autobiography, fictional narrative, a diary entry – whatever – you probably really do need to have a writing implement in hand and something to write on, there and then. When you do not have these tools, you cannot really write.[72]

---

[68] Robert Bloomfield, *The Farmer's Boy. A Rural Poem*, Vernor and Hood, London, 1800; B. C. Bloomfield, 'The publication of *The Farmer's Boy* by Robert Bloomfield', *The Library*, 6th ser., 15:2 (1993), 75–94; also Robert Bloomfield, *Selected Poems*, John Goodridge and John Lucas (eds.), Nottingham Trent University, 1998. For shoemaker poets, Bridget Keegan, 'Cobbling verse: Shoemaker poets of the long eighteenth century', *The Eighteenth Century. Theory and Interpretation*, 42:3 (2001), 195–217.

[69] Bloomfield, 'The publication of *The Farmer's Boy*', p. 78.

[70] British Library, BL Add MS 28.266; 83–4, 85–6; Letters quoted in Bloomfield, 'The publication of *The Farmer's Boy*'. Of course, had Bloomfield read one of the many technical guides to English prosody available, he would have known that whilst the five stress line of English blank verse *may* have ten syllables, that is not the task-efficient way of analysing it, which is by stress: five strong stresses make an iambic line, each strong stress preceded by a weak one. James Beattie, *The Theory of Language. In Two Parts. Of the Origin and General Nature of Speech...* , Strahan, Cadell and Creech, Edinburgh,1788; Anon., *The Art of Poetry on a New Plan. Illustrated with a great Variety of Examples from the best English Poets, and of Translations from the Ancients*, 2 vols., J. Newbery, London, 1762. Also Thomas Carper and Derek Attridge, *Meter and Meaning: An introduction to rhythm in poetry*, Routledge, London, 1995.

[71] Ruth H. Finnegan, *Oral Poetry: Its nature, significance, and social context*, University of Indiana Press, Bloomington, 1992, pp. 72, 90–102, for memory and memorisation in oral poetry.

[72] Carolyn Steedman, *The Radical Soldier's Tale*, Rivers Oram, London, pp. 62–86. One could ask why folk and fairy tales, which circulated in chap-book form, especially among children and young men, did not perform the same transitional role between pre-literacy and literacy for worker-writers. Perhaps they did; but with them so much more has to be known (implicitly) about narrative form and structure than with a poem. Stories are much harder to imitate than poetry.

Most proletarian poets 'wrote' like this. John Clare did not take paper and portable ink-pot to the field or the limekiln (though he once, memorably, wrote a fragment on his hat-band – with a pencil we must presume – whilst in a field).[73] Labour occupies hands; you must compose in your head, using aural memory rather than visual memory; this is what Bloomfield said. And it was the same for the ploughman, the thresher, the journeyman weaver, the young woman dusting the wainscotting, the cook making a ragout of veal. But in the kitchen, there were surfaces to rest on; there was paper of a sort around and perhaps something to write with (anyway, she could always whip up a little ersatz ink, from soot, or a little scraping from an iron pot and some very strong tea) alongside the elderflower champagne. And the gall bladder of a recently eviscerated chicken would have been of use in fixing her ink. There was always something else to be getting on with whilst the basic beef stock (Elizabeth Raffald's 'gravy') took its three hours on the fire; but cooking processes are irregularly timed and leave moments for composition.[74] No wonder that it was the cook who wrote.

Blank verse had very high status in eighteenth-century English culture; when its splendours were extolled it was usual to remind readers that it was the form of choice for Shakespeare and Milton. Elizabeth Hands's *Death of Amnon* commanded attention because the unrhymed pentameters suggested – as the *Coventry Mercury* pointed out – 'elevated genius' in one so low, and it was on her ability to sustain the heroic style that her reviewers judged her: 'if here and there an unequal line has insinuated itself into the five cantos of this heroic poem, which is written in blank verse, we must pardon the inexperienced Muse, and consider it as more than compensated by the sentiments conveyed in the whole'.[75] The rest of the volume, its 'miscellaneous articles' (*not* in blank verse), including the two 'Suppositions' would be read by Mrs Hands's subscribers 'without the severity of criticism' – meaning exactly the opposite.

Eighteenth-century society provided hierarchies of knowledge about the rhythmic patterns and rhyme schemes chosen by its poets, labouring or otherwise. This was information transmitted in a highly codified technical language, that needed instruction to be understood (tetrameter, pentameter, trimeter, etc.; trochee, dactyl . . . etc.). Scholars writing recipes for poetry still think, as they did in the eighteenth century, that these descriptive terms are necessary (or perhaps actually useful) for conveying knowledge about poetic techniques. From 1771 onwards

---

[73] Bate, *John Clare*, pp. 89–109 for his early strategies of writing.
[74] Raffald, *Experienced English Housekeeper*, p. 3.
[75] 'Review of New Publications', *Gentleman's Magazine*, p. 540.

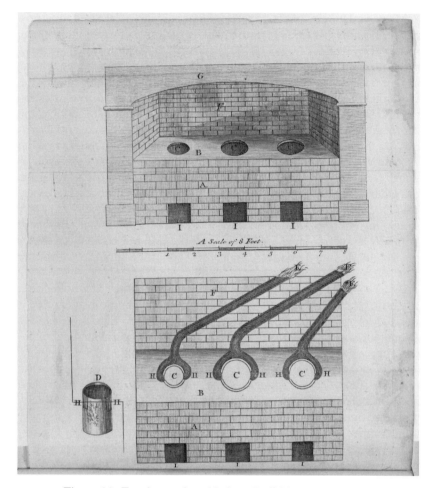

Figure 22. For the modern kitchen. Raffald recommended this stove
for health and safety reasons. See note 35.

there was available the hymn of praise to the rhythmic resources of the
English language to be found in the *Encyclopaedia Britannica*: there is
just *so much* cadence, rhythm, stress, so many words and sounds available to English-language poets. The availability of emphasis (stress) in
English was the means 'whereof... a necessary union between sounds
and sense... in versification, unknown to the ancients' was effected.[76]
Thus a certain sneering at the demotic four-beat tetrameter ('sing-song')

[76] *Encyclopaedia Britannica*, 'Poetry'.

line that Hands used in her 'Suppositions'.[77] Not all of her gentry
gathered in the drawing room are quite up to date in their literary criticism (or perhaps the old Rector retains his own strong links with oral
poetry and commonsense critical principles):

> 'That "Amnon," you can't call it poetry neither,
> There's no flights of fancy, nor imagery either;
> You may style it prosaic, blank verse at the best;
> Some pointed reflections, indeed, are expressed;
> The narrative lines are exceedingly poor...'.[78]

The eruption into printed and published verse of a resonant and still
largely shared oral culture by the socially despised tetrameter was com-
mented on by Hands when she has Lady Pedigree ask 'Who can this girl
be?'

> 'I know something of her', says Mrs Devoir;
> 'She lived with my friend Jack Faddle, Esq.
> 'Tis some time ago, though; her mistress said then
> The girl was excessively fond of a pen;
> I saw her, but never conversed with her, *though*:
> One can't make acquaintance with servants, you know'.
> ''Tis a pity the girl was not bred to high life',
> Says Mr Fribello. – 'Yes, – then', says his wife,
> 'She doubtless might have wrote something worth notice'.
> ''Tis pity', says one – says another, 'and so 'tis'.
> 'O law!' says young Seagram, 'I've seen the book, now
> I remember; there's something about a mad cow'.
> 'A mad cow! – ha, ha, ha', returned half the room.
> 'What can y'expect better?', says Madam du Bloom.[79]

And perhaps Hands hints at misbehaviour among the better sort here,
as so many of them had loudly and rudely denigrated maidservants for
their supposed loose ways. Why is Jacky Faddle Mrs Devoir's 'friend'?
Why does she slip – so effortlessly that you have to pay it attention – from
Mr to Mrs Faddle, as if trying to cover something up? *Why is Jack Faddle
called Jacky Faddle in the first place?* (To faddle: v tr., v. intr., – To pet, to
fondle, to make much of; to play about with [1755].)

---

[77] On the other hand, Frances Hamilton's favourite philosopher did not sneer at the four-
beat line, but tried to understand why it was so pleasing to the common people. Duguld
Stewart, *Elements of the Philosophy of the Human Mind*, 3 vols., A. Strahan, and T. Cadell,
London and W. Creech, Edinburgh, 1792–1827 (vol. 1, 1792), pp. 299–304.

[78] Hands, 'Supposition II', l. 102–7.

[79] Hands, 'Supposition I', l. 72–91. For 'Written, originally extempore, on seeing a Mad
Heifer run through the Village where the Author lives', Hands, *Amnon*.

Technical knowledge about poetry was available to those (like Robert Bloomfield and Elizabeth Hands) who did not read the manuals and guides provided by high literary culture. As poets they discovered, or intuited this knowledge for themselves, out of their experiences in literacy learning, in all its aspects. The four-beat line was the form of popular verse, and of many hymns. The syllabic method of reading teaching drew attention to the rhythmic potentialities of everyday speech. In describing the technical and scientific knowledge that underpinned industrial revolution in England, Joel Mokyr has said that it does not matter if propositional knowledge is incorrect by later standards: if you can japan a piece of metal, lustre the motif on a teacup, or write a poem by that knowledge (the last not one of his examples, though perhaps it should be), then it is good enough to be going on with. The 'new' story of the Industrial Revolution is of 'a small group of at most a few thousand people who formed a creative community based on the exchange of knowledge'.[80] For the economic historian, he says, what counts is *collective* knowledge: 'even if a very few individuals in a society know quantum mechanics, the practical fruits of the insights of this knowledge to technology may still be available just as if everyone had been taught advanced physics'.[81] This is a point well made by some historians of literacy: the thirty per cent of good, bad or indifferent readers in any late seventeenth- or eighteenth-century community, effectively made it a literate one, with as much access to the printed word, and a world of propositional and prescriptive knowledge, as if every man, woman, and child could read really well.[82] And Elizabeth Hands's knowledge of poetry as a technology of language *may* have come from her reading: she and several commentators mentioned the free access she had been given to household libraries in her various places. But her knowledge (her technical know-how) also came from her own reflection on the language system she employed and the heightened cognitive means that a poetic system (oral or written) provides for doing this.

From the time of classical antiquity, commentators have bemoaned the inadequacies of writing for expressing meaning.[83] A piece of written language may be a reasonable model of what a speaker said, but it is pretty useless for conveying what the speaker *meant*. Writing systems have

---

[80] Mokyr, *Gifts of Athena*, p. 65.   [81] Mokyr, *Gifts of Athena*, p. 7.
[82] David Cressy, *Literacy and the Social Order: Reading and writing in Tudor and Stuart England*, Cambridge University Press, Cambridge, 1980; Margaret Spufford, 'First steps in literacy. The reading and writing experiences of the humblest seventeenth-century spiritual autobiographers', *Social History*, 4:3 (1979), 125–50. Cressy and Spufford do not actually describe their findings thus; but Mokyr's account of the way 'really useful knowledge' *works* perhaps allows us to.
[83] Olson, *World on Paper*, pp. 89–92, summarises this cultural commentary.

great difficulty in capturing the prosodic features of speech – intonation, loudness or softness of volume, voice quality etc. Spoken utterances imply, hint, insinuate; they also assert and define. Written language can do the last two; it cannot easily do the first three. It cannot readily indicate its hidden and intended meanings, as speech can. Writing, to say it at its most definitive and forceful, lacks illocutionary force.[84] Or does it?

> 'Some whimsical trollop most like', says Miss Prim,
> 'Has been scribbling of nonsense, just out of a whim,
> And, conscious it neither is witty or pretty,
> Conceals her true name, and ascribes it to Betty'.

The illocutionary force here comes from the device of irony, to be sure; but also from the present-ness, the now-ness, that the rhythmic structure (those insistent four-beats) forces out of this utterance.

Elizabeth Hands's poetry gives us access to a ferment of inquiry and investigation into language and the question of *how it worked* (and how it had worked; these investigations were conducted, by scholars at least, with a highly historicised sensibility). Know-how (technical knowledge) to do with poetry was rapidly transmitted across the society. Elizabeth Hands may have had access to this knowledge, by reading or by over-hearing; but her verse is also highly articulate evidence of the ways in which craftsmen and women, exercising their skills (in weaving, cooking and versification) could increase their own knowledge and make technical discoveries, that they were not actively prevented from trying out. Indeed, Hands received a good deal of encouragement to do what she did, though we do not know what that encouragement *meant*. What *were* they up to, the Warwickshire *bon ton*, the Midlands *tout monde*, in letting a serving maid get away with it?

In this poetry and in these satires, social prejudice and social resentment was voiced, from both sides of the domestic service relationship. Following William Godwin, and using his perceptions, we could argue for a nascent language of class feeling, even though 'class' was not yet fully developed as a social form. We are not used to looking to either poetry or to kitchens for these phenomena, but perhaps we should. Employers expressed most anxiety and resentment about – used their most outrageous and denigrating terms about – servants in the kitchen. They could not really police what happened here, in the workplace that produced the means of their material existence on a daily basis, though Hamilton's housekeeping books, the insistence that Mrs Tousey record every farthing she spent, are testaments to their determined attempts to do so. The kitchen was not the employer's premises, as a parlour for

---

[84] Olson, *World on Paper*, pp. 92, 154–5.

example, remained, even as the maidservant passed through it with a broom. The better sort sometimes described opening the kitchen door and finding another life enacted there; it is a trope of eighteenth-century journal writing.[85] James Boswell descends to Dr Johnson's kitchen and by the light of the fire discovers Frank Barber and all his friends drinking round the kitchen table (one of the few fragments of evidence we have of networking among London's black servants).[86] The farce *High Life Below Stairs* was the theatrical formalisation of this kitchen scene.[87] There is always a flash of dislocating *astonishment* as the door is opened and employer and servants look at each other. As far as fiction is concerned, and for the nineteenth-century, Bruce Robbins proposes this kind of recognition scene between master and servant as an 'abridged, transient utopia – a place of displacement, a "nowhere" emerging within ideology and yet prefiguring very different social arrangements'.[88]

Certainly, the kitchen was not the master's premises – it was a Nowhere – but neither was it the servants': they were birds of passage in all the rooms of a house; the kitchen just happened to be the Nowhere-place in which they served out most of their time, which, it should be noted, William Godwin did not visit in anatomizing the footman's class melancholy in 1797. The household he imagined for his analysis of class feeling as it affected individual psychologies, was of the grander sort, where a footman might really be what he was called, and have little to do with a kitchen. Godwin did go as far as the footman's bedroom, which was dank and slovenly: a true expression of his state of mind.[89] Had he gone to the kitchen, in a more typical servant-employing household, he might have seen enough to advise the footman to *write back*: to write his way out of depression.

When one footman did this in 1766 – write back – one of his sarcastic, inverted directions to his aristocratic master was to ignore the home labour market and take pains to ensure that 'his porter be Swiss, his cook French, his valet German'.[90] But no one, neither servants nor employers, was very likely to encounter a Man-cook in real life, except working at an

---

[85] See for example, Francis Griffin Stokes (ed.), *The Bletchley Diary of the Reverend William Cole, MA, FSA, 1765–67*, Constable, London, 1931, p. 163.

[86] Aleyn Lyell, Reade, *Johnsonian Gleanings. Part II: Francis Barber, the Doctor's negro servant*, privately printed, London, 1952, p. 15.

[87] James Townley, *High Life Below Stairs. A Farce of two Acts. As it is performed at the Theatre-Royal in Drury-Lane*, J. Newbery, London, 1759.

[88] Robbins, *Servant's Hand*, p. 32

[89] William Godwin, 'Of Servants' (1797), Essay IV, in Pamela Clemit (ed.), *The Enquirer. Reflections on Education, Manners and Literature: Political and philosophical writings of William Godwin*, vol. 5, Educational and Literary Writings, Pickering and Chatto, London, 1993, pp. 167–71.

[90] Anon., *Directions*, p. 15.

inn, or in the kitchens of the nobility (though cookery was recommended as a good job for a boy, in the mid-century[91]). Yet Man-cooks had an amazing cultural presence. They were to be found littering the comic stage; in all sorts of novel, from the historical, through the gothic, to the sentimental; high-profile trials provided them in abundance for use in the law reports and scandal sheets; they were figures for discussion of moral standards and social conduct, and in essays and anecdotes. Above all, they were popular characters in the joke book, where they are presented as rather fine (and finely set-up) fellows with a nice line in self-confidence (the joke about one of them telling a duke that he must leave his service or be forever deskilled, was repeated over fifty years).[92] They are not mocked at all, in this literature; indeed, their presence sets more hearts a-flutter than a kitchen maid's. It is their employers who are derided, for their social pretensions in employing anything so grand. The Man-cook's presence in these texts is always noted among a 'numerous retinue of fashionable domestics', who in their collectivity are the very mark of tasteless ostentation in the employer who, when he is named, will be called something like 'Sir Solomon Mushroom', from Mrs Bennett's *The Beggar Girl* of 1797.[93] Productive thought on these questions, a form of social analysis, was more likely to be developed by the maidservant, alone in the kitchen among her dripping pans and dish-clouts (and sometimes, with her pen). The particularities of kitchen labour and the thought processes it gave rise to, will be discussed as the conclusion to this book.

---

[91] Anon., *A General Description of all Trades, digested in alphabetical Order: by which Parents, Guardians, and Trustees, may, with greater Ease and Certainty, make Choice of Trades agreeable to the Capacity, Education, Inclination, Strength, and Fortune of the Youth under their Care...*, T. Waller, London, 1747, p. 109.

[92] Merry Martin, *The Royal Jester, or Cream of the Jest*, F. Stamper, London, 1751, pp. 28–9; Anon., *The Genuine Edition of Joe Miller's Jests: or, Wits Vade-mecum Revived*, n.i. (London?, 1790?), p. 107.

[93] Anon., *Modern Courtship, a Comedy, in two Acts*, J. Coote, London, 1768, p. 36; Thomas Horde, jun., *The Pretended Puritan. A Farce of two Acts*, privately printed, Oxford, 1779, p. 16; Thomas, Holcroft, *The School for Arrogance: a Comedy. As it is acted at the Theatre Royal, Covent Garden*, P. Wogan, P. Byrne, J. Moore, J. Jones, A. Grueber..., Dublin, 1791, p. 10; Anon., *The Frolics of an Hour. A Musical Interlude. As performed at the Theatre-Royal, Covent-Garden*, Minerva Press, London, 1795, p. 15; Agnes Maria Bennett, *The Beggar Girl and her Benefactors. In seven Volumes*, Minerva Press, London, 1797, vol. 2, p. 146; Sarah Green, *Court Intrigue, or the Victim of Constancy, an Historical Romance. In two volumes*, printed at the Minerva-Press, for William Lane, London, 1799, vol. 1, p. 190; George Anne Bellamy, *An Apology for the Life of George Anne Bellamy... written by Herself*, 4th edn, 5 vols., privately printed, London, 1786, vol. 2, p. 125; Country Curate, *Directions to all Masters and Mistresses of Families, and to their Sons and Daughters, in several Chapters, containing their Duties in their various Stations of Life*, M. Cooper, London, 1746, p. 35; George Colman, *Prose on several Occasions; accompanied with some Pieces in Verse*, 3 vols., T. Cadel, London, 1787, vol. 1, p. 92.

11   A servant's wages

The maid's wages for a year is £8 8s. She has lived with me from 13th July to 25th December inclusive, how much is due to her? Answer £3 15s 11¼d

The Young Lady's New Guide to Arithmetic (1800)

'Tis a notorious Fault among Servants that they have a Custom of demanding Wages.

Directions to Lords, and Ladies, Masters and Mistresses (1766)

The footman who wrote a book of instructions for employers was being sarcastic when he pointed to the strange habit of domestics, in expecting wages to be paid. This pretend anthropological observation was a prolegomenon to a page of mock advice on how to get rid of servants without paying them (invent broken china; exclaim over a missing ring . . .), and his disparagement of *soi-disant* persons of quality, who refused to pay the trifling sum (for them) of £25 at a year's end.[1] The first economy to be devised by those of uncertain fortune, was simply not to pay; so believed servants, and some magistrates. When Nottingham MP Daniel Coke introduced his bill for regulating domestic service wage disputes in 1800, he spoke of the many 'imposters and swindlers' among masters he had encountered in his justicing room, who refused to pay their servants what was due. His proposal – it signally failed, as has been noted – was

---

[1] Anon., *Directions to Lords, and Ladies, Masters and Mistresses, for the Improvement of their Conduct to servants and Tenants, Tradesmen, and humble Friends and Cousins. Design'd as a Return for their Impertinent Directions to Servants*, M. Cooper, London, 1766, p. 28.

that JPs be able to commit employers ('but not in the first instance') for non-payment of wages.[2]

The minute calculations that employers and servants made in determining wages were formalised in many ready-reckoners made available from the mid-century onwards. In his *Young Lady's New Guide to Arithmetic*, the stern John Greig provided no table for reckoning them up, but rather expected the Young Lady to work it out for herself. Calculating the maid's wages was set as an arithmetic exercise, one of forty mental tests, the most practical of them, and one of the mere three that asked her to operate with farthings. (The most pertinent calculations for a woman in her situation in life were probably: 'What can I spend daily out of an income of £300 a year after paying £80 taxes and laying up £50 at the year's end?'; and 'My char woman has 1s 11d per day and I employ her 2 days a week, how much is that for a year?').[3] Greig's *Arithmetic* was a highly formalised guide to thinking about servants' wages and wages in general, inviting readers to consider the payments they made in the context of total annual expenditure. Published advice on book keeping – the kind that informed Frances Hamilton's minute recording of household expenditure in late century Somerset – offered a different arithmetical model for thinking about labour and other commodities purchased by the employer, a key difference between the two being the narrative element – the stress on time and duration – involved in daily recording, and periodic recalculation and reordering of entries across several volumes. Greig's Young Lady was invited to think in more global terms, of large sums of money, rendered down into daily payments to a charwoman, or into the portion due to the assessed taxes collector. For these situations, Greig taught her to calculate by the rule of three, that is, by working out from three numbers (quantities) given, what the fourth must be.[4] There are other ways, taught in other educational systems, for finding the answer to the arithmetical questions posed by the charwoman, the maid, and the tax collector: by calculating in base four (four farthings to a penny) for example; in base twelve (twelve pennies to a shilling) and twenty (twenty shillings in a pound), procedures which practically involve the learning of multiplication tables. This became almost universally the method taught to schoolchildren after the coming of compulsory education at the end of

[2] *The Parliamentary Register; or, the History of the Proceedings and Debates of the House of Commons*, J. Debrett, London, 1797–1800, vol. 11, pp. 4–5.

[3] John Greig, *The Young Lady's New Guide to Arithmetic. Being a short and useful Selection, containing, besides the common and necessary Rules, the Application of each Rule, by a Variety of Practical Questions, chiefly on Domestic Affairs . . .* , 2nd edn, privately printed, London, 1800, pp. 46, 51.

[4] Greig, *Young Lady's New Guide*, pp. 48–59.

the nineteenth century.[5] But this was not how Greig went about things (though he did provide a multiplication and division table for learning their rules);[6] rather, the invitation was to think of whole sums of money and periods of time, in proportion to each other.

We have very little knowledge of everyday arithmetical thinking in the eighteenth century, but whatever form it took, it was largely dependent on instruction and experience – on people being taught to perform calculations in particular ways, doing so, or deviating from that teaching. And we know less than nothing about forms of thinking among the poorer sort. The kitchen accounts of Christian Tousey, for example, or the women before Justice Parker, giving detailed accounts of what they were owed up to a week last Friday, suggest that they operated rather like Frances Hamilton, building up larger entities (sums of money owed them) from minute parts – from half-pennies and farthings (though in order to know that an agreement for £5 a year brought them in the equivalent of $3\frac{1}{4}$d a day, they would have had to perform some mental operation that moved from the whole to the part, or had a good look at Madam Johnson's *Young Woman's Companion*, with its useful 'Table to cast up . . . Wages').[7]

Arithmetical calculation was just one way of thinking about servants' wages, and the idea of the wage in general. There were many other means to conceptualisation available, not least the one that passed into later economic, sociological and historical discourse, that of Adam Smith in *The Wealth of Nations* (1777). Smith's theory of labour, its origins and remarkable longevity, has been considered throughout this book, and subjected to much analysis elsewhere. Richard Biernacki for example, has pointed to Smith's recognition of 'a divergence between fact and organising model'. His theory was constructed in a context where labour power had already become a formally marketable commodity, but even as he developed a model of labour as embodied – Biernacki's term is 'incarcerated' – in a finished article made by a small producer Smith 'acknowledged that nearly all [people] worked in the service of a master, not as independent artificers'. Smith's social model, or model of society,

---

[5] Susan Cunnington, *The Story of Arithmetic. A Short History of Its Origin and Development*, Swan Sonenchein, London, 1904; Louis Charles Kapinski, *The History of Arithmetic*, Russell and Russell, New York, 1925; Leo Rogers, 'The mathematical curriculum and pedagogy in England, 1780–1900: Social and cultural origins', *Histoire et épistémologie dans l'éducation mathematique*, REM de Montpellier (1995), pp. 401–12; John Hersee, 'Multiplication is vexation', *paradigm*, 24 (1997), 24–33. Also the British Society for the History of Mathematics, bshm.org.uk.

[6] Greig, *Young Lady's New Guide*, p. 21.

[7] Mary Johnson, *Madam Johnson's Present: or every Young Woman's Companion, in Useful and Universal Knowledge*, 4th edn, W. Nicholl, London, 1766, p. 190. Chapter 6 for sleights of hand passed off in this ready-reckoner.

was late seventeenth- and early eighteenth-century England, says Biernacki, when 'the bulk of the working population was excluded from the paradigm of commercial labor'.[8] This book has attempted to show the profound repercussions of Smith's view of labour for the legal, social and historical understanding of domestic service. As Biernacki also points out, his focus on human labour – but not domestic servants' labour – as both the generator and the regulator of value in eighteenth-century Britain 'coincided with the consecration of market categories as an effective ideology – that is, as the source of operative schemata of everyday practice'.

Smith's was by no means the first theory of the wage, but it is the theory that became rapidly an orthodoxy and that is still used and contested by historians attempting to disinter the actual level of wages and the experience of getting, earning, and spending in eighteenth-century England.[9] It was rooted in the same philosophic and social ground as his labour theory.[10] His account of society and economy discounted menial servants; to note that they are similarly absent from his discussion of wages for labour underlines that absence. Servants' wages do not figure in Smith's argument except as an index of prosperity (or luxury) in a landlord, annuitant, or monied man, who 'when [he] . . . has . . . sufficient to maintain his own family . . . employs either the whole or the part of the surplus in maintaining one or more menial servants. Increase this surplus, and he will naturally increase the number of those servants'.[11]

Smith's story of the wage was a historical one; that is, it began in the conjectural realm 'of the original state of things', before the appropriation

[8] Richard Biernacki, *The Fabrication of Labour: Germany and Britain, 1640–1914*, University of California Press, Los Angeles and London, 1995, pp. 475–7.

[9] Ernest Henry Phelps Brown and Sheila V. Hopkins, *A Perspective of Wages and Prices*, Methuen, 1981; Nicholas Crafts, 'English Workers' Real Wages during the Industrial Revolution: some remaining problems'; with a reply by Peter Lindert and Jeffrey Williamson, *Journal of Economic History*, 45 (1985), 139–53; Peter Lindert, 'English population wages and prices, 1541–1913' in R. I. Rotberg, and Theodore Kwasnik Rabb (eds.), *Population and History: From the traditional to the modern world*, Cambridge University Press, Cambridge, 1986, pp. 49–74; Charles H. Feinstein, 'Pessimism perpetuated: Real wages and the standard of living in Britain during and after the Industrial Revolution', *Journal of Economic History*, (1998), 625–58; Gregory Clark, 'The condition of the working class in England, 1209–2004', *Journal of Political Economy*, 116:6 (2005), pp. 1307–40.

[10] Another – and more engaging – way of putting this: '*The Wealth of Nations* is a great book – the greatest book ever written about economic life – in part because it is a book about old times'. Emma Rothschild and Amartya Sen, 'Adam Smith's economics' in Knud Haakonssen (ed.) *The Cambridge Companion to Adam Smith*, Cambridge University Press, Cambridge, 2006, pp. 319–65.

[11] Adam Smith, *The Wealth of Nations: Books I–III* (1776), Penguin, London, 1997, pp. 171–2.

of land and the accumulation of stock, when each man earned his own 'wage', or rather earned the produce of his own labour. There always had been 'wages' in this sense; wages were what (whatever) people got from labour; everything that a person might obtain by his or her own bodily exertions. In this conjectural past, something quite other than money-wages pertained; nevertheless there always had been some form of token for obtaining what one needed from another. For, as Smith said, had things gone on in the manner he described, a division of labour would have naturally taken place, more things would have been produced by a smaller expenditure of labour, and 'all things would have gradually become cheaper'. In describing remote and primitive times, Smith's language was strongly inflected by experience of a modern money economy; but 'cheap', 'expensive' and 'wage' did not have the direct conceptual connections with cash that they have since acquired. (And Smith's history was not 'history' in the modern sense; it was an imagined past, made ever present as a series of images for the purposes of explanation and theory-construction.)

This original state of things could not long survive the inauguration of private property, Smith continued. Soon, the appropriator and owner demanded the greater part of what was produced from his land by a labourer – who now makes an appearance. The labourer did not have the wherewithal to maintain himself (did not have the means of subsistence) during the long months before harvest. The farmer, or the master, advanced him those means from his own stock or accumulated hoard of goods. This advance was a wage (though Smith did not call it that, at this stage of the argument). The master/owner/landlord would have absolutely no interest in making this advance, did he not believe he would get the greater part of the harvest; that what he had advanced would be returned to him with profit. The labourer (now he clearly exists) thus had two deductions made from what he produced from the earth, said Smith: the first was the rent demanded by the owner; the second was the taking of the greater part of the produce of his labour by the master. The wage was thus the means to live over a period of time, advanced by the master. It is the same now, in the mid-eighteenth century, said Smith. Nearly all workmen need a master to advance them things to work on, and they need their maintenance until the work is completed, and the master appropriates his profit. What these wages (the means to live) actually are, is determined by a contract made between the two parties, in the light of local conditions and customs. The interests of these two contracting parties were 'by no means the same', said Smith. The worker wants to 'get as much, the masters to give as little as possible'. Smith discussed in some detail the legislation (we have already encountered it) that made combination among workers to raise wages a criminal offence, but that ignored frequent combinations among masters to keep things as they were: 'who ever imagines . . . that masters rarely combine, is as ignorant of the world as the subject. Masters are always and everywhere in a sort of tacit, but constant and uniform combination, not to raise the wages of labour above their actual rate . . . it is the natural state of things, which nobody ever hears of.'[12]

The connection of the wage (the means to continue existence) to the productivity of the labourer was made, as we have come to expect, by analogy with the slave. Smith cited French research suggesting that the labour of an able-bodied slave was worth twice what it cost the slave-holder to keep him or her, a calculation that had led Richard Cantillon to suppose that even 'the lowest species of [European] labourers' earned at least double their own maintenance, otherwise they would not be able 'one with another', to bring up two children. The woman could only earn a limited amount because of her child-care duties. But together, the pair had to be able to gain more than what was necessary to survival, in order to bring up their small family.[13] It was commonly held, said Smith, that 'the wear and tear' of workers was borne by themselves, whilst the slave owner bore all the expense of reproducing the slave. Smith thought this not to be the case, and that where non-enslaved labour was employed, the master bore it also through the medium of the wage, which had to be sufficient for the labourer to reproduce himself on a daily basis (to eat, sleep, survive sickness, clothe himself and keep warm), and to produce children – 'to continue the race of journeymen and servants'. Ensuring this by the payment of wages was cheaper than bearing the cost of slave reproduction (in both meanings), partly because the subjectivity, intentions and desires of free men and women entered the equation (Smith did not use these terms): in the economic management of their own lives labourers of all sorts exercised a 'strict frugality and parsimonious attention' he said; they invested their energies and intelligence in survival, and in the dim prospect of enjoying life.[14] Good wages – 'the liberal reward of labour' – in a society advancing towards greater acquisition and prosperity (as was eighteenth-century Britain), provided the greatest happiness and comfort for the labouring poor. In such a progressive state, good wages encouraged propagation and increased the industry of the common people. A 'plentiful subsistence' increased the bodily strength of the

[12] Smith, *Wealth of Nations*, pp. 167–70.
[13] Smith, *Wealth of Nations*, p. 171; Richard Cantillon, *Essai sur la nature du commerce en général. Traduit de l'anglois*, chez Fletcher Gyles, Paris, 1755; trans. H. Higgs (ed.), Macmillan, London, 1931.
[14] Smith, *Wealth of Nations*, pp. 183–4.

labourer, and gave him or her hope of improvement in everyday life, and of a comfortable old age. Good wages made good workers; they were the very measure of a prosperous and well-managed (well-policed) state.

The wage contract, or hiring – the agreement to labour consistently over a period of time – was important to this argument, which Smith conducted by condemning piece work. Payment by the piece or the job encouraged workers to over extend themselves, 'ruin their health and constitution', to disobey (though Smith did not put it like this, in the Lockean manner) the great Christian injunction, to preserve the life given by God. He noted that the best bargains for labour, from the master's perspective, were made in bad times for the worker, when provisions were dear. This proposition had been long discussed by political economists, and would be much debated in the crisis years of the 1790s, as we have seen, when many proposals for wage supplements and family allowances, turned on the relationship of the wage to the price of provisions. Fifteen years on from the publication of *The Wealth of Nations*, Thomas Ruggles thought that the current alarmed attention to discrepancies between wages and the price of life's necessities, was very new. He quoted Smith's formula that 'the money price of corn regulates that of all other . . . commodities', in order to align him with thinkers stretching back to the sixteenth century. He pointed out that, like the relatively recent Dr Burn, they had made no argument at all for rise in the wages of labour in relationship to the price of bread, even though they had lived through times in which there had been 'as great a disproportion between the price of corn and the price of labour as at present' (1793–4). Ruggles placed Smith in line with those writers whose silence on this question could be taken to mean that 'no foundation of complaint existed'.[15] Smith had said that in 1770s Britain the wages of labour did not, and never had, fluctuated with the price of provisions. The price of foodstuffs and other goods changed from month to month, but in most parts of the country the price of labour held steady, 'sometimes for a half century together'. If the labouring poor could maintain their families in expensive years, then 'they must be at their ease in times of moderate plenty, and in affluence in those of extraordinary cheapness'. The economic system thus described involved the will and volition of the labourer: people must save, in order to see themselves through both the regular lean months of winter, and times of more extended deprivation. This was, thought Smith, a mark of their

---

[15] Thomas Ruggles, *The History of the Poor; their Rights, Duties, and the Laws respecting Them*, 2 vols., J. Deighton, London, 1793–4, vol. 2, pp. 113–23; Jean Meuvret, 'Les Oscillations des prix des céréales aux 17e et 18e siècles en Angleterre et dans les pays du bassin parisien' [The oscillation of cereal prices in England and the Paris Basin in the 17th and 18th centuries], *Revue d'histoire moderne et contemporaine*, 16 (1969), 540–54.

freedom: 'a slave . . . would not be treated in this manner. His daily sub-sistence would be proportioned to his daily necessities . . . '. It was clear to him, that in this society of Great Britain at least, wages were not for-mally or informally regulated by the price of food and other necessities, 'but by the quantity and supposed value of the work'.[16]

Smith's account of the wage form and its history was one of many available. When he wrote that 'a man must always live by his labour, and his wages must be sufficient to maintain him', he evoked in many readers' mind the godly duty to labour, even though his discussion was conducted with no reference at all to the great Author of Nature.[17] On Thomas Ruggles's list of authorities who had pronounced on the wage question since the sixteenth century, not one of them assumed a necessary connection between 'wages' and cash payment – though to say that is to interpret their (and Smith's) understanding by much later criteria. Smith did not discuss cash wages, nor assume that a wage was always paid with money, because for him, as for his contemporaries, 'wage' meant all of what was got by labour (*including* money; sometimes a new pair of stays); something very like what the Wiltshire maidservant meant when she said that it was 'avery hard thing to take apore girls bread away from her' by dismissing her.[18]

Smith's historical account of the development of the wage was not as detailed – nor as sociological – as that of John Millar, for example, who described the period after the barbarian sack of Rome and conse-quent social and economic changes in master/slave (bondsman) relations across the small scattered settlements of northern Europe. Here, believed Millar, small gratuities to bondsmen for particular work performed, had slowly evolved into regular payments.[19] But Smith, like all the Enlight-enment philosophic historians, explained current circumstances by an account of an original state of things necessarily giving rise to the rela-tionship between eighteenth-century propertied and poor. Smith told the same story, of the 'natural Course of Human Affairs', in which it 'must naturally happen, that some of Mankind will live in Plenty and Opu-lence, and others reduced to state of Indigence and Poverty' even though that was not his intention in writing about 'the wages of labour'.[20] But

---

[16] Smith, *Wealth of Nations*, pp. 176–7.
[17] Smith, *Wealth of Nations*, p. 170.   [18] See Chapters 7 and 9.
[19] John Millar, *The Origin of the Distinction of Ranks; or, An Inquiry into the Circumstances which give Rise to Influence and Authority in the Different Members of Society*, 3rd edn, James Murray, London, 1781, p. 323.
[20] David Fordyce, *The Elements of Moral Philosophy. In Three Books*, R. and J. Dodsley, London, 1754, pp. 88–9. This was available in several forms in the later eighteenth century, including an entry in the *Encyclopaedia Britannica*, and in many editions of

because of the reading experience of his various audiences, Smith also pronounced (was understood as pronouncing) on 'this mutual Necessity' that was the foundation of society and the means for thinking about all social relations.

It was impossible *not* to write about the origin of social order and social division in this way. At the beginning of things, 'it was found that a part only of society was sufficient to provide by their annual labour for the necessary subsistence of all'. Thus was labour allocated to one part of society, and the cultivation of the human mind to the other. This was the schematic world history that underpinned Blackstone's *Commentaries on the Laws of England*.[21] John Vancouver quoted Blackstone in 1796, when he wrote his treatise on labour as a form of property, a kind of possession of the labourer. But in *The Wealth of Nations*, labour is that which is performed for oneself, or for others, in exchange for wages (in the old and the modern sense); it is an activity, or a quality, that gains the wages of existence: gains bread. It belongs to no one, in Smith's scheme; only the things that are produced by it are forms of possession. By the 1790s, if this long-established conjectural history was used to explain the current state of society, then it was done at second hand, as Vancouver did. History no longer *explained* Vancouver's subject, which was the poverty of the labouring class, the inadequacy of their wages in the face of increased living costs and ways of getting more cash – more money – into their hands, so that they might provide for themselves. There is a hint in Thomas Ruggles's discussion of poverty, wages and prices (a discussion conducted in close textual association with his summary of *The Wealth of Nations*) that the conceptual shift from 'wage' as that which the labouring poor got by labour (the means for living), to wage as monetary or cash payment, was influenced by experience of the poor-law dole, or cash payment in relief – a system that Vancouver wanted to vastly extend and formalise in a system of cash allowances to labourers with families.

As far as Adam Smith is concerned, this book has focused on one of the absences in social history and social thought that his work bequeathed to the nineteenth and twentieth centuries, that is, the absence of domestic servants from our accounts of modern English society and economy. Smith's silence on servants was explained as early as 1929, when Isaac

The Preceptor: 'Moral Philosophy', *The Preceptor: containing a general Course of Education. Wherein the first Principles of Polite Learning are laid down in a Way most suitable for trying the Genius, and advancing the Instruction of Youth. In twelve parts*, 5th edn, 2 vols., J. Dodsley, London, 1769, vol. 2, p. 315.
21 William Blackstone, *Commentaries on the Laws of England*, 2nd edn, Clarendon Press, Oxford, 1766–7, vol. 2, p. 8.

Rubin pointed out that according to Smith's theory, all agricultural and industrial labour was productive when it was exchanged directly for capital and earned the capitalist a profit. It was on this basis said Rubin, that the labour of a worker hired to perform services was deemed unproductive, whilst the very same worker, doing very similar work that did make the master a profit, was 'productive'. Rubin's example was a cook, hired to labour in a private kitchen, and then in the kitchen of a restaurant owned by the same master. Examples culled from the enormous pile of appeals against the servant tax would look very similar: many of them hinged on the distinction between the man hired to run errands for an apothecary, sweep and clean the shop, pound up the remedies in a mortar, fetch water for bottling, serve behind the counter; and the very same man, at work in the kitchen, bringing in water for cooking, cleaning the knives, sweeping up, carrying dishes to the dining table. For Rubin, the problem was – Adam Smith's problem had been – that he derived the distinction between productive and unproductive labour 'from their different *social forms*, rather than from their material properties'. In the case of his cook 'the servant's labour is identical in both cases [but] they both entail different social and production relations between people, productive in the one case and unproductive in the other'. But in his view Smith failed 'to reach such a correct conclusion and prove[d] unable to differentiate labour's social form from its material content'.[22] Or perhaps it would be better to say that there was no confusion, rather that Smith chose to describe the social form of labour.

In this book so far, and in a variety of ways, we have considered the certain – perhaps great – change in ways of conceptualising labour that took place in the second half of the eighteenth century, from a social form (a form of relationship) depicted by so many philosophic and conjectural historians, to some notion of labour as a material thing, that could be owned, and perhaps *was* actually owned by the worker, as a form of property, and that was located in his or her body. Smith's discussion of the worker's labour and the worker's wages, gives access to these transitions, to these processes of thought, and to the material labour thought about, by a very wide range of people, from maidservant to renowned political economist and philosopher. Looking more closely at the domestic servant's wage, and that wage as an exchange for labour, will help the inquiry further – though in fact the example above of the shopman as kitchen boy is an indicator of all the complications (and insights) that are bound to follow on the endeavour. His master pleads to

---

[22] Isaac Ilych Rubin, *A History of Economic Thought* (1929), trans. Donald Filzer (ed.), Ink Links, London, 1979, p. 214.

the assessed taxes appeal commissioners that the man was hired to serve in his shop, and that the legislation particularly exempts from tax the employment of anyone by whom he makes a living or profit. It was not the intention of the legislature to tax labour anyway. The male servant tax, inaugurated in 1777, was *intended* to tax the ostentatious display of luxury by means of a liveried man-servant. But by exempting those who employed others in their business, the tax took on the form of a labour tax, if only by omission. And if in this case the judges declared that the shopman was a servant 'within the meaning of the Act', then it is productive labour that will be taxed (and will go on being taxed, in a minor way, until 1937). And in order to determine what the law was not interested in the first place, that is productive labour, the commissioners and High Court judges will go on paying minute attention to the material content of labour – to what it was hired hands like the shopmen actually do, and what the difference between bringing water to the kitchen, and water to the shop, between cleaning the table knives, and cleaning out the apothecary's mortar, actually is. And wages – the judges make this point often – *cash* wages make no difference to the status of domestic servant. In law, you can be a servant without any wages at all; what makes a servant is the hiring, the agreement to work over a period of time. But perhaps that point only applies to the operation of settlement law, where a year served earns a settlement, said Lord Mansfield (and others), and wages, their existence or non-existence, their expression in a bushel of potatoes, or '2 yds of body lining for the gowns of my washerWomen',[23] are quite immaterial. And all of this tax-law deliberation – the judges contemplating the difference between the servant lifting potatoes for the family's use, and lifting potatoes for the employers' sale of them (perhaps on the same morning, gathered into the same basket), and which of those actions make the man or woman doing the lifting, a menial servant or not – will not enter any philosopher's understanding of the relationship between productive and unproductive labour, between labour as a social form, and labour as a material activity.

Except that, the point must surely be that people knew what they were talking about when they used the term 'wages', whether they were paying them out or complaining for them before a magistrate. By 1800, Frances Hamilton, like many who employed agricultural labour, kept a specific wages book, in which she recorded weekly payments to the men and women who worked her land. Here also, as wages, she recorded the days and hours undertaken by washerwomen, the men and women who gardened for her, the children who ran errands, the village people

---

[23] SCRO, DD/FS 5/7, 25 Aug. 1789

who looked after her poultry, those who came in to brew or to clean. This was a minute accounting, with daily or hourly entries, so that she could calculate a sum of money to pay them, either on Saturday or at the end of the time the job agreed had taken. When she paid them in part with potatoes, wheat, or barley – food stuffs they had usually already had – she noted this, with the monetary equivalent of the goods deducted from the wage. When she fed her workers in her own kitchen (this is information from her earlier account books) she did not note the cash equivalent of their breakfast, or their dinner. On the other hand, when she provided drink, or cash for drink, she calculated it in money terms. In one household enterprise, the complex network of lending and borrowing, credit, promise and obligation by which the wider economy was managed, is minutely detailed.

Before 1800 and the opening of the 'Wages' ledger, Hamilton had kept note of payments like these in her farm and household account books, which is where she also recorded payment to her domestic servants. The last was a much simpler financial arrangement, easy of calculation; there was no need for the *aide memoire* that the farm wages books provided her with. Payment to domestic servants constituted one of the most common wage systems in the society, and it was a highly satisfying one, easy of management (perhaps more satisfying to the employer than to the servant, though I believe there is much evidence to suggest that domestic workers found it so too). Their wages were agreed at the hiring, when the length of service time was also agreed. This was nearly always for a year. A master or mistress might evade a clear verbal statement of time, using formulations like 'a month in the first instance . . . see if we like one another . . . see if he suits . . . '. High Court judges, contemplating many examples of obfuscation and uncertainty of contract in the disputed settlement cases that came before them, believed that this was universally done to defeat the servant's settlement. Even as late as 1821, employers and servants were still being instructed in the determination of many an eighteenth-century judge, that 'If there be a hiring, it shall be presumed to be hiring for a year, unless something appear to shew that the contrary was intended'.[24] By now, the advice was powerfully to abandon *parole* contracts, and to put all such agreements in writing.

---

[24] County Magistrate, *A Letter Addressed to the Agriculturalists in general, and to the Magistrates and Clergy in Particular throughout the Kingdom, on the Subjects of Hiring, Service and Character, to which are added Printed Forms of Contract between the Master and Servant, designed to be filled up by the contracting parties, and calculated to prevent disputes about wages, and lessen the number of appeals to Quarter Sessions . . .*, Longman and Whitaker, London, 1821, pp. 6–7.

The annual contract was most profoundly what most employers wanted, even though some of them tried to get away with 364 days for poor-law purposes. As Stephen Caunce says of nineteenth-century echoes of this 'tight' service contract, it was 'intended to be long-term and to reflect a particular commitment to an employer'. It was a highly effective means of keeping a worker, and of placing legal restraints on his or her leaving. This was 'the essence of service', he further remarks; it was not a paternalistic, cordial relationship, but a labour and wage form that provided for the retention of labour, and which the law powerfully upheld. It could deliver a reliable paid workforce, and motivate it. In English law 'it was *servant* contracts which were central to permanent and regular paid work', he says, not the daily or hourly rates to weeders and washers that someone like Frances Hamilton spent so much effort tracking over her quarter-century of farming.[25] Discussing agricultural service rather than domestic service, Caunce argues that the contractual year was not an archaic arrangement, but 'seems rather to have actively promoted the spread of both market-orientated and capitalist farming'. It was the labour contract that shaped this modern workforce, whether it was for agricultural or domestic employment; 'service in the form of an annual hiring was socially and legally the most significant form of wage labour for most of the eighteenth century'.[26]

By-passing this, the most common form of wage-paying in eighteenth-century England, historians have sometimes evoked an image of the North African or 'Oriental bazaar' labour market, as did Mike Sonenscher in discussing eighteenth-century French trades: all sorts of workers paid in 'a bewildering variety of ways: by the day, the month, with meals or without meals, by the piece'. He described wage-forms 'typical of a world of short-term arrangements, fleeting opportunities and brief association'.[27] Our knowledge of how English workers managed household economies under the 'bazaar' regime, through elaborate, extensive and long-term systems of credit, promise and obligation, in a situation where cash money circulated uncertainly or not at all, has recently been vastly extended by the work of Margot Finn and Deborah Valenze.[28] The

---

[25] Stephen Caunce, 'Farm servants and the development of capitalism in English agriculture', *Agricultural History Review*, 45 (1997), 49–60, esp. 50–3.

[26] Simon Deakin and Frank Wilkinson, *The Law of the Labour Market: Industrialization, employment and legal evolution*, Oxford University Press, Oxford, 2005, p. 45.

[27] Michael Sonenscher, *Work and Wages: Natural law, politics and the eighteenth-century French trades*, Cambridge University Press, Cambridge, 1989, pp. 23–7.

[28] Margot Finn, *The Character of Credit: Personal debt in English culture, 1740–1914*, Cambridge, Cambridge University Press, 2003; Deborah Valenze, *The Social Life of Money in the English Past*, Cambridge University Press, Cambridge, 2006. See also Jane Humphries and Sara Horrell, '"The Exploitation of Little Children": Child labour

many informal means by which the poorer sort of household sustained itself – got the means of subsistence – has long been acknowledged. Common rights, scavenging, the availability of forest food and payment in kind for a wide variety of small jobs, from errand-running by children to charring work by women (and some boys and men) underlie historians' use of the wage series that are available.[29] The household budgets that the Reverend Davies collected in the 1780s and 1790s for his account of agricultural labour in England, are generally accepted as the most reliable by historians, though it is always pointed out that his work mainly concerned the southern counties and that the monetary calculations he recorded cannot provide a full account of what went into a household by way of food, firing and clothing over any one year.[30] Thomas Beddoes thought that all of his contemporaries inquiring into the state of the poor – 'the highly commendable pains . . . taken by Ruggles, Davies, Eden, and others' – had proceeded by asking the wrong questions.[31] As far as he was concerned, the right questions were to do with the effects of material deprivation on the living system of the labourer's body. He invented a fictional farm labourer, Isaac Jenkins, to make his point.[32]

The 'County Magistrate' who urged written contracts on employers in 1821 had spent many a long year on the bench, dealing with the uncertain memory and outright lying of masters and servants disputing the terms of their particular labour arrangement. Yet during the preceding century, many hiring agreements were written down by the employer; there were printed forms available for very efficient employers, though

and the family economy in the Industrial Revolution', *Explorations in Economic History*, 22 (1995), 485–516.

[29] John Rule, *The Experience of Labour in Eighteenth-century Industry*, Croom Helm, London, 1981; Jeanette Neeson, *Commoners: Common Right, enclosure and social change in England, 1700–1820*, Cambridge University Press, Cambridge, 1993; Craig Muldrew and Stephen King, 'Cash, wages and the economy of makeshifts in England, 1650–1800' in Peter Scholliers and Leonard Schwarz (eds.), *Experiencing Wages: Social and cultural aspects of wage forms in Europe since 1500*, Berghahn, New York and Oxford, 2003, pp. 155–82; Penelope Lane, Neil Raven and Keith Snell (eds.), *Women, Work and Wages in England, 1600–1850*, Boydell, Woodbridge, 2004.

[30] K. D. M. Snell, *Annals of the Labouring Poor: Social change and agrarian England 1660–1900*, Cambridge University Press, Cambridge, 1985, p. 56; David Davies, *The Case of Labourers in Husbandry Stated and Considered in three Parts*, G. G. and J. Robinson, London, 1795.

[31] Thomas Beddoes, *A Lecture Introductory to a Course of Popular Instruction on the Constitution and Management of the Human Body*, J. Johnson, London, Joseph Cottle, Bristol, 1797, p. 69; Ruggles, *History of the Poor*; Davies, *Case of Labourers in Husbandry*; Frederick Morton Eden, *The State of the Poor: or, an History of the Labouring Classes in England, from the Conquest to the present Period . . . together with Parochial Reports . . . in three volumes . . .*, B. and J. White; G. G. and J. Robinson and others, London, 1797.

[32] See Chapter 9; Thomas Beddoes, *The History of Isaac Jenkins and of the Sickness of Sarah his Wife, and their three Children*, privately printed, Madeley, 1792, p. 42.

most appear not to have used them. A commercial *pro forma* did not allow them to specify the odd details of their own particular case and special arrangements (and in any case they were expensive).[33] Frances Hamilton always recorded her hiring agreements in one of her ledgers or daybooks. Where expensive clothing was concerned she was very clear in her recording, as was Thomas Cooper (East Sussex):

1794 Agreed with James Fuller for One Yr from Lady : next, for Nine Guineas; to give him a Coat and Waste Coat, Leather Breeches, Boots & Hat, and Great Coat; if he lives with us the Yr out, but not otherwise, all is to be his Property; (Except the Great Coat) & that is not to be his Property until he has lived with us two years; – He is to be in the Capacity of a Footman, & Groom &c; he is to do as follows: waite at Table, Clean Knives & Forks Bootes & Shoes; Brew the Beer, Pump the Water, fetch in Wood & Coale; Clean the Chaise and Harness; Clean out Chaise House & Coach Yard; Look after Horses, Bridles and Sadles; and do anything I shall require of him.[34]

It was best to be very clear anyway, and to know what other family members were up to in the hiring and use of domestic labour. A Norfolk father wrote to his son in 1789 about the 'extraordinary mistake subsisting between us and Ann Black, respecting the wages she was hired for. I am obliged to refer the matter to you, because she acknowledges the agreement to have been between you and her, without the concurrence of your mother...'.[35] Apart from arrangements over clothing, many employers noted how a replacement servant's duties differed from those of the last one, and any new special arrangements, particularly over tea: 'Hired Amy Green for a year. £3.5.0 no tea money... Susan Ward for a year. £3.0.0 – tea allowance 10/-'; 'hired Martha Goal in a Cookmaid's place. She to have after the rate of twelve pounds a year wages to clean all the rooms below Chambers'; 'Ann Wages till Martinmass 3.0.0 & ten shillings additional for cleaning Shoes – a Months Wage or a Months Warning the Agreement'; '1804 23 [Feb.] Ann Graham Wages 6.16.6 & one Pound more if she waits at Table during the Year instead of a Boy...'.[36] There

---

[33] Attorney at Law, *The Attorney's Complete Pocket Book*, 3rd edn, Henry Lintot, London, 1751.

[34] East Sussex County Record Office (ESCRO), AMS 6191, Household account book of Thomas Cooper of New Place Farm in Guestling, 1788–1824, pp. 212–13.

[35] Norfolk Record Office (NRO), BOL 2/105, Leathes family papers in the Bolingbroke Collection, BOL 2/105/5, 14, J. A. Reading to his son (10 Oct. 1789).

[36] Mary Hardy, *Mary Hardy's Diary: With an introduction by B Cozent Hardy*, Norfolk Record Society, vol. 37, 1968, p. 73; Warwickshire County Record Office (WCRO), CR 1711, 58, John Ward Boughton-Lee, 1791–1868, Notes on servants hired 1785–7; West Yorkshire Archives (WYAS), Bradford District, BAR/3/a/2, George Baron, wool merchant of Woodhouse in Leeds, accounts for servants' wages, 1791–1828; Cheshire County Record Office (CCRO), DAR/G/60, Aderne Collection, Accounts of servants

were strategies for making the agreement more formal, perhaps bringing it within the purview of the law. Sometimes the servant signed, or marked a contract (Hannah Burston was the only one of Hamilton's female servants who signed the agreement and on receipt of wages). Between 1761 and 1770, the Beach family of Keevil, Somerset, recorded thirty contracts with live-in domestic servants (some of these were renegotiated contracts, when a servant stayed beyond the year). Twenty-two of them made their mark; none of them signed. The other eight, with 'gone' entered by their name, suggest that in this household at least, a servant was tried out for a period, before the formal agreement was made.[37] Some employers required a form of receipt when wages were paid. John Adherne of Cheshire required a signature from the servant where this was possible, using the formula 'paid Samuel... witness his hand'. Thirteen servants passed through his household in twelve years in order to maintain an establishment of three – if the ones living with him when he either died or stopped keeping accounts, are anything to go by. Five of them signed on the receipt of wages and three made their mark; the rest were short-term servants. He did not require a written acknowledgement of the hiring agreement.[38] Board, lodging and washing were implied in these contracts, and rarely noted by employers, though George Baron, wool merchant of Leeds did note one agreement to 'allow Ann Maude 10s 6d per week from 7th May 1816 when at Home but only her Wages of 14s per month to be allowed her when she lives with me'. Ann Maude had been employed by the Barons since at least 1811. Here they calculated the cost of her living in the house at something between 18s and £1 per month.[39] What was more usually noted was the requirement that a man live out, as in 'agreed with Mr ward to find me a pair of good Coach horses and a good driver to take care that my carriage and Harness in good order and I to allow towards the Coachman's board 4s per week he is not to have his Board here, not to be in the house'.[40] Presents to servants were sometimes also noted in the employer's account book, tagged on to the original agreement. Amanda Vickery's discussion of Elizabeth Shackelton's spending on her 'ungrateful girl' Nanny Nutter between 1772–5 is a monument to the elision of maintenance (the clothing she

wages 1792–1806; ESCRO, AMS 6191, Household account book of Thomas Cooper of New Place Farm in Guestling, 1788–1824.

[37] Wiltshire Record Office (WRO), 1665/4, Household account book of the Beach Family of Keevil, Fittleton and Widcombe (Somerset).

[38] CCRO, DAR/G/60, Aderne Collection, Accounts of servants wages, 1792–1806.

[39] 'Paid her a quarter in advance May 7th... Sarah Baron'. WYAS, Bradford District, BAR/3/a/2, George Baron, merchant of Woodhouse in Leeds, Accounts for servants's wages, 1791–1828.

[40] WCRO, CR 1711/58 (17 Oct. 1786).

considered it her obligation to provide) with gift-giving. The sections in *The Ladies Own Memorandum-Book* that Shackleton used were far too small to add 128 entries (85 items of everyday wearing apparel, 43 gifts to Nanny and her family, the ones to her of the most fashionable and generous kind) to the original note of her arrival in January 1772. They were spread throughout the little volume, just as Frances Hamilton recorded her purchase of clothing, fairings and other treats for her servants and apprentices, across all her household account books.[41]

A domestic servant entered employment under a legally binding hiring agreement, with terms and conditions – at least theoretically – agreed, and in anticipation of wages that had – in theory again – been discussed. The most common arrangement was for wages to be paid at the end of the agreement year, though many employers of the later century paid quarterly. Except in very large or exceptionally strictly managed households, there was near universal borrowing from the employer against the annual wage. For those who could write and had the means to keep accounts (the employer, for the main part) the noting of small sums borrowed was important. The reckoning day was when the employer paid back the servant what he or she had borrowed as well. Frances Hamilton relied on her maids to pay for foodstuffs delivered to the door and purchased in Lydeards; they had their own cash in hand, and she made use of it, at regular intervals. On the anniversary of the hiring, a new arrangement might be made for the coming year, as the Reverend Murgatroyd of Slaithwaite did every August for seventeen years with his servant: 'I reckoned with Phebe; she paid me all due to Me so we begin again.'[42] Here, in the 1790s West Yorkshire worsted field, one employer at least, started to record the wage agreed at the hiring with his maidservants in terms of a weekly equivalent. Robert Heaton, merchant manufacturer of Ponden Hall near Haworth noted thirty service contracts in his account books between 1768 and 1792. Eighteen of them recorded payment by

---

[41] Amanda Vickery, *The Gentleman's Daughter*, Yale University Press, New Haven and London, 1998, pp. 143–5. Lancashire County Record Office (LCRO), DDB 81/15, Parker of Brownsholme, Notebooks and memoranda, 1772–5. This is a pocket diary for 1772, used over the next three years. What *are* the implications of putting all and everything to do with this infuriating girl in one place and then moving her out of time, so that what Shackleton spent on her (£11 9s 6d, according to her own reckoning, though the sum says nothing of the gifts) became a marker of chronology and the life Shackleton lived between 1772 and 1775? The monetary outlay and the gifts to Nanny are interspersed with long accounts of the doings of her dysfunctional family. She bears all the marks of a poor child put on the Shackletons as apprentice (though she was not). She was paid no wage, was given clothes and presents (as were Frances Hamilton's Boys, though many more and luxurious) and was as maddening to Shackleton as Hamilton's apprentices were to her.

[42] WYAS, Kirklees District, KC242/2, Diary of Revd John Murgatroyd (7 Aug. 1794).

the week, a practice started in the early 1770s. This could have been a highly elaborate means for getting round the settlement question, though to do that he would have had to renegotiate, or at least make, a new hiring agreement, every single week (there is no evidence that the parish of Haworth was tougher than any other on settlement by service). Moreover, should either party have taken this arrangement before a magistrate, and that magistrate been willing to act in the case of a domestic, the principle that where no length of time was mentioned at the hiring, a year should be assumed, should have held good. (Which is not to say that it would have held good, had labour law been tested as settlement law. But all of this is hypothetical in the case of Robert Heaton and his maidservants.) What is striking about the weekly sum he recorded was that it was the exact equivalent of what a woman working full-time at worsted spinning in an outputting system might expect to receive during these years – 1s 2d a week.[43] It is unlikely that 1s 2d was handed over once a week, rather that this was some expression of a local female wage, familiar to servant and employer (Heaton after all, ran a worsted and cotton enterprise). In 1784 the annual wage of £3 was recorded against Mary Greenwood's name. This was the equivalent of 1s 2d a week (or as near as dammit; the *Young Lady's Companion* gives the sum of 1s 1³/₄d). Against her name is also recorded expenditure totalling £5 17s 7d (for 'clogs cloging . . . cash to Haworth fair . . . a Neckcloth . . . Gown mending . . . apron dying . . . shallon gown & Dying . . . a pair of old Stays . . . scarlet sowing silk . . . a scarlet clook dying . . . ', and more). All other things being equal, this was not a bad job for a girl, especially if at the end of her term she got the stays, bonnets, ribbons, gowns and designer buttons, with which Heaton's servants so liberally provided themselves on his credit.

This was a relatively certain method of wage-payment, from a servant's perspective. Many examples of employers refusing to pay them, out of unwillingness, inability or meanness, have been noted in this book; but out of the total number of female domestic service contracts operative in society as a whole (we can take as a minimum the 90,000 mentioned by William Pitt in 1792), they were a very small number. Of course, many unpaid domestic servants, believing perhaps, in the letter of the Statute of Artificers, that a magistrate had no jurisdiction in their case, may have left without contemplating recourse to one, and without wages. But this is an imponderable question. It was a relatively certain payment method, because it was pre-arranged, and there was thus more chance of an employer having money in the house for reckoning day. Although

---

[43] Carolyn Steedman, *Love and Labour in the English Industrial Age*, Cambridge University Press, Cambridge, 2007, Chapters 2 and 4.

Frances Hamilton was a dutiful payer of wages to her farm workers, she was frequently a month late in paying her maidservants, waiting on the collection of cash from Taunton, either from the sale of produce at market, or from her bankers; perhaps she assumed that the servants could wait for theirs, as they were not going anywhere, were getting fed, and had not a household to maintain. The certainty of the system was promoted to servants, though saving, which this form of wage payment could provide, was rarely underscored, either because commentators assumed that this was what all servants did, or, more likely, knew from their own experience how much of an annual wage dripped away in advances and subventions before pay day came round. In 1801, in York, a four-page flyer – 'A Friendly Address to Female Housekeepers, Apprentices, Servants, and Others' – was distributed by a benefit society, originally formed for spinners ten years before. In this year of bread shortages and high prices, it was relaunching itself, hoping for a wider membership among those willing to put by for 4s a week when bed-ridden, and 2s a week when convalescent. Its first pitch was to female housekeepers of the poorer sort (they were urged not to keep running off to the shop for small quantities of food – 'buy their potatoes and other necessaries a week beforehand at the Market'); the second address was to 'Young Women who are in service, [who] . . . have no such excuse [of poverty] to plead' for not joining. They were addressed directly, and told that 'You feel none of the difficulties of the times under which House-keepers labour. Your wages are not lessened. You have no sacrifices to make, unless it can be called one, to save a Part of your wages for your own future benefit, instead of laying out the whole in dress as is too often done at present'. Young domestics could provide against sickness and old age, and 'lay by something to furnish a House or a Room against they marry, or become unable to continue in Service'.[44]

A negotiated wage rate and periodic and certain payment in cash was a mark of a modern labour force. So was the formula 'month's wages or a month's warning'. Some said that this was a metropolitan device, evolved to cope with London's volatile service sector. 'Commonly they are in the country hired for the year; but in London, though they are hired for the year, it is with proviso, to give a month's warning, or a month's wages; and even though it is not mentioned in the agreement, it is by custom a law', said John Breues in 1754. And 'What is the meaning of a

<hr />

[44] WYAS, Bradford District, 16D86/0646, Benson Family, Papers of Miss Benson re the York Female Benefit Club. Includes rules, 'Address to the Club', 'A Friendly Address to Female House-Keepers by a Townswoman'.

month's warning, or a month's wages?' asks William, one of the recipients
of his advice in *The Fortune Hunters*. He is told in detail about what
happens in London.[45] But it was a provincial practice as well, the formula
sporadically noted by a variety of provincial employers from the 1770s
onwards. By 1785 (possibly earlier) it had reached the theatrical stage. In
the play *Fashionable Levities* it is explained by a 'foreign' servant, symbol
of metropolitan glamour and opulence, not by the earnest young men
trying to make their way in the world whom Breues used as exposition.[46]
Thomas Netherton Parker encouraged use of the wages/warning system
in early nineteenth-century Shropshire when he helped renegotiate a
domestic service contract. Summarising a century's development, an
anonymous *Laws Respecting Masters and Servants* (1831) said that 'this
mode of hiring has been now so long sanctioned by all powerful custom,
that the law courts do not hesitate to recognise it as binding on both
parties'.[47]

In the fictional realm, a good servant always gave warning, even in
circumstances of the utmost emergency and melodrama, and where so
doing added to the improbabilities and oddities of a plot-line.[48] But
not all employers liked the system. It was 'a manifest Disadvantage to
both Parties, and is attended by very evil Consequences, and often the
Occasion of Servants having unjust Characters', said one in 1767, not

---

[45] John Breues, *The Fortune Hunters: shewing (from experience) 1. How People may improve
their Fortunes, and raise themselves in London . . .* , privately printed, London, 1754,
pp. 17–22. Breues provided a ready-reckoner for servants, 'for the immediate knowledge of wages due to you for days, weeks, and months, at any sum, from four to ten
Pounds a year . . . N.B Any other sum may be found by Adding, Dividing, or Multi-
plying . . . '. See also the table in Anon., *The Complete Man and Maid Servant: containing Plain and Easy Instructions for Servants of both Sexes . . .* , J. Cooke, London, 1764,
pp. 9–35.

[46] Leonard MacNally, *Fashionable Levities, a Comedy. In Five Acts*, G. G. and J. Robinson,
London, 1785, p. 68: 'zo master, — our bargain is this, a month's warning, or a month's
wages; zo, pay me, and I'll go . . . '.

[47] Anon., *A Familiar Summary of the Laws Respecting Masters and Servants, Apprentices,
Journeymen, Artificers and Labourers . . .* , Henry Washbourne, London, 1831, p. 21. See
also Samuel Clapham, *A Collection of the Several Points of Sessions Law, Alphabetically
Arranged contained in Burns and Williams on the office of a Justice, Blackstone's Commentaries, East and Hawkins on Crown Law, Addington's Penal Statutes and Const and Nolan
on the Poor Laws; Designed To assist Magistrates to refer to these several Authorities; to supply the Clergy with professional Information; and to enable Vestries to transact the Business
of their Respective Parishes. The Statutes continued to 57 Geo. III 1817, inclusive*, 2 vols.,
Butterworth and Clarke, London, 1818, vol. 2, pp. 83–6.

[48] Elizabeth Helme, *Louisa; or, The Cottage on the Moor. In two volumes*, G. Kearsley,
London, 1787, vol. 1, pp. 108–9. Frances Hamilton did not enjoy novels, but she read
this one in 1787, all the way through, evidently not finding it quite so silly as Miss
Palmer's *Female Stability*. SCRO, DD/FS 6/3 (15 Sep. 1787).

mentioning the disadvantage to him of not being able to get rid of servants when he wanted.[49] Most literature, from the legal sort to compendiums of advice to domestics, assumed like *The Fortune Hunters*, that it was a customary practice of more value to servants than to masters. This was Mrs Taylor's point in 1816, when she wrote of servants' 'habit' of giving warning 'in order that they may be invited to stay another year, and thereby obtain an opportunity of behaving amiss, from the value that seems to be put upon them'. (There is tension in this advice book, between the tenaciously held belief that you must never give an inch in approbation – never respond to the servant's warning – and its major moan about teaching a girl *everything*, from how to clean a copper pan to the correct method for washing an oaken staircase, who then just ups and goes, taking her carefully inculcated skills with her.)[50] The merest hint of a warning allowed the novelist to perform the comic turn that *was* the servant, at least in the recent historical past, according to Catherine Thompson. Writing in the 1830s she set her *Constance* fifty years back, in 1780s Warwickshire – Elizabeth Hands territory – opening with the ejaculation of a mistress to her servant: '"Thomas . . . this water don't boil, Thomas".' (Tea-time was a pregnant hour in 1780s mid-Warwickshire, as Elizabeth Hands taught.) The narrator continues:

The words conveyed no very important meaning, but they were uttered in a tone so different to the apathetic manner habitual to Mrs Cattell, that her consequential domestic, humoured, as servants were wont to be fifty years ago, did condescend, as he was quitting the room, to turn round and look at her. "She is in a fuss – a miff about something," was Thomas's internal ejaculation, while his audible expostulation consisted of this laconic reply, "This here water *do* boil, ma'am" . . . .

'"Thomas won't stand it long, I can tell you, my dear; he's not a man to be run after, nor interfered with"', says her husband; to which she replies '"Bless me, Mr. Cattell, he's stood it these fifteen year" . . . "And if I don't give you satisfaction, – ma'am -" said Thomas, re-entering the room. Thomas well knew that those words always brought his mistress to reason; and setting down the toast at the same time, he retreated, having said, he thought, just enough'.[51]

[49] Gentleman of the Inner Temple, *Laws Concerning Master and Servants*, W. Owen, London, 1767, p. 27.
[50] Ann Taylor, *The Present of a Mother to a Young Servant: Consisting of Friendly Advice and Real Histories*, 2nd edn, Taylor and Hessey, London, 1816, pp. 7–9.
[51] Katherine Thomson, *Constance. A Novel. In Three Volumes*, Richard Bentley, London, 1833, vol. 1, pp. 1–3. Rosemary Mitchell, 'Thomson, Katherine (1797–1862)' in *Oxford*

The warning was an aspect of the wage system in domestic service, a further example of its regulated nature. Early nineteenth-century magistrates, judges and other legal commentators discussed it as a customary practice that had acquired formal legal status by their cognizance of it, over half a century. Masters and mistresses thought of it as a convention to the advantage of the servant; the servant's opinion is difficult to discern. It was one of the means by which servants could claim, and often get, cash wages due, in the context of all that had been got during a period of employment. The resentment of an employer like Taylor may have had a source in her calculation of the rewards to labour already made before they handed over the cash: the food consumed, the small beer drunk, the laundry done, the stays mended, the shoes tapped, the stuff for a gown bought, and the dressmaker already paid. To say nothing of the skills taught. These could not be taken back (except the clothes, of course); they had already been consumed and incorporated in the labouring body. Who might not think of cash as an expendable reward, when settling day came round?[52]

Recent discussion of wage differentials between men and women from the medieval through to the modern period, has calculated the ratio of difference between the monies received by them to be between one-third and one-half.[53] New histories of eighteenth-century household economies have emerged, that stress the contribution of women and children to family income. The logic of wage differences between the sexes has been hotly debated: do we fall back on the notion of 'custom' in paying women less than men, for very similar work? Or attempt to discover whether or not women worked a shorter day than men, in agricultural field work, for example? Or think that employers made the judgement that women's productivity was less than that of men; or that they had fewer powers of endurance than men, and that they thus set wages accordingly? Or is it, and was it, always and everywhere the case that women's labour has

Dictionary of National Biography, Oxford University Press, 2004, www.oxforddnb.com/view/article/27319, accessed 28 Feb. 2007.

52 Some magistrates' notebooks detail complaints from servants about their clothes being withheld after leaving. Alan F. Cirket (ed.), *Samuel Whitbread's Notebooks, 1810–11, 1813–14*, Bedfordshire Historical Record Society, Ampthill, (case no. 1070); Shropshire Records (SR), 1060/168, Justices of the Peace, Justicing notebook of Thos. N. Parker, 1805–40 (9 Apr. 1805, 8 Sep. 1807).

53 Penelope Lane, 'A customary or a market wage? Women and work in the East Midlands, c. 1700–1840' in Penelope Lane, Neil Raven and K. D. M. Snell (eds.), *Women, Work and Wages in England, 1600–1850*, Boydell, Woodbridge, 2004, pp. 102–18; Joyce Burnette, 'An investigation of the female-male wage gap during the Industrial Revolution in Britain', *Economic History Review*, 2nd ser., 50 (1997), 257–81.

been undervalued, and that sexual discrimination was expressed in wage differentials?

As far as eighteenth-century England is concerned, these questions have been asked in relation to agricultural work in general, and to harvest work in the grain growing areas in particular, where male labour provided normative standards for contemporaries and for historians thinking about them. It has been unusual to ask these same questions of domestic servants, as Penelope Lane has done. She has considered female and male servants' annual wages in one elite household between 1693 and 1783, and found that the ratio between wages for similar work performed (between a footman and a housemaid, between a butler and a housekeeper, between a man cook and a woman cook, for example) to range between one-quarter and three-quarters for all coincidental periods of service calculated over these years.[54] She argues that as men were employed for the purposes of prestige – 'luxury' in contemporary terms – it is not possible to say, as some have done, that they were paid disproportionately on the basis of their productivity differences from women. She concludes that 'women received a lower wage because they were women and of less value'.

But Donington Park, Leicestershire, was a highly unusual household: it employed a hierarchal retinue of servants. In the sketchy calculations that the servant tax returns allow, households with more than three domestics represented perhaps 5 per cent of servant-employing households across the country. This is to extrapolate from Doncaster (a far cry from rural Leicestershire!) and to leave out all of the innumerable factors (children under fourteen in the house, tax-free girls and elderly women as servants) that we have already dwelt upon. Perhaps it is only possible to say that Donington Park was not the common type of eighteenth-century household employing one or two female servants. Taxpayers who did employ 'official' servants between 1785 and 1792 employed women far more than they did men, at the rate (Doncaster again) of four to one (the actual ratio was almost certainly higher). Why make these points? Because of course, on the evidence of many household account books, women *were* paid less than men for domestic work, not in that rather small number that employed servants of both sexes, but in comparison between households across the country. Wages paid in eight different (non-elite) households in the north and south of the country between 1780 and 1820, suggest that a woman's wages were between one-third and two-thirds of a man-servant's:

---

[54] Lane, 'Customary or market wage', pp. 116–17.

Table 11.1 *Wages (weekly equivalent) for women and men servants in eight non-elite households, 1780–1820*

	1781–1785	1786–1790	1791–1795	1796–1800	1801–1805	1806–1810	1811–1815	1816–1820
Maidservant	1s *a*	1s 5d *a*	1s 2d *a*	2s 1d *b*	2s 8d *e*	3s 10d *c*	4s 2d *c*	3s 4d *c*
	1s 3d *a*	2s 8d *b*	2s 6d *c*	2s 3d *b*	2s 11d *f*	1s 9d *c*	1s 3d *c*	3s 6d *c*
	1s 5d *a*	1s 9d *b*	2s 8d *c*	2s 6d *e*				
Child-maid			1s 3d *d*	1s 9d *d*	10d *d*			
Cookmaid		3s 6d *d*	3s 6d *d*	2s 11d *d*	1s 3d *h* 3s *d*			
Footman/Man-servant	2s 3d *b*		3s 10d *d* 7s 1d *e*		12s 6d *e*	3s 6d *c*		

Sources:

a WYAS, Bradford District, Heaton B149, Account book of Robert Heaton, 1764–92

b SCRO, DD/SF 5/7, 5/8, Bishops Lydeard farming accounts

c WYAS, Bradford District,16D86/temp.0440, Francis Sharp Bridges of Horton Old Hall, Bradford, Account book with payments for domestic duties and wages, 1802–43

d ESCRO, AMS 6191, Household account book of Thomas Cooper of New Place Farm in Guestling, 1788–1824

e CCA, DAR/G/60, Adherne Collection, Account of servants' wages, John Adherne. 1 Vol., 1792–1804

f WYAS, Bradford District, BAR/3/a/2, George Baron, wool merchant of Woodhouse in Leeds. Accounts for Servants's Wages, 1791–1828

g WRO, 1665/4. Household account book of the Beach Family of Keevil, Fittleton and Widcome (Somerset)

h Mary Hardy, *Mary Hardy's Diary: With an introduction by B Cozent Hardy*, Norfolk Record Society, vol. 37, 1968, p. 131

These weekly rates cannot be used to judge whether wages increased or decreased, for men or for women, and they concern different households. Footmen were increasingly rare items as the eighteenth-century passed. There was wide variation between households and in the years of employment that these fragmentary figures represent. A maid at 4 guineas a year might leave, to be replaced by one at £3 10s 6d, or £5. We are not here calculating the wage (and its fluctuation) that any one individual maidservant or footman received, only supporting Lane's finding that female domestic workers were paid less than men, though the discrepancy between the two may have been less in this kind of non-elite household.

But, in fact, there is a good deal of point to removing payment to female domestic servants from the comparative perspective that has dominated discussion of the female wage in England's past. Domestic servants constituted a predominantly female workforce; we have seen them discussed *as* a workforce, at the highest levels. They were the largest female workforce in the society. They *were* the norm, in their line of work. When domestic work was performed as piece work – charring – the local female rate for casual farm work seems to have set the pay level for both men and women, as Frances Hamilton's account books attest. Men as well as women bought in to perform the same household tasks, tended to be paid the same rate; it could be called the 'female' rate. There certainly were a great many more women in the agricultural labour force than we used to think there were, as a great deal of recent scholarship attests; the male farm worker (labourer or servant) and his wage constitute the measure of a woman worker's earning capacity for historians because it did so in the eighteenth century, for employers and workers. But the 'useless old man' or the jobbing woman bought in by Frances Hamilton to shovel out the necessary house were paid at the same rate.

It was unusual for a maidservant to work alongside a man. In Doncaster in 1788–9 only 20 per cent of taxpayers employed both men and women (and if the unknown but certain employment of non-taxable female servants is taken into account, then working alone, or with one other woman must have accounted for more than 80 per cent of female work experience). However, in 1790s East Sussex, there were comparisons to be made. When Thomas Cooper replaced his footman with first Elizabeth Stocks (1792–3) and then Elizabeth Dink (1793–4) as 'Waiting Maid or Footman' he paid them each £5 a year, compared with the 9 guineas he agreed with James Fuller, who followed them both in 1794.[55] Stocks had

---

[55] This rearrangement probably had something to do with the end of the maidservant tax, in 1792, but it was a common economy to use a maid as a Man: WYAS, Bradford District, BAR/3/a/2, George Baron, wool merchant of Woodhouse in Leeds, Accounts

been elevated from child-maid at only £3, and was not around in 1794 to feel resentment at what Fuller got. So too did Elizabeth Dink leave her place before Fuller's arrival ('Upper House Maid Or Waiting. . . 1794 to Lady D[ay] 1795 kept none having an Footman').[56] Penelope Lane mentions the possession of greater cultural capital, literacy in particular, in a man-servant as a possible reason for their higher rate of pay. But as she also points out, female servants were as likely, if not more likely, to be able to read than their male counterparts.[57] In elite households, and on the point of human capital in general, a footman's wage *might* reflect a well-turned calf, the skill of lounging around gracefully in livery clothes, and the ability to deliver a plot-summary of *Don Quixote* to guests in the dining room, as Hester Thrale's servants did in December 1778.[58] But Thomas Cooper required none of these things. Rather he wanted a man who could multitask, in the kitchen and the stables as well as wait at table, and we must assume that the 9 guineas was seen by him as the correct wage for a wider set of skills than those he asked of Elizabeth Dink.

In an ordinary Doncaster kitchen – and many others – there were not the pressing examples of men being paid more to do exactly what women were doing, as there were in a harvest field. But we are not to know if servants saw things that way. None of the invented servants of the bourgeois imagination – all the voices with dialect and demotic uncertain, but heroically rendered by their creators – ever complain about wages, or about gender-based wage discrimination. Their loud and long (invented) complaints about working conditions take up many pages of books targeted at children, and the lifestyle advice market. (Usually, their complaints are about the behaviour of the horrid children of the household – the intended readers of the book they are in.) But a complaint about wages, or pay differential, could scarcely be invented (nor in real life, heard) by a lady and a writer, who had not only created fictional servants for didactic purposes, but who had also set her own, actually existing, servants' pay level. Gentry women, in a position to think about paying well, did consider the reward to skills and abilities in their maidservants, including

for servants' wages, 1791–1828: '1804 23 February Ann Graham wages £6 16s 6d & one pound more if she Waits at Table during the Year instead of a Boy – Let her have £2 2s 0d then [she] left –'.

56 ESCRO, AMS 6191, Household account book of Thomas Cooper of New Place Farm in Guestling, 1788–1824 (25 Mar. 1794).

57 Lane, 'Customary or market wage', p. 117.

58 Katharine C. Balderson (ed.), *The Diary of Mrs Hester Lynch Thrale (Later Mrs Piozzi) 1778–1809*, 2 vols. (1941), Clarendon Press, Oxford, 1951, vol. 1, pp. 354–5. Thrale was pleased to note that the women came off rather better than the men on this occasion: 'Old Nurse, the Nursery Maid, the Dairy Maid, my own Maid & Mr Thrales Valet had all read the Book'.

Figure 23. 'Progress of the Toilet. The Stays'.

their possession of cultural capital; or at least, the Stanley ladies of Alderley, Cheshire did: one wrote from London in 1797, telling how 'we left two she servants [at home], one by name Betty Holt, who takes charge of the linen and the stores, and can make preserves and pickles, and is not above cleaning the rooms. Her wages are £12 12s; Fanny's £6 6s . . .'.[59] But the human capital asset of appealing face and figure that

[59] Jane H. Adeane, *The Early Married Life of Maria Josepha Lady Stanley, with extracts from Sir John Stanley's 'Praeterita': Edited by one of their grandchildren*, Longman, Green, London, New York, Bombay, 1899, pp. 127–8.

Lane suggests was rewarded in the men-servants of Donington Park was not highly rated by these correspondents. 'Milady has taken nobody to Town but Miss Quinn and the Kitchin Maid', reported another in 1795. 'Mrs Q I think will not stay long, and I am sure I hope not, she is as idle in the way of work, as it is possible [to be] . . . and she is much too pretty in my estimation, and knows it too well'.[60] A good pair of stays may well have contributed to Quinn's appeal and her own confidence in it. If so, they came as part of her wages – in the Smithian and historical sense – as part of the everything she got in exchange for her labour. It is to stays as an aspect of the wage form, and their social meaning, that we now turn.

[60] Adeane, *Early Married Life*, p. 237.

Stays

Eighteenth-century domestic servants have been allowed to dream by their recent historians – to dream in the sense of desiring, or wanting. They made up a large part of the customer-base for ready-made clothing and other fashionable items; they are John Styles's example of a kind of involuntary consumer – perhaps made into involuntary and inadvertent dreamers in this way.[61] We cannot be sure if dreams of possessing (consumer desire for) buttons, buckles and painted silk gowns, were really *their* dreams. And stays – a pair of stays – which some of them also acquired, will complicate any dreams that historians allow them to have had. What follows is about stays, dreams, and our theory-construction concerning the wishes and desires of eighteenth-century working people, especially domestic servants.

Englishwomen wore stays – all sorts of women, from the lowest to the highest – according to foreign observers of their habits and manners. A contrast was drawn between them and their continental sisters in this regard.[62] The appearance of women wearing stays was one of the ways in which Englishness was identified according to Paul Langford, and a kind of otherness put in place by European travel writers.[63] So frequent was this observation, that it became an item of self-identity. 'Whence came the Custom of wearing Stays . . . in England, unknown to many foreign Nations?' asked Mr George Brown of Oxford composing a Notes and Queries page for *The Gentleman and Lady's Palladium* in 1754. Answers before Candlemas would win a prize.[64]

---

[61] John Styles (2001) 'Involuntary consumers? Servants and their clothes in eighteenth-century England', *Textile History*, 33:1, 2002, pp. 9–21.

[62] Jacques-Henri Meister, *Letters written during a Residence in England. Translated from the French . . . Together with a Letter from the Margravine of Anspach to the Author*, T. N. Longman and O. Rees, London, 1799, pp. xx, 311.

[63] Paul Langford, *Englishness Identified*, Oxford University Press, Oxford, 2000, pp. 164–5.

[64] Robert Heath, *The Gentleman and Lady's Palladium for the Year of our Lord 1754; containing (besides what is usual) the Abuse and Use of History; an Account of the Origin and Family of Pride; on Drunkenness and Gaming; a Dream; the Muses [sic] Banquet; of Story-telling*

Stays then, have a minor role in modern historical accounts of nation and social identity-formation. Yet as objects (and objects of desire) they oscillate wildly between the categories we have put in place for the reconstruction of consumer identity in the past. They were practical objects, a form of work-wear; they played a part in the wage-economy of household service; they were utterly necessary to the women who wore them (all women), and also deeply connected to the project of self-fashioning (much more than is their closest modern equivalent, the brassiere). They provided – for those who got a fine new pair – a new shape, a new figure in the world. They were part of all that might be got by the exercise of the servant's labour.

Stays are among the many accessories and items of clothing discussed by Styles in his description of one northern household of the late eighteenth century and its servants' access to the world of fashionable goods.[65] The account books of the Heaton family, cotton and worsted manufacturers of Ponden Mill, Stanbury near Haworth, records in very great detail the buckles, buttons, hats and hat-boxes, lengths of cloth and laces, bought on the Heatons' credit by the young women who worked as their household servants between 1768 and 1794.[66] 'With only one exception', says Styles, 'all Heaton's female servants, irrespective of whether they were in debt or credit at the end of their hiring, devoted the bulk of what they spent out of their wages to the purchase of clothing... eighty-six percent of their spending went on clothes, clothing materials and the upkeep of clothing'. These items were bought from local shops and from 'the Scotchman', or travelling salesman. Betty Mason ('came to live here Feb: 28th 1786 on a Tuesday to have 1s 2d a week') got plated buckles in 1786; Nancy Holmes ('Entered her Second year July 31st 1782 to have 1s 3d') a new painted gown at 18s in her first year, and a paper box for her hats the next. Were buckles and hat-boxes means to imagining other communities, in the way that Benedict Anderson has suggested we understand the printed goods that the Scotchman also carried

---

and Satyr . . . For the Benefit of both Sexes, and Use of Schools. The sixth number published. By the late author of The Ladies Diary, J. Fuller, London, 1754, p. 11.

[65] Styles, 'Involuntary consumers?'; also 'Custom or consumption? Plebeian fashion in eighteenth-century England', Paper presented to the Conference on Luxury and the Marketplace in Eighteenth-century Europe, University of Warwick, 1998 (cited with permission of the author); 'Clothing the North. The supply of non-elite clothing in the eighteenth-century North of England', *Textile History* 25: 2 (1994), 139–66.

[66] West Yorkshire Archives Service (WYAS), Bradford District, HEATON B149, 'Account book of Robert Heaton giving names of servants employed and wages paid'; Styles, 'Involuntary consumers'.

on his cart?[67] The question is irrelevant perhaps in the case of the fine lawn that Nancy Holmes got for 10½d in 1781 to sew into caps for herself, because near Haworth she knew how fine linen was woven (though her direct experience was to do with cotton, serge and worsted). But it is a pertinent question as far as mass-produced items – buckles, buttons, fancy paper goods – are concerned, whose production process might be only dimly understood, taking place somewhere else, but where people like the maidservant but whom she would never meet, sewed on the same scarlet buttons and fixed the same plated buckles to their shoes. *Can* mass-produced items of clothing and haberdashery, as opposed to novels and newspapers, produce an act of imagining an unknown other *like Nancy Holmes* tightening her stays with new scarlet laces, adorning the new shape with buttons and ribbon tied into bows?

The printed goods assigned the historical role of allowing these imaginative processes spread along the same routes as the ribbons, tapes, kerchiefs, lace and laces, that tied up, bound, held together, kept in place and decorated the longer lengths of fabrics that constituted 'the great reclothing of rural England', from the end of the sixteenth century onwards. Margaret Spufford describes the variety of cloth and ready-made clothing in the pedlar's pack.[68] She suggests the existence of a mass market among the poorer sort ('among wage-labourers, cottagers and small-holders') by the beginning of the eighteenth century.[69] In *Small Books and Pleasant Histories*, Spufford has direct testimony from the poorer sort who bought and read the chapman's penny 'histories', and scandal-sheets.[70] But there is no testimony to what 'Callimanco gown old one', 'cloth for sleives', 'painted Gown' meant to the Heaton servants, or to anybody else.

Sometimes the book trade established the route and the distribution network for these goods, and the haberdashery, calicos and linens followed; sometimes it was the other way round. The Scotchman (or probably, several Scotchman) who called at Ponden Hall between 1768 and 1794 were part of the great descent from the mountainous regions of Europe to sell petty wares that Laurence Fontaine describes in her *History of Pedlars in Europe*. The Scots found a new English market to

---

[67] Benedict Anderson, *Imagined Communities: Reflections on the origin and spread of nationalism* (1983), Verso, London, 1991, pp. 37–46.

[68] Margaret Spufford, *The Great Reclothing of Rural England: Petty chapmen and their wares in the seventeenth century*, Hambledon, London, 1984.

[69] The dating of this development is contested. See Spufford, *Great Reclothing*, pp. 1–22; Lorna Weatherill, *Consumer Behaviour and Material Culture in Britain, 1660–1760*, Methuen, London, 1988, pp. 192–4.

[70] Margaret Spufford, *Small Books and Pleasant Histories: Popular fiction and its readership in seventeenth-century England*, Cambridge University Press, Cambridge, 1981.

open up after the Act of Union in 1703, though British peddling was less dominated by the highlands than was mainland Europe because of the very early existence of trading networks organised around the industrial zones. Nevertheless, says Fontaine, 'Scotland invariably accounted for [its] largest number of pedlars', even in the later eighteenth century, which also saw the emergence of a new type of petty trader, 'the "Manchester Man"', working for a single firm on an exclusive basis.[71] The Scotchman who took in Haworth and its environs on his route was probably what Fontaine calls a 'regular pedlar', with established suppliers, faithful customers, enough capital to guarantee credit and to manage a repayment timetable drawn up for his customers. A different kind of salesman – the 'destitute pedlar' – catered to their imagination rather than their consumer desires.[72] Half-beggar, half-tramp, says Fontaine, a destitute pedlar 'put on a show, and sold dreams'. He was an intermediary between his public and other worlds, took his audiences into 'the realms of the imaginary, into other ways of knowing oneself, to other places, and to new understandings'. He 'crooned his wares and the new fashions' says Fontaine; fashions that 'opened windows onto other ways of knowing oneself, other ways of life'.[73]

Perhaps all pedlars, respectable or not, belonged to another world, sold both 'the stuff of everyday life, and the stuff of dreams'.[74] What kind of dreams might these have been? What imaginings were provoked in the Heatons' servant Nelly Coats ('came to live here the 26th Septr 1791 to have 1s 2d a week') when she got 'Muffs and Lawn', 'a new Gown & Sundreys', and 'a blew Sarge petticoat'? Servants are the workers that labour and that social historians have been most embarrassed about, and, at the same time, the category around which they have constructed most of their theories of consumption. Colin Campbell is particularly sharp on our blithe and uncomplicated use of eighteenth-century employers' routine condemnation of maidservants' aping the dress, manners and desires of their superiors. When we consider the buying and ownership of things in the past, he says we should abandon ideas like these about social emulation, vaguely based on Thorstein Veblen's notion of conspicuous consumption.[75] Rather we should look at eighteenth-century vocabularies of self-construction that prompted

---

[71] Laurence Fontaine, *The History of Pedlars in Europe*, Polity, Cambridge, 1996, pp. 92–3.
[72] Margot Finn, *The Character of Credit: Personal debt in English culture, 1740–1914*, Cambridge University Press, Cambridge, 2003, pp. 93–5 for types of pedlar and credit.
[73] Fontaine, *History of Pedlars*, pp. 81–2.   [74] Fontaine, *History of Pedlars*, p. 2.
[75] Thorstein Veblen, *The Theory of the Leisure Class : An economic study of institutions*, Allen and Unwin, London, 1925.

desire for particular types of object.[76] Following Campbell, we might also consider the proposition that dress, and the little things that hold dress together and adorn it, are means to *imagine yourself*, rather than others, in new ways. Fontaine says as much, when she describes pedlars offering 'objects and ideas which helped the recipient to consider his or her own personality and to mould it. Ultimately, whatever the manner in which these objects were used . . . they provided one and all with the opportunity of expressing his or her irreducible individuality.' This was 'something new and radical'.[77]

In the Heaton account book, thirty female servants' acquisitions were recorded. Stays (new – mostly new – or second-hand) were got by 15 of them. New ones were expensive, ranging in price from 18s to £1 4s 6d. Ann Proctor's new painted gown and lining only put 17s 6d on the Heaton tally sheet in 1792.[78] But stays do not belong to the same category as painted gowns and black silk hats: they only partly belong to the world of *fashion* items. They were 'fundamental to the eighteenth-century . . . fashionable silhouette' as Styles says, and they could indeed change shape and appearance, perhaps allow a young woman to see herself (not often literally, in a mirror) in a new way, a self and shape she may have dreamed of being, before their purchase and fitting. But stays are strange, hybrid items (not entirely underwear or outer wear) and they belonged to other economies besides the economy of dreams, imaginings and desires. For many employers besides the Heatons, stays were a taken-for-granted of the domestic-service economy. Down the Pennine Ridge from Haworth, 14 miles away in Slaithwaite near Huddersfield, the Reverend John Murgatroyd noted in May 1790 that his neighbour and 'her two promising Daughters walk to Hudd.[ersfield] today – Our Servant Phoebe goes with em to buy stays &c'. Eighteen months later they needed mending: on his shopping list for a visit to Halifax was the purchase of 'some leather for her to mend her stays'.[79] Stays were to do with the servant's labour as far as Hannah Glasse, writing *The Servants' Directory* in 1760, was concerned. She addresses her directly: 'Now . . . my little young House

---

[76] Colin Campbell, 'Understanding the traditional and modern patterns of consumption in eighteenth-century England: a character-action approach' in John Brewer and Roy Porter (eds.) *Consumption and the World of Goods*, Routledge, London, 1993, pp. 40–57.

[77] Fontaine, *History of Pedlars*, p. 201.

[78] For the production and consumption of ready-made clothes by working women, see Beverly Lemire, '"In the Hands of Workwomen": English markets, cheap clothing and female labour', *Costume*, 33 (1999), 23–35.

[79] WYAS, Kirklees Office, KC242/1, Murgatroyd Diary (1 May 1790, 17 Dec. 1791).

maid . . . take care to be up very early in the morning . . . lace on your Stays and pin your things very well tight around you, or you never can work well'.[80] A chambermaid should be 'dressed accordingly [for dirty work]', said an anonymous guide of 1800; 'but should, nevertheless, be tight and decent'; she should be wearing her stays.[81] Glasse's mid-century advice is much of a muchness with that delivered a few years later by Wetenhall Wilkes to young ladies about to enter the married state: 'Never appear in company without your stays', he wrote; 'Make it your general rule, to lace in the morning, before you leave your chamber. The neglect of this, is liable to the censure of indolence, supiness of thought, sluttishness – and very often worse . . . '.[82] Both advisers emphasised a woman's work, albeit of a rather different kind. Frances Hamilton kitted out her little apprentice girl with a pair in 1778; the ladies of Hertingfordbury, advising on cutting out apparel for the poor in 1789 provided three patterns for 'Stays for Girls' cut with darts and gussets, and so bang up-to-the-minute in design. The ladies suggested making them from Duck (strong linen, lighter than canvas), using 'cane split once' instead of whalebone, and purchasing coloured laces.[83]

In 1792 Dr Walter Vaughan mused on the vast number of fellow medical men (antedating even John Locke) who had fulminated about them; but '*Stays* have been so long in Use and so often condemned, that I cannot flatter myself our Ladies will be persuaded by me to throw them aside.'[84] He thought that in less polished times they had indeed been work wear, originally intended for protection of the breasts whilst labouring. Eager of inquiry, he got a lady friend to lace him up, and described the effects for his readers.[85] *This* reader cannot detect the slightest sexual thrill in this experiment, only a concern to describe discomfort and restriction,

[80] Hannah Glasse, *The Servant's Directory, or, Housekeeper's Companion*, W. Johnston, London, 1760, p. 23.

[81] Anon., *Domestic Management, or the Art of Conducting a Family with Instructions to . . . Servants in General, Addressed to Young Housekeepers*, H. D. Symonds, London, 1800, p. 57.

[82] Wetenhall Wilkes, *A Letter of Genteel and Moral Advice to a Young Lady*, 8th edn, L. Hawes, London, 1766, pp. 211–12.

[83] Somerset County Record Office (SCRO), DD/FS 6/3, '26 Aug 1778 . . . 3yds 7$\frac{1}{2}$ of Cloath a[t] 18d 5s 3d . . . 1$\frac{1}{4}$ lining [at] 13$\frac{1}{2}$d 1s 5d . . . Hat 6d . . . Stays 2s 6d . . . '; Anon., *Instructions for Cutting out Apparel for the Poor; principally intended for the Assistance of Patronesses of Sunday Schools . . . But useful in all Families. . . . Published for the Benefit of the Sunday School Children at Hertingfordbury in the Country of Hertford*, J. Walter, London, 1789, pp. 32–5.

[84] Walter Vaughan MD, *An Essay Philosophical and Medical, Concerning Modern Clothing*, W. Gilman, Rochester, 1792, pp. 66–76, 'On Stays'.

[85] Vaughan, *An Essay*, pp. 70–2.

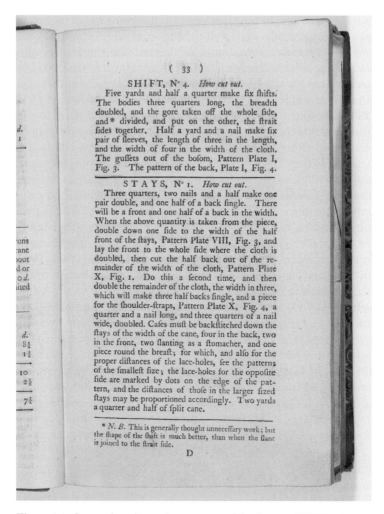

Figure 24. *Instructions for cutting out apparel for the poor* (1789).

though that this amiable Kentish medical man thought to do such a thing – inhabit the somatic and sexual space of another – is perhaps a points of origin for corset-erotics, which reached its full flowering in the mid-nineteenth century. But if we look back through the fog of tight-lacing and fetishism which is its historical legacy and through which the corset-question has usually been addressed, we will never find meaning in Hannah Glasse's injunction to her 'little house maid', nor to the place of so many new and second-hand ones in the wage economy of Ponden

Hall.[86] The very least we can discern is that stays cannot have restricted movement, nor breathing, nor effort, very much (obviously, if you can lace tight, you can lace loose). The Ponden Hall young women wanted a pair of stays for reasons of practicality and comfort, as well as the foundation upon which a contemporary sexiness *à la mode* could be fashioned. They were underwear in an important sense; they provided an extra layer of warmth around the middle body area; they did not get really dirty, as they were universally worn over a shift.[87] They could be altered in length and width, professionally or by their owner; women could make their own, from some stout canvas and split reeds; they were handed down, inherited, and sold onto the second-hand market.[88] They fitted as well or as ill as the brassieres that a majority of modern British women report as uncomfortable, and that professionals say are ill-fitting. From the 1780s onwards stays may actually have increased in comfort, with cutting on the bias and the introduction of gores, darting, flares, and 'slopes' added to their construction.[89] Even the straight up-and-down stays of the earlier century (no shaping, no darting) held the breasts in place, stopped them bouncing around as you worked, and perhaps prevented the irritating sticky band of sweat that develops beneath them, and that is now

[86] For the fetishism – of extraordinarily long standing – provoked by stays and corsets, see Peter Farrer, *Tight Lacing: A bibliography of articles and letters concerning stays and corsets for men and women: Part I, 1828–1880*, Kahn, Liverpool, 1999; Colin McDowell (ed.), *The Pimlico Companion to Fashion*, Pimlico, London, 1998, pp. 346–7; David Kunzle, *Fashion and Fetishism: A social history of the corset, tight-lacing and other forms of body-sculpture in the West*, Rowan and Littlefield, Totowa, 1982; Michael Colmer, *Whalebone to See-through: A history of body packaging*, Johnston and Bacon, London, 1979; F. Libron et H. Clouzot, *Le Corset dans l'art et les moeurs, du XIIIe au XXe siècle*, Libron, Paris, 1933; Docteur O'Followell, *Le Corset. Histoire, médicine, hygeine. Etudes historiques*, A. Maloine, Leoty, Paris, 1893; Ernest Leoty, *Le Corset à travers les ages*, Ollendorce, Paris, 1893; Anon., *The Freaks of Fashion: With illustrations of the changes in the corset and the crinoline, from remote periods to the present time*, Lock and Taylor, London, 1868. Or type 'a pair of stays' into an internet search engine.

[87] Which perhaps accounts for their absence from contemporary manuals of cleaning techniques. William Tucker, 'late Dyer and Scourer in the Metropolis' advised how to clean 'Every Article of Dress, Bed and Window Furnishing, Silks, Bonnets, Feathers etc. whether made of Flax, Silk, Cotton, Wool or Hair; also Carpets, Counterpanes, and Hearth-Rugs, Ensuring a Saving of Eighty percent'; but not a word on stays. *The Family Dyer and Scourer, Being a Complete Treatise on the Arts of Dying and Cleaning*, 2nd edn, Sherwood, Neely and Jones, London, 1818.

[88] For the second-hand clothing trade, Beverly Lemire, *Dress, Culture and Commerce: The English clothing trade before the factory*, Macmillan, Basingstoke, 1997; for home-made stays, John Keane, *Tom Paine: A political life*, Bloomsbury, London, 1995, pp. 29–31.

[89] C. Willett and Phillis Cunnington, *The History of Underclothes*, Michael Joseph, London, 1951, pp. 37–8, 115–18; Norah Waugh, *Corsets and Crinolines*, Batsford, London, 1954, pp. 74–85; Lynne Sorge, 'Eighteenth-century stays: Their origins and creators', *Costume*, 32 (1998), 18–32.

absorbed by the bra, wired or not.[90] No wonder that Hannah Glasse connected stays with working hard and efficiently.

By the logic of the argument about the contents of the pedlar's pack (the argument about dreams, imagination, identity and consumption) stays could have brought English whaling ships on the high Atlantic seas to the mind of the Ponden Hall servants. Or the east coast ports. Or the baleen whale industries of Aberdeen and further north.[91] But as a form of work-wear, stays were probably not the vehicle of that kind of dream. If the Haworth Scotchman also carried the scurrilous and satirical balladry that sneered at a former stay-maker for having something to say about the constitution, *that* might have produced political reverie in its purchasers. In 1791–2, according to his detractors, Tom Paine had turned 'From moulding forms and bolst'ring shapes . . . to shaping Laws, Sir' ('To be sung to the Tune of Bow, wow, wow!').[92] *Tom the Boddice Maker* and possibly, *The Rights of Man*, may have reached Keighley and other Pennine metropole by 1793.[93] Books and pamphlets could do the work of identity formation and make dreams in a way that a pair of stays could not.

[90] Waugh, *Corsets and Crinolines*, pp. 152–5.

[91] Edourd A. Stackpole, *Whales and Destiny: The rivalry between America, France and Britain for control of the southern whale fishery, 1785–1825*, University of Massachusetts Press, Amherst MASS, 1972, pp. 386–7; W. R. H. Duncan, 'Aberdeen and the early development of the whaling industry, 1750–1800', *Northern Scotland*, 3:1 (1977–8), 47–59; Ole Lindquist, 'The Auskerry whale, 1777: Processing and economy', *Northern Scotland*, 17 (1997), 17–32; Lynne Sorge, '"29 Doz and 11 Best Cutt Bone": The trade in whalebone and stays in eighteenth-century London', *Textile History*, 36:1 (2005), 20–45.

[92] Anon., *Pour Commençer. Tom the Bodice-maker. To the Tune of Bow! Wow! Wow!*, n.i., 1792; Anon., *Life and Character of Mr Thomas Paine, put in Metre and inscribed to the Society against Levellers and Republicans*, n.i., 1793; Anon., *Tom the Boddicemaker. A Satirical Song*, n.i., 1793; Anon., *Tom Paine, the Staymaker*, n.i., 1793. See Keane, *Tom Paine*, pp. 29–31; 36–7; 267–344. In fact, there was surprisingly little scurrility found by his detractors in Paine's stay-making past – rather more to do with his denying Mrs Paine 'The Rights of Man' (or, Woman – they meant). See Anon., *Life and Character of Mr Thomas Paine put in Metre*, n.i., 1793?

[93] The Heaton servants often went over to Keighley, to visit family or the Fair, go shopping, perhaps (the account book is unclear) collect a pair of stays. But there was no stay-maker in town; or rather, no stay-maker who insured their business with the Royal Exchange; indeed, there were no insured stay-makers in the whole of Yorkshire, though they clearly existed. Insured businesses were found in London, and in the coastal counties where the last stages of whalebone processing took place. Royal Exchange and Sun Fire Insurance Register, Indexes 1775–87. Trade index, p. 652, p. 125; Place index, p. 461, p. 339. (WCRO, CR 811/293). Deborah Oxley counts female stay-makers among her early nineteenth-century 'convict maids'. *Convict Maids: The forced migration of women to Australia*, Cambridge University Press, Cambridge, 1996, pp. 118–23. See John Rule, *The Experience of Labour in Eighteenth-century Industry*, Croom Helm, London, 1981, p. 41. Chapter 5 for parliamentary attention to female stay-makers.

Dreams are about the material world, or more precisely, use the objects of the material world to do their work. There is nothing else for them *to be about* for the modern reader, who has long abandoned the idea of a dream as some visitation from another, unseen, world. Whether it is Sigmund Freud or brain neuro-chemistry that tells us this, it is not a knowledge that we can refuse to have.[94] Words, fragments of words, hats, hatboxes, buckles, stays . . . are inverted, turned upside down, do weird things in dreams, but they do not stop being the things themselves. They keep their own edges. The dreamer's knowledge of the world is laboured on to produce a new and strange account of how things are, and how they might be. The dreamer needs some kind of knowledge or information to do this work, knowledge that is not imbricated in a pair of stays in the same way it is in the one-sheet *Tom Paine, the Staymaker*. What stays held was labour: the labour that went into their making; the reward for labour that a pair of stays represented for a working woman; and all the scrubbing and pounding she was about to do wearing them.

[94] Duguld Stewart told Frances Hamilton (and many other readers) this in 1792: 'the same laws of association which regulate the train of our thoughts while we are awake, continue to operate during sleep'. *Elements of the Philosophy of the Human Mind*, 3 vols., A. Strahan, and T. Cadell, London and W. Creech, Edinburgh, 1792–1827 (vol. 1, 1792), pp. 327–39.

12   Conclusion: The needs of things

In the 1980s, E. P. Thompson edited Stephen Duck's *The Thresher's Labour* (1730) and Mary Collier's *The Woman's Labour* (1739). This was the first time the two poems had appeared together, even though Collier intended hers to be read as a sardonic response to Duck 'in Answer to his late Poem'.[1] It was 'so-what?' and more, to Duck's account of the village field hands who were called on at particularly intense times of the agricultural year. Collier's response details the female field labourer's double burden: the children fed and dressed, the beds made, the dinner cooked against the thresher's return – all of this as well as the reaping and haymaking she undertakes for cash. The women are waged domestic workers as well, says Collier to Duck: she writes of charring and laundry work at the big house, where 'The Washing is not all we have to do:/We oft change Work for Work as well as you.' Both Thompson and Donna Landry draw our attention to Collier's 'effective critique of the hard-nosed middle class mistress for whom poor women "char"'. Thompson said that with charring 'we enter another world in which we are situated within the perceptions of an underpaid and overworked labouring woman who is confronting an over privileged Mistress and sees her not only in her role as an employer, but as another woman'. This

---

[1] *The Thresher's Labour by Stephen Duck, The Woman's Labour by Mary Collier: Two eighteenth century poems*, Intro. E. P. Thompson, Merlin Press, London, 1989. Also *The Thresher's Labour and The Woman's Labour*, Augustan Reprint Society, no. 230, Andrews Clark Memorial Library, Los Angeles, 1985.

account of 'washing, cleaning, brewing . . . at the houses of the wealthy, is unfamiliar, and . . . probably unique'.[2]

Collier presents charring as antiphonal to the domestic servant's work. Early on a winter's morning, the village women rise by prior arrangement ('our Work appointed') and go to the big House for the wash. They can't get in, for the maidservant is tired out 'with work the day before', and it takes a while to rouse her. The wash ('Cambricks and Muslins . . . Laces and Edgings . . . Ruffles and Fringes') takes all day, for the consumer revolution has already changed the nature of the servant's work. (There is no mention of dirty clouts.) The mistress of the house appears at noon, with *perhaps* a mug of ale for the women, but mainly to nag about being gentle with ruffles and lace, sparing with fire and soap, and to complain about items lost in former washes. The women work until dusk, sometimes having to 'piece the Summer's day with Candle-light'; by now 'Blood runs trickling down/Our wrists and fingers'.

Thompson noted differences between Duck and Collier in their depiction of the labour relationship. Duck's farmer also 'calls his Threshers forth'; the men are clearly tied to him by bonds of obligation and need; they appear to be paid by the day or the week; work discipline is maintained 'by the direct surveillance of the employer'. But the men are more aware of their vulnerability to dismissal than the women are. The women have sold their labour to the farmer for just a few weeks, at the time of year when it is indispensable, during the hay and cereal harvests. They 'were, in a sense, in a stronger position' than the men, whose day-in, day-out labour is husbandry. Perhaps this is the reason said Thompson, for the women's lack of deference in the field, and the men's greater sensitivity to the farmer's disapproval, as both poets describe it.[3] Duck describes how the threshers submit to their master's curses 'just like School-boys', as when 'th'angry Master views the blotted Book'. Thompson remarked that the employer is 'defined by his role', a 'scarcely-personal element in the labourer's situation, like the weather'.

Thompson's reading of poetry as social text can be deepened and expanded, by noting that the threshers do not appear to have a personal position on, or feelings about, being denigrated or verbally abused as workers: there is no analysis of the employment relationship by the men. The world goes on – Things as They Are – as it always has, in unquestioned ways, and the men are infantilised within it. No so with

---

[2] Donna Landry, *The Muses of Resistance. Labouring-Class Women's Poetry in Britain, 1739–1796,* Cambridge University Press, Cambridge, 1990, p. 59; Duck, Collier, *Thresher's . . . Woman's Labour,* pp. x–xii.

[3] Duck, Collier, *Thresher's . . . Woman's Labour,* p. xi.

Collier. You know what Collier thinks about her mistress: there is Collier's analysis of the mistress's motivation, Collier's feelings about expending her own 'Strength and Patience' on 'Cambrick and Muslins, which our Ladies wear', and, if you wish to hear it, her dismissive opinion of complicated furbelows, 'Fashions which our Forefathers never knew'. Neither does Collier think very much of the mistress's *batterie de cuisine*. It is not just that she and the other women have been all day at the other task she calls them in for, the 'hard and tiresome' job of pewter cleaning, not just that as night comes on, they are so tired that they 'scarce can count' the 'pots, kettles, sauce-pans, skillets' they have scoured, but because then, to make a long day longer, 'Skimmers and ladles and such Trumpery/[Are] brought in to complete our Slavery'. Rubbishy, ridiculous things, Collier allows us to hear her think, like the useless, fussy trimmings on the linen they have washed so many times. We have seen Elizabeth Hands express – also in verse – her very similar disparagement of her employers' cuisine, and their literary taste.

Thompson noted class feeling, articulated in kitchens, wash houses and brew houses, around things, and between women. He remarked that Collier's 'language implies questions as to the humanity of class divisions, and as to the rationality of luxuries which depend upon the degrading labour of others'.[4] We can take the perception further than that and say that the experience of the woman with whose labour Collier's poem deals – her experience with ladles and laundry and with her employer – allow her to *think* about these processes, in the way that a flail and a barn full of wheat or barley, does not allow the thresher the same kind of cognition. That is the conclusion that these two poems push us towards. Moreover, whilst Duck does inscribe the capitalist wage relationship in his poem – knows that each sheaf of corn represents the farmer's greater or lesser profit for the year – his view of the whole task – from cutting, through threshing, to storing, to harvest feast – is framed by the *master's* perspective. It is the farmer who, his landlord's rent threatening, inaugurates the harvest; it is the farmer who rejoices in his profit with a feast for his workers. It is the master's language that becomes the threshers' very consciousness: 'These words, or words like these, disclose his Mind:/ So dry the Corn was carried from the Field,/ So easily 'twill thresh, so well 'twill yield. /Sure large day's Work I may well hope for now; /Come, strip, and try, let's see what you can do.' There are no inverted commas to mark the boundary between the thresher's thoughts and those of his master. This is a far cry from Collier's brisk assessment of the wage relationship, made in her own voice: 'And after

[4] Duck, Collier, *Thresher's . . . Woman's Labour*, p. xii.

all our Toil and Labour past,/Sixpence or Eightpence pays us off at last'. Not only does she mention cash payment (as Duck does not) but also suggests that it isn't enough.

Thinking was done in kitchens, brew houses and laundry rooms by servants like Mary Collier and Mary Leapor, and with kitchens – the idea of the kitchen – by the employing classes, in many kinds of text. What kind of space – literary and social – was the kitchen? In the literary realm we have seen fictional servants sit round kitchen fires to discuss in detail and at length the shortcomings of their employers' children (and their parents) for the purposes of infant improvement.[5] For the same purposes, extremely recalcitrant (fictional) children are banished to the kitchen, to eat with the servants.[6] Famous misers demonstrate their extreme meanness over money by living in the kitchen with their one servant.[7] Popular history shows an early modern English king to be as useless in the kitchen as was Alfred the Great.[8] An Irish heiress, caught up in revolutionary turmoil in Paris and reduced to poor lodgings, articulates her feelings about having to play the role of maid of all work, 'sweeping rooms, making beds &c' whilst her husband cleans knives and nurses the baby in the kitchen. (But this is an Irish novel, with a Catholic heroine to boot, and things could happen with servants and the idea of service here, that could never happen in an English one.)[9] In popular 'travelling-tales', pins and pennies make fictional journeys through entire social orders, spending much time in kitchens and holding conversations with many servants there. But in that nowhere space, few of them contemplate social division in relation to commodities as Collier did, even though the pin's first social identity *was* commodity.[10] In the

---

[5] For Kilner, see Chapters 1, 8; also Anon., *The Adventures of a Pin, supposed to be related by Himself, Herself, or Itself*, J. Lee, London, 1790, pp. 40–50.

[6] Richard Johnson, *Tea-table Dialogues, between a Governess, and Mary Sensible . . . and Emma Tempest*, Darton and Harvey, London, 1796, p. 77.

[7] Edward Topham, *The Life of Mr. Elwes, the celebrated Miser. With singular Anecdotes, &c*, D. Brewman, and W. Locke, London, 1792, p. 37.

[8] Anon., *A Third Collection of Scarce and Valuable Tracts, on the most interesting and entertaining Subjects: but chiefly such as relate to the History and Constitution of these Kingdoms. . . . Particularly . . . of the late Lord Somers. Revised by eminent Hands*, 4 vols., F. Cogan, London, 1751, vol. 2, p. 317.

[9] F. C. Patrick, *The Irish Heiress, a Novel, in three volumes*, Minerva Press, London, 1797, vol. 3, p. 70. For the representational opportunities provided by the Irish novel as far as servants were concerned, Maria Edgeworth, *Castle Rackrent* (1800).

[10] Anon., *Adventures of a Pin*, 1790; Miss Smythies, *The History of a Pin, as related by Itself. . . . By the Author of The Brothers, a Tale for Children*, E. Newbery, London, 1798. The pin maybe the first commodity of the economic imagination, but both of these fictional Pins spring fully formed into a social world and into the text. They are orphan Pins, having no memory of their birth in the eighteen-stage labour (process) of *The Wealth of Nations*. Nor do they know their own sexual identity. Mrs Midnight's 'Oration'

autobiographical realm a (non-fictional) Nigerian prince, house-slave in New York, is frightened by tales of the devil told by another black servant in the kitchen. He thus inscribes his autobiography in relation to the most repeated childhood experience of the Lockean person, who only grows successfully to man's estate if kept away from servants' kitchen-stories of Raw-bones and bugaboos.[11] So the philosophical history of civil society and the modern, possessive individual is discussed in kitchens; in a wide range of eighteenth-century texts kitchens are the site for articulating economic and social theory. At the same time, kitchens are liminal places, to which no one and nothing belongs.

Servants did not belong in kitchens, in either the social or literary realm. For the main part, servants *emerge* from them, into the narrative of many novels. In the eighteenth century, the footman is not the 'silent messenger . . . with murder on his face as he takes orders for tea' of later fictions. He is perhaps the modern (eighteenth-century) device that medieval stagecraft inaugurated with the idea of 'place' (here, a kitchen), somewhere far away from the audience, a *locus* where 'the "real-ist" convention of ignoring the audience first develops, and with it the need to provide psychological motives for the movements of the actors'. That was 'the birthplace of the representational', says Bruce Robbins; the servant in eighteenth-century novels frequently re-enacts that birth by his 'presentation of essential information, particularly about what has occurred *prior*'. A literary function and more, enters the parlour with the tea urn.[12] In all sorts of fiction, even in the further gothic reaches of the Minerva Press, maidservants pause in their dusting to relate dramatic circumstances to their employers, or to rehearse a family genealogy that makes (nearly) all clear. Or, dusting a desk, she will uncover – her eyes will fall upon – a letter, a message, a signature – that is equally the story of

---

of 1763 does have the kind of conversation in a kitchen that you might expect a commodity to have: a Tea-pot and a Scrubbing Brush discuss social division in relation to the production and ownership of household things, in rhyming tetrameters. *Mrs. Midnight's Oration's [sic]; and other Select Pieces; as they were spoken at the Oratory in the Hay-market*, London, privately printed, 1763, pp. 56–8. See Deborah Valenze on travelling coins as economic theory in *The Social Life of Money in the English Past*, Cambridge University Press, Cambridge, 2006, pp. 81–88.

[11] James Albert Gronniosaw, *A Narrative of the most remarkable Particulars in the Life of James Albert Ukawsaw Gronniosaw, an African Prince, as related by Himself*, S. Hazard, Bath, T. Mills, Bristol; S. Chirm, London, W. Walker, Ashburn, [1780?], pp. 18–19. Vincent Carretta, 'Gronniosaw, Ukawsaw (b. 1710–14, d. after 1772)', *Oxford Dictionary of National Biography*, Oxford University Press, 2004, www.oxforddnb.com/view/article/71634, accessed 7 Mar. 2007.

[12] Bruce Robbins, *The Servant's Hand: English fiction from below*, Duke University Press (1986), 1993, Duke University Press, Durham SC and London, pp. 54, 112, 123.

what *has* happened, and of what now *must* follow.[13] Social verisimilitude, even in the most exotic realms, demands that the maid is dusting in a house place, not scouring the kitchen floor, for that is where standing, she encounters her betters, and has conversation with them. She is a plot mechanism, for fiction and the stage. Even the most *jejune* actress, of no matter how uncertain gentility, will not appear on her knees, with scrubbing brush in hand.[14] Indeed, dusting, being a relatively clean and genteel task, is something that young ladies in instructional literature may themselves attempt, though they needs must be reduced to an orphan state before undertaking it.[15] Very occasionally, a maidservant in a novel may be espied sweeping, but in this activity she is rarely engaged in conversation by her social superiors, even though her presence is the mark of some plot development, or some moment of revelation (as in 'That is Clarinda's maid! So this is her mansion!') to the gentleman or lady doing the observing.[16] Sweeping a floor simply does not allow for the richness of event, sequence, timing and history, that can flow from a dusting

---

[13] Miss Smythies, *The Brothers. In two volumes. By the Author of The Stage-coach and Lucy Wellers*, 2nd edn, 2 vols., R. and J. Dodsley, London, W. Reymer, Colchester, 1759, vol. 2, p. 219; Susannah Gunning, *Family Pictures, a Novel. Containing Curious and Interesting Memoirs of Several Persons of Fashion in W——re. By a Lady. In two volumes*, P. Wilson etc, Dublin, 1764, vol. 2, pp. 22–32; *Louisa Matthews. By an Eminent Lady*, 3 vols., J. Lackington, London, 1793, vol. 2, pp. 209–10; Mary de Crespigny, *The Pavilion. A Novel. In four volumes*, William Lane at the Minerva Press, London, 1796, vol. 2, p. 105; Anon., *Agatha; or, a Narrative of Recent Events. A novel, in three volumes . . .*, printed for the author, London, 1796, vol. 2, pp. 4–5; Fanny Burney, *Camilla: or, a Picture of Youth. By the Author of Evelina and Cecilia. In five volumes. . . .*, T. Payne, T. Cadell Jun. and W. Davies, London, 1796, vol. 2, p. 63; Anon., *Human Vicissitudes; or, Travels into Unexplored Regions . . .* 2 vols., G. G. and J. Robinson, London, 1798, vol. 1, p. 171; Mrs Showes, *The Restless Matron. A Legendary Tale. In three volumes*, the Minerva Press for William Lane, London, 1799, vol. 1, pp. 119–30; John O'Keeffe, 'The Doldrum, or, 1803', *The Dramatic Works of John O'Keeffe, Esq. Published under the gracious patronage of His Royal Highness the Prince of Wales. Prepared for the press by the author. In four volumes*, T. Woodfall, London, 1798, vol. 4, pp. 463–505 (Act I, Scenes II and III).

[14] Anon., *The Complete Letter-writer. Containing familiar Letters on the most common Occasions in life. Also a Variety of elegant Letters for the Direction and embellishment of style, on business, duty, amusement, love, courtship, marriage, friendship, and other subjects . . .*, W. Darling, Edinburgh, 1768, pp. 27–8.

[15] Mary Pilkington, *Tales of the Cottage; or Stories, Moral and Amusing, for Young Persons. Written on the plan of . . . Les veillees du chateau, by Madam Genlis*, Vernor and Hood, London, 1799, p. 139; Anon., 'No. 79 . . . To the Author of the Lounger', *The Lounger. A Periodical Paper published at Edinburgh in the Years 1785 and 1786* , 3 vols., Strahan and Cadell, London, William Creech, Edinburgh, vol. 3, 1787, pp. 96–100. This interesting tale (a purported autobiography) of service in reduced circumstances and social attitude constructed around household and personal objects, went into six editions (all published in London) in ten years, and was liberally extracted from and anthologised.

[16] As in Eliza Haywood, *The Invisible Spy. By Explorabilis. In two volumes*, 3rd edn, L. Gardner, London, 1767.

session – in the novel, or on the stage. However, in an eighteenth-century theatre, a male servant might sweep, the activity providing for some interesting stage business; or a whole group of servants might appear to signal status and wealth of domicile ('Castle discovered; servants entering with scrubbing-brushes, brooms, &c.').[17]

Domestic servants knew all about these *things* – household and extra-household objects – commodities or not, fictional or real. In the advice literature directed at but not often read by them, they were counselled so frequently about the care of things that the response 'It just came apart in my hands', became a kind of catch phrase attributed to them, and the motor of a joke told over fifty years.[18] Servants spent half their life cleaning, scouring, pounding, washing, scraping, chopping, cooking, making... things. They knew their contours, and their crevices, the place dirt collected in them; knew their interior spaces, and what was and was not seen of them; they knew cracked china and bent forks, the difference between the appearance of cleanliness and the back-and-forth movement of the human body with a rag that produced it in actuality; knew of burned wooden spoons, and how you might use one to get the worst off before you boiled the baby's clouts. When servants wrote about their experience of life and labour, all these things made up long lists – of things and activities with things – stretching into eternity. There is no end, ever, to dishes to be washed and ironing to be done, as the 1970s wages for housework movement so eloquently described. It is endless – the world's work – but there is also, in the writing of it by the few eighteenth-century maidservants we have considered here, a kind of staccato, almost-hysterical cheerfulness about it all. This is not just because of the verse-form (the demotic iambic tetrameter in which most of them chose to write) but because the things upon which they exercised

---

[17] Miles Peter Andrews, *The Baron Kinkvervankotsdorsprakingatchdern. A New Musical Comedy.* As performed at the Theatre-Royal in the Hay-Market, T. Cadell, London, 1781, p. 8.

[18] Sarah Trimmer, *The Servant's Friend, an Exemplary Tale; Designed to Enforce the Religious Instructions Given at Sunday and Other Charity Schools, by Pointing Out the Practical Application of them in a State of Servitude*, 2nd edn, T. Longman, London, 1787, p. 66; John Trusler, *Trusler's Domestic Management, or the Art of Conducting a Family, with Economy, Frugality and Method*, J. Souter, London, 1819, p. xv; the law had very clear things to say about servants' breaking of china. Anon., *Domestic Management; or the Art of Conducting a Family with Instructions to ... Servants in General, Addressed to Young Housekeepers*, H. D. Symonds at the Literary Press, London, 1800, pp. 84–6, for the advice that servants are responsible for goods if they have been told they are; if they lose them, the law obliges them to replace them; they are not compelled to make good breakages of china, unless it was done deliberately, and the servant had agreed to pay for them at the hiring. Also Anon., *A Letter from Betty to Sally, with the Answer...*, Fielding and Walker, London, 1781, p. 6: 'If china's broke, or spoons are lost,/ You're sure to hear what either cost'.

their labour and their intelligence, were *small* things, and the small – the miniature – has an irreducible connection to the comic, in most forms of representation, at least in the modern period.[19] All of these household things could be held in the hand, or could be worked upon by a human hand equipped with a hand-tool, like a duster or a mop. And not even Longleat's ballroom floor was as big as a field of barley waiting for the reapers. In any case, the kind of maidservants with whom we have not been much concerned in this book, those who laboured as a unit in the menial train of an aristocratic establishment, were not set alone to clean such a floor. Rather, a small army of them moved across it with mops and pails.

In a fine moment, John Hatcher argues with all the eighteenth-century philosophers who attempted such elaborate explanations for the worker's unwillingness to work (his or her poor productivity, failure to turn up on Monday, failure to finish the job; working only when there was something to spend the money on . . . going slow . . .). He inscribes the materiality of all work, whilst underscoring the simple factors that eighteenth-century gentlemen commentators did not take into account: malnourishment, physical weakness, and the terrible nature of all physical labour.[20] As a swift route to empathy in the historian, he asks his student readers to recall their own need to expiate bodily tension in drink after a long night spent essay writing, a tension that is particularly acute when hand, eye and body have performed minute operations, relentlessly, over many hours. Equally, we could reconstruct the cookmaid's experience of cutting six pounds of carrots into little, regular batons for a dish of beef in the French manner, a task that – after washing and scraping them – produces a similar insanity in the worker and the pressing need for a stiff drink.[21] And they are not *her* carrots, but Frances Hamilton's . . . . Or sticking twenty-five rolls with almond slivers (she's already slivered them) for the hedgehog

---

[19] Steven Millhauser, 'The fascination of the miniature', *Grand Street*, 2 (1983), 128–35; E. Liebs, 'Some remarks on the dialectic of GREAT and SMALL in literature', *Phaedrus*, 13 (1980), 56–60; Frances Armstrong, 'Gender and miniaturization: Games of littleness in nineteenth-century fiction', *English Studies in Canada*, 16 (1990), 403–16; Jillian Heydt-Stevenson, *Austen's Unbecoming Conjunctions: Subversive laughter, embodied history*, Palgrave Macmillan, 2005.

[20] John Hatcher, 'Labour, leisure and economic thought before the nineteenth century', *Past and Present*, 160 (1998), 64–115.

[21] Bath and West of England Society for the Encouragement of Agriculture, Arts, Manufacture and Commerce, *Letters and Papers on Agriculture, Planting, &c Selected from the Correspondence of the Society*, The Society, Bath, 1792–3, vol. 6, p. 245 said something similar about concentrated energy expenditure and the need for alcohol.

soup that She, or They, have decided to serve to a party at dinner this day.[22]

As well as offering access to the experience of labour in the past, and to articulated thoughts about it, these little things – kitchen things in particular – present a problem in historical methodology (as well as the advantages enumerated above). Dozens of lemons, pounds of butter, eggs, barm, pigeons, treacle, mace, anchovies and crabs, flowed into the Bishops Lydeard kitchen, to be worked on and processed by Frances Hamilton's maids. The historian believes she understands; perhaps a spurious kind of intimacy with the cook is forged. I understand why she's dealing with such immense quantities of butchers' meat, which cuts were for the likes of her and the farm labourers and which were for Hamilton's dinner guests; I know how it was cooked; I know what the mace and lemons and anchovies were for, and a globalised history of trade and commodity consumption (and consumer desire) that brought non-native products like these to Taunton market. I know exactly what the maids did after the men killed a pig (Elizabeth Raffald told them – and tells me – *how* to kill the pig in the first place[23]). I could walk into the Bishops Lydeard kitchen and cook what Hamilton's maidservants cooked; I could use the open fire, the same iron pots and earthenware crocks, and the new cook stove Hamilton later purchased. Raffald's was the best-selling of all eighteenth-century cookbooks, its culinary style translated for the twentieth century through Elizabeth David's work for the main part, which provided me with my own apprenticeship in cooking.[24] Raffald's way (with the addition of Mediterranean ingredients – but then Hamilton purchased those too . . . olive oil, lemons . . .) is how I cook. That, I think, is the nodal point of my intimacy with the Bishops Lydeard kitchen; it comes from the charm of recognition; the materiality of processes and procedures stretching back over two hundred years has the power to entrance. I chop (anyone cooking chops) an onion, scrape a nutmeg on

[22] Raffald, *The Experienced English Housekeeper, for the Use and Ease of Ladies, House-keepers, Cooks, &c*, 2nd edn, R. Baldwin for the Author, London, 1771, pp. 7–8. See Chapter 10.

[23] Raffald, *Experienced English Housekeeper*, pp. 55–6: 'To roast a Pig. Stick your pig just above the breast-bone, run your knife to the heart, when it is dead, put it in cold water for a few minutes . . . '. In William Augustus Henderson, *The Housekeeper's Instructor; or, Universal Family Cook*, 5th edn, W. and J. Stratford, London, 1795, p. 49, the addressee is the servant, so 'it may not be improper to inform her . . . how to proceed. Stick the pig just above the breastbone . . . '.

[24] From the David corpus, see in particular Elizabeth David, *Salt, Spices and Aromatics in the English Kitchen*, Penguin, Harmondsworth, 1970. Jane Grigson was a more overt transmitter of Raffald's work. *English Food*, orig. pub. 1974, Penguin, Harmondsworth, 1977, pp. 214–16 and passim.

a grater, in the same way. It is a very great pleasure to contemplate what is *in* this kind of physical activity. Physical activity carries the past and something of everyone who has ever sliced a lemon in half for squeezing, stripped the yellowing leaves from a Savoy cabbage, or come to their own conclusion that the best way to peel a parsnip is to boil it first.[25] And yet they were not the cook's cabbages and parsnips; not *her* knife; not *her* kitchen. They belonged to her employer. I have developed great intimacy with Frances Hamilton, as reader, as intellectual, as account keeper and sardonic observer of the comedy of domestic life. But as I am not certain that this woman about whom I know so much ever peeled a parsnip or squeezed a lemon, and am certain that the servants (about whom I know next to nothing) did chop and squeeze – and pare and boil – their way through their years in her house, identification with the servant implodes, or disperses itself. There is nowhere for it *to be*.

Nevertheless, it is with this kind of activity either depicted or undertaken, that you may find yourself in the greatest closeness with the dead and gone. In Paul Connerton's *How Societies Remember*, bodily movement is deeply implicated in the process of social memory.[26] There is something here about the extraordinarily *limited* ways you can cut a lemon, given the shape of the fruit and the existence of carbon steel knives; and the repetition of those actions, again and again, across the centuries. The way in which the lemon or the cabbage (or whatever) *is*, dictates the work that is to be done on it. The anthropologist Tim Ingold describes weaving a basket (in many cultures: his is a kind of universal coiled basket, and 'weaving' the very epitome of all human technical activity). He rejects the epistemologies of other anthropologists who have understood the basket as a thing made by the operation of culture on nature; for him, all craftsmen are *in* the things they make: they work from 'within the world, not upon it'.[27] The world includes the basket *and* the basket-maker. They are both in it together. The artefact shows the way it will be made, as each coil or plait of the fibre ineluctably suggests the next movement of the hand, the next coil and loop.[28] In this schema, the basket has its own time, which is the time of its making.[29]

But we know too much now, about the historical experience of work for this fine depiction of the somatic and emotional states produced by

[25] Raffald, *Experienced English Housekeeper*, pp. 76, 79.
[26] Paul Connerton, *How Societies Remember*, Cambridge University Press, Cambridge, 1989.
[27] Tim Ingold, 'On weaving a basket' in *The Perception of the Environment: Essays in livelihood, dwelling and skill*, Routledge, London and New York, 2000, pp. 339–48, 346–7.
[28] Ingold, 'Of string and birds nests' in *Perception*, pp. 349–61, 356.
[29] Ingold, *Perception*, pp. 326–7.

making something, to have much purchase on our reconstructions of it.[30] If you are going to cook with them, a pound of carrots do indeed suggest and make the cook enact the next operation: they *need to be* topped and tailed, peeled and sliced. The lemon is particularly insistent in its demand to be held down on a surface and sliced in half. But *six pounds* of carrots (soon to be amalgamated with the beef in the pot, and consumed by the company in the dining room)? Six pounds of carrots invite a different approach and relationship from the worker, as does the eighteenth part of processing one pin, repeated again and again; or the million brass valves produced during the course of a life ('the foreman picked up a valve between finger and thumb and spun it into the air. "Eh you must have made a forever of 'em... I bet they'd stretch from 'ere to 'ell!" "Aye... and back"').[31] As one washerwoman of the Edwardian period remarked 'Christ!... Wash, wash, wash; it's like washing your guts away. Stand, stand, stand; I want six pairs of feet; and then I'd have to stand on my head to give them a rest.'[32] (I am sorry to use twentieth-century evidence here, though Kathleen Woodward's mother said pretty much the same thing about laundry work as Mary Collier did in the 1740s.) Stephen Duck did not discuss his relationship with a shed of barley; we have no evidence about the *experience* of making them from eighteenth-century pin-makers, male or female.[33] But Mary Collier *did* discuss her relationship with a boiling vat of linen (Ann Vines, from Bermondsey, June 1800, articulated something of the same. Of course, it would have been better for the child Esther Dandy had she written a poem about it... Who would deny that?).

The basket, the carrots, the pins and brass mushrooms, the dirty clouts, all have their wants: they tell the worker what needs doing to them. It is the same with the field of standing corn – it needs harvesting; earlier in the year, the same field needed weeding; the heap of barley mutely waits for the thresher to do with it what needs to be done. The language used here to describe the relationship between the worker and the object on which he or she exercises her labour ('This shift wants washing'; 'this raspberry bush needs some manure') seems only to have

[30] Ronald Fraser, *Work: Twenty personal accounts*, 2 vols., Penguin Books with New Left Review, Harmondsworth, 1968–9 and in particular the concluding essays by Raymond Williams and Alvin Gouldner in vols. 1 and 2 respectively; R. E. Pahl, *Divisions of Labour*, Basil Blackwell, Oxford, 1984; Patrick Joyce (ed.), *The Historical Meanings of Work*, Cambridge University Press, Cambridge, 1987.

[31] Robert Roberts, 'Bronze mushrooms' in *The Classic Slum: Salford life in the first quarter of the century*, Manchester University Press, Manchester, 1971, pp. 207–9.

[32] Kathleen Woodward, *Jipping Street* (1928), Virago, London, 1983, p. 12.

[33] But see Maxine Berg, *The Age of Manufactures, 1700–1820*, Fontana, London, 1985, pp. 75, 84, 90.

emerged towards the end of the period covered by this book. At the end of the eighteenth-century, farriers, agriculturalists and naval men spoke – wrote – of livestock, stables and ships needing (or wanting) cleaning and washing (souls had always wanted washing in the Blood of the Lamb, but that injunction did not imply an actual, material activity). So too did public buildings occasionally want cleaning; and in the agricultural guide Frances Hamilton owned, Bradley's *Treatise of Husbandry and Gardening* (1726), land wanted manuring. But she never used the terms 'needs' or 'wants' about material things, in all her vast recording of the production, care, and maintenance of her household and farm property. Her instruction to her household and farm servants during her absence in 1788 were not expressed as the needs of raspberry bushes, bees, cattle or cow-dung, but as direct instructions to work with those things ('Mere & Thos: to Stake the Apple Tree, remove the Apple Tree that is too near the Horsery. To get Furze to put round the Stem . . . '). I am not sure about the implications of this linguistic usage. We could say that all of Hamilton's workers mediated between her and the material source of her living and her profit, and thus reiterated the Lockean and legal fiction that the servant was a mere aspect of the mistress's legal personality, exercising her own God-given (but unused) capacity to stake fruit trees and collect furze. But to say this we would probably have to link the emergence of 'those apple trees need staking' in the 1830s, to a considerable number of the better sort doing their own orchard work and washing; which patently did not happen. Anyway, it is a very grave error in theoretical linguistics to link language change to changes in material practices in this way. We are taught to attribute linguistic change to the internal dynamics of the system itself. Nevertheless, over a longer time span than is covered by this book, these things became the workers' (verbal) things, as in Mary Leapor's 'my Pigs . . . my hungry Chickens', or the modern 'I've still got my stairs to do', or 'I'm just finishing my carrots'. At some point between the end of the eighteenth and the mid-twentieth century, domestic workers took the things they laboured on into their verbal possession, whether they owned the objects themselves or were working on them for wages, as in 'Do me work and my washing and bleeding ironing'.[34]

Without a late eighteenth-century vocabulary for saying this, we are left with a universe of material objects and entities pressing their needs, not upon their owners, but upon those whose energies and time had been purchased for their production, processing, maintenance and care. The

---

[34] Nell Dunn, *Poor Cow* (1967), Virago, London, 1994, p. 2; May Hobbs, *Born to Struggle*, Quartet Books, London, 1973; Dolores Hayden and Gwendolyn Wright, 'The new scholarship: Review essays', *Architecture and Urban Planning*, *Signs*, 1:4 (1976), 923–33.

servant's labour was work; and work is – work. Hard, exhausting, what has to be done to get a living. You are not pounding your own clouts, not heaving, pushing, carrying, carting, scrubbing, peeling, something for yourself, but for another, who has bought your energies, for ditch digging in clayey soil in a cold rain, for driving the cart of household shit to the town gully, for scraping it (surely she must have scraped, preliminary to soaking?) from the baby's clouts, in a back yard, somewhere... everywhere. By means of these activities and entities, social relationships between masters and mistresses and their servants, were negotiated, rethought, and remade, on a daily basis. What historians have taken from social and cultural anthropology over the last half-century is the symbolic or representational aspect of things (carrots and clouts) in determining their meaning for historical actors and for ourselves. What this book has urged is a dual approach, in which things certainly may have – and did – represent *something else*, but with that something else dependent on the thing itself; the way it was; its thing-ness.

Historians have recently been urged to turn away from notions of a coherent social totality in delivering their explanations of the pasts they conjure before the eyes of their readers. In *Reassembling the Social*, Bruno Latour describes a century of social-science writing in which 'society' or 'the social' figured as the explanation for the very social phenomena under discussion. The word 'social' has been used as if it described a material, actually existing thing, rather as the adjectives 'wooden' and 'furry' are used to describe buildings or animals. The 'social' is conceived of as a stable thing, or bundle of things, that will later be used to describe something else. Latour has proposed 'reassembling' the social, by retracing all the networks and associations that we call (and have for a long time called) 'society'.[35] Historians are invited to make a conceptual departure: to see 'the social' as 'performed by material things just as much as by humans'.[36] Labelling one thing a person and one a machine, for example, 'is not given in the order of things, but is itself a product of the ordering of people and things that make up "the social" in the first place'. There is not – there never was – a social realm lying outside 'the actors and networks in which it is located'.[37] It is – we can conceptualise

---

[35] Bruno Latour, *Reassembling the Social: An introduction to actor-network-theory*, Oxford University Press, Oxford, 2005.

[36] Patrick Joyce, 'The necessity of social history: Putting the social back in social history', forthcoming. 'This does not mean that inanimate objects should be given agency *per se*, but that historians should unravel the ways in which the interaction between person, object and language constructs historical meaning.' Giorgio Riello, 'Things that shape history: The material culture of historical narratives' in Karen Harvey (ed.), *Practical Matters: History and material culture*, Routledge, London, 2009 (forthcoming).

[37] Joyce, 'Necessity'.

it as – a flat kind of social rather than as a social with surface/depth, or base/superstructure. Then accounts of social life can be given 'in terms of the specific forms of interaction at work in this flat social, where the affordances of material things translate human intentions and shape human uses'.[38] Or six pounds of carrots shape the next hour of a cook's labour, or a horse is used as a measure of her energies expended in labour (as well as contributing to a market-garden economy by production of its manure. Or maybe the horse pulled the cart containing the carrots to market . . .).

It is a strange labour to have written a book that appears to have done something of what has been asked of historians, in reassembling the concept of the social! But all the information presented in this book, about law and labour and carrots and cooks, must refine and complicate the agenda of the new materialists. First, in the English eighteenth century, society *was* a totality, not because it was used to explain other phenomena, but in the way in which it was conceptualised as the setting, given by God, for all human endeavour and animal activity, past and present. Second, the affordances of horses and hand tools shaped human uses by means of *ideas, thoughts* and *language,* as well as by the horse-ness of the horse, and the shape of the kitchen knife and the carrot. The law in particular, on the page and in use by maids, magistrates and all manner of people, was a particularly potent expression of these ideas. Ideas, thoughts, novels, jokes, volumes of verse and the verse itself, should be added to the list of *things* – entities – that made and remade social relationships on a daily basis, in courtrooms and kitchens, and in the moment snatched by the servant to *say* something about it all, by means of her pen. These things – stories in the broadest sense – had discernable effects on the world as it was and as it has been described. After all, we would have a very different history of this time and place if Adam Smith had not said that the servant's work was *not* work and if Karl Marx had not followed him, and said that we could discount service labour in our accounts of capitalist modernity.

Writing of English literature, Bruce Robbins said that the between-the-lines presence of servants signalled the *absence* of what could not be represented, that is, the people. But he was describing their absence (and weird presence) in the novel, and the nineteenth-century novel to boot, in an argument that draws a distinction between the material world and

[38] John Frow, 'Matter and materialism: A brief pre-history of the present' in Tony Bennett and Patrick Joyce (eds.), *Material Powers: Essays beyond cultural materialism*, Routledge, London, forthcoming.

representation of it.[39] Things shift if you understand the novel – and the ideas about servants they contain – as a thing, or entity, fully part of the material world. Ideas, figures, propositions, the texts that carried them and the human voices that contested them, shaped human uses. Servants were not signposts left at random in the no-man's land between what could and could not be represented. Inside texts and outside texts, in the imaginings of their employers, and in their own, they demonstrate that for all manner of thinker, including themselves, they *were* the people – or, if you will have it this way, the working class.

[39] Bruce Robbins, *The Servant's Hand: English fiction from below* (1986), Duke University Press, 1993, p. 27.

Bibliography

ARCHIVAL DOCUMENTS

BERKSHIRE COUNTY RECORD OFFICE (BCRO), READING

D/ED 031–3, Papers of Robert Lee and William Trumbull as justices (the former acting in Surrey as well as Berks), 1735–9.
D/EPb A5, Account Book of Philip Slott of Duntsbourn (Abbots) Glos., 1768.
D/ESv(M) B19–21, Stevens Papers, Correspondence of a Servants' Agency at Woodstock.

BIRMINGHAM CENTRAL LIBRARY ARCHIVES (BCLA), BIRMINGHAM

Homer 425, Accounts of the ... Children of the Rd Henry Secheverell Homer, Rector of Birdingbury, & Vicar of Willoughby, Warwickshire.
Hutton 12, Hutton Family, Letters and Papers.

BIRMINGHAM UNIVERSITY LIBRARY (BUL), BIRMINGHAM

Special Collections, 1956/V27–27A, Philip Bracebridge Homer, Letters, Papers.

BRITISH LIBRARY (BL), LONDON

Add MS 28.266; 83–4, 85–6 (Robert Bloomfield).

CAMBRIDGESHIRE RECORD OFFICE (CRO), CAMBRIDGE

P 135/12, Royston Parish Records, Accounts, 'Account of Rents for the several Houses Belonging to the Parish of Royston'; with details of receipts and payments.

CHESHIRE AND CHESTER ARCHIVES AND LOCAL STUDIES SERVICE (CCA), CHESTER

DAR/G/60, Aderne Collection, Accounts of servants wages 1792–1806.
DSA 59, Stanley of Alderley, Maria Josepha Stanley, Letters to Moomie, 1808–50.

DSA 60, Stanley of Alderley, Letters from Moomie, 1811, 1828, 1829.
P 88/13/3, Macclesfield Parish, Macclesfield Forest with Wildboar Clough.

DERBYSHIRE COUNTY RECORD OFFICE (DCRO), MATLOCK

D239, M/0134, 0138, Sir William Fitzherbert, JP, Recorder of Derby.
M77, Vol. 2, Parish Records, Ashover Parish Register.
Q/SO 1/9, Quarter Sessions Records, Order books, 1774–80.

DEVON RECORD OFFICE (DRO), EXETER

818A/PZ 44, Notice showing rates of rewards payable to informers about houses, windows, servants, horses, carriages, etc., 1785.

DONCASTER METROPOLITAN ARCHIVES (DMA), DONCASTER

AB 6/8/56 (formerly AB6/2/13), An Assessment made ... A Duty Upon all Servants ... for One Year commencing the 25th day of March 1779.
AB 6/8/57 (formerly AB6/2/14) Windows, House and Servants Tax 1781.
AB6/8/59 (formerly AB6/2/16) An assessment made upon the township of Doncaster ... for the year 1788 ending Ladyday 1789.
AB 6/8/60 (formerly AB6/2/18) Windows etc. Duty 1790.
AB6/8/62 (formerly AB6/2/19) An assessment made upon the several inhabitants of the township of Doncaster.... from 5th April 1791 to the 5th of April 1792.
AB6/8/63 (formerly AB6/2/20) An assessment made upon the several inhabitants of the township of Doncaster.... from 5th April 1792 to the 5th of April 1793.
DD.DC/H7/1/1, Davies-Cooke of Ouston, Mrs Mary Cooke, Copy letter book, 1 vol. 1763–7.
HP/27/4, Records of the Warde Family of Hooton Pagnel.

EAST SUSSEX COUNTY RECORD OFFICE (ESCRO), LEWES

AMA 6192/1, Notebook of Richard Stileman of Winchelsea, JP, 1819–27.
AMS 6191, Household account book of Thomas Cooper of New Place Farm in Guestling, 1788–1824.

HERTFORDSHIRE COUNTY RECORD OFFICE (HCRO), HERTFORD

D/EX3/3, Diaries of John Carrington Snr, vol. 3, May 1800–Dec. 1800.
D/P/18/1, Royston Parish Records, Correspondence concerning placing of paupers as apprentices and servants and notebook containing addresses to which servants were sent, 1784–1804.
D/P87/1/1, Royston Parish Records, Register of Baptisms.
D/P87/1/22, Royston Parish Records, Register of Marriages.
D/P87/11/2 and 3, Poor Rate Assessments, 1793–1803.
QSR/48, Quarter Sessions Rolls 1779–1802, Accounts, 145.

C. HOARE AND CO., BANKERS, LONDON

46/303, Customers' ledgers.

KEELE UNIVERSITY SPECIAL COLLECTIONS AND ARCHIVES, KEELE

W/M 1116, Wedgewood Manuscripts, Josiah Wedgewood II, 'Hints on the Management of the Children', 1797–8.

LANCASHIRE RECORD OFFICE (LRO), PRESTON

DDB 81/15, Parker of Brownsholme, Notebooks and memoranda, 1772–5.
DDKE.acc 7840, Lloyd Kenyon, 1st Baron Kenyon, Diaries, 1767 to 1802.
Correspondence in quarto boxes, 1–26 (1753–1802), box 23, 1800.
Folio Boxes, 'Briefs Cases Opinions 1783–1800'.

LINCOLN'S INN LIBRARY (LIL), LONDON

Dampier Manuscripts, A. P. B., 19.
Dampier Manuscripts, B. P. B., 377.
Dampier Manuscripts, L. P. B., 104.

LONDON METROPOLITAN ARCHIVES (LMA), LONDON

P74/LUK/111, St Luke's Chelsea, Workhouse and Discharge Register, Jan. 1782–Dec. 1800.

NATIONAL MARITIME MUSEUM (NMM), GREENWICH

ADM. L/T84, Lieutenants' Logs.

NORFOLK COUNTY RECORD OFFICE (NCRO), NORWICH

BOL 2/113, 2/15, Bolingbroke Collection, Leathes family papers.

NOTTINGHAMSHIRE ARCHIVES (NA), NOTTINGHAM

311/1–6, Diary of Joseph Woolley, framework knitter, for 1801, 1803, 1804, 1809, 1813, 1815.
DD 871/1, Male servants tax return, 1780.
M 8050, M 8051, Notebooks of Sir Gervase Clifton JP, 1772–1812, 1805–10.
PR 2728, Taxation, Servants, Cuckney, 1777–8.
PR 2731, Norton Cuckney, Assessment for bachelors, houses, window shop, servant, horse, carriage taxes, 1785–92, 1794, 1795, 1802.
PR 2131, Edwinstowe Parish Account Book, 1778–1807.

SCONE PALACE (SP), FIFE

NRA(S) 0776, Second series, Bundle 54, Accounts and vouchers 1774–8 [this is in error for 1798].
NRA(S) 0776, Murray Family Papers, Earls of Mansfield, Second series, bundle 2346.
NRA(S) 0776, Murray Family Papers, Earls of Mansfield, Box 68, King's Bench papers, 1782–5.

SHROPSHIRE ARCHIVES (SA), SHREWSBURY

1060/168–171, Justices of the Peace, Justicing notebooks of Thos. N. Parker, 1805–40.
3365/274, Shrewsbury Borough Records, Taxes (shops, servants, carriages and horses), 1778–9, 1780 and 1786.
QS/3/1, Quarter Sessions Records, 1708–1800, Sessions minutes.

SOMERSET COUNTY RECORD OFFICE (SCRO), TAUNTON

DD/CH Bx 16, Copy of the will and codicils of Mrs Frances Hamilton.
DD/FS 5/1, Bishops Lydeard household and farm accounts, farm account book kept by Frances Hamilton (1792–1801).
DD/FS 5/2, Bishops Lydeard household and farm accounts, farm diary, with memoranda of addresses and at the back of the volume a list of books (1791–6).
DD/ FS 5/3, Bishops Lydeard household and farm accounts, farm diary, indexed, kept by Frances Hamilton (1797–1800).
DD/FS 5/4, Bishops Lydeard household and farm accounts, estate and farm account book kept by Frances Coles [Hamilton], reusing her arithmetic exercise book 1767 (1765–77).
DD/FS 5/7, Bishops Lydeard household and farm accounts, account book of Francis Hamilton (1778–91), showing personal and incidental expenses; wages for casual work. At back of volume note on defence of reason and freedom and list of seven wise men of Greece (1788–91).
DD/FS 5/8, Bishops Lydeard household and farm accounts, account book of Francis Hamilton. A continuation of 5/7, but showing fewer personal expenses (1791–8).
DD/FS 5/9, Bishops Lydeard household and farm accounts, housekeeping account book kept by Frances Hamilton reusing a receipt book kept by the executors of Sir John Trevelyan Bt.
DD/FS 6/1, Bishops Lydeard household and farm accounts, concerning farm produce; book list at back of volume (1792–1801).
DD/FS 6/3, Bishops Lydeard household and farm accounts, household and farm account book kept by Frances Hamilton, using book kept as administrator to her husband (1779–85).
DD/FS 7/1, Bishops Lydeard household and farm accounts, general account book kept by Frances Hamilton, reusing a doctor's prescription book (1776–9).

DD/ FS 7/2, Bishops Lydeard household and farm accounts, farm and general diary, partly indexed, kept by Frances Hamilton, reusing a lawyer's bill book (1787–8).

DD/FS 7/3, Bishops Lydeard household and farm accounts, general account book, partly indexed (1797–1800).

DD/FS 7/4, Bishops Lydeard household and farm accounts, wage book kept by Frances Hamilton, reusing a volume of inventories for 1779–1802 (1801–2).

DD/GB, 148–149, Gore Family Papers, 1521–1814.

DD/SF, 1678 (1)–(137), Sandford Mss, Parliamentary papers and pamphlets of Edward Clarke, MP for Taunton . . . late 17th–early 18th century.

DD/SF, 2918, Testimonial from B. Limbry, Exeter for Biddy Page a servant.

DD/SF 3304/15/4, Sanford Mss., 3077, 3109.

DD/X/MAY 13 1786, Letter by Joshua Toulmin (1740–1815).

SURREY HISTORY CENTRE (SHC), WOKING

2568/7/4, Thames Ditton Parish Records, Baptisms.

2568/7/4, Thames Ditton Parish Records, Poor rate assessment for Thames Ditton.

2568/7/4, Thames Ditton Parish Records, Poor rate assessment and vestry minutes, 1778–96.

2568/8/4, Thames Ditton Parish Records, Overseers accounts, 1773–1805.

QS2/6/ Surrey Quarter Sessions, Order book.

THE NATIONAL ARCHIVES, KEW

TNA ADM 1/1906, Captains' letters 1780–1, 28, Tyringham Howe.

TNA ADM 25/101, Half-Pay Registers Jul.–Dec. 1781.

TNA ADM 34/774, Ships' Pay Books, Treasury Pay Books for *The Thames*, 27 Aug. 1776–Sep. 1781.

TNA ADM 36/8282, Thames Muster Table 11 Aug.–20 Sep. 1781, Compleat Book.

TNA ADM 36/10121, Navy Transports 1 Jan. 1775–27 Mar. 1785.

TNA ADM 49/2, Transports and Tenders and Employed, Promiscuous Papers Relative to . . . the American War.

TNA ADM 51/982, Captains' Logs, Part 10.

TNA ADM 52/2036, *The Thames*, Master's Log and Journal, 9 Nov. 1780–21 Sep. 1781, 2036 Part 3 Log Book, 2036 Part 4 Journal.

TNA ASSI 5 97/4, English Assize Records, 1559–1971, Criminal Trial Records, Gloucestershire Indictments, Lent 1777.

TNA ASSI 31/18 folio 280, Crown Minute Book for the Home and South Eastern Circuit, for the Summer Assizes in 1800.

TNA ASSI 94/1497, English Assize Records, 1559–1971, Criminal Trial Records, Herts. Indictments, Summer Assizes 40 Geo. III 1800, Hertfordshire, Felony File.

TNA ASSI 31/18 folio 280, Crown Minute Book for the Home and South Eastern Circuit, for the Summer Assizes in 1800.

TNA ASSI 94/1497, English Assize Records, 1559–1971, Criminal Trial Records, Herts. Indictments, Summer Assizes 40 Geo. III 1800, Hertfordshire, Felony File.

TNA E 102/70, Land Tax, Property Tax, Assessed Taxes Letter Book, 1777–1805.

TNA KB 16/18/1, Records of Orders Files, 17 Geo. III, 1776–1777.

TNA KB 16/19/5, Records of Orders Files, 25 Geo. III, 1784–1785.

TNA IR 70/3, Assessed Taxes and Inhabited Houses Duties. Judges Opinions, 1805–30, vol. 3, Feb. 1810–Jun. 1813.

TNA IR 70/5, Assessed Taxes and Inhabited Houses Duties. Judges Opinions, 1805–30, vol. 5, Mar. 1817–Dec. 1819.

TNA IR 70/6, Assessed Taxes and Inhabited Houses Duties. Judges Opinions, 1805–30, vol. 6, Dec. 1819–Jul. 1822.

TNA IR 71/2, Board of Taxes, Miscellaneous, Entry Book of Law Opinions, 1780–1823.

TNA IR 83/131, Appeals before Commissioners, 1770–15.

TNA PROB 11/1106; 11/1142; 11/1167.

TNA SP 78/273, 276, 296, State Papers Foreign, France; Letters from British residents in France.

TNA T1 542/191–196, Letters from Tax Office.

TNA T1/577/200, To Lords Commissioners of the Treasury, Memorandum of the Commissioners of Excise respecting the duties on chocolate and also in regard to the duty on male servants, dated 15 Mar. 1782.

TNA T1 577/198–199, To Lords Commissioners of the Treasury, from the Board of Taxes, a report respecting the defects in the laws at present in force for the collection of the revenue under the management of the Board of Taxes.

TNA T1 609/36–37, Tax office and suggestions regarding taxes, proposal to put a tax akin to rates on houses and a tax on furniture.

TNA T1 609/111–112, Tax office and suggestions regarding taxes.

TNA T1 609/395–399, Tax Office and suggestions regarding taxes, proposal for increasing the tax on servants.

TNA T1 610/404–426, Tax Office and various proposals upon the new tax on hats.

TNA T 1/624/118–121, Letters regarding a riot in Tavistock.

TNA T 1 624/397–398, Tax Office, letter from William Pratt regarding his suggestions on tax and hoping for reward.

TNA T 1 7000/45–48, Tax office and suggestions concerning a tax on bakers, Thos Stone to Tax Office, 12 Feb. 1791.

TNA T 1 700/49–50, Account of the annual produce of the duties upon female servants under the Act of the twenty-fifth of George the Third for four years ending 5th Apr. 1791.

TNA T 1 915/55–71, Letters from Treasury Chambers.

TNA T 22/7–9, Treasury Out-letters concerning stamps, taxes and other matters, 1777–1805.

TNA T 22/8, Land tax, property tax, assessed taxes' letter book, 1777–1805.

WARWICKSHIRE COUNTY RECORD OFFICE (WCRO)

CR 136/A [565], Newdigate of Arbury, Notebook of books received and sent out.

CR 136/A [621], Newdigate of Arbury, Appointment and memorandum diaries.

CR 1707, Heber-Percy of Guys Cliffe, 1759–1826, Diaries of Bertie Greatheed.

CR 1711/ 58, John Ward Boughton-Lee, 1791–1868.

CR 656/36, Holbech of Farnborough, Volume containing cuttings from newspapers mainly eighteenth century, printed ephemera and various letters or copies of letters.

WEST YORKSHIRE ARCHIVE SERVICE (WYAS) BRADFORD DISTRICT, BRADFORD

16D86/temp.0440, Francis Sharp Bridges of Horton Old Hall, Bradford, Account book with payments for domestic duties and wages, 1802–43.

16D86/1150, Sharp Bridges accounts, 'Brief To Doncaster Sessions 20 Janry 1768'.

BAR/3/a/2, George Baron, wool merchant of Woodhouse in Leeds, Accounts for servants' wages, 1791–1828.

HEATON/B149, Account book of Robert Heaton, 1764–92.

16D86/temp.0440, Francis Sharp Bridges of Horton Old Hall, Bradford, Account book with payments for domestic duties and wages, 1802–43.

16D86/0646, Benson Family, Papers of Miss Benson re the York Female Benefit Club.

WEST YORKSHIRE ARCHIVE SERVICES (WYAS), KIRKLEES DISTRICT, HUDDERSFIELD

KC242, Diaries of the Reverend John Murgatroyd.

WEST YORKSHIRE ARCHIVE SERVICES (WYAS), WAKEFIELD DISTRICT, WAKEFIELD

QS1/107/3–8, West Riding of Yorkshire, Quarter Sessions Rolls, Orders.

QS10/25, Quarter Sessions, Order books, 1767–9.

WILTSHIRE AND SWINDON RECORD OFFICE (WSRO), TROWBRIDGE

9/35/62, Ailesbury of Savernake, about 100 letters on the employment and dismissal of employees, 1714–1829.

635/152, Murder of Catherine Pierce Ashe A'Court (Gloucester) by a family servant, 1776.

776/922A, Household account book, kept by Christine Tousey of Salisbury.
1665/4, Household account book of the Beach Family of Keevil, Fittleton and Widcombe (Somerset).

GOVERNMENT REPORTS AND PUBLICATIONS, PARLIAMENTARY PAPERS AND OTHER REPORTS OF PARLIAMENTARY PROCEEDINGS

Board of Agriculture, *Communications to the Board of Agriculture; on Subjects Relative to the Husbandry and Internal Improvement of the Country*, vol. 1, W. Bulmer, London, 1797.
Great Britain, Parliament, House of Commons, *Select Committee on Finance. First [-twenty-second] Report from the Select Committee on Finance*, 2 vols., 1797.
Parliamentary History of England.
Parliamentary Register; or, the History of the Proceedings and Debates of the House of Commons.
The Senator; or, Parliamentary Chronicle

FICTION, POETRY, DRAMA AND JEST BOOKS

Andrews, Miles Peter, *The Baron Kinkvervankotsdorsprakingatchdern. A New Musical Comedy. As performed at the Theatre-Royal in the Hay-Market*, T. Cadell, London, 1781.
Anon., *Modern Courtship, a Comedy, in two Acts*, J. Coote, London, 1768.
  A Letter from Betty to Sally, with the Answer; a New Year's Gift. Recommended to be learnt by every Servant in the Three Kingdoms. Read once by every Mistress of a Family, in the Hearing of every Master, whose Fortune does not exceed Three Hundred a Year, Fielding and Walker, London, 1781.
  'Qualifications of a Modern Maidservant', *The Wit's Magazine . . .* , 2 vols., London, 1784–5; vol. 2 (Dec. 1784), p. 466.
  The Widow of Kent; or, the History of Mrs Rowley. A Novel in Two Volumes, F. Noble, London, 1788.
  The Genuine Edition of Joe Miller's Jests: or, Wits Vade-mecum Revived, n.i., [London?, 1790?].
  The Adventures of a Pin, supposed to be related by Himself, Herself, or Itself, J. Lee, London, 1790.
  The Frolics of an Hour. A Musical Interlude. As performed at the Theatre-Royal, Covent-Garden, Minerva Press, London, 1795.
  The Trial Of Betty the Cook-maid, Before the Worshipful Justice Feeler, for Laying a Bed in the Morning, 'printed and sold in London', 1795.
  Agatha; or, a Narrative of Recent Events. A novel, in three volumes . . . , printed for the author, London, 1796.
  Human Vicissitudes; or, Travels into Unexplored Regions . . . , 2 vols., G. G. and J. Robinson, London, 1798.
Austen, Jane, *Mansfield Park* (1814), Penguin, Harmondsworth, 1986.

Bellamy, George Anne, *An Apology for the Life of George Anne Bellamy . . . written by Herself. To which is annexed, her original letter to John Calcraft, Esq; advertised to be published in October, 1767*, 4th edn, 5 vols., printed for the author, London, 1786.

Bennett, Agnes Maria, *The Beggar Girl and her Benefactors. In seven Volumes*, printed for William Lane, at the Minerva Press, London, 1797.

Blake, Joseph, alias Blueskin, Foot-pad, and John Sheppard, *The History of the Lives and Actions of Jonathan Wild, Thief-taker . . . Housebreaker*, Edward Midwinter, London, 1725.

Bloomfield, Robert, *The Farmer's Boy. A Rural Poem*, Vernor and Hood, London, 1800.

Selected Poems, John Goodridge and John Lucas (eds.), Intro. John Lucas, Nottingham Trent University, 1998.

Burney, Fanny, *Camilla: or, a Picture of Youth. By the Author of Evelina and Cecilia. In five volumes. . . .*, T. Payne; and T. Cadell Jun. and W. Davies, London, 1796.

Carr, John, *The Life and Opinions of Tristram Shandy, Gentleman*, privately printed, London, 1760.

Clement, Jennifer, *A True Story Based on Lies*, Canongate, Edinburgh, 2001.

Collier, Mary, *The Woman's Labour. An Epistle to Mr. Stephen Duck; in answer to his late poem, called The Thresher's Labour . . .*, printed for the author, London, 1739.

Colman, George, *Prose on several Occasions; accompanied with some Pieces in Verse*, 3 vols., T. Cadel, London, 1787.

Cunningham, Peter, *Peter Cunningham's New Jest Book; or, Modern High Life Below Stairs*, Funny Joe, London, 1785.

de Crespigny, Mary, *The Pavilion. A Novel. In four volumes*, William Lane at the Minerva Press, London, 1796.

Dickens, Charles, *Barnaby Rudge* (1841), Penguin, London, 1973.

Duck, Stephen, *Curious Poems on several Occasions. Viz. I. On Poverty. II. The Thresher's Labour. III. The Shunamite*, John Lewis, London, 1738.

Dunn, Nell, *Poor Cow* (1967), Virago, London, 1994.

Eminent Lady, *Louisa Matthews. By an Eminent Lady*, 3 vols., J. Lackington, London, 1793.

Fielding, Henry, *The History of Tom Jones, a Foundling. In three volumes*, John Smith, Dublin, 1749.

Gee, Maggie, *My Cleaner*, SAQI, London, 2005.

von Goethe, Johann Wolfgang, *Wilhelm Meister's Theatrical Mission*, trans. Gregory A. Page, Heinemann, London, 1913.

Green, Sarah, *Court Intrigue, or the Victim of Constancy, an Historical Romance. In two volumes. By the author of Mental Improvement*, printed at the Minerva-Press, for William Lane, London, 1799.

Gunning, Susannah, *Family Pictures, a Novel. Containing Curious and Interesting Memoirs of Several Persons of Fashion in W——re. By a Lady. In two volumes*, P. Wilson etc, Dublin, 1764.

Hands, Elizabeth, *The Death of Amnon. A Poem with an Appendix: containing Pastoral and Other Poetical Pieces*, N. Rollason, Coventry, 1789.

Haywood, Eliza, *The Invisible Spy. By Explorabilis. In two volumes*, 3rd edn, L. Gardner, London, 1767.

Helme, Elizabeth, *Louisa; or, The Cottage on the Moor. In two volumes*, G. Kearsley, London, 1787.

Holcroft, Thomas, *The School for Arrogance: a Comedy. As it is acted at the Theatre Royal, Covent Garden*, P. Wogan, P. Byrne, J. Moore, J. Jones, A. Grueber and others, Dublin, 1791.

Homer, Philip Bracebridge, *The Garland; A Collection of Poems*, C. S. Rann, Oxford, n.d. (1783?).

Horde, Thomas, *The Pretended Puritan. A Farce of two Acts*, printed for the author, Oxford, 1779.

Johnson, Richard, *Tea-table Dialogues, between a Governess, and Mary Sensible... and Emma Tempest*, Darton and Harvey, London, 1796.

Jones, Charles, *The Miscellaneous Poetic Attempts of C. Jones. An Uneducated Journeyman-Woolcomber*, printed for the author by R. Trewman, London, 1781.

Kilner, Dorothy, *Life and Perambulations of a Mouse*, John Marshall, London, 1783.

The Life and Perambulations of a Mouse, 2nd edn, John Marshall, London, 1787.

Leapor, Mary, *The Works of Mary Leapor*, Richard Greene and Ann Messenger (eds), Oxford University Press, Oxford, 2003.

Lennox, Charlotte, *The Female Quixote, or, the Adventures of Arabella* (1752), Oxford University Press, Oxford, 1989.

Lonsdale, Roger (ed.), *Eighteenth-Century Women Poets*, Oxford University Press, Oxford, 1990.

MacNally, Leonard, *Fashionable Levities, a Comedy. In Five Acts*, G. G. and J. Robinson, London, 1785.

Mansfield, Katherine, 'The-Child-Who-Was-Tired' in *In a German Pension* (1911), Penguin, Harmondsworth, 1964.

Martin, Merry, *The Royal Jester, or Cream of the Jest*, F. Stamper, London, 1751.

Midnight, Mrs, *Mrs Midnight's Oration's [sic]; and other Select Pieces; as they were spoken at the Oratory in the Hay-market*, London, privately printed, 1763.

O'Keeffe, John, 'The Doldrum, or, 1803' in *The Dramatic Works of John O'Keeffe, Esq. Published under the gracious patronage of His Royal Highness the Prince of Wales. Prepared for the press by the author*. In four volumes, printed for the author, by T. Woodfall, London, 1798.

Pasquin, Anthony, *Poems: by Anthony Pasquin*, 2 vols., J. Strahan, London, W. Creech, Edinburgh; J. Exshaw, Dublin, 1789.

Patrick, F. C., *The Irish Heiress, a Novel, in three volumes*, Minerva Press, London, 1797.

Pilkington, Mary, *Tales of the Cottage; or Stories, Moral and Amusing, for Young Persons. Written on the plan of... Les veillees du chateau, by Madam Genlis*, Vernor and Hood, London, 1799.

Showes, Mrs, *The Restless Matron. A Legendary Tale. In three volumes*, the Minerva Press, for William Lane, London, 1799.

Smythies, Miss, *The Brothers. In two volumes. By the Author of The Stage-coach and Lucy Wellers*, 2nd edn, 2 vols., R. and J. Dodsley, London, W. Reymer, Colchester, 1759.

The History of a Pin, as related by Itself.... By the Author of The Brothers, a Tale for Children, E. Newbery, London, 1798.

Thomson, Katherine, *Constance. A Novel. In Three Volumes*, Richard Bentley, London, 1833.

Topham, Edward, *The Life of Mr. Elwes, the celebrated Miser. With singular Anecdotes, &c*, D. Brewman, and W. Locke, London, 1792.

Townley, James, *High Life Below Stairs. A Farce of two Acts. As it is performed at the Theatre-Royal in Drury-Lane*, J. Newbery, London, 1759.

Trimmer, Sarah, *The Servant's Friend, an Exemplary Tale; Designed to Enforce the Religious Instructions Given at Sunday and Other Charity Schools, by Pointing Out the Practical Application of them in a State of Servitude*, 2nd edn, T. Longman, London, 1787.

Updike, John, *Memoirs of the Ford Administration* (1993), Penguin, London, 2007.

Upstairs, Downstairs, 1971, dirs. Bill Bain and Derek Bennett [TV Series 1971–5].

Weldon, Fay, *She May Not Leave* (2005), Harper, London, 2006.

Wollstonecraft, Mary, *The Works of Mary Wollstonecraft*, Janet Todd and Marilyn Butler (eds), 7 vols., Pickering, London, 1989.

The Wrongs of Woman; or Maria (1798), Oxford University Press, 1976.

Yearsley, Ann, *Poems on Various Subject. A second Book of Poems... by Ann Yearsley*, G. G. J. and J. Robinson, London, 1787.

Young, Mary Julia, *The Family Party. In three volumes*, Minerva Press for William Lane, London, 1791.

PRIMARY TRACTS, TREATISES AND OTHER PUBLICATIONS, PRE-1900

Adams, George, *Lectures on Natural and Experimental Philosophy considered in its present State of Improvement*, 2nd edn, J. Dillon, London, 1799.

Adams, Samuel and Sarah, *The Complete Servant; Being a Practical Guide to the Peculiar Duties and Business of all Descriptions of Servants from the Housekeeper to the Servant of All-Work, and from the Land Steward to the Footboy; with Useful Receipts and Tables*, Knight and Lacy, London, 1825.

Adeane, Jane H., *The Early Married Life of Maria Josepha Lady Stanley, with Extracts from Sir John Stanley's 'Praeterita': Edited by one of their grandchildren*, Longman, Green, London, New York, Bombay, 1899.

Anderson, John, *Institutes of Physics*, 3rd edn, 3 vols., Robert Chapman, Glasgow, 1777.

Annual Register, or a View of the History, Politicks, and Literature, of the Year 1762, R. and J. Dodsley, London, 1763, 1767, 1780, 1787.

Anon., *The Trial of Mrs. Branch, and her Daughter, for the Murder of Jane Buttersworth, before the Hon. Mr. Justice Chapple, at Somerset Assizes, March 31, 1740.... To which are added, true Copies of some very material Informations,... With a just Account of the Prisoners behaviour at their Trial;... and at the Place of Execution*, James Leake, Bath, 1740.

The Cruel Mistress; being, the genuine Trial of Elizabeth Branch, and her own Daughter; for the murder of Jane Buttersworth, their Servant Maid: who were executed on Saturday, May 3. 1740. . . . Together with an Account of their Lives, C. Simpson, London, 1740.

A General Description of all Trades, digested in alphabetical Order: by which Parents, Guardians, and Trustees, may, with greater Ease and Certainty, make Choice of Trades agreeable to the Capacity, Education, Inclination, Strength, and Fortune of the Youth under their Care. . . . To which is prefixed, an Essay on Divinity, Law, and Physic, T. Waller, London, 1747.

A Third Collection of Scarce and Valuable Tracts, on the most interesting and entertaining Subjects: but chiefly such as relate to the History and Constitution of these Kingdoms. . . . Particularly . . . of the late Lord Somers. Revised by eminent Hands, 4 vols., F. Cogan, London, 1751.

A Modern Dissertation on a Certain Necessary Piece of Household Furniture, H. Kent, London, 1752.

A Proposal for the Amendment and Encouragement of Servants, J. Shuckburgh, London, 1752.

Public Nuisances considered under the Several Heads of Bad Pavements, Butchers, infesting the Streets, the Inconveniences to the Publick occasioned by the present Method of Billetting the Foot-guards, and the Insolence of Household Servants . . . by a Gentleman of the Temple, E. Withers, London, 1754.

The Laws Relating to Masters and Servants: With Brief Notes and Explanations to Render them easy and intelligible to the meanest Capacity. Necessary to be had in all Families, Henry Lintot, London, 1755.

The Art of Poetry on a New Plan. Illustrated with a great Variety of Examples from the best English Poets, and of Translations from the Ancients, 2 vols., J. Newbery, London, 1762.

The Complete Man and Maid Servant: containing Plain and Easy Instructions for Servants of both Sexes . . . , J. Cooke, London, 1764.

Remarkable Trials and interesting Memoirs, of the most noted Criminals, who have been convicted at the Assizes, the King's-Bench Bar, Guildhall, &c. . . . From the year 1740, to 1764. . . . In two volumes. . . . , vol. 1, W. Nicoll, 1765.

Directions to Lords, and Ladies, Masters and Mistresses, for the Improvement of their Conduct to servants and Tenants, Tradesmen and humble Friends and Cousins. Design'd as a Return for their Impertinent Directions to Servants, M. Cooper, London, 1766.

An Appeal to Humanity, in an Account of the Life and cruel Actions of Elizabeth Brownrigg. Who was tried at the Old Bailey on the 12th of September 1767, . . . To which is added the Trial of Elizabeth Branch and her Daughter, Harrison and Ward, London, 1767.

The Complete Letter-writer. Containing familiar Letters on the most common Occasions in life. Also a Variety of elegant Letters for the Direction and embellishment of style, on business, duty, amusement, love, courtship, marriage, friendship, and other subjects . . . , W. Darling, Edinburgh, 1768.

The Tyburn Chronicle: or, Villainy display'd in all its Branches. Containing an authentic Account of the Lives, Adventures, Tryals, . . . of the most notorious Malefactors. . . . From the year 1700, to the present Time, J. Cooke, London, 1768.

An Essay on Trade and Commerce: Containing Observations on Taxes, As they are supposed to affect the Price of Labour in our Manufactures: Together with some interesting Reflections on the Importance of Our Trade to America. To which is added the Out-lines, or Sketch, of a Scheme for the Maintenance and Employment of the Poor, the Prevention of Vagrancy, and the Decrease of the Poor Rates. By the Author of Considerations on Taxes, S. Hooper, London, 1770.

A View of Real Grievances, with the Remedies Proposed for Redressing them, printed for the author, London, 1772.

Directions to Servants; particularly those who have the Care of Children, G. Kearsley, E. and C. Dodd, London, 1779.

The Malefactor's Register; or, the Newgate and Tyburn Calendar. Containing the authentic Lives, Trials, Accounts of Executions, and dying Speeches, of the most notorious Violators of the Laws of their Country; . . . from the Year 1700 to Lady-Day 1779. . . . Embellished with a most elegant and superb set of copper plates, 5 vol., Alexander Hogg, London, 1779.

(Mrs Newbery), *The Housekeeper's Accompt-Book for the Year 1782; or an Easy, Concise, and Clear Method of Keeping an Exact Account of every Article Made Use of in Every Family throughout the Year*, R. Cruttwell, London, and W. Taylor, Bath, 1782.

[H. C. Jennings], *A Free Inquiry into the Enormous Increase of Attornies, with Some Reflections on the Abuse of our Laws. By an Unfeigned Admirer of Genuine British Jurisprudence*, W. Clacher, Chelmsford, 1785.

'No. 79. Saturday August 5. 1786' in *The Lounger. A Periodical Paper published at Edinburgh in the Year 1785 and 1786*, 3 vols., Strahan and Cadell, London, William Creed, Edinburgh, 1786, vol. 3, pp. 96–110.

Instructions for Cutting Out Apparel for the Poor; principally intended for the Assistance of Patronesses of Sunday Schools . . . But Useful in all Families . . . Published for the Benefit of the Sunday School Children at Hertingfordbury in the County of Hertford, J. Walter, London, 1789.

A Present for Servants, from their Ministers, Masters, or Other Friends, 10th edn, J. F. and C. Rivington, for the SPCK, London, 1787.

The Natural History of Insects, compiled from Swammerdam, Brookes, Goldsmith, &c. Embellished with copper-plates, Morison, Perth, G. Mudie, Edinburgh, W. Coke, Leith, 1792.

Cries of the Afflicted . . . Being a faithful Account of the Sufferings of Mary Mitchell, Mary Jones and Mary Clifford, Apprentices to Mrs Elizabeth Brownrigg, a Painter's Wife in Fetter Lane, Fleet Street, London, 1795.

'No. 79 . . . To the Author of the Lounger' in *The Lounger. A Periodical Paper published at Edinburgh in the Years 1785 and 1786*, 3 vols., Strahan and Cadell, London, William Creech, Edinburgh, vol. 3, 1787, pp. 96–100.

The Connexion between Industry and Property; or a Proposal to make a fixed and permanent Allowance to Labourers for the Maintenance of their Children. Addressed to the Society for bettering the Condition and increasing the Comforts of the Poor, Trewman, Exeter, 1798.

A Full and Particular Account, of the Wonderful Apparition of Mary Nicholson which appeared to two Men her intimate Friends and Acquaintance, at a Village near

Durham, during the late ahunder [sic] Storm; and an account of her meditations after the Rope Broke, n.i., Durham, 1799.

Hints to Masters and Mistresses, Respecting Female Servants, Darnton and Harvey, London, 1800.

Reflections on the Relative Situations of Master and Servant, Historically and Politically Considered; the Irregularities of Servants; the Employment of Foreigners; and the General Inconveniencies Resulting from the Want of Proper Regulations, W. Miller, London, 1800.

Summary Trial of the King v. S. F. Waddington . . . , Crosby and Letterman, London, 1800.

A General View of the Agriculture of Hertfordshire, Drawn up for the Consideration of the Board of Agriculture and General Improvement, by the Secretary of the Board, B. McMillan, London, 1804.

The History of Oswestry, From the Earliest Period; its Antiquities and Customs: With a Short Account of the Neighbourhood, William Price, Oswestry, 1815.

The Housekeeper's Account Book for the Year 1820, Cruttwell, Longman, Hurst, Rees, Orme and Brown, Bath and London, 1820.

Remarks on the Present State of the Poor, privately printed, Oswestry, 1826.

A Familiar Summary of the Laws Respecting Masters and Servants, Apprentices Journeymen, Artificers and Labourers, by the Author of 'Plain Instructions to Executors and Administrators', 'Plain Advice on Wills . . . ', Henry Washbourne, London, 1831.

'The Journal of a Gloucestershire Justice, A. D. 1715–1756. Journal of the Rev. Francis Welles, Vicar of Presbury, Gloucestershire, and Justice of the Peace for the County of Gloucester, A. D. 1715 to 1756. Folio. MS', *The Law Magazine and Law Review or Quarterly Journal of Jurisprudence*, 11 (1861), 125–42; 12 (1861), 125–42; 13 (1862), 247–91.

The Date Book for Lincoln, and Neighbourhood, from the Earliest Time to the Present; collected with Care and from the most authentic Sources, R. E. Leary, Lincoln, 1866.

d'Arnay, Jean Rodolphe, *The Private Life of the Romans. Translated from the French of M. D'Arnay*, printed for the translator, Edinburgh, 1761.

Astle, Thomas, *The Origin and Progress of Writing, as well hieroglyphic as elementary, &c*, privately printed for the author, London, 1784.

Attorney at Law, *The Attorney's Complete Pocket Book*, 3rd edn, Henry Lintot, London, 1751.

Bailey, Nathan, *Dictionarium Domesticum, being a new and compleat household Dictionary. For the Use both of City and Country*, C. Hitch, C. Davis and S. Austen, London, 1736.

Baker, Henry, *Of Microscopes, and the Discoveries made thereby. Illustrated with many Copper Plates. In Two Volumes*, J. Dodsley, London, 1785.

Barclay, David, *Advice to Servants*, privately printed, London, 1800?

Baretti, Joseph, 'On Signora Piozzi's Publication of Dr. Johnson's Letters. Stricture the First', *European Magazine and London Review*, 13 (May 1788), 313–17, 'Stricture the Second', 14 (Jun. 1788), 393–9; 'Stricture the Third', 14 (Aug. 1788), 89–99.

The Sentimental Mother. A Comedy in Five Acts; the Legacy of an Old Friend, and his Last Moral Lesson to Mrs Hester Lynch Thrale, now Mrs Hester Lynch Piozzi, James Ridgeway, London, 1788.

Barker, Anne, *The Complete Servant Maid: or Young Woman's Best Companion*, 6th edn, J. Cooke, Dublin, 1770.

Bath and West of England Society for the Encouragement of Agriculture, Arts, Manufacture and Commerce, *Letters and Papers on Agriculture, Planting, &c*, 6 vols., The Society, Bath, 1792–3.

Bayntun-Rolt, Andrew, *The Trial of the Right Honourable Lady Maria Bayntun . . . in the Arches Court at Doctors Commons, for committing the Crime of Adultery, To which is added, a very pathetic and affecting Letter, from Lady Maria to her Husband*, printed for the editor, London, 1781.

Beattie, James, *The Theory of Language. In Two Parts. Of the Origin and General Nature of Speech . . .* , Strahan, Cadell and Creech, Edinburgh, 1788.

Beddoes, Thomas, *The History of Isaac Jenkins and of the Sickness of Sarah his Wife, and their three Children*, privately printed, Madeley, 1792.

A Lecture Introductory to a Course of Popular Instruction on the Constitution and Management of the Human Body, J. Johnson, London, Joseph Cottle, Bristol, 1797.

Bedford, W. K. Riland, *Three Hundred Years of a Family Living: Being a history of the Rilands of Sutton Coldfield*, Cornish, Birmingham, 1889.

Belsham, William, *Remarks on the Bill for the better Support and Maintenance of the Poor, now depending in the House of Commons*, G. G. and J. Robinson, London, 1797.

Billingsley, John, *General View of the Agriculture of the County of Somerset, with Observations on the Means of Its Improvement, drawn up in the year 1795, for the Consideration of the Board of Agriculture and Internal Improvement*, 3rd edn, R. Cruttwell, Bath, 1798.

Bird, James Barry, *Laws Respecting Masters and Servants, Articled Clerks, Apprentices, Manufacturers, Labourers and Journeymen*, 3rd edn, W. Clarke, London, 1799.

Blackstone, William, *Commentaries on the Laws of England. Book the First*, 3rd edn, 4 vols., John Exshaw etc, Dublin, 1769.

Commentaries on the Laws of England. In Four Books (1765), 6th edn, Company of Booksellers, Dublin, 1775.

Reports of Cases determined in the several Courts of Westminster-Hall, from 1746 to 1779. Taken and compiled by the Honourable Sir William Blackstone, 2 vols., His Majesty's Law Printers for W. Strahan, T. Cadell, London, 1781.

Commentaries on the Laws of England, 12th edn, Edward Christian (ed.), 4 vols., T. Cadell, London, 1793–5 (1796).

Boswell, James, *Life of Samuel Johnson, LL.D, comprehending an account of his studies and numerous works, . . . In two volumes*, Charles Dilly, London, 1791.

Boswell, John, *A Method of Study: or, an useful Library. In two Parts. Part I. Containing short Directions and a Catalogue of Books for the Study of several valuable Parts of Learning, viz. Geography, Chronology, History, Classical Learning, Natural Philosophy, &c. Part II. Containing some Directions for the Study of Divinity*, printed for the author, London, 1738–43.

Bott, Edmund, *Digest of the Laws Relating to the Poor, by Francis Const*, 3 vols., Strahan, London, 1800.

The Laws relating to the Poor in which the Statutes and Cases to Easter Term 1807, are arranged under their respective Heads; and the whole System of the Poor's Laws, including the Collections originally made by E. Bott, together with many cases never before published, are arranged under their respective Heads... and the whole... placed in one clear and perspicacious View, 3 vols., J. Butterworth, London, 1807.

Bouyer, Reynold Gideon, *An Account of the Origin, Proceedings, and Intentions of the Society for the Promotion of Industry, in the Southern District of the Parts of Lindsey, in the County of Lincoln.... The third edition.... To this edition is also added, a Report of the Board of Trade to the Lords Justices,... by Mr. John Locke*, privately printed, Louth, 1789.

Bradley Martha, *The British Housewife: or, the Cook, Housekeeper's and Gardiner's Companion* (1756), Prospect Books, Totnes, 1996.

Bradley, R., *A General Treatise of Husbandry and Gardening; containing a new System of Vegetation: illustrated with many Observations and Experiments. In two Volumes. Formerly publish'd monthly, and now methodiz'd and digested under proper heads, with additions and great alterations. In four parts. ... Adorn'd with cuts*, T. Woodward and J. Peele, London, 1726.

Breues, John, *The Fortune Hunters: shewing (from experience) 1. How People may improve their Fortunes, and raise themselves in London...*, privately printed, London, 1754.

Brooke, William, *The True Cause of our Present Distress for Provisions; with a natural, easy, and effectual Plan for the future Prevention of so great a Calamity. With some Hints respecting the absolute Necessity of an encreased Population*, H. D. Symonds etc, London, 1800.

Brown, John, *The Elements of Medicine of John Brown, MD. Translated from the Latin, with comments and illustrations, by the Author. A New Edition, revised and corrected, with a Biographical Preface, by Thomas Beddoes, MD*, 2 vols., J. Johnson, London, 1795.

Brown, Sarah, *Letter to a Lady on the Management of the Infant*, Baker and Galabin, London, 1779.

Broughton, Thomas, *Serious Advice and Warning to Servants, More Especially Those of the Nobility and Gentry*, 4th edn, J. Rivington for the SPCK, London, 1743.

Browne's General Law-list; for the year 1779, 3rd edn, privately printed, London, 1778.

Bryant, Jacob, *A New System, or, an Analysis of Ancient Mythology: wherein an Attempt is made to divest Tradition of Fable; and to reduce the Truth to its original Purity*, 2nd edn, 2 vols., T. Payne; P. Elmsly; B. White; and J. Walter, London, 1775.

Buchan, William, *Observations concerning the Diet of the Common People, recommending a Method of Living less Expensive and more conducive to Health than the Present*, A. Strahan and T. Cadell, London, 1797.

Builder's Magazine: or Monthly Companion for Architects, Carpenters, Masons, Bricklayers, &c..., F. Newbery, London, 1774.

Buller, Francis, *An Introduction to the Law relative to Trials at nisi prius. The sixth edition, corrected*, R. Pheney, London, 1793.

Burchell, Joseph, *Arrangement and Digest of the Law in Cases Adjudged in the King's Bench and Common Pleas from the Year 1756 to 1794, inclusive*, T. Jones, London, 1796.

Buret, Antoine Eugène, *De la Misère des classes labourieuses en Angleterre et en France*, 2 vols., privately printed, Paris, 1840.

Burke, Edmund, *Thoughts and Details on Scarcity, Originally presented to the Right. Hon. William Pitt, in the Month of November, 1795*, J. F. and C. Rivington, London, 1800.

Burn, Richard, *The History of the Poor Laws: With Observations* (1764), Augustus M. Kelly, Clifton NJ, 1973.

The Justice of the Peace and Parish Officer... In Four Volumes, 15th edn, A. Strahan and W. Woodfall, London, 1785.

Blank Precedents Relating to the Office of Justice of the Peace, Settled by Doctor Burn, and printed for by the King's Law-Printers..., T. Cadell, London, 1787.

A New Law Dictionary. Intended for General use, as well as for Gentlemen of the Profession, Continued to the Present Time by his Son, John Burn, 2 vols., Strahan and Woodfall, London, 1792.

The Justice of the Peace and Parish Officer. Continued to the Present Time by John Burn, Esq. his Son, 17th edn, 4 vols., A. Strahan and W. Woodfall, London, 1793.

The Justice of the Peace and Parish Officer, 19th edn, 4 vols., T. Cadell, W. Davies, J. Butterworth, 1800.

Burrow, James, *Reports of Cases adjudged in the Court of King's Bench, since the Death of Lord Raymond, in March 1732, to June 1776, inclusive, during which Time Lord Hardwick, Dudley Ryder, and Lord Mansfield presided...*, 2nd edn, 5 vols., London, 1790.

Caldecott, Thomas, *Reports of Cases Relative to the Duty and Office of a Justice of the Peace, from Michaelmas Term 1776, inclusive, to Trinity Term 1785, inclusive*, Strahan, London, 1785.

Candidus, *A Letter to Philo Africanus upon Slavery, in Answer to his of the 22nd November in the General Evening Post; together with the Opinions of Sir John Strange, and other Lawyers upon the Subject, with the Sentence of Lord Mansfield in the Case of Somerset and Knowles...*, W. Brown, London, 1788.

Cantillon, Richard, *Essai sur la nature du commerce en général. Traduit de l'anglois*, chez Fletcher Gyles, Paris, 1755, trans. H. Higgs (ed.), Macmillan, London, 1931.

Carter, Susannah, *The Frugal Housewife, or, Complete Woman Cook. Wherein the art of dressing all sorts of viands with cleanliness, decency and elegance, is explained in five hundred approved receipts... To which are added twelve new prints, exhibiting a proper arrangement of dinners, two courses for every month in the year*, E. Newbery, London, 1795.

Caulfield, James, *Blackguardiana: or, a Dictionary of Rogues, Bawds, Pimps, Whores, Pickpockets, Shoplifters... Illustrated with eighteen Portraits of the most remarkable Professors in every Species of Villainy. Interspersed with many Curious*

Anecdotes, Cant Terms, Flash Songs, &c. The whole intended to put Society on their Guard against Depredators, printed for the author, Bagshot, 1793.

Chubbe, William, *A Few Words to the Labourers of Great-Britain*, R. Loder, Woodbridge, 1793.

Clapham, Samuel, *A Collection of Several Points of Sessions Law, Alphabetically Arranged*, 2 vols., Butterworth and Clarke, London, 1818.

Clarkson, Thomas, *An Essay on the Slavery and Commerce of the Human Species, particularly the African, translated from a Latin Dissertation, which was honoured with the first Prize in the University of Cambridge, for the year 1785*, T. Cadell and J. Phillips, London, 1786.

Cole, Mary, *The Lady's Complete Guide; or Cookery and Confectionary in all their Branches*, G. Kearsley, London, 1789.

Colquhoun, Patrick, *A Treatise on Indigence; Exhibiting a General View of the National Resource for Productive Labour...*, J. Hatchard, London, 1806.

Commissioners of Excise, *Abstract of Cases and Decisions on Appeals Relating to the Tax on Servants*, T. Longman and T. Cadell, London, 1781.

Const, Francis, *Decisions of the Court of the King's Bench, Upon the Laws Relating to the Poor, Originally Published by Edmund Bott Esq. of the Inner Temple, Barrister at Law. Revised... by Francis Cost Esq. of the Middle Temple*, 3rd edn, 2 vols., Whieldon and Butterworth, London, 1793.

Cooper, Thomas, *Letters on the Slave Trade: first published in Wheeler's Manchester Chronicle; and since re-printed with additions and alterations*, C. Wheeler, Manchester, 1787.

Country Curate, *Directions to all Masters and Mistresses of Families, and to their Sons and Daughters, in several Chapters, containing their Duties in their various Stations of Life*, M. Cooper, London, 1746.

Country Magistrate (Samuel Glasse), *The Magistrate's Assistant; or, a Summary of Those Laws which immediately respect the Conduct of a Justice of the Peace: to the end of the Fifth Session of the Sixteenth Parliament of Great-Britain, viz., to July 12, 1788*, 2nd edn, R. Raikes, Gloucester, 1788.

County Magistrate, *A Letter addressed to the Agriculturalists in general, and to the Magistrates and Clergy in particular throughout the Kingdom, on the Subjects of Hiring, Service and Character*, Longman and Whittaker, London, 1821.

Crunden, John, *Convenient and Ornamental Architecture, consisting of Original Design, for Plans, Elevations and Sections; beginning with the Farm House, and regularly ascending to the grand and magnificent Villa...*, Henry Webley, London, 1767.

Dalton, Michael, *The Country Justice. Containing the Practice, Duty and Power of the Justices of the Peace, as well as in as out of their Sessions*, Henry Lintot, London, 1742.

Davies, David, *The Case of Labourers in Husbandry Stated and Considered in three Parts*, G. G. and J. Robinson, London, 1795.

Davy, Humphrey, *Elements of Agricultural Chemistry, in a Course of Lectures for the Board of Agriculture*, Longman, Hurst, Rees, Orme and Brown, London, 1813.

Day, Thomas, *Dialogue between a Justice of the Peace and a Farmer*, 2nd edn, John Stockdale, London, 1785.

Dogherty, Thomas, *The Crown Circuit Assistant: being a Collection of Precedents of Indictments, Informations, . . . in criminal and penal Proceedings*, London, 1787.

Douglas, Sylvester, *Report of Cases Argued and Determined in the Court of the King's Bench*, vol. 4 (1784–5), Sweet and Stevens, London, Milliken, Dublin, 1831.

Durnford, Charles and Edward Hyde East, *Term Reports in the Court of the King's Bench*, vol. 7 (1794–6), Butterworth and Cooke, London and Dublin, 1817.

Eden, Frederic Morton, *The State of the Poor: or, an History of the Labouring Classes in England, from the Conquest to the Present Period; . . . together with Parochial Reports . . . In three volumes*, B. and J. White; G. G. and J. Robinson; T. Payne and others, London, 1797.

Ellis, William, *The Modern Husbandman, complete in eight volumes*, published for the author, London, 1750.

Emerson, William, *Mechanics; or, the Doctrine of Motion*, J. Nourse, London, 1769.

The Principles of Mechanics. Explaining and demonstrating the general Laws of Motion . . . A Work very necessary to be had by all Gentlemen . . . and extremely useful to all sorts of Artificers, 5th edn, G. Robinson, London, 1800.

Encyclopaedia Britannica; or, a Dictionary of Arts and Sciences, Compiled Upon a New Plan, Edinburgh, 1771.

Ferguson, Adam, *An Essay on the History of Civil Society*, Boulter Grierson, Dublin, 1767.

Ferguson, James, 'Useful Projects' in *Annual Register, or a View of the History, Politics, for the year 1771*, 4th edn, J. Dodsley, London, 1786.

Lectures on Select Subjects in Mechanics, Hydrostatics, Hydraulics, Pneumatics and Optics, 8th edn, T. Longman, London, 1793.

The Principles of Mechanics. Explaining and demonstrating the general Laws of Motion . . . A work very necessary to be had by all gentlemen . . . and extremely useful to all sorts of articers [sic], 5th edn, G. Robinson, London, 1800.

Fielding, John, *A Plan of the Universal Register-Office, Opposite Cecil-Street in the Strand & of That in Bishops Gate-Street the Corner of Cornhill. Both by the Same Proprietors*, privately printed, London, 1752.

Fordyce, David, *The Elements of Moral Philosophy. In Three Books*, R. and J. Dodsley, London, 1754.

[Fordyce, David], 'Moral Philosophy' in *The Preceptor: containing a general Course of Education. Wherein the first Principles of Polite Learning are laid down in a Way most suitable for trying the Genius, and advancing the Instruction of Youth. In twelve parts*, 5th edn, 2 vols., J. Dodsley, London, 1769, vol. 2, p. 315.

Fothergill, A. *Cautions to the Heads of Families, in three Essays: I. On Cyder-Wine, prepared in Copper Vessels; with Hints for the Improvement of Cyder, Perry, and other Fruit Liquors. II. On the Poison of Lead – Method of Detecting it in various Liquors, Foods, Medicines, Cosmetiks &c. with general Indications of Cure. III. On the Poison of Copper – How it may be discovered though in very minute Quantity – Methods of Cure*, R. Cruttwell, Bath, 1790.

Gentleman of Experience, *The Economist. Shewing, in a variety of Estimates, from Fourscore Pounds a Year to upwards of £800, how comfortably and genteely a*

Family may live with Frugality for a little Money, 15th edn, privately printed, London, 1781.

Gentleman of the Inner Temple, *Laws Concerning Master and Servants*, W. Owen, London, 1767.

Law Concerning Master and Servants, Viz Clerks to Attornies and Solicitors . . . Apprentices . . . Menial Servants . . . Labourers, Journeymen, Artificers, Handicraftmen and other Workmen, His Majesty's Law Printer, London, 1785.

A Concise Abstract of the most important Clauses in the following interesting acts of Parliament, passed in the Session of 1785 . . ., J. Walker, London, 1785.

Gilbert, Thomas, *A Plan of Police: exhibiting the Causes of the present Increase of the Poor, and proposing a Mode for their future more effectual Relief and Support*, privately printed, London, 1781.

A Bill, intended to be Offered to Parliament, for the better Relief and Employment of the Poor, and for the Improvement of the Police of this Country, Harrop, Manchester, 1787.

Gisborne, Thomas, *The Principles of Moral Philosophy Investigated, and briefly applied to the Constitution of Civil Society: together with Remarks . . .*, The second edition, corrected and enlarged, B. White, London, 1790.

An Inquiry into the Duties of Men in the Higher and Middle Classes of Society in Great Britain, Resulting from their Respective Stations, Professions and Employments, 2nd edn, 2 vols., B. and J. White, London, 1795.

Glasse, Hannah, *A Servant's Directory, or House-keeper's Companion Wherein the Duties of Chamber-maid, House-maid, Laundry-maid, Scullion or Under-cook, Are fully and distinctly explained. To which is annexed a Diary, or House-keeper's Pocket Book for the Whole Year with Directions for keeping Accounts with Tradesmen, and many other Particulars, fit to be known by the Mistress of a Family*, W. Johnson, London, 1760.

Godschall, William Man, *A General Plan of Parochial and Provincial Police*, T. Payne, London, 1787.

Godwin, William, *The Enquirer. Reflections on Education, Manners, and Literature. In a Series of Essays*, G. G. and J. Robinson, London, 1797.

Good, John Mason, *Dissertation on the best Means of Maintaining and Employing the Poor in Parish Work-houses. Published at the Request of the Society for the Encouragement of Arts, Manufactures, and Commerce: having obtained the Premium offered by the Society for the best Treatise on this Subject*, Cadell and Davis and Morton, London, 1798.

Greig, John, *The Young Lady's New Guide to Arithmetic. Being a short and useful Selection, containing, besides the common and necessary Rules, the Application of each Rule, by a Variety of Practical Questions, chiefly on Domestic Affairs . . .*, 2nd edn, privately printed, London, 1800.

Gronniosaw, James Albert, *A Narrative of the most remarkable Particulars in the Life of James Albert Ukawsaw Gronniosaw, an African Prince, as related by Himself*, S. Hazard, Bath, T. Mills, Bristol, S. Chirm, London, W. Walker, Ashburn, [1780?].

Hanway, Joseph, *Virtue in Humble Life; containing Reflections on the Reciprocal Duties of the Wealthy and the Indigent, the Master and the Servant: Thoughts on the various Situations, Passions, Prejudices, and Virtues of Mankind, drawn from real Characters: Fables applicable to the Subjects: Anecdotes of the Living and the Dead: the Result of long Experience and Observation. In a Dialogue between a Father and his Daughter, in rural Scenes. A Manual of Devotion, comprehending Extracts from Eminent Poets. In two Volumes*, J. Dodley, Brotherton and Sewell, London, 1774.

Harcourt, Leverson Vernon, *The Diaries and Correspondence of the Right Hon. George Rose. Containing Original Letters of the most distinguished Statesmen of his Day. In Two Volumes*, Richard Bentley, London, 1860.

Harris, Raymund, *Scriptural Researches on the Licitness of the Slave-trade, shewing its Conformity with the Principles of Natural and Revealed Religion, delineated in the Sacred Writings of the Word of God*, John Stockdale, London, 1788.

Haweis, Thomas, *Hints Respecting the Poor: submitted to the Consideration of the Humane and Intelligent*, C. Dilly, London, 1788.

Hayes, Richard, *Interest at one View, calculated to a Farthing: at 2$^{1}/_{2}$, 3, 3$^{1}/_{2}$, 4, 5, 6, 7, and 8 per cent. For 1000£. to 1£. for 1 day to 96 days;... The fifteenth edition, with additions. Carefully calculated and examined from the press by Richard Hayes*, G. Keith, London, 1771.

Heathcote, Ralph, *The Irenach: or, Justice of the Peace's Manual. II Miscellaneous Reflections upon Laws, Policy, Manners &etc &etc. In a Dedication to William Lord Mansfield. III An Assize Sermon Preached at Leicester, 12 Aug. 1756*, privately printed, London, 1781.

Henderson, William Augustus, *The Housekeeper's Instructor; or, Universal Family Cook*, 5th edn, W. and J. Stratford, London, 1795.

Holliday, John, *The Life of William Late Earl of Mansfield*, P. Elmsly and D. Bremner, London, 1797.

Hughes, William, *A Discourse in Favour of the Abolition of Slavery in the British West Indies. Preached on the first Sunday in Lent, in the Parish Church of Ware, Herts.*, T. Cadell, London, 1788.

An Answer to the Rev. Mr Harris's 'Scriptural Researches....', T. Cadell, London, 1788.

Huntingford, James, *An Account of the Proceedings, Intentions, Rules, & Orders of the Society for the Encouragement of Agriculture and Industry, instituted at Odiham in Hampshire. To which is added, A List of the Society's Premiums, the Society's Queries, and the Names of Servants that have obtained Certificates of Good Characters...*, Frys and Couchman, London, 1785 (1786).

Huntingford, John, *The Laws of Masters and Servants Considered; with Observations on a Bill intended to be offered to Parliament, to prevent the forging and counter-feiting of Certificates of Servants [sic] Characters. To which is added an Account of a Society formed for the Encrease and Encouragement of Good Servants*, privately printed, London, 1792.

Hutchinson, Peter O., *The Diary and Letters of Thomas Hutchinson. Compiled from the Original Documents*, Sampson and Low, 2 vols., London, 1883–6.

Imlay, Gilbert, *A Topographical Description of the Western Territory of North America: containing a succinct Account of its Soil, Climate, Natural History, Population, Agriculture, Manners, Customs... to which are added, the Discovery, Settlement, and present State of Kentucky, and an Essay towards the Topography and Natural History of that important Country by John Filson, to which is* added, I. The Adventures of Col. Daniel Boone... II. The Minutes of the Piankashaw Council... III. An Account of the Indian Nations inhabiting within the Limits of the thirteen United States... by George [i.e. Gilbert] Imlay, 2nd edn, J. Debrett, London, 1793.

Impey, John, The Practice of the Office of Sherrif... also The Practice of the Office of Coroner... with a Copious Appendix of Useful Precedents, 5th edn, J. and W. T. Clarke, London, 1822.

Jackson, William, The New and complete Newgate Calendar; or, Villany displayed in all its Branches.... containing the most faithful Narratives ever yet published of the various Executions, and other exemplary punishments,... from the year 1700, to the end of the Year 1795, 6 vols., Alexander Hogg, London, 1795.

J. B., Brother of the Cloath, The Footmans Looking-glass; or, Proposals to the Livery Servants of London and Westminster, &c. for bettering their Situations in Life, and securing their Credit in the World. To which is added, an humble Representation to Masters and Mistresses, M. Cooper, London, 1747.

Jenks, Benjamin, The Glorious Victory of Chastity, in Joseph's Hard Conflict, and His Happy Escape, while he was a Servant unto Potiphar, an Officer of Pharoah's, in Egypt, W. Rogers and B. Tooke, London, 1707.

Johnson, Mary, Madam Johnson's Present: or every Young Woman's Companion, in Useful and Universal Knowledge, 4th edn, W. Nicholl, London, 1766.

Jones, Charles, The History of Charles Jones, the Footman. Written by Himself, J. Marshall, London, 1796.

Latham, Frank, The Sanitation of Domestic Buildings, Sanitary Publishing Company, London, 1898.

Locke, John, An Essay Concerning Human Understanding. In four books (1689), 7th edn, J. Churchill; and Samuel Manship, London, 1715–16.
    Two Treatise on Government (1689), Dent, London, 1993.
    Two Treatises of Government (1690), Cambridge University Press, Cambridge, 1993.
    Some Thoughts Concerning Education, A. and J. Churchill, London, 1693.
    Some Thoughts concerning Education, 10th edn, George Risk and others, Dublin, 1737.

Maddock, James, The Florist's Directory; or a Treatise on the Culture of Flowers: to which is added A supplementary Dissertation on Soils, Manures etc, privately printed, London, 1792.

Marshall, John, Five Cases of Recovery from the Effects of Arsenic..., privately printed, London, 1815.
    Remarks on Arsenic, considered as a Poison and a Medicine..., Callow, London, 1817.

Marx, Karl, 'Wage Labour and Capital' (1849), Karl Marx and Frederick Engels, Selected Works. In Two Volumes, Progress Press, Moscow, 1962.
    'The Eighteenth Brumaire of Louis Bonaparte' (1859) in David McLellan (ed.), Selected Writings, Oxford University Press, Oxford, 1977.

Matthews, John, A Voyage to the River Sierra-Leone on the Coast of Africa,... With an Additional Letter on the Subject of the Slave Trade, White, London, 1791.

Metyard, Sarah, *The Last dying Speech (and last Farewell to the World) of Sarah Metyard, and her own Daughter Sarah Morgan Metyard*, n.i., London, 1762.

Mickleborough, John, *The Great Duty of Labour and Work, and the Necessity there is at present for agreeing and fixing upon some Plan for a general Workhouse for the Poor of this Place; Urged and Illustrated in a Sermon before the Corporation of Cambridge in the Parish Church of St. Andrew the Great January 27 AD 1751*, J. Bentham, Cambridge, 1751.

Middleton, Erasmus, *The New Complete Dictionary of Arts and Sciences*, 2 vols., privately printed, London, 1778.

Millar, John, *The Origin of the Distinction of Ranks; or, An Inquiry into the Circumstances which give Rise to Influence and Authority in the Different Members of Society*, 3rd edn, John Murray, London, 1781.

Montagu, James, *The Old Bailey Chronicle; containing a circumstantial Account of the Lives, Trials, and Confessions of the most notorious Offenders*, 4 vols., London, 1788.

Moss, Hugh, *Essay on the Management, Nursing and Diseases of Children*, 2nd edn, C. Boult, London, 1794.

Neale, Erskine, *Experiences of a Gaol Chaplain; comprising Recollections of Ministerial Intercourse with Criminals of Various Classes, with their Confessions*, 3 vols., Richard Bentley, London, 1847.

Neild, James, *Account of the Rise Progress, and Present State of the Society for the Discharge and Relief of Persons Imprisoned for Small Debts throughout England*, privately printed, London, 1802.

State of the Prisons in England, Scotland and Wales . . . not for the Debtor only, but for Felons also . . . , J. Nichols, London, 1812.

Nolan, Michael, *A Treatise of the Laws for the Settlement of the Poor*, 2 vols., J. Butterworth, London, 1805.

Oswestry Society for Bettering the Condition and Increasing the Comforts of the Poor, *The Family Receipt Book, or, the Cottager's Cook, Doctor, and Friend*, privately printed, Oswestry, 1817.

Pain, William, *Pain's British Palladi: or the Builder's General Assistant . . .* , William and James Pain, London, 1788.

Parker, Thomas N., *An Essay on the Construction, Hanging and Fastening of Gates*, 2nd edn, Lackington, Allen, London, 1804.

Parkes, Mrs William, *Domestic Duties; or, Instructions to Young Married Ladies, on the Management of their Households, and the Regulation of their Conduct in the Various Relations and Duties of Married Life*, Longman, Hurst, Rees, Orme, Brown and Green, London, 1825.

Parkyns, Thomas, *A Method Proposed, For the Recording of Servants in Husbandry, Arts, Mysteries, &etc.*, printed for the author, London, 1724.

Pashley, Robert, *Pauperism and Poor Laws*, Longman Brown Green and Longman, London, 1852.

Pearson, Richard, *An Account of a particular Preparation of Salted Fish to be used with Boiled Rice, or Potatoes, for the purpose of lessening the Consumption of Wheaten Bread*, Rivington, Reading, 1812.

Peckham, Ann, *The Complete English Cook; or, Prudent Housewife*, 2nd edn, Griffith Wright for the author, Leeds, 1771.

Philo-Africanus, *A Letter to Wm. Wilberforce*, J. Debrett, London, 1790.

Piozzi, Hester Lynch, *Anecdotes of the Late Samuel Johnson, LL.D during the last Twenty years of his Life*, Moncrieffe, White, Byrne, Cash, W. Porter and others, Dublin, 1786.

Potter, R. *Observations on the Poor Laws, on the Present State of the Poor, and on Houses of Industry*, J. Wilkie, London, 1775.

Poulter, Edmund, *Address and Report on the Enquiry into the General State of the Poor. Instituted by Order of the last Epiphany General Quarter Session for the County of Hampshire*, Robbins, Winchester, 1795.

Powell, John, *A View of Real Grievances: or a Dissertation Upon the State of the Poor in this Kingdom, Shewing by what Means the Poor Rates have grown to such enormous Heights, with Remedies proposed for redressing them*, 2nd edn, W. Whittingham, London, 1786.

Priestley, Joseph, *A Sermon on the Subject of the Slave Trade; delivered to a Society of Protestant Dissenters, at the New Meeting, in Birmingham; and published at their Request*, Pearson and Rollason, Birmingham, 1788.

Raffald, Elizabeth, *The Experienced English Housekeeper, for the Use and Ease of Ladies, Housekeepers, Cooks, &c*, 2nd edn, R. Baldwin for the Author, London, 1771.

The Experienced English Housekeeper, 8th edn, R. Baldwin, London, 1782.

Ramsay, James, *An Essay on the Treatment and Conversion of African Slaves in the British Sugar Colonies*, James Phillips, London, 1784.

Robinson, Robert, *Slavery Inconsistent with the Spirit of Christianity. A Sermon preached at Cambridge, on Sunday, Feb. 10, 1788*, Robbinson, Bowtell and Cowper, Cambridge; Dilly, London, 1788.

Rolleston, Samuel, *A Philosophical Dialogue concerning Decency. To which is added a critical and historical Dissertation on Places of Retirement for necessary Occasions... By the Author of the Dissertation on Barley Wine*, James Fletcher, Oxford, London, 1751.

Roscoe, William, *A General View of the African Slave-trade, demonstrating its Injustice and Impolicy: with Hints towards a Bill for its Abolition*, R. Faulder, London, 1788.

Rose, George, *A Brief Examination into the Increase of the Revenue, Commerce and Navigation of Great Britain, from 1792 to 1799*, Graisberry and Campbell, Dublin, 1799.

Rousseau, Jean-Jacques, *A Discourse on Inequality* (1755), Penguin, Harmondsworth, 1984.

On the Origin of Language: Two essays, Jean Jacques Rousseau and Johann Gottfried Herder (Rousseau, 1781), University of Chicago Press Chicago, 1966.

Ruggles, Thomas, *The History of the Poor; their Rights, Duties, and the Laws respecting Them*, 2 vols., J. Deighton, London, 1793.

The History of the Poor; their Rights, Duties, and the Laws Respecting Them. A New Edition Corrected, and continued to the present Time, W. Richardson, 2 vols., London, 1797.

Rumford, Benjamin, Count of, *Essays, Political, Economical and Philosophical*, vol. 1, T. Cadell, London, 1796.

Sabatier, William, *A Treatise on Poverty, its Consequences and Remedies*, John Stockdale, London, 1797.

Scott, John, *Observations on the Present State of the Parochial and Vagrant Poor*, Dilly, London, 1773.

Sharp, Granville, *A Representation of the Injustice and Dangerous Tendency of Tolerating Slavery; or of Admitting the Least Claim of Private Property in the Persons of Men, in England. In four parts*, Benjamin White and Robert, London, 1769.

Serious Reflections on the Slave Trade. Wrote in March 1797, W. Calvert, London, 1785.

Short Sketch of Temporary Regulations (until better shall be proposed) for the intended Settlement on the Grain Coast of Africa, near Sierra Leona, H. Baldwin, London, 1786.

Sheppard, William, *A Grand Abridgment of the Common and Statute Law of England alphabetically digested under proper heads . . .* , Richard and Edward Atkyns, London, 1675.

Simpson, David, *A Discourse on Dreams and Night Visions, with numerous Examples Ancient and Modern*, Edward Bayley, Macclesfield, 1791.

Sinclair, John, *The History of the Public Revenue of the British Empire. Containing an Account of the Public Income and Expenditure from the remotest Periods recorded in History, to Michaelmas 1802. With a Review of the Financial Administration of the Right Honourable William Pitt*, A. Strahan, London, 1803–4.

Smee, John, *A Complete Collection of Abstracts of Acts of Parliament and Cases with Opinions of the Judges upon the following Taxes Viz, upon Houses, Windows, Servants . . .* , 2 vols., J. Butterworth, London, 1797.

Smith, Adam, *The Wealth of Nations: Books I–III* (1776), Penguin, London, 1986.

Smith, Hugh, *Letters to Married Women, on Nursing and the Management of Children*, 6th ed, C. and G. Kearsley, London, 1792.

Smith, Samuel Stanhope, *An Essay on the Causes of the Variety of Complexion and Figure in the Human Species. To which are Added, Strictures on Lord Kames's Discourse on the original Diversity of Mankind. A new edition. With some additional Notes, by a gentleman of the University of Edinburgh*, Philadelphia printed and Edinburgh reprinted, for C. Elliot; and C. Elliot and T. Kay, London, 1788.

Smollett, Tobias, *The Miscellaneous Works of Tobias Smollett, M. D. with Memoirs of his Life and Writings*, 2nd edn, Robert Anderson (ed.), 6 vols., Mundell, Edinburgh, 1800.

Society for Bettering the Condition of the Poor, *Information for Cottagers, Collected from the Reports of the Society . . .* , privately printed, London, 1800.

Spike, Edward, *The Law of Master and Servant in regard to Domestic Servants and Clerks. Chiefly Designed for the Use of Families*, Shaw, London, 1839.

Stevens, George Alexander, *A Lecture on Heads with Additions by Mr. Pilon; as delivered by Mr. Charles Lee Lewis . . . To which is added An Essay on Satire*, William Lane, London, 1795.

Stewart, Duguld, *Elements of the Philosophy of the Human Mind*, 3 vols., A. Strahan and T. Cadell, London and W. Creech, Edinburgh, 1792–1827.

Swift, Jonathan, *Polite Conversation, consisting of smart, witty, droll, and whimsical Sayings collected for his Amusement, and made into a regular Dialogue*, Joseph Wenman, London, 1783.

Symmons, John, *Thoughts on the Present Price of Provisions, their Causes and Remedies; addressed to all ranks of people. By an Independent Gentleman*, T. Reynolds, London, 1800.

Taylor, Anne, *The Present of a Mother to a Young Servant: Consisting of Friendly Advice and Real Histories*, 2nd edn, Taylor and Hessey, London, 1816.

Taylor, John, *Elements of the Civil Law*, privately printed, Cambridge, 1767.

Theobald, John, *The Young Wife's Guide, in the Management of her Children*, W. Griffin and G. Kearsley, London, 1764.

Thompson, Jonathan, *The Commutation Act candidly considered, in its Principles and Operations. To which is annexed, an Address to the Freeholders of Northumberland, assembled in the Town-Hall, in Morpeth, January 21 1789 . . . addressed to Gawen Aynsley, Esq.*, T. Reynolds, London, 1800.

Townsend, Joseph, *A Guide to Health; being Cautions and Directions in the Treatment of Diseases*, Cox, London, 1795, p. 317.

Trusler, John, *The Way to be Rich and Respectable, addressed to Men of small Fortune*, 6th edn, privately printed, London, 1787.

Trusler's Domestic Management, or the Art of Conducting a Family, with Economy Frugality & Method, J. Souter, London, 1819.

Vancouver, George, *A Voyage of Discovery to the North Pacific Ocean, and round the World*, John Vancouver (ed.), 3 vols., G. G. and J. Robinson, London, 1798.

Vancouver, John, *An Enquiry into the Causes and Production of Poverty, and the State of the Poor: together with the proposed Means for their Effectual Relief*, R. Edwards, London, 1796.

Villette, John, *The Annals of Newgate; or, Malefactors Register. Containing a particular and circumstantial Account of the Lives, Transactions, and Trials of the . . .* , 4 vols., J. Wenman, London, 1776.

Wade, John, *History of the Middle and Working Classes: with a popular Exposition of the economical and political Principles which have influenced the past and present Condition of the Industrious Orders*, E. Wilson, London, 1833.

Walker, Ann, *A Complete Guide for a Servant Maid; or, the Sure Means of Gaining Love and Esteem*, T. Sabine, London, 1787.

Waller, George, *Abstract of the several Acts of Parliament passed in this Kingdom from the 33d of His late Majesty King George the 2d. for the better regulating the Collection of the Revenue, and for preventing of Frauds therein*, George Grierson, Dublin, 1784.

Watkins, John, *The Important Results of an Elabourate Investigation . . .* , William Hone, London, 1815.

West Indian (Samuel Estwick LL.D), *Considerations on the Negroe Cause, Commonly so Called. Addressed to the Right Honourable Lord Mansfield. Lord Chief Justice of the Court of the King's Bench, &c. By a West Indian*, J. Dodsley, London, 1772.

West-India Planter, *Considerations on the State of the Sugar Islands, and on the Policy of enabling Foreigners to lend Money on real Securities in those Colonies. In a Letter addressed to the Right Hon. Lord North; by a West-India Planter*, S. Bladon, London, 1773.

Considerations on the Emancipation of Negroes and on the Abolition of the Slave-trade, J. Johnson and J. Debrett, London, 1788.

Williams, Thomas Walter, *The Whole Law Relative to the Duty and Office of a Justice of the Peace*, 4 vols., John Stockdale, London, 1812.

Wingrave, John, *A Narrative of the many horrid Cruelties inflicted by Elizabeth Brownrigg upon the Body of Mary Clifford, deceased; and for which the said Elizabeth received Sentence of Death, on Saturday the 12th of September 1767*, privately printed, London, 1767.

Witherspoon, John, *The History of a Corporation of Servants. Discovered a few Years ago in the Interior Parts of South America. Containing some very surprising Events and Extraordinary Characters*, John Gilmour, Glasgow, 1765.

Wollstonecraft, Mary, *Thoughts on the Education of Daughters: with Reflections on Female Conduct, in the more important Duties of Life*, Joseph Johnson, London, 1787.

Wood, I. *A Letter to Sir William Pulteney Bart . . . containing some Observations on the Bill . . . presented to the House of Commons by the Right Honourable William Pitt*, privately printed, Shrewsbury, 1797.

Wright, Mrs, *An Essay to Instruct Women how to Protect themselves in a State of Pregnancy . . . Also, Some Observations on the Treatment of Children, which, if attended to, may ward off Dangerous Disease, and prevent future Evils*, privately printed, London, 1798.

Zouch, Henry, *Hints Respecting the Public Police, Published at the Request of the Court of Quarter Sessions held at Pontefract, April 24, 1786*, John Stockdale, London, 1786.

SECONDARY SOURCES

Adams, Gene, 'Dido Elizabeth Belle. A black girl at Kenwood: An account of a protegée of the 1st Lord Mansfield', *Camden History Review*, 12 (1984), 10–14.

Allen, Margaret, 'Frances Hamilton of Bishops Lydeard', *Notes and Queries for Somerset and Dorset*, 31 (1983), 259–72.

Anderson, Bridget, *Doing the Dirty Work? The Global Politics of Domestic Labour*, Zed Books, London, 2000.

Armstrong, Frances, 'Gender and miniaturization: Games of littleness in nineteenth-century fiction', *English Studies in Canada*, 16 (1990), 403–16.

Bailey, Margaret (ed.), *Boswell's Column: Being his seventy contributions to the London Magazine, under the pseudonym The Hypochondriac from 1777–1783*, William Kimber, London, 1951.

Balderson, Katharine C. (ed.), *The Diary of Mrs Hester Lynch Thrale (Later Mrs Piozzi) 1778–1809* (1941), 2 vols., Clarendon Press, Oxford, 1951.

Bate, Jonathan, *John Clare*, Picador, London, 2003.

Batt, John, '"United to Support But Not Combined to Injure": Public order, trade unions and the repeal of the Combination Acts of 1799–1800', *International Review of Social History*, 31:2 (1986), 185–203.

Beattie, J. M. *Crime and the Courts in England, 1660–1800*, Clarendon Press, Oxford, 1986.

Beckett, J. V. 'Land tax or excise: The levying of taxation in seventeenth- and eighteenth-century England', *English Historical Review*, 100 (1985), 285–308.

Beckett, J. V. and Michael Turner, 'Taxation and economic growth in eighteenth-century England', *Economic History Review*, 43: 3 (1990), 377–403.

Bendix, Reinhard, 'Inequality and social structure: A comparison of Marx and Weber', *American Sociological Review*, 39: 2 (1974), 149–61.

Berg, Maxine, *The Age of Manufactures, 1700–1820*, Fontana, London, 1985.
Luxury and Pleasure in Eighteenth-century Britain, Oxford University Press, Oxford, 2005.

Berg, Maxine, and Helen Clifford (ed.), *Consumers and Luxury: Consumer culture in Europe 1650–1850*, Manchester University Press, Manchester, 1999.

Berry, Christopher, *The Idea of Luxury: A conceptual and historical investigation*, Cambridge University Press, Cambridge, 1994.

Biernacki, Richard, *The Fabrication of Labour: Germany and Britain, 1640–1914*, University of California Press Berkeley, Los Angeles and London, 1995.

Birch, William Russell, *The Life of William Russell Birch, Enamel Painter, Written by Himself*, privately printed, Philadelphia, 1927.

Blackburn, Robin, *The Making of New World Slavery: From the baroque to the modern, 1492–1800*, Verso, London and New York, 1997.

Block, Fred and Margaret Somers, 'In the shadow of Speenhamland: Social policy and the old poor law', *Politics and Society*, 31:2 (2003), 283–323.

Bloom, Edward A. and Bloom, Lillian D. *The Piozzi Letters: Correspondence of Hester Lynch Piozzi, 1784–1821 (formerly Mrs Thrale)*, 3 vols., University of Delaware Press: Associated University Press, Cranbery NJ, 1989–93.

Bloomington, Anne, *The Clifton Dynasty: A chronicle of the Cliftons of Clifton Hall, Nottinghamshire*, Authorhouse, Bloomington, IA, 2005.

Branch-Johnson, W. *The Carrington Diary, 1797–1810*, Christopher Johnson, London, 1956.

Branwell, Eric Benjamin, *The Ludford Journals of Ansley Hall*, privately printed, no place of publication, 1988.

Braverman, Harry, *Labor and Monopoly Capitalism: The degradation of work in the twentieth century*, Monthly Review Press, New York and London, 1974.

Brewer, John, *The Sinews of Power: War, money and the English state, 1688–1783*, Unwin Hyman, London, 1989.
Pleasures of the Imagination: English culture in the eighteenth century, Harper Collins, London, 1997.

Brissenden, R. F. *Virtue in Distress: Studies in the novel of sentiment from Richardson to de Sade*, Macmillan, London, 1974.

Brown, Ernest Henry Phelps and Sheila V. Hopkins, *A Perspective of Wages and Prices*, Methuen, 1981.

Brown, Richard, 'Work histories, career strategies and the class structure' in Anthony Giddens and Gavin MacKensie (eds), *Social Class and the Division of Labour*, Cambridge University Press, Cambridge, 1982, pp. 119–36.

Brown, Susan E. 'Assessing men and maids: The female servant tax and meanings of productive labour in late-eighteenth-century Britain', *Left History*, 12:2 (2008), 11–32.

Bryceson, Deborah Fahy and Ulla Vuovela, 'Outside the domestic labour debate: Towards a theory of modes of human reproduction', *Review of Radical Political Economies*, 16:2/3 (1984), 137–66.

Burke, Tim (ed.), *Eighteenth-Century Labouring Class Poets*, vol. III, *1700–1800*, Pickering and Chatto, London, 2003.

Burnette, Joyce, 'An investigation of the female-male wage gap during the Industrial Revolution in Britain', *Economic History Review*, 2nd ser., 50 (1997), 257–81.

'The wages and employment of female day-labourers in English agriculture,1740–1850', *Economic History Review*, 57:4 (2004), 664–90.

Burney, Ian A. *Poison, Detection and the Victorian Imagination*, Manchester University Press, Manchester, 2007.

Burton, Elizabeth, *The Georgians at Home, 1741–1830*, Longman, London, 1967.

Cardwell, D. S. L. *From Watt to Clausius: The rise of thermodynamics in the early industrial age*, Heinemann, London, 1971.

Carpenter, Kenneth J. *Protein and Energy: A study of changing ideas in nutrition*, Cambridge University Press, Cambridge, 1994.

Casswell, J. D. *The Law of Domestic Servants: With a chapter on the National Insurance Act, 1911*, Jordan, London, 1913.

Caunce, Stephen, 'Farm servants and the development of capitalism in English agriculture', *Agricultural History Review*, 45 (1997), 49–60.

Chappell, Vere (ed.), *The Cambridge Companion to Locke*, Cambridge University Press, Cambridge, 1999.

Chartier, Roger, 'Labourers and voyagers: From the text to the reader', *Diacritics*, 22;2 (1992), 49–61.

Christmas, William J. *The Lab'ring Muse: Work, writing and the social order in English plebeian poetry, 1730–1830*, University of Delaware Press, Newark, 2001.

Christopher, Emma, *Slave Ship Sailors and Their Captive Cargoes, 1730–1807*, Cambridge University Press, Cambridge, 2006.

Cirket, Alan F. (ed.), *Samuel Whitbread's Notebooks, 1810–11, 1813–14*, Bedfordshire Historical Record Society, Ampthill, 1971.

Clanchy, Kate, *What Is She Doing Here? A refugee's story*, Picador, London, 2008.

Clark, Anna, *The Struggle for the Breeches: Gender and the making of the British working class*, University of California Press, Berkeley, Los Angeles and London, 1995.

'The Chevalier d'Eon and Wilkes: Masculinity and politics in the eighteenth century', *Eighteenth-Century Studies*, 32.1 (1998), 19–48.

Clark, Gregory, Michael Huberman and Peter H. Lindert, 'A British food puzzle, 1770–1850', *Economic History Review*, 48:2 (1995), 215–37.

Clark, Gregory, 'The condition of the working class in England,1209–2004', *Journal of Political Economy*, 116:6 (2005), 1307–40.

Clark, Lorenne M. G. 'Women and John Locke: or, Who owns the apples in the Garden of Eden', *Canadian Journal of Philosophy*, 7 (1977), 699–724.

Clarke, Bridget, 'Huguenot tutors and the family of Edward and Mary Clarke of Chipley, 1687–1710', *Proceedings of the Huguenot Society of Great Britain and Ireland*, 27:4 (2001), 527–42.

Connerton, Paul, *How Societies Remember*, Cambridge University Press, Cambridge, 1989.

Cook, Elizabeth Heckendorn, *Epistolary Bodies: Gender and genre in the eighteenth-century republic of letters*, University of California Press, Stanford CA, 1991.

Cottrell, *Energy and Society: The relations between energy, social change and economic development*, McGraw Hill, New York, Toronto, London, 1955.

Cox, Rosie, *The Servant Problem: Domestic employment in a global economy*, I. B Tauris, London, 2006.

Crafts, Nick, 'British economic growth, 1700–1831: A review of the evidence', *Economic History Review*, 2nd ser., 36 (1983), 177–99.

'English workers' real wages during the Industrial Revolution: Some remaining problems'; with a reply by Peter Lindert and Jeffrey Williamson, *Journal of Economic History*, 45 (1985), 139–53.

Cranston, Maurice, *John Locke: A Biography*, Longmans, Green, London, 1957.

Crittall, Elizabeth (ed.), *The Justicing Notebook of William Hunt, 1744–1749*, Wiltshire Record Society, vol. 37, Devizes, 1982.

Cullwick, Hannah, *The Diaries of Hannah Cullwick*, Intro. by Liz Stanley (ed.), Virago, London, 1984.

Cunnington, Susan, *The Story of Arithmetic: A short history of its origin and development*, Swan Sonenchein, London, 1904.

Curwen Archives Texts, *Vital Statistics: The Westmorland 'Census' of 1787*, Curwen Archives Trust, Berwick, 1992.

Dalla Costa, Maria, *The Power of Women and the Subversion of the Community*, Falling Wall Press, Bristol, 1974.

Dalporto, Jeannie, 'Landscape, labor and the ideology of improvement in Mary Leapor's "Crumble Hall"', *The Eighteenth Century. Theory and Interpretation*, 42:3 (2001), 228–44.

Daunton, Martin, *Trusting Leviathan: The politics of taxation in Britain, 1799–1914*, Cambridge University Press, Cambridge, 2001.

David, Elizabeth, *Salt, Spices and Aromatics in the English Kitchen*, Penguin, Harmondsworth, 1970.

Davidoff, Leonore, 'Mastered for Life: Servant and wife in Victorian and Edwardian England', *Journal of Social History*, 7:4 (1974), 406–20.

'The rationalization of housework' in *Worlds Between. Historical Perspectives on Gender and Class*, Polity, Cambridge, 1995.

Deakin, Simon and Frank Wilkinson, *The Law of the Labour Market: Industrialization, employment and legal evolution*, Oxford University Press, Oxford, 2005.

Dean, Mitchell, *The Constitution of Poverty: Towards a genealogy of liberal governance*, Routledge, London, 1991.

De Beer, E. S. *The Correspondence of John Locke*, 8 vols., Clarendon Press, Oxford, 1976.

Dereli, Cynthia, 'In search of a poet: The Life and work of Elizabeth Hands', *Women's Writing*, 8 (2001), 169–82.

Derrida, Jacques, *Spectres of Marx: The state of the debt, the work of mourning, and the New International* (1993), Routledge, London, 1994.

Douglas, Lorimer,'Black slaves and English liberty: A re-examination of racial slavery in England', *Immigrants and Minorities*, 3 (1984), 121–50.

Drescher, Seymour, 'Manumission in a society without slave law', *Slavery and Abolition*, 10 (1989), 85–101.

Duck, Stephen and Mary Collier, *The Thresher's Labour and The Woman's Labour*, Augustan Reprint Society, no. 230, Andrews Clark Memorial Library, Los Angeles, 1985.

The Thresher's Labour... The Woman's Labour... Two Eighteenth Century Poems, Intro. E. P. Thompson, Merlin Press, London, 1989.

Earle, Peter, 'The female labour market in London in the late seventeenth and early eighteenth centuries', *Economic History Review*, 42:3 (1989), 328–53.

A City Full of People: Men and women of London, 1650–1750, Methuen, London, 1994.

Eastwood, David, *Governing Rural England: Tradition and transformation in local government 1780–1840*, Oxford University Press, Oxford, 1994.

Ehrenreich, Barbara and Arlie Russell Hochschild, *Global Woman: Nannies, maids and sex workers in the new economy*, Granta, London, 2003.

Eley, Geoff, and Keith Nield, *The Future of Class in History: What's left of the social?*, University of Michigan Press, Ann Arbor, 2007.

Emsley, Clive, *British Society and the French Wars*, Macmillan, Basingstoke, 1979.

Fairchilds, Cissie, *Domestic Enemies: Servants and their masters in old regime France*, Johns Hopkins University Press, Baltimore and London, 1984.

Fauve-Chamoux, Antoinette, *Domestic Service and the Formation of European Identity: Understanding the globalization of domestic work, 16th–21st Centuries*, Peter Lang, New York and Oxford, 2004.

Federici, Sylvia, 'Wages against housework' in Ellen Malos (ed.), *The Politics of Housework*, New Clarion Press, New York, 1975, pp. 187–94.

Feinstein, Charles H. 'Pessimism perpetuated: Real wages and the standard of living in Britain during and after the Industrial Revolution', *Journal of Economic History*, (1998), 625–58.

Ferber, Marianne A. and Julie A. Nelson, *Beyond Economic Man: Feminist theory and economics*, University of Chicago, Chicago, 1993.

Fergus, Jan, 'Provincial servants' reading in the late eighteenth century' in *The Practice and Representation of Reading in England*, James Raven, Helen Small and Naomi Tadmor (eds.), Cambridge University Press, Cambridge, 1996, pp. 202–25.

Provincial Readers in Eighteenth-Century England, Oxford University Press, Oxford, 2006.

Ferguson, Adam, *An Essay on the History of Civil Society* (1767), Edinburgh University Press, Edinburgh, 1966.

Finch, Lynette, *The Classing Gaze: Sexuality, class and surveillance*, Allen and Unwin, St Leonards NSW, 1993.

Finn, Margot, *The Character of Credit: Personal debt in English culture, 1740–1914*, Cambridge, Cambridge University Press, 2003.

Finnegan, Ruth H. *Oral Poetry: Its nature, significance, and social context*, University of Indiana Press, Bloomington, 1992.

Ford, Charles Howard, *Hannah More: A critical biography*, Peter Lang, New York, 1996.

Fortunati, Leopoldina, *The Arcane of Reproduction: Housework, prostitution, labor and capital* (1981), Autonomedia, New York, 1995.

Franklin, Caroline (ed.), *The Romantics: Women poets 1770–1830. The Death of Amnon, A Poem Elizabeth Hands*, Routledge, London, 1996.

Fraser, Ronald, *Work: Twenty Personal Accounts. Vol. 1 . . . with a concluding essay by Raymond Williams . . . Vol. 2 with a concluding Essay by Alvin Gouldner*, Penguin Books with New Left Review, Harmondsworth, 1968–9.

Frey, Sylvia R. *Water from the Rock: Black resistance in a revolutionary age*, Princeton University Press, Princeton NJ, 1991.

Fryer, Peter, *Staying Power: The history of black people in Britain*, Pluto, London, 1984.

Furniss, Edgar S. *The Position of the Laborer in a System of Nationalism: A study in the labor theory of the later English mercantilists* (1920), Augustus M. Kelly, New York, 1965.

Gagen, N. V. *Hanged at Lincoln, 1716–1961*, privately printed, Welton, Lincoln, 1998.

Gatrell, V. A. C. *The Hanging Tree: Execution and the English people, 1770–1868*, Oxford University Press, Oxford, 1994.

Gerhold, Dorian, 'Packhorses and wheeled vehicles in England, 1550–1800', *Journal of Transport History*, 14:1 (1993), 1–26.

Gilboy, Elizabeth W. *Wages in Eighteenth Century England*, Harvard University Press, Cambridge, MA, 1934.

Gilmour, Ian, *Riot, Rising and Revolution: Governance and violence in eighteenth-century England*, Pimlico, London, 1992.

Gobetti, Daniela, *Private and Public: Individuals households and body Politic in Locke and Hutcheson*, Routledge, London, 1992.

Godwin, William, *Collected Novels and Memoirs of William Godwin*, Pamela Clemit (ed.), 6 vols., Pickering and Chatto, London, 1992–3.

Goody, Jack, *Cooking, Cuisine and Class: A Study in comparative sociology*, Cambridge University Press, Cambridge, 1982.

The Interface Between the Written and the Oral, Cambridge University Press, Cambridge, 1987.

Gorz, André, *Farewell to the Working Class: An essay on post-industrial socialism*, Pluto, London, 1982.

Graham, Elspeth, *et al.*, *Her Own Life: Autobiographical writings by seventeenth-century English women*, Routledge, London, 1989.

Graham, Sandra Lauderdale, *House and Street: The domestic world of servants in nineteenth-century Rio de Janeiro*, Cambridge University Press, Cambridge, 1988.

Gregson, Nicky and Michelle Lowe, *Servicing the Middle Class: Class, gender and waged domestic labour in contemporary Britain*, Routledge, London, 1994.

Grigson, Jane, *English Food*, (1974), Penguin, Harmondsworth, 1977.

Haakonssen, Knud (ed.), *The Cambridge Companion to Adam Smith*, Cambridge University Press, Cambridge, 2006.

Hall, Catherine, 'The tale of Samuel and Jemima: Gender and working class culture in nineteenth-century England' in Harvey J. Kaye and Keith

McClelland (eds.), *E. P. Thompson: Critical perspectives*, Polity, Cambridge, 1990, pp. 78–102.

Hargrove, James L. 'History of the calorie in nutrition', *Journal of Nutrition*, 136 (2006), 2957–61.

Harvey, David, *The Limits to Capital*, Basil Blackwell, Oxford, 1999.

Hatcher, John, 'Labour, leisure and economic thought before the nineteenth century', *Past and Present*, 160 (1998), 64–118.

Hay, Doug, 'The state and the market in 1800: Lord Kenyon and Mr Waddington', *Past and Present*, 162 (1999), 100–62.

'England, 1562–1875: The law and its uses' in Paul Craven and Douglas Hay (eds.), *Masters, Servants and Magistrates in Britain and the Empire, 1562–1955*, University of North Carolina Press, Chapel Hill, 2004, pp. 59–116.

Hayden, Dolores, and Gwendolyn Wright, 'The new scholarship: Review essays', *Architecture and Urban Planning*, *Signs*, 1:4 (1976), 923–33.

Hecht, J. Jean, *The Domestic Servant Class in Eighteenth Century England*, Routledge and Kegan Paul, London, 1956.

Hemlow, Joyce (ed.), *The Journals and Letters of Fanny Burney (Madame d'Arblay)*, vol. 1, *1791–1792*, Oxford University Press, Oxford, 1972.

Hersee, John, 'Multiplication is Vexation', *paradigm*, 24 (1997), 24–33.

Heslop, Joe, *According to Local Custom: Waste disposal in Hull from the middle ages to the end of the eighteenth century*, Local History Archives, Hull College of Further Education, Hull, 1990.

Heydt-Stevenson, Jillian, *Austen's Unbecoming Conjunctions: Subversive laughter, embodied history*, Palgrave Macmillan, 2005.

Heward, Edmund, *Lord Mansfield*, Rose, Chichester and London, 1979.

Higgs, Edward, 'Domestic servants and households in Victorian England', *Social History*, 8:2 (1983), 201–10.

Hill, Bridget, *Women, Work and Sexual Politics in Eighteenth-Century England*, Basil Blackwell, Oxford, 1989.

Servants: English domestics in the eighteenth century, Clarendon Press, Oxford, 1996.

Hilton, Boyd, *A Mad, Bad, and Dangerous People? England 1783–1846*, Oxford University Press, Oxford, 2006.

Hobbs, May, *Born to Struggle*, Quartet Books, London, 1973.

Hobsbawm, Eric, *Worlds of Labour: Further studies in the history of labour*, Weidenfeld and Nicolson, London, 1984.

Hochschild, Arlie Russell, *The Commercialisation of Intimate Life: Notes from home and work*, University of California Press, Berkeley, Los Angeles and London, 2003.

Holdsworth, William, *A History of the English Law*, 17 vols., Methuen, London, 1936–72.

Horne, Thomas A. *Property Rights and Poverty: Political argument in Britain, 1605–1834*, University of North Carolina Press, Chapel Hill and London, 1990.

Hudson, Derek, *Munby, Man of Two Worlds: The life and diaries of Arthur J. Munby, 1828–1910*, John Murray, London, 1972.

Hughes, Kathryn, *The Victorian Governess*, Hambledon, London, 1993.

The Short Life and Long Times of Mrs Beeton, Fourth Estate, London, 2005.

Humphries, Jane, and Sara Horrell, '"The Exploitation of Little Children": Child labour and the family economy in the Industrial Revolution', *Explorations in Economic History*, 22 (1995), 485–516.

'Women's labour force participation and the transition to the male breadwinner family, 1790–1865', *Economic History Review*, 98 (1995) 89–117.

Hunt, E. K. 'Marx's theory of property and alienation' in Parel and Flanagan (eds), *Theories of Property: Aristotle to the present*, Wilfrid Laurier for the Calgary Institute for the Humanities, Waterloo, Ontario, 1979, pp. 283–315.

Hunt, Lynne, *The Family Romance of the French Revolution*, Routledge, London, 1992.

Hyde, Mary, *The Thrales of Streatham Park*, Harvard University Press, Cambridge, MA and London, 1977.

Ingold, Tim, *The Perception of the Environment: Essays in livelihood, dwelling and skill*, Routledge, London and New York, 2000.

Innes, Joanna, 'Parliament and the shaping of eighteenth-century social policy', *Transactions of the Royal Historical Society*, 5th ser., 40 (1990), 63–92.

'Politics and morals: The late eighteenth-century reformation of manners' in E. Hellmuth (ed.), *The Transformation of Political Culture: Late eighteenth-century England and Germany*, Oxford University Press for the German Historical Institute, Oxford 1990, pp. 57–118.

'The state and the poor: Eighteenth-century England in European perspective' in John Brewer and Ekhart Hellmuth (eds.), *Rethinking Leviathan: The eighteenth-century state in Britain and Germany*, Oxford University Press, Oxford, 1999, pp. 225–80.

'Origins of the Factory Acts: The Health and Morals of Apprentices Act 1802' in Norma Landau (ed.), *Law, Crime and English Society, 1660–1830*, Cambridge University Press, 2002, pp. 203–55.

'Changing perceptions of the state in the late eighteenth and early nineteenth centuries', *Journal of Historical Sociology*, 15:1 (2002), 107–13.

Jackson, Mark, *New-Born Child Murder: Women, illegitimacy and the courts in eighteenth-century England*, Manchester University Press, Manchester and New York, 1996.

Janowitz, Anne, *Lyric and Labour in the Romantic Tradition*, Cambridge University Press, Cambridge, 1998.

Joyce, Patrick, 'The necessity of social history: Putting the social back in social history', forthcoming.

(ed.), *The Historical Meanings of Work*, Cambridge University Press, Cambridge, 1987.

(ed.), *Class*, Oxford University Press, Oxford, 1995.

Kahn, Madeleine, 'Hannah More and Ann Yearsley: A collaboration across the class divide', *Studies in Eighteenth-century Culture*, 25 (1996), 203–23.

Kamminga, Harmke and Andrew Cunningham, *The Science and Culture of Nutrition, 1840–1940*, Rodopi, Amsterdam and Atlanta, GA, 1995.

Kapinski, Louis Charles, *The History of Arithmetic*, Russell and Russell, New York, 1925.

Karsten, Peter, *Between Law and Custom: "High" and "low" legal cultures in the lands of the British diaspora – the United States, Canada, Australia, and New Zealand, 1600–1900*, Cambridge University Press, Cambridge, 2002.

Kaye, Harvey J. and Keith McClelland (eds.), *E. P. Thompson: Critical perspectives*, Polity, Cambridge, 1990.

Keane, John, *Tom Paine: A political life*, Bloomsbury, London, 1995.

Keegan, Bridget, 'Cobbling verse: Shoemaker poets of the long eighteenth century', *The Eighteenth Century. Theory and Interpretation*, 42:3 (2001), 195–217.

Keeton, G. W. *Guilty but Insane*, Macdonald, London, 1961.

Kennedy, William, *English Taxation, 1640–1799: An essay on policy and opinion*, Bell, London, 1913.

Kent, D. A. 'Ubiquitous but invisible: Female domestic servants in mid-eighteenth-century London', *History Workshop Journal*, 28 (1989), 111–28.

King, Peter, 'The summary courts and social relations in eighteenth-century England', *Past and Present*, 183 (2004), 125–72.

Kiple, Kenneth F. *The Caribbean Slave: A biological history*, Cambridge University Press, Cambridge, 1984.

Kramer, Matthew H. *John Locke and the Origins of Private Property: Philosophical explorations of individualism, community and equality*, Cambridge University Press, Cambridge, 1997.

Kuhn, W. E. *The Evolution of Economic Thought*, South Western Publishing, Cincinnati, 1963.

Lana, Renata, 'Women and the Foxite strategy in the election of 1784', *Eighteenth-Century Life*, 26:1 (2002), 46–69.

Landau, Norma *The Justices of the Peace, 1679–1760*, University of California Press, Berkeley, 1985.

'Going local: The social history of Stuart and Hanoverian England', *Journal of British Studies*, 24 (1985), 273–81.

'Laws of Settlement and the surveillance of immigration in eighteenth-century Kent', *Continuity and Change*, 3 (1988), 391–420.

'The eighteenth-century context of the Laws of Settlement', *Continuity and Change*, 6 (1991), 417–39.

Landes, David S. *The Unbound Prometheus: Technological change and industrial development in Western Europe from 1750 to the present* (1969), Cambridge University Press, Cambridge, 2003.

Landry, Donna, *The Muses of Resistance: Labouring class women's poetry in Britain, 1739–1796*, Cambridge University Press, Cambridge, 1990.

'The labouring class women poets: "Hard Labour we most chearfully pursue"' in Sarah Prescott and David E. Shuttleton (eds.), *Women and Poetry, 1660–1750*, Palgrave Macmillan, Basingstoke, 2003, pp. 223–43.

Lane, Joan, *Apprenticeship in England, 1600–1914*, UCL Press, London 1996.

Lane, Penelope, 'Work on the margins: Poor women and the informal economy of eighteenth and early nineteenth-century Leicestershire', *Midland History*, 22 (1997), 88–99.

'A customary or a market wage? Women and Work in the East Midlands, c. 1700–1840' in Penelope Lane, Neil Raven and K. D. M. Snell (eds.), *Women, Work and Wages in England, 1600–1850*, Boydell, Woodbridge, 2004, pp. 102–18.

Langford, Paul, 'The management of the eighteenth-century state: Perceptions and Implications', *Journal of Historical Sociology*, 15;1 (2002), 102–6.

Laslett, Peter, (ed. with the assistance of Richard Wall), *Household and Family in Past Time*, Cambridge University Press, Cambridge, 1972.

Latour, Bruno, *Reassembling the Social: An introduction to actor-network-theory*, Oxford University Press, Oxford, 2005.

Laurence-Anderson, Judith, 'Changing affective life in eighteenth century England and Samuel Richardson's *Pamela*,' *Studies in Eighteenth Century Culture*, 10 (1981), 445–56.

Lazear, Edward P. 'Salaries and piece work', *Journal of Business*, 59:3 (1986), 405–37.

Lebovics, Herman, 'The uses of America in Locke's *Second Treatise of Government*', *Journal of the History of Ideas*, 47:4 (1986), 567–81.

Lees, Lynn Hollen, *The Solidarities of Strangers: The English poor laws and the people, 1700–1948*, Cambridge University Press, Cambridge, 1998.

Lehmann, Gilly, 'Women's cookery in eighteenth-century England: Authors, attitudes, culinary styles', *Studies on Voltaire and the Eighteenth Century*, 305 (1992), 1737–9.

Levi-Strauss, Claude, *Totemism*, Beacon Press, Boston, 1963.

Lieberman, David, 'Property, commerce, and the common law: Attitudes to legal change in the eighteenth century' in John Brewer and Susan Staves (eds.), *Early Modern Conceptions of Property*, Routledge, London, 1995.

Liebs, Elke, 'Between *Gulliver* and *Alice*: Some remarks on the dialectic of GREAT and SMALL in literature', *Phaedrus*, 13 (1980), 56–60.

Light, Alison, *Mrs Woolf and the Servants*, Fig Tree, London, 2007.

Lindert, Peter, 'English population wages and prices, 1541–1913' in R. I. Rotberg and Theodore Kwasnik Rabb (eds.), *Population and History: From the traditional to the modern world*, Cambridge University Press, Cambridge, 1986, pp. 49–74.

Lloyd, Sarah, '"Pleasure's Golden Bait": Prostitution, poverty and the Magdalen Hospital in eighteenth-century London', *History Workshop Journal*, 41 (1996), 50–70.

Loftis, John,'Whig oratory on stage: Sheridan's *Pizarro*, *Eighteenth-Century Studies*, 8:4 (1975), 454–72.

Lorimer, Douglas A. 'Black slaves and English liberty: A re-examination of racial slavery in England', *Immigrants and Minorities*, 3 (1984), 121–50.

Lukás, Georg, *History and Class Consciousness: Studies in Marxist dialectics*, Merlin Press, London, 1968.

MacPherson, C. B. 'Servants and labourers in seventeenth-century England', *Democratic Theory: Essays in retrieval*, Clarendon Press, Oxford, 1973.

Magnusson, Lars, *Mercantilism: The shaping of an economic language*, Routledge, New York, 1994.

de Marchi, Neil, 'Smith on ingenuity, pleasure and the imitative arts' in Knud Haakonssen (ed.), *The Cambridge Companion to Adam Smith*, Cambridge University Press, Cambridge, 2006.

Mascuch, Michael, *Origins of the Individual Self: Autobiography and self-identity in England, 1591–1791*, Cambridge University Press, Cambridge, 1997.

Maza, Sarah, *Servants and Masters in Eighteenth-century France: The uses of loyalty*, Princeton University Press, Princeton and Guildford, 1983.

McBride, Theresa, *The Domestic Revolution: The modernization of household service in England and France, 1820–1920*, Croom Helm, London, 1976.

McDonagh, Josephine, *Child Murder and British Culture, 1720–1900*, Cambridge University Press, Cambridge, 2003.

McGarvie, Michael (ed.), *The King's Peace: The justice's notebook of Thomas Horner, of Mells, 1770–1777*, Frome Society for Local Study, Frome, 1997.

McIntosh, Carey, *Common and Courtly Language: The stylistics of social class in eighteenth-century British literature*, University of Pennsylvania Press, Philadelphia, 1986.

McKeown, Michael, *The Origins of the English Novel, 1600–1740*, Johns Hopkins University Press, Baltimore, 1987.

Meldrum, Tim, *Domestic Service and Gender, 1660–1750: Life and work in the London household*, Longman, London, 2000.

Meuvret, Jean, 'Les Oscillations des prix des céréales aux 17e et 18e siècles en Angleterre et dans les pays du bassin parisien', *Revue d'histoire moderne et contemporaine*, 16 (1969), 540–54.

Michael, Ian, *The Teaching of English from the Sixteenth Century to the Present Day*, Cambridge University Press, Cambridge, 1987.

Millhauser, Steven, 'The Fascination of the miniature', *Grand Street*, 2 (1983), 128–35.

Ministry of Agriculture, Fisheries and Food, *Manual of Nutrition*, 10th edn, HMSO, London, 1995.

Mitchell, Ian, 'Pitt's shop tax in the history of retailing', *Local Historian*, 14:6 (1981), 348–51.

Mokyr, Joel, *The Gifts of Athena: Historical origins of the knowledge economy*, Princeton University Press, Princeton and Oxford, 2002.

'Accounting for the Industrial Revolution', *The Cambridge Economic History of Modern Britain*, vol. 1, *Industrialisation, 1700–1860*, Roderick Floud and Paul Johnson (eds.), Cambridge, Cambridge University Press, 2004.

Morris, R. J. *Class and Class Consciousness in the Industrial Revolution, 1789–1850*, Macmillan, London, 1979.

Muldrew, Craig, and Stephen King, 'Cash, wages and the economy of makeshifts in England,1650–1800' in Peter Scholliers and Leonard Schwarz (eds.), *Experiencing Wages: Social and cultural aspects of wage forms in Europe since 1500*, Berghahn, New York and Oxford, 2003, pp. 155–82.

Myers, Mitzi, '"Servants as They are now Educated": Women writers and Georgian pedagogy', *Essays in Literature*, 16 (1989), 51–69.

Myers, Norma, 'Servant, sailor, soldier, beggarman: Black survival in white society, 1780–1830', *Immigrants and Minorities*, 12 (1993), 47–74.

Namier, Lewis and John Brooke, *Charles Townshend*, Macmillan, London, 1964.

Neale, R. S. *Class in English History, 1680–1850*, Basil Blackwell, Oxford, 1981.

Neeson, Jeanette, *Commoners: Common right, enclosure and social change in England, 1700–1820*, Cambridge University Press, Cambridge, 1993.

Newman, Gerald, *The Rise of English Nationalism: A cultural history 1740–1830*, Macmillan, Basingstoke, 1997.

Nussbaum, Felicity, *The Autobiographical Subject*, Johns Hopkins University Press, Baltimore, 1989.

Oakley, Ann, *Woman's Work: The housewife past and present* (1974), Vintage, New York, 1976.

The Sociology of Housework (1974), Basil Blackwell, Oxford, 1985.

O'Brien, Patrick K. 'The political economy of British taxation, 1660–1815', *Economic History Review*, 2nd ser., 41 (1988), 1–32.

'Public finance and the wars with France,1793–1815' in H. T. Dickinson (ed.), *Britain and the French Revolution, 1789–1815*, Macmillan, Basingstoke, 1989, pp. 165–87.

O'Brien, Patrick and Phillip Hunt, 'The rise of the fiscal state in England, 1485–1815', *Historical Research* (1993), 66–176.

O'Brien, Patrick Karl, 'The triumph and denouement of the British fiscal state: Taxation for the wars Against Revolutionary and Napoleonic France, 1793–1815', Working Paper No. 99/07, London School of Economics, 2007.

Ogborn, Miles, *Spaces of Modernity: London's geographies, 1680–1780*, Guilford Press, New York, London, 1998.

Oldham, James, 'New light on Mansfield and slavery', *Journal of British Studies*, 27 (1988), 45–68.

The Mansfield Manuscripts and the Growth of the English Law in the Eighteenth Century, 2 vols., Chapel Hill, NC and London, 1992.

Olson, David R. *The World on Paper: The conceptual and cognitive implications of writing and reading*, Cambridge University Press, Cambridge, 1994.

Orth, John V. 'English Combination Acts of the eighteenth century', *Law and History Review*, 5:1 (1987), 175–211.

Pahl, R. E. *Divisions of Labour*, Basil Blackwell, Oxford, 1984.

Paine, Thomas, *The Rights of Man (1792), Common Sense and Other Political Writings*, Mark Philp (ed.), Oxford University Press, Oxford, 1995.

Parel, Anthony and Thomas Flanagan (eds.), *Theories of Property: Aristotle to the present*, Wilfrid Laurier for the Calgary Institute for the Humanities, Waterloo, Ontario, 1977.

Parsons, Talcott, 'The social structure of the family' in Ruth N. Ashen (ed.), *The Family: Its Functions and Destiny*, Harper, New York, 1949.

Pateman, Carol, *The Sexual Contract*, Polity, Cambridge, 1988.

Patterson, Orlando, *Slavery and Social Death: A comparative study*, Harvard University Press, Cambridge, MA and London, 1982.

Phillips, Anne and Barbara Taylor, 'Sex and skill: Notes towards a feminist economics', *Feminist Review*, 6 (1980), 79–88.

Phillips, Mark, 'Adam Smith, Bellelettrist' in Knud Haakonssen (ed.), *The Cambridge Companion to Adam Smith*, Cambridge University Press, Cambridge, 2006, pp. 57–78.

Pocock, J. G. A. 'The mobility of property and the rise of eighteenth-century sociology' in Anthony Parel and Thomas Flanagan (eds.), *Theories of Property: Aristotle to the Present*, Calgary Institute for the Humanities, Waterloo, Ontario, 1979.

'The myth of John Locke and the obsession with liberalism' in J. G. A. Pocock and Richard Ashcraft (eds.), *John Locke: Papers read at a Clark Library Seminar, 10 December 1977*, William Andrews Clark Memorial Library, University of California, Los Angeles, 1980, pp. 3–24.

'Adam Smith and History' in Knud Haakonssen (ed.), *The Cambridge Companion to Adam Smith*, Cambridge University Press, Cambridge, 2006, pp. 270–87.

Poovey, Mary, *Uneven Developments: The ideological work of gender in mid-Victorian England*, University of Chicago Press, Chicago 1988.

Poulantzas, Nicos, *Classes in Contemporary Capitalism*, New Left Books, London, 1975.

Poynter, John Riddoch, *Society and Pauperism*, Routledge and Kegan Paul, London, 1969.

Quah, Euston, 'Persistent problems in measuring household production', *American Journal of Economics and Sociology*, 45:2 (1986), 235–46.

Radin, Margaret Jane, 'Property and personhood', *Stanford Law Review*, 34 (1981–1982), 957–1015.

Rand, Benjamin, *The Correspondence of John Locke and Edward Clarke*, Harvard University Press, Cambridge, MA, 1927.

Rathbun, Ted A. and Richard H. Steckel, 'The health of slaves and free blacks in the East' in Richard H. Steckel, and Jerome C. Rose (eds.), *The Backbone of History: Health and nutrition in the Western Hemisphere*, Cambridge University Press, Cambridge, 2002, pp. 208–25.

Rawley, James A. *The Transatlantic Slave Trade: A history*, Norton, New York, 1981.

Reade, Aleyn Lyell, *Johnsonian Gleanings: Part II: Francis Barber, the Doctor's negro servant*, privately printed, London, 1952.

Reay, Barry, *Watching Hannah: Sexuality, horror and bodily de-formation in Victorian England*, Reaktion, London, 2002.

Richardson, Samuel, *Selected Letters*, Intro. John Carroll (ed.), Clarendon Press, Oxford, 1964.

Rizzo, Betty, 'The patron as poet maker: The politics of benefaction', *Studies in Eighteenth-century Culture*, 20 (1990), 241–66.

Robbins, Bruce, *The Servant's Hand: English fiction from below* (1986), Duke University Press, Durham, SC and London, 1993.

Roberts, Michael, '"To Bridle the falsehood of unconscionable workers, and for her own satisfaction": What the Jacobean housewife needed to know about men's work, and why', *Labour History Review*, 63:1 (1998), 4–30.

Roberts, Robert, 'Bronze mushrooms' in *The Classic Slum: Salford life in the first quarter of the century*, Manchester University Press, Manchester, 1971.

Rosenthal, Laura J. *Infamous Commerce: Prostitution in eighteenth-century British literature and culture*, Cornell University Press, Ithaca and London, 2006.

Ross, Ian Simpson, *The Life of Adam Smith*, Clarendon Press, Oxford, 1995.

Rothschild, Emma and Amartya Sen, 'Adam Smith's economics' in Knud Haakonssen (ed.), *The Cambridge Companion to Adam Smith*, Cambridge University Press, Cambridge, 2006, pp. 319–65.

Rubin, Isaac Ilych, *A History of Economic Thought* (1929), Ink Links, London, 1979.

Rule, John, *The Experience of Labour in Eighteenth-century Industry*, Croom Helm, London, 1981.

'The property of skill in the period of manufacture' in Patrick Joyce (ed.), *The Historical Meanings of Work*, Cambridge University Press, Cambridge, 1987.

Rutherford, Thomas, *Institutes of Natural Law, being the Substance of a Course of Lectures on Grotius de Jure Belli et Pacis*, 2 vols., J. Bentham, Cambridge, 1754–6.

Ryan, Alan, *Property and Political Theory*, Basil Blackwell, Oxford, 1984.

Said, Edward, *Culture and Imperialism*, Chatto and Windus, London, 1993.

Sambrook, Pamela A. *The Country House Servant*, Sutton in association with the National Trust, Stroud, 1999.

Schama, Simon, *Rough Crossings: Britain, the slaves and the American Revolution*, BBC Publications, 2006.

Schwarz, Leonard, 'English servants and their employers during the eighteenth and nineteenth centuries', *Economic History Review*, 52:2 (1999).

Scott, Joan Wallach, *Gender and the Politics of History*, Columbia University Press, New York and London, 1988.

Sekora, John, *Luxury: The concept in Western thought: Eden to Smollett*, Johns Hopkins University Press, Baltimore, 1977.

Sewell, William H. Jnr, 'How classes are made: Critical reflections on E. P. Thompson's theory of working-class formation' in Harvey J. Kaye and Keith McClelland (eds.), *E. P. Thompson: Critical perspectives*, Polity, Cambridge, 1990, pp. 50–77.

Sharpe, Pamela, 'Bigamy among the labouring poor in Essex, 1754–1857', *Local Historian*, 24 (1994), 139–44.

Adapting to Capitalism: Working women in the English economy, 1700–1850, Macmillan, Basingstoke, 1996.

'"The Bowels of Compation": A labouring family and the law, c. 1790–1834' in Tim Hitchcock, Peter King and Pamela Sharpe (eds.), *Chronicling Poverty: The voices and strategies of the English poor, 1640–1840*, Macmillan, Basingstoke, 1997.

Shyllon, Folarin Olawale, *James Ramsay: The unknown abolitionist*, Canongate, Edinburgh, 1977.

Silverthorne, Elizabeth, *The Deposition Book of Richard Wyatt, JP, 1767–1776*, Surrey Record Society, vol. 30, Guildford, 1978.

Siskin, Clifford, *The Work of Writing: Literature and social change in Britain, 1700–1830*, Johns Hopkins University Press, Baltimore and London, 1998.

Sisman, Adam, *Boswell's Presumptuous Task: Writing the Life of Dr Johnson*, Penguin, London, 2001.

Skeggs, Beverley, *Formations of Class and Gender: Becoming respectable*, Sage, London, 1997.

'The making of class through visualising moral subject formation', *Sociology*, 39:5 (2005), 965–82.

Slack, Paul, *The English Poor Law, 1531–1782*, Cambridge University Press, Cambridge, 1996.

Smith, Adam, *The Correspondence of Adam Smith*, Ernest Campbell Mossner and Ian Simpson Ross (eds.), Clarendon Press, Oxford, 1977.

Lectures on Jurisprudence: Glasgow edition of the works and correspondence of Adam Smith, R. L. Meek, D. D. Raphael, P. G. Stein (eds.), Clarendon Press, Oxford, 1978.

Snell, K. D. M. *Annals of the Labouring Poor: Social change and agrarian England 1660–1900*, Cambridge University Press, Cambridge, 1985.

Snell, Keith, 'Pauper settlements and the right to relief in England and Wales', *Continuity and Change*, 6 (1991), 375–439.

'The apprenticeship system in British history: The fragmentation of a cultural institution', *History of Education*, 25 (1996), 303–21.

Sonenscher, Michael, *Work and Wages: Natural law, politics and the eighteenth-century French trades*, Cambridge University Press, Cambridge, 1989.

Sorge, Lynn, 'Eighteenth-century stays: Their origins and creators', *Costume*, 32 (1998), 18–32.

'"29 Doz and 11 Best Cutt Bone": The trade in whalebone and stays in eighteenth-century London', *Textile History*, 36:1 (2005), 20–45.

Spellman, W. M. *John Locke*, Macmillan, Basingstoke and London, 1997.

Spencer, M. G. 'Pursuing Pamela, 1740–1750', *Eighteenth Century Life*, 26:2 (2002), 96–100.

Stapleton, Barry, 'Inherited poverty and life-cycle poverty: Odiham, Hampshire, 1650–1850', *Social History*, 18:3 (1993), 339–55.

Staves, Susan, *Married Women's Separate Property in England, 1660–1833*, Harvard University Press, Cambridge, MA and London, 1990.

Steedman, Carolyn, *Landscape for a Good Woman*, Virago, London, 1986.

'Enforced narratives: Stories of another self' in Tess Cosslett, Celia Lury and Penny Summerfield (eds.), *Feminism and Autobiography: Texts, theories, methods*, Routledge, London, 2000, pp. 25–39.

'Servants and their relationship to the unconscious', *Journal of British Studies*, 42 (2003), 316–50.

'The servant's labour. The business of life, England 1760–1820', *Social History*, 29:1 (2004), 1–29.

Master and Servant: Love and labour in the English industrial age, Cambridge University Press, Cambridge, 2007.

Steinfeld, Robert J. *The Invention of Free Labour: The employment relation in English and American law and culture, 1350–1870*, University of North Carolina Press, Chapel Hill and London, 1991.

Stevenson, John, *Popular Disturbance in England, 1700–1832*, 2nd edn, Longman, London, 1992.

Stokes, Francis Griffin (ed.), *The Blecheley Diary of the Reverend William Cole, MA, FSA, 1765–67*, Constable, London, 1931.

Stott, Anne, *Hannah More: The first Victorian*, Oxford University Press, Oxford, 2003.

Stone, Laurence, *Uncertain Unions: Marriage in England 1660–1753*, Oxford University Press, Oxford, 1992.

Road to Divorce: England 1530–1987, Oxford University Press, Oxford, 1990.

Styles, John, 'Involuntary consumers? Servants and their clothes in eighteenth-century England', *Textile History*, 33:1 (2002), 9–21.

Symons, Michael, *A History of Cooks and Cooking*, Prospect Books, Totnes, 2001.

Tadmor, Naomi, '"Family" and "Friend" in *Pamela*: A case-study in the history of the family in eighteenth-century England', *Social History* 14;3 (1989), 289–306.

Family and Friends in Eighteenth-Century England: Household, kinship and patronage, Cambridge University Press, Cambridge, 2001.

Taylor, Barbara, *Mary Wollstonecraft and the Feminist Imagination*, Cambridge University Press, Cambridge, 2003.

Taylor, James Stephan, *Poverty, Migration and Settlement in the Industrial Revolution: Sojourners' narratives*, Society for the Promotion of Science and Scholarship, Palo Alto, CA, 1989.

Thaddeus, Janet, 'Swift's Directions to Servants', *Studies in Eighteenth-Century Culture*, 16 (1986), 107–23.

Thomas, Hugh, *The Slave Trade: The history of the Atlantic slave trade 1440–1870*, Picador, London, 1997.

Thomas, R. D. *Industries of the Morda Valley: Life and labour in the 19th century*, Woodhall, Minshall and Thomas, Oswestry, 1939.

Thompson, E. P. *The Making of the English Working Class* (1963), Penguin, Harmondsworth, 1968.

'The crime of anonymity', in Douglas Hay *et al.* (eds.), *Albion's Fatal Tree*, Allen Lane, London, 1976.

Whigs and Hunters: The origins of the Black Act, Allen Lane, London, 1975.

Thomson, George Derwent, *Aeschylus and Athens: A study in the origins of drama* (1946), 4th edn, Lawrence and Wishart, London, 1973.

Tinsman, Heidi, 'The indispensable service of sisters: Considering domestic service in United States and Latin American studies', *Journal of Women's History*, 4:1 (1992), 37–59.

Todd, Janet, *Mary Wollstonecraft: A revolutionary life*, Weidenfeld and Nicholson, London, 2000.

Todd, Selina, *Young Women, Work, and Family in England, 1918–1950*, Oxford University Press, Oxford, 2005.

Tully, James, *A Discourse on Property: John Locke and his adversaries*, Cambridge University Press, Cambridge, 1980.

Trainor, Richard H. *Black Country Elites: The exercise of authority in an industrialised area 1830–1900*, Clarendon Press, Oxford, 1993.

Tribe, Keith, *Land, Labour and Economic Discourse*, Routledge and Kegan Paul, London, 1978.

Turner, M. E., J. V. Beckett and B. Afton, 'Taking stock: Farmers, farm records, and agricultural output in England,1700–1850', *Agricultural History Review*, 44 (1996), 21–34.

Turner, Michael, 'Counting sheep: Waking up to new estimates of livestock numbers in England c. 1800', *Agricultural History Review*, 46:2 (1998), 142–61.

Uglow, Jenny, *Nature's Engraver: A life of Thomas Bewisk*, Faber and Faber, London, 2006.

Valenze, Deborah, *The First Industrial Woman*, Oxford University Press, Oxford and New York, 1995.

The Social Life of Money in the English Past, Cambridge University Press, Cambridge, 2006.

Verdon, Nicola,'"A Much Neglected Historical Source": The uses and limitations of farm account books to historians of rural women's work', *Women's History Notebook*, 8 (2001), 5–12.

Rural Women Workers in Nineteenth-century England: Gender, work and wages, Boydell Press, Woodbridge, 2003.

Vickery, Amanda, 'Women and the world of goods: A Lancashire consumer and her possessions, 1751–81' in John Brewer and Roy Porter (eds.), *Consumption and the World of Goods: Consumption and society in the seventeenth and eighteenth centuries*, Routledge, London, 1993, pp. 274–301.

The Gentleman's Daughter: Women's lives in Georgian England, Yale University Press, New Haven, 1998.

Vincent, David, *The Rise of Mass Literacy: Reading and writing in modern Europe*, Polity, Cambridge, 2000.

Wadsworth, Michael, *The Imprint of Time: Childhood, history, and adult life*, Clarendon Press, Oxford, 1991.

Wahrman, Dror, 'Percy's prologue: From gender play to gender panic in eighteenth-century England', *Past and Present*, 159 (1998), 113–60.

The Making of the Modern Self: Identity and culture in eighteenth-century England, Yale University Press, New Haven and London, 2004.

Waldron, Jeremy, '"The Turfs My Servant Has Cut"', *Locke Newsletter*, 13 (1982), 1–20.

Walvin, James, *The Trader, The Owner, The Slave*, Vintage, London, 2008.

Ward, W. R. *The English Land Tax in the Eighteenth Century*, Oxford University Press, London, 1953.

Wardle, Ralph M. (ed.), *Godwin and Mary: Letters of William Godwin and Mary Wollstonecraft*, University of Kansas Press, 1967.

Watson, William, *Textile Design: Colour, elementary weaves and figured fabric*, Longman, Green, London, 1912.

Watt, Sir James, 'The voyage of Captain George Vancouver 1791–95: The interplay of physical and psychological pressures', *CBMH/BCHM*, 4 (1987), 31–51.

Webb, Sidney and Beatrice, *English Local Government*, vol. 1, *The Parish and the County* (1906), Cass, London, 1963.

Weber, Max, *Economy and Society: An outline of interpretive sociology* (1925), Guenther Roth and Claus Wittich (eds.), 2 vols., Bedminster Press, New York, 1968.

'Class, status and party' (1924) in H. Gerth and C. W. Mills (eds.), *From Max Weber: Essays in sociology*, Routledge and Kegan Paul, London, 1991, pp. 180–95.

Wells, Roger, *Wretched Faces: Famine in wartime England, 1798–1801*, Alan Sutton, Gloucester, 1988.

'The development of the English rural proletariat and social protest, 1700–1850' in Mick Reed and Roger Wells (eds.), *Class, Conflict and Protest in the English Countryside, 1700–1880*, Frank Cass, London, 1990, pp. 29–53.

'Social protest, class, conflict and consciousness, in the English countryside 1700–1880', idem., pp. 121–214.

Wiesenthal, Christine S. 'Representation and experimentation in the major comedies of Richard Brinsley Sheridan', *Eighteenth-Century Studies* 25:3 (1992), 309–30.

Williams, Raymond, *Writing in Society*, Verso, London, 1983.

Willk-Brocard, Nicole, *Une dynastie Les Hallé*, Arthena, Paris, 1995.

Whatman, Susanna, *The Housekeeping Book of Susanna Whatman, 1776–1800*, Intro. Christina Hardyment, National Trust, London, 2000.

Wokler, Robert, 'Anthropology and conjectural history in the Enlightenment', Christopher Fox, Roy Porter and Robert Wokler (eds.), *Inventing Human Science. Eighteenth-century domains*, University of California Press, Berkeley, 1995.

Woodward, Kathleen, *Jipping Street* (1928), Virago, London, 1983.

Woolhouse, Roger, *Locke: A biography*, Cambridge University Press, Cambridge, 2007.

Wright, Araminta, *Ripped and Torn: Levi's, Latin America and the blue jean dream*, Ebury Press, London, 2006.

Wrigley, E. A. *Continuity, Chance and Change: The character of the Industrial Revolution in England*, Cambridge University Press, Cambridge, 1988.

Poverty, Progress and Population, Cambridge University Press, Cambridge, 2004.

Wrigley, E. A. and R. S. Schofield, *The Population History of England, 1541–1871: A reconstruction*, Cambridge University Press, Cambridge, 1989.

Wrigley, Julia, 'Feminists and domestic workers', *Feminist Studies*, 17;2 (1991), 317–29.

NEWSPAPERS AND PERIODICALS

Analytical Review
Cambridgeshire Chronicle and Journal
Cambridge Intelligencer
County Chronicle for and Weekly Advertiser for Essex, Hertfordshire, Kent etc
Courier and Evening Gazette (London)
Gentleman's Magazine
Jopson's Coventry Mercury
Leicester and Nottingham Journal
Lloyd's Evening Post and British Chronicle (London)
London Chronicle

Northampton Mercury
Nottingham Journal
Observer (London)
Trewman's Exeter Flying Post; or Plymouth and Cornish Advertiser
Western Flying Post; or Sherbourne and Yeovill Mercury
Whitehall Evening Post

UNPUBLISHED THESES

Adams, Matthew, 'Imagining Britain: The formation of British national identity during the eighteenth century', PhD, University of Warwick, 2002.

Bellingham, R. A. 'Demographic, economic and social change in the later eighteenth and early nineteenth centuries: Some conclusions from a study of four small towns in Yorkshire from circa 1750 to circa 1830', PhD, University of Leicester, 2000.

Handley, Sasha, '"Visions of an Unseen World": The production and consumption of English ghost stories, c. 1660–1800', PhD, University of Warwick, 2005.

Roberts, Michael, 'Wages and wage-earners in England: The evidence of the wage assessments, 1563–1725', DPhil, University of Oxford, 1982.

WEBSITES AND ELECTRONIC RESOURCES

British Society for the History of Mathematics, *www.bshm.org.uk*.

Ferguson, Ann, 'Feminist perspectives on class and work', *Stanford Encyclopedia of Philosophy*, *www.plato.stanford.edu/archives/fall2004/entries/ferguson/*.

International Labour Organisation, ISCO 9131, 'Domestic helpers and cleaners', *www.ilo.org/public/english/pureau/stat/isco88/9131,*
www.lse.ac.uk/collections/economicHistory/pdf/WP99.pdf.

Index